Environmental Governance and Decentralisation

NEW HORIZONS IN ENVIRONMENTAL ECONOMICS

This important series is designed to make a significant contribution to the development of the principles and practices of environmental economics. It includes both theoretical and empirical work. International in scope, it addresses issues of current and future concern in both East and West and in developed and developing countries.

The main purpose of the series is to create a forum for the publication of high quality work and to show how economic analysis can make a contribution to understanding and resolving the environmental problems confronting the world in the twenty-first century.

Recent titles in the series include:

Choice Modelling and the Transfer of Environmental Values
Edited by John Rolfe and Jeff Bennett

The Impact of Climate Change on Regional Systems
A Comprehensive Analysis of California
Edited by Joel Smith and Robert Mendelsohn

Explorations in Environmental and Natural Resource Economics
Essays in Honor of Gardner M. Brown, Jr.
Edited by Robert Halvorsen and David Layton

Using Experimental Methods in Environmental and Resource Economics
Edited by John A. List

Economic Modelling of Climate Change and Energy Policies
Carlos de Miguel, Xavier Labandeira and Baltasar Manzano

The Economics of Global Environmental Change
International Cooperation for Sustainability
Edited by Mario Cogoy and Karl W. Steininger

Redesigning Environmental Valuation
Mixing Methods within Stated Preference Techniques
Neil A. Powe

Economic Valuation of River Systems
Edited by Fred J. Hitzhusen

Scarcity, Entitlements and the Economics of Water in Developing Countries
P.B. Anand

Technological Change and Environmental Policy
A Study of Depletion in the Oil and Gas Industry
Shunsuke Managi

Environmental Governance and Decentralisation
Edited by Albert Breton, Giorgio Brosio, Silvana Dalmazzone and Giovanna Garrone

Environmental Governance and Decentralisation

Edited by

Albert Breton
University of Toronto, Canada

Giorgio Brosio
University of Turin, Italy

Silvana Dalmazzone
University of Turin, Italy

Giovanna Garrone
University of Turin, Italy

NEW HORIZONS IN ENVIRONMENTAL ECONOMICS

Edward Elgar
Cheltenham, UK • Northampton, MA, USA

Published by
Edward Elgar Publishing Limited
Glensanda House
Montpellier Parade
Cheltenham
Glos GL50 1UA
UK

Edward Elgar Publishing, Inc.
William Pratt House
9 Dewey Court
Northampton
Massachusetts 01060
USA

A catalogue record for this book
is available from the British Library

Library of Congress Cataloguing in Publication Data

Environmental governance and decentralisation / edited by Albert Breton . . . [et al.].
p. cm.—(New horizons in environmental economics series)
Includes bibliographical references and index.
1. Environmental policy. 2. Intergovernmental cooperation. I. Breton, Albert.
HC79.E5E5775 2007
337.7—dc22

2007025583

ISBN 978 1 84720 398 4

Printed and bound in Great Britain by MPG Books Ltd, Bodmin, Cornwall

Contents

Contributors

Mikael Skou Andersen
Department of Policy Analysis
National Environmental Research Institute (NERI)
University of Aarhus
Kalø, Rønde (Denmark)
Email: msa@DMU.dk

Felix Ankomah Asante
Institute of Statistical, Social and Economic Research (ISSER)
University of Ghana
Legon, Accra (Ghana)
Email: fasante@ug.edu.gh

Gedion Asfaw
Green Vision Plc
Addis Ababa (Ethiopia)
Email: gedion48@yahoo.com

Albert Breton
Department of Economics
University of Toronto
Toronto, Ontario (Canada)
Email: albert@albertbreton.com

Giorgio Brosio
Department of Economics
University of Turin
Turin (Italy)
Email: giorgio.brosio@unito.it

Ivana Capozza
Evaluation Unit, Ministry of Economic Development
Rome (Italy)
Email: ivana.capozza@tesoro.it

Clóvis Cavalcanti
Federal University of Pernambuco and Institute for Social Research, Joaquim Nabuco Foundation
Recife (Brazil)
Email: clovati@fundaj.gov.br

Tommaso Chiamparino
Department of Political Science and Sociology
University of Florence (Italy)
Email: tommaso.chiamparino@gmail.com

Silvana Dalmazzone
Department of Economics
University of Turin
Turin (Italy)
Email: silvana.dalmazzone@unito.it

Sebsebe Demissew
Science Faculty
Addis Ababa University
Addis Ababa (Ethiopia)
Email: s_demissew@yahoo.com

Stefanie Engel
Institute for Environmental Decisions
ETH Zurich (Switzerland)
Email: stefanie.engel@env.ethz.ch

Giovanna Garrone
Department of Economics
University of Turin
Turin (Italy)
Email: giovanna.garrone@unito.it

Pavel V. Kasyanov
Environmental consultancy company FRECOM Ltd.
Moscow (Russia)
Email: p.kasyanov@frecom.ru

Kifle Lemma Woldesemayat
Addis Ababa (Ethiopia)
Email: wonderer@ethionet.et

Duncan Liefferink
Department of Political Sciences of the Environment
Radboud University Nijmegen
Nijmegen (The Netherlands)
Email: d.liefferink@fm.ru.nl

Subrata Mandal
National Institute of Public Finance and Policy
New Delhi (India)
Email: subrata_mn@hotmail.com

Jeffrey D. Petchey
Federal and Regional Economics Research Unit
School of Economics and Finance
Curtin University, Perth (Australia)
Email: Jeff.Petchey@cbs.curtin.edu.au

Laura Piazza
Bocconi University
Milan (Italy)
Email: la.piazz@gmail.com

M. Govinda Rao
National Institute of Public Finance and Policy
New Delhi (India)
Email: mgr@nipfp.org.in

Pierre Salmon
Laboratoire d'Economie et de Gestion
Université de Bourgogne
Dijon (France)
Email: pierresalmon@compuserve.com

Jason F. Shogren
Department of Economics and Finance
University of Wyoming
Laramie (USA)
Email: JRamses@uwyo.edu

Stephen Smith
Department of Economics
University College London
London (UK)
Email: stephen.smith@ucl.ac.uk

Aliona V. Stovpivskaya
Russia

Marcia Valiante
Faculty of Law
University of Windsor
Windsor, Ontario (Canada)
Email: mvalian@uwindsor.ca

Irene Venturello
Environment Park
Turin (Italy)
Email: irene.venturello@gmail.com

Hua Wang
World Bank
Washington, DC (USA)
Email: Hwang 1@worldbank.org

Mark Wiering
Department of Political Sciences of the Environment
Radboud University Nijmegen
Nijmegen (The Netherlands)
Email: m.wiering@fm.ru.nl

Changhua Wu
The Climate Group
Shanghai (China)
Email: cwu@theclimategroup.org

Melanie Zimmermann
Center for Development Research (ZEF)
Department of Economics and Technological Change
University of Bonn (Germany)
Email: melanie.zimmermann@uni-bonn.de

Anthony R. Zito
Department of Politics
Newcastle University
Newcastle upon Tyne (UK)
Email: A.R.Zito@newcastle.ac.uk

Preface

This research is part of a broader program on environmental governance in decentralized government systems, based in the Department of Economics at the University of Torino, which has been funded by the Compagnia di San Paolo of Torino. The editors would like to express their gratitude to the Compagnia for its sensitivity to the issues we proposed to address in the research program and for its generous financial help.

This volume is the end product of the first of a two-stage process. A few chapters were discussed at a Seminar held in Cogne in May 2003. The results of that Seminar served to define in a more precise way what we could expect from country studies. A first version of all the studies was then presented and discussed at a Symposium held in Alghero in March 2004.

We would also like to thank Silvio Funtowicz (Institute for the Protection and Security of the Citizen – IPSC, EC-JRC), Jeffrey Huntington (European Environmental Agency), Francesco La Camera (former Director for Sustainable Development at the Italian Ministry for the Environment), Alan Nymark (at the time Deputy Minister of Environment Canada) and Anthony Scott (University of British Columbia, Vancouver), who acted as discussants during the seminars and helped give direction to the debate, and Lopamudra Patnaik Saxena for careful copy-editing. We also thank the Department of Economics 'Cognetti de Martiis' of the University of Torino for a contribution to the publication cost of this volume.

1. Introduction

Albert Breton, Giorgio Brosio, Silvana Dalmazzone and Giovanna Garrone

With the pressures of population, economic growth, and the movement of people and commodities reaching a scale which threatens the regenerative and assimilative capacities of the biosphere, environmental conservation has come to be recognized as a pre-eminent global challenge. Concerns for the environment, at the level of research and of policy-making, have been significant, but, it seemed to us, have been mainly cast in a framework that conceives of environmental problems as problems of degradation through pollution and over-exploitation. Such an approach reflects a view of an environment made of unconnected or disjointed components – urban spaces, alpine ecosystems, blue whales, or the Amazonian forest as isolated fragments.

This conventional view identifies as 'environment' what are in effect only a few of its attributes, typically the ones perceived as most directly related to the immediate well-being of western, urbanized populations – air and water quality in cities, the availability of parks and other recreational sites, the conservation of a few charismatic or symbolic species. These attributes and others like them are important, but are essentially derivative of more general properties of the natural ecosystems on which economies and societies rely. Indeed, we now know that the biosphere consists of highly interrelated and complex components, where even elements and species performing similar ecological functions are generally important in maintaining the capacity of the overall system to operate, to absorb shocks and stress, and to support life.

The complexity of ecological systems implies that decisions concerning a specific natural resource generally affect more than one ecological component, although the impact is often lagged and difficult to predict. Environmental policy-making, in turn, does not emanate from a single unitary authority, but is rather the outcome of a multi-layered structure mainly designed by history to deal with the large number of different and sometimes conflicting demands that citizens place on their governments. The complexity of nature therefore poses a difficult problem of assignment of powers over the environment: at what level of government – global, national, regional, local – should the responsibility over the various environmental issues be placed? Are there governments at different jurisdictional levels that have a comparative advantage in dealing with long-term, spatially intertwined, uncertain or irreversible environmental issues? Through what mechanisms can coordination be achieved?

The interdependence between environmental media and systems would seem to dictate the necessity of a highly centralized regulatory structure for the protection of those different components. However, if costs of coordination between governments located at different jurisdictional levels are not excessive, decentralization could bring about benefits such as a more direct access to local information, recognition of heterogeneous local preferences and socio-economic conditions, as well as promotion of initiative and creativity on the part of the citizenry and sub-national governments. Moreover, a multi-layered governmental system has the power to unleash the forces of competition among its units, forces which allow these to adjust automatically, to a degree at least, to exogenous changes. This capacity to adjust is especially important for structures generating environmental policy processes that need to be adaptive and flexible to be able to respond to a continuing flow of new evidence and scientific information.

Several questions posed by the assignment of powers over the environment have been considered in the environmental federalism literature (well summarized in Oates and Portney, 2001), but largely ignored in conventional environmental economics. A number of other questions, essential to an understanding of the way policies are designed and implemented as well as to a discussion of how the policy process can be improved, have not yet received much attention. For example, the existing research on the division of powers over environmental issues in decentralized governmental structures is set in a framework that takes for granted that the relevant structure is federal.[1] What applies to federal states may not apply in the same way in decentralized unitary states: the theory of federalism and the theory of decentralization do not, indeed, fully coincide.[2] Furthermore, there now exists a governmental structure of growing importance on the international stage, namely the EU, which is neither a federal nor a unitary state. In that case also, the existing models dealing with environmental policy-making in federal countries cannot be mechanically applied.

In conventional economic, political science, and legal-constitutional approaches to the division of powers between jurisdictional tiers, the focus is often on the norms or criteria that should govern the assignment of powers: the degree of responsiveness to citizens' preferences of governments inhabiting different jurisdictional tiers, the capacity of differentially located governments to minimize the risks associated with innovating, the size and nature of interjurisdictional spillovers originating in consumption and production activities, and others. Such criteria point to the conclusion that assignments, once determined, tend to be permanent: the degree of responsiveness will always be higher the lower in the hierarchy a government is located, the size of spillovers will remain the same unless there are radical changes in technology and/or in the nature of the goods and services supplied by public bodies, and so on. For the same reasons, assignments would be essentially similar in countries that are more or less similarly decentralized.

In less conventional work, the attention is placed on the organizational costs associated with different assignments. Some of these costs, especially coordination costs, are a function of the size of spillovers, others are a function of the difficulty of eliciting information regarding the preferences of citizens.[3] Until recently that approach was based on the assumption that those who have the responsibility for assigning powers would act to make these costs as small as possible. Lately, models have been developed in which cost minimization is the result of vertical competition between levels of government. This literature tends to emphasize that assignments do change over time under the impact of changes in the relevant exogenous factors, in particular those affecting coordination costs, and that they will vary across countries.

Actual assignments of environmental powers do vary significantly across countries. One objective of our research has been to understand the nature of the variation, that is, how different countries actually define and address environmental issues with specific attention to intergovernmental relations: what institutions have been created, what assignment of powers have been chosen, what has been done when these assignments needed to be changed, what solutions have been tried and with what success. We also wanted to investigate whether a systemic view of the environment had percolated to the level of policy-making. The adopted perspective has been as broad as possible, with the inclusion of 16 countries in six continents and of the European Union, analysed by scholars from different disciplines – economics, political science, environmental science and law. The country studies have produced interesting material in respect of a number of issues that are not part of the conventional treatment of the environment and of decentralization, at least in the economics literature.

The chapters are assembled in two parts. Part I contains the studies on a set of federal countries plus that on the European Union. Part II brings together the studies on non-federal countries. In both instances, the selection reflects three basic criteria, the result being a compromise between our ambitions and what we were able to secure: identifying a sample of countries (i) covering all continents; (ii) reflecting socio-economic, political and environmental diversity; and (iii) characterized by some degree of decentralization.

The ultimate goal of our research programme is to explore how a systemic view of the environment – one that recognizes the need for policies aimed not only at controlling pollution and conserving a few charismatic species but at protecting the integrity of ecological systems and functions at local, regional, national and global levels – would affect the assignment of powers and the design of environmental institutions. The structure of the country studies reflects that goal. The areas of environmental policy studied include pollution control, ecosystem protection and natural resource management, highlighting innovative approaches, notable failures and major changes that make it possible to compare the effectiveness of different institutional arrangements or policy tools. The analyses concern the definition of environmental areas of responsibility, the institutional set-up at all governance levels (supranational, national, state/regional, local/municipal), the policy tools and the enforcement procedures – on paper and in practice.

Other matters which receive attention are the mechanisms introduced to deal with incomplete information, the use of scientific expertise in the policy process, the existence of integration between environmental and other economic (transport, energy, regional development, industrial, trade) policies, the use of complementary powers (for example a 'clean water' policy or regulation implemented through the fisheries power) or general powers (for example environmental policies put in place through broad powers such as criminal law powers, trade and commerce powers, and so on), the existence of powers that are not exercised (environmental legislation on the books that is not enforced). The above themes run across the various studies, although each one looks at environmental governance from an angle that reflects the specificity of national situations and the background of authors.

In Chapter 2, Jeffrey Petchey provides an analysis of how Australia is responding to the threats to native biodiversity and to the management of a limited water supply. To that effect, the chapter discusses the assignment of environmental powers with special emphasis on the centralist interpretation of the Constitution by the High Court of Australia. Petchey also underlines that in addressing environmental issues – in particular that of water supply – the approach adopted has been one of cooperation. The policies developed under the 'umbrella of cooperation' are monitored by the National Competition Council, a national body with the power (effectively used) to levy financial penalties for non-compliance. The chapter underlines the increasing role played by indigenous people in preserving biodiversity.

Conservation of its huge endowment of natural resources is not only a domestic issue for Brazil (Chapter 3). The international community is exerting increasing pressure on this country, in particular for the preservation of the Amazonian forests. Partly in response to this pressure, the federal parliament has introduced in the recent past progressive legislation that is based on a broad sustainability perspective and on a participative approach. The responsibility for its implementation falls mainly on state and local governments. A fairly complex network of consultative and executive bodies has been set up at every level of government to devise specific policies and to monitor their implementation. Results, however, are still unsatisfactory. According to Clóvis Cavalcanti, this is because the assignment of responsibilities is quite intricate, and society's commitment to environmental sustainability is partial. Extreme poverty still affects large segments of the population and many areas of the country. These factors weaken the capacity of the public sector as a whole to resist the pressures of powerful private lobbies that oppose more stringent environmental policies.

In Chapter 4, Marcia Valiante argues that environmental governance in Canada is the result of a complex and dynamic structure. Constitutional authority is divided between the federal and provincial governments, but international institutions, municipalities, Aboriginal peoples, industry and non-governmental groups play important roles (in some cases increasingly crucial ones) in shaping the direction of Canada's policies. Overlapping powers between orders of government and the consequent uncertainty result in delays and inaction. Valiante highlights that while coordination is necessary, it entails significant costs which slow down the policy-making process. The recent trend has been toward a greater decentralization. Implementation of environmental policies occurs primarily through traditional regulatory instruments at the provincial level. The command-and-control approach is gradually being supplemented by information-based schemes, economic instruments and voluntary initiatives. Valiante claims that whereas this system has achieved important reductions in industrial pollution, frustratingly little progress has been made in addressing more complex environmental challenges, such as meeting Kyoto protocol targets and moving toward sustainable development. Over the last decades, governmental activity on the environment has cyclically intensified and declined in response to changing levels of public concern.

In Ethiopia (Chapter 5), which has a federal constitution, the system of government is articulated into nine regional governments each having legislative, executive and judicial powers. The states are structured into a number of levels of local government. The implementation of constitutional mandates referring to sub-national governments has been slow, and only in 2003 were elections of local governments held. The Conservation Strategy of Ethiopia sets the framework for environmental policy. It intends to bring about sustainable management of natural resources in the context of development. The launch of the Conservation Strategy has been prompted, according to Gedion Asfaw, Sebsebe Demissew and Kifle Lemma Woldesemayat, by the recognition that most of the horrors of the 1984/85 famine were attributable to environmental mismanagement, which caused deterioration of natural resources and of the urban environment, and accelerated soil erosion and biodiversity loss. Ethiopia has also set up a system of environmental protection agencies operating at the different layers of government. The authors stress that while Ethiopia has introduced good policies and strategies both at the federal and at regional levels, the implementation of policies leaves a lot to be desired. Different priorities have prevailed and the pursuit of environmental goals has been displaced by events such as external wars.

The European Union is the most macroscopic example in history of transfers of competencies – *inter alia*, in environmental matters – to a supranational entity. Given its power to impose direct obligations to individuals and firms, it shares significant features with federal systems. Anthony Zito (Chapter 6) provides an analytical overview of the European Union's environmental policy process, addressing a number of governance components: institutional structure and policy style, the content of the European Community legislation, and the instruments used to implement legislation.

Although the EU, over the last three decades, has developed an extensive array of legislation across a number of environmental areas, implementation and other governance problems present significant challenges for the future. The European Community decision-making processes have to accommodate a number of tensions inherent in the complex array of positions and institutions present. The Commission shares executive functions, that is policy leadership, with the Council of Ministers, and implementation with the member states. This, added to the sharing of the traditional legislative functions of ratification and accountability between the European Parliament and the Council of Ministers, creates a complex political system, which makes forming decisional consensus difficult. The EU leaders have agreed on a draft of a New Constitutional Treaty that changes some institutional elements in the direction of amalgamating the three pillars, but it is not clear yet whether all the member states will ratify the Treaty and, if so, how this will reflect on environmental governance. The dissimilarity of views across member states is obviously a powerful hindering factor in the creation of new common institutions; an important example is the 1993 outcome of the argument over the European Environment Agency's functions and location, which produced an organization charged mainly with systematizing and providing environmental information – a far more limited role than the one the original proponents hoped for, and the one, for example, of the United States' EPA.

Germany has been widely considered, during the 1970s and 1980s, an international leader in environmental policy. Its predominant command-and-control approach based on the 'best available technology' has succeeded in achieving significant improvements in environmental quality, particularly with respect to emissions from major point sources. The country continues to be a leader in international environmental cooperation and an exporter of environmental technology. Stefanie Engel and Melanie Zimmermann, in Chapter 7, analyse the factors driving these successes – the visibility of several environmental problems, a high degree of public and consumer environmental awareness, the organized nature of environmental interests and their direct voice in politics thanks to the possibility of small parties (like the Green Party) entering into parliament at all political levels. Germany's leading role in the EU, particularly in pushing for harmonization measures, can also be explained by the country's export-dependant economy and its high ecological vulnerability due to its geographic position. Recently, however, the country is falling behind in the implementation of EU measures. The traditional command-and-control approach is increasingly showing its limits, in terms both of costs and of effectiveness, and the formal objective of sustainable development has not yet found its way into a real national strategy. A cross-sectoral and cross-media approach is made difficult by the prevailing asymmetry in environmental policy competences between the federal government and the states, and by the distribution of environmental policy responsibilities between several federal ministries. Vertical and horizontal policy coordination is hampered by conflicts among and between federal and Länder authorities within the decentralized system, and the bicameral system tends to favour more incremental policy evolution over major policy change.

In Chapter 8, Subrata Mandal and Govinda Rao focus on the assignment of powers and on implementation in regard to water, air and forests in India. The analysis is not restricted to the division of powers among different levels of government, but addresses also that between the executive and the judiciary. On this last issue, the authors argue that judicial intervention in environmental matters can be construed as part of the checks and balances characteristic of federal arrangements if it does not become a substitute for a failure of the executive to act. Mandal and Rao insist that even if in the short-term decisions of the Courts are beneficial, their effects in the longer run are not known and are just as likely to be negative as positive. Indeed, the authors' judgement is that the last outcome is the most likely. The authors then make the point that despite a reasonably clear division of powers the implementation of environmental policies has not been very satisfactory. Two factors are at play: one, the incentives facing policy-makers and bureaucrats cause them to be susceptible to the influence of polluters; the other, the lack of adequate resources and of modern technology to measure pollution levels.

Ineffectiveness of environmental governance also characterizes the Russian federation (Chapter 9). The legacy inherited from the Soviet Union is difficult to overcome. Environmental degradation characterizes large areas of the country, and the transition to a rule-based system is slow and painful. In recent years the Russian parliament has passed a number of sector laws aimed at bringing the legal framework on environmental governance up to the standards prevailing in industrial democracies. The assignment of tasks between layers of government is broadly in line with that prevailing in developed countries, where standards and broad policies are determined at the central level, while regions are responsible for detailed regulations and implementation of legislation. However, according to the authors, Pavel Kasyanov and Aliona Stovpivskaya, many weaknesses exist. Discrepancies between federal and regional legislation and regulations are frequent. The federal government has resisted devolution of tasks to the regions, but is not capable of controlling them. Lack of clarity permeates the assignment of responsibilities for the implementation of legislation, and monitoring is ineffectual. These weaknesses are exploited by powerful private economic groups active in sectors, such as the oil sector, that are crucial for environmental governance. The authors also decry the reliance on command-and-control instruments at the expense of economic ones.

The core element in the United States' environmental and natural resource policy is the role of the federal government in setting national pollution standards that are to be implemented at the state level. The on-going challenge is to find the appropriate way to share authority in the design and implementation of policy across levels of government – to find an effective balance between centralized policies that address national health concerns versus decentralized polices that address local physical and social conditions. In Chapter 10, Jason Shogren first presents an overview of the political economy of environmental policy in the United States over the last three decades, discussing the federalist institutional framework used to create and implement environmental policy and the major federal environmental regulations. He then considers in detail three policy tools used in the US – citizen suits, collaboration, and market-based instruments. Finally, he explores several on-going debates over environmental policy in the US, including clean air, climate change, Superfund, endangered species protection, and children's health. It appears that many environmental policy innovations come from the bottom-up regulatory approaches of the states, and officials of state governments constantly demand greater authority in environmental policy-making, especially for those regulations initially designed to be implemented at the federal level which in several cases (for example, endangered species, Superfund) show a relatively poor record of performance.

The next eight chapters in Part II of the volume deal with non-federal states. Chile is not only a unitary state, it is also still a very centralized one. As in other South American countries, the burden of the recent dictatorial experience on governmental institutions is still clearly apparent. With the return to democratic government in 1990, an Environmental Framework Law was introduced. The law assigns most responsibilities concerning the environment to the central government. A specialized body has been set up to prepare legislation, to promote implementation and to coordinate actions of the various stakeholders. Municipalities, the core of decentralized government, have minor responsibilities in regard to environmental issues. While the framework law assigns most of the monitoring tasks to municipalities, deconcentrated bodies created by sector ministries have supplanted the former. Fostering of popular participation has been practically abandoned, despite initial claims. Although democratic governments have shown some activism on the environment, an increasing pessimism is emerging in the society about the capacity and the willingness of government to solve environmental issues. In Chapter 11, Tommaso Chiamparino, Laura Piazza and Irene Venturello note that the legislation is new and the implementation instruments are recent, making their evaluation difficult. A notable aspect of the chapter is the analysis of the impact of international trade agreements – particularly, the agreement between Chile and Canada – on the implementation of domestic norms and the activation of policies.

China is undergoing a process of government decentralization and of reforms in environmental governance. Changhua Wu and Hua Wang, in Chapter 12, argue that on the one hand environmental quality, despite improvements in some parts of the country, has been continuously deteriorating with the progress of decentralization. On the other hand those reforms have indeed brought fundamental changes in environmental policy, for example by strengthening local administrations responsible for environmental protection. The international dimension and the increasing degree of openness of the Chinese economy have an impact on environmental policy not only through the ratification of environmental multilateral agreements but also through specific environmental legislation or regulation developed in relation to import or export activities. In the face of increasing tension between the development and the environmental agendas, the reforms carried out so far do not seem to provide adequate cross-sectoral and inter-jurisdictional coordination mechanisms. Wu and Wang argue that increasing the decentralization could help address this issue, as well as the problem of the conflicting mandates of some specialized agencies. They also call for enhanced public participation.

In Chapter 13, Mikael Skou Andersen remarks that even if Denmark is a unitary state, the economic independence of municipalities is revealed in their power to levy income and property taxes and in their responsibility, in environmental matters, for sewage treatment and waste disposal. If there is a perception of a persistent deficit in municipal environmental management, it is not only due to the globalization of environmental issues, Andersen argues, but is also a consequence of the inability of municipalities to regulate polluters. Despite the introduction in the 1990s of a policy giving the centre the power to levy environmental taxes and to grant subsidies, the municipalities continue to play a central role in environmental management. The author imputes this fact to a general consensus in Denmark regarding decentralization. The preponderant 'municipalization of environmental administration' exacerbates three problems: that of scale, related to the inadequate size of some local administrations relative to technical requirements; that of subsidization, which leads to the support of local enterprises rather than to a focus on compliance with regulation; and that of capacity, which refers to a lack of expertise to deal with technically complex environmental issues.

In Chapter 14, Albert Breton and Pierre Salmon emphasize that in France, the present balance between centralization and decentralization is the result of permanent structural features of the French governmental system on the one hand, and of recent developments in that system and in environmental concerns and priorities on the other. The authors make the point that the capacity of the central government to adapt to spatial heterogeneity applies to all policy areas, but is particularly pertinent in the case of environmental policies. Breton and Salmon go on to argue that the decentralization instituted in the early 1980s enhanced the responsibilities, authority and ambitions of sub-central governments, so that many tasks can now be undertaken by these governments and not only by the central government.

Breton and Salmon then turn their attention to the demand for environmental policy. They note that if populations are still concerned with the effects of pollution and industrial hazards on their health and safety, scientific information has persuaded them that some negative consequences of human activities are now more global than local. In other words, in regard to some important substances, populations know that what counts is their aggregate emissions, possibly at the world level, but certainly at the national level. The important role played by the directives from the European Union and by international commitments in shaping demand is underlined. A last influence on demand, which the authors mention, is the growing awareness by populations of the importance of the preservation of nature, landscape and biodiversity. The authors then argue that changes in supply and demand have sometimes circumscribed the role of the central government and enhanced that of sub-national governments.

Felix Ankomah Asante (Chapter 15) focuses on the capacity and constraints of local governments in implementing environmental policies in Ghana. The structural changes needed to enable the local level of government to deal with increasingly severe environmental problems – deforestation, biodiversity loss, soil erosion and land degradation due to overgrazing and inappropriate agricultural practices, pollution and waste disposal – require involving a wider range of organizations and decentralizing authority and responsibility. The efforts at decentralization that started to materialize around the mid-1970s succeeded in strengthening the regions, but largely failed to produce an effective transfer of power to lower tiers of government. The functions which were transferred to the District Councils were not accompanied by a simultaneous transfer of competences and means required for effective decentralization. There have been attempts to involve community groups and non-governmental organizations in the environmental policy process, but as yet the impact of these efforts remains limited.

Environmental policy in Italy has had a late start. However, the last 15 years have seen a dramatic improvement of the legal framework, mainly prompted by the need to comply with European Union requirements. In fact, the EU acts as a stimulus compensating for the relative weakness of the priority given to environmental issues in the agendas of the various political parties and of the pressure exerted by public opinion. Italy is a regional state undergoing a process of quasi federalization. While many competences over the environment have been shifted to regional and local governments, the central government retains a number of regulatory responsibilities as well as coordination and control powers. In spite of these reforms, however, the assignment of powers and the legislative framework remain unclear and fragmented. The establishment of a system of environmental agencies has caused a noticeable progress in monitoring and reporting, but implementation and enforcement are still weak. Moreover, the effectiveness of environmental governance suffers from persistent regional disparities and limited coordination among administrations. Various forms of contractual agreements between administrations and among public agencies and private entities are emerging as a response to the latter problem. The environmental policy toolbox is also evolving, with voluntary approaches playing an increasing role. Ivana Capozza and Giovanna Garrone (Chapter 16) argue that behind the relative success of voluntary and participatory instruments there is often a more or less direct form of public subsidy. Indeed, the command-and-control approach still prevails. A few economic taxes and charges are used, but they are usually not intended as environmental measures and are not designed in a way as to induce behavioural changes.

The Netherlands (Chapter 17) have a reputation of being one of the more progressive states in Europe when it comes to environmental policy. Traditionally, this country has had to face huge environmental challenges. It is a small, very densely populated country, with large industries. It is also, despite its tiny size, the third largest exporter of agricultural products in the world. Consistent with these peculiarities, the chapter focuses on industry-related pollution control, agricultural pollution control, and water management.

The 1990s witnessed increased governmental activism in environmental governance. Three main trends can be observed. The first is a trend to move from top-down regulation, where the regulated parties are merely passive subjects, to a more inclusive, cooperative 'governance' system, where stakeholders take part in designing the regulation. Voluntary agreements have been a main ingredient of this shift. The second trend consists in the move from compartmentalization and differentiation to integration (multi-sector). The third one is towards multi-level governance, notably the growing role of the EU, combined with a certain shift of responsibilities from the national towards the regional and local levels (multi-level). In some areas, such as ecosystem protection, water, and rural and spatial planning, either decentralization or Europeanization appears to have resulted in a certain degree of erosion of state-level powers.

An interesting feature of the chapter concerns the impact of EU policies on the effectiveness of domestic policy. Duncan Liefferink and Mark Wiering maintain that in some cases, such as the Water Framework Directive, the EU has clearly stimulated and supported domestic developments. Other EU policies, for instance the Packaging, Habitats and Nitrates Directives, have somewhat negatively interfered with Dutch policies and to some extent even frustrated novel, integrative approaches.

The authors also attempt to evaluate the impact of observed policy changes on the quality of the environment. It appears that the emissions of several major pollutants have decreased in absolute terms over the past few decades. Thus, a decoupling of economic growth and environmental pressure seems to have taken place. According to the authors, this is largely due to the increasing involvement of target groups in environmental policy-making, a dominant feature of Dutch political culture which has also led to successful cases of voluntary approaches and public–private agreements.

The UK is a highly centralized political system, in which the central government has substantial decisive power. Territorial decentralization (with the exception of the recent devolution in Scotland and Wales) is very limited, with no democratically elected regional level of government, and a system of local governments under tight central control. In the analysis of Stephen Smith (Chapter 18), the increasing significance of the international level of government (international agreements and the EU) in most areas of policy appears to be the only marked general trend in terms of changes in the assignment of environmental powers. There has probably been, however, some general tendency for further centralization of land use and planning decisions, especially through appeals against local authority decisions.

Privatization of the water industry has led to the creation of a separate water regulator, a form of functional decentralization to a specialized regulatory agency. Indeed, a distinctive feature of the UK over the past 20 years has been the move towards specialized agencies created by the central government, and away from direct implementation of policy by central government departments themselves. This has been accompanied, in recent years, by a significant shift in the style of UK environmental policy, away from case-by-case negotiation of pollution consents between the regulator and individual enterprises, towards a more rule-based regulatory approach. Most of the initiatives towards 'modernization' of regulatory approaches and the adoption of a limited number of incentive-based regulatory mechanisms have come from the central government.

The last chapter provides a synthesis on the current trends in the development of governance structures for environmental protection, which draws heavily on the evidence from the 17 countries included in our sample. It focuses on aspects identified as fundamental in describing how environmental governance is unfolding, globally, in the twenty-first century: the widespread shift from command-and-control policy tools towards both voluntary approaches and market-based instruments, the role played by contractual agreements between administrations as instruments in ordering intergovernmental relations in environmental policy, the worldwide trend towards privatizations in the provision of environmental services such as water distribution, sewage and waste disposal, the diffusion of Environmental Protection Agencies, the role played by the judiciary in a number of countries as a major environmental player, the allocation of enactment and enforcement powers between different levels of government, the role of indigenous people and local communities in environmental management. It also tries to ascertain the ground actually gained by a sustainability approach aiming at a growing integration of environmental policy-making with other policy sectors.

NOTES

1. See, for example, Butler and Macey (1996), Revesz (1992, 1996), Ulph (1998) and Scott (2000).

2. That literature is reviewed and referenced in Breton (1996), Breton et al. (1998), Brosio (1994), Litvack et al. (1998) and Oates (1999).
3. See Breton and Scott (1978) and Inman and Rubinfeld (1997).

REFERENCES

Breton, Albert (1996), *Competitive Governments. An Economic Theory of Politics and Public Finance*, New York: Cambridge University Press.

Breton, Albert and Anthony Scott (1978), *The Economic Constitution of Federal States*, Toronto: University of Toronto Press.

Breton, Albert, Alberto Cassone and Angela Fraschini (1998), 'Decentralization and subsidiarity: Toward a theoretical reconciliation', *University of Pennsylvania Journal of International Economic Law*, **19**(1), Spring, 21–51.

Brosio, Giorgio (1994), *Equilibri instabili. Politica ed economia nell'evoluzione dei sistemi federali*, Turin: Bollati Boringhieri.

Butler, Henry N. and Jonathan R. Macey (1996), *Using Federalism to Improve Environmental Policy*, Washington DC: American Enterprise Institute.

Inman, Robert P. and Daniel L. Rubinfeld (1997), 'The political economy of federalism', in Dennis C. Mueller (ed.), *Perspectives on Public Choice*, New York: Cambridge University Press, pp. 73–105.

Litvack, Jennie, Junaid Ahmad and Richard Bird (1998), *Rethinking Decentralization in Developing Countries*, Washington DC: World Bank.

Oates, Wallace E. (1999), 'An essay on fiscal federalism', *Journal of Economic Literature*, **37**(3), September, 1120–49.

Oates, Wallace E. and Paul R. Portney (2001), 'The political economy of environmental policy', Discussion Paper 01-55, November, *Resources for the Future*, http://www.rff.org.

Revesz, Richard L. (1992), 'Rehabilitating interstate competition: Rethinking the "race-to-the-bottom" rationale for federal environmental regulation', *New York University Law Review*, **67**(4), October, 1210–54.

Revesz, Richard L. (1996), 'Federalism and interstate environmental externalities', *University of Pennsylvania Law Review*, **144**(6), June, 2341–416.

Scott, Anthony D. (2000), 'Assigning powers over the Canadian environment', in Gianluigi Galeotti, Pierre Salmon and Ronald Wintrobe (eds), *Competition and Structure. The Political Economy of Collective Decisions: Essays in Honor of Albert Breton*, New York: Cambridge University Press, pp. 174–219.

Ulph, Alistair (1998), 'Political institutions and the design of environmental policy in a federal system with asymmetric information', paper presented at the *European Economic Association* Meeting, August–September.

PART I

Federal and supranational systems

2. Australia: Preserving biodiversity and managing water resources

Jeffrey D. Petchey

1. INTRODUCTION

Australia is a vast, dry continent with a fragile ecology. European settlement, with the associated farming and economic practices, is only two hundred years old, yet the landscape has changed beyond recognition from the one which greeted the first Europeans. Much of this change has been for the worse. Australia now faces environmental challenges, mainly to do with threats to biodiversity (for example the threatened extinction of many endangered native species) and management of a limited water supply in the face of a growing population, partly due to continued immigration.

The aim of this chapter is to provide a selective analysis of how Australia is responding to these challenges and to draw out implications for environmental policy in regional unions of States such as the European Union (EU). The outline is as follows. Section 2 provides an overview of the assignment of environmental policy, constitutionally, and in practice. The discussion here examines trends in centralisation and inter-governmental cooperation. It also examines why Australia has adopted a cooperative approach to environmental issues. Section 3 examines international assessment of Australia's environmental performance using the Environmental Sustainability Index (ESI) published by the Yale Centre for Environmental Law. Here the conclusions are that Australia scores very highly overall on environmental issues, certainly much higher than major European countries such as France, Germany, the UK and Italy, but has a particular problem with biodiversity and water supply. These results are well known in Australia and have been the focus of environmental policy over the last decade. For these reasons, section 4 provides a detailed examination of current policies developed to address problems of biodiversity and water supply. It is noted that indigenous people play an increasing role in preserving biodiversity through joint management of some of Australia's largest and ecologically most significant national parks (for example the well known World Heritage listed Kakadu national park).

Section 5 summarises the key features of Australia's cooperative policy approach and asks whether this model could be transferred to regional unions such as the EU. Generally, the answer reached is no, principally because the EU does not have a strong central authority with the ability to impose effective financial penalties for non-compliance. Conclusions are presented in section 6.

2. ASSIGNMENT

Since federation in 1901 Australia has become a prosperous democratic federation with three features that distinguish its fiscal arrangements: (i) State financial dependence because of highly centralised tax powers combined with relative decentralised expenditure powers; (ii) a High Court which has favoured centralist interpretations of the Constitution; and (iii) an emphasis on inter-State equity through a comprehensive equalisation scheme that measures both expenditure and revenue disabilities. The 104 years since federation in 1901 has seen the national government (known from now on as the Commonwealth) use its financial powers, supported by centralist Constitutional interpretations by the High Court, to increase greatly central control of most areas of public policy. This zero sum inter-governmental game has weakened the power of the States to the point where some question whether Australia needs States at all.[1]

2.1 Centralisation

Being part of these broader trends, environmental policy became increasingly centralised, at least up until the early 1990s. This is despite the fact that management of environmental assets is constitutionally a State responsibility. However, the Commonwealth has been able to intervene increasingly in State policy-making using three of its constitutional powers. First, Section 51 (xxix) of the Constitution gives the Commonwealth the power to legislate to enact international agreements binding on Australia (for example the Commonwealth has the power to nominate land for World Heritage status; see Box 2.1 for a list of the major international agreements to which Australia is a signatory). The Constitution also gives the Commonwealth exclusive power over commerce and trade policy, as well as over policy directed towards corporations (for example taxation and regulation of corporations is an exclusive Commonwealth power). Finally, Section 109 of the Constitution says that State legislation not consistent with Commonwealth legislation is invalid. Thus, where there is a conflict between Commonwealth and State laws, the Commonwealth law overrides the State law.

BOX 2.1 AUSTRALIA'S MAJOR INTERNATIONAL AGREEMENTS

Australia is a signatory or party to international agreements on the environment including the following:

- Agreement on the Conservation of Albatrosses and Petrels, 2001.
- Basel Convention on the Control of Trans-boundary Movements of Hazardous Wastes and their Disposal, 1989.
- Convention on Biological Diversity, 1992.
- Convention on International Trade in Endangered Species of Wild Fauna and Flora, 1972.
- Convention on the Conservation of Migratory Species of Wild Animals, 1979.
- Kyoto Protocol.
- Montreal Protocol for the Ozone Layer, 1987.
- Rotterdam Convention on the Prior Informed Consent Procedure for Certain Hazardous Chemicals and Pesticides in International Trade, 1998.
- Stockholm Convention on Persistent Organic Pollutants, 2001.
- UN Convention to Combat Desertification, 1994.
- UN Convention on Climate Change, 1992.

In addition, Australia is a signatory or party to major treaties on the law of the sea (e.g: UN Convention on the Law of the Sea, 1982), and treaties relating to the Antarctic (e.g. Antarctic marine resources – such as seals) as well as pollution at sea. Such agreements impinge in general and specific ways on domestic policy for ecosystem protection, resource management and pollution control.

The implication is that the Commonwealth has, to a substantial degree, been able to use the Constitution to centralise power over environmental policy. For example, it has (increasingly) signed international agreements on the environment and then used the obligations created under such agreements as a pretext to make national policies that override State policy (using Sections 51 (xxix) and 109). An example here is the so-called Franklin Dam issue. In this case, during the early 1980s the State of Tasmania wanted to build a dam across the Franklin River, an ecologically significant river system in a pristine forest with high environmental value. The resulting protests and outcry from environmentalists stimulated a reaction from the Commonwealth: though it could not intervene directly, it ultimately used its foreign affairs power to stop the project (with compensating side payments to Tasmania).

This case was a watershed. People increasingly realised that Commonwealth intervention using its Constitutional powers (for example foreign affairs) was ad hoc, produced tension between the States and the Commonwealth and created confusion over the assignment of powers with consequent uncertainty for investment in environmentally sensitive resource projects. These problems in turn had adverse economic implications (for example for mineral exploration). Given the importance of resource exports to the Australian economy, this became a serious issue.

Thus, unlike other countries included in this study (for example Canada), if the Commonwealth becomes a signatory to international treaties that affect State responsibilities, it has the Constitutional power to force the States to comply with the obligations created through the international agreements. In addition, as noted above, the Commonwealth has substantial financial powers and it is able to use these powers to ensure compliance by the States.

2.2 Cooperation

Concerns over the adverse economic impacts of growing central intervention led to the adoption of a more cooperative approach to environmental policy through a new body set up specifically to foster 'cooperative federalism'. This body, the Council of Australian Governments (COAG), was given a major role in the development and implementation of environmental policy. There have been at least two important environmental initiatives undertaken through COAG since the early 1990s. The first was an agreement, signed by the Commonwealth and the States, that set out, among other things, a formal assignment of environmental powers between the two levels of government. It seems that this was designed to reduce uncertainty over the division of powers and to minimise the chances of another Franklin Dam fiasco, thus making up for the lack of any explicit assignment in the Constitution. The second initiative of significance was the signing of an agreement on water reform. Each is briefly outlined below.

COAG's first major initiative was to implement the Intergovernmental Agreement on the Environment (IAGE) in May 1992. Voluntarily agreed to by all States, Territories, the Commonwealth and local governments (though the latter have limited or no power over environmental issues), the aims of the IAGE are to:

- Provide the basis for inter-governmental cooperation on the environment.
- Identify the *responsibilities* of each level of government. For example:
  - The Commonwealth was made responsible for ensuring that international agreements are met, cross-border externality issues, maritime areas within Australia's jurisdiction, developing national environmental standards.
  - The States were made responsible for anything that does not impinge on Commonwealth responsibilities and where there are no inter-State externalities, living and non-living natural resources, and participation in the development of national standards.
- Devise principles to guide environmental policy, including:
  - Ecologically sustainable development.
  - Integration of environmental considerations into public policy.
  - Precautionary principle.
  - Inter-generational equity.
  - Retention of biological diversity and ecological integrity.
  - Better valuation, pricing and evaluation mechanisms (for example, polluter pays and user pays for provision of services using natural resources).

The environmental principles are to apply to:

- Land use decisions, approval processes for resource projects.
- Environmental impact assessments.
- Measures to address climate change.

The IAGE also established a National Environmental Protection Council (NEPC) whose powers are limited to developing National Environmental Protection Measures (NEPMs), setting uniform standards which requires a two-thirds majority of Council members (States and the Commonwealth each have one representative – the Environment Minister in each case – and one vote).

The NEPC does not have the power of a federal environmental protection agency and is only a cooperative body. For example, NEPMs can only be adopted with a two-thirds majority vote. The intention is that States would enact legislation to implement the NEPMs within their jurisdiction. The NEPMs would also apply to Commonwealth activities within each State.

In practice, the adoption of NEPMs by the States has been variable and more limited than originally intended. For example, Western Australia has continually argued against uniform standards which do not take account of different inter-State production technologies (for example, due to different resource endowments), population densities, preferences and so on. So, although States signed the IAGE, in practice they have disliked the uniform standards implied by implementing NEPMs, and this has limited their compliance with the spirit of the agreement. States that have enacted enabling legislation to implement NEPMs have often adopted different standards. In its own enabling legislation the Commonwealth has been forced to adopt these different standards in different States.

In June 2001, the NEPC was reconstituted as the Environmental Protection and Heritage Council (EPHC) with more emphasis on monitoring and inclusion of heritage issues. Responsibilities of the EPHC include:

- Environmental protection.
- Heritage (natural, historical and indigenous).
- Air, water and soil quality.
- NEPMs implemented by COAG.
- Environmental performance of industry.
- Hazardous wastes.
- Environmental indicators and monitoring.
- Data on releases of chemicals and wastes.
- International aspects of environmental protection.
- Development of policy tools for the above.
- Natural and cultural heritage.

NEPMs have been made for the following:

- Ambient air quality.
- Diesel emissions (discussed in section 4).
- Site contamination.
- Used packaging materials.
- Movement of wastes.
- National Pollution Inventory.

NEPMs currently under development (2003) include:

- Ambient air quality particle standards.
- Ambient air toxins.

Each State has also agreed to produce reports on how these NEPMs are being implemented within their jurisdictions, on an annual basis, but there is no enforcement. Reports are publicly available but the process still relies on State voluntary reporting of compliance with NEPMs.

Another major initiative of COAG on environmental matters is the Water Reform Agreement of 1994. The aim of the Agreement is to improve the efficiency of Australia's water supply and waste-water industries and create sustainable water management practices that take account of all water users' needs, including those of the environment.[2]

Interestingly, progress towards the goals set out by COAG (and subsequently modified and expanded through the years through additional policies such as the National Water Initiative of 2003, is monitored by the National Competition Council (NCC), a body set up specifically to assess governments' progress on a range of reform obligations created through COAG (not just environmental issues). Through this process, progress on reform is linked to so-called National Competition Policy (NCP) Payments made by the Commonwealth to the States to 'reward' State compliance with COAG reform obligations. Withholding these payments also acts as a 'stick' with which to punish States for non-compliance. This is an effective tool to use in Australia given the reliance of the States on Commonwealth funding (as discussed previously). More detail is provided on the Water Reform Agreement in section 4.

Since the IAGE set out inter-governmental responsibilities, the Commonwealth has subsequently pursued its own policy in areas assigned to it by the Agreement. An excellent example of such policy is the recent introduction by the Commonwealth of legislation designed to address national biodiversity and ecological issues. These policies are discussed in section 4.

In summary, the issue of assignment has been reasonably well settled in Australia through the IAGE. This has allowed a clear role for the Commonwealth in areas where there is a national interest (that is inter-State externalities) and the Commonwealth is able to act independently. It has also given clear roles to the States in areas of specific State interests only (that is no inter-State externalities), and has facilitated cooperative action in areas where the levels of government have joint interests. Interestingly, such an assignment is in line with what one might expect from basic fiscal federalism principles.

2.3 The Assignment of Particular Policies

The current assignment of particular environmental policies in the fields of ecosystem production, resource management and pollution is summarised in Table 2.1. One can see from the table the separate roles of the States, for example in managing national parks, and the shared or cooperative roles with regard to the Environment Protection and Biodiversity Conservation (EPBC) Act and forest policy.

Table 2.1 Environmental responsibilities of each level of government[a]

Field		Resource management		Pollution control
	(1) Ecosystem Protection	(2) Forests	(3) Water	(4) Air
Level				
1. National	(i) EPBC Act: (biodiversity) (ii) Joint management of large parks (e.g. Kakadu) with indigenous owners	(i) Forest Policy Statement (ii) RFAs (iii) LandCare	(i) Water Reform Agreement	(i) National fuel quality standards
2. State/ Territory	(i) State EPAs conduct impact studies for development project (e.g. marine resorts, mining) and act as agents for the EPBC Act	(i) Parks (ii) Policy for forests outside of parks (iii) Forest Policy Statement (iv) RFAs	(i) Water Reform Agreement (ii) Water provision (households, firms and agriculture) (iii) Waste water	(i) Air pollution standards for industry, fines, fees (ii) Monitoring of air quality standards
3. Regional	NA	(i) RFAs	(i) Murray–Darling Basin Commission	NA
4. Local	(i) Land use zoning laws (ii) Waste management	(i) Local reserves	NA	NA

Note: [a] Australia is also a signatory to many international agreements (see Box 2.1).

Under field 1 – ecosystem protection – the main national policy is the previously mentioned EPBC Act. The States also have a key role in ecosystem protection through the State Environment Protection Authorities (EPAs) established under State legislation with widespread environmental policy, implementation and enforcement powers. One of the major functions of the EPAs is to assess the environmental implications of major development projects. Indeed, State approval for many such projects is contingent on advice from the relevant EPA. In addition, State EPAs play a role in the EPBC Act, mainly as agents for the Commonwealth (see later discussion). Local governments have a role to play in ecosystem protection in the sense that they are responsible for land zoning (for example residential, agricultural), waste management (for example rubbish removal from homes and processing of the rubbish) and management of local reserves.

In relation to field 2 – forests – the Forest Policy Statement, an intergovernmental agreement signed under the auspices of COAG in 1992, sets the overall background for policy on forests in Australia. In more recent years Regional Forest Agreements (RFAs) have also been developed. These are 20-year plans for the conservation of native forests within parks and reserves, and the sustainable management of forests outside of the parks and reserves. Criticism of the RFAs has come from environmental groups for not setting aside enough old growth forests in parks, while industry groups claim the opposite, that too much forest has been locked away. Nevertheless, the RFAs are based on the results of years of scientific research by bodies such as the prestigious Commonwealth Science and Industrial Research Organisation (CSIRO). Given the predictable reaction of stakeholder groups, the balance struck is probably reasonable.[3] So far, RFAs have been signed between the Commonwealth and four States, Western Australia, Victoria, Tasmania and New South Wales. One of the commitments made under the agreements is to preserve in parks 15 per cent of the native forest that existed at the time of European arrival in Australia. This commitment exceeds targets for forest retention established under international conventions by a considerable amount. Finally, the LandCare programme, funded by the Commonwealth, has provided extensive funding for reforestation on private and public lands. It relies on tree planting on a large scale by voluntary local community groups.[4]

For field 3 – water – most of Australia's water policy over the last decade has been developed under the umbrella of the Water Reform Agreement signed by all States through COAG. This Agreement is discussed in considerable depth later on in the chapter. The State too has a strong role to play under this agreement as well as direct responsibility for water provision (through State public utilities) and waste water management. Water policy is also developed and implemented at a regional level where river catchments cross a number of State boundaries. The best example here is the Murray–Darling Basin Commission.

Finally, air pollution policy is developed at State and national levels. For example, the Commonwealth has recently introduced national standards for fuel (including diesel) which will indirectly have an effect on air quality. States also have responsibility for air pollution standards, mainly for industry. The States also have a regime of taxes and fines for violation of air quality standards (for example for factory pollution).

2.4 Why Cooperation?

Discovering what has driven policy-makers to arrive at such an assignment, and in particular cooperative arrangements, is a separate project in itself and beyond the scope of this chapter. However, one can say that since the 1970s voters have demanded more action by governments to fix environmental problems, as the environment has come under greater stress because of population and economic growth. These demands have been reflected at local, State and national levels with the rise of 'green' parties and the so-called 'green vote'. States have responded to these demands in areas under their own control: for example, it was during the 1980s that most States created the EPAs with powers to assess industrial and general development proposals.

As already noted, the Commonwealth also responded to voter pressures, but since the States have most of the responsibilities for environmental policy-making it could only respond to these pressures through ad hoc intervention at the State level, mostly through the use of its Constitutional powers. The Commonwealth has also shown a willingness to use its financial hold over the States, at times refusing to provide grants if States do not act according to its wishes, and at other times offering financial incentives. Eventually this approach became counter-productive because of its economic consequences, and this has led both the Commonwealth and States to realise that inter-governmental cooperation is a more reasonable approach.

The standard problems with coordination, namely coordination costs, problems associated with monitoring and compliance, have not really been seen in Australia. This is because the number of States is small (limiting coordination costs and the possibilities for sub-coalitions of break-away States forming), there is a separate national body (the National Competition Council (NCC)) with extensive and clear powers relating to information gathering and monitoring, and because the Commonwealth has the financial powers to ensure compliance (carrots and sticks). In addition, the national body set up to facilitate coordination, COAG, has also proved to be an effective body, generally well supported by all participating governments.

3. PERFORMANCE ASSESSMENT

Research by international groups/agencies provides some evidence of relative success/failure of Australian environmental policy, though it is impossible to draw any conclusions from such work about the success of specific policies, such as those to be discussed below. The Environmental Sustainability Index

(ESI) constructed by the Yale Centre for Environmental Law provides an interesting assessment of Australia's environmental performance relative to its peers, namely, developed economies with incomes greater than US$14 171.

At the most aggregate level, the ESI for 2002 ranked Australia 16th of 142 countries.[5] The only countries ranked ahead of Australia were: Finland (1), Norway (2), Sweden (3), Canada (4), Switzerland (5), Uruguay (6), Austria (7), Iceland (8), Costa Rica (9), Latvia (10), Hungary (11), Croatia (12), Botswana (13), Slovakia (14) and Argentina (15). Only six of these countries would be classed as high income (peer group) countries. This puts Australia well ahead of other high income countries such as France (33), USA (45), Germany (50), Japan (78), Italy (84) and the UK (91). At an aggregate level this provides qualified evidence that Australia is performing relatively well in environmental policy and outcomes.

Table 2.2 provides more detailed information on Australia's performance on each of the underlying indicators used to construct the aggregate ESI index, relative to the average score for all countries in Australia's peer group. Specifically, column 2 shows Australia's standardised Z-score for each indicator, while column 3 shows the average for all countries in the peer group for the variables that make up the particular indicator. A higher score represents higher levels of relative performance.

The indicators for which Australia scores a significantly higher value than its peer group include, air quality, land, reducing water stress, reducing ecosystem stress, science and technology and capacity for debate. The apparent success in reducing water stress relates to relatively good outcomes in the following areas:

- Fertilizer consumption per capita and industrial water pollutants.
- Pesticide use and percentage of the country under water stress.

The relative success in reducing ecosystem stress results from good performance in the following fields:

- Changes in forest cover since 1990–95.
- Percentage of country with acidification exceedence.

Indicators for which Australia scores relatively poor results include:

- Water quantity and quality.
- Biodiversity.
- Reducing air pollution.
- Governance.

Table 2.2 Australia's ESI performance relative to its peers

Indicators	Value for Australia	Average value for peer group
Air quality	1.41	0.68
Water quantity	−0.44	−0.17
Water quality	0.33	0.58
Biodiversity	−0.73	−0.44
Land	1.50	−0.58
Reducing air pollution	−1.22	−0.98
Reducing water stress	0.38	−0.61
Reducing ecosystem stress	0.26	−0.13
Reducing waste and consumption pressures	−0.92	−1.19
Reducing population growth	0.71	0.79
Basic human sustenance	1.06	0.9
Environmental health	1.01	0.97
Science/Technology	1.52	1.15
Capacity for debate	0.96	0.38
Governance	0.23	0.67
Private sector responsiveness	0.35	0.69
Eco-efficiency	−0.35	−0.11
Participation in international cooperative efforts	0.86	0.63
Reducing GHG emissions	−1.74	−0.61
Reducing trans-boundary environmental pressures	0.03	−0.33
Overall ESI	60.3	54.5

Source: Yale Centre for Environmental Law (2002).

- Private sector responsiveness.
- Eco-efficiency.
- Reducing greenhouse gas emissions.

The outcome for water quantity is simply a reflection of the fact that Australia has limited water resources, while the result for water quality is a reflection of relatively high scores for variables such as oxygen concentration, phosphorous, suspended solids and electrical conductivity. The outcome for biodiversity is a result of Australia having a relatively high proportion of mammals and breeding birds under threat of extinction. As will be seen below, the EPBC Act is designed to address this problem. The result for air pollution reduction is due to relatively poor results for coal consumption. The outcome for eco-efficiency is a result of Australia's relatively high energy consumption per unit of GDP, and relatively low use of renewable energy as a percentage of total energy production. This is in part due to the fact that Australia is a comparatively large and efficient producer of natural resources such as coal and relies heavily on such resources for the production of electricity. The poor result for greenhouse gas emissions is the result of Australia's failure to meet emission targets set under international agreements.

In summary, the Yale Centre results provide evidence that Australia compares well in terms of outcomes at an aggregate level, but that there are serious problems with biodiversity and water quality/quantity. These results confirm what is already known in Australia: that much of our water supply system is under severe stress due to growth in demand for water and declining supplies due to climate change, and that development is now placing severe stress on biodiversity. Indeed, these are generally seen as our two biggest environmental problems and challenges. For this reason, the following section provides a detailed discussion of the most recent policies directed towards these problems. Of course, it is not possible to provide evidence of any scientific assessment of the success of these policies, since they are very recent developments.

4. BIODIVERSITY, WATER RESOURCE AND POLLUTION POLICIES

As noted in the introduction, Australia is a dry continent with a high per capita income and a relatively large agricultural sector. Despite this, its people live almost exclusively in urban areas: indeed, Australia is one of the most highly urbanised countries in the world. Because of these factors, by the end of the 1980s it was increasingly clear that many of the continent's water systems (for example the Murray–Darling Basin) were under intense stress in the sense that environmental flows were too low to continue to sustain marine life and surrounding ecosystems, and consumption of water by agriculture and urban communities was correspondingly too high. Water salinity problems, in particular, became a serious issue in many major water systems.

Other serious and related environmental issues to emerge included soil salinity, caused by 'over-clearing' of land based on European farming experience, and ecosystem destruction. Australia has one of the most diverse and prolific biodiversities on earth but it also has comparatively high rates of land clearing (in some States, such as Queensland, this is for tourism development and pastoral activities) and many endangered species. Pollution (air, water and noise), though an issue in particular parts of major urban areas, and for particular river systems in terms of salinity, has not become the significant issue that it is in, say, Europe or North America. This is due largely to Australia's size and relatively small population.

In the following discussion, environmental policy is divided into three areas: ecosystem protection, natural resource management and pollution control. Australia has many policies that fall under each heading, and reviewing each of them is beyond the scope of this chapter. Given its special problems, under the heading of ecosystem protection the discussion concentrates on biodiversity. The discussion here highlights the role of indigenous people through an Advisory Committee and joint management of environmentally significant national parks. For resource management the discussion focuses on water, and for pollution control the emphasis is on air pollution.

4.1 Ecosystem Protection and Biodiversity[6]

At the beginning of 2000 the power to implement policies directed towards the protection of habitat, biodiversity, land use and ecological functions with national significance was granted almost exclusively to the Commonwealth through the passing of the EPBC Act.[7] The purpose of this Act, effective from 16 July 2000, is to make any actions (for example by individuals, firms or government agencies) that may have national environmental consequences subject to an assessment and review process either by the Commonwealth, or, through delegation under the terms of Commonwealth/State agreements, by a State environmental agency.[8] Though the ultimate policy-making power under this Act resides with the Commonwealth, as will be seen below, the Commonwealth can, if it wishes, delegate such power to the States.

The EPBC Act concentrates on biodiversity protection and contains provisions which deal with:

- Identification and monitoring of biodiversity and preparation of regional plans.
- Listing of threatened species and ecological communities, migratory species and marine species.
- Preparation of regional recovery and conservation plans for listed species and special protection for such species on Commonwealth owned land.
- Identification of major processes threatening biodiversity and the construction of abatement plans for such processes.
- Establishment of the Australian Whale Sanctuary Zone.
- Access to biological resources on Commonwealth owned land.
- Invasive species (e.g. introduced weeds and feral animals such as rabbits and foxes).

- Voluntary conservation agreements covering private land (including indigenous land).
- Protection and management of protected areas including Commonwealth national parks, World Heritage listed areas, Ramsar wetlands and Biosphere reserves.

The following discussion deals with how the Act sets up the assessment and approval process, the role of bilateral agreements with the States, the mechanism for dealing with threatened species and communities and enforcement issues.

Assessment and approval

Whenever an individual plans to undertake an action that is likely to have national environmental implications, the EPBC Act requires that the action be assessed (and approved or disapproved) prior to the action being undertaken. The 'triggers' that bring the Act into play include any activity that has an impact on:

- World Heritage listed lands.
- Ramsar wetlands.
- Nationally threatened species and ecological communities.
- Migratory species (e.g. birds).
- Commonwealth marine areas.
- Nuclear actions including uranium mining (Australia is a major exporter of uranium).

For example, a private developer with existing accommodation facilities within a park which has World Heritage status would need to have any proposal for an expansion of activities assessed and approved (or otherwise) under the terms of the Act. The process for obtaining approval has three stages.

Under the first stage, the individual(s) planning the action must refer their proposals to the Commonwealth Minister for the Environment who must make a decision as to whether the action needs to be assessed under the terms of the Act. The Minister must then advise the individual(s) officially within 20 working days on whether assessment and approval is, or is not, required. This is important since it reduces investors' uncertainty. For example, if the Minister advises that the proposed action does not require assessment, then a proposal can proceed without any further delay (apart from requiring other normal planning approvals).

If the Minister decides that the Act is triggered by a proposed action, then an assessment must be undertaken (stage 2). If the Commonwealth has a bilateral agreement with a State on the matter in question (discussed further below) then the relevant State may assess the proposal. Alternatively, if there is a Ministerial Declaration in place that allows another Commonwealth agency to assess the proposal, then the Minister may direct that the agency in question undertake the assessment. If none of these arrangements are in place, then stage 3 of the process applies; the Minister's own agency, the Commonwealth Department of the Environment and Heritage (otherwise known as Environment Australia) undertakes the assessment process using four possible approaches:

1. Assessment based on documentation supplied by the proponent.
2. A public environment report (PER).
3. Environmental impact statement (EIS).
4. Public inquiry.

The first three approaches involve publication of the draft assessment documents, a period for public comment and finalisation of documentation which take public comments into account. During these steps the individuals proposing the action must also be consulted. Once these steps are completed, the Secretary of Environment Australia prepares a final assessment report for the Minister, who must then make a decision on approval or rejection. In making this decision, the Act requires that the Minister take into account the following principles:

- Ecologically sustainable development.
- The assessment report on the impact of the proposed action.
- Any other information about the proposed action.
- Comments from other Ministers (e.g. comments from the Treasury Department on economic consequences).

In addition, the Commonwealth Minister cannot make a decision until advice has been received from the State(s) affected by the proposal. This advice must make it clear that all environmental impacts of the proposal other than those of national interest have been assessed (for example matters of local environmental concern). The Commonwealth Minister is also permitted under the Act to take into account a proponent's history with regard to environmental matters.

In summary, the Act places considerable discretionary power in the hands of the Commonwealth Minister for the Environment, though it does seek to impose constraints on his/her decision-making from the States and in terms of the principles of environmental best practice. However, there seems to be no requirement that proposals should be referred to Federal

Cabinet for consideration/decisions, or that they be tabled and debated in Parliament (either the lower House or the Senate).

Commonwealth/State bilateral agreements

As noted above, the Commonwealth may rely on State agencies for assessment, and also for approval/rejection, even though the matters being considered are of national significance. This is done through bilateral agreements negotiated between the Commonwealth and the States. However, while the Commonwealth Minister and States are free to negotiate such 'accreditation' agreements, the EPBC Act places limits on the scope of agreements and provides minimum standards that need to be observed. For example, to be accredited, a State agency must meet 'best practice' criteria in its assessment processes.

Broadly, there are two types of agreement. One, an 'assessment bilateral', allows the State agency to assess the proposal, with ultimate power to approve or reject lying with the Commonwealth Minister. The other, an 'approval bilateral', allows the State agency to assess and approve or reject the proposal. Bilateral agreements may also cover matters other than issues dealt with under the EPBC Act. For instance, they may cover broader environmental issues such as management plans for World Heritage listed areas or cooperation over monitoring and enforcement. They also last for a period of five years and prior to expiry must be reviewed. Also, at any time during the operation of the bilateral agreement, the Commonwealth Minister has the power to cancel or suspend the agreement if he or she believes that the State has not complied with the agreement and/or the spirit of the EPBC Act. Thus, much of the real power in these agreements lies with the Commonwealth.

Threatened species

As noted, the EPBC Act also requires the listing of:

- Nationally threatened native species and ecological communities.
- Internationally protected migratory species.
- Marine species.

Activities that pose threats to native species must also be listed. The Commonwealth Minister is required to construct and maintain a register that lists critical habitat, threatened species and ecological communities. The Minister is also required to develop a recovery plan for each threatened species and ecological community, and construct threat abatement plans for the threatening activities. These plans must be developed in cooperation with the States, and if State plans meet standards set out in the Act, they can be adopted as appropriate threat abatement plans.

This part of the Act establishes the Australian Whale Sanctuary, covering Australia's entire exclusive economic zone and coastal waters. The Sanctuary grants protection to whales, dolphins and porpoises, and is a contribution to establishing a world-wide whale protection zone.

The Act also allows for regulations with regard to non-native species that may threaten Australia's biodiversity. These regulations can limit trade in such species and allow the Commonwealth to develop plans to limit the spread of these species within Australia (for example foxes, feral cats and rabbits).

Conservation agreements

Conservation agreements between the Commonwealth and individuals can also be made for the protection of biodiversity. This is one tool that the Commonwealth can use to protect biodiversity outside of parks and reserves. Under such agreements, the Commonwealth can provide financial assistance to individuals to pay for fencing of remnant native vegetation.

Monitoring and enforcement

Provisions for monitoring compliance with approvals granted under the auspices of the Act are weak. One potential avenue for monitoring, though indirect, may occur through three advisory committees established by the Act. These are:

- *The Threatened Species Scientific Committee*: advises the Minister on listing of threatened species and plans for such species.
- *The Biological Diversity Advisory Committee*: advises the Minister on biodiversity issues.
- *The Indigenous Advisory Committee*: advises the Minister on the operation of the Act taking account of the knowledge of indigenous people; in particular, their understanding of the land, conservation and biodiversity.[9]

The other opportunity afforded by the Act for monitoring is provided by a requirement that the Commonwealth must provide regular reports on the environment and sustainable development. For example, the Commonwealth Minister is required to prepare a State of the Environment Report every five years. In addition, all Commonwealth Government agencies must report on an annual basis on their implementation of ecologically sustainable development.

However, other than these relatively 'soft' mechanisms, there is no evidence of any attempt to monitor compliance with the approvals process, and to measure achievements against any quantifiable environmental targets.

Despite this, there are explicit penalties for non-compliance with any approvals given under the Act and for any developments made without approval. Specifically, the Commonwealth Minister may conduct environmental 'audits' if there are grounds to suspect that an individual has not complied with an approval made under the Act (though how such information is to be made available in the absence of formal monitoring mechanisms is unclear). Civil and criminal penalties may also apply to individuals or corporations that are found to have breached the conditions placed on approvals, or who proceed to undertake actions that have national environmental consequences without seeking approval under the auspices of the Act (there are fines of up to $5.5 million for such actions). Penalties and fines can also be brought to bear on those who provide false information during the assessment process. Individuals found to have acted in this way may be required to correct any environmental damage at their own cost.

Indigenous people, biodiversity and joint park management

Indigenous people play a role in environmental policy, not just through their role on the Indigenous Advisory Committee under the EPBC Act, but also through land management projects on indigenous lands, managing indigenous protected areas, and through shared management of some of Australia's most important national parks, including Kakadu National Park, Uluru-Kata Tjuta and Booderee parks.

For example, Kakadu National Park, located in the tropical regions of northern Australia, comprises an area of 19 804 square kilometres, an area larger than many countries. Kakadu is rich in biological diversity and is seen as one the few remaining wilderness areas on earth. The wetlands in Kakadu are recognised under the international Convention on Wetlands (Ramsar Convention), and the park is one of only 22 World Heritage areas listed for its natural and cultural significance. Indeed, aboriginal people have occupied this area for about 50 000 years. The park is separately proclaimed under the EPBC Act and is managed jointly by Aboriginal traditional owners and the Director of National Parks (Commonwealth). About half of the land in the park is currently designated as Aboriginal land and much of the remainder of the park is subject to land claims by Aboriginal people. Interestingly, the existing Aboriginal land within the park is owned by Aboriginal land trusts which have leased the land to the Commonwealth Director of National Parks so that tourists and Australians generally can access the park. There is a view that the traditional Aboriginal owners see having their land as part of a national park as protection from competing demands from alternative uses such as mining.

Joint management is undertaken through a Board of Management with majority Aboriginal representation. The powers of the Board include preparing management plans for the park. The current plan is the fourth: it contains strategies for ensuring that the interests of traditional owners are protected, the cultural values are preserved and that biodiversity is maintained.[10]

Summary

The EPBC Act is an attempt to develop a comprehensive and consistent policy framework to deal with the protection of ecosystems of national significance and make a significant attempt to involve indigenous people in this process. Criticisms of the approach include:

(i) The degree of central control Though cloaked in the guise of a cooperative approach with the States, the Act vests all of the discretionary power over policy with the Commonwealth. It is a centralised approach to dealing with ecosystem protection where the States really only play the role of agents of the central government. One could argue, using the ideas of fiscal federalism, that a genuine 'cooperative federalism' approach would be more effective.

(ii) Ministerial discretionary power The constraints on the power of the Commonwealth Minister seem relatively weak. Though the Act itself provides general constraints on the power of the Minister, ultimately the power to approve or reject proposals lies in the hands of one person, without any explicit parliamentary scrutiny. It is not clear, for example, whether there are sufficient constraints on the activities of a pro-development Minister.

(iii) Lack of monitoring As discussed, there are no formal monitoring mechanisms established, nor are there any quantifiable targets established with assessments of how well these targets are being achieved over time. This is in contrast to the efforts made in respect to air pollution (discussed above).

4.2 Natural (Renewable) Resource Management

The most important policy with regard to natural resource management in Australia in recent times is the Water Reform Agreement agreed to by the State and Commonwealth Governments, through COAG, in 1994. This Agreement sets out strategies for the long term management of Australia's water resources with a view to improve the efficiency and equity involved in the allocation of water for both economic and environmental use. The Agreement, which has evolved over the years, and is still a major policy initiative today, involves many innovative arrangements, and has achieved notable successes. In contrast to the centralised approach to biodiversity and ecosystem protection, water reform is being undertaken cooperatively between the States and the Commonwealth.

One novelty of the Water Reform Agreement, and a major reason for its relative success, is that it is part of another major COAG reform programme designed to improve economic efficiency within the public sector. This initiative, formally known as the National Competition Policy, was formalised by COAG in 1995 in: The Agreement to Implement the National Competition Policy and Related Reforms. Moreover, all obligations made by the Commonwealth and the States under this Agreement to undertake public sector efficiency reforms are monitored by the NCC, which, as noted in section 2, was set up specifically for this purpose.

As part of the National Competition Policy, the Commonwealth makes special payments to the States based on whether they have implemented obligations agreed to under the National Competition Policy. In other words, the Commonwealth can reward States for carrying out their reform obligations, or penalise them by withholding the special payments if reforms have not been achieved. And the decision on whether to make or withhold payments is made on the basis of the assessments made by the NCC. By integrating the Water Reform Agreement into this broader reform agenda, progress on reform in water management and the associated environmental issues have become linked to National Competition Policy payments. Thus, progress on the Water Reform Agreement is monitored by an independent referee, and enforcement is provided for through financial incentives.

Generally, senior COAG officials (from the States and the Commonwealth) decide on what reforms will be assessed by the NCC in each year. All State Governments, and the Commonwealth, are required to provide an annual progress report to the NCC on the reforms to be assessed. The NCC uses this information, as well as its own research, to provide its final assessment of progress by each Government. In addition, interested parties can make independent submissions to the Council on Governments' progress on water reform. In 2001, the NCC made a full assessment of all reforms from 1994 to that year, and in 2005 it will assess compliance with the whole reform programme, from 1994 to 2004. Hence, the monitoring process does not rely purely on information provided by the States and the Commonwealth, though this is used as an input into the monitoring process.

The Murray–Darling Basin Commission

Before commencing discussion of the Water Reform Agreement in detail, it should be noted that one of Australia's most important water catchment/river systems is the Murray–Darling Basin, which cuts across several different

States (including New South Wales, Victoria and South Australia). This river system has, over many years, suffered from decline in the quality of the water due to salinity problems generated by drawing too much water for irrigation. As a consequence, ecosystems that depend on adequate water flow are under considerable stress. Many of the problems are due to externalities, namely, up-stream States tend to 'over-use' the water because the costs of such use are borne by down-stream residents in other States.

These problems were recognised by the States and the Commonwealth, leading to the creation of the Murray–Darling Basin Commission, an inter-State body designed to manage the river system in terms of setting allocations for environmental flows, monitoring water quality and setting the rules for water rights allocations to irrigators. The Commission, and its operations, is a major example in Australia of how States and the Commonwealth have responded to water-related inter-State externality problems, that is, through a cooperative approach between States.

The COAG Water Reform Agreement also applies, in large part, to the operations of the Murray–Darling Basin Commission. Indeed, the Commission's progress in implementing the Agreement reforms is also monitored by the NCC, almost as if it were a separate State.

The water reform obligations[11]

Under the Water Reform Agreement, Governments committed to implement a wide range of reforms, including:

- *Pricing:* Pricing water on the basis of economic principles (rather than property values).
- *Regulation:* Creating regulatory arrangements for water providers.
- *Water rights:* Introducing water allocation entitlements that are independent of land ownership.
- *Trading water rights:* Facilitating the creation of a national market for the trading of water rights.
- *Environmental allocations:* Making allocations of water to the environment in recognition that it is a legitimate user of water in order to maintain sustainability of ecosystems.
- *Investment:* Any new investment in water infrastructure to be subject to cost–benefit analysis, including analysis of ecological sustainability.
- *Management:* Integration of water management with resource management generally.
- *Standards:* Using market-based and regulatory measures to improve water quality standards.
- *Functions:* More clearly defining the function of water service providers (e.g. State-run monopolies providing urban and rural

water) and separating out the activities of standard-setting and monitoring to minimise conflicts of interest.
- *Commercial focus:* Giving a more commercial focus to water service providers.
- *Devolution:* Decentralising responsibility for management of irrigation systems to local bodies.

The following discussion examines progress (to 2003/04) on a selection of these obligations, namely, water pricing, water rights, water allocation to the environment, and trading in water rights (these are some of the obligations to be assessed by the NCC in 2004).

Water pricing
The Water Reform Agreement requires that water service providers (State monopolies) be regulated by a regulator to be nominated by each State Government, and that the regulator has the responsibility for determining water prices using the following principles:

- *Asset valuation:* Assets to be valued using a deprival valuation method.
- *Replacement/maintenance:* Use of an annuity approach to determine long-run cash requirements for asset replacement/maintenance.
- *Cost structure:* Water suppliers must not recover (as revenue) anything in excess of operational, maintenance and administrative costs, externalities, taxes, the cost of capital and dividends (set at commercial levels). These costs will determine the marginal cost curve for a water supplier.
- *Transparency:* Prices set should reflect efficient resource use (based on social marginal benefit) and marginal costs as calculated above. The Agreement requires that community service obligations (e.g. subsidies to particular water users), externalities and taxes be separately identified in the pricing structure.

Basically, the pricing principles come down to a requirement that water suppliers use marginal cost pricing, that the supply curve include all relevant externality costs of water usage, and that price also reflect social marginal benefits of water usage. In combination, the principles are designed to ensure efficient water allocation where all social costs and benefits are taken account of. The provisions also allow for phase-in periods for the new pricing structure.

To date, five States and Territories have fulfilled the obligation to subject their monopoly water businesses to price regulation by a regulator. The remaining three States appear to have plans in place to do so by 2004/05. The pricing principles have also been applied, to varying extents, for urban water providers. However, for rural water providers the situation is less clear. States are being required to report to the NCC, in their 2004 reports, on progress towards achieving both urban and rural water pricing reform. Their National Competition Policy payments for 2004/05 will be dependent, in part, on success in introducing such reform.

There is an example here that shows that the NCC, and the monitoring and enforcement process that it presides over, has some effectiveness in ensuring compliance. The example is the State of Western Australia, and the slowness it has shown in meeting its obligations with respect to water pricing and regulation. By 2003/04, the State had still not met its pricing obligations, or established a regulator for its water providers. As a result, the NCC recommended (in its 2003/04 assessment) the suspension of 10 per cent of the State's National Competition Policy payment. The Commonwealth Treasurer followed this recommendation, and the State was financially penalised in 2003/04 for failure to fulfil its water pricing and regulatory obligations.

Subsequently, the State has established (January 2004) the Economic Regulation Authority (ERA). The onus is now on the State to show that it is meeting its water pricing and regulatory obligations in order to have the suspended Competition Policy payment reinstated. South Australia is another State that has been slow to reform water pricing and will need to demonstrate much greater progress during 2004 if its Competition Policy payments are to be secured. It is doubtful that such States would comply with pricing and regulatory obligations under the Water Reform Agreement without the enforcement afforded by financial penalties and rewards.

The new system of water rights

As noted above, the Water Reform Agreement requires the separation of rights over the use of water from land ownership, and the formal recognition that the environment is a legitimate user of water. The amount to be made available for environmental needs is to be determined on the basis of scientific advice, and the remainder is to be allocated to competing users, ultimately, in a national water rights market. To date, all States and Territories have introduced new legislation to ensure that water rights are separate from land ownership.

However, progress towards converting existing allocations of water rights to the new system, creating a registration process, and developing water management plans to determine environmental allocations from different water systems, is on-going, and overall progress will be assessed by the NCC in its 2004 reports. To facilitate this, in 2003 COAG developed a

National Water Initiative that includes a framework for creating a national market in water rights.[12] One aspect of this market that needs to be dealt with is the possibility that future access to water will change to cater for revised allocations to the environment. This means that measures have to be put in place to share the risk of such changes between Governments and the holders of tradable water rights. Without such arrangements, it is possible that a market for water rights might not result in efficient trading.

The 2004 assessment by the NCC will concentrate on looking at progress by the States in implementing water entitlement arrangements. They will be required to report on how they have progressed with implementing water management plans to define environmental allocations of water, progress with converting existing water allocations to the new system, and how they are proposing to register new entitlements.[13]

Providing water for the environment

As discussed, the Water Reform Agreement requires Governments to treat the environment as a user of water, and to include these environmental allocations within water management plans for each major waterway/catchment and river system. This raises the question of what is the appropriate amount of water required by the environment, with the answer determining the amount that is available for human use. In 1999 a tripartite meeting on water for the environment agreed that the amount required for the environment should be based on principles provided by the Agricultural and Resource Management Council of Australia and New Zealand/Australian and New Zealand Environment and Conservation Council (ARMCANZ/ANZECC). The objective of these principles is to ensure that the environment is allocated sufficient water to maintain ecosystems and biodiversity in river and water catchment systems.[14]

When it assesses Governments' progress towards implementing these goals, the NCC will use a rough rule of thumb which defines a 'healthy working river' as one in which at least two-thirds of the natural flow is retained, and human activities take at most one-third of the natural flow for economic uses.[15] The (at most) one-third that is taken for economic activities will then be allocated among competing users using markets in which water rights are traded, and the water is allocated efficiently to highest valued users.

There is already an upper limit on the amount of water that can be taken from the Murray–Darling system based on scientific advice on what such a limit should be if specific ecological attributes of the system are to be maintained.[16] In 2004, the NCC will assess how this cap is being implemented, and how the Murray–Darling Basin Commission is monitoring compliance by irrigators.

A national market for trading water rights

The Water Reform Agreement stipulated that Governments were to implement water trading subject to satisfactory arrangements being put in place for water rights allocations (as noted above, this process is not yet complete and the NCC will be reviewing water rights allocations in its 2004 assessment of progress on water reform). Moreover, the intention is that the market for trading in water rights be a national one. This was designed to ensure that trade could take place across State borders where catchments and river systems are contained within more than one sub-national jurisdiction. As noted in National Competition Council (2003, p. 46):

> In most jurisdictions, water entitlements may be traded temporarily (for an agreed number of seasons, including consecutive seasonal assignments) or permanently. In some jurisdictions, it is also possible to lease entitlements with no limit on the duration of the lease. The water management arrangements being developed under State and Territory legislation establish the quantum of tradable volumetric allocations and set the rules for governing trading.

COAG, and the NCC, have both expressed a strong desire to see a national market for trading water rights substantially in place by 2005. Indeed, the 2004 NCC assessment will include a major review of progress towards the creation of a national water rights market.

Summary

The Water Reform Agreement is an attempt to ensure that adequate supplies of water are allocated to the environment in the interests of ecological sustainability, and that the water that is allocated to human use is used efficiently. The portion to be allocated to the environment is being determined using the best scientific evidence available, while economic principles are being applied to ensure that what is available for humans is allocated to the highest valued users. This latter goal is to be achieved through two policies. One is to make water suppliers responsive to market signals (including externalities) without generating monopoly profits (through regulation). The other is to create a national system for trading water rights. In addition, standards are being put in place for water quality (see under 'Water pollution' below), and institutional changes are being made to facilitate the above reforms.

However, even with monitoring and enforcement through formal incentives/penalties, the reforms have proceeded much more slowly than originally envisaged by COAG in 1994. This has been due to various problems encountered by the States, including resistance to change by special interest groups and the (unforeseen) magnitude of some of the technical and legal issues encountered. Nevertheless, the experience in Australia with water reform might be a useful benchmark for other countries, or regional unions of countries, such as the European Union, facing similar problems of how to deal with cross-border water allocation problems, ensuring adequate supplies of water for ecological sustainability, and creating economically and socially efficient use of the water available for human use.

4.3 Pollution Control

The following discussion examines recent attempts in Australia to deal with issues related to pollution control. The discussion is restricted to initiatives on air and water pollution.

Air pollution

There are on-going initiatives in Australia at present to reduce urban air pollution. The first is the NEPM on ambient air quality and the second is the development of national standards for the supply of petrol and diesel fuels. The last of these policies is discussed below.

During 2002 Australia introduced its first national standards for petrol and diesel fuel.[17] These standards are designed to bring Australia into line with international standards for the supply and use of petrol and diesel fuels. Indeed, there were two major initiatives designed to improve air quality in urban areas. They are:

- the Fuel Standard (Petrol) Determination 2001; and
- the Fuel Standard (Automotive Diesel) Determination 2001.

Both determinations were made under the auspices of the (Commonwealth) Fuel Quality Standards Act 2000. The Act prohibits the sale of petrol and diesel fuels which do not comply with the standards set out in the Determinations.

The Commonwealth Department of the Environment and Heritage (also known as Environment Australia) monitors compliance with the fuel standards and has developed extensive enforcement mechanisms. There are three aspects to monitoring, enforcement and compliance. First, the Act requires that fuel suppliers provide documentation to the Department of the Environment and Heritage regarding the quality of the fuel being supplied and how the fuel complies with the standards (self-regulation). This requirement is placed on importers and producers, distributors, service station outlets and large-scale vehicle fleet operators.

Second, in each State there is a team of Commonwealth inspectors who conduct sampling along the entire fuel supply chain. These samples are tested at independent accredited testing facilities to check for compliance with the standards. Initially, sampling was done on a random basis. However, increasingly sampling is done using the information provided by firms. For example, if sampling shows results different from the information provided by a supplier, then this provides a trigger for inspectors to examine the affairs of the firm in more detail. The Fuel Quality Standards Act 2000 is quite proscriptive in setting out the powers of fuel inspectors. Using warrants or with consent, they can conduct searches, inspect, measure and test any fuel found (including additives) and examine documentation.

Third, the Department of the Environment and Heritage has established mechanisms for information sharing with motoring clubs, consumer affairs organisations, State departments of fair trading and State environmental protection agencies. These agencies collect considerable information, based on complaints and their own investigations, about fuel quality issues.

The Department of the Environment and Heritage produces public information on its monitoring and enforcement of the standards, as well as how standards are being achieved, and is required to present this information to Parliament in its Annual Report. Standards for many other fuels, such as liquefied natural gas (LPG), compressed natural gas (CNG), biodiesel and diesohol, are expected to come into force in the near future.

Water pollution

The COAG Water Reform Agreement also deals with water quality, and requires Governments to support the National Water Quality Management Strategy (NWQMS). This strategy contains guidelines for water quality monitoring and reporting, as well as standards for fresh and marine water quality.[18] The NCC notes that it (National Competition Council (2003), pp. 61–2): 'expected State and Territory governments to have largely implemented the NWQMS by the 2003 NCP assessment. Most governments have some elements remaining: in particular, Western Australia had scheduled significant elements of the NWQMS for implementation in 2003–04.'

By including water quality standards within the Water Reform Agreement the NCC is able to monitor and enforce reforms and eventual adherence to the standards.

5. IMPLICATIONS FOR THE EU

Can such a cooperative approach be transferred to other federations or regional unions of States, such as the EU? This may be problematic for the following reasons. First, Australia has relatively few States so the costs of coordination are relatively low and the potential for blocking sub-coalitions forming is relatively small. Second, this approach 'works' in Australia because the national government is financially dominant and is supported by a centralist High Court. Third, there is effective monitoring of agreements by an independent body with substantial powers to collect information. Finally, the financial power of the national government means that it has effective instruments to punish non-compliance, or alternatively, to reward compliance. So monitoring and compliance are effective to some degree.

Do these conditions exist in the EU? One issue is that there are 25 highly independent nation states within the EU so the potential costs of coordinating are higher. Also, the potential for sub-coalitions of nation states forming, and blocking agreements, is higher. So if unanimity is required, agreement may be difficult. Some say this is already happening with the formation of a grouping of the three most powerful states: Germany, the UK and France. The distribution of financial power within a regional union such as the EU is also the reverse of a highly centralised federation like Australia: namely, the centre is (relatively) financially weak, and the nation states are comparatively strong. Thus, the EU lacks a central government with strong financial and constitutional powers to penalise states for non-compliance, or to reward them for compliance with agreements/treaties made between member states. Witness, for example, the problems the EU is currently experiencing with French and German non-compliance during 2002 over budget deficit rules as a percentage of GDP. If such open non-compliance occurred in Australia, the offending States would have financial penalties imposed quickly without resort to the legislature or even Parliament. Finally, though the EU could establish a monitoring body (like the Australian NCC), without the ability to impose financial sanctions/rewards, the value of such a body is doubtful. It could only shame recalcitrant states into complying with agreements.

6. CONCLUDING REMARKS

Australian States are financially dependent on the central government, and the High Court of Australia has consistently made centralist interpretations of the Constitution. Combined, these facts imply that the Commonwealth has considerable power to intervene in State policy-making, and environmental policy is no exception. However, in recent years the Commonwealth's power has been used to enforce a 'cooperative' approach to many inter-governmental issues including environmental matters. State (and Commonwealth) compliance with policies developed under the umbrella of cooperation have been monitored by a separate national body, the NCC. This body has powers to obtain information from the States in determining compliance, and in addition can recommend various sanctions in the form of financial penalties for non-compliance. This is not just an empty threat either: there are several cases where financial grants have been withheld from States not complying with commonly agreed cooperative policies on the environment.

Two of the most pressing problems, threats to biodiversity and water supply, have been discussed in depth. The first problem is being addressed mainly through central action, with State support, while water supply problems are being addressed through genuine cooperative action, mainly, it seems, because the States own the infrastructure for the supply of water to industry, irrigators and households. With regard to biodiversity, indigenous people are now playing an increasing role in policy-making, both through the Indigenous Advisory Committee under the auspices of the EPBC Act, and through joint management of some of Australia's major World Heritage listed parks. This is an important development since indigenous people have a unique understanding of much of the Australian environment, particularly as it existed prior to European settlement.

Australia has also tended to rely on policy instruments other than taxes/subsidies (or fees). The main instruments of choice have been standards developed on the basis of best scientific practice (for example on air quality and water), environmental plans which set down codes of conduct for economic activities, and, as the example of water reform shows, the implementation of economic principles (for example marginal cost water pricing that includes externality costs and the creation of a national market for trading water rights). Thus, Australian policy-makers have turned to scientists to set appropriate standards, for example, for river flow rates consistent with sustainability, and economics to develop the principles for allocating scarce environmental inputs in a sustainable fashion.

Finally, it is suggested that this approach to environmental policy might not be easily transplanted to regional unions of States where the centre is relatively weak and it is more difficult to enforce compliance.

NOTES

1. For a detailed discussion of fiscal relations in Australia see Petchey and Wells (2004).
2. See Council of Australian Governments (2004).
3. See websites of the Department of Agriculture, Fisheries and Forestry – Australia, and the Department of the Environment and Heritage, for background scientific and other documents that form the basis of the RFAs.
4. States are responsible for most national parks with the exception of large parks of national significance, such as Kakadu, which are managed jointly with indigenous people (see later discussion).

5. See www.yale.edu/envirocenter/.
6. The discussion of the EPBC Act is based, in part, on Environment Australia (2003a).
7. This has some economic logic since one might expect, from the ideas of fiscal federalism, matters with predominately national significance to be central government responsibilities.
8. The Act replaced the following Commonwealth Acts relating to the environment, some of which dated back to the 1970s: Environment Protection (Impact of Proposals) Act 1974, Endangered Species Protection Act 1992, National Parks and Wildlife Conservation Act 1975, World Heritage Properties Conservation Act 1983 and the Whale Protection Act 1980.
9. See www.deh.gov.au/indigenous/iac.html for more details on the role of the Committee.
10. For more information on joint management of Kakadu see: www.deh.gov.au/parks/kakadu/parkjointmang/index.html.
11. The following discussion draws, in part, on National Competition Council (2001, 2003).
12. See Council of Australian Governments (2003).
13. See National Competition Council (2003) pp. 31–32.
14. See National Competition Council (2003) p. 37 for listing of the principles.
15. As noted in National Competition Council (2003), this working notion of a healthy river was developed by the Expert Reference Panel (ERP) of scientists under the 'Living Murray Initiative'.
16. Such limits are analysed in the draft report of the Scientific Reference Panel (2003).
17. See Environment Australia (2003b).
18. See National Water Quality Management Strategy (1998).

BIBLIOGRAPHY

ARMCANZ (Agriculture and Resource Management Council of Australia and New Zealand) and ANZECC (Australian and New Zealand Environment and Conservation Council) (1996), 'National principles for the provision of water for ecosystems', *Occasional Paper SWR No.3*, Sustainable Land and Water Resources Management Committee, Subcommittee on Water Resources, Sydney.

Council of Australian Governments (2003), *Communiqué*, http:/www.dpmc.gov.au/docs/coag 290803.cfm.

Council of Australian Governments (2004), *Water Reform Framework*, http:/www.deh.gov.au/water/policy/coag.html.

Environment Australia (2003a), *An Overview of the Environment Protection and Biodiversity Conservation Act, 1999*, October.

Environment Australia (2003b), *National Standards for Fuel Quality*, http:/www.deh.gov.au/atmosphere/cleaner-fuels/information.html.

National Competition Council (2001), 'Assessment of governments' progress in implementing the National Competition Policy and related reforms', June, Canberra: AusInfo.

National Competition Council (2003), *Water Reform Assessment Framework: 2004*, December, Canberra: AusInfo.

National Water Quality Management Strategy (1998), *Implementation Guidelines*, Australia: Agriculture and Resource Management Council of Australia.

Petchey, J.D. and S. Levtchenkova (2004), 'Fiscal equalisation in Australia: Proposals for an efficiency-based system', *Economic Papers*, **23**(2), 189–200.

Petchey, J.D. and G. Wells (2004), 'Australia's federal experience', in M. Baimbridge and P. Whyman (eds), *Fiscal Federalism and European Economic Integration*, London: Routledge.

Scientific Reference Panel (Chair: Gary Jones) (2003), 'Ecological assessment of environmental flow reference points for the River Murray system', Interim report prepared for the Murray–Darling Basin Commission Living Murray Initiative, Canberra: Cooperative Research Centre for Freshwater Ecology (draft report).

Shah, A. (1994), 'The reform of intergovernmental fiscal relations in developing and emerging market economies', The World Bank Policy and Research Series, 23, Washington, DC: World Bank.

Walsh, C. (1993), 'Vertical fiscal imbalance: The issues', in D.J. Collins (ed.), *Vertical Fiscal Imbalance*, Australian Tax Research Foundation, Conference Series No. 13, pp. 31–53.

Walsh, C. (1996), 'Refocusing Commonwealth–State financial relations: Tax powers, microeconomic reform and intergovernmental relations', in P. Boothe (ed.), *Reforming Fiscal Federalism for Global Competition*, Edmonton, Canada: University of Alberta Press.

Yale Centre for Environmental Law (2002), *Report on Country Profiles – Section Two*, www.ciesin.columbia.edu/indicators/ESI/ESI2002_21Mar 02b.pdf.

3. Economic growth and environmental protection in Brazil: An unfavourable trade-off

Clóvis Cavalcanti

1. INTRODUCTION

A characteristic of Brazil's history over the last 500 years[1] is that it has produced a succession of actions with huge negative environmental implications (Viola, 1987; Cavalcanti, 1991). The present picture conveys a sense of the irresponsibility with which the natural resources of the country have been systematically exploited since the conquest. Moreover, it also exhibits instances of many of the same evils which afflict ecosystems throughout the world – slash-and-burn agriculture, soil degradation (recently accelerated by the expansion of the cultivation of soyabeans in Amazonia, preceded by deforestation and logging), contaminated water, and so on. In the Brazilian case, the problem is aggravated by the 'pollution of misery' and a very unequal income distribution. These problems, by the way, were presented in the Stockholm UN Conference (1972) as arguments justifying more pollution of the conventional type (Viola, 1987: 83–4). The military who ruled the country at that time, and had a nationalist project of development, justified the need for polluting industries to move to Brazil on grounds that, although they polluted, they also raised the prospects of rapid growth.

The international press and the literature on environmental issues do not exaggerate when they offer dramatic information about the relationship between Brazil and its ecology. This has been especially true in the last decades with problems such as those we have witnessed in the Amazon. Frontier expansion in that unique region stimulated by the opening of new roads has brought in the business-as-usual scenario of rapid deforestation, with the release of several billion tons of carbon to the atmosphere, more accidental forest fires, species loss, deforestation-driven rainfall inhibition, and so on (Nepstad et al., 2002). Between 1992 and 2000, 157 000 km^2 of forest, equivalent to almost half the area of Italy, were deforested (Camargo et al., 2002). These problems are now exacerbated by the fact that, today, the pressure for the expansion of the soyabean sector[2] represents a serious threat to environmental governance. The case of shrimp farming and the concomitant destruction of mangroves and estuarine areas that it brings about should also be noted (Varela, 2003). In short, the process of development in Brazil has provoked a series of grave ecological problems which can be summarised as follows: biodiversity loss with deforestation due to subsidised cattle-raising and large-scale agricultural projects; desertification processes mainly in the north-east region, but even in Amazonia; ecosystem destruction such as in the case of mangroves; a lack of observance of environment protection laws and rules; deterioration of urban living conditions; urban violence, and so on (Cavalcanti, 1991: 476). In other words, the process of development in Brazil has not taken into account its ecological or social costs. In the words of a biologist in the Ministry of the Environment, whose work is related to the Convention on Biological Diversity, 'The traditional model of exploitation of natural resources in Brazil is extractivist, predatory and colonialist' (Dias, 2002: 140).

It is worth noting, however, that this phenomenon of environmental degradation has been accompanied by meaningful efforts to create a legal framework to protect the integrity of ecosystems. At the same time, Brazilian society seems to be incorporating new attitudes concerning the importance of the environment. A national opinion poll conducted on three different occasions – 1992, 1997 and 2002 – indicates, for example, some meaningful changes of perception in recent times. There has been a broader diffusion of environmental notions and policies in the public agenda, and people feel more and more committed to the solution of environmental problems (ISER, 2003). The problem is that, parallel to this, faith in the idea of unlimited economic growth appears to be particularly ingrained in the Brazilian collective mind, penetrating even the world of the 'critical intellectual elite' (Viola, 1987: 85).[3] In a supposedly pro-environment sphere, such as that encompassing the preparation of the Brazilian Agenda 21, such thinking can be encountered, as is shown in this statement from a document of the group in charge of Agenda 21: 'The resumption of growth during the decade 2002–2012 should not be inferior to 5% per year' (CPDS, 2002: 7).[4] What else but faith could justify such a confident declaration? As a Brazilian environmental scientist says, the economy of Brazil since the 1930s has been submitted to a process of development 'amply dominated by the developmental belief that it is worth incurring any costs to grow economically' (Drummond, 1998–1999: 128).

The faith in the indispensability of growth can explain the waste of resources in Amazonia as if they had no limits (Allegretti, 2001: 41). It has also dominated the orientation of the government of president Luiz Inácio Lula da Silva (who was inaugurated in January 2003) in its first two years.

Short-run considerations determine what is undertaken, especially in connection with economic decisions and their environmental consequences (SENAC, 2003). This is particularly true in the conspicuous case of soyabeans, whose expansion has been one of the factors responsible for the great increase in Brazil's export earnings in recent years. In the logic of the Ministry of Agriculture, which tends to be ruled by the agribusiness sector (to the chagrin of people in the Ministry of the Environment, with a great presence of NGOs and environmentalists), all efforts must be concentrated on increasing the area cultivated with soy. This involves creating appropriately 'favourable' conditions, no matter how detrimental they are to the natural environment. Hence the pressure for paving roads and building a system of modern waterways in the Amazon, besides other controversial initiatives (see Kohlhepp, 2001). Governor Maggi, of the state of Mato Grosso (where over 4.5 million hectares of land are cultivated with soyabeans), in the Centre-West region, has openly argued for deforestation, saying that the Amazon biome can easily bear the loss of 40 per cent of its forest cover[5] (SENAC, 2003: 29).

Against public opinion and a system of rules that favour conservation, the tendency in Brazil has been to give in to powerful predatory lobbies. The above-mentioned 1992–2002 opinion poll shows that, in 1997, 49 per cent of all Brazilians thought that the level of deforestation allowed to landowners in Amazonia (20 per cent) should be reduced. This proportion rose to 58 per cent in 2002 (Camargo et al., 2002: 37). Nonetheless, the core strategy of Amazonian (and Brazilian) development persists in its bias in favour of supplying massive subsidies to large domestic investors and favourable terms for foreign investors (Torras, 2003: 6). In the post-1992 period, the evolution of indicators of eight central problems for the sustainable development of Brazil – namely, biomes, agriculture, biodiversity, water resources, energy, urban development, consumption, and the social responsibility of enterprises – indicate that the relevant problems continue characteristically unsolved and that, in many cases, they have become even more serious (Camargo et al., 2002: 24). The result is that, as a recent study has shown (Torras, 2003: 129), 'There is considerable evidence that Brazilian living standards worsened from 1965 to 1998, at least for the poorest members of society' and that, even more serious, 'green income was invariably negative for the poorest quintile – and at times for the second- and third-poorest as well'.

2. EARLY INITIATIVES TOWARDS FORMAL ENVIRONMENTAL GOVERNANCE IN BRAZIL

Drummond (1998–1999: 129) remarks that the crucial point to remember in attempting to understand the history of the environmental legislation and institutional set-up in Brazil is the country's chronic lack of control, until recent times, by the federal government over public lands, combined with the total lack of a democratic land policy. This lack of control led to the overexploitation and degradation of resources, until its formal, though not effective, interruption by a constitutional amendment in 1964. Without control over public lands, and with little power to intervene in the use of private land, no serious environmental policies – if any were contemplated – could be undertaken by the central government. An exception to that situation was the treatment traditionally given to coastal areas, in relation to which the Portuguese practice, inherited by Brazil, was to limit property rights: those lands subject to the tide regime remained under the public domain. This principle continues to prevail in Brazil, where 'Public access to the maritime littoral is a sacred principle' (Drummond, 1998–1999: 131).

The situation of neglect depicted above begins to change a little from 1934 onwards. In 1934 Brazilian legislation produced two important landmarks, the Forest Code and the Water Code, the intention of which was not to promote the ecologically sound management of resources, but rather their 'rational' control by planners in the federal bureaucracy (Drummond, 1998–1999: 132). The first of these two laws attempted (unsuccessfully) to dissociate the full right of use of the native flora from the ownership of the land in which the forest was located. In spite of the existence of this new law, landowners and settlers continued to fell trees at will, invoking the necessity of opening new tracts for agricultural purposes.[6] However, some conservationist practices were introduced – at least, landowners felt somehow restrained – and the Forest Code led to the creation of the first national parks. This law was modified, and strengthened, in 1965 under the name New Forest Code. The Water Code, more successfully, determined the dissociation of the ownership of a piece of land from the ownership of the water and mineral resources on or under that land. In Brazil, since 1934, the purchase of land excludes in principle the right of the landowner to exploit the water and minerals existing on or under that land (considered national patrimony). This, however, has not prevented those resources from being abusively exploited directly by, or under concession of, the national authority.

The early initiatives for the establishment of a framework of rules and institutions to manage environmental resources in Brazil were extended in 1964 by a constitutional amendment which removed public lands from the domain of the states, and placed them under the control of the central government. The Land Act, issued by the military regime at the same time, established that private land ownership would fulfil its full social function only if it combined fair distribution, adequate use and, as an innovation, the conservation of natural resources (Drummond, 1998–1999: 137).

At the state level[7] things had not been stagnating. In effect, various undertakings in favour of a more solidified form of environmental governance had been promoted since the early 1960s. Councils, commissions, agencies, and so on concerned with the environment gradually sprang up in states such as São Paulo, Rio de Janeiro, Pernambuco and Bahia, introducing new approaches to the management of resources and pollution control. Their impact was never impressive, contributing though to the formation of technical bodies with a beneficial involvement in environmental issues.

3. NEW ATTITUDES TOWARDS THE ASSIGNMENT OF POWERS

It is the year 1972, however, that constitutes a reference point for the introduction of an integrated approach to environmental governance in Brazil, with some influence from the experience in the 1960s of the US Environmental Protection Agency (EPA) (Mattos de Lemos, 2002: 31; Egler, 2002: 117). It was felt then that the existing policies, institutions and norms had been formulated in a segmented fashion, chiefly with respect to the use and conservation of natural resources. This led gradually to new attitudes. Despite the fact that Brazil officially assumed an anti-environmentalist position at the Stockholm Conference, the Brazilian delegate subscribed the pro-environment Stockholm Declaration and a growing conservationist consciousness formed within the federal government.

In October 1973 this led to the creation, within the Ministry of the Interior, of the Special Secretariat of the Environment (SEMA). To head the new agency, whose activities can be considered to have been somewhat successful from the start, a respected natural scientist from São Paulo, Paulo Nogueira Neto, though not exactly a popular or unanimous name inside the ecological movement, was appointed. He was to remain in that position, against the odds, for 12 years which made possible SEMA's safer evolution and consolidation. During Nogueira Neto's mandate, Brazil's environmental situation became ever more critical. Economic growth – then, as today, the real sacred cow – was proceeding at a rapid pace (with rates of GDP increase above 5 per cent per year in 1973–1981), without any corresponding commitment to sustainable processes in ecological terms. The costs of growth – in accordance with a long-standing tradition of the economics profession – were simply ignored.

The great moment for the new paradigm of environmental governance in Brazil arrived in August 1981, with the approval of the National Environmental Policy Act. This was as a consequence of SEMA's work – supported by CETESB (São Paulo State Company of Basic Sanitation

Technology) and FEEMA (Rio de Janeiro Foundation for Environmental Engineering) – and the actions of many groups in society (Mattos de Lemos, 2002: 42). This Act is considered the most important piece of environmental legislation issued in the country up to the present time (Drummond, 1998–1999: 141). In fact, it sets up both the legal basis and the institutional framework for policy-making concerning the environment at all levels of government (see Figure 3.1) (Medauar, 2003: 671–80). That law gave SEMA a central role in the newly-created National Environment System (SISNAMA), which is made up of Brazil's different levels of environmental governance and the powerful National Council of the Environment (CONAMA). What makes this law outstanding, however, is the nature of its objectives, which in essence require that socio-economic development be compatible with a high quality of life and ecological equilibrium. To that end the environment is considered to be a public patrimony

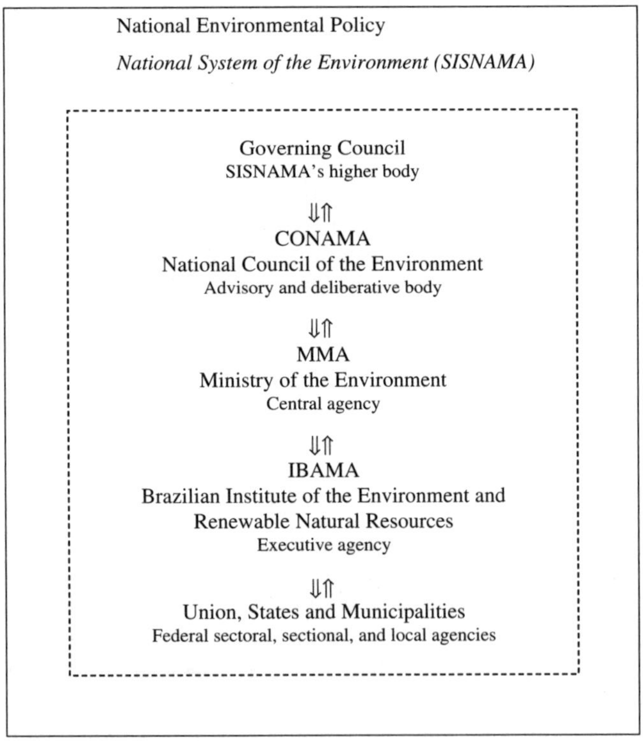

Source: Mattos de Lemos (2002: 44).

Figure 3.1 Brazil's national environmental policy framework: an overview

which must be guaranteed and protected with a view to its collective use on a sound basis and without imperilling its permanent availability.

The National Environment Policy Act, which establishes directives to be observed by the states and *municípios* (municipalities), accepts the polluter-pays principle as the way of recognising guilt, and sets up the obligation of those who cause damage to repair it. It also determines the obligation to produce assessment studies, and their respective reports, of environmental impact in the relevant cases. In sum, it constitutes a move away from a narrow pollution-control model of environmental policy towards a more comprehensive, systemic approach, although it has not had the power – nor is it its intent – to assuage the widespread, even mystical, belief in the enhancing powers of economic growth.

4. THE NATIONAL ENVIRONMENT SYSTEM

As Figure 3.1 suggests, the National Environment Policy Act, which has suffered some slight modifications in its lifetime, including adaptation to the 1988 Constitution, governs SISNAMA's structure. It establishes concepts, principles, objectives, mechanisms of application and formulation, instruments and penalties in relation to policy-making in environmental questions and the management of natural resources in Brazil. It also sets up an articulated set of agencies, entities, rules and practices responsible for the protection and improvement of the quality of the environment, whose structure is roughly depicted in Figure 3.1. At the highest level of SISNAMA sits the Governing Council, formed by all federal ministers under the coordination of the Civil House (a kind of super-ministry or a *primus inter pares*), whose function is to provide advice and basic guidelines to the President of the Republic (who heads the federal government) on the formulation of policy.

CONAMA, the National Council of the Environment, constitutes the advisory and deliberative instance of SISNAMA. It is its true heart (M. Ribeiro, 2002: 89) and a kind of environmental parliament (Mattos de Lemos, 2002: 52), with regulatory powers ceded by Congress through legislation with respect to national environmental policy initiatives. Its composition, originally of 36 people, has grown continually. It is now much larger: 101 members (called 'councíllors') who represent the federal government (32 people), the states (27), the *municípios* (8), civil society (22), and the productive sector (8), plus an honorary member and three non-voting others. Civil society, whose participation in CONAMA has always been highly active and appreciated, is represented by 11 NGOs, three people freely chosen by the President of the Republic, three indicated by professional societies and trade unions, and one each from the indigenous communities, traditional peoples (like riverine inhabitants of the Amazon, and the so-called *caiçaras*[8] in the south-east), state-level military police and fire departments, the scientific community and the Brazilian Foundation for the Conservation of Nature.

Depending on the complexity and volume of the problems it must deal with, CONAMA has recourse to a number of technical chambers (ten of which function on a permanent basis, and a few others which function temporarily according to need). In the technical chambers, proposals for environmental regulation and the sustainable use of natural resources are presented for examination by the councillors. To be adopted, they must be supported by a sound justification. Stakeholders represented within CONAMA are also required to be heard before a process is concluded. It is the chambers' role to furnish reliable technical references for the CONAMA plenary to make its decisions. To that effect they can establish working groups with specific missions. As an illustration, in 2002 the permanent Technical Chamber for Environmental Control had 21 working groups dealing with subjects such as asbestos, agrarian reform, environmental auditing, civil construction, incinerators, ozone, and so forth (Mattos de Lemos, 2002: 61–2). The working groups must be made up of experts, who are normally appointed from technical bodies and academia. Their qualifications ensure that adequate information is supplied, rigorous scientific analyses are elaborated, consultation with concerned parties are made, and that proposals are duly prepared for adoption by CONAMA's assembly. The working groups serve as advisory bodies to improve the quality of CONAMA's decisions. They consult frequently on a case-by-case basis with the scientific community. However, there are no big projects contracted out to academia. A shortage of funds and the low status attributed to the environment within the government are the main reasons for this. A number of Brazilian federal public bodies traditionally produce environmental knowledge. Two important research organisations in the Amazon, INPA (the National Institute for Research in Amazonia) and the Goeldi Museum (a pioneer in ethnoecology), deal specifically, among other subjects, with ecology. Work also exists in many universities, such as the well-known Federal University of São Carlos in São Paulo state. But this work is part of the regular activities of those universities.

SISNAMA's central organ is the Ministry of the Environment (MMA), created in September 1992, whose responsibility is to plan, coordinate, supervise and control all actions of environmental policy at the federal level. CONAMA deals instead with *national* policy issues, thus embodying all levels of government – federal as well as state and municipal. The role of executing directly, and commanding the execution by other bodies, of the policies and guidelines related to the environment, belongs to IBAMA, the Brazilian Institute of the Environment and Renewable Natural Resources, an agency with a certain autonomy under the authority of the Ministry of the Environment. When the National Environment Policy Act was enacted, that role was performed by SEMA. IBAMA was created in 1989, but the organ from which it was transformed, the Brazilian Institute of Forestry Development (IBDF) dates back to 1967, reflecting that moment's almost exclusive preoccupation with forest protection.[9]

5. ASSIGNMENT OF POWERS OVER THE ENVIRONMENT: AREAS OF RESPONSIBILITY

Sectoral bodies of an executive character in all federal ministries, national public enterprises and foundations, whose activities are associated with the protection of environmental quality or the enforcement of environmental norms and regulations, together with sectional (state) and local (municipal) agencies with the same profile, form the next level of SISNAMA (see also Table 3.1). Their function, either at the federal, state or local level, in their respective jurisdictions, is to carry out environmental programmes and

Table 3.1 National System of the Environment (SISNAMA) by government level

Level	Council	Executive Agency
Municipality	Municipal Council of the Environment (*only 22.2% active ones*)	Secretariat or municipal executive agency of the environment (*almost all do not have secretariat status*)
State	State Council of the Environment (*all state councils are active with different functioning patterns*)	Secretariat or state executive agency of the environment (*in general, environment is part of a secretariat covering other areas such as planning or science and technology*)
Federal	National Council of the Environment (CONAMA) (*very active*)	Brazilian Institute of the Environment and Renewable Natural Resources (IBAMA) / Ministry of the Environment

projects, and to take charge of supervising, monitoring, controlling and inspecting activities that may cause impairment to the environment. It is important to point out that, in conformity with the Constitution of the Brazilian federation, states and municipalities have the competence to supplement federal legislation by legislating about subjects of their interest. Following the pattern set up by CONAMA, all 26 states and the Federal District (Brasília, the country's capital) created their own councils of the environment, although the shape, mission and purpose of each of these differ, sometimes noticeably. In the small (46 184 km^2) Espírito Santo state, for instance, it was decided that in addition to the state council, six regional councils should be established, one for each of its river basins. The rhythm and regularity with which the state councils exercise their mission are not uniform, either. In 2001, for example, Amazonas (which has 1 577 820 km^2) had only one meeting, while Acre had four, and Santa Catarina seven (J.C. Ribeiro, 2002).

At the municipal level, the picture is rather different, as can be seen in Table 3.2. In 2001 only 22.2 per cent of *municípios* possessed 'active' local councils, a situation that has probably not changed significantly today. Note that the number of active councils presented in Table 3.2 is based on the criterion that a council is considered active if it had at least one meeting in 2001. These councils have an irregular existence (Carvalho et al., 2003; Siviero, 1995). Many are created and then put in quarantine just to satisfy the requirements of lines of credit to the *município* from agencies such as the World Bank or the Interamerican Development Bank (IDB) (Sobreira de Moura, 2002: 216). It should be underlined here that the role of the *municípios* in formal environmental governance in Brazil was fortified in the last two decades as a result of principles established by the National Environment Policy Act of 1981. According to this law, the *municípios* may elaborate and enforce environmental norms, a possibility that was enhanced by the 1988 Constitution. The latter, in addition to having a long article (number 225) focusing on environmental issues, also introduced a tax reform giving new powers to local governments. This reflects a more decentralised model brought in by the 1988 Constitution, not only in relation to the environment but to many other sectors of social life as well, with the intention of involving the population more effectively in the decision-making process.

To put these new environmental provisions into action, local governments may create councils, environmental or other, may establish special environmental funds – to promote better use of natural resources, or support local projects, for example – and may issue special legislation to promote sustainable practices, specific uses of the soil, or to protect areas of particular interest (a landscape, cultural heritage, and so on). The function of licensing may

Table 3.2 *The Brazilian federation (states, municipalities) and some elements of the municipalities' framework of formal environmental governance*

Regions	No. of states	No. of municipalities	Municipalities (2001) having (% of total municipalities)			
			Active council (A)	Environm'l fund (B)	Legislation* (C)	A, B, C
North (Amazon)	7	449	15.6	5.3	7.8	9
North-east	9	1,792	10.7	2.7	7.0	7
South-east	4	1,668	29.3	5.8	18.0	2.3
South	3	1,189	31.0	13.2	19.5	4.5
Centre-West	3	463	25.5	9.1	12.3	3.3
Total	26	5,561	22.2	6.6	13.5	2.2
Federal District	1					

Note: * Legislation on special-interest areas for preservation purposes.

Sources: IBGE – Brazilian Institute of Geography and Statistics; Carvalho et al. (2003).

be a source of finance for a *município* to promote initiatives that protect the local environment. However, to be implemented, it requires the previous existence of the municipal council. For the receipts to remain in the coffers of the local treasury, in turn, the government of the *município* must create a special fund or similar mechanism. Otherwise, the money is transferred to the state or federal government, following a principle that was introduced by the 1998 Law of Environmental Crimes. Where environmental councils formally exist, their success depends on the body's political weight (or on the intensity of green sentiments) inside the local administration as well as on resources, which are not always available. This problem can vary significantly, as the policy directions of local administrations tend to oscillate considerably over time. Sometimes they give priority status to the environment, sometimes they turn their back on it. In certain places, there are strong social movements, while in others people are not organised, and so on. Everywhere, the lack of environmental education is a factor that contributes to hold back the advance of sound practices of governance. Table 3.2 shows, for instance, that only 2.2 per cent of Brazilian *municípios* have local environment councils as well as special environmental funds and legislation on special interest areas. This means that a very small proportion of local governments in Brazil actually implement a conscious, integrated environmental policy (Carvalho et al., 2003).

6. CENTRALISATION AND DECENTRALISATION TRENDS IN THE FORMAL ENVIRONMENTAL GOVERNANCE

As a result of the 1988 Brazilian Constitution,[10] powers are well established in the country concerning the way the federation and its constituent units deal with environmental, and all other relevant, matters – although Brazil still lacks a complementary law detailing the competence of each level of government (Mattos de Lemos, 2002: 67). In effect, there is a legislative vacuum regulating co-operation among the entities of the Brazilian federation. This has provoked serious stalemates in the definition and reach of the actions of each one of these bodies (Souza et al., 2003: 65). The Constitution, however, requires that all international treaties signed by Brazil and ratified by the national Parliament be obeyed as laws, with which states and municipalities have to comply. The Constitution stipulated that the states had a one-year time limit after its promulgation to write their own constitutions in accordance with the principles it enshrined. This was done. The *municípios* were then given six months after the approval of their respective state constitutions to produce the laws which would serve as their municipal constitutions (called 'organic law'), and which were in turn required to be compatible with the federal and state constitutions. This was done as well. The end result is that the specific assignment of responsibilities among federal, state and local governments regarding the environment is that anticipated in the national basic law, supplemented by routine legislation.

In the case of industrial zoning for pollution control, for instance, basic directives are set up at the federal level, which consider the compatibility of environmental protection with the needs of manufacturing activities – a point that is the subject of the 1980 Industrial Zoning Bill. The states then indicate places where factories can be built, and issue licensing. The states are also responsible for enforcing legislation in general, and for assuring compliance with the norms. The municipalities observe if there is compliance with specific local rules, such as those concerning residential areas as against industrial parks, and issue final permits for the factories to be located at the designated places – or deny them. Any conflicts concerning clashing levels of government are solved by the judiciary system. In the case of chemicals used in agriculture, the 1989 Agrotoxics Act establishes that it is the competence of federal legislation to define agrotoxics, and the conditions under which they can be produced, marketed, used, transported and exported. The states also rule on the conditions under which agrochemicals can be produced, employed, and so on, and are responsible for enforcement. To the municipalities is ascribed the duty of issuing supplementary legislation on the use and storage of agrotoxics and their components.

The Union establishes general norms with respect to competing legislation. In those cases in which general rules are lacking, the states have full autonomy to set up their own legal framework, the validity of which will depend on its compatibility with the federal Constitution. To the *municípios* is reserved the authority to legislate on subjects of local interest, supplementing federal and state legislation. The Supreme Federal Tribunal, the highest court in Brazil, is the arbiter in the resolution of conflicts concerning the interpretation of the federal Constitution. The pattern of state and local governments' involvement in specific environmental policies is thus shaped by the way power is assigned for specific questions. Air pollution, for example, is controlled at the federal level, while sewage has traditionally been a responsibility of the states, as has the distribution of water (although the latter is now being assumed somewhat timidly by some municipalities). Waste collection, in turn, is undertaken only by local governments. Figure 3.2 tries to convey a concise picture of both centralising and decentralising trends with regard to environmental politics in Brazil. The existence of an international level to orient the country's policy-making does

Field→ ↓Level	Industrial pollution	Ecosystem protection	Agriculture	Forests	Water	Implementation & Enforcement
International		Convention on Biological Diversity (CBD)		(CBD); Convention on Climate Change		International treaties (Montreal and Kyoto Protocols, etc.)
National	National Environment Policy Act (LPNMA); Industrial Zoning Bill	LPNMA; SISNAMA; CONAMA's resolutions	LPNMA; CONAMA's resolutions; Agrotoxics Act	LPNMA; Forest Code	LPNMA; Water Code; National Water Agency (ANA); Water Resources Nat'l. Policy	CONAMA; Public Office of the Prosecution
State	State councils For the environment directives; State executive agencies; Permits, licensing	State councils For the environment directives; State executive agencies	State legislation; State executive agencies; Labelling	State councils For the environment directives; State executive agencies	River basin committees; State secretariats for water resources	State attorneys' offices; State executive agencies
Local	Municipal environm. agencies and councils; Municipal chambers of councillors; Licensing		Municipal inspection		Municipal environm. agencies and councils; Municipal chambers of councillors	Municipal environm. agencies and public attorneys; Municipal chambers of councillors

↑ centralisation ⇩ decentralisation

Figure 3.2 Centralisation/decentralisation trends in Brazilian environmental politics

not represent a strong determinant. Brazil complies with treaties and conventions it signs, but it is domestic legislation that provides the main frame of reference for environmental purposes. This is particularly meaningful in terms of federal and state institutions and norms, enforcement having a strong local element.

7. BASIC FEATURES OF THE ENVIRONMENTAL POLICY PROCESS

According to the SISNAMA model, Brazil's Ministry of the Environment (MMA) must plan, coordinate, supervise and control the implementation of the country's federal environmental policy, as well as set up governmental guidelines for a balanced, harmonious use of the environment. In principle, all sectors of the government should follow those orientations, there being ample room for autonomous initiatives at the state and local levels within the contexts of their jurisdictions. A central aspect of SISNAMA is precisely its sharing of functions in a decentralised way with other units of the Brazilian federation. The states are especially well prepared to participate in this interaction. The *municípios*, however (see Table 3.2), still lack more involvement in the process (MMA, 2003). This is mostly due to a shortage of financial resources and technical expertise, as well as to insufficient knowledge of, or commitment to, the principles of sustainable development. But the lack of laws complementing the 1988 Constitution and specifying competences among the federal bodies has led to many conflicts. It is routine for contradictory, even antagonistic, measures to be taken up by the municipalities under the aegis of insufficient characterisation of what the norms call 'local interests' (Souza et al., 2003: 66–7).

Within SISNAMA, several instruments, essentially of a command-and-control nature, were created in the last two decades. In spite of its lack of infrastructure and financial resources, CONAMA contributed to their appearance through its rigorous normative resolutions (M. Ribeiro, 2002: 95). The instruments introduced by CONAMA include environmental impact evaluations for all those activities which are potentially damaging to the environment, as a result of which the presentation of assessments and reports of environmental impact (known as the EIA–RIMA instruments) is now obligatory. The instruments also include the federal technical register of activities of significant environmental impact, licensing, labelling, environmental zoning, and so on. In addition, CONAMA has the mission to establish patterns of environmental quality, limits to polluting activities, and less environmentally aggressive technological alternatives. It has the power to institute fines and control fiscal benefits to polluting activities. An important point on CONAMA's trajectory was the establishment, in 1987, of the public-hearing tool, whose democratic nature makes it the most criticised of the juridical instruments for the defence of the environment in Brazil (Antunes, 2000: 239). Public hearings were conceived to inform citizens about the contents of the EIA–RIMAs, and to provide the authorities with a measure of the repercussions of the projects involved. A point to be stressed here is that the large majority of EIAs in Brazil are more an instrument for justifying decisions already made than the opening of a negotiation process.[11] They 'are couched in a rhetoric aimed at convincing the public that all possible precautions have been taken to protect the environment' (Leis, 2000: 99).

The legal framework that sets the pattern for environmental politics in Brazil, with the important support of the current Brazilian Constitution, was the result of a great mobilisation of the environmental movement. The latter was able to count on almost 60 of the 550 members of the constituent assembly to form an ecologist front, led by São Paulo deputy Fábio Feldman (Drummond, 1998–1999: 144). A chapter on the environment was conceived, and for the first time included in a Brazilian constitution. Its fundamental tenet is to recognise the right of the population to an ecologically-balanced environment as a common good, essential to a sane quality of life. The duty of the government, together with society, to defend and preserve the environment for the sake of the present and future generations, is also inscribed in it.

BOX 3.1 PHASES IN BRAZILIAN ENVIRONMENTAL LEGISLATION

The evolution of the Brazilian environmental legislation over time may be summarised as follows (see Projeto GEO Cidades, 2002: annex 5):

(a) Up to the 1970s (mainly from the 1930s on): An environmental component was inserted in a range of legal documents on a sector-by-sector basis (Water Code, Forest Code, for example); control institutions like the IBDF appeared. There was no consistent effort to protect or preserve nature through legislation.

(b) 1970s: Social mobilisation, with some influence from abroad, chiefly after 1972; specific norms begin to be introduced (minerals, nuclear sector, tourist areas, urban development, etc.), but without a comprehensive approach; creation of SEMA (1973) at the federal level, and new agencies at the state level (such as FEEMA in Rio de Janeiro).

(c) 1980s: National Environment Policy Act (1981), Public Civil Action Act (1985), Coastal Management Act (1988), Agrotoxics Act (1989). New treatment of the environment in the 1988 Federal Constitution (with a new role for municipalities, as federative units). Creation of SISNAMA–CONAMA (1981), and of a new executive agency inside the Ministry of the Environment, IBAMA (1989).

(d) 1990s: New approach to problems, although more rhetorical than effective, with the appearance of the concept of sustainable development, adopted in 1992; consolidation both of CONAMA – whose resolutions have the force of law – and SISNAMA. Public hearings and participation of the population are strengthened. Law of Environmental Crimes is approved in 1998, transforming environmental damage into punishable crime, and giving polluters penal responsibility. National Water Resources Policy Act, or Law of the Waters, is issued (1997), introducing the concept of participatory committees for the management of river basins; Environmental Education Law also issued (1999).

(e) From 2000 on: The Agenda-21 process is resumed at the national level (concluded in 2002), and in several states and some municipalities. Creation of the Environmental Control and Inspection Fee (2000) on potentially polluting and environmental-resources-intensive activities, whose proceeds, together with the income from environmental fines, form the financial basis of the National Environmental Fund (FNMA). At the state and municipal levels similar funds exist, though not universally. The resources of such funds are reserved for projects to recuperate degraded areas, ameliorate environmental quality and promote environmental education. Law of the Statute of the City is approved (2001) establishing norms for environmentally-sound urban development. After an ample consultation process, the National Biodiversity Policy is instituted by decree (2002).

Viewing the recent Brazilian history of environmental governance in a wider context, the items of basic legislation which were passed following the National Environment Policy Act of 1981 include the Public Civil Action Act (1985), the Coastal Management Act (1988), the IBAMA Law

(1989), the Agrotoxics Act (1989), the Water Resources Act (1997), and the Environmental Crimes Law (1998). According to a proviso of the 1988 Constitution (third paragraph of article 225, on the environment), the last of these falls within the domain of criminal law. It is probably the most important in the above list. It had a long, complex, and difficult passage through Congress. Before this law, many serious crimes were punished with light sentences, while illicit acts of more debatable dimensions were severely punished. As a result of the law, public agents are to be relentlessly and criminally prosecuted when they waive the need for environmental impact assessments in inappropriate situations, or accept insufficiently complete EIAs.

8. PARTICIPATORY CHARACTERISTICS OF THE ENVIRONMENTAL POLICY PROCESS

In Brazil the effective use of participatory practices in the environmental arena has been promoted by the creation of both SISNAMA and CONAMA (Mattos de Lemos, 2002: 71). This has occurred mostly at the national and state levels. At the local level, there has not been so much participation in the environmental sphere, as pressures from society have not been as common in this field as they are in fields such as health, rural development, rights of the child and the adolescent, municipal budgets, and so on. Overall, however, participation in ecological issues has developed considerably during the last decade. The construction of Brazil's Agenda 21, for instance, followed the participatory model, and the resulting mobilisation of society in many parts of the country taught important lessons and produced meaningful results.

Participation of civil society in formulating policy is a crucial feature of the SISNAMA model (Camargo et al., 2002: 34–5). This is based on the premise that stakeholders not only want a say, but are also prepared to share the responsibility of decision-making. The principle of social control in the definition of directives and priorities for environmental policy is fundamental in that conception. Civil society has been called to participate effectively through NGOs and social movements. Its response to, and presence in, the process of environmental policy formulation in Brazil has been impressive. Groups from civil society play a fundamental role in the discussion of problems, in devising alternative solutions, and in finding the measures that can lead towards their adoption by SISNAMA. CONAMA's assembly, by the way, is the oldest and largest body with such a profile in Brazil.

The adoption of the participatory model by the state of Pernambuco for the preparation of its Agenda 21 constitutes a valuable case study (see Pernambuco, 2003). During the period 1999–2002, several rounds of discussion and consultation took place throughout the eleven development regions of the state. A state forum was set up to coordinate the process. Civil society had a great involvement in this, indicating priorities and directions for the process's final product.[12] The increasing role of participation in democratic spaces has given more openness to the formulation of environmental policy in Brazil. Stakeholders' participation is a particularly significant feature of some procedures of the country's formal environmental governance – the composition of CONAMA and similar bodies serving as proof of this. Participation was particularly intense during the preparation and final realisation, in November 2003, of the first National Conference of the Environment, convened by MMA. This was a truly democratic forum with all the tensions and drawbacks of a gathering of almost 2000 delegates chosen during pre-conferences at the state level, in addition to CONAMA's members.[13]

Greater participation on the part of the private sector – which is duly represented in CONAMA – has also been a feature of environmental politics in recent times. There has been an increasing tendency to involve the business sector in the arena of environmental issues, through calls for responsible behaviour. The year 1992 may be cited as a landmark with respect to these new attitudes, with Brazilian enterprises assuming the need for more co-operative government–private sector arrangements (Almeida, 2002). A manifestation of the adoption of such new attitudes can be seen in the area of social care which has been taken up by many enterprises (Camargo et al., 2002: 34). This is a sphere in which both negotiated agreements with industry, and voluntary or non-regulatory initiatives, have been implemented. The powerful National Bank for Economic and Social Development (BNDES), a public bank which has a function within Brazil similar to the global one of the World Bank, has played an important role in this context. It has emitted signals to which the reactions from industry show that there is receptivity to the concepts of precaution and prevention, as opposed to remedial solutions, as basic principles for dealing with the issue of environmental impact (Kishiname et al., 2002: 379–80).

An instance of this is the 1995 Green Protocol, a federal government initiative to internalise the environment as a variable to be taken into account in lending by the official banks – of which there are a number in Brazil. The BNDES has attempted, in fact, to induce an environmentally-friendly modernisation process. It has promoted, for example, the replacement of the technology for cellulose whitening, the utilisation of gas from coke-making to generate electricity, environmental certification, and so on. An indicator of the objective interest of enterprises in new, more accountable, systems of environmental management is the growth in the number of

ISO 14001 certifications in Brazil. In 1998, 101 certifications were issued. This number increased to 359 in 2001 (Kishiname et al., 2002: 380). The great change in corporate behaviour may be ascribed to the approval in 1998 of the Environmental Crimes Law, which introduced the notion of corporate penal responsibility for damage caused to the natural environment. As a result, many programmes of environmental education, preservation of natural resources, recycling and recovery of degraded areas (with reforesting), have been undertaken by the corporate segment, within which the Brazilian Business Council for Sustainable Development (CEBDS) has represented a paradigm change (Almeida, 2002).

9. FURTHER RELATED QUESTIONS

Water resources management is an area in which new rules for environmental governance have been implemented since the 1988 Constitution. The 1997 Law of the Waters instituted the national water resources policy, the management system of which employs both participation and decentralisation, with river basins serving as the basic unit of planning. The mechanism of river basin management has assumed the form of committees, many of which have been created since the new water law was approved. Besides the basin committees, the scheme as a whole also embraces the National Water Resources Council, its counterparts at state level, and the water agencies, under the command of ANA, the National Water Agency, created in 2000. The committees are made up of users, civil society and representatives of the three levels of government (federal, state, local) – in proportions that may be criticised, as many people have done, chiefly on account of an insufficient representation of civil society (Ribeiro and Galizoni, 2002–2003: 133). Their powers include voting and monitoring the water resources plan of the corresponding basin, setting up mechanisms for charging for water use, and arbitrating conflicts related to water resources. Together with the MMA, the federal and state water councils, and ANA, the committees compose a system which has been somewhat successful in establishing the rules for managing water resources, although it is felt that the power of the committees is compromised by the fact that ANA has the final say in basin projects (Ribeiro and Galizoni, 2002–2003; Pagnoccheschi, 2003). Although charging for water use is a central feature of the system, this rule has not yet been applied in a generalised manner. It is, however, a new parameter to be taken into account, and one which the basin committees are trying to implement under the umbrella of the polluter-pays principle. It has already been implemented in a few places, such as the valley of the River Paraíba (Rio de Janeiro and São Paulo states). Tapped water and sanitation, in turn, are segments which have been undergoing a somewhat controversial privatisation process. Because of a number of conflicts of interests between the states and municipalities there is a need for a federal law to be approved in Congress before these services can be privatised. The national executive has sent a project to that effect, but the debate has been politicised (Tucci, 2002: 276). On the whole, no major tendency for the privatisation of environmental services exists in Brazil at the present time.

A particularly distinguishing trait of formal environmental governance in Brazil is the role assigned to public attorneys. In accordance with Brazilian law, public attorneys (in the Public Office of the Prosecution) have the function 'to promote civil inquiries and public civil actions for the protection of public and social patrimony, the environment and other diffuse and collective interests' (article 129-III, Brazilian Constitution). This means that they can act independently (*ex-officio*) of lawsuits introduced by offended parties. They can initiate civil enquiries, penal actions and any other administrative procedure upon being notified of environmental violations. They act on the principle that violators are to be made responsible for damage caused, on both penal and civil counts. In CONAMA there are two non-voting members from the Public Office of the Prosecution, one representing the federal branch and the other the state branches.

The constitutional organisation of Brazil's Public Office of the Prosecution, with its ample autonomy and independence, does not, according to Antunes (2000: 416), have a parallel in any other country. In effect, the attorneys are subject to no one except the law and their own conscience. Moreover, diverse laws have attributed extra-judicial functions to the Office of the Prosecution in relation to the protection of a wide range of diffuse interests. This means that public attorneys have also become an important agent of policy-making (Souza et al., 2003: 84). Protected by their ample shield, they have taken up the task of promoting lawsuits by themselves, or induced by public demand, in defence of the environment, with impressive results. In Recife, for example, they won a fight against big contractors who (in alliance with the local government) were constructing buildings without respecting a minimum 30-metre distance from the river waterline. An indication that the attorneys have been truly effective in enforcing environmental regulation is that some people want to introduce a constitutional amendment to reduce their powers.

The above analysis has focused only on the formal process of environmental governance in Brazil. This should not be taken as an indication of neglect regarding the practices and knowledge of the country's traditional and indigenous peoples. In fact, both the natives – some of them still living in isolation in the Amazonian rainforest – and traditional inhabitants, such as the riparian populations of the Amazon and *caiçaras* from the south-east, offer a sound reference in terms of their interactions with the environment (see, for example, Posey, 1995). An example of indigenous practices in the Amazon are the 'forest islands', called *apetê* by the Kayapó tribe and studied by Posey (1995). Silva and Begossi (2004) refer to the sound ways in which the traditional peoples of the Amazon manage their fishing resources, and the bad consequences they are experiencing as a result of the intensification of commercial fisheries and the expansion of large land-holdings in their territories in recent decades. In spite of the interest aroused by the study of traditional ecological knowledge and its applications (Cavalcanti, 2002), what effectively drives environmental governance in Brazil is what is being done on the modern side of Brazilian society. Nonetheless, the study of indigenous practices, as the work of people like Begossi (2004) and McGrath et al. (1999) has shown, is a field in itself for the understanding of the challenges of environmental governance in general.

10. RHETORIC AND REALITY

The real problem of environmental governance in Brazil lies in its implementation, since the core of Brazil's political system remains addicted to growth, and extremely vulnerable (or sympathetic, to say the least) to powerful economic lobbying. As a matter of fact, policy-making in general does not combine at all well with the commitments of SISNAMA and the MMA. There is a great abyss between the (dominant) perspective of the politically-strong Ministries of Planning and Finance, on the one hand, and the marginalised Ministry of the Environment, on the other (Kohlhepp, 2001: 28). This is a situation where decentralisation does not work, and where bottom-up strategies seldom have a chance of being adopted. Just to give an illustration of the problem: in 2001, the breakdown of authorised federal expenditure in the Amazon shows an allocation of 85 per cent of the total to infrastructure, 9 per cent to military activities, and only 6 per cent to environmental protection (Allegretti, 2001: 49). The crux of the matter is that the environment has a marginal presence in the bigger scenario, as if it were a subset of society and the economy (in the same category of transport, energy, communications, foreign trade). In this model, what deserves care, attention, protection, priority treatment, is none other than the economy (Viola, 1998–1999).

Essentially, SISNAMA's actions are geared towards public initiatives for the maintenance of ecological equilibrium, and the compatibility of socio-economic development with the preservation of nature. It is a different approach from that of the hard core of the government (the Ministries of Planning, Finance, Economic Development, Agriculture), since for SISNAMA the interpretation that ought to prevail, correctly, from a biophysical perspective, is to consider the environment as the larger envelope within which all human activity takes place. This view seems to orientate the MMA in its efforts to coordinate policy at the state and federal levels. The MMA has also tried to include environmental criteria in the formulation of all government policy (the so-called transversality principle), with the goal of minimising negative environmental impacts.

At the same time, the enforcement apparatus of environmental governance is, or is made to be, inefficient, because it is hostage to incongruous legislation and short-run sectoral policies. In sum, the predatory, traditional sectors end up prevailing over the environment. This was clear in 1995 when the government should have implemented the Inter-Ministerial Commission for Sustainable Development (CIDES), created by President Itamar Franco, after some hesitation, in mid-1994. CIDES was to report directly to the head of government, and its role was to give sustainable features to the general process of policy-making. But it suffered a silent veto. In its stead, the government finally set up, in 1997, the lower-graded Commission of Policies for Sustainable Development and Brazilian Agenda 21, subordinated to the Chamber of Natural Resource Policies, the latter in turn being an arm of the federal Council of Government.

Environmental politics seemed to evolve favourably in 2003 with the appointment by president Lula of Marina Silva[14] as Brazil's minister of the environment. This antecedent appeared to outline a commitment by the new administration to promote economic development while simultaneously respecting and preserving the environment, as assumed in the official discourse on sustainable development. Minister Marina Silva intended especially to preserve biodiversity in the Amazon as well as the traditional way of exploiting the rainforest represented by the successful extractivist-reserves model. In her new post, she tried in fact to introduce a new perspective for policy-making at the federal level.

As a basic component of her programme as minister she conceived the first National Conference of the Environment, which took place in November 2003 in Brasília, after a series of preliminary activities mobilising civil society and governmental sectors all over the country. At the closing of the conference (30 November), the minister said: 'Implementation is the catchword. The guideline of our government . . . is to lead by example.' This also reflected the conference's spirit, as indicated by the fact that four-fifths of the proposals submitted to the pre-conference assemblies in the states, and later forwarded to the national event, asked for compliance with the legislation and the norms of environmental control.

Despite having a rigorous and well-conceived legislation, considered by some as one of the most advanced in the world (Drummond, 1998–1999: 145; Antunes, 2000: 43; Mattos de Lemos, 2002: 71–2), the fact is that the Brazilian state has not succeeded in putting it into effect. A permanent struggle exists between those, like Marina Silva, who recognise the necessity of applying the existing rules of environmental governance, and the flock of supporters of the idea of economic development at any cost. The latter have been victorious so far. In the aftermath of the Rio-92 summit, the economicist hegemony prevailed, with economic reforms dominating everything else according to the basic tenets of neoliberal policy. Environmental considerations were not removed from the official discourse, but any emphasis on the environment had little more than a symbolic function, as a sort of pledge in favour of sustainable development, to assuage public opinion (Camargo et al., 2002: 23). Today, this situation continues to be a strong feature of Brazilian reality. Not that there is a complete paralysis of effective environmental governance in Brazil. Many of CONAMA's resolutions,[15] for instance, are concretely applied. Public hearings are constantly being implemented. And, above all, public attorneys, with functions strengthened by the 1988 Constitution, have played an important role in assuring that the legislation is observed (Saint-Clair dos Santos, 2002).

The sad fact remains, however, that what is occurring in Brazil, even now, contradicts the principles and references of good environmental governance. Although it is not easy to build a framework of legislation, rules and institutions of environmental governance like that which Brazil now possesses (including those to protect the native people's way of environmental governance), this is not enough, because what matters is the effective application of the existing norms. One example of the inadequacy of effective governance in Brazil is the continuation of Cardoso's policies in Amazonia. The question is that the same narrow short-run perspective which renders the economy more important than anything else has infiltrated all relevant levels of government in Brazil. A general fear of contradicting the expectations of the market leads to the triumph of the short-sighted, production-oriented view, against the feelings of the ecologically-minded community centred around the commitments of sustainable development.

NOTES

1. The country, inhabited by indigenous tribes speaking over 4000 languages, was conquered by the Portuguese in April 1500. Until then the native population (somewhere

between 6 and 8 million people in an area of around 8.5 million sq km) had used the resources of nature in a well-balanced way, as Pero Vaz de Caminha, the scribe of the discoverers' fleet, seems to have been somewhat aware (see Cortesão, 1943, *A carta de Pero Vaz de Caminha*, Rio de Janeiro: Edições Livros de Portugal).

2. The governor of the state of Mato Grosso, where the soyabean sector has become dominant in the economy, is Blairo Maggi, Brazil's biggest soyabean producer. Likewise, the Brazilian Minister of Agriculture, Roberto Rodrigues, is an important soyabean grower.
3. This certainly mirrors, using Joseph Schumpeter's terminology, the 'pre-analytic view' of conventional economics which considers the environment not as the whole but as a sector of society (see Daly, 1996). I follow the same line of Daly's reasoning, namely, that the economy is a subsystem of the ecological subsystem. This means that there are limits to growth, regardless of how desirable it might be.
4. Typically, the state of Pernambuco's Agenda-21 document on a sustainable economy (basic to the process), places first, among the five items in the section entitled 'Philosophical north – the principles of sustainability', the item: 'More growth, sustained and shared by all' (CENTRU – Centro de Educação e Cultura do Trabalhador Rural, 2002, *Projeto Construir: construindo a Agenda 21 no Estado de Pernambuco*. Recife: CENTRU, first version: 7).
5. Presently, landowners there are allowed to cut up to 20 per cent of the forest in their legal plots for agricultural purposes. A law has been proposed in Congress to increase this fraction to 50 per cent, but it has not been accepted so far.
6. Writing about forest law in Brazil in 1950, Osny Duarte Pereira, a lawyer and judge, pointed out: 'The laws were never observed, and today we regret the integral disappearance of brazil-wood and other hardwoods' (quoted by Antunes, 2000: 256).
7. Brazil since 1889 has been a federation, now with 26 states and a Federal District (see Table 3.2). The 1988 Federal Constitution, restoring a condition that existed until 1967, raised the status of Brazil's 5561 municipalities to the level of federative entities, giving them a series of attributions, including the defence of the environment.
8. *Caiçara* is a backwoodsman dwelling on the seacoast of the states of Rio de Janeiro and São Paulo.
9. In August 2007, Congress approved a new arrangement of environmental powers, reducing the extent of IBAMA's attributions, and splitting it into two. This occurred due to pressures from the powerful economic sectors within the federal government to speed up the licensing of controversial big hydroelectric projects in the Amazon.
10. The 1988 Constitution has an admirable democratic record. It was the result of a Constituent Assembly convened in 1986, after the return of Brazil to civilian rule in 1985. During the process of its elaboration, serious discussion took place on the nature of the Brazilian Federation. Although this led to a more solid understanding in relation to the assignment of powers among the federal units, the resulting constitution is not free of controversies.
11. To close this loophole, the environmentalist deputy Fernando Gabeira has proposed a new clause to be added to the National Environment Policy Act requiring that strategic environmental assessments of policies and programmes affecting the environment are prepared at their planning level. The proposal is following its course in Congress.
12. This author was invited to participate on several occasions. These included participation in the seminar (August 2002) which determined the final document of Pernambuco's Agenda 21.
13. This author also took part in the Pernambuco state pre-conference.
14. Marina Silva is a senator from the Amazon state of Acre. She has an admirable ecological background, including a close association with the well-known Brazilian environmentalist Chico Mendes who fought for the poor until his murder by unscrupulous big landowners in 1988.
15. To be fair, it must be said that CONAMA has suffered a certain paralysis since the beginning of 2003 which was still continuing at the end of 2004.

REFERENCES

Allegretti, Mary Helena (2001), 'Políticas do governo federal frente a problemas ambientais', *Cadernos Adenauer*, **2**(4), 39–50.

Almeida, Fernando (2002), 'A participação empresarial na Agenda 21', *Meio Ambiente e Desenvolvimento Sustentável* (Ministry of the Environment), special edition, August, pp. 34–9.

Antunes, Paulo de Bessa (2000), *Direito Ambiental*, 4th edn, Rio de Janeiro: Editora Lumen Juris.

Begossi, Alpina (ed.) (2004), *Ecologia de pescadores da Mata Atlântica e da Amazônia*, São Paulo: Hucitec, Fapesp, NUPAUB/USP; Campinas: NEPAM/UNICAMP.

Camargo, Aspásia, João Paulo Capobianco and José Antonio Puppim de Oliveira (2002), 'Os desafios da sustentabilidade no período pós-Rio-92: uma avaliação da situação brasileira', part I in Aspásia Camargo, João Paulo Capobianco and José Antonio Puppim de Oliveira (eds), *Meio Ambiente Brasil: Avanços e Obstáculos pós-Rio-92*, São Paulo: Estação Liberdade, Instituto Socioambiental; Rio de Janeiro: Fundação Getúlio Vargas.

Carvalho, Paulo Gonzaga M. de, Sonia Maria de Oliveira and Frederico Cavadas Barcellos (2003), 'Instrumentos de gestão local e meio ambiente', paper delivered at the V Biennial Meeting of the Brazilian Society for Ecological Economics (ECOECO), Caxias do Sul (Rio Grande do Sul), 3–6 September.

Cavalcanti, Clóvis (1991), 'Government policy and ecological concerns: some lessons from the Brazilian experience', Chapter 31 in Robert Costanza (ed.), *Ecological Economics: The Science and Management of Sustainability*, New York: Columbia University Press.

Cavalcanti, Clóvis (2002), 'Economic thinking, traditional ecological knowledge and ethnoeconomics', *Current Sociology*, **50**(1), 39–56.

CPDS – Comissão de Políticas de Desenvolvimento Sustentável e Agenda 21 Nacional (2002), 'Agenda 21 Brasileira: Plataforma de Ação da CPDS', *Texto para Discussão*, Brasília: CPDS.

Daly, Herman (1996), *Beyond Growth: The Economics of Sustainable Development*, Boston: Beacon Press.

Dias, Bráulio F. de Souza (2002), 'Biosegurança, bioética e biodiversidade', in Fábio Feldman (ed.), *Rio+10: Uma Década de Transformações*, Rio de Janeiro: Instituto de Estudos da Religião – ISER.

Drummond, José Augusto (1998–1999), 'A legislação ambiental brasileira de 1934 a 1998: comentários de um cientista ambiental simpático ao conservacionismo', *Ambiente e Sociedade*, **2**(3–4), 127–50.

Egler, Paulo (2002), 'Gestão ambiental integrada', in Wilhelm Hofmeister (ed.), *Rio + 10 = Joanesburgo: Rumos Para o Desenvolvimento Sustentável*, Fortaleza: Fundação Konrad Adenauer.

ISER – Instituto de Estudos da Religião (2003), *What Brazilians think about Environment and Sustainable Development: Survey with Leaders*, Rio de Janeiro: ISER; Brasília: Ministry of the Environment.

Kishiname, Roberto, Oded Grajew, Paulo Itacarambi and Carmen Weingrill (2002), 'Artigo-base sobre responsabilidade socioambiental das empresas', in Aspásia Camargo, João Paulo Capobianco and José Antonio Puppim de Oliveira (eds), *Meio Ambiente Brasil: Avanços e Obstáculos pós-Rio-92*, São Paulo: Estação Liberdade, Instituto Socioambiental; Rio de Janeiro: Fundação Getúlio Vargas.

Kohlhepp, Gerd (2001), 'A Amazônia frente a um novo desafio: o desenvolvimento sustentável e o programa Avança Brasil', *Cadernos Adenauer*, **2**(4), 9–38.

Leis, Héctor R. (2000), 'A politico-communicative model to overcome the impasse of the current politico-technical model of environmental negotiation in Brazil', in Clóvis Cavalcanti (ed.), *The Environment, Sustainable Development and Public Policies: Building Sustainability in Brazil*, Cheltenham, UK and Northampton, MA, USA: Edward Elgar.

Mattos de Lemos, Haroldo (2002), 'O sistema nacional do meio ambiente e o conselho nacional do meio ambiente no Brasil: seu impacto na qualidade de vida', 2nd part of Chapter II in Banco Interamericano de Desenvolvimento/Ministério do Meio Ambiente do Brasil, *Diálogos de Política Social e Ambiental: Aprendendo com os Conselhos Ambientais Brasileiros*, Brasília: Interamerican Development Bank.

McGrath, David G., F. Castro, E. Câmara and C. Futema (1999), 'Community management of floodplain lakes and the sustainable development of Amazonian fisheries', in C. Padoch et al. (eds), *Várzea: Diversity, Development, and Conservation of Amazonia's Whitewaterfloodplain*, New York: The New York Botanical Garden Press, pp. 59–82.

Medauar, Odete (ed.) (2003), *Constituição Federal. Coletânea de Legislação de Direito Ambiental*, São Paulo: Editora Revista dos Tribunais.

MMA – Ministério do Meio Ambiente, Conferência Nacional do Meio Ambiente (2003), *Vamos cuidar do Brasil: Fortalecendo o Sistema Nacional do Meio Ambiente*, texto-base (basic paper), Brasília: MMA.

Nepstad, Daniel, J.P. Capobianco, Ana C. Barros, Georgia Carvalho, Paulo Moutinho, Urbano Lopes and Paul Lefebvre (2001), *Avança Brasil: os Custos Ambientais para a Amazônia*, 2nd edn, Belém, Pará: IPAM – Instituto de Pesquisa Ambiental da Amazônia; Gráfica e Editora Alves; São Paulo: Instituto Socioambiental.

Nepstad, Daniel, D. McGrath, A. Alencar, A.C. Barros, G. Carvalho, M. Santilli and M. del C. Vera Díaz (2002), 'Frontier governance in Amazonia', *Science*, **295**, 629–31.

Pagnoccheschi, Bruno (2003), 'Política Nacional de Recursos Hídricos', in Paul E. Little (ed.), *Políticas Ambientais no Brasil: Análise, Instrumentos e Experiências*, São Paulo: Peirópolis; Brasília: IIEB.

Pernambuco, Fórum Estadual da Agenda 21 (2003), *Agenda 21 do Estado de Pernambuco*, Recife: Secretaria de Ciência Tecnologia e Meio Ambiente.

Posey, Darrell (1995), 'Conseqüências ecológicas da presença do Índio Kayapó na Amazônia: recursos antropológicos e direitos de recursos tradicionais', in Clóvis Cavalcanti (ed.), *Desenvolvimento e Natureza: Estudos para uma Sociedade Sustentável*, São Paulo: Cortez; Recife: Fundação Joaquim Nabuco.

Projeto Geo Cidades (2002), *Relatório Ambiental Urbano Integrado: Informe GEO Rio de Janeiro*, Rio de Janeiro: Consórcio Parceria 21 IBAM/ISER/REDEH.

Ribeiro, Eduardo Magalhães and Flávia Maria Galizoni (2002–2003), 'Água, população rural e políticas de gestão: o caso do vale do Jequitinhonha, Minas Gerais', *Ambiente e Sociedade*, **V**(2), August/December; **VI**(1), January/July, pp. 129–46.

Ribeiro, José Cláudio J. (2002), 'Os conselhos ambientais estaduais e municipais e seus resultados', in Banco Interamericano de Desenvolvimento/Ministério do Meio Ambiente do Brasil, *Diálogos de Política Social e Ambiental: Aprendendo com os Conselhos Ambientais Brasileiros*, Brasília: Interamerican Development Bank.

Ribeiro, Maurício Andrés (2002), 'A arquitetura da gestão ambiental colegiada', in Banco Interamericano de Desenvolvimento/Ministério do Meio Ambiente do Brasil, *Diálogos de Política Social e Ambiental: Aprendendo com os Conselhos Ambientais Brasileiros*, Brasília: Interamerican Development Bank.

Saint-Clair dos Santos, Honorato (2002), 'Ministério Público e a proteção ao meio ambiente: participação no Conselho Nacional do Meio Ambiente', in Banco Interamericano de Desenvolvimento/Ministério do Meio Ambiente do Brasil, *Diálogos de Política Social e Ambiental: Aprendendo com os Conselhos Ambientais Brasileiros*, Brasília: Interamerican Development Bank.

SENAC (2003), 'Meio ambiente lança desafio ao governo', *SENAC e Educação Ambiental*, **12**(3), 28–30.

Silva, Andréa Leme and Alpina Begossi (2004), 'Uso de recursos por ribeirinhos no Médio Rio Negro', in Alpina Begossi (ed.), *Ecologia de Pescadores da Mata Atlântica e da Amazônia*, São Paulo: Hucitec, Fapesp, NUPAUB/USP; Campinas: NEPAM/UNICAMP.

Siviero, Simone de Oliveira (1995), 'A política ambiental e o poder local', in 35 NEPAM – Núcleo de Estudos e Pesquisas Ambientais, *A Questão Ambiental: Cenário de Pesquisa*, Campinas: UNICAMP: pp. 253–74.

Sobreira de Moura, Alexandrina (2002), 'A perspectiva dos Estados', in Banco Interamericano de Desenvolvimento/Ministério do Meio Ambiente do Brasil, *Diálogos de Política Social e Ambiental: Aprendendo com os Conselhos Ambientais Brasileiros*, Brasília: Interamerican Development Bank.

Souza, Elaine Castelo Branco et al. (2003), 'Desafio da gestão ambiental nos municípios', in Paul E. Little (ed.), *Políticas Ambientais no Brasil: Análise, Instrumentos e Experiências*, São Paulo: Peirópolis; Brasília: IIEB.

Torras, Mariano (2003), *Welfare, Inequality and Resource Depletion: a Reassessment of Brazilian Economic Growth*, Aldershot, UK and Burlington, VT, USA: Ashgate Publishing.

Tucci, Carlos E.M. (2002), 'Recursos hídricos', in Aspásia Camargo, João Paulo Capobianco and José Antonio Puppim de Oliveira (eds), *Meio Ambiente Brasil: Avanços e Obstáculos pós-Rio-92*, São Paulo: Estação Liberdade, Instituto Socioambiental; Rio de Janeiro: Fundação Getúlio Vargas.

Varela, Jorge (2003), 'The shrimp pond threat to coastal ecosystems', paper delivered at the Mangrove 2003 Conference 'Connecting research and participative management of estuaries and mangroves', Salvador (Bahia), 20–24 May.

Viola, Eduardo (1987), 'O movimento ecológico no Brasil (1974–1986): do ambientalismo à ecopolítica', in J.A. Pádua (ed.), *Ecologia e Política no Brasil*, Rio de Janeiro: Espaço e Tempo: pp. 63–110.

Viola, Eduardo (1998–1999), 'As políticas públicas do primeiro governo Cardoso sob a ótica da sustentabilidade', *Ambiente e Sociedade*, **II**(3&4), 195–204.

4. Interdependence and coordination in the Canadian environmental policy process

Marcia Valiante

1. INTRODUCTION

Canada is a large, industrialized country with a relatively small population and a highly decentralized governance structure. It has an image, both inside and outside the country, of the active pursuit of environmental protection and sustainable development. This study reviews the development and implementation of environmental and sustainable development policies in Canada, with an emphasis on the legal, political and institutional framework within which such policies are adopted and carried out. It is not intended as a comprehensive treatment of all aspects of environmental policy but as a general overview. It is hoped that this will provide both a general understanding of how the structures influence the direction of environmental policies and some assessment of the effectiveness of those policies.

2. STRUCTURAL FOUNDATIONS OF CANADIAN ENVIRONMENTAL POLICY

2.1 The Constitution

The usual starting point for an understanding of Canadian environmental policy-making structures is the Constitution.[1] In the Canadian Constitution, the power to legislate over all subjects is divided between two levels of government, federal and provincial.[2] Although it was last amended in 1982, the Constitution does not refer to the environment. Rather, 'the environment' is viewed by the courts broadly, as a 'diffuse subject matter' that touches on many powers of both the federal and the ten provincial governments. Thus, it is 'not an independent matter of legislation under the *Constitution Act, 1867* . . . it is a constitutionally abstruse matter which does not comfortably fit within the existing division of powers without considerable overlap and uncertainty.'[3] This means that environmental regulation is a matter of shared jurisdiction between the federal and provincial governments and that any analysis of that division of authority is complex and lacks definitiveness.

Certain powers to affect the environment flow from how the Constitution divides ownership of public lands and resources between the two levels of government. Generally speaking, public lands and resources located within the territory of a province are owned by the province.[4] Some lands within each province[5] and lands and resources in the three northern territories and the offshore are federally-owned. As a result, provinces control access to, the pace of exploitation or conservation of, and royalties derived from, all natural resources within their boundaries.[6]

Federal *legislative* power includes some specific subjects, including fisheries, navigation, Aboriginal lands and interprovincial transportation and works, and more general matters that can embrace a wide range of issues and responses: matters of 'national concern'[7] or national emergency, criminal law,[8] 'trade and commerce', taxation and spending.

Provincial legislative power encompasses the subjects of 'property and civil rights' (which includes the regulation of businesses in the province), local works, the management of public lands, non-renewable natural resources, municipal issues, direct taxation (which restricts the kinds of economic instruments available to provincial regulators), and 'generally all matters of a local or private nature'. Provinces are limited in their authority to affect extraprovincial matters, and it has been suggested that the federal government alone would have authority over interprovincial pollution.[9] Nevertheless, most environmental regulation in Canada is provincial.

Agriculture and health are subjects of concurrent jurisdiction. International relations are generally a matter within federal competence, but not exclusively. Treaty negotiation is an executive function, but implementation is a legislative one, resulting in implementation of international treaties being divided, depending on the subject matter.[10] Thus, even though the federal government negotiates treaties, it may have little or no ability to implement them if they deal with matters within provincial jurisdiction. The current example of Canada's support for the Kyoto Protocol illustrates this dilemma: Canada was an international leader in shaping the Protocol, the federal government ratified it and now faces enormous political backlash at home in getting provincial support for implementation.[11]

Because of the nature of environmental issues, it is clear from this catalogue that there could be considerable fragmentation, inconsistency or duplication in Canada's environmental policy. Even with respect to provincial resources, federal authority over trade and commerce, fisheries and taxation can have significant impacts on their development and use, and the associated environmental implications. In defining the boundary between each level's authority, the Supreme Court's approach has been to review regulations on a case-by-case basis, rather than making general pronouncements. Even though the Court has been supportive of a strong federal role in environmental protection, the federal government has not tested the full limits of its authority. It is, therefore, difficult to predict with certainty which level of government would have jurisdiction to address a particular environmental issue, and the limits on that authority, for example, when an environmental problem might become a matter of 'national concern'. This uncertainty creates some degree of risk for the government that acts in response to an environmental problem that its action will be challenged and it will lose.[12] However, the Supreme Court has repeatedly upheld environmental measures by the federal, provincial and municipal governments, stating that environmental concerns are of 'superordinate importance' and a 'major challenge of our time' requiring 'action by governments at all levels'. Despite this, the federal government in particular has taken a narrow view of its jurisdiction and has been reluctant to push the limits of its role. The Supreme Court has also made it clear that '[d]ifferent types of legislative powers may support different types of environmental provisions'.[13]

In Canada over the last 30 years, governments have experimented with a range of mechanisms to overcome the legal uncertainty of shared authority and have developed practical methods for coordinating their actions directed toward environmental protection.[14] The federal and provincial governments have gone through several cycles of conflict and cooperation, occasionally competing with each other for public credit for decisive environmental action. Particularly active periods occurred in the early 1970s and in the late 1980s and early 1990s, and led to significant conflicts between governments, but at the same time to advances in environmental protection. More commonly, however, governments have worked cooperatively either to jointly address problems or to divide up, or 'rationalize', responsibility. These relationships and efforts have varied greatly over time and between issues (Harrison, 2002). As well, relationships have been more strained between the federal government and certain provinces, such as Alberta and Quebec, than with other provinces, but not with respect to all issues (Skogstad, 1996):

> There is little doubt that the general federal–provincial domain of environmental policy is extraordinarily multi-faceted. The [federal Environment] ministers' various briefing books over the years reveal at any given time, and with each province, dozens of ongoing issues, from small to large. Most are resolved as a

> matter of course. Some become test cases for the practice of intergovernmental warfare or for the studied art of deflecting blame onto someone else. (Doern and Conway, 1994: 94)

The most sustained effort to recast the federal–provincial relationship on environmental issues commenced in the early 1990s and culminated in the adoption of the Canada-Wide Accord on Environmental Harmonization in 1998 by all provinces, territories and the federal government, except Quebec.[15] The Accord itself is a framework agreement containing broad principles and objectives, and will be implemented through a series of sub-agreements. The existing sub-agreements divide roles and responsibilities according to which order of government is 'best situated'.[16] In most cases, that will mean the development of national, or 'Canada-wide', standards by consensus of the 13 participating governments and implementation of those standards by the provinces. Once a government has been assigned a role, the other government agrees not to act in that role (Canadian Council of Ministers of the Environment, 1998).

Although it is a political, rather than legally-binding agreement, in Winfield's view the Harmonization Accord has 'fundamentally restructured national environmental policy-making in Canada' (Winfield, 2002). The major expected effect is to dilute the role of the federal government on national environmental policy and to move primary control over implementation to the provinces. The major achievement of the Accord's first six years has been the successful development of a number of Canada-wide standards; however, implementation of the standards has been slow and there are as yet few positive environmental results.[17] An increased 'spirit of cooperation' has prevailed, but the process has required significant amounts of time and resources on the part of all participants. Governments have committed to continue to work through this process.

2.2 Actors and Institutions

There are a very large number of actors involved in environmental policy in Canada. These include governmental, inter-governmental and non-governmental agencies and organizations. The most important ones and their roles are discussed in this section.

At the federal level, environmental legislation is adopted by Parliament, first by the House of Commons, then by the non-elected Senate. There are more than 50 federal laws that affect the environment in some way. Within the structures of Parliament, the shape of legislation is largely due to the governing party's preferences but can be affected by the legislative hearing process run by the House of Commons Standing Committee on the

Environment and Sustainable Development. This process provides a public forum for interested groups and individuals to express their opinions on draft legislation which the Committee then considers as it recommends amendments prior to a final vote in Parliament. In recent years, this Committee has been quite aggressive in its reports, pushing for stronger legislation and a stronger federal role in environmental protection. However, it has not been supported by the governing party on a number of significant issues.

Executive responsibility for setting the policy agenda, developing strategies and implementing environmental programmes is not centralized but is spread across a number of departments, including Environment, Natural Resources, Health, Industry, Fisheries and Oceans, Agriculture, Indian and Northern Affairs and Transport. Environment Canada is the lead federal agency. It has a broad and growing mandate but has always had to compete with other departments for resources and influence. Its history has been one of internal conflicts about direction, inconsistent leadership, lack of power relative to other departments, successive reorganizations, and resistance to progressive action from both inside and outside government.[18] Governmental activity on environmental issues went through at least two cycles of 'rise and fall', usually associated with changing levels of public concern (Harrison, 1996). Environment Canada's fortunes rose and fell in tandem with these shifts in public opinion. By the mid-1990s, as public concern shifted to the economy, the government's response to the recession was to cut the department's budget by 30 per cent, despite new legislative mandates requiring greater resources for implementation.

A new institution, independent of the government in power, was created in 1996 within the Office of the Auditor General. The Commissioner for the Environment and Sustainable Development was given the mandate to 'ensure the federal government is accountable for greening its policies, operations and programs'. To do this, it conducts environmental audits of the government's activities, monitors implementation of the 'sustainable development strategies' of 25 federal departments and agencies, manages a public petitions process, and reports on all to Parliament.[19] The Commissioner's reports have had a positive impact: they 'play an important role in providing and disseminating information, raising public awareness and providing recommendations for policy reform to the departments concerned' (Vourc'h, 2001: 7).

The courts have helped shape environmental policy to a limited extent. On constitutional challenges, the Supreme Court of Canada in particular has upheld almost all the environmental laws of all levels of government that came before it within the last 30 years. The Supreme Court has clarified that there is a strong constitutional basis for an active federal role in environmental protection. In a parliamentary system, where the legislature and executive are fused, legislation tends to give a great deal of discretion to the executive departments. Thus, laws generally give a minister or official the power to act, but not the duty to do so. This gives relatively little room for judicial review.[20] In addition, enforcement decisions are at the discretion of the Crown and cannot be challenged (see discussion in Benidickson, 2002: 154–6). However, in the 1980s, a series of court decisions relaxed traditional standing rules, allowing citizens and non-governmental organizations to bring legal challenges to governmental action, both constitutional challenges and judicial review of administrative action.[21] Since then, litigation has become a more common strategy of environmental groups, but has never become a central determinant of Canadian environmental policy.[22]

At the provincial level, there are parallels to the federal legislative and executive institutions, but with a lot of variety between provinces. As at the federal level, environmental activities are spread across a number of departments, requiring coordination. Several provinces have large, diverse, professional ministries of the environment that are responsible for developing and implementing environmental policy with other functions such as resource management assigned to other departments. Other provinces have amalgamated their environmental protection and environmental conservation programmes into a single ministry. Provinces have taken on the lion's share of regulation and this has meant that each ministry includes a large scientific and technical staff plus inspectors, investigators and lawyers. As well, there are appeal tribunals and other agencies charged with carrying out specific tasks. Ontario established the independent Environmental Commissioner of Ontario in 1994 as part of a package of reforms intended to expand public participation rights and government accountability.[23]

Coordination of inter-governmental environmental policy and action is the responsibility of the Canadian Council of Ministers of the Environment (CCME), which is comprised of the Environment Ministers of each of the provinces, territories and federal government. Similar inter-ministerial councils are organized around wildlife, forestry, energy, agriculture and other issues.[24] The CCME has become a major focal point for environmental decision-making over the last ten years, particularly since adoption of the Harmonization Accord in 1998. There are regular meetings of the ministers, but the CCME's ongoing work is managed by a committee of deputy ministers and a full-time national secretariat and is carried out by committees and work groups comprised of technical staff representing governmental members.[25] Ministerial decisions are by consensus, effectively giving each jurisdiction a veto over every policy decision. Recently, consensus has been difficult to achieve on some important but controversial issues.[26] However, on low profile issues, much progress has been made in developing national guidelines, codes of practice, action plans, and so on.

Aboriginal peoples, long marginalized in Canadian politics generally and ignored in decisions affecting their traditional lands, are becoming important actors in environmental protection at the national, provincial and territorial levels. They act as individual bands or communities and through collective organizations such as the Assembly of First Nations. Through a series of legal and political changes, including Constitutional recognition of 'existing Aboriginal and treaty rights', and negotiation of comprehensive claims agreements, self-government initiatives and co-management arrangements,[27] First Nations and other Aboriginal communities are taking on governmental powers that recognize their authority to affect resource development and the environment.[28] A common pattern in these agreements is for land and water use, environmental impact assessment and resource and wildlife management to be planned and implemented by joint committees that include a guaranteed number of Aboriginal seats, but with final decisions the responsibility of the federal or provincial minister.[29] Most of these committees have only been operating for a few years, so it is difficult to evaluate their impact. Certainly, their mandates focus on sustainable development and conservation. However, there is little evidence that these co-management regimes have as yet truly incorporated traditional knowledge and customary management practices. A few studies have been done assessing the differences in approach between Aboriginal and non-Aboriginal resource development methods and outcomes. They indicate that: 'Even in a modern context, where neoclassical market incentives are pervasive, Aboriginal resource extraction is often both radically different from non-Aboriginal extraction and consistent with customary norms promoting sustainability and resource conservation' (Keay and Metcalf, 2004: 8).

However, there are cases demonstrating that this is not always so, and should not be assumed (Poelzer, 2002). Also, because of their need to secure their economic future, Aboriginal communities will often support resource development and find themselves at odds with the interests of environmental groups promoting preservation.

As a result of a series of Supreme Court of Canada decisions recognizing their land and resource rights and governments' fiduciary obligations to them, Aboriginal peoples must at a minimum be consulted on any initiative that has the potential to interfere with their rights. If their rights are more seriously interfered with, consent of the affected community and payment of compensation will also be required.[30] Historical, political and cultural factors make this a complex task, and governments are struggling with how to ensure these obligations are effectively met.[31]

Municipal governments are created by and carry out powers delegated to them from provincial governments. With respect to the environment, this includes responsibility for waste disposal and recycling, sewers and sewage treatment, and land-use planning. Although they have limited legal powers and limited sources of revenue, recent changes have expanded their powers somewhat, allowing for a more expansive role in protecting local public health and welfare.[32] Associations of municipalities, such as the Federation of Canadian Municipalities, are increasingly important forces in national environmental policy-making. There is much diversity among municipal governments with respect to resources and the capacity to develop and carry out environmental policy; however, there have been many innovative programmes that have emerged out of municipal governments.[33] The large, 'international' cities, including Toronto, Montreal and Vancouver, have effectively pushed their interests onto the national political agenda and have received commitments from the Prime Minister for a greater share of revenue.

Business and industry are active participants in all aspects of environmental policy in Canada, both as individual firms and through industrial and business associations that are well-organized, well-resourced, and influential. According to Boyd, the most powerful association is the Canadian Council of Chief Executives, comprised of the Chief Executive Officers from Canada's 150 largest corporations (Boyd, 2003: 223–5). This council, and other industry associations, through their lobbying efforts and through participation in the public policy development processes, have been successful in shaping both the substance of legislation and the regulatory methods used to pursue implementation.[34] It is also widely accepted that resource-based industries and other important economic interests have a dominant, restraining, influence on environmental policies, particularly those of provincial governments (Holland, 2000: 8 and Paehlke, 2000). On the other hand, insurance and banking interests have had a significant positive effect on the environmental performance of their customers with respect to the clean-up of contaminated sites.

National environmental NGOs that are active on a range of broad policy issues are relatively few in number. However, over the last three decades they have matured into skilled and professional organizations that are active and influential on major policy debates in Ottawa and provincial capitals. These groups use many different techniques and often work together in coalitions, often successfully influencing decision-makers. 'No one can deny that [the environmental movement's] record is full of great achievements. The entire structure of federal and provincial laws governing the use of Canadian land, water and air bears the strong imprint of environmental organizations' (Wilson, 2002: 62). However, many of the goals of these groups have not been achieved, as will be discussed below.

In addition to the national NGOs, 'there exists a sprawling, ever-evolving, and thriving collection of smaller organizations' at the local and regional level in Canada (Wilson, 2002: 59). These groups work mostly on a very diverse range of local issues, but also participate in networks addressing regional, national or international concerns.[35]

3. THE DEVELOPMENT AND IMPLEMENTATION OF CANADIAN ENVIRONMENTAL POLICY

Of course, even having clear authority to regulate does not guarantee that governments will respond. They are influenced by many factors, including the nature and scope of the environmental problem, the intensity of international pressures and domestic public concern, the larger political context of federal–provincial relations, the values of the governing parties, economic implications, competing policy priorities, and so on.

Given the above discussion, it should be obvious that environmental policy-making and implementation can be quite complex and fragmented in Canada with a multiplicity of relevant actors and interests varying considerably issue-by-issue. The following discussion attempts to draw out the general nature of these endeavours.

3.1 Environmental Policy Formulation

In Canada, environmental policy emerges at all levels, from the local to the national and beyond. In the past, the Canadian 'policy style' was to formulate policy in a 'process of closed door negotiation between regulators and the polluting industry in which the latter, having greater technical expertise, strong motivation and ample opportunities for delay, [held] the upper hand' (Macdonald, 2002: 69). Over the last 20 years, this bilateral process has been opened up to a broader spectrum of interests and now includes institutionalized consultative mechanisms. All levels of government have laws and policies in place that require public participation, particularly at the stage of policy formulation.

In Canada, this structured participation usually takes the form of involvement by organized groups: environmental and health NGOs, industry associations, labour unions, Aboriginal communities, professional associations, and so on. These opportunities are widely used by the environmental community, increasingly through 'coordinated efforts by a network of organizations' (Wilson, 2002: 53), but are less well-known in the general public.

However, individuals and smaller community groups are more active at the local level. Increased participation has brought about important changes:

> The evolution of multistakeholder forums involves structural changes in participation. These bodies accommodate a greater range of interests and to some degree even reflect a transformation in philosophical attitudes to the policy-making process. In particular, the state is no longer the exclusive representative of environmental interests; instead, environmental groups and individuals have assumed direct involvement. (Benidickson, 2002: 289)

At times of intense public concern, environmental group influence was high and all governments competed for public credit and blame avoidance.[36] At other times, it is 'more normal that both levels are hesitant' (Paehlke, 2001: 89). Since the mid-1990s, environmental groups have succeeded in getting and keeping issues on the public agenda but have been less successful in shaping the resulting policies as priorities shifted toward economic issues. This is because the Canadian system has 'structured the influence of various ideas and interests on environmental policy. The ideas and goals of political elites and territorially dominant economic interests have been promoted, and those of nonterritorially specific environmental groups have been weakened' (Skogstad, 1996: 105).

The process of environmental policy-making also involves consultation between levels of government. National policy formulation is now done largely through the CCME process in which the federal environment minister is but one of 14, all of whom must agree. Disagreements between federal and provincial governments occur regularly, but become particularly acute when proposed federal environmental policies are perceived as threatening dominant economic interests in a province, for example, oil and gas in Alberta, or as threatening the overall balance of power in the Canadian federation, for example, with Quebec (Doern and Conway, 1994, ch. 4). 'Under the constraints of executive federalism, however – including the requirement of unanimity among the participating ministers for many decisions – federal–provincial conflict continues to lead to "buck-passing", delays, inaction, rigidity, and piece-meal solutions' (Holland, 2000: 8). Where federal and provincial governments worked together, important progress was made (for example, acid rain); where they didn't, there was conflict, delay and inaction (for example, climate change and smog). 'The implication of this is that the reasons for the shifting balance of federal and provincial roles and for adoption of different intergovernmental arrangements over time may owe less to theoretical debates about the strengths and weaknesses of alternative federal–provincial models than to shifting political winds . . .' (Harrison, 2002: 134). On less visible and more routine issues, there is a lot of cooperation and coordination between Canadian governments.

Provinces undertake policy development with little input from other provinces or the federal government on issues clearly within their authority. There are significant disparities between provinces in terms of commitment to environmental protection and infrastructure to develop and carry out policy.[37] Certain provinces have played leadership roles from time to time, but not consistently. Thus, despite having plenary power within their territory and a growing influence over national policy, provinces have only occasionally experimented with innovative approaches to environmental regulation (Rabe, 1999). It has been suggested that the reason for this lack of innovation is, contrary to conventional wisdom, the high degree of decentralization in environmental policy-making in Canada.[38]

Environmental policy formulation is heavily dependent on science to help identify issues and solutions. In Canada, there has traditionally been a very strong scientific capability in government, particularly at the federal level;[39] however, there is a sense that budget reductions and government reorganization have affected this capability. Some provinces have extensive, professional staff but others have more limited resources.[40] The federal government is both the primary funder of scientific research in Canada and a performer of research. Funding goes to university scientists through a number of programmes and to government research institutes. Government scientists are involved in doing basic research – what Doern calls 'patient science' – and in policy-related science. The latter includes studies to support standards and regulations, product review and approval processes, monitoring and assessment for compliance and general ambient monitoring.[41] Concerns have been expressed about the lack of independence of government scientists (see Schrecker, 2001) and about their ability to keep up with a mandate that is expanding into areas of greater complexity and uncertainty, with fewer resources and personnel. Recent initiatives have been undertaken to guide the role of government scientists and to provide a consistent structure for the use of science in public policy.[42]

Increasingly, Canadian environmental policy is being driven by global pressures, though in seemingly conflicting directions. On the one hand, Canada is active in supporting the adoption of strong environmental commitments made at the international level. As a result, Canada's central policy objective has shifted to achievement of sustainable development. On the other hand, Canada is more and more pressured by the demands, concerns and constraints of economic globalization and Canada's active participation in free trade arrangements which have linked the economy ever more closely with the United States. Economic globalization has come to dominate not just economic policy but also policy direction in other areas, including the environment, to support a competitive economic climate for Canadian business and industry.[43] Effects include growing pressure to further exploit natural resources and a corresponding resistance to further environmental regulation, greater restrictions on national policy autonomy, and pressure toward a convergence of Canadian environmental policy with that in other jurisdictions, in particular the United States (see Hoberg, 1997 and Paehlke, 2001).

In the midst of the shift to globalization, there is a trend in Canada to greater decentralization in environmental administration in what was already a highly decentralized system (Paehlke, 2000). In response to fiscal demands and national unity considerations – and not to environmental considerations – the federal government agreed to a harmonization arrangement that moves more control to the provinces and requires it to act with self-restraint. This occurred within the larger context of pressure to 're-invent government' and to allow greater self-regulation of industry:

> The reform effort includes a preoccupation with streamlining operations, integrated service delivery, greater efficiency, and a stronger focus on 'clients' or 'customers'. The reforms also involve identifying those activities and policy areas that are part of the core activities of a given order of government and those activities that can or should be devolved to another government or to the private sector. (Fafard, 1998: 215)

For the provinces it also involved downloading responsibility to municipalities. 'National environmental policy in Canada is thus caught between centrifugal and centripetal forces, between globalization and decentralization' (Paehlke, 2000).

3.2 Implementation of Environmental Policy

In Canada, governments employ a range of instruments and tools to implement environmental policy. Howlett argues that governments exhibit a particular implementation style involving 'characteristic and long-lasting patterns in both the types of policy instrument chosen to implement policy as well as the manner in which they are implemented' (Howlett, 2002: 25). He terms the Canadian style 'consultative regulation'. That is, although other instruments are growing in importance, governments use regulation as the primary policy instrument, but the process for developing and enforcing regulations is a consultative one. In the 1970s and 1980s, consultation was a closed bargaining process with industry; since then, the process has been opened up to broader, 'multi-stakeholder' consultations.[44] Over the 1990s, however, the federal government pulled back from an exclusive reliance on regulation 'in response to a combination of declining public attention to environmental issues, budgetary restraints, concern for economic competitiveness, and pressure for devolution in response to the national unity agenda' (Harrison, 1999: 122). At the same time, provincial governments reduced spending on traditional environmental programmes.[45] As a result, regulatory instruments were increasingly supplemented by the growing use of non-regulatory agreements, economic instruments and information-based strategies. Until now, the choice of instrument was largely ad hoc. Since 2003, however, the federal government has been developing a 'smart regulation' strategy for the design of a national regulatory system 'that will promote health and sustainability, contribute to economic growth and reduce the regulatory burden on business and other stakeholders'. One important goal of this exercise is to identify the range of policy tools available and better define when each is appropriate: 'the objective is to enrich the use of the instrument mix and, where possible, use regulation more sparingly. There are also alternative approaches to regulation that should be considered to introduce appropriate flexibility and reduce regulatory burden'.[46]

Regulatory instruments

At the federal level, implementation of environmental goals has always been measured, due in no small part to the resistance of provinces to an active federal role. Thus, despite the appearance of coercive 'command and control' legislation, in reality there have always been 'few commands and limited control' (Harrison, 1999). Even in recent years, with the federal government taking on new regulatory mandates, there has been a tendency to devote enormous time and effort to negotiations and consultations toward the development of policy and much less success in implementing those agreements. The OECD has termed this a 'tendency to "talk" rather than "act" . . . After a long and comprehensive consultation process, ambitious strategies do not necessarily result in concrete action' (OECD, 2002a: 44). Similarly, the recurring message of the Commissioner for Environment and Sustainable Development is that the federal government is failing to meet its commitments on environmental protection and sustainable development. Lee and Perl attribute this 'integrity gap' to a number of factors including jurisdictional overlap, the lack of political will to impose some costs on powerful resource industries, and the tension between environmental goals and economic competitiveness and growth, among others (Lee and Perl, 2003: 21).

The regulatory approach used in Canada involves several components: standard-setting, licensing, and enforcement/compliance. It is the provinces that carry out the bulk of this regulation as it applies to industrial pollution control. While policies appear superficially similar between provinces, there are great differences between them in terms of their commitment to, and capacity for, implementation (see VanNijnatten, 2002).

There are no comprehensive national air or water standards in Canada. In the past, the federal government set a number of ambient objectives for conventional pollutants that were intended to serve as models for adoption by the provinces (VanNijnatten, 2002). In addition, the federal government issued guidelines for specific industry sectors intended to guide provinces in establishing regulatory requirements. These are now developed through the CCME and adopted under the Canadian Environmental Protection Act, (CEPA) which allows for input and agreement from the provinces and territories.[47]

The federal government's regulatory role is quite targeted. A limited number of industries are directly subject to enforceable federal standards: for example, quantitative effluent standards are directed at six industrial sectors under the Fisheries Act, with pulp and paper mills singled out for more detailed measures under both the Fisheries Act and CEPA.[48] In addition, there are general prohibitions on depositing toxic substances in water 'frequented by fish' and on altering fish habitat. Historically, these Fisheries Act provisions have been the federal government's strongest tool in protecting water quality and have led to dramatic improvements in certain industries, but enforcement was often delegated to the provinces.[49] With respect to air pollution, there are only four sectors targeted.[50] Powers within federal legislation that authorize federal control of sources having transboundary effects have never been used.

The federal government takes the lead on regulating mobile sources of air pollution, through a combination of methods. For motor vehicles, the federal government establishes emission standards for new vehicles being sold throughout the country. Once sold, vehicles become subject to provincial regulations that prohibit tampering with pollution control equipment and that in some cases enforce continued compliance with the initial standards through Inspection and Maintenance programmes. Other forms of transportation – shipping, railways, aircraft – are regulated under specialized federal legislation. An important aspect of the regulation of transportation emissions is the regulation of fuel content, which is done by the federal government under authority in CEPA. Using these provisions, the quantities of lead, sulphur and benzene in gasoline and diesel fuel have been limited. The federal government also regulates the import and export of toxic substances and hazardous waste and the international and interprovincial movement of dangerous goods.

In addition to discharge standards, the federal government uses 'product' standards, restricting the manufacture, sale or use of certain products or regulating their contents. These often work in conjunction with provincial regulations. For example, pesticides are registered for use in Canada at the federal level through the Pesticide Review Management Agency of Health

Canada and the provinces then regulate how and by whom those pesticides are used. To fulfil its obligations under the Montreal Protocol, Canadian governments coordinated their regulations to phase out the use of ozone-depleting substances. Under CEPA, federal regulations limit the manufacture, use, sale, import and export of ozone-depleting substances. Complementary provincial regulations deal with other sources of ozone-depleting substances (such as in air conditioners and refrigeration) by preventing their release to the environment and regulating their recycling and disposal. This combined approach has been quite successful in effectively reducing production, use and emissions (Office of the Auditor General of Canada, 2000).

The federal government also coordinates a number of ecosystem-based programmes, providing research, technical assistance and funding, in partnership with provincial and local interest. These Ecosystem Initiatives include programmes focused on the Georgia Basin, the Great Lakes, the St Lawrence River, northern ecosystems, the western boreal forest and the Atlantic coast.

Each province manages development of its energy, mineral and forestry resources and regulates pollution through comprehensive regulatory regimes. There is a lot of variation in the details between provinces, but a common 'command and control' framework for stationary sources is used whereby provinces set quantitative medium-specific standards (typically discharge standards) and license the operations of industrial facilities to ensure compliance with the standards. All provinces also have comprehensive regulations for the management of municipal solid and hazardous waste. These provincial regulatory activities are largely independent of federal oversight or involvement, although guidance comes through the work of CCME work groups.

All provinces and the federal government have environmental impact assessment (EIA) laws that require certain new facilities to undergo extensive evaluation prior to construction. The requirements vary greatly between jurisdictions in terms of what projects must be assessed, the criteria for evaluation, and the degree of formality of the process. This has given rise to problems when projects trigger the EIA process in more than one jurisdiction. A classic federal–provincial battle erupted when environmental groups went to court to force the federal government to follow its process with respect to provincial government projects.[51] Since then, much work has gone into developing joint processes and harmonizing EIA requirements.[52]

Municipalities regulate the majority of industrial effluents through sewer use by-laws. More industrial effluent goes into sewers than directly into receiving waters, leaving municipalities responsible for controlling what is discharged to sewers and for treating effluent at their sewage treatment plants. The success that municipal governments have in achieving this control is quite mixed. Many large cities have the resources to provide effective sewage treatment and even to implement pollution prevention initiatives. However, some large cities in Canada, including Halifax, St John's, Quebec City and Victoria, have no sewage treatment at all and thus dump untreated sewage into receiving waters. Many smaller municipalities struggle with limited resources to provide minimal treatment. The result is that seven of the ten largest toxic dischargers in Canada are municipal sewage treatment plants. Such plants also routinely violate provincial laws and the federal Fisheries Act, but are rarely prosecuted (see discussion in Boyd, 2003: 35–6).

Another key municipal role is the management of municipal solid waste. In Canada, local and regional governments are mandated to provide for the collection, recycling and disposal of household waste. Regulations are set by the provinces and carried out by municipalities or through contractors. In 2002, Ontario turned over coordination and financing of recycling programmes to a non-governmental corporation, Waste Diversion Ontario, run by representatives from industry, municipalities and non-governmental groups and supervised by the Ministry of the Environment (MOE).

Municipalities also play an important role in decisions about the siting of industrial and other environmentally relevant facilities through local control of the land-use planning process. Local planning decisions also identify and protect natural areas and water sources. A growing concern is 'sprawl' around major urban centres that is triggered through a combination of economic and demographic factors and inadequate planning laws.

Economic instruments

In addition to regulatory instruments, there is increasing interest at all levels in the use of economic instruments for achieving environmental protection and sustainable development. In the past, economic tools were used to promote resource exploitation. Such policies at both the federal and provincial level included preferential tax treatment for development of the oil and gas, mining, agriculture, fisheries and forestry sectors (Vourc'h, 2001: 8) and contributed to over-exploitation of resources and to environmental pollution. In recent years, efforts have been made to 'level the playing field' for energy investments by increasing tax assistance to renewable energy; however, significant subsidies remain for oil sands and nuclear technology.

Canadian governments have recognized the potential of green taxes and other financial incentives 'to align economic and environmental signals', and have repeatedly expressed interest in expanding their use. However, they have been slow to shift toward them and their use is neither comprehensive nor strategic.[53] Some recent federal tax measures that promote more responsible environmental behaviour include:

- tax incentives and subsidies for renewable energy and energy efficiency;
- accelerated depreciation for electricity generated from wind power;
- exemptions from the federal excise tax on fuel for ethanol or methanol blended gasoline; and
- tax incentives promoting donations or conservation easements of privately owned ecologically sensitive land.[54]

Provinces have more limited taxation powers but use sales taxes and regulatory charges,[55] for example on fuels, tyres, batteries, and pesticide and paint containers, to promote environmental objectives.

In addition to taxes, Canadian governments provide subsidies,[56] grants[57] and other funding,[58] and rebates[59] to support environmental goals. Financial assurance is required under provincial laws for certain activities, such as landfills, mine reclamation and transportation of hazardous goods, which create particular risks, and most provinces use deposit-refund systems for beverage containers. The federal government is proposing to use a combination of publicly funded stewardship programmes and compensation for private landowners as the key instruments for implementation of the recently adopted Species At Risk Act.

Canadian governments have repeatedly expressed interest in the use of tradable permits but, again, there has been little use of them in practice. At the federal level, amendments to CEPA in 1999 added authority for the Minister of the Environment to use a tradable allowance system to achieve the Act's objectives, but to date, the technique has only been used to help achieve the phase-out of the use of methyl bromide (see Madé, 2001). Although effective, enabling a 'smoother, less costly transition' for industry, the administration costs were 'higher than those associated with a regulatory approach' (Madé, 2001). Tradable permits are now being touted as a key tool in Canada's strategy for meeting its greenhouse gas reduction targets under the Kyoto Protocol.

At the provincial level, Ontario experimented with tradable permits for several years through a pilot project. Then in 2001, the provincial government brought in a regularized system of tradable permits for NO_x and SO_2 emissions from the electricity sector as a device to help reduce acid rain and smog. The system is a 'cap, credit and trade' system that commenced operations as of 31 December, 2001. A web-based registry was established, allowing participants and the public to track progress.[60] The system was expanded to include seven major industrial sectors in 2005.

'Voluntary' initiatives

Although Canadian environmental management is based on the use of regulatory instruments, there has been a shift over the last 10 years toward greater use of 'voluntary' or non-regulatory approaches, at both the federal and provincial levels.[61] Starting in the late 1980s, the chemical industry began pushing for recognition of a programme of voluntary compliance as a way of forestalling imposition of new regulations and improving its public image. Environment ministries, faced with declining capacity due to significant budget reductions, embraced the idea as an efficient and effective method of shifting some responsibility for environmental protection onto industry.[62] Since then, their use has expanded.

Voluntary initiatives used in Canada include negotiated agreements between governments and industry. Several memoranda of understanding (MOU) were negotiated by the federal government with specific companies or sectors in the 1990s,[63] but it was not until 2001 that Environment Canada developed a 'Policy Framework' establishing principles and design criteria to guide its participation in such agreements.[64] In a similar vein, Ontario recently inaugurated a pilot project for the negotiation of 'cooperative agreements' that will follow set criteria.[65] With the establishment of these policy frameworks, agreements should become more consistent, have greater public input, require results to be reported and verified and provide some (still limited) enforcement mechanisms. This should improve their effectiveness and credibility in the future.

Canada also uses the 'voluntary challenge', in which governments invite industrial polluters to reduce their discharges below regulated limits and report on their progress. The best known of these is called the 'Accelerated Reduction/Elimination of Toxics' or ARET Challenge. ARET developed out of a multi-stakeholder network, known as the New Directions Group, that was seeking innovative ways of accelerating the reduction or elimination of toxic discharges. With support of Environment Canada, a committee was formed in 1992 that developed a list of priority substances but disagreed on goals and methods. Environmental and labour groups left the committee in 1993, but industry carried on with continuing government support. A challenge was issued and, eventually companies representing 40 per cent of industrial production participated. ARET claims success in reducing toxic emissions significantly, but it has been plagued by a number of issues that undermine its public credibility.[66] Reductions cannot be causally linked to ARET, and most would have likely happened anyway as a result of more stringent regulations (see discussion in OECD, 2003: 30).

A voluntary challenge was the centre-piece in Canada's initial strategy to reduce greenhouse gas emissions. Known as 'National Climate Change Voluntary Challenge and Registry Programme,' or 'VCR', the programme challenged corporations to reduce GHG emissions voluntarily. They were required to register, submit action plans to reduce emissions, then carry out the plans. By most accounts, this programme was a failure and did not achieve noticeable reductions in GHG emissions.[67] A similar programme is used in Ontario to reduce smog precursor emissions. With no threat of sanctions for failure to reduce emissions, there is no incentive for companies to pursue significant reductions that are not otherwise required.

Another type of voluntary initiative used in Canada is the environmental management system.[68] One example is the self-regulatory industry code of practice, best represented by the 'Responsible Care' Programme of the Canadian Chemical Producers' Association (CCPA), initiated in the late 1980s in Canada and now used in many other countries. Responsible Care is a set of principles and practices that has evolved to guide the chemical industry in its environmental performance, including a commitment to continuous improvement and product stewardship.[69] The CCPA represents 63 companies, accounting for 90 per cent of Canada's chemical industry and has made adherence to the programme a condition of membership. Verification of compliance with the Responsible Care ethic and codes of practice is now required every three years.[70] This programme represents a large investment of resources by CCPA and individual companies, and has resulted in significant reductions in toxic discharges, largely through the application of pollution prevention techniques, and in reductions in workplace injuries.[71] Other aspects of the programme, such as community relations and product stewardship, have been less successful. Participation in Responsible Care is no guarantee of compliance with existing regulations and many members have been prosecuted for violations since the programme's inception, but participation has raised the standard by which industry members are judged. CCPA has improved its relations with governments because of its commitment to Responsible Care and has had success in influencing government policy.[72]

Most voluntary initiatives have not proved to be effective.[73] The evidence suggests that they have had little success in achieving real reductions in emissions that would not have happened anyway. As well, the administrative costs associated with them are often significant, particularly compared with the use of economic instruments.[74] Nevertheless, they have gained a foothold in Canadian environmental practice, and efforts are underway to improve them and better structure the role they will play in the future.

Information-based instruments and strategies

Information requirements form an important part of regulatory strategies. For example, requirements for companies to monitor and report their discharge data as a condition of provincial authorizations are routine. In addition, the federal government requires companies releasing specified toxic substances to report annually. These data are compiled and made available on the Internet, by individual facility and aggregated by location. Known as the National Pollutant Release Inventory (NPRI), this database is intended to influence environmental and community groups, governments, investors and lenders and thereby to induce emission reductions by reporting companies.[75] Because significant reductions in reported emissions have been achieved through the use of these registries in other jurisdictions, many commentators consider them highly effective in improving environmental quality (see citations in Harrison and Antweiler, 2001: 2). There are few analyses of the impact of the NPRI, but it appears that effectiveness claims are exaggerated: emissions have been shifted to other streams and most of the overall reductions achieved so far have been the result of governments using traditional regulatory methods rather than community or investor pressure or the desire of corporate executives to avoid public shaming (Harrison and Antweiler, 2001).

Information is also provided by government to industry and the public to try to influence their behaviour. This is seen in a number of governmental initiatives in Canada and is the cornerstone for governments' approach to achieving pollution prevention. Pollution prevention was adopted as the key objective of the CEPA 1999 amendments, but rather than mandate pollution prevention planning or toxics use reduction across the board,[76] the focus has been on providing relevant information, technical support and training to industry to remove a central obstacle to adoption of pollution prevention. These activities are carried out through Environment Canada's National Office of Pollution Prevention, the CCME, and the Canadian Centre for Pollution Prevention, a non-profit corporation established by a federal grant in 1994 but now supported through contracts and fees.

Information about the environmental impact of consumer products and services is provided to the public through an eco-labelling initiative, known as 'Environmental Choice'.[77] Established in 1988 by Environment Canada, the programme certifies a growing range of products and services that meet its criteria, allowing them to use the programme's logo. The hope is that consumers will rely on the certification and change their purchasing behaviour accordingly. Labelling is also used to provide information to consumers about the energy efficiency of appliances and the fuel efficiency of automobiles as a means of assisting them in making more environmentally-friendly purchases.

Enforcement

Canadian environmental law at all levels provides a wide range of administrative and legal tools to ensure compliance with regulatory requirements.

Governments operate under written compliance policies, and, though in principle compliance with the law is mandatory, regulators have unfettered discretion in whether and how they will respond to incidents of non-compliance.

Non-compliance is detected in a number of ways. Under provincial regulatory schemes, conditions on licences or approvals usually require that facilities monitor and report to the ministry on their discharges on a regular basis and immediately if an incident or spill occurs. Provincial environment ministries also have authority to inspect regulated facilities to ensure compliance and so maintain staff for this purpose. For most provinces, the number of inspectors and the number of inspections fell significantly during the 1990s as a result of budget cuts. For example, in Ontario, inspections overall dropped by 50 per cent from 1995 to 1998, and after 1998 the Ministry decided that inspections of municipal waterworks in particular would thenceforth be optional (Ontario, Ministry of the Attorney General, 2002). Since 2000, in Ontario in response to death and illness from tainted municipal drinking water, there has been an increase in the number of inspectors and a more aggressive inspection policy has been pursued.[78]

At the federal level, inspections to ensure compliance with the Canadian Environmental Protection Act are carried out by regional staff of Environment Canada. Following a 1998 report that highlighted the lack of resources in the department for enforcement (House of Commons Standing Committee on Environment and Sustainable Development, 1998), the number of enforcement staff was increased nation-wide from 60 to about 100. Environment Canada's policy is not to enforce all of its regulations all of the time; rather, it develops a national inspection plan every year that establishes priorities, identifying the regulations that will be enforced the following year.[79]

Environment Canada is also responsible for enforcing the pollution provisions and regulations under the Fisheries Act. There is a long tradition of delegating enforcement of these regulations to the provinces[80] but there is a poor track record in some provinces with fulfilling that responsibility,[81] and, with the exception of British Columbia, the federal government has not filled the void.[82] Yet this forms the model for the Inspections and Enforcement Sub-agreement under the Harmonization Accord.

If non-compliance is detected, the information is usually turned over to investigators, who will attempt to obtain evidence that is usable in court. Once an investigator has reasonable and probable grounds to believe an offence has been committed, the task is treated as a search, which is highly structured due to constitutional protections against 'unreasonable search and seizure'.[83] All prosecutions will go through this stage but prosecution is not the only route available if non-compliance is found.

When facilities are found to be out of compliance, each province and the federal government has a comprehensive set of administrative orders and prosecution available with which to respond. Compliance policies vary considerably between jurisdictions and over time, but in all cases negotiation and administrative approaches are usually pursued first with non-complying facilities. Prosecution is considered a last resort. In addition to administrative orders, governments can impose administrative penalties[84] and issue tickets for some minor offences. Under CEPA 1999, there are now 'alternative measures' available for those who are in violation of the Act but instead of a formal prosecution, an agreement is negotiated to bring the facility into compliance and usually pay an amount into an environmental damages fund.

Environmental offences are usually not treated as true crimes but as 'regulatory offences', allowing for a defence of due diligence, even though criminal procedure is followed. All jurisdictions in Canada have recently moved to raise fines and add jail as penalties for those convicted of environmental offences. Yet prosecutions at the federal level average only a handful.[85] There is a great deal of difference between provinces, with the number of charges ranging from fewer than a hundred to more than a thousand per year.[86] These numbers also change over time, depending on the compliance policy being pursued. Ontario has followed a roller coaster, moving from a 'mandatory' abatement strategy to voluntary abatement after 1995 and back to mandatory abatement in 2000 following the deaths in Walkerton. There are more than 6000 violations forwarded from inspectors to investigators every year and the number of charges laid has fluctuated from more than 2000 in 1992 to 758 in 1996 and back up to more than 1700 in 2000.[87]

Overall, there has been a drop in the use of prosecution in recent years, reflecting a debate about how best to achieve compliance.[88] Numerous petitions regarding the failure to enforce environmental laws have been made to the federal environment commissioner, the Environmental Commissioner of Ontario and the Commission for Environmental Cooperation, and studies have questioned the capacity and commitment of governments to respond to non-compliance. Citizen suits are generally not available and, where they are, they are quite restrictive; private prosecution is possible in some provinces but is used only occasionally (see Valiante, 2002b).

4. CONCLUSIONS

Canada's approach to the development and implementation of environmental policy is structurally decentralized, with provinces having significant powers, but with overlapping authority between orders of government. The uncertainty in environmental powers is a recurring theme that is exploited by certain interests, resulting in delays and inaction. This decentralized structure is further decentralizing through a formal process of harmonization that was adopted in response to several factors including global economic changes, fiscal pressures, national unity concerns and shifting political values. The result has been a restrained federal presence, particularly in implementation of environmental policy, but without compensating strong or innovative leadership from the provinces. Generating a strong federal stance has also been hampered because of internal government structures that limit the influence of Environment Canada and make it vulnerable to fluctuating short-term priorities.

Environmental policy-making is quite open to diverse interests, both formally and informally, and NGOs play an important role in goading government action. However, as public attention to environmental issues wanes, governments have tended to pull back from assertive roles, and the nature of the structures makes this retreat difficult to resist. Over time, economic interests have proved more influential in shaping the substance of environmental policy, particularly with provincial governments, but also federally.

Policy implementation favours the use of traditional regulatory measures, but there is growing interest and experience with economic measures, information-based instruments and non-regulatory measures. There has been reluctance to expand the use of these alternatives more broadly, with industry resisting economic instruments and NGOs resisting 'voluntary' measures, which demands governmental leadership if these alternatives are to be pursued in appropriate and optimal combinations. As understanding of these measures grows, attitudes will shift and their use will increase.

Generally speaking, Canadian pollution control measures have been successful in reducing major point source discharges to water, but have been less successful in controlling pollution from municipal wastewater treatment plants and have generally focused little on non-point source pollution. As a result of air pollution regulations, ambient air quality has improved, and there have been major successes in reducing lead exposure and phasing out ozone-depleting substances. However, 'Canada remains one of the top emitters among OECD countries, per capita and per unit of GDP, for SO_x, NO_x and CO_2, and there are still areas where air quality is inadequate for human health and ecosystems' (OECD, 2002c). Significant policy failures have occurred over the regulation of smog and greenhouse gas emissions and in the management of fish stocks. Achieving sustainable development has proved even more elusive, with waste generation and energy usage rates remaining amongst the highest in the world and rampant suburban sprawl.

Perhaps the most frustrating characteristic of Canadian environmental management is the gap between commitment and implementation, the tendency to talk rather than act. The effort to coordinate decisions takes a lot of time and resources and often results in little action. Despite significant technical capability, wealth, political stability, and an educated and informed citizenry, the fulfilment of international obligations and domestic policy objectives has stalled. The environmental challenges that lie ahead are ever more complex, and without the commitment of all governments, organizations and citizens, Canada runs the risk of falling behind in achieving its commitments to sustainable development and environmental protection.

NOTES

1. Constitution Act 1867 (UK) (30 & 31 Vict c 3). The Canadian Constitution is not found in a single document but is divided amongst a number of instruments, adopted over more than a hundred years.
2. Only two levels of government are recognized in the Constitution. Powers exercised by territorial governments are delegated by the federal government and municipalities exercise powers delegated by provincial governments.
3. *Friends of the Oldman River Society v Canada (Minister of Transport and Minister of Fisheries and Oceans)*, [1992] 1 SCR 3, at 64, per LaForest, J.
4. Constitution Act 1867 s 109 and Natural Resource Transfer Agreements, affirmed by Constitution Act 1930 (UK), (20–21 Geo V c 26), reprinted in RSC 1985, Appendix II.
5. Including harbours, canals, lighthouses, military bases, national parks and government buildings.
6. The production and export of natural resources continues to be a major source of economic wealth across Canada, and provinces are very protective of their locally dominant industries. Perhaps because of abundant resources, Canadians are large consumers of energy, water, etc. and 'consequently, large generator[s] of pollution and waste' (Vourc'h, 2001: 25).
7. Regulation of the dumping of contaminants into marine waters (even where those waters are considered part of a province) was upheld as a matter of national concern in *R v Crown Zellerbach Canada Ltd* [1988] 1 SCR 401. This power requires that the subject of regulation be definable in a discrete manner, be of national rather than just local concern and not be too disruptive to the balance of authority between the federal and provincial governments. All aspects of nuclear power are within federal authority, both as a matter of national concern and as a matter declared to be 'for the general advantage of Canada' under s 92(10)(c) of the Constitution: *Ontario Hydro v Ontario (Labour Relations Board)*, [1993] 3 SCR 327.
8. Regulation of toxic substances has been upheld as a matter of criminal law: *Canada (Procureure générale) c Hydro-Québec*, [1997] 3 SCR 213. This case expanded the legitimate purposes of the criminal law power to include environmental protection, even where not directly related to public health, and expanded the form of criminal law to include more regulatory measures, even though they must still be accompanied by prohibitions and penal sanctions.
9. *Interprovincial Cooperatives Ltd v R*, [1976] 1 SCR 477. There were no federal regulations of interprovincial pollution at issue in that case, but all judgments considered that this would be a matter of federal jurisdiction. Interprovincial pollution has not been a major issue in Canada.

10. *A.G. Canada. A.G. Ontario ('Labour Conventions'),* [1937] AC 326 (PC). To get around this problem, the federal government usually consults with the provinces while developing its position for international treaty negotiations.
11. The Canadian negotiators went beyond what had been agreed to with the provinces in order to achieve agreement at the international level. Now, with implementation shared by both levels, there is significant resistance to the Kyoto targets by many provincial governments, led by Alberta, whose economy is heavily dependent on oil and gas development.
12. Note that almost every constitutional challenge to Canadian environmental legislation has been brought by either industry or environmental groups, and not by another level of government.
13. *Canada (Procureure générale) c Hydro-Québec, supra* note 9, paragraph 114, per LaForest, J. For example, in this case, the criminal law power required a particular form of legislation (prohibitions plus sanctions) that would not be required if legislation flowed from a different power.
14. Examples include the use of 'mirror legislation', whereby all governments adopt virtually identical laws – this was used in regulating the transportation of dangerous goods; a division of labour – used with pesticide regulation; the delegation of administrative duties or enforcement – used with fisheries enforcement; prior consultation requirements – used in toxic substance regulation; joint decision-making processes – used in environmental assessment; and inter-governmental, collaborative decision-making. This latter is referred to as 'executive federalism' and is characteristic of the Canadian federal system generally: see Meekison et al. (2003).
15. The initial effort, known as the Environmental Management Framework Agreement, was pushed by provinces concerned about containing an expanding federal role resulting from a surge of federal interest and from several court decisions recognizing broad federal powers. The effort failed because the federal Cabinet was split over the extent of proposed restrictions on the federal role. See Fafard (1998). By the mid-1990s, the federal government had shifted its focus to deficit-cutting, and was motivated by the need to demonstrate the flexibility of federalism to Quebec in the wake of the closely contested 1995 sovereignty referendum. The Prime Minister put pressure on his officials to reach an agreement as part of a 'renewal of the federation' process. Although Quebec participated in the negotiations, it refused to sign the Accord because it wanted the federal government to go further and amend its legislation to prevent it from ever acting on environmental matters within the province. The Harmonization Accord illustrates a more general trend in federal–provincial relations, characterized as 'collaborative federalism', an alternative to constitutional change that recognizes the increased power and maturity of provincial governments, whereby national goals are achieved through collective action of the federal and provincial governments. See Cameron and Simeon (2002).
16. The sub-agreements include the Canada-Wide Standards Sub-Agreement, the Environmental Assessment Sub-Agreement and the Inspections and Enforcement Sub-Agreement. In addition, there is an Annex to the Accord on stakeholder participation and government accountability and a Statement of Principles to Guide Cooperative Arrangements on Monitoring and Reporting. See www.ccme.ca. The federal government will take the lead on scientific research, product standards, international and transboundary issues, federal lands and operations.
17. CCME (2003). Standards have been agreed to for six priority contaminants. CCME admits to the lack of 'transparency' in implementation: 'While the implementation of the Canada-Wide Standards is apparently reasonably moving forward, there is no easily available method to ascertain this.' Under the agreements, provinces can use a wide range of tools for implementation; there is no requirement that they adopt them into legally-binding regulations. There are also new bilateral agreements on environmental assessment and some increased coordination of inspections and monitoring.
18. The leading study of the department's history over its first 20 years is Doern and Conway (1994).

19. Amendments to the Auditor General Act, SC 1995, c 43, s 5. As Canada's largest employer, landlord and purchaser, the government can play an important leadership role through the rules it follows with respect to its own property and operations.
20. See examples and discussion in Boyd (2003), pp. 231–3. Also see Elgie (1993), pp. 185–224.
21. In federal environmental law, the greatest scope for judicial review has been with respect to environmental assessment requirements.
22. In contrast with the United States: see Hoberg (1997).
23. Environmental Bill of Rights 1993, SO 1993, c 28. The Commissioner plays a number of roles including presenting an annual review of the government's compliance with its obligations to the Legislature and facilitating citizen participation in requests for reviews of policies, laws and instruments and for investigations of alleged non-compliance.
24. Principles to govern action on climate change were agreed to by a joint meeting of the CCME and the Council of Energy Ministers. Consultations and policy development were then pursued and coordinated by a newly organized National Climate Change secretariat: www.nccp.ca.
25. CCME is the focus for development of Canada-Wide Standards under the Accord and has been responsible for development of a toxic substances management policy, a national packaging protocol, a national system for classifying contaminated sites and principles to guide contaminated site liability, a national action plan on municipal water use, among many other initiatives. Quebec actively participates in the CCME, but does not officially participate in actions under the Harmonization Accord.
26. For example, Canada-Wide Standards for mercury emissions from coal-fired power plants have been delayed for several years because of the resistance of some governments. In addition, implementation of efforts to reduce smog are stalled. Climate change negotiations are not being coordinated through the CCME.
27. There are more than a dozen final agreements between federal, provincial, territorial governments and Aboriginal communities, largely in northern Canada and British Columbia. One such agreement resulted in the creation of a new territory, Nunavut, in 1999.
28. See discussion in Doyle-Bedwell and Cohen (2001), pp. 169–206, in Poelzer (2002) and in Valiante (2002a).
29. For example, under the 'Nisga'a Final Agreement' in British Columbia, fisheries, forestry, wildlife and parks are jointly managed by the Nisga'a and the province (and the federal government in the case of fisheries). See Nisga'a Final Agreement (2002). In the Gwich'in Comprehensive Land Claim Agreement, land-use planning, environmental impact assessment, wildlife, water and renewable resource management are conducted through joint structures. See Gwich'in Comprehensive Land Claim Agreement (2002).
30. *Delgamuukw v British Columbia*, [1997] 3 SCR 1010.
31. Recent cases have taken a broad view of the consultation obligation: *Taku River Tlingit First Nation v Tulsequah Chief Mine Project*, (2002), 211 DLR (4th) 89 (BCCA) and *Haida Nation v B.C. (Min. of Forests)*, *#1*, (2002), 99 BCLR (3d) 209 (BCCA), *#2*, (2002), BCJ 1882 (BCCA). See discussion in Borrows (1997) and Lawrence and Macklem (2000). The Canadian Environmental Assessment Act allows for the consideration of traditional ecological knowledge in decisions about projects covered by the Act. The Canadian Environmental Assessment Agency has recently drafted an interim set of principles to guide use of traditional knowledge in its decisions: CEAA (2004).
32. Alberta and Ontario have modified their municipal legislation; also see *114957 Canada Ltée (Spraytech, Société d'arrosage) v Hudson (Town)*, [2001] SCJ No. 42, endorsing an active local role in the protection of public health.
33. Including action on air pollution, water conservation, recycling and composting, energy efficiency, pesticide use reduction. Some examples are cited in Boyd (2003), pp. 220–21.
34. Examples include the changes to the Canadian Environmental Protection Act and the Species at Risk Act. See discussion in Amos et al. (2001) and in Macdonald (2002), pp. 66–86.
35. There is a national network of more than 800 environmental groups, known as the Canadian Environment Network, and affiliated provincial networks.

36. Harrison (1996). For example, in the early 1970s and again in the late 1980s/early 1990s, all governments were active in developing policy on toxic substance management, environmental assessment and acid rain.
37. See comments in OECD (2002a), p. 21.
38. Rabe (1999) and Rabe (1997). Rabe argues that in the highly decentralized federalism found in Canada, the federal government is unlikely to contribute to policy innovation because it defers to the provinces, and the provinces are reluctant to do so because of the potential impacts on economic development.
39. About 70 per cent of Environment Canada's staff are scientific and technical personnel, and the overwhelming share of the department's budget goes to scientific and technical expenditures: Doern (2000). Other federal departments, in particular Health Canada, are involved in environmentally relevant science. Doern suggests that Canada's scientific strength has given it clout with the US on controversial issues such as acid rain, and credibility in international environmental negotiations.
40. One of the important benefits of the CCME coordinated process has been to compensate for the lack of resources in the smaller, poorer provinces, contributing to the professional development of their staff.
41. Much of the data for policy science comes from regulated companies, for example, product studies, monitoring of discharges.
42. See, for example, Government of Canada, Council of Science and Technology Advisors (1999); Industry Canada (2000); Treasury Board Secretariat (2000); Privy Council Office (2003).
43. Parson (2001). Also see Canada, External Advisory Committee on Smart Regulation (2003a).
44. Stakeholders do express frustration with Environment Canada's consultations, including inadequate opportunities to participate, differential weighting of comments from different participants and the perception that comments do not influence outcomes. See OECD (2002b).
45. See discussion in Boyd (2003), pp. 240–41, and in Krajnc (2000). In Ontario's case, the cuts to the MOE and the regulatory changes were pursued as part of a political shift to the right when a new provincial government was elected in 1995.
46. Canada, External Advisory Committee on Smart Regulation (2003b). The strategy is expected to be released by the end of 2004.
47. Guidelines and Codes of Practice are found on the CEPA Environmental Registry: www.ec.gc.ca/CEPARegistry.
48. Even though set by the federal government, the regulations were developed in consultation with the provinces, industry, and, in recent years, the NGOs. See discussion in Webb (2000).
49. Any prohibitions using this power have to be clearly linked to protection of fish: *Fowler v R*, [1980] 2 SCR 213. When Environment Canada was first established, the Environmental Protection Service was staffed largely with former fisheries officers, knowledgeable and concerned to protect fish and fishing communities from industrial pollution. They were instrumental in the department taking a strong national position, using the clear authority of the Fisheries Act. In the late 1970s, a proposal to enhance federal regulations on protection of fish habitat created a great deal of conflict with a number of provinces, and the federal government pulled back. In a period of intense regulation making, the federal government once again used the Fisheries Act (and the then new CEPA) as the bases for controlling toxic effluent from pulp and paper mills, at the time some of the worst toxic polluters across Canada. See Doern and Conway (1994). Enforcement is discussed below.
50. These are lead from secondary lead smelters, vinyl chloride from VC and PVC manufacturing, asbestos from mining and milling operations, and mercury from chlor-alkali plants. These regulations were all adopted in the 1970s and brought under the Canadian Environmental Protection Act 1988 upon proclamation.
51. The issue eventually went to the Supreme Court of Canada in the case of *Friends of the Oldman River Society v Canada, supra* note 3. This case recognized broad federal authority

over the environment, and led to the development of the present federal legislation, the Canadian Environmental Assessment Act, SC 1992, c 37.

52. Coordination of EIA was an important provincial objective of the Harmonization Accord. See Kennett (2000), pp. 105–32.
53. See discussion in Barg (2000). Barg suggests that the barriers to greater use include the attitudes and a low level of understanding of key decision-makers.
54. See OECD, *Environmentally Related Taxes Database*, www.oecd.org. Government support for energy is discussed in Commissioner of the Environment and Sustainable Development, *2000 Annual Report*, ch. 3.
55. Quebec in particular uses pollution charges as a disincentive.
56. For example, for soil conservation and reforestation.
57. For example, for construction or upgrading of municipal wastewater treatment plants, treatment of agricultural waste and tyre recycling.
58. Examples include funding for innovation provided by Industry Canada and Sustainable Development Technology Canada; for projects through the Climate Change Action Fund, Great Lakes Sustainability Fund, Habitat Stewardship Program and Eco-action.
59. Examples include Ontario's rebate programme for the purchase of energy efficient appliances and the Ontario Tax for Fuel Conservation, a graduated sales tax imposed on fuel-inefficient vehicles that provides a 'feebate' of the tax for the most efficient cars.
60. See Ontario Air Emissions Trading Registry, www.oetr.on.ca.
61. The OECD identifies four types of 'voluntary approaches': unilateral commitments by polluters, private agreements between polluters and pollutees, environmental agreements between industry and public authorities, and voluntary programmes initiated by government where individual firms are invited to participate: OECD (2003).
62. See discussion in Macdonald (2002). A number of cooperative government–private sector arrangements are discussed in Commissioner for the Environment and Sustainable Development, *2000 Annual Report*, ch. 8.
63. Nine MOUs were entered into, including agreements with the Canadian Chemical Producers' Association, steel maker Dofasco Inc., and Algoma Steel Inc. The Dofasco agreement grew out of the 'strategic options process' in which industry and environmental stakeholders developed options for managing substances considered toxic under the Canadian Environmental Protection Act. The key outcome was that industry pursue reductions in the use or discharge of these substances through 'enhanced voluntary measures'. Dofasco was the first company to agree to significant reductions in benzene and PAHs and entered into an agreement with Environment Canada and the Ontario Ministry of the Environment to formalize this and other commitments. See discussion in Lukasik (1999).
64. Environment Canada, *Policy Framework for Environmental Performance Agreements* (June, 2001). This policy framework was developed to reduce inconsistency and improve effectiveness and accountability, in response to recommendations by the Commissioner for the Environment and Sustainable Development: see *1999 Annual Report*, ch. 4. The framework details the conditions under which the department will enter into an agreement, the principles to be followed in negotiation, and the role of the department in their implementation. Since then, agreements have been signed with the Refractory Ceramic Fibre Industry, the Automotive Parts Manufacturers' Association and Dow Chemical Canada Inc.
65. This is now known as the 'Environmental Leaders Program'. Two agreements, consistent with the 'Framework for Ontario's Cooperative Agreements' were concluded in 2003: one with the Automotive Parts Manufacturers' Association and one with the Canadian Chemical Producers' Association. Individual facilities within these associations will be accepted into the programme if they fulfil specified criteria and then work with the MOE to develop a reduction plan for priority toxic substances. Progress must be reported annually and be independently verified. The MOE in return provides a 'suite of incentives', including preferential review, and 'greater regulatory certainty' – which is not clearly defined. Both agreements authorize the MOE to impose 'appropriate sanctions'

in one case and 'appropriate consequences' in the other for a facility's failure to meet its commitments. See: www.ene.gov.on.ca.

66. For example, there is only self-reporting but no standard reporting protocol, no third party verification, lack of participation by important facilities, no consequences for failure to reduce. See VanNijnatten (1999).
67. Hornung (1999). In fact, GHG emissions in Canada have increased 18 per cent since 1990.
68. Some international environmental management systems, including ISO 14000 and the Forest Stewardship Council's Principles of Management, are used in Canada.
69. Detailed information can be found at www.ccpa.ca.
70. The verification process includes a community and public participant. For those not fully compliant or for the few 'laggards' who have resisted verification, the CCPA has not revoked membership, their ultimate sanction.
71. These are in part reductions that would not have happened otherwise, although some consider them 'low hanging fruit', so that further reductions will be more difficult to achieve without more radical changes in industry attitudes and practices. See discussion in Moffet and Bregha (1999).
72. See examples in Moffet and Bregha (1999). One recurring criticism of CCPA is a lack of 'congruence' between its Responsible Care ethic and its lobbying positions, such as on the proposed amendments to CEPA and on ratification of Kyoto. This contributes to a continuing public credibility problem.
73. See Harrison (2001), and Vourc'h (2001), at p. 43.
74. OECD (2003). Other problems include the absence of any incentive to innovate, significant free riding, and lack of credibility. The better programmes involve commitment of significant resources on the part of both governments and industry.
75. For example, the North American Commission for Environmental Cooperation uses NPRI data in its annual report comparing US, Canadian and Mexican jurisdictions.
76. The federal government can mandate preparation of a pollution prevention plan for specified chemicals and specified facilities. It has done so in only a very few cases.
77. See www.environmentalchoice.ca.
78. Ontario created an inspection and enforcement 'SWAT Team' in 2000 to complement the regular Ministry inspection effort. The team has focused on particular sectors each year and in its first two years found an average non-compliance rate of 70 per cent, ranging from 45 per cent to 100 per cent non-compliance. See www.ene.gov.on.ca/envision/swat/.
79. Environment Canada (2002). For 2002/03, this plan focused on three regulations, out of at least 20 that the department is responsible for enforcing.
80. Webb (2000). Bilateral agreements were entered into with seven provinces; the others were treated similarly. These agreements lapsed and others were negotiated. The agreements provide for a one-window approach with a lead role for the province. Provinces agreed to include federal standards in provincial authorizations/permits and to take the lead on inspections and enforcement; assistance for the extra costs was provided by the federal government. The federal government retained residual enforcement power, which it has used from time to time. These arrangements allow provincial officials to proceed under either federal or provincial law.
81. See discussion in House of Commons Standing Committee on Environment and Sustainable Development (1998).
82. Provincial staff apparently 'actively discourage' federal enforcement even when evidence of contraventions is substantial because federal enforcement makes the provincial agency 'look bad' and because they prefer to rely on provincial law with which they are more familiar: Environmental Commissioner of Ontario (2002), p. 62.
83. Section 8 of the Charter of Rights and Freedoms. Warrants must be obtained at this point to enter the facility, interview employees, and so on: *R v Inco*, (2001), 54 OR(3d) 495. See discussion in Benidickson (2002), pp. 151–4.
84. These have been used in Alberta since 1995 and were recently adopted in Ontario.
85. For example, in 2002/03, there were only four prosecutions under CEPA; in 2001/02 there were nine federally-launched prosecutions under the Fisheries Act. See www.ec.gc.ca.

86. See Boyd (2003), pp. 237–45. Alberta, for example, laid 129 charges during 2002/03: Alberta Environment (2003). Many facilities will face multiple charges in one prosecution.
87. Environmental Commissioner of Ontario (2001), p. 82. In one investigation looking at Ontario's enforcement of water quality laws, Ontario (through the Ministry of Natural Resources) pursued 47 charges under the federal Fisheries Act over the six-year period ending in 2001, virtually all of which related to deposits of silt and sediment rather than chemical contaminants. At the same time, MOE did not enforce the provincial act 'with vigour in the last six years. Indeed . . . [it] launched only 11 prosecutions for alleged contraventions of the OWRA between 1995 and 1999, despite evidence – contained in more than 10,000 MOEE exceedance reports issued during this four-year period – of thousands of potential contraventions of the Act, its regulations and facility approvals'. Environmental Commissioner of Ontario (2002), p. 61.
88. While governments have increasingly favoured 'voluntary' compliance, many commentators suggest that without a credible threat of prosecution, compliance will suffer. See Duncan (2003).

REFERENCES

Alberta Environment (2003), *Compliance Assessment and Enforcement Initiatives, Annual Report, April 1, 2002–March 31, 2003.*

Amos, William, Kathryn Harrison and George Hoberg (2001), 'In search of a minimum winning coalition: The politics of species-at-risk legislation in Canada', in K. Beazley and R. Boardman (eds), *Politics of the Wild: Canada and Endangered Species*, Don Mills, Ont.: Oxford University Press, pp. 137–66.

Barg, Stephan (2000), 'Economic instruments for environmental policy making in Ontario', in Ontario Ministry of the Environment, *Managing the Environment Report*, Volume II, Research Papers, December 2000.

Benidickson, Jamie (2002), *Essentials of Canadian Law: Environmental Law*, 2nd edn, Toronto: Irwin Law.

Borrows, John (1997), 'Living between water and rocks – first nations, environmental planning and democracy', *University of Toronto Law Journal*, **47**(4), 417–68.

Boyd, David (2003), *Unnatural Law: Rethinking Canadian Environmental Law and Policy*, Vancouver: UBC Press.

Cameron, David and Richard Simeon (2002), 'Intergovernmental relations in Canada: The emergence of collaborative federalism', *Publius: The Journal of Federalism*, **32**(2), 49–71.

Canada, External Advisory Committee on Smart Regulation (2003a), *Regulating in the 21st Century: Global Changes and Implications for Regulation*, September.

Canada, External Advisory Committee on Smart Regulation (2003b), *The Regulatory Process: Enabling Smart Regulation; A Dialogue with Stakeholders*, September.

Canadian Council of Ministers of the Environment (1998), 'Canada-Wide Accord on Environmental Harmonization', www.ccme.ca/assets/pdf/accord_harmonization_e.pdf.

CCME (2003), *Five-Year Review of the Harmonization Accord*, October.

CEAA (2004), *Considering Aboriginal Traditional Knowledge in Environmental Assessments under the Canadian Environmental Assessment Act: Interim Principles*.

Doern, G. Bruce (2000), 'Patient science versus science on demand: The stretching of green science at environment Canada', in G.B. Doern and T. Reed (eds), *Risky Business: Canada's Changing Science-Based Policy and Regulatory Regime*, Toronto: University of Toronto Press, pp. 286–306.

Doern, G. Bruce and Thomas Conway (1994), *The Greening of Canada: Federal Institutions and Decisions*, Toronto: University of Toronto Press.

Doyle-Bedwell, Patricia and Fay G. Cohen (2001), 'Aboriginal peoples in Canada: Their role in shaping environmental trends in the twenty-first century', in Edward A. Parson (ed.), *Governing the Environment: Persistent Challenges, Uncertain Innovations*, Toronto: University of Toronto Press, pp. 169–206.

Duncan, Linda (2003), 'Enforcement and compliance', in E. Hughes, A. Lucas and W. Tilleman (eds), *Environmental Law and Policy*, 3rd edn, Toronto: Emond Montgomery.

Elgie, Stewart A.G. (1993), 'Environmental groups and the courts: 1970–1992', in G. Thompson, M.L. McConnell and L.B. Heustis (eds), *Environmental Law and Business in Canada*, Toronto: Canada Law Book.

Environment Canada (2001), *Policy Framework for Environmental Performance Agreements* (June), Ottawa.

Environment Canada (2002), *CEPA Annual Report: April 2001–March 2002.*

Environmental Commissioner of Ontario (2001), *2000/2001 Annual Report.*

Environmental Commissioner of Ontario (2002), *Developing Sustainability: 2001–2002 Annual Report* (September).

Fafard, Patrick (1998), 'Green harmonization: The success and failure of recent environmental intergovernmental relations', in H. Lazar (ed.), *Canada: The State of the Federation, 1997, Non-Constitutional Renewal*, Montreal: McGill-Queen's University Press.

Government of Canada, Council of Science and Technology Advisors (1999), *Building Excellence in Science and Technology: The Federal Roles in Performing Science and Technology*.

Gwich'in Comprehensive Land Claim Agreement (2002), 'Annual Report of the Implementation Committee. April 1, 2001–March 31, 2002', www.ainc-inac.gc.ca/pr/agr/gwich/anrh_e.pdf.

Harrison, Kathryn (1996), *Passing the Buck: Federalism and Canadian Environmental Policy*, Vancouver: UBC Press.

Harrison, Kathryn (1999), 'Retreat from regulation: The evolution of the Canadian environmental regulatory regime', in G. Bruce Doern, M. Hill, M.J. Prince and R.J. Schultz (eds), *Changing the Rules: Canadian Regulatory Regimes and Institutions*, Toronto: University of Toronto Press, pp. 122–42.

Harrison, Kathryn (2001), 'Voluntarism and environmental governance', in Edward A. Parson (ed.), *Governing the Environment: Persistent Challenges, Uncertain Innovations*, Toronto: University of Toronto Press, pp. 207–46.

Harrison, Kathryn (2002), 'Federal–provincial relations and the environment: Unilateralism, collaboration, and rationalization', in Debora L. VanNijnatten and Robert Boardman (eds), *Canadian Environmental Policy: Context and Cases*, 2nd edn, Don Mills, Ont.: Oxford University Press, ch. 7.

Harrison, Kathryn and Werner Antweiler (2001), 'Environmental regulation vs. environmental information: A view from Canada's national pollutant release inventory', 25 January, www.policy.ca.

Hoberg, George (1997), 'Governing the environment: Comparing Canada and the United States', in Keith Banting, George Hoberg and Richard Simeon (eds),

Degrees of Freedom: Canada and the United States in a Changing World, Montreal: McGill-Queen's, ch. 9.

Holland, Kenneth M. (2000), 'Introduction', in Kenneth M. Holland, F.L. Morton and Brian Galligan (eds), *Federalism and the Environment: Environmental Policymaking in Australia, Canada and the United States*, Westport, Conn.: Greenwood Press.

Hornung, Robert (1999), 'The VCR doesn't work', in Robert Gibson (ed.), *Voluntary Initiatives: The New Politics of Corporate Greening*, Peterborough, Ont.: Broadview Press, pp. 134–40.

House of Commons Standing Committee on Environment and Sustainable Development (1998), *Enforcing Canada's Pollution Laws: The Public Interest Must Come First!*, Third Report, May 1998.

Howlett, Michael (2002), 'Policy instruments and implementation styles: The evolution of instrument choice in Canadian environmental policy', in Debora L. VanNijnatten and Robert Boardman (eds), *Canadian Environmental Policy: Context and Cases*, 2nd edn, Don Mills, Ont.: Oxford University Press.

Industry Canada (2000), *A Framework for Science and Technology Advice: Principles and Guidelines for the Effective Use of Science and Technology in Government Decision Making*, May.

Keay, Ian and Cherie Metcalf (2004), 'Aboriginal rights, customary law and the economics of renewable resource exploitation', *Canadian Public Policy-Analyse de Politiques*, **30**(1), 1–22.

Kennett, Steven A. (2000), 'Meeting the intergovernmental challenge of environmental assessment', Patrick C. Fafard and Kathryn Harrison (eds), *Managing the Environmental Union: Intergovernmental Relations and Environmental Policy in Canada*, Kingston: School of Policy Studies, Queen's University, pp. 105–32.

Krajnc, Anita (2000), 'Wither Ontario's environment? Neo-Conservatism and the decline of the environment ministry', *Canadian Public Policy*, **26**(1), 111–27.

Lawrence, Sonia and Patrick Macklem (2000), 'From consultation to reconciliation: Aboriginal rights and the crown's duty to consult', Canadian Bar Review, **79**, p. 252.

Lee, Eugene and Anthony Perl (2003), 'Introduction: Institutions and the integrity gap in Canadian environmental policy', in E. Lee and A. Perl (eds), *The Integrity Gap: Canada's Environmental Policy and Institutions*, Vancouver: UBC Press.

Lukasik, Linda (1999), 'The Dofasco deal', in Robert Gibson (ed.), *Voluntary Initiatives: The New Politics of Corporate Greening*, Peterborough, Ont.: Broadview Press, pp. 141–8.

Macdonald, Douglas (2002), 'The business response to environmentalism', in Debora L. VanNijnatten and Robert Boardman (eds), *Canadian Environmental Policy: Context and Cases*, 2nd edn, Don Mills, Ont.: Oxford University Press, pp. 66–86.

Madé, Bernard (2001), 'Experience using tradable permits to eliminate methyl bromide', in Environment Canada, *Supporting a Sustainable Future: Making Dollars and Sense*; An International Conference on the Use of Economic Incentives and Instruments in Environmental Policy: Conference Summary and Analysis.

Meekison, J. Peter, Hamish Telford and Harvey Lazar (2003), 'The institutions of executive federalism: Myths and realities', in J. Peter Meekison et al. (eds), *Canada: The State of the Federation, 2002, Reconsidering the Institutions of Canadian Federalism*, Montreal: McGill-Queen's University Press.

Moffet, John and François Bregha (1999), 'Responsible care: Canada's most influential initiative offers many lessons but its biggest challenges may lie ahead', in Robert Gibson (ed.), *Voluntary Initiatives: The New Politics of Corporate Greening*, Peterborough, Ont.: Broadview Press, pp. 69–92.

Nisga'a Final Agreement (2002), 'Annual Report', www.ainc-inac.gc.ca/pr/agr/nsga/.

OECD (2002a), *Governance for Sustainable Development: Five OECD Case Studies*, Paris: OECD.

OECD (2002b), *Reviews of Regulatory Reform: Canada: Maintaining Leadership Through Innovation*, Paris: OECD.

OECD (2002c), *Canada. Country Performance Review*, Paris: OECD.

OECD (2003), *Voluntary Approaches for Environmental Policy: Effectiveness, Efficiency and Usage in Policy Mixes*, Paris: OECD.

Office of the Auditor General of Canada (2000), *2000 Report of the Commissioner of the Environment and Sustainable Development*, Ottawa.

Ontario, Ministry of the Attorney General (2002), *Report of the Walkerton Inquiry, Part One*, Toronto: Queen's Printer.

Paehlke, Robert (2000), 'Environmentalism in one country: Canadian environmental policy in an era of globalization', *Policy Studies Journal*, **28**(1), 160–75.

Paehlke, Robert (2001), 'Spatial proportionality: Right sizing environmental decision-making', in Edward A. Parson (ed.), *Governing the Environment: Persistent Challenges, Uncertain Innovations*, Toronto: University of Toronto Press.

Parson, Edward A. (2001), 'Persistent challenges, uncertain innovations: A synthesis', in Edward A. Parson (ed.), *Governing the Environment: Persistent Challenges, Uncertain Innovations*, Toronto: University of Toronto Press, pp. 345–89.

Poelzer, Greg (2002), 'Aboriginal peoples and environmental policy in Canada: No longer at the margins', in Debora L. VanNijnatten and Robert Boardman (eds), *Canadian Environmental Policy: Context and Cases*, 2nd edn, Don Mills, Ont.: Oxford University Press, pp. 87–106.

Privy Council Office (2003), *A Framework for the Application of Precaution in Science-based Decision Making about Risk*.

Rabe, Barry G. (1997), 'The politics of sustainable development: impediments to pollution prevention and policy integration in Canada', *Canadian Public Administration*, **40**(3), 415–35.

Rabe, Barry G. (1999), 'Federalism and entrepreneurship: Explaining American and Canadian innovation in pollution prevention and regulation integration', *Policy Studies Journal*, **27**, 288–306.

Schrecker, Ted (2001), 'Using science in environmental policy: Can Canada do better?', in Edward A. Parson (ed.), *Governing the Environment: Persistent Challenges, Uncertain Innovations*, Toronto: University of Toronto Press, pp. 31–72.

Skogstad, Grace (1996), 'Intergovernmental relations and the politics of environmental protection in Canada', in Kenneth M. Holland, F.L. Morton and Brian Galligan (eds), *Federalism and the Environment: Environmental Policymaking in Australia, Canada and the United States*, Westport, Conn.: Greenwood Press, ch. 5.

Treasury Board Secretariat (2000), *The Integrated Risk Management Framework*.

Valiante, Marcia (2002a), 'Legal foundations of Canadian environmental policy: Underlining our values in a shifting landscape', in Debora L. VanNijnatten and Robert Boardman (eds), *Canadian Environmental Policy: Context and Cases*, 2nd edn, Don Mills, Ont.: Oxford University Press, pp. 3–24.

Valiante, Marcia (2002b), '"Welcomed participants" or "environmental vigilantes"? The CEPA environmental protection action and the role of citizen suits in Canadian environmental law', *Dalhousie Law Journal*, **25**, 81–111.

VanNijnatten, Debora L. (1999), 'The ARET challenge', in Robert Gibson (ed.), *Voluntary Initiatives: The New Politics of Corporate Greening*, Peterborough, Ont.: Broadview Press, pp. 93–100.

VanNijnatten, Debora L. (2002), 'The bumpy journey ahead: Provincial environmental policies and national environmental standards', in Debora L. VanNijnatten and Robert Boardman (eds), *Canadian Environmental Policy: Context and Cases*, 2nd edn, Don Mills, Ont.: Oxford University Press, ch. 8.

Vourc'h, Ann (2001), 'Encouraging sustainable growth in Canada', Working Paper No. 290, Paris: OECD.

Webb, Kernaghan (2000), 'Gorillas in closets? Federal–provincial Fisheries Act pollution control enforcement', in Patrick C. Fafard and Kathryn Harrison (eds), *Managing the Environmental Union: Intergovernmental Relations and Environmental Policy in Canada*, Kingston: School of Policy Studies, Queen's University, ch. 7.

Wilson, Jeremy (2002), 'Continuity and change in the Canadian environmental movement: Assessing the effects of institutionalization', in Debora L. VanNijnatten and Robert Boardman (eds), *Canadian Environmental Policy: Context and Cases*, 2nd edn, Don Mills, Ont.: Oxford University Press, pp. 46–65.

Winfield, Mark S. (2002), 'Environmental policy and federalism', in Herman Bakvis and Grace Skogstad (eds), *Canadian Federalism: Performance, Effectiveness and Legitimacy*, Don Mills, Ont.: Oxford University Press, ch. 7.

5. Ethiopia: Protecting nature in a developing decentralized country

Gedion Asfaw, Kifle Lemma Woldesemayat and Sebsebe Demissew

1. INTRODUCTION

Ethiopia is located between 3° and 15°N latitudes and 33° and 48°E longitudes, with an area of 1.1 million km^2. It has immense geographical and ecological diversity. It is richly endowed with natural resources such as flora, fauna, minerals and water. It is primarily an agrarian country.

2. INSTITUTIONAL BACKGROUND

2.1 The Federal Level

Ethiopia, a parliamentary democracy, has a federal system based on nine regional states (hereafter regions) constructed on the basis of the settlement patterns, language, identity and consent of the concerned communities in Articles 45, 46, 47 of the Federal Constitution (Proclamation No. 1, 1995). The federal and the regional governments each have a legislative, an executive and a judicial branch. Regional councils have the power to legislate on matters falling under their jurisdiction. They also have the power to draft, adopt and amend their constitutions.

In addition to the overall mandate of the federal government to formulate and implement policies, strategies and plans in respect of economic, social and development matters, there are distinct provisions in the Federal Constitution which assign responsibilities for natural resources to the federal government. These include the protection and preservation of cultural and historical heritage and utilization and conservation of land and other natural resources. The federal government also has jurisdiction on the utilization of the water of rivers and other water bodies situated across two or more regions, or crossing the national boundaries (Article 51). In addition, the federal constitution enshrines the important principle that all persons have the right to a clean and healthy environment and that all persons who have been displaced, or whose livelihoods have been adversely affected as a result of state programmes, have the right to commensurate monetary (or alternative means of) compensation, including relocation with adequate assistance (Article 44 (1)).

The federal government may delegate its powers to the regions. It is a constitutional principle that what is not specifically assigned to the federal jurisdiction falls within the jurisdiction of the regions. Furthermore, the Federal Constitution mandates that adequate power shall be granted to the lowest units of government to enable the people to participate directly in the administration units (Article 50).

The Federal Constitution establishes that all nationals have the right to participate in national development and, in particular, to be consulted with respect to 'policies and projects affecting their community' (Article 43 (2)). This is a principle that should also be embraced by the regions. It is one of the major advantages of a decentralized system of governance. Its full realization, however, requires an efficient judiciary system, a capacity for solving conflicts peacefully, the existence of an enlightened bureaucracy and communities as well as a fully-fledged democracy. In this respect the country still has a long way to go, but there should be an unflinching resolve on the part of the people to influence the state to work relentlessly for the full application of these guiding principles.

The constitution also mandates that all international agreements and relations shall protect and ensure Ethiopia's right to sustainable development (Article 43 (3)). It is implicit in this provision that international interdependence is unavoidable, including in the environmental area, and that every effort should be made to ensure that the country's interests are protected within the framework of such interdependence.

2.2 The Regional Level

The regional states are subdivided into Woredas and the Kebelles, which have their own elected councils and administrative organs. It should be noted that the federal and the regional constitutions recognize the possibility of establishing intermediate deconcentrated levels of government between the regions and the Woredas, such as the Zones. However, a reform undertaken in 2003 has drastically reduced the role of the Zones by transferring most of their responsibilities to the Woredas. Municipalities are responsible for the provision of public services in the urban centres.

As stated above (section 2.1), all powers not assigned, exclusively, or concurrently, to the federal government are reserved for the regions. Thus, these states have the power to legislate, to formulate, and to execute their economic, social and development policies. However, they can manage land and other natural resources only in accordance with federal laws (Article 52). They have the power to collect royalties from forest resources and are entitled to share royalties from mining, gas and petroleum with the federal government.

The Woredas

The Woredas are subordinate to the regions. They are responsible for economic development and for the provision of social services. They have specific responsibilities concerning agricultural development and the conservation and management of natural resources. Their budget is funded by grants from regional governments but they also have the authority to levy their own revenue. While the utilization of the grants is subject to supervision and control by regional governments, funds generated from their own sources are free from regional scrutiny. They formulate and approve their own budget.

Obviously, the more powers and responsibilities are devolved downwards, the more opportunities there will be for local communities to participate in their governance through elected councils. However, the challenge is to ensure that the institutions at Woreda and Sub-Woreda level have adequate institutional strength and resources to carry out their newly acquired powers and responsibilities effectively. Considerable effort has to be made to build the professional, technical and administrative expertise that is required. Personnel will have to be transferred from zonal offices to the Woredas, and additional staff, where available, will have to be recruited. It will take a considerable time to fulfil the needs of human and other resources of the Woredas and of the government units below them.

The Kebelles

The Kebelles are accountable to the Woreda or the town council within which they are located. They have a council, an executive body and Social Courts. They can issue local regulations regarding social affairs and have the power to pursue policies of local interest.

Development and Environment rights defined in the regional constitutions are similar to those enshrined in the Federal one (Articles 43 and 44). In a few cases, however, regional constitutions are quite specific as regards the environment. For example, in the Amhara Constitution it is stated that 'People have the full right to full consultation and to the expression of their views in the planning and implementation of environmental policies and projects that affect them directly' and that the regional state and the inhabitants of the region shall have the duty to protect the environment (Article 113 of the Amhara National Regional State Constitution).

This decentralized system of government is expected to facilitate environmental governance through its highly autonomous regional governments and the units operating at the sub-regional level. This devolution of power is designed to ensure that citizens at all levels, particularly at community and village levels, are empowered in the political, economic and social spheres as the prime movers of development in their areas. The various levels of government and their responsibilities are shown in Table 5.1.

Figure 5.1 shows the main trends in the devolution of environmental management responsibilities resulting, particularly, from the decentralization measures taken in 2003. Decentralization started in Ethiopia in 1992 when the country moved from the highly centralized military government of the Dergue era to the federal system of government presently in place. This led to the establishment of highly autonomous regional governments. However, the need to devolve power and responsibilities still further down in view of a more effective and participatory implementation of development programmes prompted the second major decentralization step undertaken in 2003. Sub-regional levels of government (Woredas and below) have been increasingly taking over responsibilities for planning and implementing local level environmental policies and other local development activities as well. Important planning and implementation responsibilities which were assigned to the Zones before the year 2003 have been devolved to the Woredas. Zones are now restricted to facilitation and coordination activities.

Ethiopia is predominantly an agricultural country dependent on renewable resources, such as water, soil and forests. Devolving the responsibility for the management and protection of these resources to the lowest feasible (community) level together with the necessary empowerment appears to be a move in the right direction. This is particularly so since millions of Ethiopian farmers and pastoralists dependent on the renewable resources have a large impact on the resource base. Unless they are empowered and given the responsibility to ensure that the resource base is constantly renovated, their livelihood could be gravely affected and ultimately destroyed.

Obviously, it will take some time before local governments and communities will be able to carry out their newly acquired powers and responsibilities effectively. For example, many Woredas initially suffered a shortage of technical and professional personnel. Although the situation appears to be gradually improving, some time will still elapse before the country has at its disposal the necessary skilled human resources (particularly at middle and lower echelons). Before this capacity is built across the whole country, there is no doubt that federal and regional tutelage will have to be provided. However, this tutelage is expected to decrease and become less obtrusive in the long term.

Table 5.1 Levels of government and responsibilities

Level of government	Hierarchy of government	Responsibilities in environmental affairs
Federal	• House of People's Representatives (Standing Committee for Natural Resources and Environment) • House of Federation • Council of ministers and various line ministries • Environmental Protection Authority	• Approval of laws, federal policies, establishment of agencies • Approval of regional subsidies, amendment of constitutional provisions • Implementation of policies, enactment of regulations • Preparation of policies, coordination and regulation, as well as some implementation of policies, legislation, EIA, public awareness
Regional	• Regional Council • Regional Administration and various line bureaux • Environment Protection Agency	• Approval of regional laws and regulations • Implementation of policies; Preparation and implementation of development plans • Preparation, coordination & regulation, as well as some implementation of regional conservation strategies, public awareness, EIA
Zonal	Zonal Council	• Coordination of Woredas
Woreda	• Woreda Council • Woreda Administration	• Approval of Woreda development plans • Preparation and implementation of Woreda development plans
Kebelle	• Kebelle Council • Kebelle Administration	• Community level actions
Sub/Kebelles/ Communities	• Community associations • Community representatives	• Social affairs • Development activities

Level	Industrial Pollution	Ecosystem Protection	Agriculture	Forests	Water
International/ Regional	Climate Change Convention	Various Conventions: –Climate change –Biodiversity –Desertification			–Multicountry organizations
Federal	–Overall Minimum Standards –Permits –Capacity Building for States	–Capacity Building & Budget Subsidy for States		– Capacity Building & Budget Subsidy for States – National priority forests	–River Basin management
States	–State Specific Standards –Permits –Monitoring	–State policies –Budget –Capacity building for lower levels		– Forests conservation – Afforestation	–Urban water supply
Zonal					
Woreda	–Land allocation	–Planning, resources mobilization and budgeting for local level eco-system management –Local/community technical support		– Planning, resources mobilization and budgeting for local forestation – Forest products control/ check points – Local/community technical support	–Planning, resources mobilization and budgeting for Rural Water Supply –Local/community technical support
Kebelle	–Participatory monitoring & reporting	–Participation in planning and implementing local level eco-system management activities		– Participation in planning and implementing local level community forestation	–Participation in planning, constructing, operating and maintenance of rural community water supply (Water Committees)

Figure 5.1 Trends in centralization/decentralization in environmental governance

3. ENVIRONMENTAL POLICY FRAMEWORK

The Environmental Policy of Ethiopia (EPE) emanates from the Conservation Strategy of Ethiopia (CSE). The CSE is intended to bring about sustainable management of natural resources in the context of development. It is designed to integrate environmental concerns into development. Its objective is to improve human and ecological conditions and help make the transition to a sustainable society. The main reasons which prompted the launch of the CSE process are as follows:

- the horrors of the 1984/85 famine created a consensus opinion among technocrats and politicians that environmental mismanagement was amongst the crucial causes for that famine;
- an international situation which was conducive to making intense efforts towards finding solutions to food insecurity and to live up to the expectations of the Brundtland Commission's report, *Our Common Future*; and,
- the existence of a powerful entity – the 'Zemecha Memria' – with a mandate to make decisions on policy and strategy issues.

Thus, the CSE was the result of both internal and external pressures, with external sources providing the funding for the exercise (Asfaw, 1998). Internally, the process of identifying and agreeing on the major environmental issues included: (a) discussions with a number of local communities; (b) the carrying out of assessments at the zonal level; (c) conducting a series of workshops and conferences; and, (d) undertaking a comprehensive review of the relevant literature. On the basis of the findings from the consultations and the review of the literature, a number of major problems were identified and subsequently outlined in the environmental policy.

3.1 Economic Context and Environmental Constraints

Stagnation of GDP, predominance and decline of agriculture

Economic growth stagnated over many years. In fact, per capita GDP declined from 255 Birr in 1986/87 to 233 Birr in 1994/95. This was because of stagnation in the dominant agricultural sector brought about by policy failures, recurrent droughts, civil wars, resource degradation and poor infrastructure. By itself, predominance of agriculture is not, and should not be, a problem, if only agriculture were capable of improving the standard of living of the farmers and were able to feed the nation (CSA, 1998).

The view that agricultural predominance is a problem stems from several factors: (a) Ethiopian peasants have remained very poor with no change in their living standard for many decades; (b) subsistence farming persists with no sign of a shift to modernization; and, (c) reliance on extensive agriculture requires large swathes of farming and grazing land which results in deforestation and soil erosion.

Deterioration of renewable natural resources

Depletion of indigenous forests continues to take place due to absence of the necessary environmental conditions for regeneration. Water flows out of the country at the rate of more than 100 billion cubic metres per year without being put to use, and taking with it billions of tons of fertile soil.

Burning of dung

Dung is by far the most readily available energy resource for cooking in rural Ethiopia. A major factor which impacts on the use of dung for fuel is deforestation, which has made it increasingly difficult to get wood near rural villages. It has been estimated that the burning of dung instead of using it as fertilizer causes an annual reduction in grain production by some 550 000 tons. The annual consumption of fuel from animal-waste was estimated to be 3.942 million metric tons or 13 797 Tcal (CSE, 1997).

Accelerated soil erosion

Soil erosion resulted in a loss of grain production estimated at around 40 000 tons in 1990. The permanent loss in soil resources' value caused by erosion was estimated to be 59 million Birr in 1990 (EPA, 1997). Deforestation and poor farming practices which cause soil erosion are by and large behavioural issues. They require constant attention from policy makers, and concern and engagement by farmers. The CSA agricultural survey indicates that in 1997/98 there were 9.3 million agricultural households in the country, of which 8.3 million (89 per cent) were recorded in Oromia, Amhara and SNNP regional states; 6.4 million had 4 to 9 family members, 6.9 million (74 per cent) were illiterate, and 86 per cent had a plot of land of 0.10 to 2 hectares. These figures vividly show the extent of land ownership fragmentation. The problems are compounded by the large size of households, a lack of education, a low awareness level and deficiencies in soil management practices.

Low utilization of some natural resources

Resource utilization in the country has been exploitative and destructive in some cases and unacceptably low in other cases. No more than 1 per cent of water resources are put to use. Irrigated land is less than 4 per cent of potential. Less than 30 per cent of the population has access to potable water, while only 2 per cent of the hydro-power potential is being used. The contribution of mining is minimal, accounting for less than 3 per cent of GDP in 1985 (CSE, 1997). The contribution of tourism to GDP generation is extremely low when compared to the potential and to that of neighbouring countries.

Erosion of biodiversity

The decline in biodiversity is driven by the following factors: disruptive interventions by the state, the weakening of local management in the face of an expanding population, and the increasing needs of agriculture. Disruptive interventions by the state include expansion of state farms and unpopular settlement programmes in densely forested areas and its focus on mono-cropping of exotic trees. Weakening of local management stems from a decision-making process which excludes the participation of communities in the affected areas. It also derives from the formulation of directives at the centre which disregard local conditions.

Erosion of biodiversity also takes place as a result of the total reliance of the population on biomass for its energy needs.

Deterioration of the urban environment

Fifteen per cent of the population lives in the urban centres. The stock and quality of urban houses is very poor. Access to potable water and sanitation services is very low. About 31 per cent of the households in Addis Ababa have no sanitation facilities. In other urban areas the proportion is about 48 per cent (CSE, 1997). Migration from rural areas to the urban centres has been increasing, leading to unemployment and an ever-increasing number of street children and beggars. Industrial pollution is increasing in and around Addis Ababa and some other urban centres.

3.2 The Policies

Environmental policies which emanate from the Conservation Strategy of Ethiopia (CSE) developed in 1997 are influenced by the definition of sustainable development brought forward by the Brundtland Commission. As noted earlier, the CSE is intended to foster sustainable management of natural resources in the context of development. It is designed to integrate environmental and development concerns within a holistic approach. The Ethiopian environmental policies have also drawn substantially from international initiatives, such as the UN's Agenda 21 and the IUCN's Caring for Earth. The policies have adapted the principles contained in these initiatives to the Ethiopian conditions. The main goals are:

- improve and enhance the health and quality of life of all Ethiopians;
- promote sustainable social and economic development;

- foster sound management and use of the environment;
- meet the needs of present and future generations.

This is a major departure from the traditional approach which focused on preserving the environment. Here the focus is on improvement and enhancement of the health conditions and the quality of life for all Ethiopians.

The regions have their own Regional Conservation Strategies (RCSs) tailored to their specific needs but consistent with the Environmental Policy of Ethiopia (EPE)/Conservation Strategy of Ethiopia (CSE). The CSE and the RCSs consist of policies, strategies, institutional frameworks and action plans. Their implementation is expected to be supported by a legal framework which creates the proper conditions for formulating, reviewing and updating sectoral regulations and procedures. The current legal framework consists of laws and regulations issued by the EPA, other federal and regional sector agencies and the regional states. General civil and criminal law provisions enable both government and the society at large to prevent environmental abuses. Violations of transboundary environmental agreements are normally dealt with via inter-governmental consultation instruments, such as border commissions and the like.

Ethiopia's environmental management is also influenced by international agreements to which it is a party including the Convention on Biological Diversity (CBD), the Framework Convention for Climate Change (FCCC), the Convention to Combat Desertification (CCD), the Bamako Convention and the Lusaka Agreement. The New Partnership for African Development (NEPAD) also has an environmental component.

3.3 Federal and Regional Institutions for Environmental Management

The EPE/CSE prescribes the establishment, by law, of coordination and management bodies from the federal level down to the community level to handle sectoral and cross-sectoral planning and implementation of policies. These institutions will consist of coordinating committees/councils with a secretariat at the regional, zonal and Woreda level. At the community level, only a secretary who takes minutes and records the decisions made by the community is envisaged. The committees at the various levels will include community, NGO, private sector, as well as government representatives.

The main federal environmental institution is the Environmental Protection Authority (EPA) established in 1995 (Proclamation No. 9, 1995). Its powers and duties have recently been revised (Proclamation No. 295, 2002). The EPA has an Environmental Protection Council (EPC). The EPA's objective is to formulate policies, strategies, laws and standards, which foster social and economic development in a manner that enhances the welfare of citizens and the sustainability of the environment (Proclamation 295, 2002). Its specific duties and responsibilities include the following:

- to coordinate measures that ensure the implementation of environmental objectives enshrined in the Federal Constitution and the basic principles set out in the EPE;
- to liaise with competent agencies in the field of environmental protection and rehabilitation and to support the capacity development of these agencies;
- to establish a system for the assessment of the environmental impact of public and private projects;
- to define social and economic development policies, strategies and programmes;
- to review environmental impact studies of projects subject to federal licensing, and their auditing;
- to set environmental standards and ensure their compliance;
- to participate in the negotiation of international environmental agreements ensuring their ratification by the national instances;
- to initiate and formulate the policies, strategies, laws and programmes that are needed to implement international environmental agreements;
- to formulate incentives for the prevention of environmental degradation or pollution and disincentives to discourage those practices that endanger the sustainable use of natural resources;
- to formulate directives for implementing environmental protection laws and to oversee their implementation;
- to provide advice and support to competent agencies regarding their obligations under the laws pertaining to environmental protection; and, when required, to formulate recommendations to the government regarding measures to ensure compliance.

The EPA can also delegate some of its powers and duties to other agencies. Other governmental agencies involved in environmental management at both the federal and regional levels include the following:

- Ministry/Bureaux of Agriculture
- Ethiopian Wildlife Development and Protection Department
- The Ethiopian Agricultural Research Organization
- Regional Agricultural Research Institutions (where they exist)
- The Ethiopian Science and Technology Commission
- Ministry/Bureaux of Water Resources
- Institute of Biodiversity Conservation

- Ministry/Bureaux of Water and Mines
- Ministry/Bureaux of Labour and Social Affairs
- Disaster Prevention and Preparedness Commission
- Regional Disaster Prevention and Preparedness Bureaux
- The Rural Energy Development Promotion Centre

Most regional states have created agencies with mandates on environmental matters. The federal law requires that each regional state should establish its own independent regional environment agency based on the EPE/CSE. It also gives the regional states the option to designate an already existing agency for this purpose (Proclamation No. 295, 2002). As a result, these organs have differing status depending on their location, and their autonomy is determined within the regional administrative structure and by the scope of their mandate. A few regions have created a presence at the Woreda level (Lemma, 2004). A good example would be the Amhara region. This region has established its own Environmental Protection, Land Administration and Utilization Authority at the regional level (Proclamation No. 46, 2000) and separate Environmental Protection, Land Administration and Utilization Offices in every Woreda. The Woreda offices are part of the Department of Rural Development of the Woreda, to which they are accountable. The regional environmental agencies are not hierarchically linked to the federal organs. However, there are cases where regional environmental agencies maintain links with the federal EPA for the exchange of information and for consultation. These contacts are made on a personal basis and do not derive from legal requirements. The links between the regional environmental agencies and the environmental offices at the Woreda level are stronger because of the hierarchical links between regions and Woredas.

It has been observed that the institutional arrangements for environmental management in Ethiopia have changed over the years as many times as the whims of individuals and decision-makers permitted. In the last two decades, the management has passed on from the Forestry and Wildlife Authority, the Valleys Development Authority, the Ministry of Agriculture, the Ministry of Agriculture and Natural Resources, the Ministry of Natural Resources and Environment Protection to the current Environmental Protection Authority in succession, one replacing the other with no consideration given to the resources wasted in the process of making these changes.

There is no documented evidence that changes in the institutional arrangements have resulted in improving or worsening the environmental situation of the country. However, the establishment of the Valleys Development Authority and of the Ministry of Water Resources has enhanced the capacity of the country in drafting river basin master plans and has increased the coverage of clean water supply and the development of human resources in the field of water resources. There is also some evidence that the recent decentralization process and the establishment of environmental and land administration agencies at regional level are impacting positively on soil and water conservation and on forestation activities. Some studies indicate that in some regions there has been a substantial increase in plantations of eucalyptus trees due to encouragement of homestead plantations by the newly established agencies.

The general mandate of these regional agencies is also specified in federal law (Proclamation No. 295, 2002). Their responsibilities include the following: coordinating the formulation, implementation and review of regional conservation strategies; monitoring, regulating and protecting the environment; and, ensuring the implementation of federal environmental standards, or issuing and enforcing their own standards that are no less stringent than the federal ones. These general mandates are further elaborated in the respective regional laws establishing regional environmental organs.

Although initially an attempt was made to establish coordinating committees at the regional level, there is no information about the actual creation of these bodies and of their performances. Coordinating committees at the Woredas, Kebelles and Sub-Kebelle levels have yet to be created. Nevertheless, environment-related activities, within the context of combating poverty, improving food security and increasing agricultural productivity, continue to be carried out at Sub-Kebelle and community levels, particularly with regard to combating land degradation and the promotion of sustainable management of renewable resources. Local communities are being encouraged to take the lead and are provided with technical assistance by Development Agents (DAs). This is a completely new approach when compared with past practices based on a top-down approach and where the communities were mobilized to implement the government plans, whether they liked it or not. The top-down approach of the past has resulted in the destruction of forests, wildlife, and in the neglect of soil conservation works by peasants who resented that approach (Lemma, 2004).

At the supra-national level, Ethiopia is a member of a number of subregional, regional and international organizations. It is a party to treaties and agreements dealing directly or indirectly with environmental matters. At the sub-regional level it is a member of the Inter-Governmental Authority on Drought and Development (IGADD), while at the regional/continental level it is a member of the African Union, the Economic Commission for Africa and Inter-ministerial bodies, such as the African Ministerial Conference on Environment (AMCEN). At the international level the country is a member of UNEP and UNDP. The supra-national bodies provide the necessary multi-level supra-national linkages as regards environmental management.

3.4 Involvement of the Civil Society

The promotion of participation and the involvement of stakeholders in the decision-making process and in the implementation of environmental activities is a standard policy of the Ethiopian government. Genuine people participation is an important principle of the EPE/CSE. This requires an understanding of the policy by the citizens, which in turn requires that the policy be communicated to the public in an understandable language. It also requires the holding of regular public discussions about the policy at hand and the role of the public in its implementation. There is a significant level of involvement of the civil society, in particular, by international and local NGOs in the field of environment. Several NGOs are active in the planning and implementation of natural resources conservation and integrated rural development projects. NGOs generally carry out these activities using participatory approaches and in collaboration with grassroots organizations. However, NGOs are not involved in systematic advocacy concerning critical environmental issues. Most local NGOs are still focused on domestic issues and are not visible in civil society movements at sub-regional, continental and international levels (Lemma, 2004).

Professional and trade associations, particularly those active in the area of natural resources management, have shown interest in carrying out research and studies in the various areas of environmental management.

3.5 Scientific Research for Environmental Management

Scientific knowledge and research on environmental management are indispensable to ensuring that decisions affecting the environment are made with full knowledge of the consequences. In recognition of this fact, the EPE provides for strengthening the development of scientific knowledge. It encourages, in particular, research through partnership between scientists and potential end users.

There are a number of governmental institutions which are involved in activities related to scientific research. The most important, at the federal level, is the Ethiopian Agricultural Research Organization. There are also regional agricultural research organizations. These regional and federal institutions carry out research in the area of improved soil (and other renewable resources) management and conservation technologies with a view to improving agricultural production.

Academic institutions, such as the Wondo Genet Forestry College, also carry out research relevant to forest management activities. However, there are no specific scientific organizations at either the regional or federal levels to provide support to environmental decision-making. In large part, federal and regional organizations with environment-related responsibilities try to satisfy their needs of scientific knowledge through their own efforts but have a very limited capacity. Instances of contracting research to the private sector do not exist, although there are a number of instances where academic institutions are involved in research which could be of relevance to environmental decision-making.

It is also important to note that EPE envisages the establishment of Science and Technology Associations in all communities to identify and support traditional systems of research. However, no such associations exist yet (Lemma, 2004).

4. ENVIRONMENT MANAGEMENT: POLICIES, RESPONSIBILITIES AND ACTIVITIES

4.1 Pollution Control

Policies

The Federal Constitution mandates that every person has the right to live in a healthy environment. This provision is a long-term one. The EPE/CSE provides the specific principles, policies and strategies for attaining the stated environmental quality objectives with respect to air, water and soil pollution. The focus, however, is solely on pollution from industries and hazardous substances. Pollution from agricultural activity is not specifically considered, as the use of chemical fertilizers, pesticides and herbicides in agriculture is still insignificant. Although control of noise pollution is not envisaged in the policy, it is being taken into account.

The 'polluter pays' and the 'precautionary' principles are the cornerstones for controlling pollution (Proclamation No. 300, 2002). An important guiding principle is that when a compromise between short-term economic growth and long-term environmental protection is necessary, then development activities have to minimize degrading and polluting impacts on ecological and other life-support systems. When working out a compromise, it is better to err on the side of caution, since rehabilitating a degraded environment is very expensive, and bringing back a species that has become extinct is impossible. The first part of this principle embodies the requirement of conducting environmental impact assessments (EIAs) for development projects. The second part is non-committal, but it recommends as far as possible, that decisions should be made in favour of protecting the environment when the impact of development activities on the environment cannot be clearly evaluated.

The mandate for issuing legislation with regard to regulating and controlling pollution is vested in the EPA. Proclamation No. 300, 2002 has been enacted to enforce policy requirements for pollution control. The EPA is also responsible for drafting regulations designed to control pollution from industrial waste. The proclamation refers to pollution in general, but it also deals with specific issues, such as the management of hazardous waste including chemical and radioactive substances and municipal waste. Its implementation is yet to commence. The law also requires the establishment of standards for the discharge of effluents into water bodies and sewerage systems, as well as soil, air, noise and noxious odour. The provision of incentives to presently operating businesses for the introduction of methods that enable the prevention or minimization of pollution is envisaged. New equipment destined for pollution control is exempt from customs duties upon verification by the EPA.

The law specifies that the regional states may adopt more stringent standards than those determined at the federal level. The EPA has currently drafted standards for water, air, soil and noise, which have yet to be approved and transformed into legislation. It is also presently engaged in the definition of the legal and institutional framework concerning the management of Persistent Organic Pollutants (POPs) (EPA, 2003).

Recently the EPA has received legal backing with the issuance of Proclamation No. 299, 2002. Despite the lack of a fully-fledged EPA legislation, however, the EPA has been reviewing Environmental Impact Statements (EISs) of development projects submitted by the Ethiopian Investment Authority and other government organizations.

Institutional responsibilities and activities

The implementation of the policies and legislation related to pollution is the responsibility of both the EPA and the regional environmental agencies. Sewage and garbage collection and disposal are the responsibility of municipal councils. In Addis Ababa, a special agency is responsible for water and sewerage services (the Addis Ababa Water and Sewerage Authority), while garbage collection is carried out by the municipality itself. However, only Addis Ababa has a sewerage system, and its coverage is very small. Liquid waste from septic tanks in other bigger towns is collected by vehicles; the same system is used for solid wastes. Most remaining towns and townships have little or no sewage and garbage collection services. As Ethiopian cities, including Addis Ababa, keep growing, the problem of the collection and disposal of both solid and liquid wastes is becoming difficult to handle by municipal authorities alone. It is interesting to note that since municipal authorities in Addis Ababa are not able to provide a house-to-house garbage collection service, in many cities the poor and unemployed youth have started setting up organizations for the provision of this service.

Institutional and legal reforms are being carried out with respect to the organization and power exercised by municipalities. There is a trend towards creating autonomous municipal enterprises, or to grant the right to run services provided by municipalities to the private sector. Indeed, in the city of Addis Ababa alone, there are already several private firms providing liquid waste collection services.

Adherence to the various standards is to be ensured through 'Environmental Inspectors' to be appointed by the respective environmental agencies. Any person dissatisfied with any decision of either the federal or the regional environmental agencies may submit a grievance notice to the heads thereof. If an agency fails to make a decision within the prescribed time, or if the decision does not satisfy the complainant, an appeal can be made to the court. The law also provides for a right to standing by allowing any person, without the need to show any vested interest, the right to lodge a complaint at the EPA, or at regional environmental agencies against any person causing actual or potential damage to the environment and the right to appeal thereafter.

The preparation of EIA legislation is the responsibility of the EPA, while implementation is the responsibility of both the federal EPA and the regional environmental agencies (Proclamation No. 295, 2002). The EPA is responsible for the review of EISs and the monitoring of their implementation, when the project is subject to licensing, execution or supervision by a federal agency, or when it is likely to produce transboundary impacts. Where projects are subject to licensing, execution or supervision by a regional agency, the regions are responsible for reviewing such EISs. It is required that the public and particularly the communities affected by the implementation of a project are involved both during the EIAs and the review of the EISs. In addition, while any person dissatisfied with the review, monitoring or any other decision of either the federal or the regional environmental agencies may submit a grievance notice to the heads thereof, interestingly no appeal thereof is provided for. It is also interesting to note that the EIA legislation does not provide for the right to standing as in the case of the pollution control legislation. In any case, the culture of using the *loci standi* provision evident in the pollution control proclamation has yet to develop in Ethiopia.

Among the projects that are relevant for pollution control and which have already been implemented or are being implemented, we can mention the following: the Project for the Control and Disposal of Expired Pesticides; Project for the Preparation of a National Chemical Handling and Registration guideline; the Ecologically Sustainable Industrial Development Project; the National Cleaner Production Center Project; the Tannery Pollution Control Project; and, the Project for the Environmental Auditing of 10 Factories (EPA, 2003).

There are also a number of programmes being carried out in relation to international conventions and agreements. After Ethiopia ratified the Framework Convention for Climate Change by Proclamation No. 97 on 2 May, 1994, capacity building and restructuring work was carried out within the National Meteorological Services Agency (NMSA) in the area of monitoring climatic change, and collecting and disseminating timely data. Within the NMSA, a Climate Change and Air Pollution Research Team has been established. Major sources of greenhouse gases in the country have been registered, and preliminary research has also been conducted to verify the effect of climatic change on the water flow of the Awash River as well as on wheat production and forest resources. Furthermore, research has been undertaken on the best possible measures to minimize greenhouse gas emissions associated with energy utilization, as well as from grazing and livestock production. It has also been possible to produce the first National Climate Change Report and submit it to the Secretariat of the Convention (EPA, 2003).

Ethiopia ratified and became a party to the Vienna Convention and the Montreal Protocol in January 1996. The NMSA has been mandated for the coordination and supervision of implementation of measures in Ethiopia under this convention. Since then a National Ozone Team has been established under the auspices of NMSA, and a programme for controlling ozone-depleting substances has been put in place. Draft legislation for the control of substances that deplete the ozone layer has been prepared and is awaiting enactment. Some projects, such as a project for the repair and re-use as well as a programme with respect to the handling of CFC-based refrigerators have been developed (EPA, 2003).

In addition to the Bamako Convention of 1991, Ethiopia has ratified the Basel Convention by Proclamation No. 192, 2000. To implement the Convention within the country, draft policies and legislation have been prepared and submitted to the government. Moreover, activities related to prior informed consent are being carried out (EPA, 2003).

In 2002 and 2003, Ethiopia fully accepted and ratified the Stockholm Convention designed to ban the use of Persistent Organic Pollutants (POPs) and the Rotterdam Convention dealing with informed consent in the context of international trade in specific hazardous chemicals and pesticides. The EPA is responsible for the domestic implementation of these conventions. Projects and programme frameworks designed to develop an appropriate system for the realization of the objectives of these Conventions are in progress (EPA, 2003).

4.2 Ecosystem Protection

Policies

Several factors affect the sustainability of ecosystems in Ethiopia. The major ones are human settlements, investment activities, the lack of land use policy as well as localized but increasing amounts of toxic substances and pollutants. As a result, various ecosystems are under enormous pressure and subject to degradation. Poverty is also a major factor, as poor people focus on the immediate satisfaction of their survival needs from the resources in ecosystems they depend on.

The general policy principle is that biological diversity should encompass natural and human managed ecosystems, species of domesticated and wild flora and fauna, and the genetic variation within individual species; and, that it should be protected and conserved, primarily, through *ex situ* and *in situ* conservation of wild and domesticated biodiversity, the establishment of protected areas and integrated biodiversity conservation outside protected areas with strategic land use plans and agricultural and pastoral production strategies. Involvement of communities, which are inside and outside Protected Areas and community sharing of the benefits of conservation programmes is an important principle.

Institutional responsibility and activities

Until 1998, the Institute of Biodiversity (IB) carried out activities related to sampling and conserving the country's plant genetic resources. Since then IB has been renamed as the Institute of Biodiversity Conservation (IBC) and given the additional responsibility for animal life and micro-organisms. Biodiversity Protection and Research Policy and Strategies are in place. An undertaking to develop a national biodiversity programme in collaboration with the relevant federal and regional institutions is being carried out. The setting up of institutional mechanisms and a legal framework for regulating access to biodiversity as well as ensuring bio-safety is in process.

The IBC is the leading agency for the implementation of biodiversity conservation activities. It carries out its responsibilities at the federal level with the cooperation of such federal organs as the Ethiopian Wildlife Development and Conservation Department (EWDCD), the Ethiopian Institute of Agricultural Research (EIAR), the EPA and the Ministry of Agriculture and Rural Development, and at the regional level, with the

Bureaux of Agriculture, the Regional Agricultural Research Institutions, the Regional Environmental Agencies and the local communities.

In as far as activities in biodiversity conservation are concerned, a number of measures are being taken. *In situ* and *ex situ* conservation is being carried out to protect and conserve biodiversity in several areas of the country. In 1994, a conservation project entitled 'A dynamic farmer based approach to conservation of Ethiopia's plant genetic resources' was implemented under the auspices of the Institute of Biodiversity Conservation with the purpose of promoting conservation of genetic resources *in situ* (at the village and farm levels). The project has resulted in the formation of Crop Conservation Associations (CCAs), which are made up of farmers and focus on 'community-gene banks' and botanical gardens. Conservation centres on cereals (teff, wheat, barley, sorghum, maize) and field-grown crops (EPA, 2003). The *ex situ* conservation of useful plants and crops aims at preventing their extinction. Currently 56 558 accessions/samples of various species are being conserved *ex situ*. In addition, a Forest Genetic Resources Conservation Project with the objective of developing a national forest genetic resources research strategy, registration of woody biomass, conducting socio-economic surveys in natural forest areas, establishing forest gene banks, compiling data on indigenous trees and shrubs, awareness creation and institutional capacity building is currently being implemented (EPA, 2003).

At the sub-regional level a Project for the Conservation and Sustainable Use of Biodiversity in the East African Rift Valley Lakes is under consideration for implementation by Ethiopia, Kenya and Tanzania. The objective of the project is to strengthen and enhance the conservation of biodiversity through sustainable use of the lakes of the Rift Valley. A particular aim of the project is the development and strengthening of appropriate protection and conservation systems for threatened ecosystems (EPA, 2003).

With regard to the protection and conservation of the country's wildlife resources, 9 national parks, 8 wild animal reserve areas, 3 wildlife sanctuaries, 18 game reserves and 51 bird areas have been designated in different parts of the country (Hillman, 1993). However, the size of these areas is shrinking as a result of human settlements around wildlife habitats and the consequent expansion of farmed land; an increase in the number of domestic animals; poaching; and forest fires. A lack of ownership rights within the concerned communities and the absence of participation and benefit-sharing arrangements in the development and protection of the wild animals are also impacting negatively.

With support from donors, a Wildlife Protection Support Programme is being implemented. Programme activities include establishment of an endowment fund, rehabilitation of infrastructure, undertaking community and tourism development in national parks as well as rehabilitating and enhancing the management of protected areas of prime importance. The programme is being implemented by the EWDCD. This organization has also been implementing a Biodiversity Protection and Conservation Support Project in important bird areas since 1999 as well as the rehabilitation of three national parks. An effort is also being made to improve household security for pastoralists and to undertake conservation and protection activities in the Awash National Park.

With respect to land use, the EPE/CSE requires that land use categories shall be recommended based on the criteria of biological, chemical and physical factors, that is, carrying capacity, vulnerability to erosion, wetland values, biodiversity values, and pollution hazards as well as social and economic considerations. The national land use plan shall be based on the land use plans to be prepared by the Regional States. Within the framework of the regional land use plans, the Woreda and community land use plans are to be prepared. Communities shall be assisted by government in the preparation of their participatory land use plans. Institutional responsibility shall be with an agency which is impartial to all.

The policy emphasizes that an uninterrupted and continuing access to the same land is indispensable for farmers to undertake soil conservation measures and investments related thereto. There are various options and arrangements for the realization of the above principle. However, uninterrupted access to a piece of land is a necessary but not a sufficient condition for building confidence among farmers. Furthermore it does not offer farmers the freedom to move to other livelihoods when conditions and opportunities arise, since they are not guaranteed to get the same value from their land as they would if they were to rent it long term or permanently transfer their holding right. The environmental policy further recommends recognition and protection, wherever possible, of customary rights of access to and use of land and natural resources, which are constitutionally acceptable, socially equitable and preferred by local communities.

In addition, maintenance of soil productivity by protecting the soil from erosion, desertification, salinization and promoting effective ground cover is an essential element of the approach to improved soil, crop and animal husbandry for sustainable agriculture. Stall-feeding to protect the soil from trampling due to grazing, and planting trees, are considered important measures for re-vegetation and for protecting and building up the soil. The policy approach to agriculture is the sustainable improvement and intensification of existing farming systems by developing and disseminating technologies which are biologically stable, appropriate under prevailing environmental and socio-cultural conditions, economically viable and environmentally beneficial. The policy recommends the use of appropriate organic matter and nutrient management for improving soil structure, nutrient status and microbiology. The integrity of soil is to be safeguarded, and its physical and biological properties are to be protected through management practices for the production of crops and livestock which pay particular attention to a proper balance in amounts of chemical fertilizers and organic ones used, including green manure, farmyard manure and compost. Indigenous systems of soil management have been given recognition in the policy as a possible foundation for improved soil conservation measures.

To combat land degradation, particularly soil erosion and loss of soil fertility, activities such as the construction of terraces, soil bunds, microbasins and cut-off drains, as well as tree planting are being carried out. The lead federal agency is the Ministry of Agriculture, while the lead agencies at the regional level are the Bureaux of Agriculture whose reach goes down to the Woreda level and from there, through Development Agents (DAs) to the Sub-Kebelle, village and household levels. Soil conservation activities are carried out by the farmers themselves with guidance from the DAs.

In Ethiopia, there is also the problem of soil salinization to deal with. This problem may become an increasing threat as irrigation expands within the country. While a number of federal and regional organizations such as the EPA, Ministry of Agriculture, Ministry of Water Resources and their regional counterparts are concerned with the question of soil salinization, their focuses of attention vary. The EPA should ensure that the policies and the laws against soil salinization are effectively implemented. On the other hand, the Ministry of Water Resources is mainly concerned about drainage in medium and small scale irrigation schemes, while the Ministry of Agriculture is mainly concerned about soil salinization that may be caused by micro-irrigation schemes mainly operated by farmers in a formally organized or unorganized fashion.

Within the context of the implementation of the Convention to Combat Desertification regarding which EPA is the lead agency, a national action programme at the federal level and at some regional state levels has been elaborated. Participatory pilot projects designed to demonstrate to communities how degraded land can be rehabilitated are underway in a number of regions with the cooperation and collaboration of the regional bureaux of agriculture and regional environmental agencies. Although the establishment of a fund for combating desertification is envisaged, action in this respect is yet to be undertaken.

4.3 Natural Resources Management

Ensuring social equity in resource use in a decentralized, ethnic-based federal set-up and in a situation where regional states have full legal powers to manage and use their natural resources within their respective boundaries is quite a challenge. However, as mentioned above, the regional states have to share with the federal government the royalties from mining and gas and petroleum operations as indicated in Article 52 (Proclamation No. 1, 1995). The assumption is that the federal government will use these resources to subsidize development in the more impoverished regional states. The current state of affairs with regards to resource use and sharing can at best be described as an unspoken gentleman's agreement among regions. Any crisis will surely precipitate the need for clearly defining the use and sharing arrangement of resources among regional states.

As regards renewable resources, the EPE/CSE deals with forest, water and mineral resources management in some detail. Although the sustainable management of wildlife resources is not dealt with separately, it can be said that it is adequately incorporated within the policies for biodiversity management. Similarly, fishery resources are not specifically treated in the policy.

Forest resources

Policies With regard to forests, EPE promotes sustainable forest management principles. This entails conservation of natural forests by management plans and determining which forests should be used for habitat protection, for conservation and for production. Uncultivable lands are to be afforested, and felling and grazing therein are to be controlled. While the formulation of forestry strategies that integrate the development, management and conservation of forest resources with those of land, water, energy, ecosystem and genetic resources, as well as with crop and livestock production is required, agricultural and other policies and programmes that reduce pressure on fragile wood land resources and ecosystems are also to be pursued.

Detailed sectoral forest policy is not presently in place, and a draft prepared a few years ago is still awaiting approval. However, there is a sectoral legislation enacted in 1992 which is considered as the governing federal law as regards the management of forestry resources (Proclamation No. 94, 1992).

Institutional responsibility and activities While the protection and management of protected forest areas is mainly regional government responsibility with the involvement of the relevant communities, the responsibility for community forests lies with the communities concerned.

The lead agency at the federal level is the Ministry of Agriculture while the lead agencies at the regional level are the Bureaux of Agriculture. An Ethiopian Forestry Action Plan had been developed some years ago but hardly any action has been taken since then to systematically implement it. The regions have also developed forestry action programmes but are faced with the same implementation shortcomings.

However, farmers are being encouraged to plant farmstead/homestead trees/woodlots for purposes of protecting the soil, meeting their firewood needs, as well as to earn supplemental income from the sale of wood. Technical assistance is provided by Development Agents to the farmers. Soil conservation activities are carried out by the farmers themselves with guidance from the Development Agents. Generally, each household is responsible for carrying out such activities on its own holding while responsibility for conserving soil on communally owned land (for grazing or as community forests) lies with the concerned communities as a whole. There are instances of positive developments in encouraging individuals and associations to plant trees on public lands through long-term free land lease arrangements. According to some studies, an overall increase in biomass is resulting from the positive policy environment and the initiatives taken by the farmers.

Major forestry-related activities include forestation and demarcation of forest reserve areas. The demarcation and inventorying of 58 natural forest priority areas totalling 4.78 million ha has already been carried out, and the conservation of priority forests is underway (EFAP, 1994).

However, the current situation where private investors are provided with various incentives to invest in the regions, especially in the peripheral ones, has resulted in unsustainable exploitation of forest resources in the name of agricultural investment. This, of course, is not the result of a deliberate policy on the part of the regional states, but rather the unintended outcome of investment policies in those regional states where environment concerns have not been integrated into development activities. As a result, cases of 'modern slash and burn' farming practices whereby investors clear a large area of forest for agriculture and abandon the cleared area on account of unsuitability of the soil for agriculture are becoming commonplace. This practice is inexcusable in that investors are expected to conduct their investment on the basis of a feasibility study among which soil suitability should be one component. If this practice is allowed to continue some regions are bound to lose both their resource base and the investment.

Water resources

Policies Although Ethiopia's water resources have significant potential for use in irrigated agriculture, hydroelectric power generation and other social and economic purposes, the use that has been made of these resources is very low. On the other hand, the water resources of the country and the related aquatic ecosystems are being affected by such factors as siltation, pollution from discharge of various wastes, and disruption in rainfall patterns.

The planning and development unit for water resources is the drainage basin, and priority is to be given to watershed management in order to control and conserve water and to regulate its flow in the catchments. Integrated Water Resources Management, which puts emphasis on multipurpose projects, has been adopted. In this connection, EPE also gives recognition to the fact that natural ecosystems, particularly wetlands and upstream forests, as well as the interface between water bodies and land (for example lake shores, river banks and wetlands) are fundamental in regulating water quality and quantity and to integrate their rehabilitation and protection into the conservation, development and management of water resources.

There are several policy prescriptions with regard to the protection of water and related flora and fauna from harmful effects. They include for instance the following: the amount of water used for irrigation should be kept at the minimum required to maintain soil conditions suitable for growth; soil shall be protected from salinization; and, any proposed introduction of exotic species into water ecosystems shall be subject to detailed ecological studies and environmental impact assessment. Furthermore, the design, construction and use of dams and irrigation systems and other water works should ensure the control of environmental health hazards.

Currently, sectoral water resources development and protection policies and strategies and water resources development action plans, including drinking water and sanitation, are in place. A legal framework for water resources legislation (Proclamation No. 197, 2000) is also in place. However, regulations for its implementation have yet to be enacted. A number of river basin development master plans also exist. In order to meet human and financial needs of the water sector, the Arba Minch Water Technology Institute and a Water Fund at federal level have been established.

Institutional responsibility and activities The federal lead agency for water resources management is the Ministry of Water Resources Development, while at the regional level the Water Mines and Energy Bureaux play the leading role. Even though the study, planning and regulating, is expected to be carried out at the river basin level, the bulk of the implementation of water development works is carried out at the regional level by the regional bureaux and their Woredal water offices with the participation of grassroots communities. At the grassroots level, water resources development through micro-irrigation schemes and water works necessary thereto (such as micro-dams, small diversion systems, and so on) are carried out with the involvement of the community members. Communities are also responsible for post-construction activities such as operation and maintenance of works. The water office staff and the agricultural office's Development Agents coordinate their activities at this level to implement agriculture-related water works.

It should be noted that both at the federal and regional levels, other sector organizations have mandates that should normally be seen as complementing that of the Ministry of Water Resources (MOWR) and the respective regional states. These complementary mandates include environment and health, water quality and standards, but these overlapping mandates pose the possibility of conflict between the MOWR, EPA and the Ministry of Health (MOH). However, due to traditional turf protection mentality these complementarities are often seen as jurisdictional overlaps and lead to conflicts. The situation is further exacerbated by badly drafted laws.

Regarding ownership and management of water supply systems, EPE stresses devolution and management autonomy to the lowest possible local level and encourages the involvement of all stakeholders, including the private sector. Currently, regional states are observed formulating and implementing their respective five-year water resources development plans and undertaking large-scale water-dependent private investment projects without giving adequate consideration to the interdependence. Together with these measures of devolution, service contracting to the private/informal sector in such areas as consultancy, construction, supply of spare parts, maintenance and operation as well as management of water supply systems is also being promoted. Urban water supply services are expected to cover all their costs (investment, operation and maintenance), while rural water supply services are expected to cover at least their operation and maintenance costs. Rural water supply remains essentially a community-run service managed by water committees elected by the communities being served.

Mineral resources

Policies Minerals are important non-renewable resources for Ethiopia. Hence, the EPE and RCS provide for mineral resources development and mining operations management. The management approach is based on integrating mineral development with that of the various mineral end-user sectors of the economy and with those sectors that provide inputs and support to the mining industry.

Institutional responsibility and activities The federal lead agency for mineral resources management is the Ministry of Mines, while at the regional level the Water Mines and Energy Bureaux manage mineral resources and regulate mining operations in accordance with federal law. Although the specific mandate to negotiate exploration and exploitation rights and to grant licences for these purposes is not specified in the federal and the regional constitutions, the direct mandate of the regional bureaux in licensing mineral exploration and exploitation appears to be limited to small scale (artisan) mining only. This conclusion is warranted from a reading of Article 98 of the federal constitution stating that the states and the federal state shall jointly levy and collect taxes on incomes derived from *large-scale mining* and all petroleum and gas operations as well as royalties on such operations.

5. CONCLUSIONS

As shown in the preceding sections, while Ethiopia has some very good policies and strategies, both at the federal and regional state levels, the situation in terms of consistent, continuous, integrated and coordinated implementation leaves a lot to be desired. The main factors affecting implementation are: a low priority given to environmental issues; weak institutional structures; lack of human, technical and material resources; weakness of civil society in Ethiopia; and a lack of advocacy on critical environmental issues to influence policies, laws and programmes. If all stakeholders (government, civil society, private sector, and so on) take a concerted action to deal with the issues mentioned above, as well as the other economic, social and environmental problems in the country, there is very good chance for the Ethiopian environment not only to be rehabilitated where such rehabilitation is essential, but to be more enhanced to provide its essential services to the citizens of the country.

BIBLIOGRAPHY

Asfaw, Gedion (1998), *Institutional Responsibilities for the Implementation of the Environmental Policy of Ethiopia*, Addis Ababa: Environmental Protection Authority.

Asfaw, Gedion (2000), 'The conservation strategy process in Ethiopia: overview and status', TEFTERO, *Quarterly Newsletter of the CSE Project*, Special Issue.

Central Statistical Authority (CSA) (1998), *Agricultural Sample Survey, 1997/98, Report on Land Utilization (Private Peasant Holdings)*, Volume IV, Addis Ababa.

Conservation Strategy of Ethiopia (CSE) (1997), *The Conservation Strategy of Ethiopia (CSE). The Resource Base, its Utilization and Planning for Sustainability*, Vol. 1: 138. Federal Democratic Republic of Ethiopia, Addis Ababa: Environmental Protection Authority.

Environmental Protection Authority (EPA) (1997), *Environmental Policy*, 2 April, Addis Ababa.

Environmental Protection Authority (EPA) (2003), *State of the Environment Report*, Mimeograph. Addis Ababa.

Ethiopia Mapping Agency (EMA) (1988), *National Atlas of Ethiopia*, Addis Ababa.

Ethiopian Forestry Action Program (EFAP) (1994), *Ethiopian Forestry Action Program (EFAP). The Challenge for Development*, Volume II, Addis Ababa: Ministry of Natural Resources Development and Environmental Protection.

Ethiopian Valleys Development Studies Authority (EVDSA) (1989), *Draft National Resources Master Plan*, Addis Ababa.

Friis, I. (1992), *Forests and Forest Trees of Northeast Tropical Africa – Their Natural Habitats and Distribution Patterns in Ethiopia, Djibouti and Somalia*, Kew Bulletin, Additional Series, No. 15, London: Her Majesty's Stationery Office.

Hillman, J.C. (1993), *Ethiopia: Compendium of Wildlife Conservation Information*, New York & Addis Ababa: The Wildlife Conservation Society International and Ethiopian Wildlife Conservation Organization.

Lemma, Kifle (2004), *A Brief Note on the Implementation of the Environmental Policy of Ethiopia and Related Institutional Issues*, Addis Ababa, unpublished.

Proclamation No. 94 (1992), *Forestry Proclamation*, Addis Ababa: Federal Negarit Gazeta of the Democratic Republic of Ethiopia.

Proclamation No. 52 (1993), *Mining Proclamation*, Addis Ababa: Federal Negarit Gazeta of the Democratic Republic of Ethiopia.

Proclamation No. 97 (1994), *Climate Change Convention Ratification Proclamation*, Addis Ababa: Federal Negarit Gazeta of the Democratic Republic of Ethiopia.

Proclamation No. 1 (1995), *Federal Constitution of Ethiopia*, Addis Ababa: Federal Negarit Gazeta of the Democratic Republic of Ethiopia.

Proclamation No. 9 (1995), *The Environmental Protection Authority Establishment Proclamation*, Addis Ababa: Federal Negarit Gazeta of the Democratic Republic of Ethiopia.

Proclamation No. 46 (2000), *Amhara Regional Rural Land Administration and Use Establishment Proclamation*, Addis Ababa: Federal Negarit Gazeta of the Democratic Republic of Ethiopia.

Proclamation No. 192 (2000), *Ratification of the Basel Convention Proclamation*, Addis Ababa: Federal Negarit Gazeta of the Democratic Republic of Ethiopia.

Proclamation No. 197 (2000), *Water Resources Management and Administration Proclamation*, Addis Ababa: Federal Negarit Gazeta of the Democratic Republic of Ethiopia.

Proclamation No. 295 (2002), *Environmental Protection Organs Establishment Proclamation*, Addis Ababa: Federal Negarit Gazeta of the Democratic Republic of Ethiopia.

Proclamation No. 299 (2002), *Environmental Impact Assessment Proclamation*, Addis Ababa: Federal Negarit Gazeta of the Democratic Republic of Ethiopia.

Proclamation No. 300 (2002), *Environmental Pollution Control Proclamation*, Addis Ababa: Federal Negarit Gazeta of the Democratic Republic of Ethiopia.
Regulation 182 (1994), *Regulations Issued for the Implementation of the Mining Proclamation of 1993*, Addis Ababa: Federal Negarit Gazeta of the Democratic Republic of Ethiopia.
Regulation 82 (1998), *Mining Works Council of Ministers*, Addis Ababa: Federal Negarit Gazeta of the Democratic Republic of Ethiopia.

6. European Union: Shifting environmental governance to the supranational level

Anthony R. Zito

1. INTRODUCTION

Compared to most of the other political systems covered in this book, the European Union (EU) and its First Pillar, the European Community (EC), is a political system undergoing rapid institutional change in terms of structure and membership.[1] This situation of institutional change has increased with the accession of 2 more member states (with radically varying histories and experiences of governance and environmental protection) on 1 January 2007.

The EU's relative youth and continual evolution, combined with the relative youth of the environmental policy area, suggests a number of plausible hypotheses about EC environmental governance. For instance, this system should be more open to different actor coalitions; more innovation should be possible given the relatively shorter opportunity for entrenched interests to capture the system and the fact that the EU member states foster their own policy innovation. The reality is much more complex than these hypotheses, however. The process may see innovative policy proposals but the crucial range of instruments is largely traditional. Compared to some EU policy areas, there are less well defined and fluid opposing coalitions, but this opposition to specific proposals can be wide-ranging and embedded in the policy process while the pro-environmental constituency can be fluid and ineffectual.

This chapter examines this complex landscape, focusing on several core governance tensions operative in the EC environmental process. Compared to other EC environmental governance overviews (for example Weale et al., 2000; Lenschow, 1999; Butt Phillip, 1998), this chapter adopts both a wider and a narrower scope. It investigates a broader range of policy sectors, institutions, instruments and implementation through a much narrower analytical focus on the tensions existing in the EC institutions and policy ideas. This chapter argues that the European Union's institutional and ideational complexity leads to both regulatory and network patchworks that are at times new and other times highly traditional; the complexity provides both opportunities and constraints for the wide array of involved actors (Héritier, 1997). Actors succeed in placing innovative policies and instruments on the agenda, but the political system makes it difficult to incorporate innovation effectively. Only by addressing this complex and often highly specific EU reality can one conceptualize effective governance solutions.

The chapter's section 2 presents the theoretical framework: taking the Hall (1993) framework as an organizing device, the chapter studies the environmental sector in four sections. Section 3 investigates the overarching EC institutional structure and style that governs the EC policy area. Section 4 examines how this governance process has approached particular issues of environmental protection, such as air pollution. Section 5 identifies the actual instrument choice made in these differing policy areas while section 6 discusses the actual implementation. Finally, section 7 maps the overall EC governance trends.

2. THEORETICAL FRAMEWORK

2.1 Ideational and Institutional Perspectives

This chapter integrates a combined institutional and ideational approach. Institutional explanations emphasize that institutions are 'collections of interrelated rules and routines that define appropriate actions in terms of relations between roles and situations' (March and Olsen, 1989). Institutions provide rules and norms that create conditions under which certain policy decisions are made and others excluded (Weale, 1992). Because (1) institutional actors operate with limited information, (2) institutions can change the thinking of actors over time as they operate within the institutions and (3) institutional decisions may lead down paths that are unanticipated, it is difficult for actors to change the policy direction or the wider institutional norms (Pierson, 1996).

While institutions are important, many environmental scholars have recognized the importance of ideas (Weale, 1992). Ideas provide the means for making choices and establishing the rules of the game and serve as the focus for new policies and political coalitions (Goldstein and Keohane, 1993). In contrast to institutions, ideational explanations offer the possibility for substantial change as old ideas are challenged. Ideas can exist as a larger set of beliefs (which may be quite amorphous) or as distinct ideas operating within a particular belief system or context. Rein and Schön (1994) offer a useful conceptualization of 'policy framing': framing isolates how actors organize and interpret the complex reality confronting them in order to develop guideposts and maps for understanding and acting.

Hall (1993) provides a way of bringing these institutional and ideational elements together in differentiating three components of a policy area: the structure, style and content. For Hall, policy structure covers the government's administrative structures and procedural arrangements that develop and implement policy. Policy style refers to the normal way that EU actors go about making environmental policy decisions and how they involve other interested societal actors; this value encompasses both rules and attitudes of institutional actors. Policy content involves three aspects: (1) the policy goals, which will be centred on a framework of ideas that explain their position and the means to implement the goal; (2) the instruments for achieving the policy aims; and (3) the precise instrument calibration. Hall's concepts are heuristic notions that may overlap, but they help to pinpoint different elements of the environmental governance system and to focus our attention at what levels governance reform needs to be exercised.

Tensions

Within the EU institutional structure and governing ideas there are five key governance tensions affecting environmental policy. The first is shared by all federal systems, namely the inherent institutional and ideational tension between territorial expectations and outlooks versus the more supranational ideas and interests. While the EC has been strikingly successful in creating a supranational environmental policy area, the tensions remain and manifest themselves, for instance, in the subsidiarity debate (Golub, 1996).

Closely related to the territoriality issue is the governance issue of efficiency versus control (Kerremans, 1998). Territorial representation has been embedded consciously in all EU institutions (Sbragia, 1993). Nevertheless, and particularly with the 2004 accession of 10 enlargement states, there is a struggle to maintain the voice and control of individual states while ensuring efficiency in the decision-making process through greater qualified majority voting.

While territorial concerns define the organizational structure of many key EU institutions, the heavy EU institutional orientation towards policy sectors cuts across the territorial dimension. The EU's institutional emphasis on policy sectors allows for the possibility of specialization witnessed in the European Parliament (EP) committees, but it also creates the possibilities for struggles between different sectoral interests and bureaucratic politics (Peters, 1992). Thus the priorities and policy frames of the individual sectors shape EU institutions and actors. For example, the Finance Ministers of the ECOFIN Council often prioritize different values and goals than the Environment Council when considering the principle of environmental taxation (Hill, 1993; Zito, 1995). This sectoral tension manifests itself in many ways in EC environmental governance.

Equally one of the most difficult EU environmental objectives has been the attempt to integrate environmental considerations into other EU sectors and priorities despite its explicit eminence in EU thinking (Jordan, Schout and Zito, 2003; Schout and Jordan, 2003). The Commission has created a number of operating principles to integrate environmental concerns more effectively, but the results have been quite limited due to various administrative failings and limitations.

The policy sector issue becomes sharper when assessing 'complementary environmental policies'. In the fisheries sector, the question of over-fishing and potential remedies such as catch quotas are environmental activities, even though they are not carried out by the Directorate General for Environment (Ritchie, 2003). However, these activities, as seen in Common Agricultural Policy (CAP) and Common Fisheries Policy (CFP), often suggest that the belief system and values of the sector bureaucracy and constituency have assumed policy priority over the environment. Environmental issues and perspectives have sometimes been used as a means for enhancing and/or protecting the core policy sector priorities, which may conflict with long-term environmental goals: for example, environmental clauses have been inserted in agricultural reform to justify continuing high levels of agricultural expenditure against external pressure (Lenschow and Zito, 1998).

The specialization in EU environmental governance is necessary given the level of technical knowledge and expertise required for creating and operating regulations, such as those involving hazardous substance standards. There must be some reliance on scientific, engineering and economic knowledge in order to design appropriate measures (Majone, 1997). In addition, much of the EU policy process is conducted behind closed doors. This reality limits the non-expert ability to monitor or have a presence in such deliberations (Beetham and Lord, 1998). The perception of a democratic deficit combined with the tendency towards prioritizing expertise has forced the EC to counteract these tendencies in both institutional rules (for example, signing and implementing the Århus Convention) and instruments (for example eco-labels).

Another policy complexity that limits the influence of less organized and knowledgeable EC actors is the sheer (and growing) complexity of the process. The EC process involves a number of institutions in the creation, negotiation, decision-making and implementation stages of a policy. Both legislative and executive functions are shared. Given this complex institutional chain, it has a number of implications for placing issues on the EC environmental agenda and then manufacturing consensus over a decision. First, various actors and interest groups have a number of opportunities to find favourable institutional actors and system access points. It is easy to place new and innovative definitions of the policy problem and the solution onto the EC decisional agenda (Zito, 1995). Nevertheless, each important actor within this long policy chain is a veto point, that is any actor promoting a particular goal must build consensus and compromise across all the veto points (Weale, 1996). It is relatively easy to influence the EC agenda, but much harder to maintain the issue on the agenda and achieve agreement – the process of 'agenda maintenance' (Zito, 2000).

3. STRUCTURE: INSTITUTIONAL AND IDEATIONAL SETTING

3.1 Rules of the Game

Before examining how institutions operate to create environmental policy, it is important to understand how the EC rules of the game define what institutions do, and encompass policy frames. The EU intergovernmental process has agreed a constitution in 2004, but its uncertain ratification situation underlines the key fact that it is the founding and succeeding treaties that currently define the EC process.

The evolution of the treaties has defined environmental policy even when it made no explicit reference to it: remarkably, EC environmental policy was one of the star fields in EU integration without having a treaty mention until the ratification of the Single European Act – more than two decades after environmental policy was initiated (Hildebrand, 1993; Jordan, 1999a). Before 1987, the Commission primarily based legislation under Article 100 (harmonizing national regulations that would inhibit common market trade) or Article 235 (permitting the pursuit of Community objectives in the course of operating the common market where the treaty has not provided the necessary powers).

Consequently the environment had to be inserted into a pre-existing European Treaty and ideational/institutional structure that gave explicit priority to other objectives (Lenschow and Zito, 1998). Thus the policy frame of sustainability and environmental care has had to compete against pre-existing priorities, particularly economic ones. The evolution of the treaties has seen the inclusion of the environment and the more explicit priorities of environmental governance such as policy integration. It has also given greater power to supranational bodies, particularly the European Parliament (EP), which is seen as being a pro-green integration body.

More broadly, the inclusion in the treaty of rules and provisions to protect member state autonomy remains a significant constraint on the nature of what the EU can do, and what the institutions can implement. All fiscal matters must be decided unanimously, which can impose an enormously challenging veto point on proposals for environment taxation and so on (Zito, 1995). Significantly, member state governments retain the budget-setting powers although the other more supranational institutions have a role in utilizing this money. The environmental significance is that the EC process has been constrained to limit the EU budget; this means that the spending of EU money is quite limited – beyond certain traditional (and much older than EC environmental policy) activities, namely agricultural and regional funding. This necessarily limits the range of environmental activities the EU can undertake; furthermore it creates a political dynamic where member states are loathe to challenge EU frugality (Sbragia, 2000).

It is in this historical context that the EC treaties developed agriculture and fisheries as significant EC policy sectors, with their own constituency and interests. This occurred long before the arrival of environmental policy. Thus these policy areas with a high level of common pool resource concerns and environmental impacts were conceptualized in a manner distinct from the later formulation of environmental policy. Moreover, the EU's heavy sector orientation has meant that the key institutions have separate sub-units governing these policy areas. The attempt to integrate a more environmentalist policy frame has been difficult in these policy areas with actors holding policy priorities different from the environmental actors (Lenschow and Zito, 1998). Nevertheless, both the agricultural and fisheries sectors have had to shift towards a more sustainable, ecologically oriented approach, although this has more to do with external pressures (for example budget pressure, the World Trade Organization negotiations) and realities (for example declining fishing stocks) rather than an environmentalist triumph.

The treaties do not give a strategic and an aspirational direction for EC environmental governance. This does not really exist except in the form of the Environmental Action Programmes (the current Sixth Programme covers 2001–2012) that the Commission develops for set time periods. While these Action Programmes often reflect the policy frame change concerning environmental governance, the fact remains that these documents have the status of White Papers authored by the Commission. Thus they may persuade by inspiration, but do not give any legal mandate, although the Council does take a formal decision on the document.

3.2 Governance by Institutions

This chapter emphasizes the regional/supranational policy process that creates EC outputs, but it is important to realize the influence of both more local and more international political actors and processes. National and local governments (this can include states and municipal governments as well as water boards and other responsible public, or quasi-public, authorities) are critical to the implementation and monitoring of environmental quality.

In a less obvious manner, international institutions and agreements are important to EC governance (Kellow and Zito, 2002). International bodies are a source of policy ideas and knowledge which the EC utilizes for formulating its own policies. Given the complex technical nature of environmental policy-making, actors prefer not to reinvent the wheel if another organization has invested significant capital into an issue area (Kellow and Zito, 2002). Thus the EC adopted the OECD waste categorization labels. International institutions may arrive at policy solutions to issues that the EC needs to embrace, such as the Århus Convention. In many cases, if the difficult efforts to formulate policy have taken place elsewhere and a highly involved political solution has been found, then it is in the EC interest to embrace this solution. Equally, the support of an international agreement that spreads the costs across many more non-EU states will be superior to a purely regional solution. This explains partially the active leadership role that the EC has taken in trying to promote the Kyoto accord (Damro and Luaces, 2001). As seen in Table 6.1 below, a substantial amount of environmental governance is moving towards the international level.

International treaties require both EC and state engagement 'because the implementation of international environmental treaties will involve the competencies of both the Community and the member states, such agreements are signed by both the Community and the member states' (Sbragia, 1998). Known as 'mixed agreements', they further show the complexity of the EU governance process.

Turning to the EU governance institutions, it is important to recall the Treaty foundations of the environment. This history places environmental policy in the original treaties that created the European Communities and the Common Market. The most significant implication is that the three main supranational institutions are heavily involved in the EC policy process. The integration process since the Single European Act has gradually increased the EP's power. This, added to the member state institutional bodies, creates the institutional complexity that makes agenda-setting relatively easy but forming decisional consensus relatively difficult. Furthermore the Commission shares executive functions, that is policy leadership with the Council of Ministers and implementation with the member states. This and the sharing of the traditional legislative functions of ratification and accountability (between the European Parliament and the Council of Ministers) creates a more complex political system. Although the EU leaders have agreed a New Treaty in place of the Constitution; the institutional complexity that affects EC environmental governance remains.

The EU intergovernmental element, where the territorial representation of the member states exerts itself, remains important. The ultimate intergovernmental institution, the European Council, consisting of the premiers of the member states and certain presidents, does not conduct detailed policy work. However, the European Council has made numerous statements of intent that have given EC environmental policy-making strategic direction (McCormick, 2001).

In terms of actualizing specific environmental policies, the Commission must be mentioned next given its primacy in initiating policy. However, the Commission is equally important as a 'Guardian of the Treaties', ensuring that member states comply with the obligations made to the treaties and the individual EC laws.

In terms of its composition, the Commission is led by its President and a College of Commissioners; this body acts to some degree as ministers with portfolios overseeing a number of bureaucratic directorates-general. Under this Commission system, the environment Commissioner normally holds the responsibility for nuclear safety and civil protection. The emphasis on sectoralization means that both the Commissioners and the directorates will have their own specific policy duties and policy priorities. These duties and priorities will be built around particular policy frames, bureaucratic interests and policy constituencies. Within the Commission, the Environment Directorate-General is seen as one of the less influential directorates when compared to the more senior and prestigious DGs. There has also been a tendency to see this directorate-general as being co-opted by environmental interests although the reality has always been more complex (Wurzel, 2002; McCormick, 2001). These perceptions, however unfounded, decrease the directorate's prestige.

Another constraint on Commission action is the limited amount of personnel and resources available to the Commission, including the environment directorate. This forces the Commission to rely on technical support from both member state representatives and various willing interest groups. Much of the Commission activity heavily involves member state representatives who sit on advisory and other committees with the Commission representatives (Pollack, 2003). Although the Commission is both the key agenda setter and compliance monitor, it relies on the knowledge, expertise and support of the actors that it regulates. Heavy consultation and significant involvement with various interested parties also helps the Commission to build the consensus necessary to get an agreement in the Council and the Parliament where the interest groups also will lobby.

In order for the Commission proposals to be accepted, it requires approval from, first of all, the Council of Ministers which each member state chairs (acting as EU President) for six months. Although the Council represents the ministers of each country, the Council structure involves a number of working groups and committees, as well as the critical Committee of Permanent Representatives or COREPER (Hayes-Renshaw and Wallace, 1997). Excepting COREPER, which represents senior diplomats operating in Brussels, the Council, like the Commission, is heavily organized around policy sectors. Again the relatively junior position of environment ministers in member state cabinets is reflected in the relative weight of the Environment Council versus that found in the General Affairs Council (foreign ministers) and ECOFIN (Finance Ministers).

A frequent Council dynamic occurs when certain states take a particular lead on a given issue, pushing for a Council decision or for a Commission initiative (Liefferink and Andersen, 1998). Héritier et al. (1996) argue that 'regulatory competition' drives much of this process: member states seek to get their own national standards imposed at the EC level in order to minimize the costs of adjustment for their own economic sector relative to those found in the other member states. Thus it is no coincidence that the Large Combustion Plant Directive, an aspiration of the German political system, was initiated by the Commission and finally negotiated successfully while the Federal Republic of Germany was EU President (Zito, 2000). Successful 'regulatory competition' can lead to tensions as certain states are forced to 'follow' the lead adopted by the whole EC. Indeed, over the course of EC environmental policy, there has developed a tension felt particularly by the 'Southern' states: namely that the large body of EC legislation reflects a 'Northern' outlook towards goals and standards (Weale et al., 2000). Concerns about the legislative adjustment costs and the lack of concern for more Southern issues, such as desertification, has created what many see as a North–South tension (Pridham, 1994).

The only directly elected institution remains the European Parliament (EP), and its increasing policy significance means that environmental legislation must get through the Parliament, which has the ability to block legislation if it has a sufficient majority (Bomberg and Burns, 1999). The Parliament is organized by rather amorphous catch-all European groups and specialist committees that provide the specific EP policy expertise. In carving out a presence in the environment, the EP has been fortunate in having a very active and regionally respected Environment Committee (Judge, 1992). Nevertheless, the Parliament has few resources and little expertise compared to the other institutions, so that most MEPs rely on the cues provided by fellow party members in the specialist committees. Given this position and the EP's institutional role in co-decision, it largely has had to react to an environmental agenda developed elsewhere.

The last critical institution is the European Court of Justice. Although not geared to policy formulation, the Court's guardianship role in interpreting EU law has given it the opportunity to decide the shape of EC environmental law and have some influence on implementation (Koppen, 1993). Through its cases, the Court has consistently allowed an expansive interpretation of the EC environmental role before 1985. It has also allowed the EU to take a more international role on behalf of its member states in various international institutions and negotiations, including those concerned with the environment (Sbragia, 1998).

Moving beyond the major EU institutional actors involved with the environment, there is also a European Environmental Agency based in Denmark. While certain member states and Commission officials envisioned this body as having more significant monitoring and implementation powers over what occurs in the member states (more along the lines of the US Environmental Protection Agency), other member state governments wanted a more circumscribed agency. The 1993 outcome of a protracted member state argument over the Agency's role and location was an organization charged mainly with systematizing and providing environmental information. In the cause of monitoring and assessing environmental performance, this data collation role takes on some significance, but is far more limited than the hopes of the Agency's original proponents.

The Economic and Social Committee (ESC) is a purely consultative body representing various economic and civil society interests which have the opportunity to comment on proposed EC legislation. It does not have a significant role in the environmental policy process. This reveals the lack of a formal civil society presence in the EU policy system. Furthermore, the ESC reflects the initial Common Market orientation of the treaties in the organization of its membership, although the presence of the environmental groups in one of the horizontal groups and the existence of an environmental section has made the institution relatively green (Jeffrey, 2002; McCormick, 2001).

While the formal structures for civil society input are quite limited, interest group participation is important for EC environmental governance. Non-governmental organizations (NGOs), given the openness of the EC system and the limited resources available to the Commission and the

Parliament, play an important role. Indeed the Commission Directorate General for the Environment has consistently funded an environmental constituency, particularly the European Environmental Bureau (EEB). The EEB has tried to consistently represent the environmental EU perspective on a range of issues in which other NGOs are unwilling or unable to involve themselves (interview, NGO official September 2003; EEB, 2003). Despite efforts of coordination among the larger NGOs in Brussels and support of smaller NGOs at the national level, the fact remains that NGOs themselves have more limited resources than the other interest groups lobbying the Brussels process (Mazey and Richardson, 1992). Nevertheless, when the NGO effort is concentrated, NGOs can have a significant impact, belying their organizational resources. They can provide environmental information (that is an environmental perspective on an issue area) to assist in formulating a policy solution and, perhaps more importantly, to assist the Commission in evaluating the environmental situation at the member state level. Equally important is the fact that the political activity of these groups confers legitimacy to Commission proposals.

3.3 Policy Style

Policy styles are analytical constructs which give a shorthand concerning the typical approach a system is likely to take concerning any given policy problem. Jeremy Richardson has systematized this concept around two distinct dimensions: (1) a government's approach to problem solving, ranging from anticipatory/active to reactive; and (2) a government's relationship to other actors in the policy-making process, which will be shaped by the inclination of the government either to reach consensus with organized groups or to impose particular solutions (Richardson and Watts, 1985). Judging by the institutional constraints already mentioned as leading to governance tensions, the number of agenda-setting points and veto points indicates the EC's openness to groups. This is also partly due to the resource constraints that exist at the EU level compared to the sum total available in the member states. Finally, the chain of veto points requires that consensus govern this process (Weale, 1996).

The reaction–anticipation dimension is more ambiguous because the Commission and the Environment Action Programmes have emphasized the need for precautionary legislation – for example ozone depletion (Jachtenfuchs, 1990). Nevertheless, so much of EC policy tends to be reactive in nature as the complex EC system and the numerous member states need time to generate a consensus to undertake new legislation. Unless there are sudden, severe crises, the process is likely to be more deliberate and to involve pressure to respect member state interests. A number of EC proposals for legislation have tried to embrace prevention, but the realities of the policy negotiation and implementation limit this ambition.

The presence of sufficient scientific information to inform the policy-making decisions is a key element in deciding how anticipatory the EC environmental process is. The Commission Directorate General for Research has undertaken specific research projects, including some assessing global warming and energy supply models (Zito, 2000). The EP too has its own more limited bureaucracy to provide technical expertise. Nevertheless, most expertise comes from outside the Brussels institutions. As noted already, the complex issues of global warming have been addressed by international bodies, and the Commission has not hesitated to make use of this information. Occasionally the Commission seeks to control the research aims by hiring consultant groups to undertake work with a focused aim; for example the Commission hired a French firm popular with business to study the carbon energy tax proposal (Zito, 2000). Simultaneously, significant consultation occurs with member state governments and their various interest groups specifically concerned with the environmental issue. This national input continues as the Commission formulates its proposal and persists during the separate Parliament and Council consultation and negotiation processes.

Although a narrower focus than the overarching EU policy style, the concept of the regulatory state explicates why the EU gravitates towards particular kinds of policy instruments. Majone (1997) notes how the EU differs substantially from the traditional state in its highly limited budgetary powers (as well as police powers and so on – see Sbragia, 1998). EU law-making consequently has gravitated towards creating rules which require no budgetary expenditure on the actors who formulate them. Command and control instruments fit neatly within this scope.

4. POLICY CONTENT

This section examines EC environmental policy in terms of the traditional media and the issues of ecosystem protection and resource management. In creating policy responses, the 1970s EC actors focused on specific media as opposed to more integrated policy approaches. A rethink of this approach, or a new policy frame, only entered the Commission's drafting of Environment Action Programmes by the late 1980s. This was in part influenced by national action programmes, particularly the Dutch Environmental Plan (Kronsell, 1997). In this, the EC only mirrored the situation found in the member states and other OECD countries. Nevertheless, the heavy institutional emphasis of policy sectors has made more integrated solutions difficult, and kept certain policy sectors, such as fisheries, out of the environment governance scope and policy frame.

4.1 Pollution Control of the Vital Community Media

Air pollution

In comparison to water pollution policy, the EC process developed the different aspects of air quality more gradually. Due to the concerns about the legislation's economic impact (because of issues such as the oil crisis), the scope of air pollution control is more fragmented and partial in its coverage than water control (Haigh, 2003, 6.2–1). A range of substantial political battles have been fought in the 1970s and 1980s to cover this medium more systematically: large combustion plants, vehicle emissions, and so on. Originally motivated primarily from the policy frame to protect the functioning of the common market, the EC moved into a number of basic areas: limiting air emissions from vehicles, defining the content of fuel, controlling acidification, protecting the ozone layer, reducing global warming and controlling specific air particles (McCormick, 2001).

There has been a policy frame evolution in this area, recognizing the importance of transnational sources and flows, and the more nested nature of the policy problem. In addition to the increased knowledge about environmental policy and the causes of implementation failure, particular policy problems, such as acidification, served to drive this learning process. In the 1980s when forest death alarmed the German political system, the EC instigated the large combustion plant directive, an extremely significant directive in terms of its regulatory costs and political symbolism, and other measures (Zito, 2001). Even in the 1990s the issue continued to have a push effect: actors concerned with this problem, such as the Swedish representatives, pushed the EC to develop a coherent acidification strategy in 1997 (Haigh, 2003). Besides revealing the only gradual movement towards more coherent approaches to larger issues, acidification is also a clear example where negotiations and activity in other international institutions, in this case the UN Economic Commission for Europe (UNECE), played a substantial role in EC thinking (Zito, 2001). The EC strategy led to the 2001 establishment of a national emissions ceilings directive.

The heart of the policy content for air pollution is a range of directives offering largely command and control solutions. McCormick (2001) notes that the somewhat fragmented picture of air pollution control is mirrored by the rather varied types of instruments used to fulfil the regulatory objectives. Accordingly he notes the use of product quality standards for the sulphur content of liquid fuels, while air quality standards have involved the setting of limit values for the concentration of particular airborne substances such as sulphur dioxide and lead. By the 1990s the Commission had recognized that the disjointed approach of tackling individual substances and sources was not successful (Grant et al., 2000). Dissatisfaction with the member state implementation of air quality standards led the EC to agree a framework Directive 96/62 on ambient air quality and assessment in order to harmonize member state efforts (Haigh, 2003, 6.2–3). The Directive creates long term limit values that require adherence after a certain time period and active member state planning to protect the public from pollution. A critical element of the approach is the development of 'daughter directives' to tackle specific pollutants within this overall framework (Grant et al., 2000). Innovative proposals, such as the Auto-oil Directive, which sought to get industry to cooperate with each other and with the EU process, are also occurring (Wurzel, 2002).

Water pollution

In comparison to the air pollution policy area, the EC has produced a far more comprehensive body of water legislation at an earlier point of time. Generally the EC has sought marine water environmental protection through participation in international organizations and institutions, but has created extensive legislation to deal with non-marine waters (McCormick, 2001). The motivations for such comprehensive action in the 1970s sometimes differed from those found in the air, waste and noise sectors where concerns about national regulation affecting product standards and trade within the Common Market often acted as a motivating factor. Some legislation indeed was focused on creating product standards, such as detergents (Haigh, 2003, 4.2). Gehring (1997) makes the distinction between environment standards that deal with specific products and those that deal more with industrial processes and so on, arguing that process legislation is more difficult to agree. Nevertheless, the typical Common Market push (that is fear about national environmental barriers) does not explain some of the most significant sector activity.

Generally speaking, it seems that concerns about health, rather than strict environmental rationales, explain the directives' adoption. Particularly important were the Surface Water Directive (75/440), which ensured drinking water quality, and the Bathing Water Directive (76/160) (McCormick, 2001). Pollution scares such as the Seveso incident also pushed these motivations. These and other Directives typified the notion of command and control regulation, specifying environmental quality standards for water usage. Thus the Directives took a preventative/precautionary approach. The Bathing Water Directive has since become one of the great regulatory hurdles, where every member state has been found guilty of infringement, because implementing the Directive requires extensive monitoring and planning. The Directive also contained various ambiguities that were hotly contested for over three decades. In the initial phase of the 1970s, water industry was not organized or motivated to attack these initiatives, nor did some of the more sceptical governments fully understand the implications of the legislation they signed (Grant et al., 2000; Golub, 1996). In the 1970s, the European Commission also tackled the issues of source-based pollution but efforts in this direction led to only very limited legislation, essentially the Directive on Titanium Dioxide.

The late 1980s saw a clear frame evolution about this sector which led to discussions of agricultural policy from an environmental perspective. With the implementation problems, the water sector formed a strong target for the member states pushing for subsidiarity (Golub, 1996; Jordan, 1999a). Nevertheless, the Commission did not jettison its extant legislation, although proposals were modified in light of this debate. Indeed the evolution of the policy frame on water policy and the need to take a more integrated approach led the Commission to propose in the 1990s more ambitious legislation and to push for more of an emphasis on water supply sustainability (CEC, 1993). Dissatisfaction with the legislation in this area led the Council of Ministers and the EP Environment Committee to push for a more integrated approach to water legislation; the Commission itself recognized that much of the legislation of the 1970s was obsolete (Haigh, 2003, 4.2). Accordingly the Commission proposed the Water Framework Directive (2000/60). Agreed in 2000, the Directive repealed six directives and set forth a new water policy approach. It emphasized the need to undertake an integrated framework considering all the various community waters together. The Directive also seeks to link a wide range of actors. Nevertheless, the wider problems of agriculture and other policy sectors that affect water quality remain beyond the Directive's scope, which was developed in the environmental policy sector and follows an environmental frame (Grant et al., 2000).

Soil pollution

The EC has not adopted an integrated approach to the protection of soil from hazardous substances. There are policies oriented to hazardous substance regulation and others focused on material considered to be waste. The tendency is to differentiate radioactive material from other forms of waste and hazardous substances. This reflects the fact that these policy problems were defined at different times and with different policy frames. There are, generally speaking, several types of legislation in these different problem areas: regulations concerning the classification of this material, the trading of this material (as it was typically viewed as a good) and accidents concerning this material. These differing policy problems also share one common theme: there has been a considerable tension within the issue area between the policy frame focused on maintaining economic growth and trade, versus the frame prioritizing issues of health and ecological protection (Lenschow and Zito, 1998). The EU genetically-modified organism debate heavily reflects this tension.

As the EURATOM Treaty handled radioactive processes, much of this approach to these issues reflects the policy frame found in that partially successful treaty. Nevertheless, McCormick (2001) contends that the first piece of EC environmental legislation (concerning ionizing radiation) occurred here. Much of the nuclear sector effort has been an attempt to protect the health of both nuclear power employees and the general population, but these actions have environmental consequences (Haigh, 2003, 8.1).

The EC was also very early in regulating the dangerous substances area (1967), creating a policy response before most member states had developed a comprehensive national equivalent. At its core was not an environmental frame but rather a trade liberalization frame that wished to exploit this highly lucrative economic area. The Directive 67/548 on the Classification, Packaging and Labelling of Dangerous Chemicals has been amended numerous times, reflecting the fast-moving chemicals area (Haigh, 2003, 7.2). The Commission pushed forward a broader environmental programme in this area called REACH (Registration, Evaluation, Authorisation and Restriction of Chemicals), which shifts a considerable amount of the burden of assessing and managing chemical safety onto industry. The significant opposition to the proposal only managed to limit some of its regulatory scope (*ENDS Europe Daily*, 2006). In the light of major chemical accidents like Seveso, the Commission created a Directive on Accident Hazards. Pesticides follow a parallel track to chemicals policy. The EC has legislated extensively in this area, particularly focusing on human health, but has found it difficult to integrate the different national approaches (McCormick, 2001).

The EC has developed a wide range of waste policies. As seen in other policy sectors, a considerable amount of motivation focused on enhancing the Common Market and trade. This frame was reflected in the initial justification for the framework Directive 75/442 on waste and its daughter Directive 78/319 on hazardous waste. However, there was a core tension that has undermined the directive implementation from the very beginning: the definition of waste (Zito, 2000). Remarkably, after three decades the Commission, the member states and the European Court of Justice remain unable to resolve this ambiguity. At the core is the policy frame issue of what constitutes value (and therefore can be seen as a good to be traded) and notions of what 'discard' means. The initial common market focus has embedded the frame conflict in the waste legislation from the beginning.

Waste is a policy area where international efforts and negotiations (in the OECD and UN Environment Programme, for example) have also played a strong role in defining EU policy – for example, the Directive on the transboundary waste shipments (Zito, 2000).

The Commission has tried to develop a coherent strategy for waste policy in 1989 and again in 1996 (Haigh, 2003). These communications included notions of prevention and a hierarchy of waste options (Lenschow and Zito, 1998). In the late 1990s the Commission especially focused on implementation. It requested reports on member state adherence to the revised waste framework directive and hazardous waste directives, and reports on adherence to the waste oils and sewage sludge directives. Not only did some states fail to report their progress adequately within the time limit, but the Commission felt compelled to institute infringement proceedings against 13 out of 15 member states (Haigh, 2003). Again the lack of common approaches and methodologies, as reflected even in the fundamental questions of defining waste, was a critical problem (CEC, 2003a).

Noise

The EC has a substantial range of command and control legislation in this area. The motivation and focus for the bulk of the initial 1970s legislation was the free trade of products policy frame, rather than a more environmental focus on setting standards for ambient noise (Haigh, 2003). Thus directives have been created for setting product standards for cars, buses, lorries, motorcycles and aircraft. In the 1990s there has been something of a shift towards more general concerns about noise exposure, culminating in a 2002 framework directive creating common assessment methods and mapping of noise, public information instruments, and action plan requirements.

Ecosystem protection

It is not surprising that EU efforts in this area have been less extensive given the policy frame in early environmental policy-seeking to prevent trade barriers within the Common Market. For this reason, the relatively extensive 1979 legislation (Directive 79/409) on wild birds, for example, poses a puzzle (Pollack, 1994). It has been suggested that the French pushed for this legislation because of their specific troubles in this area.[2] While the Commission's case for this policy expansion did rest on a vague economic rationality, the Commission was more concerned about reacting to general public concern about the destruction happening to migratory birds (McCormick, 2001; Weale, 1999). Similar public concern led to similar whales and seals directives (Haigh, 2003, 9.1).

Since the 1970s, biodiversity concerns have received greater attention. The EC has become a party to a number of international agreements, such as CITES (Convention on International Trade of Endangered Species), and has required EC follow-up directives (Hildebrand and Sbragia, 1998). Reacting to a further Convention on Biodiversity and to learning in an international forum, the EC agreed a directive on the conservation of natural habitats and of wild fauna and flora, extending some of the Birds Directive's principles (Haigh, 2003, 9.9). The Directive protects and conserves certain 'natural habitats' and wild species based on lists of sites and flora/fauna.

Natural resource management

As argued previously, the EC has not developed a comprehensive environmental approach to this sector. The question of the water supply quality and its sustainability has been handled by the water legislation protecting the various elements that constitute the Community waters. However, many important natural resources are handled in other policy sectors that do not carry a pure environmental focus, that is the Common Fisheries Policy and the Common Agricultural Policy. In other cases, such as the issue of Forestry management, the Council has blocked the efforts of the Commission to create a community policy beyond the creation of a few specific protective measures to guard forests against acid damage and against fires (McCormick, 2001). As witnessed in the other sectors, certain member state representatives have made use of the power given to member states to block or drastically change EC proposals.

A separate policy sector conducts energy policy; the Commission Directorate General for Energy is one of the more interesting bureaucratic politics studies within the EU institutions. Its approach to the environment has waxed and waned, reflecting the fact that there is a substantial wing that follows a frame focused on maximizing energy generation while another wing of officials concern themselves with energy conservation (Interviews, Commission Officials, 1992, 2003). Much of the early thinking on energy was defined by the oil crisis, but concerns about related environmental issues, such as global warming and acidification (when caused by power plants) have triggered environmental legislation with a focus on conservation and renewable energy (Matláry, 1997).

There is some internal pressure within the Commission to integrate environmental priorities with these other policy priorities and there are external pressures, such as the fishing crisis, global warming, and World Trade Organisation (WTO) negotiations. The Agenda 2000 CAP reform led to an inclusion of provisions to help protect the environment by giving support to ecologically sensitive farming and countryside protection in poorer regions. Nevertheless, despite the pressure, the effort towards integration remains problematic (Lenschow, 1999).

5. POLICY INSTRUMENTS

Throughout the first decades of EC environmental policy, the key instrument remained the Directive. This was a piece of legislation where the EC specified the goals and objectives, allowing member states to translate these goals individually into their own national legislation. The actual EU directive could have highly detailed provisions as exemplified by the water quality directive. Nevertheless, the states retained significant scope to interpret the legislation, and the transcription and actual implementation of this legislation was extremely variable (Jordan, 1999b). Much less favoured (roughly 30 per cent of EU regulation – see McCormick, 2001) but also an important tool was the Regulation, which is directly applicable and is binding in its entirety. These tools, together with the binding Decision and the non-binding Recommendations and Opinions, are the only tools that the EU has treaty-based power to implement. Here we see the institutional mechanisms and norms working to limit the EU scope for action despite the fact that a wide range of alternatives have been discussed in the international arena (Jordan et al., 2004).

By the 1980s a wide range of actors began to question the effectiveness and economic efficiency of regulations generally. Members of industry and policy actors concerned with competitiveness argued that more consideration should be given to different types of instruments, such as voluntary agreements and eco-taxes, which were held to be less intrusive and economically burdensome (Jordan et al., 2004). Many member states, including the Netherlands and Germany, started experimenting with more intensive instruments such as voluntary agreements and eco-labels. The Fifth Action Programme likewise raises the possibilities of bringing in more diverse instruments to help policy effectiveness and integration (CEC, 1993). The discussions surrounding the Single European Act and the Maastricht Treaty led to the incorporation of the notion of subsidiarity (a highly disputed concept that certain member states pressed as a justification for states retaining a substantial policy role; see Flynn, 2003), which consequently supported this shift in thinking. During this time Britain and France in particular pushed for the recalibration of a number of the directives, particularly water quality. Note that the notion of instruments was quite easily raised on the EC agenda, but their incorporation into the actual policy of the EU was a very different story.

The Commission White Paper on Governance acknowledges the policy change, noting the need for new policy tools to produce more effective policy (CEC, 2001). The White Paper criticizes EC legislation as unnecessarily detailed, making it harder to revise and to implement. The White Paper promised that the Commission would improve on this situation by embracing certain policy principles: (1) regulation as a last resort to guarantee essential uniformity; (2) more framework Directives that define the essential policy goals but dispense with the technical details and can be implemented by a wide range of tertiary laws; (3) the use of co-regulation linking regulation to tools such as voluntary agreements; (4) the incorporation of the Open Method of Coordination (OMC) emphasizing the creation of policy benchmarking in which the member states can monitor their progress and to induce further interstate communication of information and cooperation (CEC, 2001).

Nevertheless, the actual experience of incorporating instruments suggests that the White Paper's vision will remain aspirational. The treaties limit the scope for such innovation and the EC environmental policy is a well established, institutionalized sector with detailed legislation not amenable to some of the softer legislation types such as OMC (Jordan et al., 2004). Furthermore, the EP is extremely wary of this direction. Here we see the importance of institutions and the reluctance of some member states for the EU to change direction significantly (for a very wide range of reasons).

The tremendously difficult task of reducing energy consumption, partly in order to reduce global emissions, has seen the widest range of instruments placed on the EC agenda. The difficult issue of who will pay the adjustment costs of energy consumption is fiercely contested and thus has pushed actors to consider other instruments to reach EC objectives. This issue reveals the only true environmental taxation and tradable permits proposals as well as some of the environmental financing.

Accordingly, the Commission sought to stamp a sign of its increasing global leadership in this area by establishing a carbon energy tax, which, however, created too much hostility in the Council of Ministers for its acceptance (Zito, 1995). Unanimity voting ensured that territorial voices could block this policy innovation. All that a renewed effort to create such an instrument has accomplished is a 2003 Framework directive that ECOFIN approved (*ENDS Daily*, 20/03/03). The Directive forces national tax measures towards a minimal convergence on the levels of a number of energy products. The EC agreed a Tradable Permits scheme to fulfil the EU obligations under the Kyoto Protocol. The Commission was forced to compromise on various details of the design including the role of auctioning in the allocation of carbon allowances (*ENDS Environment Daily*, 08/03/04; Jordan et al., 2004).

In order to find other mechanisms for achieving the carbon dioxide (CO_2) limitations, the EC agreed the SAVE I and II Programmes. SAVE emphasized using a number of administrative and legislative actions, but also included the provision of financial instruments and information-related measures (Haigh, 2003). SAVE II indicated the importance of creating voluntary agreements. The story of SAVE is one where the Council of Ministers, the territorial body, has severely limited the programme's financial and regulatory scope. Closely related to the SAVE programme is the ALTENER programme. ALTENER seeks to promote renewable energy sources in the Community through a combination of financial support and informational programmes. As with SAVE, the Parliament and the Council contested the funding levels for ALTENER, and the agreed amount disappointed its advocates (Haigh, 2003).

Beyond the energy sector, the use of other instrument types is more sporadic. As of 2004, the EU has managed to create roughly 12 voluntary agreements, most notably in the automobile sector with respect to CO_2 emissions and auto-oil (Jordan et al., 2004). In the area of financial tools, the EC also established a fund entitled Community Operations Concerning the Environment (COE) in 1984. It provided financial support for projects aimed at developing new technologies and protecting ecologically sensitive areas (McCormick, 2001). ACE replaced this fund in 1988, and it was replaced by ACNAT, which focused on protecting threatened habitats and endangered species (Haigh, 2003). LIFE I-III and LIFE + have all succeeded ACNAT, which set aside nearly half its funds for projects that protected endangered habitats and species.

The closest the EU comes to an environmental welfare fund that redistributes money from wealthier territories and gives it to poorer ones is the Cohesion fund. However, the primary motivation for the Cohesion fund was hardly environmental, as it was intended as a side payment to reassure (and thus secure endorsement from) the poorer countries (Greece, Ireland, Portugal and Spain) about the Economic and Monetary Union. Although the fund has supported the construction of water management and treatment facilities required to implement EU environmental directives, the Cohesion fund is seen as largely targeting large economic infrastructure projects and general macroeconomic conditions (Lenschow, 1999). The territorial concerns again have limited the scope, extent and direction of the non-command control instruments; this explains the EU institutional proclivity towards creating a regulatory state.

The EC has also sought to affect market behaviour by creating two Community information instruments: eco-labels, which give consumers information about the environmental characteristics of a product, and environment management standards or EMAS, which gives information to all actors in society about the environmental performance and objectives of the companies that adhere to the EMAS standards. Relative to the achievements in environmental taxation, EC efforts are successful here but pale in comparison to alternative versions. During the first seven years of its creation, only 41 EU eco-labels were awarded, compared to the nearly 4000 national eco-labels awarded by the German eco-label for much of the late 1990s (Jordan, Wurzel and Zito, 2003). Globally there are 3800 EMAS-registered organizations versus over 45 000 ISO (International Standards Organization) 14 001 certified organizations, and EMAS membership continues to drop (*ENDS Daily*, 19 March 2003 and 10 June 2003).

5.1 Summary Table

Surveying EC trends in Table 6.1, we see a strong centralization tendency in a number of environmental areas. Given the fact that the table has to cover 27 countries and a tremendous number of policy areas, all that the table can suggest is areas of significant policy presence at the EC and international levels. Taking the EU first, the strength of EC regulation in water, waste and air pollution is striking. Also dramatic is the importance of the EC in agriculture, although most of the EC impact comes through agricultural and structural policies rather than environmental ones. Much less significant is the EC presence in Forestry and Ecosystem Protection.

However, as Table 6.1 indicates, some of the EU activity reflects international agreements (Sbragia, 1998): the Habitat and Birds Directive, the Kyoto Protocol on climate change, the Basle Convention on the Shipment of Hazardous Wastes, the Montreal Protocol, the Convention on Air Pollution have all triggered significant pieces of EU legislation. Many corporations in the EU are using the ISO environmental management standards as the environmental guidelines for conducting their business. The international arena has had less impact on EC forests and ecosystems but has affected trade in species. International agreements on water are significant on marine waters surrounding the EU. While the WTO negotiations concerning agricultural policy reform are stalled, this centralizing pressure may work to change the EU's agricultural direction. Table 6.1 suggests that environmental protection is being internationalized in all but one category: implementation.

On the issue of implementation, Table 6.1 notes one international convention, the Århus Convention. It seeks to increase public involvement, an involvement which should improve all environmental policy action, including implementation. In signing the treaty, the EU commits itself to establishing the rights of the public to receive environmental information that is held by public authorities, the right to participate in environmental decision-making, and the right to challenge, in a court of law, decisions that have not respected the first two rights (UNECE, 1998). The Council and EP have agreed two Directives proposed by the Commission to implement the Convention: Directive 2003/4/EC on public access to environmental

Table 6.1 Centralization/decentralization trends in EC environmental governance

Field/level	Industry	Ecosystem Protection	Agriculture	Forests	Water	Implementation and Enforcement
International (Multilateral Environmental Agreements)	Kyoto Protocol; Basle Convention; Long-range Transboundary Air Pollution; Montreal Protocol; Stockholm Convention on Persistent Organic Pollutants; (significant centralization)	CITES; Convention on Biological diversity (some centralization)	World Trade Organisation negotiations for reform (some pressure for reform but EC resistance)	International Tropical Timber Agreement (not really focused on protecting EU forests)	Helsinki Convention on the Baltic Sea; the Elbe Convention; Bonn Agreement; Barcelona Convention for the Mediterranean (some centralization to protect international waters)	Århus Convention ISO 14001
European Union	Ambient Air Quality Directive; waste framework; Hazardous Substances Directive; EMAS (significant centralization)	Wild Birds, Whales and Seals Directives; Natural Habitats Directive (Mild centralization)	Common Agricultural Policy and its reform (Very strong centralization but limited in environmental focus although high impact)	(Legislation not specifically geared to forest management e.g. acid rain)	Water Framework directive (high centralization)	Limited monitoring; centralization of information; significant fines
National and below	Permits	Stronger responsibility	Planning	Main responsibility	Water planning and infrastructure	Strong emphasis on implementation

Source: The information on International agreements is taken from Directorate General for the Environment (2003).

information and Directive 2003/35/EC on public participation (CEC, 2004). The most interesting directive has been proposed but not yet adopted: namely the Directive on access to justice. Given the potential role of NGOs and other actors in pushing environmental failures in the court system as seen in the United States, which organizations will be able to seek justice is one of the contested issues in the EC formulation (Interview, NGO official, 2003). Århus has the potential for perhaps ameliorating one of the governance challenges mentioned above.

6. SETTING AND IMPLEMENTATION

The previous examination of the actual policy content and legislation has revealed a failure to implement in many areas. Commission documents such as the Action Programmes all highlight failures and the need to improve (CEC, 1993). Jordan (1999b) argues that the EU has created a tremendous policy overhang since the 1970s. The assessment of the true effectiveness of EC environmental policy rests with the actors' ability to implement what has been formulated. Despite the fact that the treaties give the Commission the power to note member state infringements and bring them before the European Court of Justice (which now has the power to fine member states and uses that power), the role of the member state authorities who must agree the regulations is essential to the execution of the policy and the Community performance monitoring. It is problematic to lay the blame for the implementation failure at the doors of one set of states. Börzel (2003) argues that leader/laggard labels are dangerous and that all EU states have problematic environmental issues. Implementation analysis must be contextual (with the policy context being the specific legislation) and therefore is even less straightforward to undertake and understand. The Commission in its annual report assesses member state performance in three league tables listing infringement cases at the end of the year: (1) failure to transpose EU measures into national law and communicate measures to the Commission within the time limit, (2) lack of conformity in the transposition, and (3) the practical failure to implement obligations contained in the legislation. Table 6.2 reproduces the infringement figures taken from the third category (practical implementation failure) contained in the Commission 2002 report.

These figures show that not even the Scandinavian states are immune to infringement cases. However, it is dangerous to read too much into them as certain member states may have derogations or a later schedule for implementation. Perhaps more revealing are the policy totals; there are more numerous instances in the water, nature and waste sectors. However, again

Table 6.2 Bad application infringement cases as of December 2002

	Au	Be	Deu	DK	Es	EL	Fr	FI	It	IR	Lu	NL	P	S	UK	To
Radiat.	0	0	0	0	0	0	0	0	1	0	0	0	0	0	0	1
Air	0	0	1	0	1	1	0	0	0	2	0	0	0	0	0	5
Waste	0	1	2	0	0	2	2	0	2	0	1	0	1	0	1	12
Nature	2	1	2	1	1	1	2	1	1	2	1	0	1	1	1	18
Water	1	6	1	0	5	2	5	0	3	3	2	2	3	2	5	40
Others	0	1	0	0	0	0	0	0	0	0	0	0	0	0	0	1
Total	3	9	6	1	7	6	9	1	7	7	4	2	5	3	7	77

Source: Reproduced from CEC, 2003a.

this may be misleading as this data will reflect recent EC efforts in these areas (CEC, 2003a).

At the implementation issue's core are a number of complex problems (Jordan, 1999b). First, there is the whole issue of incorporating EC law into member state legal and administrative procedures and bureaucratic frames; this transcription is relatively straightforward to assess. Much less straightforward is the issue of practical implementation failures beyond the issue of transcription; member states may fail to take on board key policy aspects. Some of this will be wilful but often this may be administrative incompetence. But there may also be failures to conceive the EU policy properly in the first place. Thus, as seen in the waste sector, there is often tremendous ambiguity in the legislative framing. Furthermore, the actual EU policy may be inappropriate to achieve the necessary environmental protection.

Even if the above questions were less problematic, the monitoring and sanctioning by EU authorities leaves much to be desired. The entire Commission is the size of one mid-level national ministry and it is not centrally based where the implementation is happening. The Commission is very reliant on the reporting of the member state actors about how implementation is proceeding. Thus NGO information about what is happening on the ground can be immensely useful when it gives a more fleshed out picture of the local reality. The European Court of Justice likewise has a limited size, creating a case backlog. The Commission can request that the Court impose substantial fines on member states who do not respond adequately to previous rulings, and these fines seem to have some deterrent effect. Nevertheless, the monitoring, enforcement and litigation process itself is often slow, complex and lacking in transparency. A critical reality is that the EU now performs this same monitoring and oversight for 12 much poorer countries. Obviously a number of the accession countries have made considerable strides, in part with EU financial and technical support. Nevertheless the EU's own environment budget is unlikely to increase tremendously in scope, given all of the other accession priorities the EU faces.

This governance study is seeking to gain some sense of the effectiveness of EU environmental policy. This is extremely difficult to ascertain. The implementation data itself is highly contentious and ambiguous when one allows for derogations and so on. Assessing effectiveness is even more problematic at the EU level because it goes beyond an assessment of levels of formal implementation to address questions of actual change on the environment. To calculate this change across the 27 countries, one must eliminate a host of factors that might have environmental consequences but do not reflect the specific measures of EU environmental policy. To illustrate this in terms of the 15 member states, it is difficult to give the EU substantial credit for holding carbon dioxide emissions under control when the industrial restructuring of the former East Germany and the natural conversion of the UK energy form such a substantial part of the important environmental gains; neither action was taken with EU environmental policy as the primary aim.

Another problem of measuring effectiveness is whether to judge the objectives of a policy against the original targets or in the face of new learning about the environment. For example, the EC understanding of water conditions has increased significantly, even though much of the original legislation was preventative in nature, and thus changed the understanding of how much of an impact the 1970s EC legislation could have on the actual environment. Nevertheless, the numerous implementation failures and the dissatisfaction with the EC legislation suggests that water policy is certainly one area (although arguably the most comprehensive in EC environmental policy) where effectiveness is problematic. This reflects a basic consensus of many implementation scholars that the effectiveness of the various EC legislative areas is much less than the legislative ambitions in these areas (for example Jordan 1999b, Grant et al., 2000).

The EEA (2002, 2004) has studied a number of trends in environmental data for the EU. While it is difficult to isolate fully the impact of EC legislation from the local circumstances and environmental legislation, some linkages between the effectiveness of EC legislation and the trends are plausible. With some adjusted targets for poorer countries, the EU 15 countries (that is members prior to May 2004) have met the target of recycling at least 25 per cent of all packaging waste by 2001 (EEA, 2004); however, there have been increases in the generation of municipal waste and packaging waste (EEA, 2002). Less encouraging is the clear projection that many of the EU 15 will not meet their climate change targets, with transport taking a significant level of the blame for growth. There have been some successes in the transport area as there has been a reduction in particulate emissions, carbon monoxide, nitrogen oxides, volatile organic compounds and lead (EEA, 2004). This does seem to reflect the role of regulations concerning fuel quality and vehicle emission standards. Other trends reflect the mixed impact of the EC: industries have reduced nitrogen pollution, which reflects EC regulations, but the agricultural sector continues to create large problems in terms of nitrogen concentrations in surface waters (EEA, 2002). Equally the forest area has increased but land resource pressures in the EC (in part reflecting the Common Market impact) have resulted in the loss and fragmentation of natural areas and habitats. These results suggest that while certain priorities identified by the Environmental Action Programme have been met through EC regulations, particularly in the areas concerning industrial and product emissions, some of the key areas of concern remain: transport, energy use and climate change, and land use. Thus a key legislative challenge seems to be how to integrate environmental concerns and regulations in these other EC policy sectors.

7. CONCLUSION

There is a strong danger, after discussing implementation, of ending this overview with a negative impression of EC environmental policy accomplishments. Given the limited resources available in the EU budget and the rather constrained context in which the policy was introduced to the Community, its growth has been rapid and impressive. Nevertheless, there are real questions to be raised about how effective this policy is. Implementation problems persist. Still, it has remained relatively popular with the member state populations (Weale et al., 2000).

In terms of the other analytical questions raised in the chapter and the project, the three decades of EC environmental policy have seen the creation of a network of environmental policy actors and organizations that operate within the various institutions of the EU. One of the most important developments has been the recognition of the environment as being a critical EU policy priority in its own right, and not something that is subsidiary to the free trade provisions of the Common Market. This in part reflects a greater ideational understanding of the environmental challenges and sustainability and the incorporation of these in the EU policy structure, style and content. So a more sustainability oriented policy frame has inserted itself in this policy sector.

Nevertheless, there are a number of governance problems that the EU faces in this policy sector. On the whole the overview of policy areas suggests that the EU actors have adopted a more sophisticated frame, acknowledging the linkages between different environmental issues; this has required legislative frameworks, such as the Integrated Prevention Pollution Control, which force public and private actors to link the issues in their everyday business. However, this is policy integration at the level of content. There are wider structural issues of integration that inhibit the EU from being considerably more effective in its environmental policy. Here the institutional nature of the EU with its diversity of voices, reflecting both the frames and interests of different policy priorities and interest groups and often very specific member state interests, structure the process. Time and again in this chapter we see the tension between this policy sector and the others. While the sustainability principle suggests that there is not a zero sum relationship between the environment and other policy priorities, it is still difficult to bring many of the core environmental aims into the process. Many of the key achievements in the area of water quality and air quality are contingent on policy sectors such as transport, energy and agriculture.

The tension about how much of the role the supranational body should have versus the member states continues to manifest itself in ways that damage effectiveness. Moreover this situation is only likely to increase as the EU faces an even greater difficulty of maintaining the efficiency of a system where states wish to have a distinctive voice in their own and the EU's affairs.

To counteract this reality the EU needs to act in terms of macro institutional concerns as well as more micro instrument concerns. Given the limitations in the EU budget, a greater linkage and networking with actors in civil society is important. Developing instruments that can be more easily implemented over 27 states is necessary. Nevertheless the institutional complexity and the embeddedness of territorial and sectoral interests and policy frame within the policy process resist drastic change and innovation. Engaging the public and the elite in focused policy-oriented networks promoting change looks attractive conceptually, but faces significant hurdles raised by the governance challenges in EU environmental policy.

NOTES

1. The European Community (EC) was the name of this regional political system until the Maastricht Treaty came into force on 1 November 1993. The regional body then became the European Union. The EU contains three different groupings of policies (called 'Pillars'); the pillar containing environmental policy is referred to as the European Community as it is the only Pillar using legal instruments set out in the Treaty of Rome.
2. I thank Jeffrey Huntington for clarifying this point.

BIBLIOGRAPHY

Beetham, David and Christopher Lord (1998), *Legitimacy and the EU*, London: Longman.

Bomberg, Elizabeth and Charlotte Burns (1999), 'The Environment Committee of the European Parliament: new powers, old problems', *Environmental Politics*, **8**(4), Winter: 174–9.

Börzel, Tanja (2003), *Environmental Leaders and Laggards in Europe: Why There is (not) a 'Southern Problem'*, Aldershot: Ashgate.

Butt Phillip, Alan (1998), 'The European Union: environmental policy and the prospects for sustainable development', in Kenneth Hanf and Alf-Inge Jansen (eds), *Governance and Environment in Western Europe: Politics, Policy and Administration*, Harlow, Essex: Longman, pp. 253–76.

CEC – Commission of the European Communities (1993), *Towards Sustainability. A European Community Programme of Policy and Action in Relation to the Environment and Sustainable Development*, Luxembourg: Office for Official Publications of the European Communities.

CEC – Commission of the European Communities (2001), *European Governance: a White Paper*, Luxembourg: Office for Official Publications of the European Communities.

CEC – Commission of the European Communities (2003a), *Fourth Annual Survey on the Implementation and Enforcement of Community Environmental Law*, Luxembourg: Office for Official Publications of the European Communities.

CEC – Commission of the European Communities (2003b), *Proposal for a Directive on Access to Justice in the Field of the Environment*, Luxembourg: Office for Official Publications of the European Communities.

CEC – Commission of the European Communities (2004), 'The Aarhus Convention', 2 July, http://europa.eu.int/comm/environment/aarhus/index.htm.

Corrie, Heather (1997), 'Experiences and realities of participation in regional development', in Ute Collier, Jonathan Golub and Alexander Kreher (eds), *Subsidiarity and Shared Responsibility: New Challenges for EU Environmental Policy*, Baden-Baden: Nomos Verlagsgesellschaft, pp. 135–47.

Damro, Chad and Pilar Luaces (2001), 'Emissions trading – a Kyoto NEPI: from EU resistance to union innovation', paper presented at the European Consortium for Political Research, Joint Sessions Conference, Grenoble, 6–11 April.

Directorate General for the Environment (2003), 'Multilateral Environmental Agreements to which the EC is a Contracting Party or a Signatory. http://europa.eu.int/comm/environment/international_issues/agreements_en.pdf.

EEA (2002), *EEA Signals 2002: Benchmarking the Millennium*, Copenhagen: EEA.

EEA (2004), *EEA Signals 2004*, Copenhagen: EEA.

EEB (2003), *EEB Annual Report 2002 and Plans for 2003*, Brussels: EEB.

ENDS Daily (2003), 'Concerns grow over health of EMAS scheme', Issue 1408, 19 March.

ENDS Daily (2003), 'European energy tax deal put back again', Issue 1409, 20 March.

ENDS Daily (2003), 'Europe's EMAS scheme prepares to go global', Issue 1459, 10 June.

ENDS Environment Daily (2004), 'Big energy users fear EU climate trading costs', Issue 1623, 8 March.

ENDS Europe Daily (2006), 'Industry disappointed by EU Reach deal', Issue 2220, 6 December.

Flynn, Brendan (2003), *Subsidiarity and the evolution of EU environmental policy*. Ph.D. thesis, University of Essex.

Gehring, Thomas (1997), 'Governing in nested institutions: environmental policy in the European Union and the case of packaging waste', *Journal of European Public Policy*, **4**(3), September: 337–54.

Goldstein, Judith and Robert Keohane (1993), 'Ideas and foreign policy: an analytical framework', in Judith Goldstein and Robert Keohane (eds), *Ideas and Foreign Policy: Beliefs, Institutions and Political Change*, Ithaca: Cornell University, pp. 3–30.

Golub, Jonathan (1996), 'British sovereignty and the development of EC environmental policy', *Environmental Politics*, **5**(4), Winter, 700–728.

Grant, Wyn, Duncan Matthews and Peter Newell (2000), *The Effectiveness of European Union Environmental Policy*, Houndmills, Basingstoke: Macmillan.

Haigh, Nigel (2003), *Manual of Environmental Policy: the EC and Britain*, London: Longmann.

Hall, Peter (1993), 'Policy paradigms, social learning and the state', *Comparative Politics*, **25**(3), September: 275–96.

Hayes-Renshaw, Fiona and Helen Wallace (1997), *The Council of Ministers*, Houndmills, Basingstoke: Macmillan.

Héritier, Adrienne (1997), 'Policy-making by subterfuge: interest: interest accommodation, innovation and substitute democratic legitimation in Europe – perspectives from distinct policy areas', *Journal of European Public Policy*, **4**(2), June: 171–89.

Héritier, Adrienne, Christoph Knill and Susanne Mingers (1996), *Ringing the Changes in Europe: Regulatory Competition and the Transformation of the State*, Berlin: Walter de Gruyer.

Hildebrand, Philipp (1993), 'The European Community's environmental policy, 1957 to "1992": from incidental measures to an international regime', in David Judge (ed.), *A Green Dimension for the European Community: Political Issues and Processes*, Portland: Frank Cass, pp. 13–44.

Hildebrand, Philipp and Alberta Sbragia (1998), 'The European Union and compliance: a story in the making', in Edith Brown Weiss and Harold K. Jacobson (eds), *Engaging Countries: Strengthening Compliance with International Environmental Accords*, Cambridge, MA: MIT Press, pp. 215–52.

Hill, Andrew (1993), 'EU rottweiler both petted and panned', *Financial Times*, 13 December: p. 2.

Jachtenfuchs, Markus (1990), 'The European Community and the protection of the ozone layer', *Journal of Common Market Studies*, **28**(2), June: 261–303.

Jeffrey, Charlie (2002), 'Social and regional interests: ESC and Committee of the Regions', in John Peterson and Michael Shackleton (eds), *The Institutions of the European Union*, Oxford: Oxford University Press, pp. 326–46.

Jordan, Andrew (1999a), 'Editorial introduction: the construction of a multilevel environmental governance system', *Environment and Planning* C, **17**(1), February: 1–27.

Jordan, Andrew (1999b), 'The implementation of EU environmental policy: a policy problem without a political solution?', *Environment and Planning* C, **17**(1), February: 69–90.

Jordan, Andrew, Adriaan Schout and Anthony Zito (2003), 'Coordinating environmental policy: shifting from passive to active coordination?', paper presented at a workshop on 'Co-ordinating the EU: Constructing Policy Coordination and Coherent Action in a Multi-Level System', Birkbeck College, University of London, 28–9 November.

Jordan, Andrew, Rüdiger Wurzel and Anthony Zito (2003), 'European governance and the transfer of "new" environmental policy instruments', *Public Administration*, **81**(3), 555–74.

Jordan, Andrew, Rüdiger Wurzel and Anthony Zito (2004), EU Baseline Paper for the Future Governance Project.

Judge, David (1992), ' "Predestined to save the Earth": the Environment Committee of the European Parliament', in David Judge (ed.), *A Green Dimension for the European Community: Political Issues and Processes*, Portland: Frank Cass, pp. 186–212.

Kellow, Aynsley and Anthony Zito (2002), 'Steering through complexity: EU environmental regulation in the international context', *Political Studies*, **50**(1), March: 43–60.

Kerremans, Bart (1998), 'The political and institutional consequences of widening: capacity and control in an enlarged council', in Pierre-Henri Laurent and Marc Maresceau (eds), *The State of the European Union (Vol. 4): Deepening and Widening*, Boulder: Lynne Rhienner, pp. 87–109.
Koppen, Ida (1993), 'The role of the European Court of Justice', in Duncan Liefferink, Philip Lowe and Arthur Mol (eds), *European Integration and Environmental Policy*, John Wiley & Sons, pp. 126–49.
Kronsell, Annica (1997), 'Policy innovation in the Garbage Can: the EU's Fifth Environmental Action Programme', in Duncan Liefferink and Mikael Skou Andersen (eds), *The Innovation of EU Environmental Policy*, Copenhagen: Scandinavian University Press, pp. 111–32.
Lenschow, Andrea (1999), 'Transformation in European environmental governance', in Beate Kohler-Koch and Rainer Eising (eds), *The Transformation of Governance in the European Union*, London: Routledge, pp. 39–60.
Lenschow, Andrea and Anthony Zito (1998), 'Blurring or shifting of policy frames? Institutionalization of the economic–environmental policy linkage in the European Community', *Governance*, **11**(4), October: 415–41.
Liefferink, Duncan and Mikael Skou Andersen (1998), 'Strategies of the "Green" member states in EU environmental policy-making', *Journal of European Public Policy*, **5**(2), June: 254–70.
Majone, Giandomenico (1997), 'From the positive to the regulatory state: causes and consequences of changes in the modes of governance', *Journal of Public Policy*, **17**(2), May: 139–67.
March, James and Johan Olsen (1989), *Rediscovering Institutions: the Organizational Basis of Politics*, New York: Free Press.
Matláry, Janne (1997), *Energy Policy in the European Union*, Basingstoke: Macmillan.
Mazey, Sonia and Jeremy Richardson (1992), 'Environmental groups and the EC: challenges and opportunities', *Environmental Politics*, **1**(4), Spring: 109–28.
McCormick, John (2001), *Environmental Policy in the European Union*, Basingstoke: Palgrave.
Peters, B. Guy (1992), 'Bureaucratic politics and the institutions of the European Community', in Alberta Sbragia (ed.), *Euro-politics*, Washington DC: Brooking Institute, pp. 75–122.
Pierson, Paul (1996), 'The path to European integration: a historical institutionalist analysis', *Comparative Political Studies*, **29**(2), April, 123–63.
Pollack, Mark (1994), 'Creeping competence: the expanding agenda of the European Community', *Journal of Public Policy*, **14**(2), March–June: 95–145.
Pollack, Mark (2003), 'Control mechanism or deliberative comitology? Two images of comitology', *Comparative Political Studies*, **36**(1–2), February: 125–55.
Pridham, Géoffrey (1994), 'National environmental policy-making in the European Framework: Spain, Greece and Italy in comparison', in Susan Baker, Kay Milton and Steven Yearly (eds), *Protecting the Periphery: Environmental Policy in Peripheral Regions of the European Union*, Ilford: Frank Cass, pp. 80–101.
Rein, Martin and Donald Schön (1994), *Frame Reflection: Toward the Resolution of Intractable Policy Controversies*, New York: BasicBooks.
Richardson, Jeremy and N.S.J. Watts (1985), *National Policy Styles and the Environment: Britain and West Germany Compared*, Berlin: Wissenschaftszentrum Berlin für Sozialforschung.

Ritchie, Ella (2003), 'Modes of regulation in the CFP: a moveable feast?', paper presented at the European Union Studies Association Biennial Conference, Nashville, 27 March.
Sbragia, Alberta (1992), 'Thinking about the European future: the uses of comparison', in Alberta Sbragia (ed.), *Euro-Politics*, Washington, DC: Brookings Institution, pp. 257–91.
Sbragia, Alberta (1993), 'The European Community: a balancing act', *Publius: the Journal of Federalism*, **23**, Summer: 23–38.
Sbragia, Alberta (1998), 'Institution-building from below and above: the European Community in global environmental politics', in Wayne Sandholtz and Alec Stone Sweet (eds), *European Integration and Supranational Governance*, Oxford: Oxford University Press, pp. 283–303.
Sbragia, Alberta (2000), 'The European Union as coxswain: governance by steering', in Jon Pierre (ed.), *Debating Governance*, Oxford: Oxford University Press, pp. 219–40.
Schout, Adriaan and Andrew Jordan (2003), 'Coordinating environmental policy: self-organizing or centrally steered?', manuscript.
UNECE (United Nations Economic Commission for Europe) (1998), Convention on Access to Information, Public Participation in Decision-making and Access to Justice in Environmental Matters, 25 June.
Weale, Albert (1992), *The New Politics of Pollution*, Manchester: Manchester University Press.
Weale, Albert (1996), 'Environmental rules and rule-making in the European Union', *Journal of European Public Policy*, **3**(4), December: 594–611.
Weale, Albert (1999), 'European environmental policy by stealth: the dysfunctionality of functionalism?', *Environment and Planning* C, **17**(1), February: 37–51.
Weale, Albert, Geoffrey Pridham, Michelle Cini, Dimitrios Konstadakopulos, Martin Porter and Brendan Flynn (2000), *Environmental Governance in Europe*, Oxford: Oxford University Press.
Wurzel, Rüdiger (2002), *Environmental Policy-making in Britain, Germany and the European Union; the Europeanization of Air and Water Pollution Control*, Manchester: Manchester University Press.
Zito, Anthony (1995), 'Integrating the environment into the European Union: the history of the controversial carbon tax', in Carolyn Rhodes and Sonia Mazey (eds), *The State of the European Union, Volume Three: Building a European Polity?* Boulder: Lynn Rhienner, pp. 431–48.
Zito, Anthony (2000), *Creating Environmental Policy in the European Union*, Basingstoke: Macmillan/St. Martin's Press/Palgrave.
Zito, Anthony (2001), 'Epistemic communities, collective entrepreneurship and European integration', *Journal of European Public Policy*, **8**(4), August: 585–603.

7. Environmental institutions in Germany: Leader or laggard?

Stefanie Engel and Melanie Zimmermann

1. INTRODUCTION

As a consequence of its geographic position,[1] high population density, and high degree of industrialization, environmental problems have been and continue to be considered an important issue in Germany[2] (Jänicke and Weidner, 1997). Since the late 1960s, major regulations covering nearly all areas of environmental policy have been passed. The country has established a reputation as a leader in international environmental protection initiatives as well as the development of 'green' technologies. Nevertheless, Germany has increasingly turned from a leader to a laggard. Despite impressive progress in the area of pollution control, serious environmental problems remain and the country is only slowly working towards the goal of sustainable development. Its strong economy has permitted Germany to get away with the adoption of inefficient, overly costly policy approaches for many years. Post-unification economic problems and high unemployment, however, have reinforced the need to shift towards more cost-effective measures. In this regard, Germany is lagging behind other industrialized countries, and change – although present – is slow. Pressure in the direction of 'new environmental policy instruments' has also increased on the part of international actors, including the European Union (EU), the World Bank, and the Organization for Economic Cooperation and Development (OECD) (Wurzel et al., 2003).

The objective of this chapter is to review the current institutional set-up of environmental policy in Germany, examine how and why this has changed over time, and evaluate the effectiveness of the applied policy tools. The structure of the chapter is as follows. Part 2 reviews the main institutional changes that have taken place in the area of environmental policy over the last four decades. In particular, changes in the institutional set-up, actors' constellation and predominant policy paradigm, and the forces and events driving these changes are described. Part 3 presents the current institutional set-up in detail, followed, in part 4, by an analysis of the main policy tools applied. Part 5 evaluates the results of environmental policy and highlights areas of persisting problems. Finally, part 6 concludes.

2. INSTITUTIONAL CHANGE IN ENVIRONMENTAL POLICY MAKING IN GERMANY

Environmental regulation in Germany is embodied in private, public and criminal law. Early environmental regulations, dating back to the nineteenth century, include the Water Rights Act, the Factories Act, and the Prussian Industrial Statute. These emphasized the protection of health and property from emissions by nearby industrial activities. In the 1960s, air pollution laws existed at the state level only. In general, the period before 1969 can, however, be called one of 'environmental ignorance' (Jänicke and Weidner, 1997). In this section we discuss the main institutional changes and paradigm shifts that have characterized German environmental policy from 1969 until today. Our presentation largely follows the analyses of Jänicke et al. (1999, ch. 1), Weidner (1995), and Jänicke and Weidner (1997), but with several changes and additions. In general, six policy phases can be distinguished. Table 7.1 summarizes the main features of each phase in terms of the driving force of institutional change, the predominant policy paradigm, and the existing actors' constellations.

2.1 Phase 1 (1969–1974): The Beginning of Systematic Environmental Policy

Environmental policy became a national policy area for the first time with the rise of the Social-Democrat (SPD)–Liberal (FDP) Coalition government in 1969. Under its rule, environmental policy was established as an independent policy area in the political and administrative system by becoming an official government programme. Interestingly, this occurred despite a lack of acute environmental crisis or noticeable pressure from public opinion or environmental organizations (EOs). In addition, the issue had not been emphasized during election campaigns (Müller, 1986). Rather, the initiative appears to have emerged from within the political system itself (Reich, 1984). It seems to have been stimulated and strongly influenced by international developments (Weidner, 1995). These developments include: (i) environmental policy initiatives in the United States[3] and Japan, (ii) activities by international organizations such as UNESCO and the European Council's water and air pollution initiatives,[4] (iii) international conferences

Table 7.1 Phases of environmental policy in Germany from 1969 to present

Duration	Main driving force of institutional change	Main actors' constellation	Policy paradigm
1969–1974	Stimuli from abroad; Rise of centre-left government	State (initiative); Industry (passive)	Dilution (high smoke stacks, thinning)
1974–1980	Oil crisis, Recession; Increase in environmental awareness	State (legislation); Industry (passive); EOs*/civil society (pressure on state)	Dilution; end-of-pipe technologies for water protection
1980–1986	Increase in environmental awareness and media coverage due to visibility of environmental problems	Cooperation and conflict between state and industry; EOs/civil society (pressure on state and industry); Media (increased coverage)	Intensive use of end-of-pipe technologies (including air pollution control); National policy drives international initiatives
1986–1994	Environmental catastrophes, emergence of a 'green market', strengthening of Green Party; German reunification	Dialogue and network building between state, industry (including 'green' industry as new actor), and EOs; Strong media coverage	Ecological modernization/Adoption of pollution-prevention technologies
1994–1998	Economic problems, high unemployment, moderate decline in public concern for environmental issues	Shift in government cooperation towards economic interests; increase in environment-minded opposition in the East	Speeding up planning and licensing procedures for large investments
1998–present	Green Party entry into government coalition; increased pressure from EU	New dynamics through green government; Increase in industry resistance; EU pressure on government	Slow shift towards adoption of market-based approaches, Ecological tax reform/Sustainable Development

Note: * EO = Environmental Organization.

Sources: Jänicke et al. (1999, ch. 1); Weidner (1995); Jänicke and Weidner (1997); Wurzel (2002); Wurzel et al. (2003).

such as the 1972 UN Conference on the Environment in Stockholm, as well as (iv) prominent publications.[5]

In 1969, responsibilities over pollution control (water, air quality, noise abatement and waste disposal) were transferred from the Federal Ministry of Health to the Ministry of the Interior. In 1970, a quick-start programme was issued, followed by the 1971 Environment Programme, which was then updated in 1976. The Environment Programme stipulates the polluter-pays principle, but also uses financial and fiscal measures to support environmental protection. The promotion of pollution-reduction technologies and environmental awareness were other stated key objectives. During the period from 1971 to 1974, several major environmental laws were passed (Jänicke and Weidner, 1997).

In 1972, an amendment to the German Constitution granted the federal government *concurrent legislative power* for statutory regulations on air pollution control, waste management, noise abatement, protection from radiation, and on criminal law relating to environmental protection, implying federal government authorization to issue detailed regulations on these issues, and that federal law overrules state law. Motivated by the US Council on Environmental Quality and Environmental Protection Agency, the German Council of Environmental Advisors (*Sachverständigenrat für Umweltfragen*) and the Federal Environmental Agency (*Umweltbundesamt*) were set up in 1971 and 1974, respectively.

These institutional reforms, especially the Federal Environment Programme, can be considered progressive and demanding for their time (Jänicke and Weidner, 1997). The fact that they passed without any major resistance from other areas of government can be attributed to several factors (Weidner, 1995). First, they were an opportunity for the Minister of the Interior, Hans Dietrich Genscher, to establish a reforming image for his liberal party. Second, they also benefited from a general reformist climate within the new government and strong backing from the Chancellor's Office. Third, at the end of the 1960s it had become widely accepted among academics and in the wider society that market corrections were needed and could be achieved through state intervention.

The period from 1969 to 1974 can be called a period of 'active policy design' where environmental policy was largely the result of government decisions (Müller, 1989, p. 23). Industry participated in some of the policy discussions, but generally took a rather passive role. Public debate as well as government legislation focused largely on visible problems, including air pollution from stationary and mobile sources, and the pollution of rivers and lakes through industrial and household effluents. The numerous laws and regulations passed within this period focused largely on the implementation of pollution-diluting technologies (for example, through higher smoke stacks and waste collection) rather than pollution prevention.

2.2 Phase 2 (1974–1980): Stagnation, Conflict, and Emergence of a Green Movement

The international oil crisis and the subsequent period of economic recession caused a period of stagnation in environmental policy in the years following 1974.[6] Industry and trade unions started to voice strong criticism of the stringent environmental legislation. A new 'anti-environment coalition', including the Federal Minister of the Economy and supported by the new Chancellor, Helmut Schmidt, promoted the relaxation of environmental requirements in the interest of economic development.

This backlash, however, met with increased public awareness, leading to a strong citizens' movement in favour of the environment, which had its roots in the anti-nuclear movement of the early 1970s. In 1972, the numerous EOs established an umbrella organization, the Federal Association of Civil Initiatives for the Environment (*Bundesverband Bürgerinitiativen Umwelt, BBU*), with the support of high-ranking officials in the Ministry of the Interior, who wanted to increase their public support (Hartkopf, 1986). In 1977, so-called 'green lists' participated for the first time in district-level parliamentary elections. In 1979, a Green Party entered the city-state parliament of Bremen, followed by further electoral successes in other states.

The resulting climate of conflict led to a slow-down in environmental policy making. Nevertheless, under the pressure of the increasingly strong environmental movement, some important legislation was passed during this period, such as, for example, the Federal Immission Control Act (1974), the Waste Water Charges Act (1976), and the Nature Conservation Act (1976). The General Paradigm remained to be one of pollution dilution, with some additional adoption of end-of-pipe treatment technology.

2.3 Phase 3 (1980–1986): Strengthening of the Green Movement and New Dynamics

In 1983, a centre-right government, consisting of a coalition of Christian Democratic Union (CDU) and FDP, returned to power. However, the Green Party also entered parliament with 5.6 per cent of the votes. This success can be explained by the public perception that the established parties had not responded adequately to the issues of environmental protection, nuclear energy, disarmament, liberal freedoms and women's rights, which were at the heart of the Environmental and Peace movements. The new government, which was traditionally expected to be pro-business, was faced with growing public discontent on environmental issues. This discontent was further fuelled by visible environmental problems, including *Waldsterben* ('dying forests') and occurrences of severe smog in parts of the country, which were increasingly covered by the media.

As early as 1980, this climate of discontent had led to a reorientation of public environmental policy, but with little immediate translation into specific regulations. Moreover, industry and trade unions weakened in their opposition to environmental protection, despite the continued resistance by some of the high-polluting sectors. First, supported by scientific results, it became accepted that environmental protection may not necessarily hamper economic growth, but may indeed improve the economic climate and structure of the economy. Second, a new branch of 'eco-industry', specializing in environmentally-friendly technologies and products started developing.

The new government quickly passed a number of strict environmental regulations, many of which had been initiated by the previous government. An example is the 1983 Ordinance on Large Combustion Plants, which set the strictest emission limits for air pollutants within Europe – despite the resistance of the strong lobby of German power companies – and became a model for other countries. The new policy was characterized by the intensive use of end-of-pipe treatment technologies. In other areas, however, the government continued to rely on often symbolic environmental regulations, which were not tied to a verifiable implementation schedule. As a consequence, environmental quality in areas other than air pollution improved only a little or even deteriorated (Weidner, 1995, p. 14).

Germany also took a leading role within Europe when it organized a multilateral environmental conference in Munich in 1984 to coordinate measures against acid rain and long-range flows of air pollutants. In this process, the developments at national level guided the government's international initiatives. The new Minister of the Interior's strong stand on air pollution reduction has been explained by the fact that his constituency was located in Bavaria where forest damage from air pollution was particularly high (Weidner, 1995, p. 14). Germany's leading role in the EU, particularly in pushing for harmonization measures, can also be explained by the country's export-dependent economy and high ecological vulnerability due to its geographic position (Wurzel, 2002).

In general, the actors' roles also changed in this period. Cooperation between state and industry gained in importance, supported by the traditionally good relation between the conservative party and the business sector. Moreover, EOs – while continuing to lobby government – also started to put pressure directly on particularly polluting industries and companies, with support from the media.

2.4 Phase 4 (1986–1994): Ecological Modernization and German Reunification

Weak environmental policy in areas other than air pollution, and failure of negotiations at the European Community (EC) on automobile emission standards led to a gradual decline in public confidence in the Minister of the Interior's competence in the environmental arena. Criticism of government environmental policy was further fuelled by the 1986 nuclear catastrophe in Chernobyl and the subsequent failure by the Ministry of the Interior to respond to concerns about a rise in radiation and the now apparent lack of protection mechanisms. In response, the Federal Ministry for the Environment, Nature Conservation, and Nuclear Safety was established within the same year. Nevertheless, some important authorities remained in other ministries.[7] The initial activities of the new ministry were largely focused on the area of nuclear safety and radiation protection, which was criticized by opposition parties, academics and EOs as attempts to ensure the political future of nuclear energy production.

In 1987, Klaus Töpfer – an environmental economist with considerable expertise in the area of environmental policy – became new Minister of the Environment. Being very active and media-oriented, he gained a reputation of competence both nationally and internationally. He contributed significantly to the further reduction in air and water pollution, the development of a concept for protecting the North and Baltic Sea, and an expansion of the scope of environmental liability legislation. In 1990, legislative and voluntary measures to reduce CO_2 emissions followed. The 1994 Closed Substance Cycle and Waste Management Act (*Kreislaufwirtschaftsgesetz*) is considered another major initiative. It stipulates a comprehensive approach to waste recycling and avoidance, including an increase in private-sector involvement (Jänicke and Weidner, 1997). Moreover, in 1994, the concept of sustainable development was incorporated in the constitution by adding the 'preservation of the means of life for future generations' to the fundamental aim of the state (Kirkpatrick et al., 2001).

The Minister, however, has also been criticized for yielding too easily to EC resistance on stringent automobile emission standards and to economic interests in general. Moreover, while Töpfer adopted the rhetoric of introducing economic instruments such as environmental charges in the 1990 state-level elections, the issue was subsequently played down. Only minor new environmental charges were introduced (for example, charges on non-deposit bottles), while some existing ones (like the sewage charge) were even weakened. Motivated by concerns that unilateral action could lead to a decrease in competitiveness, the government started to push for the EU-wide adoption of a CO_2 or energy tax (Wurzel et al., 2003).

Nevertheless, the period is widely considered as one of ecological modernization toward the use of more environmentally-friendly technologies. Major environmental catastrophes (Chernobyl, pollution incidents of the Rhine River and accidents at chemical plants) further raised public concern about the environment. Polluting companies were under increasing threat of being directly attacked by EOs and the media. In response to the emergence of a 'green market' and potential cost savings from ecological modernization, 'green' enterprises and their organizations became a powerful actor stimulating the adoption of environmentally-friendly technologies. The Green Party also became a coalition partner in several states. The threat of government intervention and consumer action, in combination with negotiation and consultation, rather than actual regulation, thus worked as a driving force of change. A new trilateral cooperation between the Ministry of the Environment, industry and EOs started emerging, including some bilateral agreements between EOs and companies.

A major event during this period was the reunification of the Federal Republic of Germany with the former German Democratic Republic (GDR). After the 'peaceful revolution' in the GDR in 1989, cooperation on environmental issues intensified when the tremendous extent of air, water and soil pollution in the East became apparent. After the formal reunification of the two German states in 1990, West German environmental legislation also became valid for the six 'new *Länder*' (federal states located in the former GDR), with a grace period of five years. Several environmental action and research programmes have been established to achieve the objective of uniform environmental conditions, including the 1991 'Cornerstones for an ecological restoration and development in the "new *Länder*"'. Substantial funds have been dedicated to environmental protection and establishment of environmental administrations in the new states.

2.5 Phase 5 (1994–1998): Economic Problems and Slowdown of Environmental Policy

After 12 years in power, in the 1994 elections, the centre-right government prevailed once again and a new Minister of the Environment was appointed. Following reunification, the economic situation in Germany, particularly in the new *Länder*, worsened, and unemployment rose dramatically. General public concern about environmental problems appears to have moderately declined (Wurzel, 2002). The '*Standort Germany*' debate raised concerns about Germany's future as a production and investment location within the global economy (Wurzel et al., 2003). As a consequence of these trends, environmental policy once again lost its momentum. The 1994 coalition agreement stated a general preference for voluntary agreements between industry and government above traditional regulatory instruments (Wurzel, 2002). The country lost its reputation of being an environmental leader and increasingly came to be seen as facing difficulties in adapting to certain EU environmental policy measures. Thus, while initially Germany had been a leader in pushing for more stringent EU environmental policy, it now itself began to come under similar pressure from the EU (Wurzel, 2002). For example, the EU Nitrate Directive of 1991 was only implemented in the 1996 Fertilization Ordinance, following a disagreement between the Ministries of Agriculture and the Environment (Weingarten, 1997).

In addition, the achievement of environmental objectives in the new *Länder* was hindered by the fact that 'the highly complex West German legal and administrative system was simply transferred to the fundamentally different legal, administrative, and economic system of the former GDR. [. . .]Sensible environmental policy instruments and structures that already exist in Eastern Germany are receiving no support and are consequently breaking down or disappearing.' (Weidner, 1995, p. 19) As a result, ecological restoration in the new *Länder* fell behind stated goals, and political conflicts between economic and ecological interests increased. In response to the increase in environmentally-motivated opposition to large public investments in the East – for example, landfills, waste incineration plants, major infrastructure – the government has passed several amendments to existing laws to speed up the planning process and licensing procedures for such investments (*streamlining legislation*). Critics see this as a way to reduce public participation rights in favour of economic interests. Moreover, the amendments apply not only in the new *Länder*, but in the entire country.

2.6 Phase 6 (1998–current): The Red–Green Coalition and Increasing Europeanization

In 1998, a new centre-left government consisting of the SPD and the Green Party replaced the old centre-right coalition, which had been in office for 16 years. This was the first time in German history that the Green Party had entered into federal government, and a representative of this party became Minister of the Environment. As a consequence, environmental policy gained new momentum. Major initiatives include an ecological tax reform (and the introduction of an 'eco-tax'), the gradual phase-out of nuclear energy production,[8] and an ambitious alternative energy programme. Most notable is the existing, although slow move towards the implementation of market-based policy instruments.

The concept of sustainable development has also finally gained some influence (SRU, 2002). However, much scepticism remains within the Ministry of the Environment due to the emphasis placed on stakeholder responsibility rather than state intervention (Wurzel et al., 2003).[9] The recently established Council for Sustainable Development provides an important forum for exploring common ground between economic, social and environmental objectives and as a venue for conflict mediation and consensus-building (OECD, 2001). Also, a new Green Cabinet[10] is intended to strengthen 'horizontal policy coordination by obliging the ministries concerned to develop sector-specific sustainable development strategies' (OECD, 2001, p. 3).

Moreover, an increasing europeanization of Germany's national environmental policy can be observed (Wurzel, 2002). Recent procedural measures put forth by the EU have triggered considerable pressure for adaptation at the national level. These measures rely heavily on informational rather than regulatory policy tools, and on an integrated pollution control approach cutting across different environmental media. Both of these measures are seen to conflict with the traditional approach. There is some concern in Germany that some of the EU measures could lead to a weakening of environmental regulation (Wurzel, 2002). In 2001, following the European Commission's proposal for an EU-wide tradable emissions permit system, the federal government set up a national working group on the issue. While attempts at the federal level to establish pilot projects within Germany failed due to strong industry opposition, some individual *Länder* have set up regional pilot schemes. In other areas, such as car emission regulations and climate change, Germany continues to be seen as an environmental leader state.

3. INSTITUTIONAL SET-UP AND MAIN ACTORS

Figure 7.1 illustrates the current institutional set-up of environmental policy making. It is comprised of a network of public and private organizations, at the national, state, and local level. In general, responsibilities for environmental policy are shared between the Federation, the individual states (*Länder*), and municipalities (UBA, n.d.). Moreover, since Germany is a member of the EU, this supranational authority has an important influence on German environmental policy. In addition, EOs and industry are important stakeholders with considerable influence over actual policy. The activities of the academic and scientific community and the media may also affect environmental policy making.

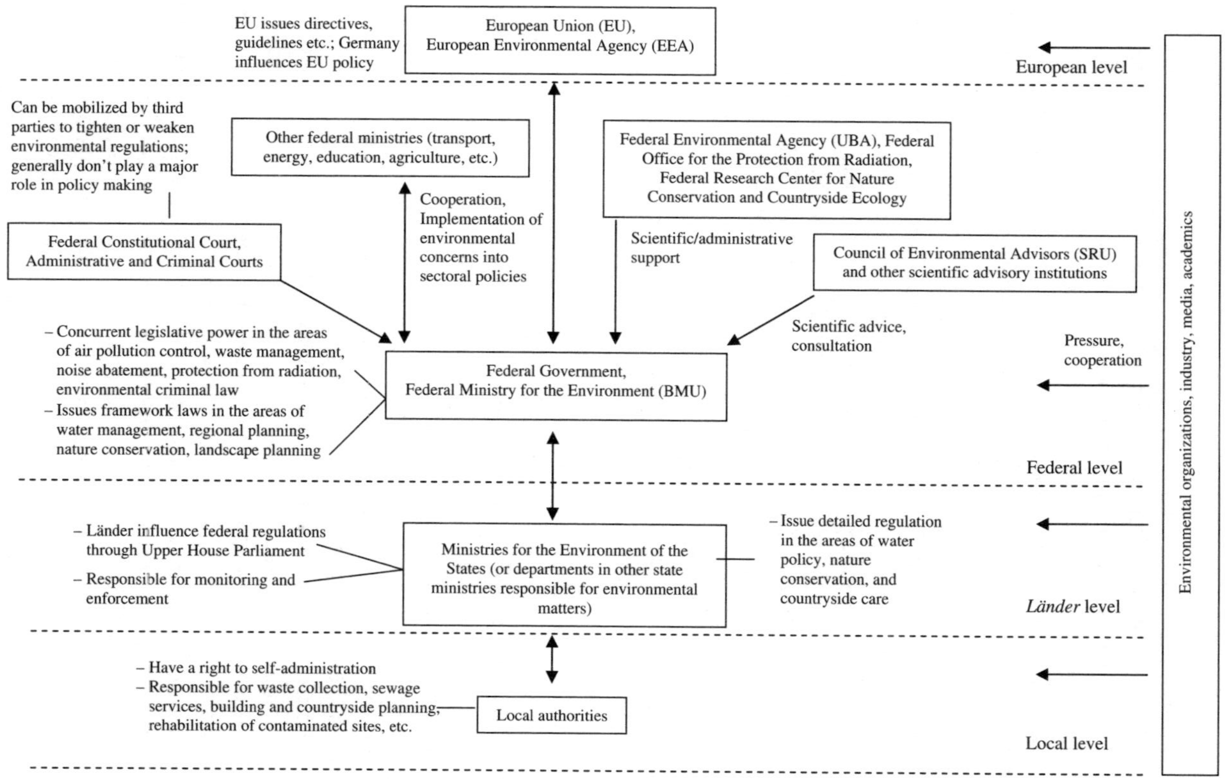

Figure 7.1 Institutional set-up for environmental policy in Germany

3.1 Public Sector Organizations

Federal level

The main organization in charge of environmental policy is the Federal Ministry for the Environment, Nature Conservation and Nuclear Safety (BMU). Technical, scientific and administrative support to the BMU are provided by several government organizations, including the Federal Environmental Agency, the Federal Office for Protection from Radiation, and the Federal Research Centre for Nature Conservation and Countryside Ecology.

Several other ministries have special environmental protection departments and have important responsibilities related to environmental policy. These are specified in Table 7.2. A dense network of inter-ministerial bodies and ad hoc working groups (for example the Interministerial Working Group CO_2 reduction) exists for the purpose of policy coordination (Kirkpatrick et al., 2001; UBA, n.d.).[11] Such coordination and cooperation mechanisms can be of benefit to environmental protection because other ministries have to take into account the impacts of their policies on the environment. However, the Ministry for the Environment is a rather weak ministry and, thus, powerful ministries, such as the Ministry for the Economy and Work, can water down environmental legislation (Günther and Krebs, 2000).

The Council of Environmental Advisors (SRU), a panel of independent experts from the social and natural sciences, is in charge of providing scientific advice to the government upon request and issues regular reports on the state of the environment. It sometimes also raises or analyses issues on its own initiative. Other scientific advisory councils with a potential influence over the debate on environmental policy include, for example, the Parliamentary Commissions of Enquiry and the German Advisory Council on Global Change.

The German Constitution stipulates that the central government is mainly responsible for the formulation of policies, while the Länder and local government organizations are in charge of policy implementation and enforcement. Some areas, such as genetic engineering, plant protection, chemicals, transboundary movement of waste, and trade with endangered species, are entirely or partly administered by federal authorities (UBA, n.d.). The 1972 amendment to the German Constitution grants the federal government concurrent legislative power for statutory regulations on air pollution control, waste management, noise abatement, protection from radiation, and on criminal law relating to environmental protection. This implies that the federal government is authorized to issue detailed regulations on these topics, and that federal law supersedes state and local

Table 7.2 Environmental responsibilities of different Federal Ministries in Germany

Ministry	Area of environmental responsibility
Ministry for the Environment, Nature Conservation and Nuclear Safety	Main organization in charge of German environmental policy
Ministry for Health	Drinking water quality and supply, projects within action programme 'Environment and Health'
Ministry of Consumer Protection, Food and Agriculture	Rural-sector water management, flood protection, coastal zone management, forestry, hunting
Ministry for Economy and Work	Energy policy, resource policy
Ministry for Transport, Building and Housing	Marine environmental protection, transport-related environmental protection, waterways, railways, regional planning, urban rehabilitation and development
Ministry for Education and Research	Environmental education, research and development on environmental issues
Ministry of Finance	Ecologically important rehabilitation measures, remediation of contaminated sites, environmental taxation
Ministry for Economic Cooperation and Development	Bilateral cooperation with developing countries in the environmental sector
Foreign Office	Involved in implementation of international environmental agreements and conferences

Sources: UBA (n.d.); Kirkpatrick et al. (2001).

decisions. In the policy areas of water management, regional planning, nature conservation, and landscape preservation, however, the Länder were able to defend their competencies, and the federal government is authorized only to issue framework laws as a basis for detailed and specific legislation to be developed by the states (Jänicke and Weidner, 1997). As a consequence, specific policies often differ between states (Weingarten, 1997). The asymmetry in environmental policy competences also helps to explain current difficulties in adopting a cross-media approach (Wurzel, 2002). On the other hand, the decentralized structure provides opportunities for implementing innovative policies in individual states first, which may later be transferred to the federal level (Wurzel et al., 2003). One example would be the 1974

Federal Immission Control Act which was heavily influenced by North-Rhine Westphalia's Immission Control Act of 1962 (Weidner, 1995).

State level

Ministries responsible for environmental issues have been instituted in all the states. In addition to their above-mentioned role in policy formulation and specification, the states are generally responsible for licensing, monitoring and enforcement (UBA, n.d.), Moreover, states are involved in national policy making directly, since Germany's bicameral system requires that major policy reform be approved by majorities in both the national parliament (*Bundestag*) and the *Bundesrat* – a chamber consisting of representatives of all federal states. Since the two chambers are often dominated by different political parties, this system tends to favour more incremental policy evolution (Wurzel et al., 2003). The *Bundesrat* also has the power to introduce its own bills.

Regional and local level

Local authorities, as stated in the German Constitution, have the right to self-administration. State legislation often sets the framework in which local authorities implement environmental policies (Kirkpatrick et al., 2001). Moreover, the states often delegate their responsibilities in policy implementation and enforcement to organizations at various regional levels (Weingarten, 1997). The specifics vary between states (Scheierling, 1994). In general, municipalities are responsible for the supervision of water and waste management, animal protection, construction, food, road infrastructure, and veterinarian matters on their territory (UBA, n.d.). Important municipal services are the provision of drinking water, the collection and treatment of wastewater, the collection, transport, and disposal of municipal waste,[12] and the provision of local public transport. They also often own and operate local energy supply (UBA, n.d.).

Many local governments have set up plans to promote sustainable development (the Agenda 21 process) (Kirkpatrick et al., 2001). Municipalities also participate in environmental impact assessment of major projects on their territory (UBA, n.d.). Other typical local initiatives include the establishment of help-lines on environmental issues and municipal environmental reports and registers (UBA, n.d.). Some German cities also play an active role in international environmental and climate protection networks (Jänicke and Weidner, 1997).

Coordination between levels

A number of committees and working groups have been created to facilitate the cooperation and coordination in environmental policy between individual states (most notably the Conference of Environmental Ministers) and between federal and state authorities (for example, the Federal/Länder Working Group Soil Protection).[13] Discussion rounds, workshops, common declarations, and financial support for research and development or investment projects are further means to promote the cooperation between federal-, state-, and local-level authorities.

Moreover, according to article 91a of the German Constitution the Federation is obligated to help with the fulfilment of tasks of the *Länder* in the form of contractual agreements (*Gemeinschaftsaufgaben*). The article stipulates that these tasks have to be of great importance to society and that the support of the Federation must be needed for the improvement of living conditions through these tasks. One of those tasks is the contractual agreement for the improvement of agricultural structure, living conditions in rural areas, and coast protection (*Gemeinschaftsaufgabe zur Verbesserung der Agrarstruktur und des Küstenschutzes*, GAK). In 2002, EU, federal and *Länder* financial means for GAK measures amounted to EUR 1.4 billion. EUR 301 million went into measures for the improvement of the rural structure (for example modernization of villages, improvement of water quality). EUR 256 million were spent on measures for the improvement of production and marketing conditions of ecologically produced agricultural products. Sustainable agricultural practices were financed with EUR 178 million (BMVEL, 2003a).

3.2 The European Union as Supranational Actor

As European integration proceeds, the EU is becoming an important actor for German environmental policy. The 1987 Single European Act introduced explicit environmental provisions into the EC Treaty. Thus, federal legislation and ordinances may be constrained by minimum standards set by the EU (Kirkpatrick et al., 2001). The role of EU policy has become particularly important since the early 1990s when EU and German environmental policy started to diverge (Wurzel, 2002).

In the past, the federal government has been accused by the states of trying to expand its competences by agreeing to EU environmental legislation (Wurzel, 2002). As a consequence, the states have often resisted implementation of EU policy measures, particularly when these fall within their areas of competence (for example water pollution and nature protection).[14] If the states fail to implement EU environmental laws correctly, the federal government can be taken to the European Court of Justice (ECJ). Since the Amsterdam Treaty, where fines were introduced as a measure to achieve member state compliance with ECJ decisions, federal government has threatened to pass on such fines to the states (as has happened lately, when the EU threatened to fine Germany for not designating enough Natura 2000 nature conservation areas) (Wurzel, 2002). The states are requesting a constitutional amendment granting them improved rights of information and involvement in EU decision-making.

3.3 Courts

Overall, courts do not play a major role in environmental policy making in Germany. Neither the Federal Constitutional Court nor criminal law courts have intervened on a massive scale (see also section 4.7). Administrative courts are responsible for the control of compliance with administrative regulations such as emission standards. They can be mobilized by third parties, for example EOs, industry, during or after the licensing or planning process and can for example stop projects or cause a tightening or weakening of environmental regulations (Jänicke and Weidner, 1997).

3.4 Environmental Organizations (EOs) and the Public

The SRU's 1996 Environmental Report stresses the significant role of EOs in operationalizing environmental protection and sustainable development in Germany. Different assessments of the role of EOs exist in the literature. Heuser (n.d.) sees the role of EOs as two-fold. First, they act as watchdogs of both environmental policy and actual compliance by industry. Through lobbying, confrontations, and information provision to the public they aim – and have often succeeded in – influencing the actions of policy makers and industry. Second, their cooperation with the same actors is seen as important for the development of new solutions to prevailing environmental problems. Weidner (1995) also describes a process of intensive formal and informal government cooperation and negotiation involving industry and environmental activists. Jänicke and Weidner (1997) highlights the fact that EOs and citizens' action groups have actively made use of participation rights, which were institutionalized early on in areas such as urban planning, nuclear energy and ambient air quality control. As mentioned earlier, these were, however, reduced to some degree by streamlining laws implemented in the 1990s. By contrast, Wurzel et al. (2003) speaks of frequent exclusion of EOs from close involvement in policy formulation and consequently a stronger reliance of EOs on court decisions during the post-decision phase. He acknowledges, however, that EOs have received active support from the government and have been closely involved in some policy initiatives, such as the national eco-labelling scheme described below.

A wide variety of environmental citizens' groups exist in Germany, with an estimated total of several thousand groups. At the national level, the most important EOs in terms of membership are Greenpeace Germany, the World Wildlife Fund, the German Federation for Environment and Nature Protection (BUND), and the German Federation for Nature Protection (*Naturschutzbund*) (Heuser, n.d.). In addition, there are many umbrella organizations and NGOs focused on specific policy fields. The German Nature Protection League (DNR) serves as an umbrella organization for approximately 100 non-governmental organizations, with a total of more than 5 million members (Heuser, n.d.). Local-level EOs include local nature conservation groups focused on specific nature conservation areas, citizen initiatives focused on specific, often short-run projects, local Agenda 21 groups, and local groups of the major national EOs. As stated earlier, the Green Party is now firmly established within the party system and has been represented in state and federal parliaments.

The federal government generally attaches great value to public opinion and participation. Every two years, a study on 'Environmental Awareness in Germany' is carried out by the Federal Environmental Agency in order to find out what the public thinks about environmental issues and policies. Government and ministries regularly advertise competitions motivating the public (from young children to adults) to present ideas for environmental protection measures and support a range of environmental education programmes in schools and other institutions. Pushed by the EU Environmental Information Directive, the government also put increased effort into widened access to and provision of environmental information. A database containing information on the condition of the environment, nature conservation and radiation protection, as well as an internet portal (GEIN) were created (BMU, 2002). Adequate and timely provision of environmental data is somewhat complicated, however, by the structure of shared responsibilities between the Federation and the states.

3.5 Industry

Eco-industry has become an active player in environmental policy. According to Jänicke and Weidner (1997), about 550 000 jobs or 2 per cent of total employment depended directly or indirectly on this area of industry, with an above-average growth rate and a dominant position in the world market. 'Green enterprises' (environmentally committed businesses) and their associations[15] have also gained importance. They have become a motor for ecological modernization by setting examples and generating environmentally-friendly demand (Jänicke and Weidner, 1997).

3.6 Scientific and Academic Sector

There is a broad range of private and public scientific institutions involved in research on environmental issues and offering policy advice to the public sector, EOs, and business interests. There are at least 80 independent research institutes for environmental issues (Jänicke and Weidner, 1997). It has become standard practice for public authorities to request complementary reports from independent research institutes on specific policy issues. Most economic research institutes now have environmental departments. While the universities in the past were often considered an unimportant or negative factor for environmental policy, today nearly all of them have special curricula for environmental protection (Jänicke and Weidner, 1997).

The SRU suggests relying more heavily on scientific expertise in areas of persistent environmental problems such as air pollution from diffuse sources. Since persistent environmental problems are often highly complex and are partly characterized by low visibility, scientific analyses can contribute to a better understanding and to an increase in awareness of such problems (SRU, 2002). Additionally, scientific analyses and recommendations can help to enforce stricter environmental policy, even against possible resistance from involved actors.

3.7 Media

The review of institutional change in the environmental arena, presented in section 2, has highlighted the important role played by the media in raising environmental awareness and mobilizing public support for environmental policy. A 'green' national daily newspaper (*Die Tageszeitung*) was founded in 1979 and now sells approximately 60 000 copies (SRU, 2002). By 1989 environmental magazines had a total circulation of around 4 million copies. The mass media also generally display a positive attitude towards environmental concerns (SRU, 2002).

3.8 Centralization vs. Decentralization Trends

Our earlier expositions indicate that, in general, a centralization of environmental policy competencies at the national and European level can be observed (see Figure 7.2). The competencies of the federal government were expanded with the 1972 amendment to the German Constitution, granting it concurrent legislative power in several policy areas, mostly related to industrial pollution. Due to difficulties in adopting a cross-media approach, EOs have been demanding that the federal government should

Level \ Field	Industry pollution	Ecosystem protection	Agriculture	Forests	Water	Implementation & Enforcement
International	• Kyoto Protocol • EU Directives	• International conventions • EU Directives	• POP Convention • Agenda 2000	• United Nations Statement on Forest Principles • UNFF	• Water Framework Directive • IMO	
National	• Federal Acts and Ordinances setting standards • VAs	• Framework legislation (Federal Nature Conservation Act)	• GAK • Federal Acts	• National Forest Programme	• Framework legislation • Federal Water Act	• Responsibilities in areas of nuclear energy, chemicals, highway planning
Länder	• Allocate construction and operation licences	• Detailed legislation • Designation of protected areas for Natura 2000	• GAK	• Manage state-owned forests • Influence on local forest administration	• Detailed legislation • Licensing of water companies	• State agencies implement and enforce federal and state laws
Local	• Monitoring environmental impact of energy production • Noise pollution measures	• Rehabilitation of contaminated areas • Building and countryside planning			• Sewage services • Water supplies	• Implement tasks under self-government principle/delegated to them by national/state governments

Figure 7.2 Centralization/decentralization trends in German environmental politics

be vested with concurrent legislative rights for the entire field of environmental protection (Koch, 2004). Up to now, however, further centralization has not taken place as the states have retained their authorities over water management, nature conservation, landscape preservation and regional planning.

With regard to implementation and enforcement of environmental laws, a decentralization trend can be observed. Specifically, a decision by the Federal Administrative Court in 1994 has provided the local level with more autonomy in their choice of implementation instruments (Weidner, 1995).

As explained earlier, environmental policies are also more and more influenced by international and European decisions. In the integration process of the EU, decisions on, for example, agri-environmental issues have increasingly been transferred from the member states to the level of the EU (Agenda 2000). The same can be said for the area of water management (EU Water Framework Directive), ecosystem protection (EU Habitats and Birds Directives), and industrial pollution (IPPC Directive). At the international level, Germany ratified several contracts (for example, the Kyoto Protocol) and is a member of various committees and forums (UN Forum on Forests).

4. POLICY TOOLS

There is no single code of environmental law (*Umweltgesetzbuch*) in Germany (Kirkpatrick et al., 2001). Instead, a large number of environmental regulations exist at the national, state and local level, turning Germany into one of the world's most complex legal systems for environmental protection. Table 7.3 lists the main areas of environmental policy and corresponding major regulations. The Environmental Programme is built on three principles intended to act as guidelines for environmental policy: (i) the precautionary principle, (ii) the cooperation principle, and (iii) the polluter-pays principle (Jänicke and Weidner, 1997). The precautionary principle is seen as the dominant one (Weidner, 1995, p. 6).

4.1 Command-and-control as the Dominant Approach

The traditional command-and-control approach, based on the principle of 'best available technology' (BAT), is by far the dominating approach applied in German environmental policy. One possible explanation is that recruitment of staff for the Ministry of Environment (and even more so, before, for the Ministry of the Interior) has focused predominantly on

Table 7.3 Major areas of environmental policy and corresponding legislation

Environmental policy area	Major legislation (year of implementation)
1) Pollution Control	
• Air pollution	Leaded Petrol Act (1971), Federal Immission Control Act (1974), Technical Instructions on Air Quality Control (*TA Luft*, 1974), Ordinance on Large Combustion Plants (1983), Programme for reducing CO_2 emissions (1990)
• Water pollution+	Federal Emission Control Act (1974), Waste Water Charges Act (1976), Federal Water Act (*Wasserhaushaltsgesetz* 1957, last amended 2001), German Fertilizer Act (1977), Fertilization Ordinance (1996), Plant Protection Act (Pesticide regulation, 1986) plus 3 related Ordinances, High Seas Dumping Act (1998), Waste Water Ordinance (1999)
• Soil pollution/Waste reduction	Waste Disposal Act (1972), DDT Act (1972), Chemicals Act (1980), Waste Avoidance and Management Act (1986, amended 1994), Packaging Ordinance (1998), Waste Transhipment Act (1994), Closed Substance Cycle and Waste Management Act (*Kreislaufwirtschaftsgesetz*, 1994), Federal Soil Protection Act (1998), Federal Ordinance on Soil Conservation and the Rehabilitation of Contaminated Sites (1999), Ordinance on Sewage Sludge (1992), Waste Storage Ordinance (2001)
• Noise pollution	Aircraft Noise Abatement Act (1971)
2) Ecosystem Protection	Plant Protection Act (1986), Federal Nature Conservation Act (1976, last amended 2002), Federal Species Protection Ordinance (1989)
3) Natural Resource Management	Federal Forests Act (1975), National Forest Programme (2003)
4) General	Energy Conservation Act (1976), Law to Combat Crimes against the Environment (1980, last amended 1994), Electricity Feed-In Act (1990), Environmental Statistics Act (1994), Environmental Impact Assessment Act (1990), Environmental Liability Act (1990), Environmental Information Act (1994), Environmental Audit Act (1995), Cornerstones for an ecological restoration and development in the 'new Länder' (1991), Renewable Energy Sources

Table 7.3 (continued)

Environmental policy area	Major legislation (year of implementation)
	Act (2000), National Organic Farming Programme (2001), National Sustainability Strategy (2001), Ordinance on Energy Saving (2001)

Note: + The division of policies between water and soil pollution is sometimes arbitrary since several laws have implications for both (e.g., the German Fertilizer Act and the Fertilization Ordinance).

lawyers and natural scientists, who tend to feel more comfortable with traditional regulatory tools, with environmental economists still being a 'rare species' in public administration (Wurzel et al., 2003). Another is that its relatively strong economic performance has allowed Germany to get away with applying cost-ineffective approaches in the past (Heuser, n.d.). Finally, traditional regulation is more easily understood and visible to the public compared to some 'new economic policy instruments' (NEPIs) (Wurzel et al., 2003).

According to Wurzel et al. (2003), German environmental regulation contains about 800 environmental laws, 2800 ordinances, and between 4700 and 35 000 technical instructions. The command-and-control approach consists mainly of standard-setting and licensing. Standards are often combined with highly technical prescriptions, and licensing of large emitting sources is made conditional on their compliance with these prescriptions. Emission standards are set for certain target groups (for example, in the Ordinance on Large Combustion Plants). In some cases, specific activities are prohibited, or the use of specific substances is restricted (for example, the use of sewage sludge in agriculture), often in combination with a step-by-step procedure for their gradual reduction or phase-out (Jänicke and Weidner, 1997). The command-and-control approach is frequently combined with subsidies, and in some cases, with charges. For example, the Federal Water Act contains provisions for compensatory payments to farmers if management restrictions within Water Protection Areas limit the 'proper use of agricultural land' (Weingarten, 1997).

The command-and-control approach is often time-consuming and involves significant administrative costs. In response to industry complaints, streamlining legislation was passed to speed up procedures for planning and industrial siting. Faced with economic problems and high unemployment the government has increasingly become more concerned about the costs of environmental policy. Also, difficulties in reaching environmental objectives with the predominant command-and-control approach became apparent.

Opposition from industry and criticism by experts that the traditional approach was inefficient and inflexible has increased. In the mid-1990s the German government began a systematic review of the command-and-control approach. As a consequence, emphasis on alternative approaches such as information provision, negotiation, and to a lesser degree, market-based instruments based on the polluter-pays principle, has increased over time. International actors such as the OECD, the EU, and the World Bank have stressed the need for Germany to increase its adoption of NEPIs (see section 4.4).

4.2 Consensus, Consultation and Liability

The German policy style in environmental regulation has been described as moderately active with heavy reliance on consensus-building and consultation, particularly of employers and trade unions (Dyson, 1982, 1992) and to some degree of EOs.

Mediation as an alternative form of dispute regulation has also gained importance. Finally, the Environmental Liability Act of 1990 is considered as an important step towards generating alternative policy approaches. It stipulates the obligation to hold environmental liability insurance, and the principle that fault or negligence are not considered in liability determination. Moreover, it partially reduces the victim's burden of proof, and extends liability to cover damages by normal, properly functioning equipment and operations.

4.3 An Environmental Media-centred Approach

Germany has not up to now implemented an integrated pollution control approach cutting across different environmental media (such as air, water and soil) (Müller, 2002). Such an approach is made difficult by the prevailing asymmetry in environmental policy competences between the federal government and the states (Wurzel et al., 2003) and by the distribution of environmental policy responsibilities between several federal ministries (Kirkpatrick et al., 2001). While the Federal Environmental Agency has conducted a major internal reorganization in the 1990s with the objective to address more successfully cross-sectoral policy issues, the Environment Ministry has resisted a similar change. Currently, the only exception is the Ministry's climate change division, which is cross-sectoral and has evolved into the main administrative unit for the implementation of NEPIs (Wurzel et al., 2003). However, some cross-media approaches have gained importance in the 1990s, including environmental liability, environmental audits and environmental impact assessment (OECD, 2001).

4.4 Subsidies and Payments for Environmental Services

Germany also has a complex system of direct and indirect subsidies to promote the adoption of environmentally-friendly technologies in the private sector, and subsidy payments have increased continuously (Jänicke and Weidner, 1997). Environmental subsidies range from research funding (for example, for research on fuel cells) to fiscal incentives for less polluting products (for example, for low-sulphur gasoline), and direct subsidies to companies and private households (for example, for renewable energy use). The EU has, however, significantly constrained the use of subsidies due to concerns about misuse for protectionist purposes (Wurzel et al., 2003).

Agri-environmental programmes are an important area of subsidies (or perhaps more correctly 'payments for environmental services'). In 1996, farmers had voluntarily adopted agri-environmental protection programmes on a total of 5 million ha or 29 per cent of the total utilized agricultural area in Germany, in return for total payments of approximately EUR 421 million.[16] Until 2000, the area managed under agri-environmental programmes had declined to 4.2 million ha, or 24.5 per cent of total utilized agricultural area. Payments, however, increased to EUR 531 million (BMVEL, 2003a). The explanation for this development is a decrease in payments for measures that vary only slightly from good professional practice standards (BMVEL, 2003a), and thus provide only a minor contribution to the improvement of environmental conditions,[17] and therewith a decline in subsidized area[18] (Schöne, n.d.). At the same time, EU financial aid to ambitious agri-environmental programmes increased (BMVEL, 2003a). The funds for agri-environmental programmes are provided jointly by the EC commission, the federal government, and state governments (Weingarten, 1997).

Generally one can say that, in the course of a turnaround in agricultural policy towards more sustainability (*Agrarwende*), the federal government adopted several measures to reduce environmentally harmful subsidies and tax concessions and to promote environmentally sound agricultural practices through fiscal incentives (that is payments for environmental services). These include cutback and redistribution of direct payments into measures for rural development including agri-environmental measures (*modulation*), promotion of ecological cultivation and production (*oekologischer Landbau*), or, from 2005 on, decoupling of direct payments from production[19] (UBA, 2003).

4.5 Use of New Economic Policy Instruments in Germany

NEPIs include market-based instruments (for example, eco-taxes, tradable permits), voluntary agreements and informational devices (for example, eco-labels and eco-audits).[20]

Market-based instruments

Early initiatives of economic policy instruments based on the polluter-pays principle were mainly limited to the areas of wastewater (effluent charges), gasoline (tax differentiation between leaded and unleaded fuel), and waste management. Some of their potential flexibility was, however, undermined by complementary command-and-control regulation (see, for example, Andersen, 1994). Moreover, they were often moderate in scope and included many exemptions (Jordan et al., 2002). A moderate water extraction charge (*Wasserpfennig*) was implemented in the state of Baden-Würtemberg in the late 1980s and adopted in several other states in the 1990s (Wurzel et al., 2003).[21] Further individual taxes have been implemented over time, but an overall strategy is lacking.

The long delay in establishing a systematic eco-tax can be partly explained by concerns about potential competitive disadvantages and a general public aversion to any type of tax (Wurzel et al., 2003). While ecological tax reform has been debated for a long time and the country in the 1980s lobbied hard for the EU-wide introduction of a CO_2 or energy tax, actual reform was only implemented when the election of a red-green government opened a new 'window of opportunity', with the Green Party and the left wing of the Social-Democratic Party strongly supporting such reform (Jordan et al., 2002). The ecological tax reform can be seen as the most important initiative towards the implementation of market-based policy instruments in Germany until today. The first reform phase was introduced in 1999, but had to be delayed by several months when the EU Commission objected to the fiscal incentives for renewable energy sources and a number of exemptions (Wurzel et al., 2003).

Specifically, the reform consists of an initial tax increase on mineral oil, gas and electricity, and four further annual increases in the taxes on electricity and fuels for transport. Tax revenues are earmarked to reduce non-wage labour costs, that is, social security and pension contributions, based on the idea of a double dividend.[22] Preferential treatment is given to cogeneration of electricity and heat at high-efficiency level, local and rail public transport, and natural gas as motor fuel. Moreover, renewable energy sources are subsidized. Several reform aspects are subject to criticism. First, industry and agriculture are subject to only 20 per cent of the standard tax rate (Kirkpatrick et al., 2001). In addition, companies can apply for refunds if their energy burden exceeds by the factor of 1.2 the reduction in social security contributions (Wurzel et al., 2003). As a consequence, the ecological impact of tax reform has been criticized as being significantly reduced and its distributional consequences being potentially severe.[23] Following a parliamentary initiative by the opposition parties demanding abolition of the eco-tax, measures were adopted to compensate socially disadvantaged and politically influential groups.[24] Second, responding to SPD fears of losing important constituency support in the coal-rich Ruhr area, taxes on coal were not increased despite its being the fuel with the highest CO_2 content. In fact, domestic coal production remains subsidized (Kirkpatrick et al., 2001).

Another important initiative is a motorway toll for trucks which was finally introduced in January 2005.[25] In waste management, a mixture of NEPI and command and control has been implemented. The 1991 Packaging Ordinance legally obliges industry and suppliers to reclaim and recycle nearly all packaging in accordance with phased-in quotas (Jänicke and Weidner, 1997). This led to the implementation of Germany's so-called 'dual system' (*Duales System*). Under this system, products are labelled with a 'green dot' (*Grüner Punkt*), in combination with a licensing fee intended to cover the costs of waste collection and recycling, under the coordination of a private enterprise. There are, however, many inefficiencies in the current system. A prominent example is the requirement under the Packaging Ordinance that packaging material be separated from other waste of the same material in the collection and sorting stages (Kirkpatrick et al., 2001).[26]

The water sector (that is supply of drinking water and sewage) is also under organizational change. This change was stimulated by international and domestic developments. At the beginning of the 1990s, Germany's water sector was criticized for not being internationally competitive and for its high prices (Kluge and Lux, 2001). The predominance of sophisticated, high-cost technology has caused a lack of funds for new investments at the municipality level and the pressure for more cost-effective management. As a consequence, municipalities are developing alternative organizational forms of water supply and wastewater disposal (BMU/UBA, 2001) (see Table 7.4). These include models of cooperation between municipalities and private firms, and forms of complete privatization, although the latter is rare and private companies must adhere to rather strict regulations in order to obtain their permit from water authorities (BMU/UBA, 2001). While the potential of privatization for higher international competitiveness and increased cost-efficiency is recognized, the process is accompanied by a debate on potential negative impacts of privatization on the environment and public health. Both advocates and opponents speak out for the need for a complementary regulatory framework and for public monitoring and enforcement of legal standards (BMU/UBA, 2001).

Although the idea of tradable emission permits has been discussed by environmental economists since the 1970s, Germany has still not attempted its implementation on a national level. Three half-hearted attempts in the 1990s to set up pilot schemes were abandoned due to industry opposition

Table 7.4 Organizational forms of water supply and wastewater disposal systems

Organizational form	Description
Municipal department	Operated by the municipality within the scope of the regular municipal administration.
Municipal utility	Operated by the municipality in a separate capacity with independent bookkeeping.
Municipal company	Private entity company in the hands of the municipality.
Joint venture	Municipal utility with the involvement of a private firm.
Operator model (BOO, BOOT, BOT, etc.)	Delegation of the plant operations to a private firm, whereas the responsibility for the fulfillment of tasks remains with the municipality.
Management and service contract	The plant property belongs to the municipality, but the operations and any further management tasks are delegated to a private firm.

Source: BMU/UBA (2001).

(Jordan et al., 2002). As stated earlier, a working group on the issue was set up in 2000. This is motivated by the realization that an EU-wide tradable permit scheme is forthcoming and the wish to take an active part in its design (Jordan et al., 2002).[27] The chemical industry, however, walked out of the working group in 2002. Some individual states within Germany have set up regional pilot schemes. In the past, there has been some resistance by EOs and the public to the idea of establishing 'rights to pollute', but recently these attitudes appear to be changing (Wurzel et al., 2003). The industry is divided on the issue, with energy-intensive and chemical industries opposing tradable permits, and other industries such as the banking sector favouring it. There is also a lot of disagreement on the best design of such a scheme, particularly with respect to the initial permit allocation, the imposition of target limits, and whether participation should be voluntary or compulsory (Wurzel et al., 2003). Some related experience that is sometimes cited is the compensation scheme implemented under the Technical Instructions for Air Pollution Control (*TA Luft*), where companies are allowed to exceed emission limits if they are compensated by overcompliance in new plants. However, this is not truly a 'market-based instrument' (Zittel, 1996).

Voluntary agreements

Voluntary agreements (VAs) between industry and public authorities or environmental organizations had already become part of the environmental paradigm early on, but have increased significantly since the 1990s. Germany is one of the countries with the highest number of VAs in the EU and the OECD, with an estimated total of 130 VAs by 2001 (Kirkpatrick et al., 2001; Wurzel et al., 2003). It also has the widest range of VAs within the EU (Wurzel et al., 2003). An example is the German car industry's voluntary agreement to take back outdated models. Similarly, the Federation of German Industry (BDI) and several umbrella organizations of specific industrial sectors have adopted VAs for the reduction of greenhouse gas emissions in 1995, 1996 and 2000. The latter are seen as a way for industry – which prefers VAs over regulation – to show that VAs can work to address complex environmental issues (Jordan et al., 2002). In the newly developed National Forest Programme (see also section 4.6), the different stakeholders such as *Länder* authorities, forest owners, forest industry and environmental organizations among others also entered into a kind of voluntary agreement. Problem areas have been defined jointly and now stakeholders begin to implement measures that protect the forest and forest biodiversity. Although legal regulation is still an instrument in the National Forest Programme, emphasis is on new policy instruments like voluntary agreements (BMVEL, 2003b).

Wurzel et al. (2003, p. 129) found that VAs have ranged from 'ad hoc informal self-declaratory statements by industry to well publicized negotiated agreements between industry and the government'. As a consequence, a standard definition of VAs is difficult. Broadly speaking, VAs include all agreements between entities with differing interests but common goals. Such entities usually comprise companies or umbrella organizations and the state, but also citizens' groups and environmental organizations (Umweltakademie, 1999). Zerle (2004) differentiates between four types of industry commitments/environmental agreements: unilateral industry declarations (not formally agreed upon by the state); bilateral agreements between industry and state that are legally non-binding; contractual agreements between state and companies (legally binding); and state-granted exemptions from regulations if industry proves that it can reach environmental goals with alternative measures (for example, in the area of waste management, Germany's dual system). Zerle argues that more ambitious environmental protection goals can only be achieved with agreements that are legally binding and backed by regulatory measures. Jänicke and Weidner (1997), however, criticize the fact that voluntary agreements in Germany are legally non-binding and do not lead to sanctions in case of non-compliance. VAs also often lack a clear definition of the obligations of individual members within sectors or organizations and of the monitoring mechanism to be applied (Jänicke and Weidner, 1997). Zerle (2004) points to the problem of free riding if VAs are not backed by monitoring and sanctioning mechanisms. Consequently, EOs have been demanding greater transparency, improvements in monitoring, and the introduction of a sanctioning mechanism. Critics have also raised concern about the potential of VAs to lead to regulatory capture and collusion between government and industry (Wurzel et al., 2003).

Zerle (2004) doubts that VAs alone are an efficient instrument in environmental policy. Many VAs are ecologically ineffective because the goals set out in the agreements do not exceed the 'business-as-usual' level firms would reach anyway. VAs can be economically inefficient due to free riding problems and unequal burden-sharing by individual firms within specific sectors (environmental protection measures are not performed cost-efficiently).

Informational devices

Germany was the first country in the world to introduce a national eco-label – the so-called *Blue Angel* – in 1978 (Wurzel, 2002). This so-called Blue Angel programme served as a model for eco-labelling schemes elsewhere, and remained the world's most widely used scheme until the late 1990s (Wurzel et al., 2003). It is a voluntary third-party scheme organized under private law. The scheme is administered by the German Institute for Quality Assurance and Labelling (RAL), which finances its operation through evaluation and licence fees. A commission consisting of a wide range of stakeholders – among which EOs have featured prominently – decide on products and services to be awarded the label (Wurzel et al., 2003). Eco-labels provide effective incentives to producers only if consumers (i) recognize the label, (ii) trust the label, and (iii) are willing to base their purchasing decisions on the label (that is, in markets with a high degree of environmental awareness and where price premia are not too high). In this regard, the label has been particularly successful for products that avoid waste (for example, recycled paper products) or save energy (for example, light bulbs, laundry machines). Recent trends towards multinational, supranational, and company eco-labelling schemes as well as additional schemes at the national level (for example in the area of food safety) are increasing the complexity of information provided to consumers and carry the risk of leading to confusion and sometimes loss of trust among consumers. Nevertheless, currently the Blue Angel scheme is still widely known and trusted (Wurzel et al., 2003). It should also be noted, however, that eco-labelling carries the potential for free-riding behaviour on the part of consumers (Kirchhoff, 2000).

German companies also make up almost two thirds of applications to the EU's environmental management and eco-audit system (EMAS) even though the government had originally opposed its adoption (Wurzel et al., 2003).

4.6 Natural Resource Management and Nature Conservation

The issue of total resource use – for example, measured as tons of aggregate material usage per unit of GDP – has dominated the debate on natural resource management in Germany (Kirkpatrick et al., 2001). Germany was a pioneer in forest management, operating on the basis of nearly equated tree-felling and regeneration rates since the nineteenth century. Forty-six per cent of the country's forests are privately owned. Of the remaining 54 per cent, 34 per cent are owned by the *Länder*, and 20 per cent by local communities. *Länder* forests are centrally managed by each individual state. The *Länder* also have some influence on local forest administration (Kirkpatrick et al., 2001).

A national forest programme (NFP), involving a strategy for biodiversity maintenance in forests, has been jointly developed by the federal government, the *Länder*, and other stakeholders between 1999 and 2003. Fields of action were defined[28] and recommendation measures developed. The recommendation measures are supposed to be implemented by the participating actors (that is, the Federal Ministry of Agriculture, *Länder* ministries, forest owners, environmental organizations, and so on) with the instruments available to them; for example at the national level, NFP recommendations will be considered in the amendment of the Federal Forest Act. It was agreed that cooperative instruments (for example VAs, participative development of forest programmes) should, whenever possible, take priority over command-and-control and process-oriented measures (*ordnungsrechtliche und prozessorientierte Steuerungsinstrumente*) such as laws and ordinances, subsidies, taxes and transfer payments. However, there is still a lack of concrete time targets, and responsible actors or institutions have only been designated in a few policy areas. During the next years, further development and implementation of the National Forest Programme will be critically monitored by all actors through progress reports and round table discussions (BMVEL, 2003b).

There are 13 national parks (of which seven are located in the new *Länder*) and 14 UNESCO biosphere reserves (OECD, 2001). About 27 per cent (OECD, 2001, p. 92) of the total land area is under some degree of protection. However, most protected areas are very small and the degree of protection is low. No national biodiversity strategy exists, nor has any nature conservation plan comprising a detailed agenda been published or adopted at the federal or state level (OECD, 2001). As Kirkpatrick et al. (2001, p. 24) notes, the polluter-pays principle does not seem to be applied in the area of biodiversity protection. Rather, current agricultural practices are seen as the status quo, with improvements to be paid for through subsidies.

With the amendment of the Federal Nature Conservation Act in 2002, the federal government directed more attention to biodiversity and nature conservation. Nature conservation has been included in good practice regulations for agriculture, forestry and fishery,[29] an expansion of agri-environmental programmes has been passed, and designation of a higher number and a connection of nature conservation areas (biotope network) has been promoted. Additionally, acknowledged environmental organizations were granted a group right of appeal at the national level (BMU, 2002). As the Council of Environmental Advisors (SRU) (2002) notes, however, the success of the new Nature Conservation Act depends upon the willingness and capacity of the *Länder* to implement the federal guidelines and recommendations.

4.7 Monitoring and Enforcement

Monitoring and enforcement is the responsibility of federal and *Länder* authorities. The different authorities run their own, mostly sector-specific monitoring programmes. This sectoral approach to environmental monitoring has been criticized since the 1970s,[30] and development and implementation of a cross-sectoral monitoring programme has been demanded (Schröder et al., 2001). Currently, BMU and UBA, together with academic research institutes, work on both vertical and horizontal harmonization and integration of monitoring activities, nationally and internationally (Schröder et al., 2001). The responsibility of data collection is delegated to public authorities, research institutes and to private firms themselves, through firm internal self-monitoring systems (BMU/UBA, 2001). If monitoring shows that firms do not comply with standards, the firm faces fines and/or licence withdrawal (BMU/UBA, 2001).

A special section in the German Criminal Code regulating crimes against the environment was established with the 1980 Law to Combat Environmental Crimes (*Gesetz zur Bekämpfung der Umweltkriminalität*), last amended in 1994. Criminal law covers the areas of water, soil and air protection, nature conservation, waste and hazardous material management, radiation protection, and hazards from the release of poison. The 1980 law pooled and harmonized environmental by-laws, which were until then part of various administrative laws (for example, the Federal Soil Protection Act). The incorporation of environmental crimes into the

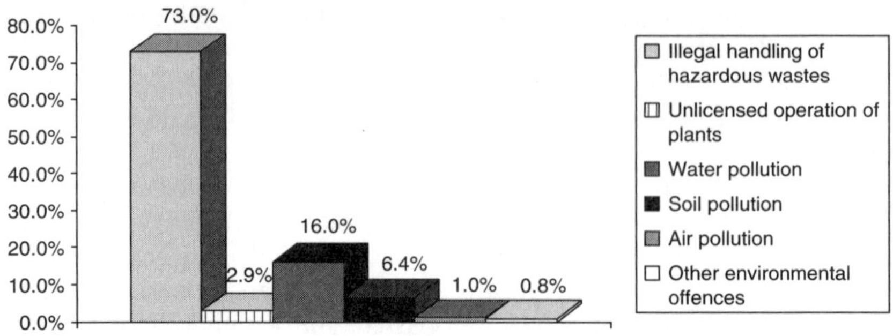

Source: Federal Environment Agency (2000)

Figure 7.3 Types of environmental crimes in 1999

Criminal Code is to create or rather increase and stabilize environmental awareness and norms on the part of the public and the courts (Kloepfer and Vierhaus, 2002). According to the Federal Environmental Agency (2000), the number of environmental crimes has decreased by 7 per cent between 1998 and 1999, from approximately 46 700 to 43 382. The percentage of cleared up cases increased from 57 per cent in 1998 to 59 per cent in 1999 (Federal Environmental Agency, 2000). (See also Figure 7.3 for figures on types of environmental crimes.) Kloepfer and Vierhaus (2002) criticize though, that, in practice, the execution of environmental criminal law is deficient. They note that the clear-up rate sank from 74 per cent in 1989 to 59 per cent in 1999, and that the number of unknown cases is probably very high since environmental crimes often lack visibility. While a relatively high number of bagatelle crimes committed by small trade and private households are being prosecuted, the number of prosecuted, severe crimes by commerce and industry is extremely low. Here, courts and prosecutors face considerable difficulties in the clear-up process and liability assignment due to lack of transparency of internal company operations. Moreover, penalty probability (only approximately 10 per cent of all suspects are being convicted) and penalty level in environmental criminal law are relatively low compared to other areas. In addition, it should be noted that environmental criminal law can only help to prevent further degradation of the environment. Therefore, according to Kloepfer and Vierhaus (2002), the main (legal) policy instrument to improve environmental conditions should be administrative law.

As mentioned before, in the case of voluntary agreements, monitoring and enforcement is more difficult, because VAs are legally non-binding, and often there is no clear specification of obligations and targets for participants. Monitoring in the National Forest Programme happens through progress reports written by stakeholders and further round table discussions. There exist no sanctioning mechanisms in the event that an actor does not implement NFP recommendations. It is hoped that pressure from other stakeholders will be incentive enough to adhere to the programme ideas.

5. EVALUATION

We now proceed to evaluate Germany's achievements and remaining challenges in terms of environmental performance.

5.1 Achievements

There is no doubt that remarkable progress has been made since the beginnings of modern environmental policy in the 1970s, particularly in terms of air and water quality improvements as well as reduction in municipal waste generation (contrary to many other industrialized countries) (Jänicke and Weidner, 1997). The environmentally damaging practices of incineration of waste on high seas and discharge of industrial wastes into oceans were abandoned in 1989. The 1993 OECD Report on Environmental Performance concluded that Germany had shown remarkable achievements in de-coupling economic growth from emissions of several major pollutants, thereby reconciling economic and environmental objectives (OECD, 1993, p. 205). The 2001 OECD Report again confirms this assessment for the period of the 1990s. It states that progress has been particularly impressive in terms of emissions to air (for example, 76 per cent reduction in SO_x emissions compared to 1990, 34 per cent for NO_x, 47 per cent for NMVOCs,[31] 52 per cent for CO), water pollution (mainly for organic pollution, to a lesser degree for nitrates, heavy metals, hazardous substances), and resource use (for example, water and energy), and that Germany has met most of its national environmental objectives and international commitments (OECD, 2001). Many rivers are now Quality Class II (suitable for human consumption) and ecological functions have been restored (Kirkpatrick et al., 2001). Several formerly endangered species have now recovered (Kirkpatrick et al., 2001).

In international comparison, the 2002 Pilot Environmental Performance Index ranks Germany as ninth among 28 (mostly developed) countries rated in terms of overall air quality and improvement in air quality, and twelfth in current air quality (World Economic Forum, 2002). The country's intensity of SO_x and NO_x emissions lies 65 per cent and 50 per cent below the OECD averages, respectively (OECD, 2001). Germany also ranks fifth among 20 (mostly European) countries in terms of current land protection status, fourth in improvement of land protection status, and second in terms of protected areas as percentage of total area (World Economic Forum, 2002).[32] The OECD states that 'having reduced CO_2 emissions by 15.5 per cent in 1999 compared with 1990 levels, Germany is one of the few countries likely to achieve the emissions goals set out in the Framework Convention on Climate Change and its Kyoto Protocol (OECD, 2001, p. 4).

Tables 7.5 to 7.8 show the development for specific pollutants and other dimensions of environmental protection over time since German reunification in 1990. Comparison of statistics before and after 1990 is obviously problematic. It should be noted that some of the achievements in environmental quality since 1990 have been the result of the restructuring of the new *Länder* (including economic contraction and changes in energy supply[33]). For example, CO_2 emissions have decreased rapidly between 1990 and 1995, but largely due to de-industrialization and ecological modernization in Eastern Germany (Kirkpatrick et al., 2001). While these are important advances, they need to be seen as a short-run window of opportunity for improvements at relatively low marginal cost, due to the desolate environmental situation in the former GDR. Therefore, the rate of improvement of the 1990s will most likely not be sustained in the future.

The 2001 OECD Report judges enforcement and compliance as generally effective in Germany, due to good monitoring and institutional capacities. It also recognizes the high amount of VAs, Germany's position as a leading exporter of environmental technology, goods and services, as well as the country's leading role in international environmental cooperation.

The ecological tax reform and the monitoring of quantitative environmental targets through the Environment Barometer – which forms part of the government's annual economic report – are seen as important advances, although room for improvement exists in both (OECD, 2001). Also, the recent climate protection programme is considered by the OECD to be 'a positive example of an integrated, cross-sectoral approach' (OECD, 2001, p. 2). The recent Renewable Energy Act, which provides for financial support to renewable energy sources, is another positive development. However, the ecological tax reform also illustrates that important challenges remain. As stated earlier, the ecological impacts of this initiative are estimated to be low, while there is reason for concern about negative distributional impacts. Also, current tax rates are likely to be inefficient because they are not based on source-specific CO_2 emissions (Kirkpatrick et al., 2001). Similarly, the taxation of electricity as an end product reduces incentives for CO_2-reducing changes in fuel composition.

Table 7.5 Air pollutant emissions in Germany, 1990–2001

Type	1990	1994	1996	1998	1999	2000*	2001*
Carbon dioxide (CO_2) (in Mt)	1014	904	921	881	855	858	871
Nitrogen oxide (NO_X) (in kt)	2729	2055	1897	1675	1619	1584	1592
Sulphur dioxide (SO_2) (in kt)	5321	2472	1340	835	738	638	650
Carbon monoxide (CO) (in kt)	11213	7064	6109	5424	5143	4868	4797
Nitrous oxide (N_2O) (in kt)	284	250	259	201	190	191	194
Ammonia (NH_3) (in kt)	736	595	608	604	604	596	607
Particulates (in kt)	1858	364	269	254	247	242	247
VOCs without methane (in kt)	3221	2159	1893	1735	1664	1605	1606
CFCs, halon (in kt)	43	8	8	8	8	n/a	n/a
Methane (CH_4) (in kt)	4813	3483	3139	2901	2825	2597	2484

Note: * preliminary numbers.

Source: Based on data from UBA Environmental Data (http://www.env-it.de/umweltdaten/jsp/dispatcher?event=WELCOME).

Table 7.6 Waste generation (in 1000 tons)

Year	1996	1997	1998	1999[1]	2000[2]
Municipal waste	44390	45593	44825	44245	45641
Industrial waste	43012	48088	48650	45952	44889
Hazardous waste	18281	18860	19473	17020	15542
Total	105683	112541	112948	107217	106072

Note: [1] preliminary numbers, [2] estimates.

Source: Based on data from UBA Environmental Data.

Table 7.7 Primary energy consumption according to energy sectors, 1990–2001 (in Peta Joule)

Energy sector	1990	1992	1994	1996	1998	2000*	2001*
Transport	2573	2661	2702	2625	2691	2744	2686
Households	2380	2435	2556	2890	2782	2599	2846
Trade, Services	1553	1468	1389	1748	1584	1483	1533
Industry	2978	2562	2462	2424	2397	2417	2391
Losses/wastages	4469	4276	4109	4106	4021	4015	4057
Total	13953	13402	13218	13793	13475	13258	13513

Note: * preliminary numbers.

Source: Based on data from UBA Environmental Data.

5.2 Problem Areas and Remaining Challenges

Despite the positive developments outlined above, important environmental problems and challenges persist (see Table 7.9 for a summary of specific OECD recommendations for environmental policy reform in Germany).

Air pollution

The OECD (2001) identifies transport-related pollution as a major problem area. Traffic-related emissions strongly increased in the 1990s, as efficiency gains in fuel use have been offset by rising transport volumes (Kirkpatrick et al., 2001). The catching up process in private car ownership following unification is one, but not the only reason behind this trend. There is also still no general speed limit for motorways in Germany. While emissions of Volatile Organic Compounds (VOCs) and NO_x have fallen during the 1980s and 1990s, they are expected to increase again, and are still contributing to

Table 7.8 Primary energy consumption according to energy source, 1990–2001 (in Peta Joule)

Energy source	1990	1992	1994	1996	1998	2000*	2002*
Mineral coal	2306	2196	2139	2090	2059	2008	1885
Lignite	3201	2176	1861	1688	1514	1547	1659
Mineral oils	5238	5628	5693	5808	5775	5500	5369
Natural gas	2316	2408	2592	3161	3048	3025	3143
Hydropower, wind power	59	62	64	73	80	106	132
Nuclear energy	1665	1732	1650	1764	1764	1849	1800
Other sources	126	135	176	181	283	310	328
External trade balance – electricity	3	–21	9	–19	–2	9	3
Total	14914	14316	14184	14746	14521	14354	14319

Note: * preliminary numbers.

Source: Based on data from UBA Environmental Data.

forest damage and summer smog (Kirkpatrick et al., 2001). Another major reason for air pollution (and health problems) is the emission of fine particles from diesel engines. The SRU therefore recommends, among other things, promoting the employment of particle filters in such engines through fiscal incentives (SRU, 2002). Air traffic and power stations continue to be major sources of air pollution. Moreover, despite lower pollution levels, forest damage has not been reduced significantly (Kirkpatrick et al., 2001). Addressing this problem requires emission reductions in a wide range of pollutants.

Moreover, improvement is required to meet challenging national and international commitments in the area of CO_2 and greenhouse gas (GHG) emissions, with current intensity of CO_2 emissions close to the OECD average (OECD, 2001). Estimates of the future development of CO_2 emissions, based on policies implemented by 1996, indicate that Germany is likely to fall far short of its 2005 target[34] (Kirkpatrick et al., 2001). Policies implemented after 1996 are not likely to change this prediction significantly. In particular, the ecological tax reform is estimated to reduce CO_2 emissions by at most 2 per cent (ZEW, 1999; RWI, 1999). The phase-out of nuclear energy will make reductions in CO_2 emissions more difficult (Kirkpatrick et al., 2001). The SRU, in contrast, believes that Germany can reach its 2005 CO_2 emission target (and even its target to reduce CO_2 emissions by 40 per cent by 2020) if it improves the weak points of the new climate protection programme (for example stricter implementation of and

Table 7.9 OECD recommendations for environmental policy reform in Germany

Policy area	Recommendation
Implementing environmental policies	Decouple growth from emissions/resource use; attention to new/unsolved challenges; development of Environmental Code; more economic instruments; more efficient/transparent services at municipal level; more effective VAs; more cost-effectiveness through more economic analyses.
Air	Reduce harmful subsidies in energy and transport sector; further limit air pollutant emissions from motor vehicle and solvent use; more rational transport pricing and taxation to further internalize costs; develop mechanisms for evaluation of cost-effectiveness of control policy options; further measures to reduce energy consumption in residential sector.
Water	Develop measures to decrease diffuse pollution of water; reduce point source pollution through investments in treatment facilities and increase in water effluent charges; address diffuse pollution by heavy metals; enhance flood prevention through partnership approaches, improve land use planning and nature conservation; pursue further efforts for water quality monitoring; work towards implementation of water resource management (river basin approach).
Waste	Improve cost-effectiveness of waste management policies and material recycling schemes: more competition in household waste management; analyse effectiveness of 'Duales System'; expand extended producer responsibility principle; better cooperation between authorities to ensure efficient treatment and disposal of waste; further upgrade landfill sites, remediate contaminated sites; improve availability and timeliness of waste data.
Nature conservation and biodiversity	Adopt set of specific national objectives and develop nature conservation plans; increase awareness and understanding by e.g. adopting a national biodiversity strategy; create new protected areas; reduce land-take rate to 30 ha/day by 2020; develop performance assessment system for spatial and landscape planning decisions; strengthen landscape protection groups' role; improve effectiveness of voluntary agri-environmental measures; encourage conservation by private landowners through economic instruments.
Integrating environmental and economic concerns	Develop national sustainable development strategy*; improve horizontal and vertical cooperation and coordination; better integrate environmental concerns in other policies; further use Environmental Barometer in policy formulation etc., especially regarding biodiversity; further

	integrate environmental concerns in fiscal policies, review problematic concessions; review and if need be phase-out environmentally harmful subsidies.
Integrating environmental and social concerns	Further examine disparities in environmental quality and impact on health and living conditions; review distributional implications of major environmental policy measures; promote local initiatives to foster progress; improve data availability and timeliness; improve access to information and to justice for stakeholders; strengthen public participation; broaden environmental education to promote change towards more sustainable consumption patterns.
Environmental governance in the new *Länder*	Improve connection to sewage and wastewater treatment facilities/cost-effective operation; continue remediation of contaminated sites; review land privatization and use practices to ensure effective management; improve integration of environmental concerns in new *Länder* policies and plans; ensure better monitoring and assessment of plans, policies; facilitate participation of NGOs/other stakeholders; launch and support partnerships for sustainable development.
International cooperation	Facilitate procedures in order to speed up implementation of EU Directives; further discuss international environmental issues especially those relating to agricultural sector; implement plans to cope with flooding in international river basins; continue cooperation with Central and Eastern European countries; increase level of official development aid.
Climate change	Further implement agreed measures taking into account phase-out of nuclear energy; continue phase-out of harmful subsidies to coal production; encourage renewable energy/energy saving; more vigorously address issues related to CO_2 emissions from transport sector; enhance carbon sinks; develop/implement additional measures in order to meet targets; make greater use of cost-effectiveness analysis.

Note: * Meanwhile, a national strategy has been developed by the Green Cabinet, with support from the Council for Sustainable Development (see p. 182).

Source: OECD (2001).

compliance with self-imposed obligations in the industrial and transport sector) and revises environmentally harmful regulations and subsidies (for example gradual phase-out of coal subsidies). According to the SRU, the phase-out of nuclear energy will not, at least until 2005, complicate the reduction of emissions, since only two smaller nuclear power stations will be turned off by then, thus not notably altering the composition of energy sources. To be able to meet the 2020 target, though, SRU recommends increasing the share of less CO_2-intensive energy sources like natural gas, and promoting energy efficiency in the areas of production and consumption (SRU, 2002).

Water and soil pollution

Wastewater treatment and disposal, strengthening of the waste and wastewater infrastructure, and clean-up of contaminated sites require further major investment effort mainly, but not exclusively, in the states of former East Germany (OECD, 2001). Nitrate pollution of rivers and groundwater is one of the major problems highlighted by the OECD. While progress on controlling water pollution from point sources has been significant, the control of non-point sources remains a challenge and is estimated to cause about 60 per cent of nitrogen load in rivers (Kirkpatrick et al., 2001). Nutrient loads from rivers and direct discharges, mainly from agriculture and sewage plants, also contribute to continued eutrophication problems, especially in the Baltic Sea. The 25 per cent reduction in nitrogen emissions from 1985 to 1995 fell short of the 50 per cent reduction target specified in the Third North Sea Conference (Kirkpatrick et al., 2001).

The SRU (2002) also criticizes erroneous trends in waste management. Widely differing waste disposal standards within Germany, conflicting regulations, and the insufficient enforcement of the Technical Instruction on Municipal Waste[35] resulted in the emergence of cheap landfill opportunities for non-preprocessed waste. Companies in particular benefited from these opportunities, thus leading to an under-utilization of cost-intensive waste disposal facilities and rising prices for households.

Nature conservation

Moreover, results of nature conservation policies are judged to be relatively limited (OECD, 2001). The EU Habitat Directive was implemented in Germany with a delay. Designation of Natura 2000 sites is behind schedule (OECD, 2001). No national strategy for biodiversity protection exists. Although Germany has a relatively high proportion of protected land, less than 3 per cent of total land area is more strictly protected.[36] A high degree of fragmentation by roads and settlements, pollutant and nutrient levels, as well as intensive agriculture, are posing major threats for nature conservation. Two thirds of the biotopes are endangered (with only 6 per cent of biotope types not endangered), and about 50 per cent of all vertebrates and one third of ferns and flowering plants are considered to be under threat (BMU, 1998; OECD, 2001). A redirection of already existing subsidies to public and private entities involved in forest management would be desirable. In particular, subsidies should be linked to the actual ecological and recreational services provided (Kirkpatrick et al., 2001). Although the amendment of the Federal Nature Conservation Act brings some improvements (see section 4.6 above), the SRU criticizes the lack of or even weakening of concrete targets and specific guidelines. This increases the danger that the *Länder* interpret the framework law in a less strict way than is desirable and thus endanger improvements in nature conservation (SRU, 2002).

Policy tools

Public expenditures on direct and indirect subsidies for environmentally-friendly activities in the private sector have increased continuously, but studies have shown that their efficiency and effectiveness is low (SRU, 1988, 1994). They have also been criticized for sending the wrong signals.

A major point continually raised by the OECD and other international organizations relates to the need to adopt more economic analysis and cost-effective approaches to environmental policy. This is particularly important because following the past progresses in both the old and the new *Länder*, the marginal cost of further improvements in environmental quality is likely to increase substantially (Buttermann and Hillebrand, 1998). Also, reducing pollution from more diffuse sources (such as those related to transport, agriculture and general consumption patterns) is particularly difficult and costly, and cannot be achieved with traditional command-and-control objectives. Economic problems and high unemployment and the fact that Germany's annual expenditure on pollution abatement and control was one of the highest among OECD countries in the 1990s[37] reinforce the need to apply more cost-effective measures.

Specific policy recommendations in this regard include the differentiation of BAT deadlines and other measures according to ecosystem characteristics, expansion of use of market-based instruments, and coordination of economic policy incentives to be consistent with environmental objectives (OECD, 2001). Also, the actual effectiveness and efficiency of VAs needs to be reviewed. Moreover, the OECD (2001) and SRU (2002) reports stress the need to reconsider the significant exemptions in the ecological tax reform and raise doubts about the cost-effectiveness of the current waste management system. In general, the regulatory framework needs to be compatible with the use of market-based instruments, a condition that is not always satisfied in current legislation.[38] Experts have proposed the development of a Code of Environmental Law (*Umweltgesetzbuch*) to synthesize current environmental policies (Kirkpatrick et al., 2001).

Sustainable development and policy integration

The establishment of a national sustainable development strategy presents a major challenge. The OECD stresses that 'at all levels of government Germany still faces significant problems that hamper better integration of economic, social and environmental concerns' (OECD, 2001, p. 3). There is a general lack of both horizontal and vertical policy integration and cooperation (that is lack of cooperation between federal ministries and lack of integration of environmental concerns into policies of other federal ministries; lack of cooperation between authorities at federal and state level, and insufficient alignment and harmonization of environmental policies) (OECD, 2001). In particular, environmental objectives need to be integrated in sectoral policies, and counterproductive incentive mechanisms (such as subsidies with environmentally harmful effects) need to be eliminated. A case in point is the existing conflict between climate policy objectives and the continued subsidization of domestic coal production. Market distortions in agriculture are another prominent example (Kirkpatrick et al., 2001).[39] Development aid per unit of GDP has declined in past years, in contrast to the increase in official development aid foreseen in the Rio declaration (OECD, 2001).

6. SUMMARY AND CONCLUSIONS

During the 1970s and 1980s, Germany was widely considered an international leader in environmental policy. Its predominant command-and-control approach based on 'best available technology' has succeeded in achieving significant improvements in environmental quality, particularly with respect to emissions from major point sources. The country continues to be a leader in international environmental cooperation and as an exporter of environmental technology, goods and services. There has also been considerable progress in the ecological restructuring of the new *Länder*, and general monitoring and enforcement capacities are satisfactory.

These successes are driven by several factors. First, Germany's geographic position, high population density and degree of industrialization have led to major and very visible environmental problems (for example, forest damage, pollution of major rivers, smog). Increased media coverage of these problems and of some major environmental catastrophes (Chernobyl, chemical accidents) have led to a high degree of public and consumer environmental awareness. Environmental interests are not only highly organized, but are also given a direct voice in politics, as the German political system permits the entry of small parties (like the Green Party) into parliament at all political levels (Schreurs, 2002). The threat of government intervention and consumer action, in combination with a strategy of negotiation and consultation, has promoted the development of a strong eco-industry, which has acted as a motor for ecological modernization. The decentralized structure provides opportunities for implementing innovative policies in individual states first, which may later be transferred to the federal level. Phases of dynamic institutional change have also been associated with a strong economic performance, a general reformist climate following changes in government administration, as well as major international developments. Sometimes, the professional background and constituency of individual politicians involved in environmental policy have contributed to positive changes as well. Germany's leading role in the EU, particularly in pushing for harmonization measures, can also be explained by the country's export-dependent economy and its high ecological vulnerability due to its geographic position.

However, over the past decade there is serious concern that Germany has turned from a leader into a laggard. While initially the country was a leader in pushing for more stringent EU environmental policy, it is now falling behind on the implementation of EU measures. Moreover, it has become evident that the command-and-control approach is not only overly costly, but also often ineffective in achieving environmental improvements. This holds particularly for emissions from more diffuse sources (for example, agriculture) or a wide range of sources (for example, CO_2 emissions, transport-related pollution). In some areas, environmental performance is falling short of existing targets (for example, for nitrate pollution in rivers and CO_2 emissions). In other areas, like urban air pollution, forest damage and global climate change, current targets appear to be insufficient (Kirkpatrick et al., 2001). Biodiversity and nature conservation is another weak chapter of German environmental policy. The concept of 'sustainable development' has been adopted as a formal government objective, and a national strategy for sustainable development has been developed. Now it is essential to incorporate the notion of sustainability into more policy areas, putting equal emphasis on economic, ecological and social concerns.

In the face of economic problems, high unemployment and globalization pressures, it is clear that more cost-effective approaches to environmental policy are needed. Internal and external pressure on the federal government to adopt NEPIs is rising. While Germany has a long tradition in the use of VAs and eco-labels, these are mainly used to supplement traditional regulatory instruments (Wurzel et al., 2003). Moreover, the actual results of

VAs in the absence of effective monitoring and sanctioning mechanisms are little understood and remain doubtful. The criticism that VAs potentially lead to regulatory capture and collusion between government and industry should also be taken seriously. Eco-labelling is unlikely to be effective as a substitute for a wider range of policies due to problems of free-riding and limited consumer capacity to process information. Progress in adopting the more promising approach of using market-based instruments, like eco-taxes and tradable permits, has been very slow, although some recent progress is to be noted. Factors hindering such change include the dominance of lawyers and natural scientists in public administration, and initial resistance by the general public and EOs. The recent ecological tax reform represents an important move in the right direction, but has been severely watered down following pressure from the industrial lobby. As in other countries, lobbying power of major industry is rising in the *vague* of globalization, a trend that can only be countered through international cooperation.

Facing the remaining environmental challenges will also require a policy approach that cuts across sectors and environmental media, and that integrates different levels of policy making. Germany so far has not succeeded in these aspects. A cross-sectoral and cross-media approach is made difficult by the prevailing asymmetry in environmental policy competences between the federal government and the states, and by the distribution of environmental policy responsibilities between several federal ministries. Vertical and horizontal policy coordination is hampered by conflicts among and between federal and *Länder* authorities within the decentralized system. Specific policies often differ between states, and the bi-cameral system tends to favour more incremental policy evolution over major policy change. The increasing 'europeanization' of environmental policy may provide an important venue for overcoming these constraints.

NOTES

1. Germany shares borders with nine other countries. Most of its rivers originate abroad. Moreover, it has a long coastline.
2. The term 'Germany' in this chapter refers to the Federal Republic of Germany, both before and after reunification.
3. For example, the US National Environmental Protection Act.
4. For example, the EU Water Charta, the 1968 Clean Air Charta and the 1970 European Nature Protection.
5. For example, Meadows et al. (1972), Carson (1962), and Ehrlich and Ehrlich (1970).
6. The political climate was further heated up by the terrorist activities of the Red Army Fraction, which reached their climax in 1977 and led to an increased voice for advocates of law and order in government and society at large.
7. See Table 7.2 and the discussion in section 3.1 for details.

8. In 2000, German government and the nuclear industry agreed to phase out all existing plants over their operating life times. The process is expected to be completed by 2032 (Schreurs, 2002).
9. The sustainable development concept was popularized by the Brundtland report in 1985 (World Commission, 1987) and later became part of the EU's Fifth Environmental Action Programme (CEC, 1993). It emphasizes a balance of environmental, social and economic concerns.
10. The Green Cabinet consists of the secretaries of state of the Department of Foreign Affairs, the Ministries of Finance, Economy and Labour, Education and Research, Consumer Protection, Food and Agriculture, Health, Transport, Economic Cooperation and Development, and Environment (Jänicke et al., 2001). With support from the Council for Sustainable Development, the Green Cabinet developed Germany's National Sustainability Strategy (Bundesregierung: Dialog Nachhaltigkeit, http://www.dialog-nachhaltigkeit.de/html/infos.htm, accessed on 14 January, 2004.)
11. According to the rules of procedure of the federal government, ministries are supposed to work together on issues that affect the jurisdiction of several ministries (as is the case with many environmental policy decisions). No binding decisions can be made unless the ministries concerned find a common position (UBA, n.d.).
12. In some cases, municipalities transfer waste disposal responsibilities to private companies.
13. In these committees and working groups the states and the federal government inform each other about urging environmental problems, scientific findings, planned measures, and so on. The German Constitution stipulates that the *Länder* should be heard before new bills are drafted, in order to find out if their interests are concerned and about their financial possibilities. Cooperation and coordination through such committees is also important to harmonize the implementation of environmental laws across Germany, that is to make sure that laws and their execution do not differ too widely (UBA, n.d.).
14. If European policy measures have an impact on areas of state competence, the federal government has to consult the states through the Upper House of parliament before signing/ratifying the treaty that contains these measures. If international treaties contain provisions that affect state competencies, the federal government should, according to the *Lindauer Abkommen*, inform the states and obtain their consent through the *Ständige Vertragskommission der Länder* (permanent commission of the states in which international treaties are being discussed) (Rengeling, 1999). However, there often remain discrepancies between states and the Federation which can, for example, result in implementation difficulties.
15. For example, BAUM, Future, and *Unternehmensgrün*.
16. Agri-environmental programmes support reductions in chemical applications, animal density, the protection of landscape and maintenance of the countryside (Frohberg, 1995). Some states also support minimum tillage and underseeding row crops to reduce erosion and nitrate leaching (Weingarten, 1997).
17. Such measures include, for example, no output of liquid manure until February, no employment of growth regulators in corn-growing.
18. In 1998, such measures were applied to approximately 1.1 million ha of land. Until 2000, this number had dropped to 159 021 ha (BMVEL, 2003a).
19. Presumably until 2005, the amount of direct payments depends on which and how much of a product a farmer produced, being an incentive for intensive land use and production. In 2005, a new law implementing thc EU resolutions on agriculture will be implemented if the German Upper House of parliament approves the draft law.
20. Jordan et al. (2002) also include traditional regulation as an additional category of NEPIs. For the purposes of this chapter, a distinction between traditional command-and-control regulation and NEPIs was thought more appropriate.
21. According to Weingarten (1997), levies were implemented in nine of the 16 states, and ranged from 0.0005 to 1.00 DM/m^3 (approx. 0.00025 to 0.5 EUR/m^3).
22. The 'double dividend' refers to the idea that a shift in taxation from economic 'goods' (for example, labour) to environmental 'bads' (such as pollution) both improves environmental performance and stimulates employment.

23. Tax reductions and exemptions for industrial users and the focus on end users (for example, tax on electricity) shift most of the tax burden to consumers and low-income groups (Klepper and Scholz, 1998).
24. Tax allowances for commuters are an example of such a measure (Jordan et al., 2002).
25. An earlier initiative for a similar road toll had been overruled by the ECJ in 1990 as it was considered to act as a discriminatory measure against foreign transport companies.
26. Consumer ignorance of this inefficient requirement caused a serious financial crisis of the *dual system* scheme in the early 1990s (Kirkpatrick et al., 2001).
27. The EU's emission trading system is supposed to start in 2005.
28. Those fields of action include: forest and society; forests and biological diversity; role of forests in the global carbon cycle; importance of wood as a renewable resource; contribution of forestry and forest industries to the development of rural areas; and forests and international cooperation/international trade (BMVEL, 2003b).
29. So far, good practice principles had only been introduced in laws and ordinances regulating fertilization, plant protection and soil conservation, but not in regulations for nature conservation (BMU, 2002).
30. See, for example, Ellenberg et al. (1978) or SRU (1983, 1988, 1991).
31. Non-methane volatile organic compounds.
32. The index of land protection status considers aspects such as glass and paper recycling, proportion of land in protected areas, and waste disposal in landfills.
33. An important change in energy supply is the reduction in the use of brown coal for domestic heating.
34. Germany aims for a reduction in CO_2 emissions of 25 per cent by 2005 (base year: 1990) (Michaelowa, 2003).
35. The Technical Instruction on Municipal Waste states that the disposal of non-preprocessed waste is only allowed in a very limited number of cases.
36. According to the World Economic Forum's Pilot Environmental Performance Index, Germany ranks second in terms of protected areas as percentage of total area (25.2 per cent in 1998) (World Economic Forum, 2002). However, IUCN Categories I to III do not exist in Germany and only three national parks meet Category IV criteria (OECD, 2001).
37. Average annual expenditures were estimated at 1.5 per cent of GDP (OECD, 2001).
38. For example, current law prevents landlords from raising rents to recover the costs of energy-saving insulation of apartments (Kirkpatrick et al., 2001).
39. Furthermore, 'flood damage has increased, resulting from a lack of integration between water management, transport policy and nature conservation objectives' (OECD, 2001, Conclusions and Recommendations, p. 4).

REFERENCES

Andersen, M.S. (1994), *Governance by Green Taxes: Making Pollution Prevention Pay*, Manchester: Manchester University Press.

BMU (1998), 'Federal Government Report under the Convention of Biological Diversity', Bonn.

BMU (2002), 'German Environmental Report 2002: Report on environmental policy in the 14th legislative period', Berlin: Federal Ministry for the Environment, Nature Conservation and Nuclear Safety.

BMU/UBA (2001), 'The German water sector – policies and experiences', Berlin, Bonn.

BMVEL (2003a), 'Ernährungs- und agrarpolitischer Bericht der Bundesregierung', Bundestagsdrucksache 15/405, Berlin: Deutscher Bundestag.

BMVEL (2003b), 'Nationales Waldprogramm Deutschland – 2. Phase: Vom nationalen Forstprogramm zum nationalen Waldprogramm', available on http://www.nwp-online.de/nwp-g 2.htm (accessed on 23 January 2004).

Bundesregierung: Dialog Nachhaltigkeit, http://www.dialog-nachhaltigkeit.de/html/infos.htm, accessed on 14 January 2004.

Buttermann, H.G. and B. Hillebrand (1998), *Carbon Dioxide-Monitoring in German Industry: Target Achievement in 1997*, Essen: RWI.

Carson, R. (1962), *Silent Spring*, Boston: Houghton Mifflin.

CEC (1993), 'Towards sustainability. A European Community programme of policy and action in relation to the environment and sustainable development', COM (94) 500, Brussels: Commission of the European Communities.

Dyson, K. (1982), 'West Germany: The search for a rationalist consensus', in J. Richardson (ed.), *Policy Styles in Western Europe*, London: George Allen & Unwin, pp. 17–46.

Dyson, K. (1992), *The Politics of German Regulation*, Aldershot: Dartmouth.

Ehrlich, P.R. and A.H. Ehrlich (1970), *Population, Resources, Environment: Issues in Human Ecology*, San Francisco/London: Freeman & Co.

Ellenberg, H., O. Fränzle and P. Müller (1978), 'Ökosystemforschung im hinblick auf umwelt- und entwicklungsplanung', Umweltforschungsplan des Bundesministers des Innern, FuE-Vorhaben 78-10104005, im Auftrag des Umweltbundesamtes, Bonn.

Federal Environmental Agency (2000), 'Environmental crime decreased significantly in 1999', Press release 52/00.

Frohberg, K. (1995), 'Programs for stimulating extensive agriculture in Germany', in M.F. Hofreither and S. Vogel (eds), *The Role of Agricultural Externalities in High Income Countries*, Kiel: Wissenschaftsverlag Vauk Kiel KG, pp. 161–79.

Günther, E. and M. Krebs (2000), 'Aufgaben- und organisationsstruktur der umweltpolitik in der Bundesrepublik Deutschland', Dresden Papers of Business Administration 40/00, Department of Economics, Dresden University of Technology.

Hartkopf, G. (1986), 'Umweltverwaltung – Eine organisatorische Herausforderung', in G. Hartkopf et al. (eds), *Umweltschutz und Verwaltung – Der öffentliche Dienst zwischen politischem Anspruch und Realisierungsnot*, Bonn: Godesberger Taschenbuch-verlag, pp. 96–119.

Heuser, T. (n.d.), 'Role and strategy of environmental NGOs in German policy', background paper for the 10th Northeast Asian Conference of Environmental Cooperation, BUND.

Jänicke, M. and H. Weidner (1997), 'Germany', in M. Jänicke and H. Weidner (eds), *National Environmental Policies: A Comparative Study of Capacity-Building*, Berlin et al.: Springer, pp. 133–55.

Jänicke, M., P. Kunig and M. Stitzel (1999), *Lern- und Arbeitsbuch Umweltpolitik: Politik, Recht und Management des Umweltschutzes in Staat und Unternehmen*, Bonn: Dietz, pp. 30–48.

Jänicke, M., H. Jörgens, K. Jörgensen and R. Nordbeck (2001), 'Governance for sustainable development in Germany: Institutions and policy making', OECD.

Jordan, A., R.K. Wurzel, A. Zito and L. Brückner (2002), 'The innovation and diffusion of "New" Environmental Policy Instruments (NEPIs) in the European Union and its member states', in F. Biermann et al. (eds), Proceedings of the 2001 Berlin Conference on the Human Dimensions of Global Environmental Change

'Global Environmental Change and the Nation State', Potsdam: Potsdam Institute for Climate Impact Research, pp. 149–59.

Kirchhoff, S. (2000), 'Green business and blue angels: A model of voluntary overcompliance with asymmetric information', *Environmental and Resource Economics*, **15**(4), 403–20.

Kirkpatrick, G., G. Klepper and R. Price (2001), 'Making growth more environmentally sustainable in Germany', Economics Department Working Papers No. 276. Paris: OECD.

Klepper, G. and C. Scholz (1998), 'Wirkung und Ausgestaltung einer Ökologischen Steuerreform', *Zeitschrift für Wirtschaftspolitik*, **47**(1).

Kloepfer, M. and H.-P. Vierhaus (2002), *Umweltstrafrecht*, Munich: Verlag C.H. Beck.

Kluge, Th. and A. Lux (2001), 'Privatisierung in der Wasserwirtschaft: Sozialökologische Forschungsperspektiven', ISOE Diskussionspapiere 17, Frankfurt-am-Mein.

Koch, H.-J. (2004), 'Naturschutz und Landschaftspflege in der Reform der bundesstaatlichen Ordnung: Rechtsgutachten im Auftrag des Bundesamtes für Naturschutz', BfN-Skripten 109, Bonn: Bundesamt für Naturschutz.

Meadows, D.H., D.L. Meadows, J. Randers and W.W. Behrens (1972), *The Limits to Growth*, New York: Universe Books.

Michaelowa, A. (2003), 'Germany – a pioneer on earthen feet', *Climate Policy*, **3**(1), 31–44.

Müller, E. (1986), *Innenwelt der Umweltpolitik. Sozial-liberale Umweltpolitik – (Ohn)Macht durch Organisation?* Opladen: Westdeutscher Verlag.

Müller, E. (1989), 'Sozial-liberale Umweltpolitik: Von der Karriere eines neuen Politikbereichs', Aus Politik und Zeitgeschichte B47–48.

Müller, E. (2002), 'Environmental policy integration as a political principle: The German case and the implications of European policy', in A. Lenschow (ed.), *Environmental Policy Integration*, London: Earthscan, pp. 57–77.

OECD (1993), *Environmental Performance Reviews: Germany*, Paris: OECD.

OECD (2001), *Environmental Performance Reviews: Germany*, Paris: OECD.

Reich, M.R. (1984), 'Mobilizing for environmental policy in Italy and Japan', *Comparative Politics*, **64**(4), 379–401.

Rengeling, H.-W. (1999), *Gesetzgebungskompetenzen für den integrierten Umweltschutz – Die Umsetzung inter- und supranationalen Umweltrechts und die Gesetzgebungskompetenzen nach dem Grundgesetz*, Cologne, Berlin, Bonn, Munich: Heymanns.

RWI (1999), 'Stellungnahme zum Entwurf eines Gesetzes zur Fortführung der ökologischen Steuerreform', Bundestagsdrucksache 14/1524.

Scheierling, S.M. (1994), 'Overcoming agricultural pollution of water: the challenge of integrating agricultural and environmental policies in the European Union', World Bank Technical Paper No.269, Washington, DC: World Bank.

Schöne, Florian (n.d.), 'Agrarumweltprogramme in Deutschland', NABU-Positionspapier, http://www.nabu.de/downloads/landwirtschaft/agrarumweltprogramme.pdf, accessed on 11 February 2004.

Schreurs, M.A. (2002), *Environmental Politics in Japan, Germany, and the United States*, Cambridge: Cambridge University Press.

Schröder, W., T. Eckstein, H. Matejka, R. Pesch and G. Schmidt (2001), 'Konkretisierung des umweltbeobachtungsprogrammes im rahmen eines stufenkonzeptes der umweltbeobachtung der bundes und der länder, teilvorhaben 3', Vechta: Institut für Umweltwissenschaften, Hochschule Vechta.

SRU (1983), *Umweltgutachten 1983*, Stuttgart: Kohlhammer.
SRU (1988), *Umweltgutachten 1987*, Stuttgart: Kohlhammer.
SRU (1991), *Allgemeine ökologische Umweltbeobachtung*, Stuttgart: Metzler-Poeschel.
SRU (1994), *Umweltgutachten 1994*, Stuttgart: Metzler-Poeschel.
SRU (1996), *Umweltgutachten 1996*, Stuttgart: Metzler-Poeschel.
SRU (2002), *Umweltgutachten 2002*, Stuttgart: Metzler-Poeschel.
UBA (Federal Environmental Agency) (2003), *Hintergrundinformation: Berücksichtigung von Umweltgesichtspunkten bei Subventionen*, Berlin: Pressestelle Umweltbundesamt.
UBA (Federal Environmental Agency) (n.d.), *A Guide to Environmental Institutions in Germany*.
Umweltakademie (Akademie für Natur und Umwelt des Landes Schleswig-Holstein) (1999), 'Akademie Aktuell', No. 5. Neumünster: Evert-Druck, p. 1.
Weidner, H. (1995), '25 Years of modern environmental policy in Germany: Treading a well-worn path to the top of the international field', discussion paper FS II 95-301, Wissenschaftszentrum Berlin für Sozialforschung.
Weingarten, P. (1997), 'Agri-environmental policy in Germany: Soil and water conservation', discussion paper No. 4, Institute of Agricultural Development in Central and Eastern Europe (IAMO).
World Commission (1987), *Our Common Future*, Oxford: Oxford University Press.
World Economic Forum (2002), 'Pilot Environmental Performance Index', in collaboration with the Yale Center for Environmental Law and Policy and the Center for International Earth Science Information Network, New Haven: Yale Center for Environmental Law and Policy.
Wurzel, K.W. (2002), 'The Europeanisation of German environmental policy: From environmental leader to member state under pressure', FFU report 09-2002. Forschungsstelle für Umweltpolitik, Freie Universität Berlin.
Wurzel, K.W., A. Jordan, A.R. Zito and L. Brückner (2003), 'From high regulatory state to social and ecological market economy? "New" environmental policy instruments in Germany', *Environmental Politics*, **12**(1), 115–36.
Zerle, P. (2004), 'Ökologische Effektivität und ökonomische Effizienz von umweltbezogenen Selbstverpflichtungen', Volkswirtschaftliche Diskussionsreihe, Beitrag No. 262, May, Universität Augsburg: Institut für Volkswirtschaftslehre.
ZEW (1999), 'Was bringt die ökologische Steuerreform der deutschen Wirtschaft?', ZEW Konjunkturreport.
Zittel, T. (1996), *Marktwirtschaftliche Instrumente in der Umweltpolitik*, Opladen: Leske & Budrich.

APPENDIX: LIST OF ACRONYMS AND GERMAN EXPRESSIONS

BAT	Best available technology
BMU	Federal Ministry for the Environment, Nature Conservation and Nuclear Safety (*Bundesministerium für Umwelt, Naturschutz und Nuklearsicherheit*)

BMVEL	Federal Ministry of Consumer Protection, Food and Agriculture (*Bundesminsterium für Verbraucherschutz, Ernährung und Landwirtschaft*)
CDU	Christian Democratic Party
ECJ	European Court of Justice
EO	Environmental Organization
FDP	Free Democratic Party
GAK	Contractual agreement for the improvement of agricultural structure and coast protection (*Gemeinschaftsaufgabe zur Verbesserung der Agrarstruktur und des Küstenschutzes*)
GDR	German Democratic Republic
IMO	International Maritime Organization
Länder	Federal states
NEPI	New economic policy instruments
NFP	National Forest Programme
SPD	Social Democratic Party
SRU	German Council of Environmental Advisors (*Sachverständigenrat für Umweltfragen*)
UBA	Federal Environmental Agency (*Umweltbundesamt*)
UNFF	United Nations Forum on Forests

8. Overlapping fiscal domains and the effectiveness of environmental policy in India

Subrata Mandal and M. Govinda Rao

1. INTRODUCTION

An important precondition for the satisfactory provision of public services is the assignment of fiscal domains to, and their implementation by, different levels of government. A clear and inextinguishable assignment system confers ownership rights and this provides incentives for making the necessary investments, and ensures efficiency and accountability in the provision of public services.

Fiscal assignments, however well construed and designed, do involve overlapping, as the geographical boundaries may not coincide with the benefits of various public services. In part, an overlapping fiscal system is the result of vertical and horizontal competition, and the competition in turn can accentuate overlapping (Breton, 1995). Satisfactory resolution of this is an important challenge in all multilevel fiscal systems. The issue is particularly relevant in the context of environmental protection, because even the issues with local environmental jurisdictions and applications have global implications.

This chapter analyses the assignment of environmental functions in Indian federalism. More specifically, it examines the assignment system and implementation aspects pertaining to three major components of environment, namely, water, air and forests. The assignment of environmental functions and its overlapping is analysed in terms not only of the different levels of government, but also between the executive and judiciary. Specifically, the chapter examines judicial intervention in environmental protection in India and argues that activism is not a solution or a substitute for the failure of the executive in undertaking the task of environmental protection.

2. THE ASSIGNMENT SYSTEM

An important dimension of federalism is the assignment of the power to own and manage natural resources. It is difficult to discern an ideal assignment system both from the viewpoint of principles and contemporary practices. The endowment of natural resources across regions is uneven, and distributional considerations dictate against the assignment of natural resource management to subnational governments. Furthermore, exploitation of important natural resources also involves significant inter-regional externalities, and their assignment to the subnational governments could lead to inefficient resource allocation (Musgrave, 1983). It could also cause significant differences in the tax effort as the state with significant natural resources may decide to use origin-based natural resource revenues rather than destination-based taxes.[1] For this reason, the Indian Constitution assigns the right to exploit major minerals to the Centre and minor minerals to the States (Rao and Singh, 2004: Ch. 10).

The Indian Constitution under Article 246, empowers the Union[2] Parliament and the State Legislatures to enact and implement laws relating to activities under their domain. The Seventh Schedule to the Constitution assigns the responsibilities of the two levels of government under the 'Union', 'State' and 'Concurrent' lists. The Central and State governments have exclusive authority over the Union and State lists respectively and both levels have jurisdiction over the activities in the Concurrent list, with the former having overriding powers. The residual power to legislate on the subjects not covered in the three lists is delegated to the Centre by Article 248. Article 249 empowers the Centre to legislate on any subject in the State list in the 'national interest'; it can also enact laws on state subjects if two or more state legislatures consent to such legislation (Article 252). Article 253 empowers the Centre to make laws necessary to implement treaties to which India is a signatory and decisions of conferences of which India is a participant. Under special or extreme situations the Centre can even dismiss a state government and take over its governance (Article 356). These features of the Constitution show centripetal bias in the Indian constitution. Such a backdrop of central dominance in policy making in general has also contributed to a dominant role of central government in matters related to environmental legislation.

The functions related to regulation and development of interstate rivers and river valleys, fishing and fisheries beyond territorial water, shipping and navigation of inland waterways, maritime shipping and navigation and entering agreements with foreign countries have been assigned to the Central Government. The State Governments are empowered to legislate on subjects related to water supplies, irrigation and canals, drainage and embankment, water storage and waterpower subject to the provisions of Entry 56 of the Union list, and fisheries. Emissions from factories and shipping and navigation on inland waterways as regards mechanically propelled vessels figure in the Concurrent list. The assignment system regarding air is much more ambiguous. Air pollution does not directly figure in any of the three lists. Regulation of mines and mineral development figures in the central list; the Central Government would therefore be responsible for air pollution related to mines. Similarly the Central Government is responsible for any pollution related to public sector industries controlled by the Central Government. Public health and sanitation figures in the State list; this empowers state governments to legislate on health aspects related to pollution. The assignment of legislative power in regard to the protection of forests and wildlife was in the State list until 1976, but was brought to the Concurrent list by an amendment (the 42nd) of the Constitution.

The third tier of government was introduced in the Indian Constitution by the 73rd and 74th amendment in 1992. The third tier comprises the local government in rural and urban areas. Rural local governments are called *Panchayats*, and they have been constituted at district, block and village levels. The urban local governments are the municipal corporations, municipalities and for smaller towns, *Nagarapalikas*. These already existed in some states, and after the amendments, these local bodies were conferred constitutional status.

The Eleventh and Twelfth Schedules to the Constitution list the subjects to be devolved to the rural and urban local governments respectively, but these are carried out concurrently with the State governments. The environmental functions listed for the rural local governments include land improvement, land consolidation and soil conservation, minor irrigation, water management and watershed development, fisheries, social forestry and farm forestry, minor forest products, drinking water, fuel and fodder, non-conventional energy sources and maintenance of community assets. For urban local bodies, the list includes subjects like water supply for domestic, industrial and commercial purposes; public health, sanitation, conservancy and solid waste management, urban forestry, protection of the environment and promotion of ecological aspects, provision of urban amenities and facilities such as parks, gardens and playgrounds are also listed.

3. ENVIRONMENTAL REGULATION IN INDIA

The UN Conference on the Human Environment held at Stockholm in 1972 exerted a major influence and has been a driving force in environmental legislation and policy making in India. The Government of India initiated a number of steps to implement the decisions taken at the Conference by means of amendments to the Constitution, new legislation relating to environmental protection, and creation of institutions for implementing legislation. In 1976, environmental protection and improvement were explicitly incorporated into the Constitution by the Constitution (42nd Amendment) Act. Specific provisions were inserted into the Directive Principle of the State Policy and Fundamental Duties. Article 48A was added to the Directive Principles, it states, 'the State shall endeavor to protect and improve the environment and to safeguard the forests and wild life of the country'. Article 51A(g) in a new chapter entitled 'Fundamental Duties', imposes a similar responsibility on every citizen 'to protect and improve the natural environment including forests, rivers, lakes and wild life and to have compassion for living creatures'. Together, these two provisions lay the foundation for jurisprudence of environmental protection. The amendment also expanded the list of concurrent powers by moving 'Forests' and 'Protection of Wild Animals and Birds' from the State List to the Concurrent List.

In 1972, Parliament enacted the Wild Life Protection Act prior to the Stockholm Conference. The Act provides for state wildlife advisory boards, regulations for hunting wild animals and birds, establishment of national parks and sanctuaries, regulations for trade in wild animals, and judicially imposed penalties for violating the Act. The Act is administered by wildlife wardens and their staff. In 1972, when the Act was introduced by the Central Government, wildlife was a State subject; in fact, 11 states introduced resolutions allowing the Central Government to legislate under Article 252(I) of the Constitution. The move for centralization of provisions for wildlife protection thus came from the States themselves. An amendment to the Act in 1982 allowed for capture and transportation of wild animals for scientific management. Another amendment in 1991 recognized the need of tribal and forest dwellers.

The core of early environmental legislation relates to forests. The State played an important role in forest management since the establishment of the Forest Department in 1864 with help from Germany, the leading European nation in forest management at the time. The colonial government immediately introduced the Indian Forest Act in 1865 and asserted propriety right of the State over forests. The Act of 1865 was made more stringent in 1878 to make a comprehensive law, which, *inter alia*, transferred the ownership and management of forests from the village level to a centralized State. The Act disregarded centuries of customary use by rural populations and alienated peasant and tribal communities. The 1878 Act was later amended to become the Indian Forest Act of 1927, which is still in force.

The significant Central Government intervention in the post-independence era was seen in the enactment of The Forest (Conservation) Act in 1980 to prevent the alarming rate of deforestation and the consequent ecological imbalance and environmental degradation by assigning a supervisory role for the Central Government. The Act was amended in 1988; it requires the approval of the Central Government if a State decides to de-reserve a reserved forest, use forest land for non-farm purposes, assign forest land to a private corporation and clear forest land for the purpose of reforestation.

The Water (Prevention and Control of Pollution) Act of 1974 was the first important environmental legislation in India. The Constitution does not unambiguously place water either as a State subject or as a Union subject. The history and the preamble of the Water Act suggest that only State governments can enact water pollution legislation. During the decade-long deliberations that preceded the introduction of the legislation in the Parliament, 12 states passed enabling resolutions urging the Centre to legislate on the subject since it involved inter-State externalities.

This Act paved the way for the creation of Central Pollution Control Boards (CPCB) and State Pollution Control Boards (SPCB). It confers regulatory authority in State Boards and empowers them to establish and enforce effluent standards for factories discharging wastewater into the water bodies. The Central Board performs these functions for Union Territories and coordinates activities among the States. These boards play an advisory role for the respective governments on matters related to location of industries and any matter related to control of pollution. The CPCB is vested with the responsibility of collecting, compiling and publishing data on water pollution and disseminating information related to treatment and disposal of sewage. It also has the mandate to carry out and sponsor investigation and research on pollution abatement. The boards were empowered to enforce the Act through criminal prosecution and injunctions to restrain polluters. Later, the Act was amended in 1988 to bolster the enforcement machinery by giving them powers to close defaulting industrial plants or to withdraw the supply of power and water by an administrative order.

The Air (Prevention and Control of Pollution) Act of 1981 was enacted under Article 253 to implement the decision taken at the United Nations Conference on Human Environment held at Stockholm in 1972. The Act expanded the authority of the Central and State Pollution Control Boards established under the Water Act to include problems of air pollution. The States that did not have a water pollution board were required to set up an air pollution board. The boards were required to prescribe emission standards for industry and automobiles after taking into account the ambient air quality standards. They were also required to issue permits to industries operating in designated air pollution control areas. To strengthen its enforcement, the Act was amended in 1987 to introduce stiffer penalties and to empower the boards to penalize the defaulting plants by requiring them to cease operation if they exceeded the emission standards, if necessary.

The Environment Protection Act of 1986 was enacted in the wake of the Bhopal gas tragedy. It is an umbrella legislation designed to provide a framework for the central government to coordinate the activities of various Central and State authorities created under the Water Act and Air Act. It delegates wide powers to the executive to enable bureaucrats to frame necessary rules and regulations. The provision of this Act and subordinate rules can override any other law. A broad rule-making power was conferred on the Central Government; it was authorized to take all measures that it deemed necessary for the purpose of protecting the environment. Some of these measures included setting new national standards for improving the quality of the environment, standards for controlling emissions and effluent discharges, to decide on industrial locations, and to establish safeguards for the prevention of accidents.

The Central Government enacted the Public Liability Insurance Act in 1991 to provide immediate relief to victims of accidents involving handling of hazardous substances. The Act requires the owner to compensate the victims irrespective of any neglect or default. The principal authority administering the Act is the district collector. The Act obligates every owner to take out an insurance policy covering potential liability from accidents. Every owner was also required to contribute to an Environmental Relief Fund established by the Central Government. The Act was amended in 1992 to introduce provisions relating to the fund and to place a cap on it of Rs 450 million (about US$10 million). The National Environmental Tribunal Act of 1995 builds on the Public Liability Insurance Act of 1991 in providing relief to victims of accidents involving hazardous substances. The Act empowers the Central Government to establish a national tribunal at New Delhi with the power to entertain applications for compensation, hold inquiries into such claims and to make an award determining the compensation to be paid. The Act imposes a bar on all civil courts from entertaining any claim that may be dealt with by the tribunal. An award may be challenged in the Supreme Court or impugned in a petition to the High Court.

The National Environment Appellate Authority Act of 1997 requires the Central Government to constitute a national environment appellate authority for hearing appeals against orders granting environmental clearance in areas where restrictions are imposed on setting up any industry or carrying out any operation or process.[3]

4. CENTRALIZATION AND DECENTRALIZATION IN INDIAN ENVIRONMENTAL POLITICS

Political factors have impacted on environmental issues to influence laws, regulations, acts, court orders, directives, conventions and formulation and implementation of policies and programmes. In particular, swings between centralization and decentralization of political power have impacted on the control and use of natural resources like water, air, forests and species of animals used in economic activities such as agriculture and industry. The attempt here is to trace the forces of centralization and decentralization at various levels of governance: national, provincial, regional and local. Figure 8.1 tries to capture these aspects in a structured manner. It looks at the aspects of industrial pollution, ecosystem protection, agriculture, forests, water and implementation and enforcement of related action plans at various levels of governance.

With regard to industrial pollution, the impact of air pollution is global, and hence we see the formation of global protocol limiting CFCs and greenhouse gases. The protocol has been implemented in India by the national government through the Air Act. The regulation of local air pollution due to vehicular use and industrial emission has come mainly from the intervention of NGOs and Public Interest Litigation (PILs)[4] in the Supreme Court. With respect to water pollution, the implications are inter-jurisdictional since it has spillover effects. The states in India voluntarily asked for a national law in such cases. At the local level too there has been PIL against pollution of local water bodies.

The case of agriculture and the issue of water use seem vexed and potentially volatile. There are big irrigation and river valley projects and dams and command area development projects mainly controlled by the Central Government and in some cases State governments. The sharing of river water has been a volatile issue involving property rights, bargaining power and with inter-jurisdictional implications. Despite legislating Central acts and establishment of tribunals, a solution to the problem has been elusive and many states in India are engaged in a bitter fight. In more recent years, however, the attempt has been to encourage decentralized systems, and the political power has shifted to the water users' associations and watershed development projects with a distinct local level component in planning and participation. This has resulted in a paradigm shift to management by pressure groups at local levels.

Deforestation is a massive problem in India, where the resource was controlled and managed by the State governments. The nexus between contractors, politicians and bureaucrats became rampant in exploiting the resource; the trend was combined with pressure from the population, which

Field/level	**Industry Pollution**	**Ecosystem Protection**	**Agriculture**	**Forests**	**Water**	**Implementation and Enforcement**
International	Montreal Protocol (CFC regulation)	CITES *		Convention on Biological Diversity	Indus Water Treaty Joint River Commission (Bangladesh)	
National	Water, Air, Environment Protection, Public Liability Insurance Acts	Wild Life Protection Act (1972) National Parks and Sanctuaries	Command Area Development River Valley Projects	The Forest Conservation Act, 1980	The Water (Prevention and Control of Pollution) Act (1974) Water Tribunals	Supreme Court Directives on air and water pollution Environmental Impact Assessment
Provincial/ State	Legislation for Central Law		Dams	Deforestation	Water Disputes, Groundwater regulations	Supreme Court Directives on ban on tree felling
Regional/ Districts			Tanks	Watershed Development	Watershed Development	
Local	NGO Action		Participatory Irrigation Management Wells	Joint Forest Management	Water Users' Association	Public Interest Litigation

Centralization ⬆ Decentralization ⇩

Note: * Convention of International Trade in Endangered Species of Wild Fauna and Flora (CITES).

Figure 8.1 Centralization and decentralization in Indian environmental politics

needs forest products but is alienated from the upkeep of the forest. The recent initiative in decentralized control, with the introduction of joint forest management between the people and the government and the formation of village forest committees, has met with some degree of success.

With regard to implementation and enforcement of regulations, the Supreme Court has been extremely active in forcing governments at the Central and State level to implement some of the regulations formed by the governments themselves by responding to PILs. The pollution control boards mandated environmental impact assessment for certain categories of industries to strengthen the regulations to control industrial pollution. The role of specialized agencies set up to regulate environment, as well as the role of the judiciary in monitoring the implementation of laws, are discussed in greater detail below.

5. ENVIRONMENTAL REGULATION IN INDIA: FORESTS

5.1 Evolution of Policy

The colonial administration declared the proprietary rights of the State over forests, and it was subsequently determined to what extent these were limited by legally existing rights of private persons or communities. After independence in 1947, the Government of India made no substantive changes to this administrative structure. The State retained exclusive control over the management and protection of forest resources. The principles, which were to guide the forest policy of independent India, were enunciated in the National Forest Policy of 1952. The policy reiterated the principles of colonial forestry, as enshrined in the earlier forest policy resolution of 1894, and reinforced the exclusive rights of the State with regard to the management and control of forest resources. A goal was adopted of bringing 60 per cent of the area in hilly tracts and 20 per cent of the area in plains (one-third of the country's total geographical area) under forest cover for ecological reasons.

5.2 Assignment of Powers

The Indian Forest Act of 1927 provides the core of regulations and institutions governing forest management and preservation. In essence, control of forests has resided with State Governments. The State Governments have appointed forest officers, a cadre of state bureaucracy, as on-the-ground implementers of forest management. A 'Secretary' who belongs to the administrative cadre heads the State Forest Administration. He is assisted by the Conservators of Forests belonging to the 'Indian Forest Service', who is technically more competent to manage forests than the officers belonging to the administrative cadre. At the district level the District Forest Officer (DFO) is the administrative head, and below him there are Range Officers (RO) who administer the forests in different ranges of a district. These officers have often functioned relatively autonomously, and their ability to control the use of the natural resource without adequate monitoring has allowed them to engage in rent seeking (Wade, 1988). Thus, collusion between state forest officers, contractors and logging companies is acknowledged to be widespread, to the detriment of forest preservation.

The Forest (Conservation) Act was passed in 1980, which gave the Central Government the power to control State Governments' decision to divert forests for non-forest uses. The administrative centralization required a recasting of the responsibilities and duties of some of the departments of the Central Governments that were responsible for forest planning. The Director General of Forests (DGF) is the administrative head of the forest and wildlife-related issues of the Union Ministry of Environment and Forests.

There are three Divisions supervised by the DGF; two of these relate to forest conservation and the third one is for wildlife protection. One division is headed by the Additional Director General of Forests (a forest service cadre) and the division coordinates its conservation programme through the seven regional offices, each headed by a chief conservator of forests. Other functions of the Division are to formulate policies, conduct surveys, conduct training programmes and undertake research and documentation. The Indian Council for Forest Research and Education (ICFRE) has been set up to facilitate research and documentation and use of scientific knowledge for the preservation of forest and wildlife. The council has set up several institutes to conduct its research activities. The forest conservation department addresses the problem of deforestation and land use changes.

The second division supervises conservation and is headed by an Additional Secretary (an administrative service cadre); this division also administers various other conservation programmes in addition to forests (like wetland, biodiversity and so on). The Additional Secretary reports to the DGF for issues related to forest conservation (called the eco-development and regeneration programme) and to the Secretary of the Ministry for all other conservation programmes. The third department under the DGF administers the protection of wildlife and maintains zoos and national parks.

The multiple actors and plethora of bureaucracy at both Central and State levels with a mix of generalists and those with specialized knowledge of forestry described above has not helped in the conservation of forest cover. The Central bureaucracy often formulates policies without proper understanding of ground realities due to its remoteness. Again, uniformity in policies may not be appropriate in a large and diverse country like India. The State bureaucracy has to deal with the Central directives besides its own rules and regulations. It is also constrained by the nexus of contractors and politicians, and often becomes a part of the axis. Thus, the coordination cost of forest conservation has been high, and, not surprisingly, the policies and institutions have led to a steady decline in the forest cover in the country.

The Central Government introduced the Forest (Conservation) Act in 1980 in response to the high rate of deforestation. The Act required that the State governments would have to obtain prior permission from a Central Committee in the Ministry, called the Forest Advisory Committee headed by the DGF, for conversion of forest land. Thus, the Government's response to declining forest cover has been to centralize decision making through increased monitoring and control. However, the deforestation problems were not due to non-optimal decisions by State Governments. The problem lies in the structure of incentives to the state-level bureaucrats and their incapacity to prevent quasi-legal or illegal logging activities or connivance with the contractors. In such cases increasing central control would do nothing to tackle the root cause. Instead, more effective local monitoring, through community and local government involvement, would seem to be the appropriate policy response. Thus, it is not suprising that the Act failed to check deforestation and the Government finally had to opt for a decentralized governance structure by involving communities for forest protection and creating the institution of joint forest management in 1990.

5.3 Stakeholders in the Forest Sector of India

Role of Central and State governments

The transfer of 'forest and wildlife' from the State list to the Concurrent list in the Constitution has given the Central Government overriding powers in formulating policies and promoting and coordinating programmes. The Ministry of Environment and Forests formulates the overall policy framework. However, implementation of measures to protect forests is the responsibility of the States. Besides, as revenue from forests accrues to the State Governments, the interests of the Central and the State Governments do not necessarily coincide, and the Centre is arguably able to take a more long-term view. Politically, the Centre responds to groups that are well represented in the national capital; in particular, conservationists, international agencies and voluntary groups have a considerable influence on the direction of policy at this level.

The responsibility for forest protection, management and utilization rests with the States. The Constitution also assigns the revenues from the forests to the State governments. Being closer to decision makers, regional and local interests influence the formulation and implementation of regulatory policies on sustainable forestry. Furthermore, priority to earning revenue could result in poor enforcement of regulations relating to the protection of forests. These have led to judicial interventions, which will be discussed below.

Other stakeholders

An important institution for the regulation and development of forests is the bureaucracy. The bureaucracy consists of field level officials of the State Forest Departments and decision makers at the policy level. They are responsible for the day-to-day management of state forests, and have maximum direct interaction with user groups. They have enjoyed considerable freedom of action in implementation because existing forest legislation gives them a great deal of discretionary control over the flow of benefits from state forests. However, in some case interference by politicians considerably constrains their ability to act independently (Vira, 1995).

Within a rural society, it is possible to distinguish groups by the extent and nature of their dependence upon natural resources. The dependence of medium and large land-owning groups on common resources is typically mediated through the market. Small and marginal farmers and the landless rural resource users depend on local commons for subsistence needs – fuel, fodder, food and basic construction timber.

Other stakeholders include manufacturers of forest-based products, and contractors. Restrictions on logging have made forest-based industry unviable. At the same time, forest contractors have been a strong force in preventing the effective implementation of restrictions on logging. Trade in non-timber forest products (NTFP) has been controlled by private contractors, who on the one hand depress wages to subsistence groups to make large profits and on the other, exploit both the forests and indigenous people living in forest. Despite the pronouncements by the National Forest Policy Resolution, 1952, and reiteration by various policy pronouncements including Plan documents, contractors remain an exploitative force in forestry operations due to their strong political links and connivance with forest bureaucracy (Guha, 1983).

The Forest Act allows the State to delegate the management of some forests, designated in such cases as village forests, to village community organizations. In practice, the weakness of local government institutions has meant that such assignments were very limited, or useless in effect. While this situation may change in the long run, with the strengthening of local governments (Wade, 1988: Ch. 13), it will require State Governments' decision makers (politicians and bureaucrats) giving up a significant source of rents. As documented by Wade (1988) in the case of irrigation, different levels of the bureaucracy and political structures also collude, and share the rents acquired from those who are given access to the resource (water or trees, as the case may be).

5.4 Features of Decentralization[5]

The increasing depletion of India's forest resources has brought into sharp focus the inherent inadequacy of traditional state-owned and operated systems of forest management in sustaining the forest resource base against the growing human and livestock population pressures, industrialization and urbanization. Apart from developmental pressures, the dependence of forest user groups is a crucial factor in the state of India's forests. Forest conservation priorities cannot be determined in isolation from local people and broader patterns of natural resource use, and this must be complemented by policies promoting sustainable and equitable development of the natural resource base as a whole. In acknowledging this factor, the Ministry of Environment and Forests, Government of India issued policy guidelines for the involvement of village communities and voluntary agencies in the regeneration of degraded forest lands on 1 June 1990 under the JFM (joint forest management) programme.

Under the JFM programme, the user (local communities) and the owner (government) manage the resource and share the cost. The effective and meaningful involvement of local communities in evolving sustainable forest management systems allows the use of indigenous knowledge about different aspects of conservation. It is well known that rural people, particularly women and indigenous tribes (also referred to as tribals), have intimate knowledge of species, their growth, utility and medicinal value. The linking of incentives and participatory forest development has been singularly instrumental in eliciting community participation. Currently, it is estimated that 10.24 million hectares of forest land are being managed under the JFM programme through 36 075 Village Forest Committees (VFCs) in 22 states.

Following the launching of the JFM programme in India in the last decade, several issues of importance have emerged, such as the diversity in institutional and benefit-sharing arrangements, development of technology and silvicultural practices to increase the productivity of degraded forests, and so on. In the current arrangement people's needs have taken centre-stage. As a result, silvicultural practices and technologies now need to be oriented not only to increasing forest productivity but also to the management of NTFP (non-timber forest products), fodder, and fuel-wood.

A review of the institutional and benefit-sharing arrangements across States that have implemented JFM has caused some serious concerns. These include inadequate funds and arbitrary allocation of the available funds, inadequate personnel to supervise, lack of coordination between the administration and field staff, and non-existence of a structure of governance to coordinate the working of VFCs with other departments to avoid a multiplicity of committees within a village. The functioning of these committees under the *Panchayats* (local governments) is also not well defined. Thus, existing legal and policy provisions relating to forests, revenue lands, rights and concessions, customary laws, traditional rights, resolution of conflicts and coordination between rural local governments and JFM lack a clear framework. There is also a plethora of ambiguous and often conflicting resolutions, laws, policies and acts. This leads to ambiguities and uncertainties, creating scope for supersession on the basis of legal technicalities. Certainly, greater coordination efforts are required among rural development and forest ministries of the State and Central governments.

Despite a reasonably successful attempt in introducing decentralized and participatory management of forests through JFM, the success of the programme depends on the way in which the Forest Department and more particularly, the Divisional Forest Officer (DFO) exercises their powers. In fact, the role assigned to the DFO is pivotal in the initiation and the success of the JFM programme. With powers to disband a badly functioning committee, cancel membership, and nominate NGOs for membership, the relationship has been criticized as being unequal, and the actual power seems to be retained by the State bureaucracy. It must also be mentioned that the JFM has been launched only in areas where natural forests are already lost and local communities require help to restore forest cover and to achieve (or regain) a more sustainable forest management system. Ironically, this has meant that those communities which have not significantly depleted their forests do not qualify for the programme.

In many areas, indigenous people have felt excluded from JFM because opportunities to participate have been monopolized by higher caste and elite groups who have been able to use their greater access to officials to secure participation in the JFM scheme. The marginalized and technically landless groups like the tribal peoples have thus seen 'degraded lands' and 'wastelands' that were important to their livelihoods annexed to JFM, leaving them further impoverished.

5.5 Intervention of the Judiciary

Despite recent efforts to increase forest cover through reforestation, there has been considerable depletion of the forest cover in India, and at present, the forest cover comprises less than 18 per cent of total land area. The actual forest area with crown density is only about 11 per cent. Despite legislation and allocation of financial resources, the forest area of the country, instead of showing an increase, has continued to deteriorate. According to the State of the Forest Report, 1997, between 1995 and 1997 more than 17 000 square kilometres of forest land was lost. Concerned with the rapid depletion of forest cover throughout the country, the Supreme Court in 1996 directed that all 'ongoing activities in any forest in any state' should be stopped forthwith. It said that no activity should be carried out without the prior permission of the Central Government under Section 2 of the Forest Conservation Act, 1980. Every state was directed to ensure immediate compliance of the direction and report to the Court within two months.

As regards tropical rain forests in Arunachal Pradesh in the districts of Tirap and Changlang, a complete ban on felling of trees was imposed. A complete ban (with the exception of defence and other government purposes) was also imposed on the movement of trees and timber from any North Eastern state to any other state. In 1998 the Supreme Court gave detailed orders on pricing of timber, licensing, forest protection, management of forests, wood-based industries and possible action against officials for neglecting duty or indulging in corrupt practices. The Court instructed all the states with rich reserves of forest on the steps to be implemented to check deforestation (Shaym Divan and Armin Rosencranz, 2001).

However, the decision of the Supreme Court has inflicted hardship on a number of State governments both by reducing the revenue earnings and by constraining the economic activities based on forest resources.

The Court's action has been effective in producing results. Latest statistics from the State of the Forest Report actually shows a net increase in the forest cover by 3896 square kilometres in the forest area assessment held between 1997 and 1999 and a further increase of 38 245 square kilometres between 1999 and 2001. Nevertheless, the appropriate course of action seems to be to have a sustainable plan for forestry rather than to persist with blanket bans.

6. ENVIRONMENTAL REGULATION IN INDIA: WATER

6.1 Evolution of Policy

The first national policy on water was formulated in 1987. The government felt that as the country prepared to enter the twenty-first century, efforts to develop, conserve, utilize and manage water resources have to be guided by national perspectives. The policy makers realized that water is a scarce and precious national resource that needs to be planned, developed and conserved as such, and on an integrated and environmentally sound basis, keeping in view the needs of the growing population. The second national policy on water was formulated in 2002. The two national policies dealt with all-important aspects of water usage, conservation and regulation.

6.2 The Assignment System

As discussed earlier, the responsibility of developing and managing the water resources has been distributed among the Central, State and Local governments in India. These responsibilities have been further delegated to different ministries, their departments, agencies and Commissions. The Union Ministry of Water Resources formed in 1985 is in charge of overall planning, policy formulation, coordination and guidance, development and regulation of water resources in the country. Prior to 1985, the focus on water-related issues was mainly on irrigation, command area development, flood control and ground water exploration. The formation of the ministry gave a new thrust to programmes on water, and a comprehensive policy was developed for the first time in 1987.

The functions of the Water Resources Ministry overlap with several other ministries since water has multidimensional aspects and uses. The Water Resources Ministry has to cooperate with the Ministry of Agriculture for the development of watersheds[6] and drip and sprinkler irrigation systems. The Central Water Commission in the Water Resources Ministry has to maintain close technical links with the Ministry of Power for the development of hydroelectricity. In matters related to water pollution the Ministry has to cooperate with the Ministry of Environment and Forests and the Central Pollution Control Board, since these organizations are responsible for maintaining the quality of water. The Ministries of Rural Development and the Ministry of Environment and Forest also have programmes for watershed development. In addition, the Ministry of Rural Development is responsible for a 'Million Wells Scheme' under which development of ground water is taken up. The National Drinking Water Mission is also under the Ministry of Rural Development and it is responsible for developing the source of drinking water in rural areas.[7] The Ministry of Industry is concerned with the planning and development of water resources for industrial use; the Ministry of Urban Development is responsible for drinking water in urban areas and the Indian Council of Agricultural Research is responsible for research on water management techniques. The Ministry of Water Resources, being the nodal agency on issues related to water, has to carefully coordinate all these ministries to ensure maximum utility from water use.

The involvement of multiple agencies for administering water use requires a well-coordinated system of governance. The Ministry of Water Resources, which is the nodal agency, has a Secretary as its administrative head. He has several commissioners below him looking after various departments such as policy planning, projects, Indus Water Treaty, command area development and water management, matters related to eastern rivers, hydrology projects and minor irrigation. The Secretary is also assisted by a financial and a coordination and evaluation advisor.

There are other organizations in the Water Resources Ministry which have been delegated responsibilities related to important aspects. These are (i) the Central Water Commission, which is a premier technical organization in the country in the field of water resources and is charged with the general responsibilities of initiating, developing and coordinating schemes for control, conservation and utilization of water resources for the purpose of flood control, irrigation, navigation, drinking water supply and water power development in consultation with the State Governments; (ii) The National Water Development Agency was set up in 1980 to promote scientific development for optimum utilization of water resources and for preparing feasibility reports for inter-basin transfer of water; (iii) The Central Ground Water Board is entrusted with the responsibilities of hydrogeological surveys, exploration, assessment, development and management of ground water resources. In addition to these national level organizations there are River Boards to look after specific river basins. Organizations such as Water and Power Consultancy Services (India) Ltd and National Projects Construction Corporations Ltd, provide technical services for development of water resources. Institutions like National Institute of Hydrology, Central Soil and Materials Research Station provide scientific inputs on water development.

As mentioned earlier, in accordance with the Constitutional provisions, some aspects of water use, regulation and development are under the charge of the State Governments. They implement two types of schemes, those with a 100 per cent grant from Central Government and those in which the States share the cost. Within States, the Department of Irrigation is in charge of developing and maintaining irrigation projects as well as ground water development. The departments of *panchayati raj* (local government) and rural development, the departments of environment and forests and science and technology and the departments of agriculture implement watershed development programmes. In addition, the departments of finance and planning oversee the work of the remote sensing agencies in different states, which are in charge of investigating and proposing areas in the states for water management, afforestation and so on.

Historically, government institutions have been formed on departmental lines rather than on a coordinated vision of resource development. They follow narrow sectoral objectives without reference to other departments working in the same area and related sectors. Most state departments of agriculture do not deal with water at all, even though agriculture consumes the largest volume of water. Further, there seems to be a disjunction of institutional responsibility between State and Local Governments. In many States the institutions related to watershed-based poverty alleviation programmes or drought-prone area programmes do not have any local presence, and the involvement of local people does not exist (James, 2003).

Another major problem in development and regulation of water resources is the plethora of bureaucracy to administer various aspects of water resources management involving heavy coordination cost. A Secretary heads the Irrigation Department of the State Governments. He is assisted by a number of bureaucrats, including the director of ground water who is usually a hydrologist or a geologist. The irrigation projects at the state level are headed by a chief engineer, who delegates responsibilities to the superintendent engineers functioning at the district level. The superintendent engineer is advised by a District Irrigation Advisory Committee headed by the district collector, who is the chief administrator of the district. At the village level (where there are existing irrigation structures or new ones being initiated) there is usually a departmental worker who liaises with the water users associations (which is an elected body of the village) and reports to the works inspector belonging to the engineering department.

At the state, district and village levels, the departments of the *panchyati raj* and rural development, environment and forest, science and technology, planning and agriculture are involved in water resource management. At the state level, the Secretary of the *panchyati raj* ministry supervises water conservation missions, rural water supply and minor irrigation. The state pollution control boards are responsible for monitoring water pollution and quality. The department of forest and environment implements afforestation and watershed projects. The state remote sensing agencies, which collect data on the availability of water, investigate and propose new areas for water management.

At the district level, the district collector is the Chairman of the District Irrigation Advisory Committee and also the Chairman of the District Watershed Advisory Committee. The district collector is assisted by a project director implementing projects related to watershed development. The chief executive officer of the *Zilla Parishads* (District Legislative

Assemblies) sanctions funds for rural water supply networks and these are constructed and maintained by the engineering department of the district headed by a Superintendent Engineer. All districts usually have an Environmental Officer functioning under the directive of the State Pollution Control Board on matters related to water pollution.

In the villages, there are *Gram Panchyats* (village local governments) with an elected head called *sarpanch* who is also the chairman of the water conservation and utilization committees, watershed committees/associations. Many states have community facilitators, social mobilizers and common interest groups working in coordination with the *gram panchyats*. Some villages also have elected water users' associations working directly with the works inspectors of the irrigation department of the states.

6.3 Issues in the Water Sector: Coordination Failures

Interstate river water disputes

A close scrutiny of Indian water dispute settlement mechanisms shows that these are ambiguous and opaque. The problems are compounded by the entanglement of interstate water disputes with more general centre-state conflicts, and with everyday political issues. These impacts can be reduced by a more efficient design of negotiating mechanisms. However, as large areas of India are relatively arid, water is critical to the welfare of the country's citizens and, obviously, it evokes a lot of emotion.

Because India is a federal democracy, and because the rivers flow across state boundaries, instituting efficient and equitable mechanisms for allocating river flows has long been an important legal and constitutional issue. Numerous interstate river-water disputes have erupted since independence. An example of the intensity of conflict relating to Cauvery river-water involving the southern States of Karnataka and Tamil Nadu may be seen from the following incident: 'A farmer jumped to his death into the Kabini reservoir on Wednesday (September 18, 2002) to protest against Karnataka's decision to release Cauvery waters into Tamil Nadu. [. . .] As news spread [. . .] spontaneous protest marches were held with 300 farmers courting arrest in Mandya' (Rediff.com/news, 19 September, 2002). This particular dispute continues to remain unresolved, and no solution acceptable to all the parties seems possible within the existing arrangements.

The phenomenon of interstate water disputes in India is still relatively little understood. Part of the difficulty is the plethora of actors and the complexity of the institutional environment within which the various parties reach (or fail to reach) agreement. Actors include state governments (which in turn must be decomposed into professional politicians, political parties and interest groups), the national parliament, central ministries, the courts, and ad hoc water tribunals. In general, river-water disputes have involved state and central politicians, as well as the courts and special tribunals and commissions set up to arbitrate. Although fairly explicit constitutional provisions govern interstate river-waters, it is unclear precisely whether existing mechanisms for adjudicating interstate water disputes are adequate. Indeed, there is growing consensus that existing institutions are increasingly unable to generate acceptable outcomes that contribute to economic growth and national welfare.

Numerous interstate river-water disputes have erupted in India since independence. The disputes persist, even though they have proved costly and the existing dispute resolution mechanisms are ambiguous, opaque and in many cases flawed (Rao and Singh, 2004). In a cooperative bargaining framework, water *can* be shared efficiently, with compensating transfers as necessary, *if* initial water rights are well-defined, and *if* institutions facilitate and implement cooperative agreements. However, when the initial allocation of rights is at stake and where the parties face a situation of pure conflict rather than one of potential gains from trade, a search for a negotiated solution may be futile, and quick movement to arbitration or adjudication may be more efficient. However, in the Indian case, not only is this process slow, but also effective binding arbitration does not exist.

Water and Indian Federalism Indian institutions for water dispute resolution are ambiguous and opaque. State governments dominate the allocation of river-waters. The InterState Water Disputes (ISWD) Act of 1956 was legislated to deal with conflicts, and included provisions for the establishment of tribunals to adjudicate where direct negotiations have failed. However, states have sometimes refused to accept the decisions of tribunals, so arbitration is not binding. Significantly, the courts have also been ignored on occasion. The Centre has sometimes intervened but in most complicated cases, it has been unsuccessful. In short, effective institutional mechanisms for settling interstate water disputes simply do not exist.

The relevant provisions of the Indian Constitution are (i) Entry 17 in the State List; (ii) Entry 56 in the Union List; and (iii) Article 262. Essentially, Indian federalism with a strong centripetal bias has consistently involved coalition building. This has meant a high level of explicit or implicit 'horse-trading' among the Centre and states that are potentially key elements of a central coalition. One possible interpretation, therefore, is that the Centre wishes to preserve a system that allows it flexibility or discretion in bargaining over Centre-state issues in general, with water being one of them. A related feature of Indian political economy is the problem of multiple vetoes (Bardhan, 1984; see also Singh, 1997), which would help explain why, with discretion preserved, it may not be used decisively. This, too, seems relevant to the case of water, where negotiations have dragged on, and where the Central Government has sometimes prolonged them, by failing to appoint a tribunal quickly, even when asked.

Disenchantment with the adjudication process for interstate river disputes led to several attempts at change. First, the National Water Development Agency (NWDA) was created in July 1982, to 'carry out the water balance and other studies . . . for optimum utilization of water resources' (National Water Development Agency, 1992). This is an institution set up by the Government of India without any statutory backing. Furthermore, its scope is technical, and separate from the institutional realities of water allocation. Second, in 1983, the National Water Resources Council (NWRC) was created by a central government resolution. Its composition includes chief ministers of states, lieutenant governors of union territories, several central government ministers, and the Prime Minister as chairman. This group met first in October 1985, and adopted a National Water Policy in 1987. Unfortunately, however, disenchantment with the adjudicative process for interstate river disputes has continued.

In summary, the resolution of water disputes is complicated by being tangled in the general difficulties of Centre-state federal issues. The wide scope for discretion, the extensive bargaining, and the multiplicity of potential vetoes work in tandem to undermine the clarity and transparency needed for speedy dispute resolution. In May 2002, the ISWD Act was amended to try to place time limits on tribunals.

Analytical Foundations of Water Disputes Economic analysis offers helpful guidance to understanding the problems of interstate water disputes. Admittedly, water has a number of features that create potential-market failure. These may include non-rivalry, non-excludability, externalities, merit good features, and significant transactions costs (Richards and Singh, 1996). The presence of these factors means that although increased reliance on market forces (for example, one state selling water to another) can contribute significantly to resolving water issues, there is no escaping from the need for parties to agree upon a set of rules, an enforcement mechanism, and a prior distribution of property rights.

Property rights have been claimed on the basis of historical use or on the basis of the 'Harmon Doctrine', that 'what falls on our roof is ours to use, without regard to any potential harm to downstream parties'. Historical use can work against trading water rights, while the Harmon Doctrine ignores externalities as well as past investments connected with water use. A third approach, that of the social contract *à la* Thomas Hobbes, holds more promise. A deal must be struck among the existing decision-making entities, such as Indian states, which (i) decides on an initial allocation of property rights and (ii) creates a mechanism to trade these rights, to regulate uses that generate externalities, and so on. Consequently, institutions that support efficient bargaining and can enforce binding agreements are essential.

Ground water

Nearly 85 per cent of ground water exploited is used only for irrigation. Besides, ground water is now the source of four-fifths of the domestic water supply in rural areas, and around half that of urban and industrial areas. Further, in drought years, it is the predominant source of irrigation. Not surprisingly, the overuse of ground water is emerging as a major concern. A burgeoning population is overdrawing aquifers in several states. The latest data indicates that in the states of Punjab, Haryana and some urban areas, water tables are falling by up to 1 metre per year. Although at the national level, only 30 per cent of the actual ground water potential has been harnessed, in states such as Punjab, against a critical level of 80 per cent, the level of exploitation is over 98 per cent. Haryana is a close second at 80 per cent, and Tamil Nadu is reaching criticality at 60 per cent. Within states there are pockets that have reached a very critical condition with respect to ground water utilization, sometimes exceeding 100 per cent. Large cities such as Ahmedabad, Jodhpur and Chennai support thriving private ground water businesses that draw water from tube wells in the neighbouring hinterlands for supply to high-income residential areas, because ground water tables in the cities are falling at a rate of 2–3 metres per year. Besides depletion, pollution of aquifers through human activity constitutes another major problem.

Most ground water structures are privately owned, and therefore are outside the purview of direct State regulation. Measures to regulate ground water extraction chiefly through restrictions on credit or electricity have had limited impact. On the other hand, wherever the water table is high, affluent farmers use diesel pumps if electricity is in short supply. In the legal framework, for the management of ground water in India, there are no *de jure* rights to ground water; *de facto*, all landowners have the right to the ground water in their land. Thus, ground water is viewed essentially as an add-on to the land. As a consequence, there is no limit to the amount of ground water a landowner can extract from his land.

Concerned at the critical situation with regard to ground water, the Supreme Court constituted the Central Ground Water Board (CGWB) as Central Ground Water Authority (CGWA) to regulate and control ground water management and its indiscriminate boring. The Authority has assessed that 310 out of 5711 blocks in the country have reached a critical situation where the rate of withdrawal is more than the rate of replenishment, and another 160 blocks are approaching such a situation. The Authority has declared several regions as notified areas for the protection and preservation of the ground water resources. In such areas, extraction of ground water without prior approval of the Authority has been prohibited. The Authority has also organized mass awareness campaigns at various locations in India.

Another problem related to ground water is the pollution and contamination of aquifers due to over-exploitation, seepage of sewer lines, disposal of chemical effluents in natural watercourses, salinity ingress in coastal areas and natural formation of arsenic, fluoride and iron. It is difficult to restore ground water quality once the aquifer is contaminated. The CGWB is mandated to develop cost effective technologies like solar stills for purifying contaminated ground water.

It is pertinent to point out here that development and monitoring of ground water needs to be done at the local level since it is the local people who use it. The cost of monitoring and generating information by a central agency like the CGWB / CGWA on ground water at the local level is higher than a local level institution like *Panchyat* in villages or municipalities, towns and cities. Moreover, ground water development plans need to be coordinated and integrated with watershed development plans which should have a specific component of ground water recharge by developing check dams. However, the watershed development programmes are planned and implemented by several central and state agencies[8] who function independently from the CGWB / CGWA. Further, at the district level there are advisory committees, and at the village level too there are committees, but there is no mechanism to coordinate among the plethora of actors and institutions. Ironically, there is an institutional disjunction or vacuum in spite of the existence of several institutions.

Surface water and irrigation

India's irrigation system is not performing anywhere near optimum capacity. The irrigation efficiencies are notoriously low, at around 35 per cent. A number of projects suffer from time and cost overruns for want of adequate financial resources to complete them. The completed projects are in a poor state of maintenance as the emphasis is on new projects rather than on properly maintaining the existing ones. The consequence of such a poor state of maintenance has resulted in a three-fold increase in waterlogged area, from 7 million hectares in 1976 to 23 million hectares in 2000.

In order to utilize the capacity created by the irrigation structure, the Command Area Development Programme (CADP) was launched in 1974–75 by the Water Resources Ministry of the Central Government. It was found in the evaluation studies of the Ministry that the progress made in the construction of field channels was inadequate due to lack of funds.

It seems difficult to carry on this programme without the involvement of the stakeholders like the water users' association, and private sector participation. The private sector has kept away from irrigation projects due to the high unit cost of development (US$2200/hectare), high gestation lag and the attitude of irrigators who are often not used to treating irrigation as a commercial service.

The Participatory Irrigation Management scheme administered by the Irrigation Department of State governments will be effective in easing the resource crunch being faced by the CADP. There is a lot of merit in coordinating the two programmes since they overlap in the same space; besides, they will promote mutual accountability between the Water Users' Association and the Irrigation Department

The CADP also envisaged integrated and coordinated development of irrigated areas along with on-farm development. However, coordination failure between the Agricultural Department of the states, which provided extension support services for on-farm development, and the Water Resources Ministry, which developed the command area, resulted in a mismatch between the place and time where the extension service and irrigation was provided.

6.4 Features of Decentralization

Watershed development and tank irrigation

One of the most undesirable features of development is that the traditions of water harvesting and tank irrigation have shown a decline in the states. Neither the Government nor the people have taken any initiative to preserve them. While the Central and State governments have focused on construction of big dams and large networks of irrigation, people have resorted to measures like ground water mining through tube wells (for example Tamil Nadu and Maharashtra and Andhra Pradesh). According to Iyer (2003) it may not be easy to revitalize these structures since the land use pattern has changed irreversibly. A more comprehensive watershed development approach is called for to rejuvenate the local systems. With the constitutional recognition accorded to rural and urban local governments in the 73rd and 74th amendment to the Constitution, the local bodies have been empowered to maintain such structures. There has also been a realization about the utility and sustainability of small locally managed water-harvesting systems with involvement of the people at the local level.

The paradigm of watershed development was initiated in India in the 1970s in the state of Haryana due to scarcity of water. Subsequently such local level initiatives were replicated in the states of Mahrashtra, Madhya

Pradesh and Rajasthan. Studies have shown that most of these initiatives have led to an increase in water availability and a noticeable increase in agricultural production (Iyer, 2003). The water harvesting structures also contributed to water recharge to the ground water aquifers that enhanced the availability of drinking water. The incidence of benefit varied across groups; most benefits accrued to the landed class with large land holdings, benefits to landless labourers and cattle grazers were not direct and assured. There is also an element of capture by the local elite even in this paradigm of development. A recent study based on primary data in the states of Karnataka and Uttaranchal has found that the local elite has benefited more than the poor (Rajashekar et al., 2004).

The country has begun to take rainwater harvesting and ground water recharge seriously at all levels under the massive Integrated Watershed Development Programme. Trends during the 1990s also suggest a progressive shift of budgetary allocation from irrigation development to water harvesting and recharge. Across India, some 6.2 million hectares of rain-fed lands are currently under treatment through 5200 micro-watersheds, at a whopping cost of Rs 8 billion ($200 million) for the year 2001–2002.

Water users' associations

In India, disappointing performances of government-owned and operated irrigation systems, mainly due to poor cost recoveries, have compelled a number of states like Maharashtra and Andhra Pradesh to transfer rights and responsibilities for management of irrigation systems from government agencies to private or local persons or organizations. Transferring responsibilities has come to be seen as a way to reduce pressures on thinly stretched government finances, while at the same time improving irrigated agricultural production and ensuring the long term sustainability of irrigation systems (Geijer, 1996; Vermillion, 1991). The intention is to encourage local initiative to take responsibility for the management of resources in the belief that beneficiaries have a greater stake and better information for making efficient resource allocations (Brewer and Kolavalli, 1998). Some states, such as Karnataka and Maharashtra, have formulated a clearly defined and codified policy, called participatory management, of promoting transfer of irrigation management responsibilities from the government to farmers.

Preliminary results indicate that, in the proper environments, participatory management increases efficiency of water use and the value of irrigated agricultural production. However, the benefits accrue mostly to the elite, and the whole system is managed and operationalized by this group.

6.5 Water Pollution

Waste disposal in rivers

Waste disposal in rivers is a big problem in India. As an illustrative case we take the river Yamuna, on which the capital city of Delhi is located. Delhi discharges more than 2000 million litres per day (mld) of waste water into the Yamuna river. Of this, about 300 mld is contributed by the industrial sector and a bulk of the pollutant comes from the untreated sewage, because the city administration lacks funds to install sufficient sewage treatment facilities. A report published by Delhi pollution control committee (1993) reveals that a mere 31.8 mld of sewage is treated sufficiently for disposal into the river. The sewage goes untreated into the river during machinery and power breakdowns, and in other cases badly silted plants get flooded during rains. As a result, though Delhi covers only 2 per cent of the length and basin area of the river, it contributes 71 per cent of the waste water discharged into the river! And since most of the Yamuna waters that flow into the city are used up to cater to Delhi's requirements, what remains of the river after Delhi is undiluted sewage. Asphyxiation of the Yamuna begins right from the entry of the river into the city, where there are 18 notorious drains, and ends up in the river at various points along the 22 km stretch through Delhi. Industrial waste from Delhi's industries flows through these drains. By the time the river leaves Delhi, the water is not fit even for bathing. The situation is worse during summer. The average annual flow in Yamuna is estimated to be about 100 billion kilolitres, of which 80 per cent is during the three monsoon months. With very little water flowing through it during the other months, the assimilation capacity of the river is considerably reduced – the river dies and turns into a sewage flow channel.

The story of the Yamuna is not unique; in fact, the entire river system in India is grossly polluted. Industries, municipal corporations, government agencies and almost everyone is responsible for polluting the river system. There is consciousness about polluted rivers, and several laws have been enacted to provide legal backing for cleaning up the system. The Ganga Action Plan (to reduce pollution in the Ganges and its tributaries) and the Yamuna Action Plan (YAP) were launched in 1984 and 1991 respectively. However, several studies conducted by the National Environmental Engineering Research Institute (NEERI) and Indian Institute of Technology point out that these Action Plans have not really reduced the level of pollution in the rivers (Shaym Divan and Armin Rosencranz, 2001).[9]

7. ENVIRONMENTAL REGULATION: CONTROLLING URBAN AIR POLLUTION

The living conditions of millions of the urban population are such that they pose a threat to their health and have potentially catastrophic social consequences. For the urban poor, the living conditions are the worst. A burgeoning urban population beyond the carrying capacity of the different components of urban ecosystems, coupled with an indifferent urban governance, are the root causes for urban environmental problems. The blood lead levels of persons in Ahmedabad, Bombay and Calcutta have been reported to be higher than the corresponding levels of persons in lead-free gasoline areas. In most of the cities, the suspended particulate matter (SPM) levels are significantly higher than the CPCB standards.

The deterioration in air quality in most Indian cities has led to an intense search for ways of controlling pollution. Tentative estimates of health costs of urban air pollution in India is US$1.4 billion (Brandon and Hommann, 1995). Vehicular emission is a major source of air pollution. For example, in Delhi, where the health incidences and the cost of air pollution is the highest in India, contribution of vehicles to the daily emission level is the highest.

Control of air pollution has to factor in the growth in the number of vehicles, congestion, poor quality of roads and quality of fuel used in vehicles. Though the history of legislation for maintenance of air quality starts with the Air (Prevention and Control of Pollution) Act, 1981, it was the Environmental (Protection) Act, 1986, that prescribed emission standards for vehicles for the first time. The prescribed standards pertained to the emission of carbon monoxide and hydrocarbons. The Act proposed to implement the standards in 1992. The responsibility of enforcing these standards was vested in the Ministry of Surface Transport (MoST).

In 1989, the Motor Vehicles Act of 1939 was amended, and the Idle Emission Regulation was enacted. In April 1990, these rules were notified to vehicle owners. The rules made it mandatory to obtain a certificate of fitness for registration of public, commercial and private vehicles older than 15 years. The rules also required all motor vehicles to comply with the laid down emission standards and to obtain a certificate of 'pollution under control' (PUC). However, the whole system of issuing the certificates needs more credibility and accountability; as a result of the lax system the maintenance of vehicles in most cases is very poor, specially in relation to pollution control. The certification authorities need to involve stakeholders like Resident Welfare Associations in the urban localities where such problems exist. At present, the PUC certification is being carried out by the motor vehicle inspectorate, known as Regional Transport Offices (RTOs), attached to the Transport Department in each state.

In 1991, Mass Emission Regulation was introduced. The legislation laid down emission standards of pollutants under specified driving conditions for vehicle manufacturers as well as for in-use vehicles. The emission rates of vehicles were checked during mass emission tests. In 1995, fitment of catalytic converters (CAT) for cars in the four metros was made compulsory. The mass emission standards were tightened in 1996 to improve the effectiveness in producing the desired result. Evaporative Emission and Crank Case Emission Regulation was introduced and emission limits of CO, HC and NO_x were lowered.

7.1 Intervention of the Judiciary

Introduction of strict norms by the Union Territory of Delhi administration did not make any difference in controlling vehicular pollution. The quality of air continued to deteriorate in Delhi; citizens found the pollution unbearable with eye and lung problems increasing sharply around the mid-1990s. On 28 July, 1998, in response to a Public Interest Litigation, the Supreme Court of India ruled that all eight-year-old buses and pre-1990 three-wheelers and taxis would have to be converted to use compressed natural gas (CNG) by 31 March, 2000. For the rest of the buses, three-wheelers and taxis, 31 March, 2001 was fixed as the deadline. This order, however, was difficult to implement. However, the Supreme Court took a strong stand and forced the Delhi Administration to implement the programme of converting the diesel-run buses to use CNG fuel, and despite opposition by various lobbies and reluctance by the government, the programme had to be implemented. Thus, the judiciary instead of the executive took the onus of implementing pollution control measures.

In May 1999, the Supreme Court of India directed that Euro-I emission norms would be effective for the National Capital Region (NCR) for registration of all private (non-commercial) vehicles with effect from 1 June, 1999 and Euro-II norms with effect from 1 April, 2000. The apex court passed these directives after detailed consideration of various options recommended by the Environmental Pollution Authority (EPA). Following the Supreme Court directives, India 2000 norms were formulated in the year 2000. These norms are significantly tighter than the mass emission standards of 1996. India 2000 norms are at least Euro-I equivalent for all four-wheelers, Euro-II equivalent for non-commercial four-wheelers in the NCR (also referred to as Bharat Stage II) and are the tightest norms in the world for two-wheelers.

It has been proposed by an Inter Ministerial Task Force Committee to review the feasibility of Euro-III emission norms for the mega cities after 2005. A CPCB Committee comprising representatives from refineries, research institutes like the Indian Institute of Petroleum, and ministries of Industry and Petroleum recommended a road map for the implementation of emission norms covering the major cities and the whole country.

8. FAILURE OF THE EXECUTIVE AND INTERVENTION OF THE JUDICIARY

8.1 Implementation of Pollution-regulating Laws

The nodal agency for implementing various laws relating to environmental protection at the Centre is the Ministry of Environment and Forest and the Central Pollution Control Board established by it. At the state level, most states have set up Departments of Environment and State Pollution Control Boards (SPCBs).

The whole issue of pollution prevention and control is dealt with mainly by command and control methods. Voluntary regulations, fiscal instruments and education and promotional measures are also being tried out. In the command and control methods the standards are determined and enforced by the central and state pollution control boards. The boards have implemented a pollution control programme whereby a total of 1551 large and medium units have been identified in the country under the 17 highly polluting industrial sectors. Such programmes need continuous monitoring until the target is attained. In order to encourage industries to manufacture their products in an environment-friendly manner, the CPCB has introduced an ECOMARK scheme to help the consumers to identify such products. As regards fiscal instruments, although the Tax Reform Committee in 1991 recommended excise taxes for dealing with externalities, the main focus of fiscal instruments has been to generate revenue rather than controlling pollution or conserving scarce resources.

Thus, despite the legislative and administrative efforts and fiscal incentives for pollution control, ambient standards of air and water pollution continue to be routinely exceeded, and in some areas the quality has even deteriorated (Mehta et al., 1996). This is attributable to the hiatus between the macro goals of our environmental policy and the micro nature of operational provisions for enforcement of the policy. Hence, though standards have been laid down for ambient air and water quality, actual enforcement relates mostly to some source emission standards laid down for individual polluters. Furthermore, the ambient and source standards are laid down independently, and unrelated in terms of the volume of pollution-generating activities. Hence, it is quite conceivable that the quality of the environment may continue to deteriorate in spite of compliance by individual polluters. Additionally, the degree of compliance may be poor.

8.2 Determination of Standards

The CPCB has stipulated baseline standards, and the SPCBs can prescribe more stringent standards depending on the particular desires and requirements. There are three types of effluent standards for discharge of effluents. These are concentration-based standards, equipment-based standards, and load- or mass-based standards. The issue, however, is not with the prescription of standards, but with their implementation. Often, an instance of dynamic instability in intergovernmental competition arises from laxity in implementing environmental standards.

Questions may be raised about the basis for setting standards and their relevance of the standard to the surrounding ecosystem. According to Sankar (1999), determination of standards should be done on the basis of detailed cost–benefit analysis. The standard-setting in India does not give any chance to the polluters or the citizens to voice their opinion. The standards in India are set on the basis of industry studies undertaken by scientific and technical institutions appointed by the CPCB. These studies provide estimates of pollution emission and abatement cost subject to the various limitations that are inherent in such exercises. These standards are often replicated identically from those existing in different parts of the world without testing their relevance to the Indian situation. Another issue at the implementation level is whether a nation-wide uniform effluent standard is desirable. The carrying capacity and the trade off between environmental quality and growth are determined and influenced by regional specificity. The standards, therefore, should vary with regions. However, fixing standards according to regional specificity may lead to the states lowering the standard to attract investment, eventually degenerating into a pollution haven. To prevent this tendency, the Environment Protection Act 1986 gives powers to the Central and State Governments to restrict or prohibit certain activities in ecologically fragile areas. The rules do not permit any State Governments or SPCBs to lower the standards fixed by the Central Government in any region. The problem of implementation is, nevertheless, critical.

It may be pertinent to mention here that in 1988 the Water Act was amended to strengthen the implementation provisions. Now, the State Boards can close a defaulting unit, the penalties are also raised and a citizen's initiative provision bolsters the enforcement machinery. In the industrialized state of Gujarat a resolution was adopted in the legislature under Article 252 not to introduce the 1988 amendments, thus continuing to allow the industries to pollute land and water-bodies. However, in 1995 this came to the notice of the Supreme Court when a writ petition was filed by a farmer against large-scale pollution of a canal called Kharicut. The petitioner complained that pollution of water had rendered irrigation practically impossible and had reduced farm productivity. The fact-finding committee appointed by the Supreme Court found that agricultural productivity had indeed reduced to 0.5 tons per acre from 2.00 tons per acre in about 8000 acres of land due to the discharge of wastewater in the canal by a number of industrial units. The court also found that Gujarat Pollution Control Board and Gujarat Industrial Development Corporation did not seriously implement the Water Act or the Environment Protection Act and only paid 'lip service' to it. The Court took a tough stand to implement the provisions of law and a cleaning operation, which included closure, fines, construction of pipeline to carry industrial wastewater to effluent treatment plants, was carried out for four years; these plans were implemented under the strict supervision of the High Court. This example clearly brings out that there is a big gap between the existence of law and its implementation. Similar instances have been reported from Tamil Nadu and Maharashtra (Shaym Divan and Armin Rosencranz, 2001). It may also be pointed out here that monitoring and enforcement through local-level institutions will be much more effective in checking such pollution; the absence of delegation of power to such institutions forms the basis of executive failure and intervention by the judiciary.

8.3 Enforcement of Standards

In India, poor enforcement of rules occurs due to unreliable information regarding quantities of effluents, emissions and solid wastes and their characteristics. There is information asymmetry, since polluters know more about the sources, magnitudes and concentration of pollutants as well as cost of controlling pollution than the regulators. It is very difficult for the regulating agencies to acquire and process information from thousands of units dispersed in their domain. The regulating agencies complain about the 'thin spread of institutions' for controlling pollution vis-à-vis the enormous spread of industrial units, which makes them very weak.[10] The SPCBs suffer from acute resource constraints. They do not have adequate technical facilities and skilled personnel for monitoring the polluting units and filing charges against them for violating standards. The amount of fines imposed is also less, and is independent of the extent of violations. The courts take many years to settle the cases due to the large number of cases pending, and that makes the dispute settlement mechanism ineffective. Penalties such as imprisonment of officials, stoppage of water and electricity and closure of units can impose hardships on the affected firms, but in a weak enforcement regime with the principal–agent problem, collusion between regulators and the regulated units is common. Since dispute settlement by going to courts is time consuming and costly, it gives the regulating officers an opportunity to indulge in rent seeking activities. Besides, the State governments can intervene and influence the decisions of the SPCBs. Even though the SPCBs are supposed to be autonomous, they depend upon the State Government for financial support, and the members owe their positions to political patronage.

8.4 Intervention of Judiciary

The inability to enforce environmental legislation has often led to affected parties, NGOs and the general public taking recourse to legal action, mostly in the form of public interest litigation. This is aided by the fact that courts have interpreted the fundamental right to life and personal liberty enshrined in Article 21 of the constitution to include the right to enjoy pollution-free air and water.

Public interest litigation in India

Public Interest Litigation (PIL) in India is working on the planned rules evolved by the Supreme Court through the various decisions pronounced by it. The need for PIL was felt by the Supreme Court when it reckoned the fact that large numbers of people in India are suffering silently in matters relating to their fundamental rights because of poverty, illiteracy and remoteness from the centre of power. The remedy available to citizens to go to the courts for the enforcement of the right to life under Article 21 and the growing environmental problems and consciousness has radically changed the situation in India. Some of the important PILs are mentioned below.

(i) *Rural Litigation and Entitlement Kendra v state of Uttar Pradesh*[11] This case is said to be the harbinger of the new trend of PILs. The Supreme Court directed the closure of mining operations in the limestone quarries of the Doon valley located in the foothills of the Himalayas when it found that it was creating an ecological imbalance and was a health hazard to the local population. It held that although closure would cause hardship to the affected parties, it was necessary for protecting and safeguarding the rights of the people to live in a healthy environment and to ensure an ecological balance. It further directed that the affected areas be restored by afforestation and a soil conservation programme to provide employment opportunities to the affected workers (Shaym Divan and Armin Rosencranz, 2001).

(ii) *M.C. Mehta v Union of India*[12] The Supreme Court directed the stoppage of operations of tanneries discharging effluents into the River Ganges if they did not set up primary effluent treatment plants. It held that financial incapacity of the tanners to set up effluent treatment plants was irrelevant.

(iii) *M.C. Mehta v Union of India*[13] The Supreme Court ordered the closing down of a chlorine plant of Shriram Industries after the oleum gas leak case. This case was decided by a five judge Constitutional Bench due to the gravity of the legal question under consideration. In this case the court ruled that there is absolute liability on hazardous industries.

(iv) *Indian Council for Enviro – legal action v Union of India*[14] In this case the Supreme Court ordered remedial action and compensation to the people affected by lethal waste left for years after chemical industries were closed. The compensation was in line with absolute liability principle.

(v) *Research Foundation for Science v Union of India* In its order on a PIL related to dumping of hazardous and noxious material by industrial units throughout India filed by Research Foundation for Science, an NGO, the Supreme Court issued a direction to the Union ministry for environment and forests to take the necessary steps within a specified time frame. The Supreme Court warned the ministry that if the top officers concerned did not measure up to their duties and enforce the provisions of the Environment Protection Act of 1986, the court would be constrained to record a 'judicial finding of failure to perform their duties against them'. The Court also threatened that the judicial finding would be recorded in their service records.

Some other important decisions of the Supreme Court are: (i) closure of 69 foundries in Howrah, in West Bengal state for their failure to install pollution control devices in 1996; (ii) closure of 39 000 illegal industrial units operating in residential areas in Delhi and shifting 513 of them to locations outside the city for causing health damage to citizens; (iii) closing of aquaculture farms within 500 metres of the sea in 1997; (iv) shifting 550 tanneries located in East Calcutta in 1997 and setting up of an environmental pollution fund, with each unit paying Rs 10 000 as a fine to be used for cleaning up the river Hoogly on the banks of which the tanneries were located; (v) ban on felling of trees and ruling that the running of saw mills of any kind, including veneer and plywood mills was, prima facie, a violation of the provisions of the Forest Conservation Act of 1980.

Taking cue from proactive judgments of the Supreme Court, High Courts of the states have also begun to invoke power of writ proceedings under Article 226 of the Constitution to deal with environmental degradation as a threat to life. In *L.K. Koolwal v State of Rajasthan*, the High Court held that according to Article 51(a), the citizens have a duty to maintain a clean environment. In another PIL challenging the environmental imbalance likely to be created by the implementation of the new water scheme in Lakshadweep Islets, the Kerala High Court ordered that the right to life is much more than the right to animal existence.

As PIL cases began crowding the court docket, often in the form of skimpy petitions based on newspaper reports, several problems have started to arise in relation to securing detailed facts, receiving expert opinion on complex social and scientific issues and ensuring the continuous supervision of judicial orders. Sometimes the official machinery is unreliable, slow and biased, and is unable to provide an impartial assessment of facts. On such occasions the Court can appoint special commissions to gather facts and data. With regard to complex scientific issues, the Supreme Court frequently relies on the National Environment Engineering Research Institute (NEERI), Nagpur. Sometimes to ease the burden of evidence the court may resort to a judicial notice of 'facts'. For example in a petition seeking to reduce pollution in the River Ganges, the Supreme Court dispensed with the need for hard scientific facts on the health effects of pollution and the damage it caused to riparian property. The Supreme Court went through certain books and writings and simply assumed that such injuries had occurred or were likely to occur, and proceeded to issue remedial action.

Frequently, environmental cases need independent scientific expertise for decision making. On such occasions the judges appoint a committee of experts to probe scientific questions and advise the court on the course of action. Like special commissions, the expert committees are appointed under the inherent powers of the Courts under Article 32 and 226 of the Constitution. The court treats the opinion of such committees with great reverence since they are eminent scientists drawn from leading institutions.[15]

The flip side of PIL is that it may be construed as an ingress into fields traditionally reserved for the executive. An example may be the Dehradun Quarrying Case, where the Supreme Court resolved the development policy which included conserving nature, preserving jobs and protecting substantial business investments while deciding to close a number of limestone quarries in the Mussoorie Hills and to allow others to operate under detailed conditions. The problem relates to the competence of the Court to review highly technical reports of various experts when they differ in their diagnosis and conclusions.

Enforcement of environmental law through the Courts has advantages as well as pitfalls. The judge who presided over the Ganges pollution case had to persistently cajole and drive recalcitrant industries and public authorities in the Ganges basin to comply with pollution norms. The polluting units included hundreds of large polluting industries in the states of Uttar Pradesh, Bihar and West Bengal, municipal corporations, the Eastern Railways, giant thermal power plants, numerous small industries and tanneries. The first task of the Court was to identify the polluters, for which it turned to the lawyer who filed the PIL. Once identified, all units were issued orders to meet effluent standards within three months or else face closure. To emphasize the urgency, the orders threatening closure were issued without hearing the companies. The Court directed the state pollution control boards to serve the notice immediately. The units had to report to the Boards. When the units reached the prescribed discharge levels, the Boards were directed by the Court to inspect the working of the emission treatment plants. The Court was clearly unhappy with the performance of the pollution control boards and regretted that the SPCBs could not perform even an elementary function. The widespread impression was that Court orders were misused by the dishonest board officials to seek rent. The Court finally entrusted the National Environmental Engineering Rcsearch Institute to perform the job.[16]

Public interest litigation and judicial activism has been extremely effective in India in dealing with the problems of executive failure, which has been so rampant in matters of environmental concerns. In many senses the courts provide a remedy to massive bureaucratization and a very non-transparent, nebulous, ineffective and corrupt administrative structure of state and central governments. Environmental conservation in India without the interference of the courts would have been a shambles. The judicial activism has been an effective remedy for administrative and executive failures. It has brought about a sense of accountability and responsibility in the otherwise lax bureaucracy. This has been an important part of 'checks and balances' in Indian federalism.

While the judicial intervention has been an effective check against executive failure, excessive intervention could result in taking over the functions of the executive by the courts and in such cases, there is no remedy for the wrong decisions. The Supreme Court's attempt to solve the environmental regulation through judicial pronouncements is certainly praiseworthy, but it basically highlights the failure of the executive to enforce environmental laws and regulations. The reluctance of the executive in environmental regulation is not due to the assignment system itself, nor can it be attributed to unstable intergovernmental competition, but seems to arise from asymmetric information and structure of incentives leading to rent seeking behaviour of the regulators. Judicial activism can not be a satisfactory solution to executive failure, because, judicial intervention can at best be an ad hoc solution and by itself, it does not help to evolve a rule-based system of environmental governance. Besides, while the Supreme Court has shown keenness to deal with environmental issues, the lower courts have been extremely reluctant to take up environmental cases. There is also a serious problem of corruption in the lower courts, which may not yield satisfactory solutions.[17] Thus, in the Indian context, rather than the assignment of the environmental function between different levels of government, the problems have centred around implementation and the overlapping roles of executive and judiciary.

9. CONCLUDING REMARKS

This chapter deals with the assignment system and implementation mechanism relating to the environmental functions in India. It analyses the effectiveness of the environmental governance in the country by examining forests, water and air. It analyses the system of assignments, problems arising from the overlapping assignments, bargaining and dispute resolution mechanisms in regard to the three elements. It also analyses the implementation aspects of environmental policy to examine the effectiveness of policies and institutions relating to environmental governance.

The assignment of environmental power in Indian federalism is reasonably clear. Broadly, while the central government has the responsibility of determining the overall policy frame, the subnational governments are involved in implementation. Thus, the assignment system attempts to minimize transaction costs by providing sufficient scope for decentralized governance of environmental functions. At the same time, the central government has overriding powers to avoid unstable competition and to institute mechanisms to resolve interstate disputes.

In implementing environmental regulations, particularly with regard to the protection of forests and management of water systems, decentralized solutions involving participatory approaches have shown promise. The institutions of JFM and Village Forest Committees have enhanced the stake of the locals in the development of forestry. Similarly, the water users' associations have helped in improved maintenance of irrigation canals. Instances of a successful decentralized approach can also be found in rainwater harvesting and watershed development. However, decentralized solutions may also lead to elite capture unless adequate safeguards are taken.

The implementation of environmental functions has been a major concern. In most cases, a critical factor impeding effective implementation is the structure of incentives to bureaucracy and policy makers and the influence of polluters on them. Besides, the environmental regulators do not have access to modern technology to measure and regulate pollution levels, and their resources are inadequate.

Although the assignment of environmental functions to different levels of government seems to be satisfactory, there is considerable overlap between the roles of executive and judiciary in the enforcement of environmental regulation. Often, we see the executive failure in environmental regulation leading to the intervention by the Supreme Court. Interpreting that access to clean water and air as a fundamental right, the courts have pronounced several judgments on the implementation of environmental regulation, often taking over the role of the executive. This has helped to resolve issues in the short term and in some cases has led to improvements in environmental quality, although it involves the risk of resulting in ad hoc and arbitrary solutions. There is also the problem of capacity of the Supreme Court to take into account changes in technology. In other words, replacement of executive action through judicial activism can not be a satisfactory solution to environmental regulation. This calls for reform of the incentive structure and institutions of governance to make the executive much more sensitive and accountable to environmental issues.

The chapter has also analysed the issues of interstate river-water disputes. The conclusion is that an effective resolution mechanism for interstate river-water disputes simply does not exist. The ruling governments at the Centre have simply used the disputes for their short-term political gains. Neither the Tribunals nor the Supreme Court order has ensured compliance by the parties to the dispute nor do they have the potential to provide an effective solution to the problem. The river-water dispute has become highly emotive, and threatens the very federal fabric of the country.

NOTES

1. For example, the province of Alberta, in Canada, gets much of its revenues from oil resources and does not impose a retail sales tax on its citizens.
2. The words 'Union' and 'Centre' are used interchangeably in this chapter.
3. There are also other Acts with implications for environmental regulations. These include the Factories Act 1948, which mandates the treatment of liquid effluents, gases and fumes generated during production process before disposal and the Insecticides Act of 1968, which regulates all aspects of use of pesticides including the monitoring of insecticides residue in the environment. There are also other Acts related to the environment such as the Prevention of Food Adulteration Act of 1954, the River Boards Act of 1956, the Mines and Minerals (Regulation and Development) Act of 1957, the Ancient Monuments and Archaeological Sites and Remains Act of 1958 and the Atomic Energy Act of 1962.
4. It may be noted that the PIL on air pollution pertained to local issues, although filed in the national court.
5. This section has been compiled on the basis of information available at the websites of ENVIS, MoEF and Sustainable Development Network Programming of National Informatics Center and of TERI, The Energy and Resource Institute, New Delhi (www.teriin.org).

6. The programmes implemented by the Ministry of Agricultural and Co-operation are National Watershed Development Projects for Rainfed Areas, Watershed Development Projects in Shifting Cultivation Areas, Integrated Watershed Development Projects, The Karnataka and Madhya Pradesh Watershed Development Projects, and the watershed projects at Tirunelveli, Ramnathapuram and Koraput.
7. The programmes under the Ministry are Desert Development Programme, Drought Prone Area Programme, and the Integrated Watershed Development Programme, which carries out water resources development activities including check dams and water harvesting structures.
8. Ministry of Rural Development and Ministry of Environment and Forest of the Central Government, Ministry of Panchayati Raj and Rural Development, Irrigation Departments of State Governments.
9. We shall come back to the issue of water pollution with respect to its regulation, enforcement of standards and institutions, in the subsequent sections. We discuss issues related to air pollution in the next section so that the common institutions which enforce pollution related regulations can be analysed with respect to both air and water pollution.
10. The total strength of employees of the Pollution Control Board in India is 600, compared to 17 000 in USEPA.
11. A.I.R. 1985 SC 652.
12. A.I.R. 1987 SC 965, 1086 and 1988 S.C.1037 and 1135.
13. A.I.R. 1987 SC 1086.
14. A.I.R.1996 SC 1037.
15. The Supreme Court accepted the Shekhar Singh Committee recommendations which was appointed by it to look into matters related to saving the fragile ecosystem of the Andaman and Nicobar Islands in spite of heavy opposition from a number of quarters.
16. Compiled from newspaper reports of the *Times of India* and *The Hindu*.
17. The Chief Justice lamented in public for his inability to prevent rampant corruption in the lower courts due to lack of effective power. See *Times of India*, 13 February, 2004.

BIBLIOGRAPHY

Alavi, H. and J. Harris (eds) (1989), *Sociology of 'Developing Societies': South Asia*, London: Macmillan.

Bardhan, P. (1984), *The Political Economy of Development in India*, Oxford: Oxford University Press.

Brandon, C. and K. Hommann (1995), *The Cost of Inaction: Valuing the Economy-wide Cost of Environmental Degradation in India*, Asia Environment Division, World Bank.

Breton, Albert (1995), *Competitive Governments: An Economic Theory of Politics and Public Finance*, Cambridge, UK: Cambridge University Press.

Breton, Albert (2002), 'An introduction to decentralization failure', in Ehtisham Ahmad and Vito Tanzi (eds), *Managing Fiscal Decentralization*, London: Routledge.

Brewer, Jeffrey D. and Shashi Kolavalli (1998), 'Assessing common property institutions', presented at 'Crossing Boundaries', the seventh annual conference of the International Association for the Study of Common Property, Vancouver, British Columbia, Canada, 10–14 June, 1998.

Coase, R. (1960), 'The problem of social cost', *Journal of Law and Economics*, **1**, 1–44.

Gadgil, M. and R. Guha (1992), *This Fissured Land: An Ecological History of India*, India: Oxford University Press.

Geijer, J.C.M.A. (1996), *Irrigation Management Transfer in Asia: Papers from the Expert Consultation on Irrigation Management Transfer in Asia*, Bangkok: RAP Publication.

Government of India (1987), *National Water Policy*, Ministry of Water Resources, New Delhi.

Government of India (1990), *National Forest Policy*, Ministry of Forest and Environment, New Delhi.

Government of India (1992), *National Perspectives for Water Resources Development*, National Water Development Agency, New Delhi.

Government of India (1993), *Reassessment of Water Resources Potential of India*, Central Water Commission, New Delhi.

Government of India (1997), *Report of the Working Group on Participatory Irrigation Management for the Ninth Plan*, Ministry of Water Resources, New Delhi.

Government of India (1999), *Report of the Working Group on Perspectives of Water Requirements* (National Commission for Integrated Water Resources Development), Government of India Ministry of Water Resources, New Delhi

Government of India (2002), *National Water Policy*, Ministry of Water Resources, New Delhi.

Guha, Ramachandra (1983), 'Forestry in British and Post-British India: A Historical Analysis', *Economic and Political Weekly*, Vol. 18.

Gupta, Shreekant (1996), 'Environmental policy and federalism in India', National Institute of Public Finance and Policy (mimeo).

Iyer, Ramaswamy R. (1999), 'Three river treaties' (mimeo).

Iyer, Ramaswamy R. (2003), *Water Perspectives, Issues, Concerns*, New Delhi: Sage Publications.

James, A.J. (2003), 'Institutional challenges for water resource management: India and South Africa, WHIRL Project Working Paper 7.

Mehta S., S. Mundle and U. Sankar (1996), *Controlling Pollution Incentives and Regulation*, New Delhi: Sage Publications.

Moench, M. (1997), 'National importance of groundwater and power supply management with particular reference to electricity pricing and supply', paper presented at the Workshop on Groundwater Regulation and Management, 17–19 February, New Delhi.

Musgrave, R.A. (1983), 'Who should tax, when and what?', in Charles McLure, Jr (ed.), *Tax Assignment in Federal Countries*, Canberra: The Australian National University Press.

Nadkarni, M.V. (1989), *The Political Economy of Forest Use and Management*, New Delhi: Sage Publications.

National Water Development Agency (1992), 'National perspectives for water resource development', National Water Development Agency, Government of India.

Oates, Wallace E. (1999), 'An essay on fiscal federalism', *Journal of Economic Literature*, **37**(3), 1120–49.

Rajasekhar, D., D.V. Gopalappa and Madhushree Sekher (2004), 'Role of local organizations in watershed development: a study in Karnataka and Uttaranchal States, India', Bangalore, India: Institute of Social and Economic Change.

Ramana, M.V.V. (1992), *Inter-State River Water Disputes in India*, Madras: Orient Longman.

Rao, Govinda M. and N. Singh (2004), *The Political Economy of Federalism in India*, New Delhi, India: Oxford University Press.
Richards, A. and N. Singh (1996), 'Water and federalism: India's institutions governing inter-State river waters', University of California (Santa Cruz), working paper.
Sankar, U. (1999), 'Laws and institutions relating to environmental protection in India', Madras School of Economics Occasional Paper No. 2.
Sankar, U. (2002), 'Design and enforcement of fiscal instruments for pollution control in India', in M. Govinda Rao (ed.), *Development, Poverty, and Fiscal Policy*, New Delhi: Oxford University Press.
Sharma, S. (2003), 'Redefining water Governance', http://pikespeak.uccs.edu.
Shaym Divan and Armin Rosencranz (2001), *Environmental Law and Policy in India*, New Delhi: Oxford University Press.
Singh, N. (1997), 'Issues in local government reforms in India', University of California (Santa Cruz), working paper.
Vermillion, Douglas (1991), 'Water user's association', International Food Policy Research Institute, working paper.
Vira, Bhaskar (1995), 'Institutional change in India's forest sector, 1976–1994: Reflections on State Policy', OCEES Research Paper No.5.
Wade, R. (1988), *Village Republics: Economic Conditions for Collective Action in South India*, Cambridge: Cambridge University Press.
World Bank (1991), *India: Irrigation Sector Review*, Washington DC.
World Bank (1998), *India – Water Resource Management Review (1998)*, Washington DC.

9. Russia: The difficult transition to stable environmental institutions

Pavel V. Kasyanov and Aliona V. Stovpivskaya

1. INTRODUCTION

The current practice of environmental protection management in Russia can be seen against the background of two main factors. One is the immense size of the country with its diverse natural conditions along with its distinctive cultural, socio-economic and civilization-specific features. The second relates to the overall system of governance in the country, which suffers from instability and institutional failure in particular with regard to environmental protection and natural resource management in the so-called 'transition' period.

It follows therefore that analysis of any administrative/governance system and prescription of measures to achieve or introduce good governance practice cannot be de-linked from the historical, cultural and other civilization-specific aspects of the country in question. If the countries are quite different, borrowing certain models and practices may produce quite unexpected and even undesirable results. It means that we should have a broader vision of the problem in dealing even with seemingly very practical issues of modern administrative or governance standards (Kasyanov 1998; Kasyanov 2000; Lukianchikov and Potravnyi 2000).

1.1 Natural Resources Profile

Russia is the world's largest country, with an area of over 17 million km^2, of which 47 per cent is covered by forests (Petrov et al. 1997), 8 per cent is arable or permanent crop land, 5 per cent is grassland, and 40 per cent has other cover. Russia is richly endowed with mineral resources. It is the world's largest producer of natural gas and the third largest producer of oil and coal. It has large reserves of iron, copper, gold, silver, diamonds and uranium. Average annual water flow amounts to 4260 km^3, and total annual water consumption averages 87.4 km^3. There are 3801 (explored/proved) deposits of underground water with the exploitation reserves of 30.4 km^3, of which

19.8 km^3 are designed for commercial use, while in fact only about 11 km^3 are used annually. Forested areas occupy approximately 1.06 billion ha, with timber resources accounting for about one fifth of the world's reserves. Annual increment of wood stock averages 871.45 million m^3, while annual allowable timber harvesting amounts to 500–510 million m^3. Fish catch amounts to nearly 200 000 tons per year, while estimated total fish stock is at a level of 16 million tons, with a potentially permissible catch of 4.3 million tons. Russia has a population of 144.5 million, with the major part living in the western section of the country. Over 70 per cent of the population lives in cities, of which Moscow, with its 10.5 million inhabitants, is the largest.

1.2 Environmental Profile

Air emissions in Russia were reduced significantly in the 1990s. Between 1991 and 1997 (a period of dramatic economic collapse) the emissions of SO_x fell by 35 per cent, NO_x by 29 per cent, CO by 24 per cent and CO_2 by 37 per cent (EIs for pollution control and Natural Resource Management: The Russian Federation). Though industrial and municipal wastewater discharges also decreased by around 20 per cent in the same period, improvement in the quality of surface water was insignificant. Despite the dramatic decline in industrial production, the quantity of industrial hazardous waste is not reported to have fallen in the period between 1993 and 1997. Large and still growing volumes of industrial waste are accumulated at industrial sites, particularly in the iron-and-steel industry and in the energy/power generation sector. Municipal waste is almost exclusively disposed of in landfills which do not meet requirements and are subject to growing capacity constraints.

Thus, despite the economic decline, the reductions in emissions were far less than the twofold decrease in GDP and industrial production, that is the pollution intensity of the economy generally increased. We can reasonably expect a further increase in pollution when the economic recovery and expansion process sets in, should additional pollution control action not be taken. It may be noted that Russian emissions of SO_x and CO_2 per capita are about the same level as in OECD countries; however, when measured per unit of GDP, emissions of these two pollutants are about 2.5 times as high in Russia as the OECD average.

A significant part of reduction in environmental impact in the 1990s had little, if anything, to do with environmental protection management per se. As we noted above, it was a natural consequence of the dramatic decline in industrial and agricultural production. What is of utmost concern is the fact that almost no replacement or capital repair of technological and specialist environmental protective equipment has been carried out in the past

10 years. Such a situation is fraught with a disproportionately high rate of emission increase when the economy starts to grow as well as an increasing risk of man-made catastrophes of different scales.

2. THE ENVIRONMENT

Until recently, pollution control, protection of ecosystems, and natural (renewable) resource management (except fisheries) and a certain level of environmental monitoring had been controlled and regulated by the Ministry of Natural Resources (MNR). MNR head-office administered its functions through regional departments in 7 federal mega-regions (*okrugs*) and in 89 regions. Other state bodies responsible for certain environmentally-related issues are mentioned below in this section and in section 3.

We look at pollution control, protection of ecosystems, and natural (renewable) resource management in detail below. The environmental policy with respect to these three aspects is regulated by different legislative, institutional, administrative, economic and other measures. The scale and success of administrative management in these three areas significantly vary for many reasons, such as, for instance, considerable variations in time and terms prescribed for addressing/dealing with different kinds of environmental impact.

2.1 Pollution Control

A major legislative act in the field of environmental protection is Federal Law No. 7-FZ On the Environment protection (FLEP) of 10.01.2002 (replacing the earlier one, of 1991) which addresses a wide range of environmental impacts.

Clause 22, item 1 establishes the following standards of permissible environmental impact:

- maximum permissible air emissions (MPE) and maximum permissible wastewater discharge (MPD)[1];
- allowed volume of generated production and consumption waste and waste disposal limits (WGDL);
- maximum permissible physical impacts (thermal, noise, vibration, ionizing radiation, electromagnetic field intensity, and other physical impacts).[2]

This clause also establishes maximum permissible amount (quotas) of withdrawal of the nature components.

Thus, the legislation and system of standards cover almost all known kinds of air, water and soil pollution, including noise pollution. As far as 'greenhouse gases' are concerned, however, although they find a mention in Russian legislation, standards are set only for those that are subject to standardization due to their toxicity (all except CO_2). As for noise standards, they were established for different types of premises: residential area, industrial area, transport zone and production facilities. However, the current legislation does not so far embrace such factors as electromagnetic fields generated by cell phones, household implements, and so on.

Clause 22 of FLEP, item 2 states that the above standards (their particular values) are established in order to provide compliance with the standards of environmental quality based on specific local conditions. It means that environmental impact standards for a certain enterprise, for example, are calculated based on the compliance of ambient environmental quality with the environmental standards, for example concentrations of contaminants in air, water, soil, water and air temperature or other kind of standards.

Item 3 of Clause 22 (Federal Law On the Environment protection) formulates (in general) liability for non-compliance with the above standards.

MPE and MPD are established for stationary, mobile and other sources based on the standards of anthropogenic environmental pressure, environmental quality standards, and technological standards. MPE and MPD are established for several hundreds of polluting substances. Technological standards are determined and set based on the best available technologies taking into account economic and social factors. In case of impossibility to comply with MPE and MPD, temporary/provisional limits can be introduced under condition of availability and actual implementation of an EAP approved by the state authorities. So, according to the legislation, the limits (that is temporarily reduced standards) are valid only if the EAP-planned activities are duly implemented. In all cases, whether the polluter should comply with MPE and MPD or with the temporary limits, the right to emit polluting substances into the environment is granted via a permit issued by the state authorities for environmental protection.

MPPI is calculated and set for each source based on standards of anthropogenic load on the environment, standards of environmental quality, and taking into account other sources of physical impacts, for example thermal conditions, noise, vibration, ionizing radiation, electromagnetic field intensity and other physical impacts.

Quotas for withdrawal of the nature/environmental components are established according to respective legislation: Forest Code, Water Code, Land Code and Federal laws On Animal Life and On Plant Life.

Standards of anthropogenic environmental pressure are determined for each type of environmental impact taking into account all sources of respective impacts located within the potentially affected area.

Amongst the major tools of pollution control and management are administrative and economic measures. Administrative control is effected through inspections (Institute of Inspectors) under MNR, SCF, SCSES and other authorities. The primary objective of carrying out inspections is to assess environmental performance of enterprises and organizations and to check compliance with the legislation and standards. As of January 2002, the MNR inspectorate was understaffed by 10 per cent and totalled 2684 officers. In 2003, the number of inspectors was reduced to almost 2000. The SCF inspectorate numbers 4000 officers. SCF includes 25 federal basin departments on the fish stock protection and renewal and fishery regulation. Basin departments, in turn, incorporate 411 inspection authorities for fish stock protection, and 248 for supervisory-and-observation ichthyological stations.

Despite weakening and near disruption of the MNR inspectorate system (primarily because of liquidation of MNR's local-municipal branches), regional inspection authorities continue their important work. They reveal numerous breaches of environmental legislation such as non-compliance with environmental standards, work without required permits, unauthorized extraction of natural resources without licences and/or other required documents, and so on.

State control and inspection of water biological resources is carried out by MNR, SCF, Border Patrol Service (BPS) and other federal bodies.

Another important tool kit is represented by environmental charges (fees) and penalties likely to be supported shortly by environmental taxes. The current system of environmental charges and penalties for air emission, water discharge and waste disposal has been in force since 1992. Air and water pollution charges were introduced for hundreds of pollutants: 217 and 198 for air emissions and water pollution respectively. Section 4 offers a detailed description of economic instruments.

2.2 Protection of Ecosystems

Apart from the above-mentioned FLEP, the following legislative acts regulate protection of ecosystems in particular: Federal laws On Animal Life and On Plant Life, Forest Code, Water Code, Land Code, and others. The major tools and measures for ecosystem protection are:

- regulation of bio-resources use, including prohibition related to endangered species, quotas and licenses for withdrawal of almost all

other species (except mushrooms, berries, some herbs, some fishes in some water bodies etc.);
- licensing fees, charges for withdrawal of one or specified quantity (or any quantity within certain period) of species, penalties for illegal hunting, fishing, tree cutting, etc.;
- a system of specially protected areas; and,
- special preventive or rehabilitation measures (tree-planting and afforestation, including targeted recovery of original ecosystems, for example, oak woods, pineries, fir-groves, cedar forests, etc.).

Nature in Russia encompasses an astounding variety of ecosystems and landscapes, from the deserts of Kalmykia and neighbouring regions to the Arctic Tundra and various marine (water) ecosystems, including the unique Baikal ecosystem, Arctic Ocean shoal ecosystem and the Far-Eastern coast, from the steppes to the taiga, from plains with large rivers and swamps to plateaux and mountains. There are vast remote territories, especially in Siberia and the European North, which have remained almost pristine. Virgin and slightly disturbed ecosystems occupy approximately 60–65 per cent of the total area of Russia. At the same time they comprise a greater part (about 80 per cent) of the Euro-Asian area of natural ecosystems, with a total area of 13 million km^2, which is the largest natural (mostly intact) ecosystem in the world. This provides natural advantage for the protection of ecosystems.

Complementing the 'passive' protection provided by remoteness and inaccessibility, special measures and actions have been undertaken for the protection of ecosystems. It is not widely known that Russia has one of the world's best systems of protected areas, which encompasses over a million square kilometres of wild landscapes nestling important habitats for a vast number of plants and animals.

The Federal Law of the Russian Federation on Specially Protected Natural Areas (SPNA) adopted on 14 March, 1995 declares that specially protected natural areas are state/public property and distinguishes between the following categories of SPNA:

- national natural reserves (wildlife sanctuaries or refuges) including biosphere preserves;
- natural parks;
- national natural reserves;
- natural monuments;
- arboretums and botanical gardens; and
- health-improvement localities and resorts.

SPNA may have federal, regional or local significance status. Amongst the most important types of SPNA are the sanctuaries, strictly protected scientific nature reserves, characterized by the highest category of nature conservation in the world (IUCN category I). National natural sanctuaries essentially target nature-protection and promote research and eco-educational institutions designed to preserve and study the natural course of natural processes, developments and events, individual species and communities of plants and animals. Sanctuaries are fully exempt from any commercial or economic use. They protect biological diversity by maintaining the natural state of existing natural complexes and objects, engage in research, keep chronicles of nature and conduct eco-monitoring within the framework of Russia's national system. Sanctuaries also take an active part in environmental education, environmental monitoring and training of nature-protection specialists.

The first state Russian sanctuary, Barguzinsky, was created in 1916 on the eastern shore of Lake Baikal. Now, 100 sanctuaries, covering more than 33.7 million hectares (82.7 million acres), protect diverse wilderness areas across the country forming a network of strictly protected areas. Sanctuaries cover a tremendous diversity of territory and play a critical role in nature conservation.

The current 'system' of Russia's sanctuaries was formerly united with similar sanctuaries of Central Asia, Ukraine, Georgia, Moldova, and other former Soviet republics. Russia also has a growing system of 35 National Parks, covering nearly 7 million hectares (17 million acres).

The system of nature and biological resource protection in the former USSR was adapted to the centralized management and strictly hierarchical governance structure. Despite its obvious technocratic orientation and weak public control, that system undoubtedly had a number of advantages, such as ensuring financing of biodiversity conservation in protected natural areas, maintenance of the Red Book, regular inventory of commercial fauna, forest and water biological resources, conservation of selection achievements in agriculture, support of scientific research, and so on. On the other hand, the environmental policy mostly relied on extensive approaches and methods, such as:

- extension of the SPNA network (even with the lack of proper financial support);
- monitoring and maintenance of the Red Book (with no serious attempts to eliminate the factors of negative impact on endangered flora and fauna species).

In the Soviet period, SPNA development was not continuously smooth: in 1951 dramatic events happened. Eighty-eight of the 128 SPNA in USSR were liquidated: 26 in Russia, 19 in the Ukraine, 16 in Georgia, 13 in

Lithuania and 14 in the other six republics. The area of 15 SPNA from the remaining 40 was cut. The total area of SPNA was reduced from 12.6 million ha to 1.38 million ha. A return to the level of 1951 was achieved again in 1985.

Changes in the political and economic situation in Russia in the early 1990s, growing sovereignty of the subjects of the Russian Federation, and decentralization of authority have seriously affected control and management of biodiversity conservation. The Russian network of specially protected natural areas was faced with challenging problems during this period. With the economic crisis and dramatic aggravation of the criminal situation, the anthropogenic pressure on sanctuaries and national parks increased and became more tangible, which drastically enhanced the ever high professional risk and physical hardships inherent in the struggle with poaching and other environmental law infringements. Highly insufficient and irregular financing of the Russian network of sanctuaries and national parks in the 1990s allowed neither equipping of the Guard Service, even to the minimum, with modern vehicles and communication means, observation devices, high-quality field and special outfit, uniforms, nor establishing of a permanently operating common federal system of guard improvement.

According to the data obtained from accounting and reporting documents of the MNR reserves, in 2002 the total budget of the entire reserve system amounted to 494 162 000 RUR against 500 758 000 in 2003, meaning merely a 1.5 per cent increase (at the annual inflation rate of 12 per cent). The budget cut included a whole range of items. Compared to 2002, in 2003 financing of two out of five reserve system items was nominally reduced; in another two cases they were reduced in real terms, and only revenues from their own activities increased both nominally and in real terms. In 2002 the annual budget of the Russian reserve averaged 5 202 000 RUR against 5 271 000 in 2003 (Financing of the state natural reserves of the MNR of Russia in 2002 and 2003).

Scientific units in all sanctuaries and national parks (especially the latter, given their short period of existence) suffered from a severe shortage of modern technical devices, scientific equipment, computers, and inadequate funds for special literature and scientific trips, which dramatically undermined the efficiency and effectiveness of scientific research activities. The lack of funds almost suspended implementation of international obligations on integrated background monitoring in biosphere sanctuaries included in the UNESCO international biosphere reserve network. Sanctuaries and national parks failed to use their capacity to develop a Unified State/Public/System of Environmental Monitoring.

With rare exceptions, sanctuaries and national parks failed to use their special capacities to establish a unique educational environment for the general public, based both on the natural, historical and cultural potential of these areas, and the available staff of qualified professionals. Social and economic changes required new approaches to environmental protection. Society came to realize the need for a new environmental policy, adequate legislative framework, new forms of government and public support to environmental activities, including essential institutional and organizational changes.

In 1995–1996, the State Duma of the Federal Assembly of the Russian Federation not only ratified the strategy for Conservation of Biological Diversity but also adopted some fundamental laws: On Specially Protected Natural Areas, On Animal Life, On the Environmental Expert Review, and On Continental Shelf Areas of the Russian Federation. In 1992–1996, the Government of the Russian Federation made decisions on the establishment of 23 new state sanctuaries with a total area of 71 000 square kilometres, 16 national parks with a total area of 31 000 square kilometres, four new federal nature *zakazniks* with a total area of 51 000 square kilometres. The territory of the other 12 sanctuaries was expanded by 25 000 square kilometres. In 1995, the Federal Target Programme on the State Support of Sanctuaries and National Parks for the period up to 2000 was approved by a Presidential Decree. The Integrated Federal Programme for the Protection of Lake Baikal, and the Federal Programme on the Protection of Amur Tiger were also approved. As of 2001, Russia had in total about 15 000 SPNAs of various status and rank with a total area exceeding 130 million ha (about 8 per cent of the Russian territory or just a little larger than the combined area of France, Germany, Italy, Denmark and the Netherlands).

As we mentioned above, the state nature sanctuaries and national parks represent the nucleus or backbone of the federal SPNA network. In early 1996, there were 93 sanctuaries with a total area of 30.1 million ha, while as of 1 January, 2002 their number grew up to 100, and the area amounted to 33.712 million ha (more than Italy plus Belgium), including the inland territory with internal water bodies amounting to 27.211 million ha, which makes up almost 1.6 per cent of the total territory of the Russian Federation. The hundredth sanctuary (Erzi) was established in 2000 in the Republic of Ingushetiya. In 1996, there were 30 national parks in the Russian Federation with the total area of 6.6 million ha, while at present their number amounts to 35 with the total area of about 7 million ha, which makes up 0.4 per cent of the Russian territory.

Notwithstanding the overall increase in terms of area, the general situation in the majority of sanctuaries is deteriorating. The scope of research and nature-protection standards are declining, primarily because of extremely scarce financing. The increasing number of people who have had to subsist mainly at the expense of taiga, forest, river and sea resources has led to greater infringements of conservation regulations and to a decline in animal populations. This, in turn, has endangered the preservation of rare and protected animal and plant species in the sanctuaries. Another problem is that the existing network of sanctuaries cannot adequately support conservation of biological diversity, since the boundaries of wildlife preserves were quite often determined without due consideration of ecosystem boundaries and ranges of populations of major protected species.

National parks are essentially nature protection, eco-educational and research institutions. Their territories include natural complexes and facilities of particular environmental, historical and aesthetical value, and are designed for nature protection, scientific, educational and cultural purposes, as well as for controlled tourism.

Preserves and sanctuaries play a major role in nature protection. However, the 'insular' location allows no coverage of the entire natural diversity found in Russia and preservation of the gene pool of all rare plant species. Dozens of rare plant species either do not occur in preserves or exist in such small quantities that do not ensure reliable preservation. Besides, numerous other natural objects requiring protection occur beyond the boundaries of preserves and sanctuaries. The most acceptable form of protected natural territories for such objects is Natural Monuments, an organizationally flexible form restricted to just several hectares, and characterized by rather strict nature protection conditions. We look at the issue of wetland conservation next.

In 1971, the Convention on Wetlands of International Importance especially as Waterfowl Habitats (the Ramsar Convention) was signed in the town of Ramsar, Iran. Russia, as a republic of the USSR, has been a party to the Ramsar Convention since 1975. The USSR had 12 designated Ramsar sites, but only three of these are situated in Russia. Since the disintegration of the USSR, the federal policy on nature conservation has been aimed at a radical improvement of the situation in Russia, and in 1994, 35 wetlands of international importance with a total area of 10.7 million hectares were designated by Decree of the Government of the Russian Federation No. 1050, 13 September, 1994.

Wetland conservation in Russia is not confined to the protection of Ramsar sites. Large wetland areas are conserved as parts of SPNA (sanctuaries, state wildlife refuges '*zakazniki*', national parks, and so on). Outside protected natural areas, wetland management is regulated by a number of laws (Water Code, Forest Code, federal laws On Animal Life, and so on). To conserve and use wetlands wisely, a national policy is needed that will formulate the main principles for interaction between society and wetlands, as specifically mentioned in the Strategic Plan of the Ramsar Convention

1997–2002. Since Russia possesses vast and relatively intact wetland resources that play an important part in oxygen regeneration and carbon sequestration, national wetland policy is of global importance.

At the moment, wetlands of international importance are the only type of important wetlands that have a legal status in Russia. Ramsar sites are designated primarily to protect biological diversity, as well as unique and typical ecological, limnological or hydrological features. The criteria for site selection and designation procedure are laid down in the Ramsar Convention and its Annexes. Proposals for the designation of new Ramsar sites may be put forward by regional authorities of the Russian Federation, governmental institutions, public organizations and individuals. At the final stage, the Government of the Russian Federation issues a decree designating the wetland as a Ramsar site, and thus, as a Contracting Party to the Convention, takes an international responsibility for the status of the wetland. Initially SCEP and now MNR and its Research Institute for Nature Conservation have been responsible for the compilation of the Ramsar Shadow List.

There exists, however, a legal contradiction in that the administrative regions of the Russian Federation have no real obligation to establish an effective system of information supply, monitoring and conservation of Ramsar sites. The lack of legal incentives does not allow expansive development of the Ramsar sites network in Russia on a regular and strategically focused basis.

Wetlands of federal importance should basically protect water and other natural resources vital for the people and the national economy. There are wetlands of regional importance too. Administrative regions of the Russian Federation have been given the right to designate wetlands as sites of regional or local importance, according to their legislation, needs and understanding of the value of their wetlands.

In general, the level of knowledge about wetlands in Russia remains extremely low. For the moment, an inventory of 35 Ramsar sites and a Shadow List of 160 sites have been made. The production of the inventory and Shadow List is only the first step towards building up public awareness of the country's wetlands, since more than 400 wetland areas meeting the Ramsar criteria have been identified in Russia, and some experts estimate that the total number of wetland areas could be several thousand!

2.3 Natural (Renewable) Resource Management

The legislative basis for natural resource management is provided mainly by the following laws: On Subsurface, Forest Code, Land Code, Water Code, FLEP, On Animal Life and a few others, along with a number of regulations, instructions, and so on. In the course of overall administrative reform a new Land Code, FLEP, Forest and Water Codes have already been adopted while a new Federal Law On Subsurface has been prepared and submitted to the State Duma (Parliament).

Forest management and protection

State management of forests and forestry is based primarily on the Forest Code, as well as FLEP, Federal Laws On Animal Life, On Plant Life and some others. The Forest Code and the Constitution of the Russian Federation provide the framework for forest management in the Russian Federation. The Forest Code defines the judicial, organizational, and economic mechanisms securing sustainable use of forests as well as the reproduction and protection of forests with respect to environmental factors.

Institutionally, forest management is currently administered by MNR, although prior to the reform of 2000 the State Forest Service (SFS, and later the State Forest Committee) was an independent federal body just like the State Committee on water resources as well as the one under MNR earlier (in 1998).

With respect to their economic and ecological characteristics, location and intended use, Russia's forests are divided (according to the Forest Code) into three groups (Forest Code; Lukianchikov and Potravnyi 2000; Petrov et al. 1997). The forests are further subdivided into different protection status classes. The three main groups were identified and recognized as early as the nineteenth century.

The first management group (Group I) comprises forests with water protection, protective, sanitation and health-improving functions. Water protection areas include forests along rivers, lakes and other water systems, and forests providing protection for waters where valuable fish species come to spawn. Large-scale harvesting is forbidden in these areas, while only improvement felling is allowed. However, the annual wood-harvesting amount should not exceed annual increment. Forests along railways and important highways protect the soils against erosion. Urban forests and parks protect the water supply and recreation areas around towns, and they have sanitary and health-improving functions. Group I also includes forests belonging to other protection categories characterized by significant environment protective, scientific-and-historical, or socio-cultural values; forest preserves, national and nature parks and other nature reserve monuments. Any commercial logging is prohibited.

The second management group (Group II) includes forests in densely populated areas with both protective and limited economic values, as well as forests characterized by insufficient timber resources and restricted forest use. Wood harvesting in Group II forests is limited to amounts equalling the annual increment. Large-scale harvesting requires special measures to be taken to ensure regeneration of the affected areas.

The third group (Group III) comprises the forests of densely-forested regions, of mainly industrial value and intended for meeting the timber requirements of the national economy without causing damage to their protective functions. The forests belonging to Group III are further subdivided into exploited forests and forests-in-reserve. The category 'forests-in-reserve' includes forests that are not utilized due to their remoteness with respect to roads or for other reasons.

Apart from the above laws, among the other essential legislation, one can mention the following: Governmental Decree 'On forest plots lease', Instructions 'On final harvesting within the European part of Russia' and 'On improvement felling within the European part of Russia'.

Changes in the political, administrative, economical, financial, social and other aspects of life in Russia in the past 10–12 years has contradictorily affected administrative management in forestry. On the one hand, the collapse of the national economy dramatically reduced volumes of logging (according to official statistics). On the other hand, illegal felling has reached a tremendous scale, especially in regions neighbouring foreign markets, like those of China, Japan, Korea and Finland. In certain regions illegal logging and export became comparable in volume with legal logging! However, illegal felling also takes place in internal regions of Russia, situated away from foreign consumers, since despite a very low stumpage fee it is still cheaper to log illegally. Illegal logging is not only damaging to the state economy but also endangers the valuable and often unique species protected by the law (to say nothing of the unpaid stumpage fees), because the loggers are not worried at all about ecological consequences. One of the negative factors is the weakening of administration and control, in other words, forestry authorities do not control the situation in many cases and many regions. The situation is aggravated by omnipresent corruption among the public officers.

Inadequate funding of local forest services (*leskhozes* – districts' subdivisions of federal forest authorities) leads to deficient law-enforcement (illegal logging) and mismanagement of forest resources (excessive sanitary cuttings). On the other hand, increased budget allocations to public services depend to a large extent on increasing economic benefits to the nation from the forestry (revenues, employment). The latter, in turn, requires efficient mechanisms for pricing forest rights (transparent bidding) and real incentives to attract new investments (secured long-term access to forest).

Improvement of the governance system is critical to sustainable management of forests. Mismanagement of public assets, such as forests and forest revenues, keeps their contribution to the national economy far below potential and reduces national interest for long-term conservation of such public assets. Clear distribution of responsibilities, rights and obligations, simple procedures and removal of economic distortions must be given priority, as well as the search for pragmatism and simplicity rather than technical perfection (Kasyanov 2000; Petrov et al. 1997).

Forests and forestry have now reached centre-stage of Russia's reform agenda, and the Government is remodelling the institutional and economic framework of this sector. The new vision is reflected in the newly approved 2003–2010 Concepts for Forest Industry (December 2002) and for Forest Development (January 2003) as well as in an influx of initiatives on new legal instruments already under development (three draft Laws on Forests, Forest Charges and Concessions).

The recently-approved Concepts and the current draft laws foresee that the Forest Fund will remain in ownership of the federal authority (92 per cent of Russian forests).[3] Other forests will remain under ownership of Municipalities and two regions (Moscow and Saint Petersburg having status of constituencies of the RF). Those documents also indicate that sustainable management of forests will increasingly rely on contractual relationships between owner and user of the forests. In accordance with civil law principles, these 'user contracts' will set the rights and obligations of both parties. The general trend is to delegate management operations and market activities to forest users while the public services will focus on strategic and regulatory core-functions. The forest user should then take responsibility for implementation of sustainable forest management plans and payment of rental fees in exchange for secured access to the resource, while the administration will focus on law enforcement.

Management of water use and protection

The management of water use and protection is currently based on the New Water Code, which was approved by the Federation Council in May 2006. The right to use surface water bodies is acquired in accordance with the procedures set by the legislation on water bodies, whereas the right to use underground water follows the procedures set by the legislation on mineral resources. The right to use water bodies is acquired either on the basis of water use agreements (contracts) or as a consequence of decisions by the relevant authority to issue a specific permit for the use of a water body. Water use contracts or use permits are not required in a number of cases, including for example the use of a water body for shipping and small craft navigation, single take-off and landing of aircrafts, withdrawal of underground water for medical purposes (for example, thermal water), withdrawal of water for fire control purposes or for preventive and response actions to other emergencies, fish breeding, watering of gardens, animal farming, and the use for domestic purposes of population in compliance with Article 6 of the new Water Code.

Water bodies are generally owned by the Russian Federation. Water use agreements and permits are issued by the state executive bodies and local government bodies respectively, within the scope of their authorities. Agreements are used to grant the right to withdraw water from the surface water bodies, use the water area for recreational purposes, and other uses of water bodies with the exclusion of electricity production. Application for an agreement can be presented by a legal entity or a private individual to (i) the Federal Water Resources Agency or its regional bodies (for water reservoirs held in federal ownership), or to (ii) the executive body of a constituent of the Russian Federation authorized to enter into water use agreements (for water reservoirs held in ownership of the constituents of the Russian Federation, or in federal ownership but located in the territory of the constituents of the Russian Federation), or (iii) local authorities (for water reservoirs owned by a municipality).

3. INSTITUTIONAL SET-UP

3.1 Historical Background

The history of natural resource management in the Russian federation can be traced back to as early as the sixteenth century. It's no surprise that natural resource management in Russia started with forest resources. However, environmental protection management per se came about much later. The state (federal) environmental protection authority was established as a separate and independent entity only in the late 1980s. Earlier, management of respective issues was carried out by the Government through sectoral ministries and departments, such as Ministry of non-ferrous metallurgy, Ministry of coal industry, Ministry of oil and petrochemical industry, Ministry of oil and gas industry, and so on. Each of the sectoral ministries had a department of environmental protection, as well as research institutes having environmental subdivisions.

A 'system' of environmental protection agencies was established in the late 1980s. To be more precise, the State Committee of USSR on the Environmental Protection was established by Decree No.32 of the Central Committee of the CPSU and USSR Council of Ministers of 7 January, 1988. It was created through integration (actual merger) of different supervisory bodies. Those also included the State Committees on Nature Protection of the USSR, RSFSR and other republics of the Soviet Union. In the first few years of the system's existence, several steps were taken for the introduction of economic management methods, amongst which were payments for nature use and environmental pollution charges.

After disintegration of the USSR, the Russian Federation Ministry for Nature Use and Environment Protection was established as a unified body responsible for integrated management, use and protection of all natural resources, as well as environmental protection. It was in 1991 that the newly formed Russian Government established, following President Yeltsin's Decree of 6 November, 1991, *Minekologia* – Ministry of Environment and Natural Resources headed by Professor V.I. Danilov-Danil'yan. Twelve former Soviet and Russian federal entities (representing six different areas of governance) were integrated in the new ministry: two ministries of environmental protection, two ministries of geology, two ministries of water resources, two forest committees, two departments of geodesy and cartography, one Soviet committee of hydrometeorology (an equivalent Russian committee didn't exist at that time), and the State Commission on mineral reserves).[4] Yet the inherited pressure and burden of narrow sectoral concerns were once again responsible for the low viability of the newly established conglomerate that shortly split almost into its initial components – Russian Committees on Subsurface, Hydrometeorology, Cartography, Forestry, and later also, Water Resources respectively.

Later, in 1998 two state committees: SC of Subsurface Use and SC on Water Resources merged and formed MNR. In 2000 two federal bodies, SCEP and SFS, were incorporated in MNR. However, it is hardly the last reorganization of the administrative structure. In the coming years the natural resource management system is likely to undergo numerous and large-scale changes, including structural ones.

Historically, the Russian governance system has been highly centralized. The federal level of administration still represents the most powerful and influential authority that commands a number of regional subdivisions apart from the central (Moscow-based) apparatus. In addition to the central state machinery, the federal system includes *okrugs* (federal mega-regions) and regions. However, the most serious step towards administrative reform has already been taken, starting with the liquidation of local subdivisions of state (federal) authorities. Now, environmental management is locally administered by municipalities, which, at least juridically, are independent of state (federal and regional) authorities.

Until recently, federal authorities had constituted a united hierarchy of bodies represented by a federal head office, 89 regional offices (in each constituency) and small subdivisions at the district (upper municipal) level. Thus, bodies located in regions (capitals of each region) and districts represented federal authorities, while the actual situation in different regions and in different periods varied from an almost total control of regional authorities over regional subdivisions of federal body, through a moderate subordination of regional subdivisions to regional authority, to almost independent functioning of regional subdivisions.

The above situation was typical of the Yeltsin period, when even the very integrity of the united Russian Federation itself was threatened. President Putin strengthened the 'vertical of authority'. One of his first steps was to establish seven federal mega-regions to provide control over regional authorities as well as regional subdivisions of federal bodies: federal ministries, committees, services, and so on. As a result, for a short period federal authorities incorporated four levels: federal as such, mega-regional (*okrugs*), regional republics (*oblasts*, *krais*, and so on) and districts.

Okrugs and their environmental and natural resource departments were established in early 2000, while the MNR district authorities were liquidated in 2002. Since then and up to now, MNR has commanded 13 types of subdivisions and subordinated organizations (including departments, inspectorates, institutes, SPNA and others) and 111 units, including seven departments of state control and perspective development in the field of natural resource use and environmental protection (one in each of seven *okrugs*), 17 water basin departments, 86 regional departments on natural resources and environmental protection, and one Head Department of National Sea in Moscow.

3.2 Current Natural Resource Management System

Supranational level

International legislation and international agreements of the RF have priority over the state legislation. Russia is a participant in, and a signatory of, numerous international bilateral and multilateral agreements (Conventions, Accords, Protocols, and so on), concerning different aspects of environmental protection and nature conservation.

A number of international entities (for instance, GEF, IUCN, IBRD, UNEP, UNDP, UNCSD, EU, TACIS, GIWA and many others) carry out with their Russian counterparts joint projects with a focus on different environmental aspects, from general issues of federal and regional environmental management, and forestry policy to specific issues, for instance wetland protection, forest disease/destruction prevention, ozone depletion, greenhouse gas emissions, and many others.

Projects of the last decade funded by international and foreign entities have played a significant role both in terms of addressing a number of specific tasks and from the viewpoint of financial support to the Russian environmental protection system, primarily providing a living and jobs for a number of scientists, researchers and practitioners dealing with different issues on environmental protection. This support was especially valuable for SPNA (within the GEF project on biodiversity conservation).

It would take several pages to simply list international projects concerning different areas of environmental protection, biodiversity conservation, natural resource use and protection, good management practices, specific issues like GHG emissions, ozone depletion, waste management, protection of certain species, and so on. We may summarize it as follows. On the one hand, the scale of international influence and assistance is rather impressive and the benefits for environmental protection are obvious in many cases. However, the effectiveness of international 'interventions' is far less than expected for numerous reasons. First of all, internally no clear strategy and/or policy for attracting international assistance have been developed. Secondly, international assistance cannot directly influence the very structure and practice (mode) of environmental protection management in Russia. Thirdly, international organizations often do not have adequate understanding of the situation in Russia; moreover, their areas of activity often overlap with other organizations which have no intention to cooperate.

National level

The Russian Federation consists of 89 regions (subjects of the federation) incorporated in seven federal mega-regions (*okrugs*), namely: Far East *okrug* (10 regions, 141 districts), Near Volga (Privoljsky) *okrug* (11 regions, 450 districts), North-West *okrug* (11 regions, 154 districts), Siberian *okrug* (16 regions, 324 districts), Urals *okrug* (6 regions, 116 districts), Central *okrug* (18 regions, 423 districts) and Southern *okrug* (13 regions, 257 districts). As mentioned above, federal ministries and committees (MNR, former SCEP, SFS, RCWR) had subdivisions not only at the regional but also at the local level. Recently local subdivisions were liquidated (regional committees existed in all 89 regions; and local committees in all the 1865 districts). Before the reform of 2004, major federal authorities managing environmental protection and natural resource use were as follows (Kasyanov 2000; Lukianchikov and Potravnyi 2000; Shevchuk 2000):

- Ministry of natural resources (MNR);
- State Committee on Fishery (SCF);
- State Committee for sanitary and epidemiological supervision (SCSES);
- Russian Committee on Hydrometeorology (RCHM);
- Border Patrol Service (BPS); and
- Ministry of Agriculture (MA).

Some functions related to nature use and environmental protection were fulfilled by the Russian Federation Ministry of Economics, Ministry of Finance, Ministry of Public Health, Ministry of Emergency Situations (*MChS*), Ministry of Defence (*Minoborony*), Ministry of Nuclear Energy (*Minatom*), and Ministry of Regional Policy (*Minregion*).

By the Presidential Decrees 'On the system and structure of federal executive authorities' of 9 March, 2004, No. 314, and 'Issues of the structure of federal executive bodies' of 20 May, 2004, No. 649, federal executive bodies were substantially restructured and the structure of bodies with powers over the environment and natural resources took the form illustrated in Figure 9.1, which is compiled on the basis of Presidential and Governmental Decrees.

Nature use and environment protection governance is also covered by the jurisdiction of the Russian Federation general governance authorities (the President, State Duma, and Government) and Russian Federation subjects and local self-governance bodies.

The central apparatus was responsible for development and implementation of environmental policy and NEAP, development of federal target programmes, legislative drafts, regulations and instructions, establishment and distribution of quotas and issue of licences (permits) for use of natural resources of federal importance (oil and gas, metals, sea fish), prohibiting of extraction of endangered species, establishment of basin quotas for water consumption, state environmental review of large scale projects, and so on, whereas the local subdivisions primarily played a very significant role in carrying out control (inspections) and monitoring functions.

The majority of 'green' activists, along with the ministerial staff, severely criticized the liquidation of local subdivisions of MNR, as well as the earlier reorganization, which delegated environmental control functions to a ministry primarily concerned with resource use/exploitation. The reason was that decentralization (see Figure 9.2) of this sort was not properly planned, and it seemed more as an effort to unload functions and a financial burden than a deliberately targeted action aimed to increase efficiency of governance. Theoretically, decentralization has been driven by two main factors: the level of centralization[5] of the former Soviet system, which was so complete that the only possible trend was decentralization; and imitation of the West, which led to adopting a much more decentralized model.

The Soviet governance system has been gradually decentralizing since the beginning of the new century. Changes at the federal level and decentralization have also affected the system of natural resource and environmental governance. Since this happened simultaneously with dramatic changes in all spheres, social, cultural, informational, economic and other aspects, many of which are wide-ranging in terms of their impact on the environmental and

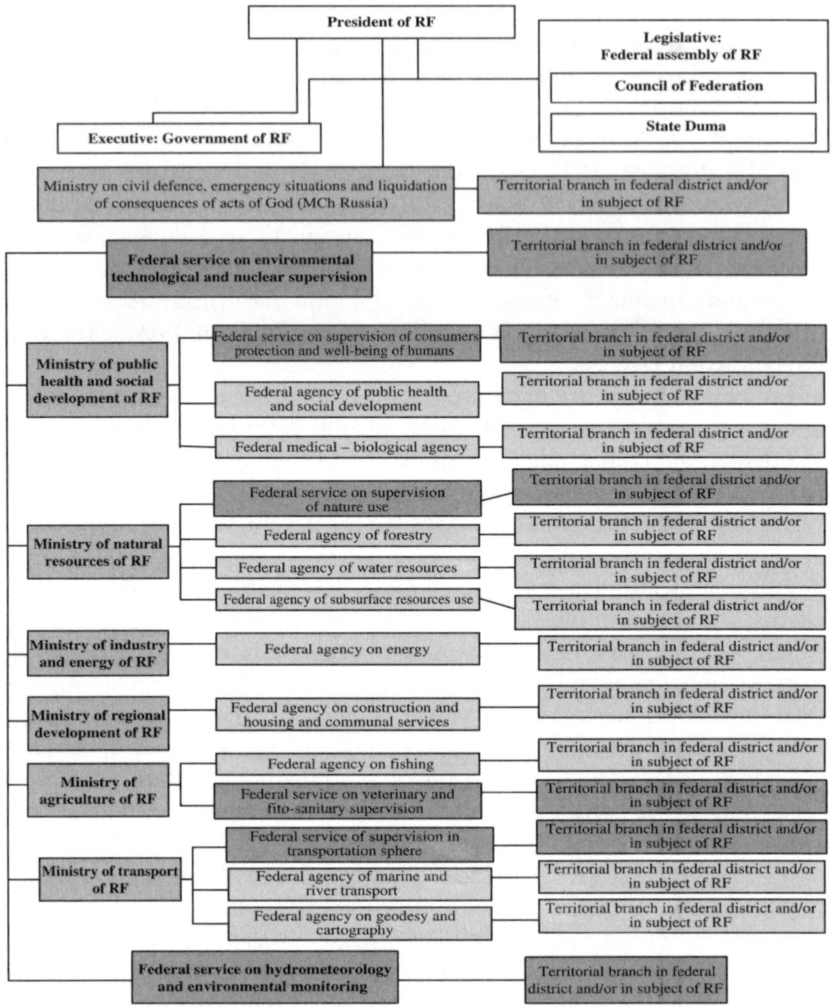

Figure 9.1 Structure of the RF public authorities in the sphere of natural resource use and environment protection

natural resource use patterns, it is too difficult, or to be more exact, even impossible to identify/reveal how the decentralization and other changes in the governance system influence the effectiveness of nature use.

The local subdivisions of federal executive bodies were liquidated, but a new level, an intermediary one, emerged between the central Moscow apparatus and the regional ones. The new establishment consists of seven mega-regional departments. Regional committees became regional departments of the Federal Ministry subordinate and accountable to the centre. They are now more dependent on the central apparatus than the earlier regional committees which depended on the regional administrations. Liquidation of local subdivisions of MNR made the establishment or/and development of municipal (local) environmental protection bodies more urgent. The major challenge faced in this regard is the lack of financial resources, since local budgets were previously not allocated to the environmental administration.

The present system of environmental and resource management combines deficiencies of the Soviet period with new ones: extremely widespread corruption often resulting in the fact that state authorities (starting from former president Yeltsin, State Duma groups, Government, Ministries and so on) come to serve private interests of companies and some top and mid-rank administrators. Since Mr Artyukhov took the Minister's chair and after his dismissal the major state executive body (MNR) has been staffed with and run mostly by top and middle-rank administrators whose educational and professional background has nothing to do with ecology and natural resources. Top posts are often assigned in exchange for large sums of money[6] which, of course, can be assumed to be compensated *n*-fold.

It was predicted by many ecologists that liquidation of an independent federal committee on the environmental protection in 2000 would mean a turning point in the environmental management evolutionary process. While until the end of the 1990s environmental protection had been progressing, though at an ever-slowing pace, since 2000 environmental protection has been undermined by the interests of ecologically 'dirty' businesses, from the nuclear lobby to the lumberers (logging companies).

It is important to mention that environmental protection authorities remained almost untouched by those forces and processes that, in the 1990s, were destroying the state governance machinery as an entity serving the welfare of the whole country. The reason is that from the first moment of the 'reforms', powerful clans (or emerging oligarchs) were fighting for the largest pieces of former Soviet assets/property. In the first half of the 1990s, the efforts of the major players – the oligarchs – focused on such authorities as the State committee of public property, the Ministry of Finance and perhaps to a greater extent, on the 'inner circle' and milieu of President Yeltsin, the Government and the State Duma (Parliament). 'Interacting' with the above-mentioned entities, oligarchs (mis)appropriated the most attractive assets of the former USSR property in Russia: oil companies (for example, YUKOS, Sibneft' and Lukoil), and metallurgical industries (Noril'sky Nikel', Aluminium sector), and so on. During this period, the Ministry of environmental protection (later reduced in status to the State committee for environmental protection) kept growing professionally, its staff consisting mostly of environmentally qualified and dedicated workers. In the late 1990s, when the oligarchs managed to solve the most important economic and political problems in favour of newly emerged large private businesses, the latter started to undertake measures to gain additional preferences and profits from appropriated assets at the exploitation/operation stage and in the meantime increase the assets' cost through further development. Among other stratagems (first of all, large-scale tax evasion), the largest companies started to actually assign and appoint their own representatives for respective positions at the ministries, including MNR.

Professor Danilov-Danilian, who had headed the ministry (and later the Committee when the ministry was reorganized into the SCEP) for a long time, was deposed in 2000. Soon the SCEP was liquidated and environmental protection subdivisions were incorporated into the MNR. Even earlier, the process of substitution of highly qualified and 'patriotic', dedicated professionals by the business-nominated officials had started within MNR. After 'annexation' of the SCEP by the MNR, the destructive process continued with removal of personnel involved in the environmental protection management.

At the beginning of 2004, on the eve of the presidential elections (parliamentary elections were held at the end of 2003 and resulted in victory for the pro-president party and candidates, the following two scenarios appeared possible. In the first, the SCEP or even the Ministry of Environmental Protection would be re-established as an independent public authority. This appeared reasonable despite the liquidation of the SCEP by President Putin's Decree. In 2000, President Putin's priorities were quite far from ecological/environmental concerns. They have hardly come to rank among his first priorities now. However, due to the fact that some important tasks of strengthening federal authority and apparent revival of the national economy have been achieved, the president will probably become more responsive to the voices of ecologists, environmentalists, professionals, researchers and practitioners. The second possible scenario is that the reform of environmental protection management (which is unavoidable) will focus on division of responsibilities and competencies between federal and regional (state/public) authorities and/or between state and municipal authorities.

Along with the regional and local subdivisions of the federal authorities (SCEP, SFS, RCWR, MNR and others), the regions and municipalities have been developing their own administrative bodies for environmental and natural resource management since the early 1990s. In the case of national republics those subdivisions were usually created on the basis of the regional subdivisions of the federal ministries (committees) transformed into republic ministries. In other regions, subdivisions of federal

Field / Level	Industry pollution	Ecosystem protection	Agriculture	Forests	Water	Implementation and enforcement
International		Habitat and Birds Directives				
National	Legislation	Legislation	Legislation	Legislation	Legislation	Legislation
Federation: Executive bodies: (Ministries, Services)	Standards, rules, taxes/charges, SER, federal programmes	SPNA	Standards, rules	Rules, Fees	Standards, rules, federal programmes	SER, Control, penalties, court
7 *Okrugs* (departments)	Supervision (over regional level)	Supervision	Supervision	Supervision	Supervision	Supervision
Large catchment areas departments					Water use Planning	
Regional departments	Permits, Control, SER, statistics			Access (auctions, licence)	Planning, Licences, Control	SER, Control, penalties
Local subdivisions	Control			Maintenance		Control
Regional		SPNA (regional)				SER, Control, penalties, court
Local			Local land Governance (except industrial, state forest, defence and some other lands)		Local spatial planning, supply and sewerage	Control, penalties, court

Figure 9.2 Decentralization trends in the Russian environmental governance

authorities operated under dual control and often depended more on the regional administration than on the respective federal ministries. In some cases the dual control or double subordination was legally fixed through agreements between regional administrations and federal authorities. However, in many regions regional subdivisions of federal authorities and environmental and natural resource departments of regional administrations or governors coexisted, their responsibilities and functions often overlapping. Similar situations were found at the municipal level.

In 2001–2002, the presidential commission was developing particular legislative proposals on reasonable division and sharing of responsibilities between different administrative levels. The work was aimed at formulation and distribution of functions in an optimal manner to exclude the overlapping of functions and responsibilities. The practical implementation of the reform has not been started yet, while some anticipatory changes already occurred prior to the commencement of the reformation. However, as stated above, major legislative acts have been already prepared.

4. POLICY INSTRUMENTS AND THEIR IMPLEMENTATION

As described in section 2, hundreds of pollutants of air, water (both drinking and natural), soil, food and other environmental media can be controlled by means of established maximum permissible concentrations (MPC). MPC values allow calculation of MPE and MPD for certain enterprises (organizations). Quotas (allowable cut, fish catch, animal extraction, water consumption) for natural resource use are determined, calculated through application of scientifically sound methodologies based on environmental (ecological) safety and renewable resource reproduction principles. Practical compliance/non-compliance with the MPC, MPE, MPD, quotas, licence conditions, lease and use agreement conditions, as well as other rules and requirements are examined by inspectors of MNR, SCF, SCSES and other state and municipal authorities.

For example, the Novgorod (Novgorod the Great) Department of MNR revealed 365 breaches of environmental legislation in 2003, that is one revealed infringement per day in the region, over 1.4 cases per working day. Leading types of breaches are as follows: 52 per cent unauthorized disposal of industrial and domestic wastes; 26 per cent breaches of water legislation; 15 per cent non-compliance with air emission standards and regulations.

4.1 Limitation and Licensing of Natural Resource Use

Limits (quotas) of natural resource use are an important instrument for effective natural resource management. While determining the limits, the relevant executive authorities should proceed from the necessity of complete quantitative and qualitative reproduction of renewable natural resources and reasonable consumption of non-renewable natural resources, along with a step-by-step reduction in adverse environmental impact/exposure to an environmentally safe level. Natural resource use and permissible environmental impact exposure limits form the baseline requirements and constraints fixed in a natural resource use licence[7] (as regards forest resources, the transition to agreement system instead of licences has been almost completed) that could be issued to any user for a planned or ongoing activity.

Two groups of limits are distinguished in the current limitation system: limits on natural resource use and those on polluting emissions (discharges) and waste disposal. The latter group, understood as permissible emission and waste disposal volumes, are fixed for a specific period to set intermediate parameters between the initial actual exposure/impact levels and the environmentally safe ones. Those limits are to be successively reduced from the initial level that exceeds the environmentally permissible standards to the ultimate environmentally safe level in accordance with the MPE, MPD and waste disposal standards defined by the regulatory documents. It should also be taken into account that such environmental standards are dictated by merely environmental requirements, while the limits are set based on a consideration of economic factors (Kasyanov 1998; Kasyanov 2000; Lukianchikov and Potravnyi 2000).

Pollution (emission, discharge, waste disposal) minimization programmes are to be developed mostly at regional level, with the exception of air emissions of greenhouse gases, ozone-depleting and other global environment-threatening substances. The dynamics of water discharges may be planned at federal, regional, trans-regional and local levels. Planning of waste disposal limitation dynamics for most types of waste should be done at regional and municipal levels. Limitation of radioactive, chemical and other highly hazardous wastes should be assigned to federal executive bodies in cooperation with regional authorities.

Actual and potential technical, economic, financial and other factors should be considered while calculating reduction in limits both regionally and individually (for a particular enterprise). State (both federal and regional) and municipal authorities, enterprises, natural resource and nature users and non-governmental organizations should take part in the preparation of environment exposure/environmental impact minimization programmes.

In future, once the rights of possession, use and disposal of biosphere assimilative capacity have been distributed between federal, regional and municipal levels, it would be reasonable to start emission trading between appropriate authorities. These allowances could then be sold by one enterprise to another (provided there is significant difference in their emission-reducing efficiency). The main goal of the limits on assimilative capacity use is to ensure the best dynamics in achieving environmental standards. After reaching the MPE (MPD) values, limits will become stable and equal to the set MPEs (MPDs) until environmental standards get higher (or, on the other hand, lower).

The second group of limits refers to renewable (in traditional understanding) natural resource use. As a rule, these limits are to be initially fixed as environmentally safe values. They refer to forests, fish, and other flora and fauna resources. In practice, when the demands of natural resource users exceed environmental standards, such limits are established not only on the basis of environmental criteria, but also with regard to the current economic situation. However, compliance with the sustainable development principles will require abandonment of this practice in future. One of the ways for solving the problem is to distribute quotas (limits) among consumers on a competitive basis within a general limit. In this connection, the issues of environmental impact limitation or quota sharing will acquire a particular world-wide significance.

4.2 Economic and Financial Tools

The economic instruments for pollution control and natural resource management in Russia were initially established at the end of the Soviet rule. In the late 1980s, the government introduced economic instruments, starting with payments for the use of natural resources, and in 1991 a comprehensive system of pollution charges. Those measures were introduced, at a time when the centralized planning system was falling apart, in the hope that they could provide viable alternatives or support to command-and-control methods.

Pollution charges

Before full-scale implementation, pollution charges were experimentally introduced in 49 constituencies of the RF in 1990. Based on those experiments, a uniform system of pollution charges was introduced in the law On Environmental Protection of 19 December, 1991. Charges were imposed based on the relative damage of the various pollutants and unit cost for waste disposal and overall revenue considerations. In total, charges were defined for 214 air pollutants and 197 water pollutants as well as for five different hazard classes of solid waste. Charge rates were also differentiated among regions by applying coefficients established at the federal level and assumed to reflect differences in environmental situations across the regions. The regional authorities also have certain rights to adjust the charge rates in response to the current environmental situation within the region. Table 9.1 represents a systematization (classification) of economic instruments for pollution control.

The newly introduced system of pollution charges was integrated into the existing system of MPE/MPD, and provisional limits were established for those enterprises which were not able to reach MPE/MPD immediately, as a transitory measure for agreed time period.[8] To provide incentives for the enterprise to reach the MPE/MPD, emissions exceeding MPE/MPD but staying within the limits, would be charged at a rate five times higher than the base rate. The emissions exceeding the limits would be chargeable at a 25-fold penalty rate.

The establishment of pollution charges was closely connected with the system of environmental funds that was created in Russia in 1989–1991. Funds were established at the federal level (federal fund), at the regional level (in all 89 constituencies of the federation), and at the local (district or municipal) level. The funds were designed to finance cross-sectoral and regional environmental activities. The activities of the funds are mainly financed through the revenues from pollution charges.

Level of charges The revenue from pollution charges has increased from 0.9 to 2.85 billion RUR in the period from 1992 to 1998. Rates have been indexed annually. In 1998 the indexation factor had a value of 60. This indexing has not been sufficient to keep up with the general price level, as, for example, the index of consumer prices reached approximately 4000 for the same period. The low level of pollution charges undermines the effectiveness of incentives for pollution control actions. However, extremely high non-compliance fees applying to emissions above the temporarily agreed pollution limits imply that significant incentives for emission reductions are still in place for heavy polluters. Implementation of other economic instruments faces similar problems related to depreciation of the real charge-rates. However, some taxes are established *ad valorem* and are automatically fully inflation indexed.[9]

Administration of payments The system of pollution charges defines charges for more than 200 air pollutants and a similar number of water pollutants. Many of those emissions cannot be measured or can be measured only at prohibitive costs. Instead, emissions are typically estimated through mass-balance, production plans and standard emission norms. Therefore air pollution charges often do not reflect actual emission levels.

Enterprises themselves are obliged to report the actual emissions to the regional authorities. The environmental authorities check those statements and undertake selective inspection of enterprises and natural resource users. If offences are discovered, fines or other sanctions may be imposed on the offender. The overall level of collection of pollution charges is estimated at around 60 per cent. But it should be noted that there are different ways of offsetting the charges through other forms of non-monetary settlements. Incomplete collection of charges concerns many other forms of taxes and this is, *inter alia*, related to the poor financial performance of many Russian enterprises.

Pollution charge offsets A specific form of non-monetary settlement or exemption from pollution charges is the so-called pollution charge offset. Enterprises may deduct costs of any activities included in an approved environmental improvement programme (environmental action plan) from pollution charges. The possibility of offsetting due payments against investments in the enterprise may have a positive effect in inducing the enterprises to undertake environmental investments where the alternative might have been no action and non-payment of the charges. The key for the evaluation of such offsets is, however, closely connected to how the system is administered in practice, in particular to effective control of environmental investments by the regional authorities.

Air pollution charges Emission charges apply to 214 different air pollutants. Charges are differentiated depending on the toxicity of the air pollutant. Emissions exceeding MPE but falling within an agreed temporary limit are charged at a rate equal to five times the base rate. For emissions above agreed limits, a non-compliance fee equal to 25 times the base rate applies. The charges are also differentiated with regard to location based on the environmental conditions in the relevant economic region. The above-mentioned rates are multiplied by a location-specific factor, normally ranging from 1 (for example in the far East) to 2 (for example in the Ural region). Within regions, further discretion exists for setting the geographical correction factor to reflect, for example, influence of local hot-spots or protected areas.

Water effluent charges The system of effluent charges forms a part of the overall system of pollution charges, and the basic principles for these charges and the non-compliance fees are the same as those described for the air emission charges. The applicable base rates for 1999 for water effluents

Table 9.1 Overview of economic instruments for pollution control

	Emission (pollution) taxes/charges	Product tax/charges	Non-compliance fees	User fees	Deposit-refund system
Air pollution (stationary sources)	Emission charges on 214 air pollutants		Yes, for above-limit emissions		
Transport related pollution	Emission charges apply also to emissions from mobile sources	Fuel taxes Taxes on cars	Yes, for above-limit emissions	Road use payments	
Water pollution	Effluent charges on 197 pollutants		Yes, for above-limit discharges	Fees for sewage and wastewater treatment	
Solid waste	Waste disposal charges		Yes, for above-limit waste generation	Fees for waste disposal and transport	Market-based system for bottle collection

range from 0.12 RUR (0.01 USD) per ton for dry residues to 13.75 million RUR (0.55 million USD) per ton for mercury. For nitrate the applicable base charge in 1999 was 15.2 RUR (0.6 USD) per ton, and for phosphate 687 RUR (27.5 USD) per ton. In 1998, the total revenues from the water effluent charges amounted to 316 million RUR in normal charges plus 382 million RUR from non-compliance fees.

Charges and fees on natural resources and services

As early as in the Soviet period, several taxes and charges directly or indirectly related to natural resource use were introduced, for example water use tariffs, stumpage fees, land taxes, payments for mineral resource reproduction (for geological prospecting/exploration), production excise taxes, and export duties. The latter two instruments are aimed at collecting mineral resource rent in an indirect way. No adequate data is available to assess the effectiveness either of individual economic instruments or of the whole system. Reforestation has been financed by the charges per cut tree, and geological prospecting payments have provided funds for the geological exploration. These instruments, however, were not intended to achieve specific environmental goals.

User charges for water supply, sewage and wastewater treatment At the municipal level, water supply, sewage and wastewater treatment are managed by public utility services, 'Vodokanals', subordinate to the municipal authorities. Vodokanals seek to cover their costs through collection of user charges for water services. Charges for water services are based on water consumption, and for the user it has little importance whether the charge covers water supply, sewage or wastewater treatment. User charges are mainly collected for cost recovery purposes. However, if actual water consumption were to be charged, user charges would also provide an incentive to reduce water consumption and, consequently, reduce generated wastewater volumes.

User charges vary across the regions (Vodokanals). For example, in 2007 the charges equal 0.09 RUR/m^3 for households and 0.4–0.7 RUR/m^3 for industrial users respectively. Industrial enterprises, thus, cross-subsidize the private households, as the costs of supplying water to industrial users are normally lower than for households. In Nizhniy Novgorod, charges are only half of those in Rostov. Metering of water consumption in private households is not common, and payments are determined based on normative consumption figures. Most industrial users, however, are metered and the relatively high charge in Rostov should have induced industrial water users to introduce water recycling and other water-saving measures.

Waste charges The main economic instrument of solid waste management is waste disposal charges, which is a form of pollution charge. In addition, there are other various forms of user charges which apply to waste management services, such as waste transportation and actual disposal in landfills. Solid waste charges were introduced as a part of the system of pollution charges that also include the air emission and water effluent charges. The basic principle is the same as in the case of pollution charges discussed above. Waste charges are levied per ton or cubic metre of solid waste. The charges vary according to the toxicity class or category (there are four classes of toxicity). In 1999, rates ranged from 0.15 RUR (0.01 USD) per ton for non-toxic waste in mineral extraction industries to 868 RUR (35 USD) per ton for waste of the highest toxicity class.

In 1998, total revenues amounted to 887 million RUR (90 million USD) collected from basic charges and 160 million RUR (16 million USD) from non-compliance fees.

Charges for hazardous waste trans-boundary transit A form of user charge has to be paid for application and issue of the permit for trans-boundary transport of hazardous waste. The level of the charge is determined based on the minimum wage, and the charges are mostly to be considered as an administrative fee with little impact on the transport of hazardous waste.

User charges for municipal waste collection and disposal User charges for domestic municipal solid waste (MSW) collection and disposal are included in housing costs and are typically around 36 roubles per ton or approximately 0.2 per cent of an average household income (compared to USD 30/ton or 1 per cent of an average household income in middle income countries, and over 60 USD/ton or less than 0.5 per cent of household income in OECD countries). Landfill disposal fees paid by commercial and industrial users of the MSW system vary according to location; from negligible amounts to around 60 RUR per ton in Moscow.

Other economic instruments

In addition to the above-mentioned economic instruments, there is also a set of indirect instruments that may create some incentives for improved environmental behaviour. This includes, for example, excise taxes on gasoline, which increase the cost of gasoline and the costs of transport. Many of these instruments have not been introduced with environmental goals in mind and the environmental authorities have typically not been involved in their design or implementation. A deposit-refund system for glass containers is also worth mentioning. Under the Soviet rule, an organized system of deposit and refunds for glass bottles functioned fairly efficiently. Since the liberalization of markets, the official system has been abolished, though lately market-based collection systems, for instance as in Moscow, have sprung up instead. Large beer producers repurchase bottles at a price that makes it worthwhile for individuals to set up collection points where consumers can sell their bottles.

Economic instruments: conclusions

Payments (taxes, charges, fees) for natural resource use are among the most important tools of environmental protection and sustainable natural resource use management. Recently they were regulated by Federal Law ‘On the environment protection’ (earlier version), Forest and Water Codes, Federal Laws ‘On land rent’, ‘On mineral resources’, ‘On animal life’, and others. Presently there is an attempt to integrate all legislative aspects of taxation in the Tax Code, which has already come into effect (Part 1). Part 2 of the Tax Code covering all environmental and natural resource taxes has been partially approved. Developers from the tax service and Ministry of Finance demonstrated a lack of understanding of the environmental and natural resource taxation (basic principles, purposes, theory of the issue, methodology approaches, and so on). On the other hand, representatives of MNR and other environment and resource-related authorities often cannot properly substantiate their vision or just lack the authority to influence decision making.

To make matters worse, that situation has proved to be quite attractive for powerful, influential industrial groups, including oil sector oligarchs, who see a possibility for further minimization of the real costs of pollution charges and other payments and for prevention of increase in environmental payments as suggested by all specialists and experts concerned with the welfare of the country. It is obvious that all environmental and natural resource payments (taxes, charges, fees) are several times or even several orders of magnitude less than economically mandated values. Environmental pollution charges were once declared unlawful and for some time no one paid them until they were rehabilitated by the Constitutional Court. However, this rehabilitation is not applicable to the indexation coefficients. Indexation of pollution charges has been lagging far behind inflation rates. As a consequence the rates of pollution charges are a thousand times lower than the economically efficient level, except perhaps in the case of emissions exceeding temporary agreed limits (see Table 9.2). Pollution charges became negligible. Today, they are regulated by the Russian Federation Tax Code and the other above-mentioned legislative acts, such as 'On mineral resources', 'On land rent', Russian Federation Forest and Water Codes, and so on. Those reflect different approaches to calculation, collection and disbursement of revenues from environmental charges, and payments for the use of natural resources.

The bulk of the Russian Federal budget revenues from profit tax, income tax, sales tax, excise and value-added tax are actually constituted by a rental income inflow from gas, oil and precious metal extraction as well as from some other resource uses. Natural resources do not yet play a dominating role in tax policy. The total direct natural resource tax does not exceed 3 per cent of the consolidated budget revenues, and environmental payments make up less than 0.1 per cent.

It is necessary to raise taxes (rental payments, charges) on the use of each natural resource so that they should be in line with the economic value of the resource. The state should fix prices for public natural resources and acquire appropriate funds to allocate them in reasonable proportions to renewable natural resource reproduction and budgets at different levels. Introduction of payments for the right of natural resource use on the basis of actual economic values should be accompanied by tax system

Table 9.2 MPCs and emission fees rates: selection of parameters

Name/formula	MPC, mg/m^3		Class of hazard	Fee rate per 1 tonne of pollutant, rubles**		
	Maximum concentration	Daily average concentration		Within MPC	Above MPC but within temporary agreed limits (×5)	Exceeding temporary agreed limits (×25)
NO_2	0.085	0.04	2	52	260	1300
NO	0.4	0.06	3	35**	175	875
$C_{20}H_{12}$ (benz(a)pyrene)	–	0.1 microgram/ 100 m^3	1	2049801	10249005	51245025
SO_2	0.5	0.05	3	21	105	525
CO	5.0	3.1		0.6	3	15
Suspended particles	0.5	0.15	3	13.7	68.5	342.5

Note: ** 1 Euro ~ 35 rubles.

restructuring, through the reduction in income, value-added and profit taxes. In addition to stimulating sustainable nature use and improving conditions for natural resource renewal, those incentives will bring about an opportunity to vitalize business, attract investments (first of all, in other sectors not linked to resource industry) and improve both the economic and technological status of enterprises. Those objectives are of a long-term character, though comprehensive substantiation of approaches to and dynamics of tax system reform should be worked out in the first place. It is necessary to elaborate a step-by-step programme for reforming the system of nature use payments and later, the entire taxation system.

5. OTHER RELEVANT ASPECTS AND CONCLUDING REMARKS

5.1 Interconnections

As stated above, environmental protection has been largely subordinated to other aspects of social life, such as political, economic and industrial activities. Under Soviet rule it was sacrificed for an acceleration of industrial and military development. In the 1990s, environmental protection (as well as other social and economic values) was sacrificed for the purposes of sharing and appropriation of assets accumulated in the Soviet era.

The low status accorded to environmental protection (formal and informal) and natural resource management (informal) authorities in the existing hierarchical executive structure poses a big problem. In a country that relied on rapid economic development in the past and depends now on natural resource use, it is of concern that environmental authorities responsible for natural resource management play a subordinate role.

5.2 Lack of Enforcement

A large portion of environmental legislation exists *de jure* but is not enforced; also a large part of it is implemented selectively. In some cases barriers are created by legislation itself. For instance, the Criminal Code establishes almost token liability for crimes against nature, environment, animals, including water bio-resources (that is penalties are very mild, and do not provide for deprivation of liberty). Moreover, criminals are able to have sentences cut by repenting, which is in fact false repentance in an overwhelming majority of cases.

Analysis of the top level of the public management system, including natural resource management, allows for the conclusion that the problem lies in the model of development currently being implemented in developed countries (which, however, shift the environmental load to the rest of the world) and, in recent years, in Russia, though with certain specific features (first of all, economic and environmental pressures primarily affect the Russian nature and population). It is characterized by the subordination of social evolution to an increasing growth of financial and, to a smaller degree, industrial capital. In terms of progress towards sustainable development, the model has no future because the interests of growth in financial and industrial capital not only differ from the interests of civilization development, but they are relatively short-term as well.

5.3 Incomplete Information

In addition to the above principal shortcomings of the natural resource management system, it is necessary to note the following: lack of efficient management in the field of natural resource use and environment protection is caused, to a great extent, by inadequate information support to the decision-making process. This concerns information on available natural resources, influence of the use of a natural resource on other environment components, and their economic valuation, which should be reflected, in our opinion, in integrated territorial cadastres (not introduced so far). Information on environmental conditions obtained through environmental monitoring does not meet effective and efficient management requirements. Besides, there are problems related to contradictory indicators controlled by different agencies and disruptions in regular and timely supply of information, its quality, presentation and communication.

5.4 Lack of Scientific Expertise in the Decision-making Process

In the 1990s the network of research institutes was destroyed: many institutes still exist but research programmes and staff have been dramatically downsized. There is a serious lack of financing for research that goes beyond the poor-quality scientific programmes of MNR and other state authorities. Remaining researchers survive owing to international or bilateral projects and grants.

The system of elaboration and implementation of federal and regional environmental action programmes and plans is far from perfect, thus reducing their efficiency to the minimum because of obsolete methods inapplicable to the new economic conditions, and inefficiency of machinery for budget allocations and control.

The existing instruments and methods for natural resource management are currently formulated in more than 30 laws of the Russian Federation adopted between 1991 and 1998. To enforce the above laws, more than 100 decrees were issued by the government of the Russian Federation.

The current system of legal acts on individual types of natural resources was generated in accordance with the sectoral practice of natural resource management intended to ensure maximum volumes of natural resource exploitation by an integral governmental enterprise on behalf of a ministry or other sectoral agency. Such a system of management is focused mostly on technical aspects and qualitative indicators, although consideration of economic and environmental issues requires a comprehensive approach to the use of nature. The modern regulatory and legislative base for environmental protection and management is deficient in the following respects:

- discord between regulatory and legal acts at federal and regional levels;
- insufficiently clear distribution of powers between the state and administrative units of the Russian Federation in the field of nature and resource use and environmental protection;
- deficient system of natural resource payments and environment pollution charges (including indexation mechanisms), and other economic and financial instruments for the use of nature;
- unclear division of functions between the bodies responsible for natural resource use management and state environmental control;
- absence of conditions for the implementation of a comprehensive approach to natural resource management;
- lack of a clearly defined scheme of disbursement of the funds earmarked for natural resource reproduction and environmental protection;
- inefficient system of information supply for state natural resource management; and,
- lack of proper laws to enact a legal base for forms of non-governmental organizations and citizens' participation in natural resource use control, reproduction and protection.

In light of the above shortcomings we may conclude that the current approach to the management of nature and of environmental protection in Russia as well as public administration in general do not meet the requirements for a smooth transition to sustainable development. Recently amended/reformed core legislative acts (like the Forest and Water Codes, Federal Law 'On subsurface' and others) may surely change the mode of administration; however, it is not clear yet whether the situation will change for the better, or, on the contrary lead to further erosion of nature use and of environmental protection governance in the Russian Federation.

NOTES

1. The new Water code of the Russian Federation and the Order No. 881 dated 30 December 2006 (on the Procedure for Setting Permissible Impact Standards for Water Bodies) introduced new standards of permissible impact on water bodies in lieu of the MPD values. The Federal Agency for Water Resources is in charge of developing and implementing the new standards, in terms of maximum permissible concentrations of chemical substances, radioactive substances, microorganisms and other water quality indicators, in accordance with methodical guidelines issued by the Ministry of Natural Resources of the Russian Federation.
2. The list is open and in principle any physical impact falls under this wording.
3. In his recent statement the Minister of Economy G. Gref said that the new Forest Code will allow privatization of forests.
4. Larin and Mnatsakanyan (2003).
5. With minor exceptions, for instance, the land issues (residential and agricultural lands) for which local administrations have been responsible, even in the Soviet period.
6. This information is based on verbal statements and general data on corruption, and is not supported by sound documented evidence. However, the situation is generally recognized in Russia; moreover, there is an official report, 'Diagnosis of corruption in Russia', prepared by the Information for Democracy Fund, which estimates an 'annual corruption turnover' at 36 billion USD in 2001, a figure comparable with the entire budget revenues.
7. It is expected that after adoption of new Water and Forest Codes, Federal Law 'On Subsurface' licences will be replaced by user agreements.
8. 'EIs for pollution control and Natural Resource Management: The Russian Federation' (P. Kasyanov actively participated in preparation of this report).
9. 'EIs for pollution control and Natural Resource Management: The Russian Federation'.

BIBLIOGRAPHY

Books: Legislation

Federal Law No. 7-FZ 'On the environment protection' of 10.01.2002.

Federal Law No. 52-FZ 'Sanitary and epidemiological health of the population' of 30.03.1999 (amended on 30.06.2003).

Federal Law No. 96-FZ 'On the air protection' of 04.05.1999.

Federal Law No. 116-FZ 'On the industrial safety for hazardous industrial sites' of 21.07.1997.

Federal Law of RF No. 89-FZ 'On the industrial and consumption waste' of 24.06.1998 (amended on 10.01.2003).

Forest Code of RF N 22-FZ of 29.01.1997.

Land code of RF (Russian Federation) No. 136-FZ of 25.10.2001 (amended version of 30.06.03).

The Russian Federation legislative foundations 'For protection of population health', No. 5487-1 of 22.07.1993 (amended on 27.02.03).

Water Code of RF No. 167-FZ of 16.11.1995 (amended version of 30.06.2003).

Other Books

Kasyanov, P.V. (1998), *Transition to Sustainable Development: Environmental and Economic Prerequisites*, Moscow: Research, Training and Methodology Centre of the State Environmental Committee (in Russian).

Kasyanov, P.V. (2000), *Ways to Reform the Natural Resource Governance*, Moscow State University, MAKS Press (in Russian).

Lukianchikov, N.N. and I.M. Potravnyi (2000), *Economical and Organisational Issues of Nature Use*, Moscow: Troika (in Russian).

Petrov, A.P., B.M. Mamaev, V.K. Tepliakov and E.A. Sh'tinsky (1997), *State Governance in the Forest Sector*, Moscow: VNIITzlesresours (in Russian).

Shevchuk, A.V. (2000), *Forming and Improvement of Economic Mechanism of Nature Use*, full doctorate thesis, Moscow: MSU (in Russian).

Internet Publications

'EIs for pollution control and Natural Resource Management: The Russian Federation', P:\50540\PDOC\Survey of Economic Instruments\Final report\CHP_50540_EI_Russian CC_final draft_en.doc.

'Financing of the state natural reserves of the MNR of Russia in 2002 and 2003: Main results', http://www.biodiversity.ru/publications/zpnp/archive/n43/st05.html).

Larin, Vladislav and Ruben Mnatsakanyan (2003), '*Goskomekologii Rossii*: from the dawn to the decline (awaiting new dawn)', *Energia* 2003, N 6. C. 42–47; No. 7. C. 16–21; No. 8. C. 11–15; No. 9. C. 30–35; No. 10. C. 30–35. http://courier.com.ru/energy/en0603larin.htm (in Russian).

Presidential Decree 'On the system and structure of federal executive bodies' No. 314 of March 9 (Version of 20 May, 2004, Presidential Decree No. 649) http://ttfoms.tomsk.ru/docs/pravit/252_04.htm.

Regulation 'On Ministry of Natural Resources of the Russian Federation' (Approved by the Governmental Decree, No. 370 of 22 July, 2004). http://www.mnr.gov.ru/part/?pid=41.

Regulation 'On Federal Service for Nature Use Supervision' (Approved by the Governmental Decree, No. 400 of 30 July, 2004. http://www.mnr.gov.ru/part/?pid=1220.

Regulation 'On Federal Agency for Water Resources' (Approved by the Governmental Decree, No. 282 of 16 June, 2004). http://www.mnr.gov.ru/part/?pid=1216.

Regulation 'On Federal Forestry Agency' (Approved by the Governmental Decree, No. 283 of 16 June, 2004). http://www.mnr.gov.ru/part/?pid=1218.

Regulation 'On Federal Agency on Subsurface Use' (Approved by the Governmental Decree, No. 293 of 17 June, 2004. http://geolog.mnr.gov.ru/part/?pid=18.

Report 'Diagnosis of corruption in Russia' prepared by the Fund 'Information for Democracy'.

APPENDIX: LIST OF ACRONYMS

BPS	Border Patrol Service
CPSU	Communist Party of the Soviet Union
EAP	Environmental Action Plan (NEAP – National EAP, REAP – regional EAP)
FACHS	Federal Agency for Construction and Housing & Communal Services
FAF	Federal Agency on Fishery
FAHSD	Federal Agency of Health and Social Development
FASU	Federal Agency on Subsurface Use
FAWR	Federal Agency for Water Resources
FFA	Federal Forestry Agency
FLEP	Federal Law No. 7-FZ 'On the environment protection' of 10.01.2002
FSETAS	Federal Service for Environmental, Technological and Atomic Supervision
FSNUS	Federal Service for Nature Use Supervision
FSHM	Federal Service for Hydrometeorology
MA	Ministry of Agriculture
MES	Ministry of Emergency Situation
MHSD	Ministry of Health and Social Development
MIE	Ministry of Industry and Energy
MNR	Ministry of Natural Resources of the Russian Federation
MPC	maximum permissible concentrations
MPE	maximum permissible emission
MPD	maximum permissible discharge
MPPI	maximum permissible physical impact
PA	protected area
RCHM	Russian Committee on Hydrometeorology (FSHM since May 2004)
RCWR	Russian Committee on Water Resources (incorporated in MNR in 1998)
RF	Russian Federation
RSFSR	Russian Soviet Federated Socialist Republic
SC	State Committee
SCEP	State Committee on the Environmental Protection (incorporated in MNR in 2000)
SCF	State Committee on Fishery (now FAF under MA)
SCSES	State Committee for sanitary and epidemiological supervision (incorporated into MHSD)
SER	State environmental review

SFS	State Forestry Service (incorporated in MNR in 2000, and transformed into FFA under MNR in 2004)
SPNA	Specially Protected Natural Area
WGDL	Allowed volume of generated wastes of production and consumption and waste disposal limits

10. The political economy of environmental governance in the United States

Jason F. Shogren

1. INTRODUCTION

In 1960 at the request of the United States Congress, the Surgeon General – the chief federal health advisor – issued a report on national environmental health. The reported stated '[i]t is not being overdramatic to suggest that threats from our environment, actual or potential, cannot only generate wholly undesirable effects on the health and well-being of isolated individuals, but under certain circumstances could affect large segments of our population and conceivably threaten the very existence of our Nation' (see Neimark and Mott, 1999, p. 184). Over the next decade, numerous other environmental warning cries were heard throughout the US, including Rachel Carson's *Silent Spring* and G. Hardin's *Tragedy of the Commons*. Reflecting the urgency of a national crisis, President Richard Nixon declared in his 1970 State of the Union message that '[r]estoring nature to its natural state is a cause beyond party and beyond factions. It has become a common cause for all the people of America.' Together Congress and President Nixon enacted a set of far-reaching federal laws and statutes aimed at protecting the environment. Starting with the federalization of environmental protection with the National Environmental Protection Act of 1969, people now approach environmental protection totally differently in decision making than they did three decades ago (see Percival et al., 1992).

Today this 1960s and 1970s sense of emergency has been replaced with the sentiment that environmental protection is an enduring US national value. The public commitment to environmental protection is revealed in the network of statutes and regulations promulgated by national and state governments and in the move toward a cleaner environment over the last three decades. The core design element in US environmental and natural resource policy is for the federal government to set national pollution standards that are to be implemented at the state level. The on-going challenge is to find the appropriate way to share authority in the design and implementation of policy across the levels of government. Finding an effective balance between centralized policies that address national health concerns versus decentralized policies that address local physical and social conditions is an unending process.

This chapter presents a brief overview of US policy for environmental protection. We discuss the federalist institutional framework used to create and implement environmental policy and the major federal environmental regulations. Next we consider three policy tools used in the US – citizen suits, collaboration and market-based instruments. Finally, we explore several on-going debates over environmental policy in the US, including clean air, climate change, Superfund, endangered species protection, and children's health.

2. INSTITUTIONS AND REGULATIONS

We begin by considering the broad institutional framework to create, administer and enforce environmental policy in the US at the federal and state level. We then discuss the major federal regulations in the development and implementation of US environmental policy.

2.1 Institutional Framework

The United States operates under a federalist system and a representative democracy. While debate continues over the appropriate degree of federalism, power is divided between the national and local units of government. The federal government as determined by the representatives of the states can assign or removes duties and responsibilities from the subordinate state governments. Up until the 1970s, the federal role in environmental policy was limited, except for the management of public lands. After the 1970s, environmental policy in the US became more centralized at the federal level. The argument for centralization is justified on three grounds. Federal regulation would prevent an environmental 'race to the bottom' by states lowering emission standards to attract new businesses; it would account for interstate externalities otherwise ignored by a state (for example, acid deposition originating in Ohio falling on New York); and it would balance out the lobbying efforts between well-funded industry and the relatively poorer environmental groups at the state level (see Revesz, 2001).

The federal government has specific powers and responsibilities, which are separated into executive, legislative and judicial branches as defined by the Constitution. This system of checks and balances is designed to guarantee no entity has too much power or control over the process. The US Congress has exclusive authority to enact federal environmental legislation. A bill specifying a new environmental law or an amendment to existing legislation originates either in the House of Representatives or the Senate, goes through committee consideration, and, provided it comes out of committee, moves to a floor debate and vote. If a bill passes both the House and Senate, the President then signs it and makes it law, does nothing (the bill either becomes law or not depending on whether Congress stays in session), or vetoes the bill. Congress can override a voted bill with at least a two-thirds majority vote in both the House and Senate.

The executive branch is responsible for implementing the environmental laws passed by the Congress. Agencies in the executive branch like the Environmental Protection Agency, Department of Interior and its Fish and Wildlife Division, Department of Agriculture and its US Forestry Service, State Department, Department of Energy, National Oceanic and Atmospheric Administration, and Department of Justice, issue rules, make adjudications, and provide guidelines based on the Administrative Procedure Act (APA). The APA says an agency decision that sets binding obligations or standards is a rule. This matters because Congress has given agencies like the EPA broad discretion to implement the environmental statutes. Administrative rules for environmental policy go through the process called notice and comment rulemaking. Before issuing most rules, the agency issues a notice of the proposed rulemaking in the Federal Register, asking for public comment. After receiving the comments, the agency issues a final rule, which has the force and effect of legislation. These administrative actions become crucial when there is a split in control over the Presidency and Congress. The Democrat Clinton Administration has been called the 'Administrative Presidency' because of its reliance on administrative rules to promote environmental policy given that Congress was controlled by the Republicans from 1994–2000. Congress has oversight responsibilities for these agencies. Some 13 Congressional committees and 30 subcommittees have some jurisdiction over the EPA's actions and activities. In addition, there are over one hundred federal trial and appellate courts that play a key role in interpreting environmental policy.

The President can also affect environmental policy by issuing an Executive Order. An EO is an official document through which the President manages the operations of the federal government. For example, President Clinton issued Executive Order 12898 of 11 February, 1994 entitled 'Federal Actions to Address Environmental Justice in Minority Populations and Low-Income Populations'. The EO ordered that all agencies shall make environmental justice part of its overall mission. An agency is ordered to identify and address whether its programs and policies could have a disproportionately high adverse affect on the health of minority and low-income populations. The EO also created an interagency environmental justice working group to oversee agency strategies and human and environmental health data collection.

Two key agencies are the Environmental Protection Agency (EPA) and Department of Interior (DOI). The EPA is the key agency responsible for pollution control; the DOI manages many of the federal land use, endangered species, and natural resource decisions. Established in 1970, the EPA's stated goal of protecting public health and the environment is to be met by guaranteeing clean air for every community, clean and safe drinking water, protected waterways, safe food, pollution prevention in homes and workplaces, better waste management, reduction of transboundary risks, increase in citizens' 'right to know' about their environment, sounder science measuring the risks and benefits, and more compliance with rules. The EPA employs about 18 000 people across the country, with its headquarters in Washington, DC, its ten regional offices in Boston, New York, Philadelphia, Atlanta, Chicago, Dallas, Kansas City, Denver, San Francisco and Seattle, and with more than a dozen research laboratories. The EPA is organized into 13 Offices: Administrator, Administration and Resources Management, Air and Radiation, Enforcement and Compliance Assurance, Environmental Information, Chief Financial Officer, General Counsel, Inspector General, International Affairs, Prevention, Pesticides, and Toxic Substances, Research and Development, Solid Waste and Emergency Response, and Water. The EPA Administrator is not a Presidential cabinet-level position, although is usually given cabinet-level status.

Established in 1849, the Department of Interior (DOI) is the main federal steward for natural resource conservation. Its stated mission is

> to protect America's treasures for future generations, provide access to our nation's natural and cultural heritage, offer recreation opportunities, honor our trust responsibilities to American Indians and Alaska Natives and our responsibilities to island communities, conduct scientific research, provide wise stewardship of energy and mineral resources, foster sound use of land and water resources, and conserve and protect fish and wildlife.

The DOI has a Secretary, which is a cabinet-level position. The Department is organized into (1) Fish, Wildlife and Parks, which includes National Park Service and Fish and Wildlife Service (FWS); (2) Land and Minerals Management, which includes Bureau of Land Management, Office of Surface Mining, and Minerals Management Service; (3) Water and Science, which includes US Geological Survey and Bureau of Reclamation; and (4) Indian Affairs. The DOI now has over 78 000 employees, and manages about 500 million acres of surface land (about one-fifth of the land in the US).

The Executive Office of the President has the Council of Environmental Quality (CEQ). The council's chair is to be the principal environmental policy advisor to the President. The CEQ's main task is to coordinate federal environmental efforts, working with other federal agencies and offices inside the White House. The CEQ manages the development of environmental policy, coordinates interagency policy implementation, and mediates disagreements among agencies, state, tribal and local governments and private citizens over the adequacy of Environmental Impact Statements (EISs). The President also has an official scientific advisor who resides in the Office of Science and Technology Policy. The science advisor gives counsel about all things scientific, ranging from human genome research to specific environmental policy questions.

Another key player on environmental policy inside the White House is the Council of Economic Advisers (CEA). While the chair of the CEA is the President's economic advisor, many economic decisions involve some impact on the environment and the associated costs and benefits. The CEA frequently takes a severe view of many environmental policy initiatives, to the point where President Clinton even publicly labeled his economic advisors 'lemon suckers'. The CEA objective is to promote efficient environment policy. The CEA supports more economic analysis of policy alternatives and greater consideration of tradeoffs in environmental policy debates. The general goal is to help guide public policy to provide more environmental protection at lower cost. The single overarching thrust is the importance of efficiency – that is, environmental policies that maximize a broad notion of net benefits to society.

In 1981, President Reagan signed Executive Order 12291, which called for federal agencies to perform a benefit–cost analysis for all federal regulations having more than a $100 million impact on the US economy. An agency could issue the regulations only if the benefits outweighed the costs. In 1993, President Clinton issue Executive Order 12866 on Regulatory Planning and Review. The EO directs agencies to guarantee that new regulations are cost-effective. In 1995, Congress passed the Unfunded Mandates Act requiring agencies to ensure their approaches meet policy targets at the lowest cost, or to explain why not.

The gatekeeper who ensures reasonable benefit–cost analysis is the Office of Information and Regulatory Affairs (OIRA), an office within the President's Office of Management and Budget (OMB). OIRA plays a key role in federal environmental policy design and implementation because it acts as the internal regulatory watchdog of the executive branch. Under Executive Order 12866, the President directed OIRA to review draft regulations proposed by agencies prior to implementation. Agencies are to follow certain principles in rulemaking, including estimating the benefits and cost of the proposed action and its alternatives. EO 12866 says agencies 'shall assess both the costs and the benefits of the intended regulation and, recognizing that some costs and benefits are difficult to quantify, propose or adopt a regulation only upon a reasoned determination that the benefits of the intended regulation justify its costs'. OIRA reviews how well the agency follows such principles. If OIRA judges that a proposed rule is inconsistent with EO 12866 principles, it 'returns' the rule to the agency for further review. For instance, if the costs and benefits estimates of the rule do not follow standard technical methods, OIRA can return the rule, requiring the agency to re-work its estimates.

Under the G.W. Bush Administration, OIRA's demand for high-quality cost–benefit analysis has increased significantly. The most contentious issue today is over valuing the benefits gained from an environmental regulation aimed at protecting life and limb, that is, the value of statistical life. The value of statistical life (VSL) is by far the largest category of benefits used to justify new federal environmental, health and safety rules. A prominent example is the EPA's application of the VSL to justify the 2000 diesel sulfur rule. Here the VSL accounted for nearly 90 per cent of the estimated annual total benefits from improved air quality, $62.6 billion out of $70.4 billion (USEPA, 2000). The political economy of the VSL is unambiguous – the larger the VSL, the more likely the benefits will justify the costs of any new regulation aimed at protecting health and safety. OIRA judges whether an agency's proposed use of the VSL is justified or not. A benefit estimate based on the VSL that does not pass OIRA standards, goes back to the agency.

At the state level, the 50 sovereign states retain important autonomy and authority over their own environmental laws and statutes and in the implementation of mandated federal policy. Powers not delegated to the federal government in the Constitution nor prohibited by it to the states, are reserved to the states, or to the people. State governments are also divided into executive, legislative and judicial branches. Established in 1993, administrators from each state environmental agency are allied through the Environmental Council of the States (ECOS). ECOS is a non-profit, nonpartisan association of state and territorial environmental commissioners in the executive branch. The key is to address the balance between general accountability for environmental policy provided at the federal level versus the flexibility of states to adjust to local conditions and preferences of its residents. In fact, many observers argue that the states have taken the lead in innovations in environmental policy, ranging from market-based instruments to voluntary action plans.

With roots in the Nixon, Reagan and Bush 41 Administrations, the pendulum of federalism began to swing back toward less federal and more state control of policy. Some policy makers pushed for the decentralization of environmental policy to the state level. The primary selling point of this New Federalism is twofold. First, different locations have different environmental conditions – a uniform treatment of heterogeneous physical environments might generate more costs than necessary. Second, local decision makers have better information on the local preferences for environmental protection. Local preferences are set by the level of knowledge about the local environment, which may be better or worse than the federal experts, depending on the type of risk (for example, water quality versus radon). National leverage over states declined during the 1990s given decreased national budgets for environmental protection, self-imposed federal restrictions on sending 'unfunded mandates' to the states, and the US Supreme Court defining new limits on Congress's constitutional authority over the states.

The aim of this New Federalism was to 'decentralize' and 'defund' federal environmental protection actions. States would have more authority to choose the federal environmental programs they wanted to keep and those they would terminate. States would also have to find the needed funding from state sources for those kept programs. Many federal environmental statutes detail how they relate to state environmental laws. These statutes can preempt state law, can create national minimum standards that states either follow or they enact tighter state standards, and can provide for grants and technical assistance to assist states in the implementation of the federal policy. Historically, the most frequent model used in the US is to establish federal standards which are to be administered and enforced at the state level. According to Rabe (2002), states issue more than 90 per cent of all environmental permits and conduct more than 75 per cent of all environmental enforcement actions.

How do the states implement (or not implement) the mandates from Washington? Each state has an agency responsible for environmental protection (see Table 10.1). This agency develops a state strategy to implement the federal statute. Each state develops its own institutional structure in the process of implementation. In Wyoming, for instance, the Department of Environmental Quality develops a strategy to implement federal air pollution policy that has to be officially approved by the Environmental Quality Council – a citizen's board appointed by the governor responsible for the promulgation of rules and regulations needed to meet state and federal policy. In Virginia, the State Air Pollution Control Board administers the implementation of federal air policy.

But inconsistencies exist in how the federal government sees the role of states in environmental policy. In 1970 under the Clean Air Act, Congress directed the EPA to set standards for ambient air quality that would apply

Table 10.1 State environmental agencies

State	Agency
Alabama	Department of Environmental Management
Alaska	Department of Environmental Conservation
Arizona	Department of Environmental Quality
Arkansas	Department of Environmental Quality
California	CA Environmental Protection Agency
Colorado	Department of Public Health and Environment
Connecticut	Department of Environmental Protection
Delaware	Department of Natural Resources and Environmental Control
Florida	Department of Environmental Protection
Georgia	Environmental Protection Division
Hawaii	HI Department of Health
Idaho	Department of Environmental Quality
Illinois	IL Environmental Protection Agency
Indiana	Department of Environmental Management
Iowa	IA Department of Natural Resources
Kansas	Department of Health and Environment
Louisiana	Department of Environmental Quality
Maine	Department of Environmental Protection
Maryland	Department of the Environment
Massachusetts	Executive Office of Environmental Affairs
Michigan	Department of Environmental Quality
Minnesota	MN Pollution Control Agency
Mississippi	Department of Environmental Quality
Missouri	Department of Natural Resources
Montana	Department of Environmental Quality
Nebraska	Department of Environmental Quality
Nevada	NV Division of Environmental Protection
New Hampshire	Department of Environmental Services
New Jersey	Department of Environmental Protection
New Mexico	NM Environment Department
New York	Department of Environmental Conservation
North Carolina	Department of Environment, Health and Natural Resources
North Dakota	ND Environmental Health Section
Ohio	OH Environmental Protection Agency
Oklahoma	Department of Environmental Quality
Oregon	Department of Environmental Quality
Pennsylvania	Department of Environmental Protection
Rhode Island	Department of Environmental Management
South Carolina	Department of Health and Environmental Control
South Dakota	Department of Environment and Natural Resources
Tennessee	Department of Environment and Conservation
Texas	TX Commission on Environmental Quality

Table 10.1 (continued)

State	Agency
Utah	Department of Environmental Quality
Vermont	VT Agency of Natural Resources
Virginia	Department of Environmental Quality
Washington	Department of Ecology
West Virginia	Department of Environmental Protection
Wisconsin	Department of Natural Resources
Wyoming	Department of Environmental Quality

to all states equally. For air quality, state environmental or health agencies are responsible for the development of state implementation plans (SIPs). A SIP details how a 'non-attainment' area plans to meet the requirements of the federal Clean Air Act. A SIP is required for each pollutant for which the non-attainment area violates the hazard air pollutants. The EPA must approve each SIP. The EPA then evaluates the progress and effectiveness of the SIP. The foundation for evaluation is an inventory conducted every three years to track the progress of emission reductions. If a SIP fails review, the EPA can either impose sanctions or assume responsibility for enforcing the federal regulations in that State.

But in 1972 under the Clean Water Act, Congress told each state to set its own standards for water quality. The Clean Water Act says:

> It is the policy of the Congress to recognize, preserve, and protect the primary responsibilities and rights of States to prevent, reduce, and eliminate pollution, to plan the development and use (including restoration, preservation, and enhancement) of land and water resources, and to consult with the Administrator (of the EPA) in the exercise of his authority under this chapter.

As Oates (2001) points out: '[i]t is not at all clear why standards for air quality should be set at a national level, while water quality standards are a matter for the states'.

States spent an estimated $15.1 billion in 2003 on environment and natural resources – the second-greatest amount the states have spent thus far. But a key sticking point in environmental federalism has been the growing gap between increasing implementation authority to the states and reducing the financial resources to meet these statutes. The states have increased their role in environmental protection over the past three decades and now implement most of the federal environmental statutes. States now operate 75 per cent of the delegable programs, up from 40 per cent in 1993.

Millimet (2003) examined how abatement expenditures were affected by the decentralized environmental policy making under Presidents Reagan and Bush 41. Examining abatement expenditures, he finds that decentralization had no impact until the mid-1980s, after which decentralization seemed to lead to a race to the top – states increased environmental abatement levels rather than lowering them as commonly feared. The caveat with this work, however, is that air quality goes beyond the limits of local jurisdictions, so disentangling federal from local policy (or something else altogether like business choices) makes this conclusion tentative at best.

Given the recent fiscal crisis in many states and the new federal environmental rules and a lack of significant new federal money, it is estimated that a $1 billion annual gap exists between the amounts states need to implement current federal law. Funding gaps raise a question about whether federal mandates that require each state to meet a national uniform standard of environmental quality is the most efficient way to spend these resources. One example is the uniform national standards for drinking water as mandated by the Safe Drinking Water Act of 1974. In general, drinking water standards matter most to local people who drink the water on a long-term basis. The Act required EPA to set national standards for about 80 pollutants. Dinan et al. (1999) estimated the inefficiencies that arise from these uniform standards. Removing pollutants from water uses treatment technologies with scale economies, in which welfare is greatest with either no control or complete control. Given that the costs of treatment per capita vary drastically across states and regions, they found the treatment costs outweighed the benefits for all small facilities.

Established in 1995, EPA started the National Environmental Performance Partnership System (NEPPS) to give states the option of more regulatory flexibility in exchange for more accountability in performance. States pushed for NEPPS for three main reasons. First, states were taking over the day-to-day management of environmental programs. Second, non-point source pollution issues (for example, agricultural runoff, transportation) were becoming relatively more prominent in environmental protection. Controlling diverse sources that are difficult to monitor requires more local regulatory interaction. Third, policy makers at all levels of government decided to manage and measure progress based on environmental outputs (for example, concentration levels) rather than just regulatory inputs (for example, number of permits, inspections, enforcement actions). This required more local monitoring efforts. In theory NEPPS makes sense; in practice, many issues remain about how to measure performance accurately, prevent inconsistent implementation, and develop stronger incentives for participation. As of 2001, 13 states still do not participate fully in the NEPPS program.

To understand state performance better, Lester (1995) developed a framework based on the capacity and will for each state to meet its environmental objectives. He grouped the 50 states into four categories based on two dimensions – the commitment to environmental protection and the strength of institutional capacity. The *Progressive* states – high commitment/strong institutions – include California, Florida, Maryland, Massachusetts, Michigan, New Jersey, New York, Oregon, Washington and Wisconsin. Here environmental quality is more likely to improve over the next decades. The *Strugglers* – high commitment/limited institutions – include Colorado, Connecticut, Delaware, Hawaii, Idaho, Iowa, Maine, Minnesota, Montana, Nevada, New Hampshire, North Carolina, North Dakota, Rhode Island and Vermont. The major challenge for these states is finding the balance between the potentially conflicting preferences of keeping governmental budgets small while wanting the public resources to protect the environment more. The *Delayers* – low commitment/strong institutions – include Alabama, Alaska, Arkansas, Georgia, Illinois, Louisiana, Missouri, Ohio, Oklahoma, Pennsylvania, South Carolina, Tennessee, Texas, Virginia and West Virginia. These states, especially those dominated by the energy industries, will maintain the status quo, but will be slow in implementing federal legislation. Finally, the *Regressives* – low commitment/limited institutions – include Arizona, Indiana, Kansas, Kentucky, Mississippi, Nebraska, New Mexico, South Dakota, Utah, and Wyoming. Historically, these states have and continue to promote commercial progress over environmental protection.

To illustrate the Regressive attitude, consider the example of coal bed methane (CBM) development in Wyoming. Coal bed methane is natural gas found in coal seams – typically saturated with ground water. Extraction of the resource requires bringing large volumes of polluted water to the surface, where it is generally discharged and allowed to pool in holding ponds. Between 1975 and 1999, about 200 discharge permits were issued annually; permits have increased to over 600 a year with the initiation of CBM. About 16 000 CBM wells have been developed in the Powder River Basin in Wyoming to date, and another 35 000 wells could be developed. The estimated amount of recoverable CBM from the Powder River Basin ranges from 8.24 to 22.42 trillion cubic feet of gas (US Geological Survey, 2003). In response to this 'boom', Wyoming's Department of Environmental Quality (DEQ) has assigned *one* person to monitor compliance with water discharge permits. 'That of course is a problem. There's a lot of activity up there, so that person is stretched pretty thin', said John Warner, administrator of DEQ's Water Quality Division (as quoted in Stark, 2004). In addition, differences exist in Montana and Wyoming on the limits to the key environmental parameters in CBM discharge water. The Montana Board of

Environmental Review approved rules in 2003, for example. The standard for the Sodium Absorption Ratio (SAR) varies between 3.0 and 4.0 for the Powder River Basin during irrigation. In contrast, Wyoming's DEQ discharge permit application specifies only that SAR will be 'Calculated as unadjusted ratio'; no numeric standard is provided (see Wyoming Department of Environmental Quality, 2003). Montana's tougher standards encourage the use of costly water re-injection technologies.

In addition, the federal and state governments work with the 562 federally recognized Tribal Entities in the process and implementation of environmental and resource policy. The unique relationship with Tribal governments rests on the Constitution, federal statues, Executive Orders and court decisions. About 56.2 million acres of land are held in trust by the federal government for various Indian tribes. In 1984, EPA implemented an 'Indian policy' – tribal self-determination in its environmental regulation on Indian lands. EPA was the first federal agency to establish a formal government-to-government working relationship with the Tribes, treating them as sovereign entities with primary authority and not a political subdivision of another governmental unit in the US. In the official declaration, the EPA states:

> In those cases where facilities owned or managed by Tribal Governments are not in compliance with federal environmental statutes, EPA will work cooperatively with Tribal leadership to develop means to achieve compliance, providing technical support and consultation as necessary to enable Tribal facilities to comply. Because of the distinct status of Indian Tribes and the complex legal issues involved, direct EPA action through the judicial or administrative process will be considered where the Agency determines, in its judgment, that: (1) a significant threat to human health or the environment exists, (2) such action would reasonably be expected to achieve effective results in a timely manner, and (3) the Federal Government cannot utilize other alternatives to correct the problem in a timely fashion.

Initiated in 1999, the National EPA-Tribal Science Council (TSC) was created to help continue building bridges and improving understanding between EPA and Indian tribes over environmental policy.

In sum, environmental policy under the pendulum of the US federalist system has led to a 'complex and fragmented patchwork of regulatory programs' (Andrews, 1999). Federal mandates implemented at the state level remains the core system. And while debates continue about whether federal or state governments should be in charge of the design and implementation of policy, the compelling question is not a dichotomous federal versus state issue. Rather the question is how best to share responsibility between the national and local level so as to increase environmental protection at lower cost. State and local authorities have and continue to adapt to cracks in the intricate structure of national environmental protection. Pragmatic ad hoc solutions have been and continue to be crafted at the state level and between the state and federal governments. Many of these solutions involve regional cooperation between states. Examplcs include watershed policy (for example, Delaware River basin, Great Lakes, Four Corners, Ozone Transport and Assessment Group (OTAG)).

2.2 Major Federal Regulations

Since Earth Day in 1970, the federal government has driven the expansion of environmental laws and statutes in the US. The US Congress has enacted several major laws and statutes that dictate the nature and extent of environmental protection and natural resource conservation. Found in title 40 of the Code of Federal Regulations, environmental regulations make up 24 volumes, which is four volumes more than that allotted to the Internal Revenue Service for tax regulation. Listed chronologically, the most significant US federal environmental laws and statutes include:

- National Environmental Policy Act of 1969 (NEPA) 42 U.S.C. 4321-4347: NEPA serves as the basic contract for environmental protection in the US.

  > The purposes of this Act are: To declare a national policy which will encourage productive and enjoyable harmony between man and his environment; to promote efforts which will prevent or eliminate damage to the environment and biosphere and stimulate the health and welfare of man; to enrich the understanding of the ecological systems and natural resources important to the Nation; and to establish a Council on Environmental Quality [CEQ].

  The power of the NEPA revolution rests not in setting standards and benchmarks, but rather in calling for a change in how the US government makes decisions. The statute forces agencies to consider the environmental ramifications of any decision by requiring detailed environmental impact assessments. By law, these environmental impact statements (EIS), must include an analysis of: (i) the environmental impact of the proposed action; (ii) any adverse environmental effects which cannot be avoided should the proposal be implemented; (iii) alternatives to the proposed action; (iv) the relationship between local short-term uses of man's environment and the maintenance and enhancement of long-term productivity; and (v) any irreversible and irretrievable commitments of resources which would be involved in the proposed action should it be implemented.

The Act offers no well-defined quantitative environmental performance standard to judge overall NEPA's success, although others have created composite 'environmental quality indices'. Jones et al. (2000) from the Fraser Institute created one such index, estimating that the overall environmental quality in the US improved by nearly 19 per cent between 1980–1995 (relative to an 18 per cent increase in Canada and a 10 per cent increase in the United Kingdom). A 25-year retrospective study conducted by the CEQ (1997) concluded 'NEPA's most enduring legacy is as a *framework for collaboration* between federal agencies and those who will bear the environmental, social, and economic impacts of agency decisions' (emphasis in original).

- Clean Air Act (CAA) 42 U.S.C. s/s 7401 et seq. (1970): Amended from the Air Quality Act of 1967, the CCA establishes the basic federal framework to address air pollution. The CAA regulates air emissions from area, stationary and mobile sources. This law directs the EPA to protect human and environmental health by establishing National Ambient Air Quality Standards (NAAQS) that would serve to protect the quality of the Nation's air resources and the public health. The goal was to set and achieve NAAQS in every state by 1975, although this has not been achieved as of 2004. The CAA directed the states to develop state implementation plans (SIPs) applicable to industrial sources in the state. The act provides means for technical and financial assistance for the states to help meet the NAAQS. The CAA also started a research and development program to achieve the prevention and control of air pollution. In 1997, the CAA was amended to set new target dates for attainment of NAAQS. The CAA encourages a regional air pollution prevention approach. The 1990 CCA amendments were added to address neglected issues like acid deposition, ground-level ozone, stratospheric ozone depletion, and air toxics. The 1990 amendments also initiated the use of tradable permits for sulfur dioxide emissions. As Portney (2000) notes, '*air quality has improved significantly in virtually every metropolitan area around the country sinces 1970*' (emphasis in original). Between 1973–1990, EPA (1999) estimated the CAA generated annual health benefits of $1.1 trillion at a cost of $37 billion – suggesting the CAA increased social welfare.
- Federal Water Pollution Control Act (Clean Water Act) PL 92-500; 33 U.S.C. 1251 et seq.: Demand for improved water quality by reducing pollution led to enactment of the Federal Water Pollution Control Act Amendments of 1972, also known as the Clean Water Act (CWA). Amended in 1977, the Act established the basic structure for regulating discharges of pollutants into the waters of the

United States. Its goal is 'to restore and maintain the chemical, physical, and biological integrity of the Nation's waters'. Seven targets and policies were announced: (1) eliminate water pollutants by 1985; (2) make waters 'fishable and swimmable'; (3) prohibit the discharge of toxic pollutants in toxic amounts, unless a permit was obtained; (4) provide federal financial assistance to construct publicly owned waste treatment works; (5) develop sewage treatment management planning processes in each state; (6) more research and demonstration efforts to develop new low-emission technology; and (7) develop programs to control non-point sources of pollution. The Clean Water Act required the federal government to set water quality standards for all contaminants in surface waters. The CWA also contains the US's most notable protection for wetlands. According to Freeman (2000), US water quality as threatened by conventional pollution has improved on net in the aggregate; healthier in some areas, deteriorating in others. Freeman concludes, however, that the costs of the Act far outweigh the perceived health benefits due in part to the use of command-and-control technological mandates.

- Federal Insecticide, Fungicide, and Rodenticide Act (FIFRA) (PL 95-516; 7 U.S.C. 136-136y): FIFRA provides the basic framework for the federal control of pesticide distribution, sale and use. The Act gave the EPA authority to study pesticide usage and potential damages, and require users like farmers, ranchers and firms to register when purchasing pesticides. After some amendments, all users now must take an exam to become a certified pesticide applicator. The EPA registers all pesticides used in the US. Registration details the requirements on how to label a pesticide, focusing on what the label says about its use, how it says it, where it is placed, legibility, misleading statements, warnings and precautionary statements.
- Endangered Species Act of 1973 (ESA): The Endangered Species Act (ESA) is one of the most comprehensive of all the US environmental laws. The ESA strengthened the Endangered Species Conservation Act of 1969, which, in turn, was passed to improve the Endangered Species Preservation Act of 1966. The act codifies the idea that species have 'ecological, educational, historical, recreational and scientific value' unaccounted for in the course of 'economic growth and development' (ESA, Sec. 2). The purpose of the act is 'to provide a means whereby the ecosystems upon which endangered species and threatened species depend may be conserved' and to provide a program to conserve these species. Thirty years ago this language seemed harmless enough to Congress – the Act passed with little or no opposition – 390–12 in the House and 92–0 in the Senate. Has the Endangered

Species Act slowed the perceived trends in extinction? The question is difficult to answer, in part because the three decades since the passage of the Act is a brief period to judge whether trends in extinction rates have changed, and because the ecological literature is by no means decided on a clear technical definition of 'recovery' (Tear et al., 1993). Since its inception, 11 species have recovered and have been removed from the list. According to the Environmental Defense Fund, less than 10 per cent of the listed species have exhibited an improved status and the status of four times that amount is declining. The ratio of declining species to improving species is 1.5 to 1 on federal lands, and 9 to 1 on private lands.

- Safe Drinking Water Act: In 1974, perhaps recognizing the challenges of moving all rivers and lakes to 'drinkable' water quality, Congress enacted the Safe Drinking Water Act. The Act is design to focus on water quality provided by public water systems. This act addresses all waters currently used or potentially targeted for drinking use, both above ground and underground. EPA is asked to establish safe health standards of purity and to require all owners or operators of public water systems to comply with these standards. These standards took the form of maximum contaminant levels (MCLs) for chemical and microbial contaminants. EPA promulgated one MCL by 1984, which prompted Congress to amend the Act in 1986, demanding MCLs for 83 contaminants within three years. The EPA did not meet the three-year deadline, but today has the mandated MCLs.
- Toxic Substances Control Act of 1976 (TSCA): Congress enacted the Toxic Substances Control Act (TSCA) of 1976, creating the authority for the federal government to track and develop data sets for the over 75 000 industrial chemicals produced or imported into the US. All chemical are screened, and some are tested for whether they pose a threat to human or environmental health. Chemicals that pose an unreasonable risk can be banned. Economic considerations are to be considered, such that restrictions on chemicals should not create unnecessary economic barriers to technological innovation. TSCA gives EPA authority to commence a civil action in a US district court to *seize* an imminently hazardous chemical substance, or for temporary or permanent *relief* as may be necessary to protect health or the environment from the unreasonable risk created by a person who manufactures, processes, distributes, uses, or disposes of, an imminently hazardous chemical substance, or both.
- Resource Conservation and Recovery Act of 1976 (RCRA): The goal of RCRA is the 'cradle to grave' control of the growing amount of

hazardous wastes generated in the US – generation, transport, treatment, storage and disposal. Hazardous implies the waste can ignite, corrode, explode or poison, such that it poses a risk to life and limb; EPA has a list of over 500 specific hazardous wastes. The general goal is to control future land disposal, discourage open land dumping, and encourage new technologies for waste reduction and recycling. The Act is to provide technical and financial assistance to state and local governments to develop waste management plans. RCRA also provides a framework to manage non-hazardous wastes. In 1986, RCRA was amended to include authority over problems arising from active and future underground storage tanks. Although waste did decline after RCRA was enacted, Sigman (2000) argues that it is 'purely speculative' to attribute all the gains to RCRA. Switches in production techniques or less output could have been driven by local NIMBY politics (not in my back yard) or state-policy-driven lawsuits.

- Comprehensive Environmental Response, Compensation, and Liability Act of 1980 (CERCLA, or Superfund): The primary purpose of CERCLA is to authorize the EPA to respond to hazardous substance emergencies and to protect public health, welfare and the environment by cleaning up the country's worst hazardous waste sites. Two financial mechanisms drive hazardous waste site clean-ups. First, liability incentives, through a broad category of responsible parties, take advantage of the 'polluter pays' principle. CERCLA § 107(a) holds liable the following: (1) the owner and operator of a vessel or a facility; (2) any person who at the time of disposal of any hazardous substance owned or operated any facility at which such hazardous substances were disposed of; (3) any person who by contract, agreement, or otherwise arranged for disposal or treatment, or arranged with a transporter for transport for disposal or treatment, of hazardous substances owned or possessed by such a person, by any other party or entity, at any facility or incineration vessel owned or operated by another party or entity and containing such hazardous substances; and (4) any person who accepts or accepted any hazardous substances for transport to disposal or treatment facilities, incineration vessels or sites selected by such a person, from which there is a release, or a threatened release which causes the incurrence of response costs, of a hazardous substance. The law seeks to make those responsible for the improper disposal of hazardous waste bear the costs and accept responsibility for their actions. Second, a trust fund, or the Superfund, financed through excise taxes on chemicals and petroleum and corporate environmental income taxes helps achieve the goal of expeditious site clean-ups.

The Superfund is used to fund clean-up at sites that require immediate remedial attention before the Department of Justice has an opportunity to seek reimbursement from responsible parties. The law was designed in this fashion so clean-up could be implemented quickly and litigation over the extent of responsibility would only take place after a site was cleaned up. The Superfund can be used to finance response actions where a liable party cannot be found or is incapable of paying clean-up costs. CERCLA § 101(24) defines response actions as remedial actions or clean-ups.

- The Superfund Amendments and Reauthorization Act (SARA); 42 U.S.C.9601 et seq. (1986): Based on the challenging experience of administering CERCLA, Congress enacted the Superfund Amendments and Reauthorization Act (SARA) to address several issues that arose. SARA focuses on permanent remedies, new technologies, more state involvement, more attention to human health risks, and greater citizen participation. SARA made significant changes to the size of the Hazardous Substances Superfund and the sources of the revenues that replenish it, as well as to the statutory criteria for selecting remedies at sites. SARA also codified the use of EPA-developed tools designed to provide incentives for responsible parties to reach settlement agreements with the government regarding the conduct of clean-ups and contributions to the cost of clean-ups. These changes are to speed settlements and reduce transaction costs. SARA amendments authorize EPA to release *de minimis* parties from liability. *De minimis* are parties found to be responsible for only a small percentage of the volume and toxicity of the hazardous substances at a hazardous waste site. SARA also permits the government to mix fund at certain sites. Mixed funding allows the government to assume some portion of the clean-up expenses, with responsible parties assuming the remainder of the costs. Finally, SARA establishes time schedules for EPA to start site studies and clean-up activities in an attempt to accelerate the pace of clean-ups.
- Emergency Planning and Community Right-to-Know Act (EPCRA): Congress enacted EPCRA, or Title III of SARA, as the national legislation on community safety. This law was designated to help local communities protect public health, safety, and the environment from chemical hazards. Congress required each state to appoint a State Emergency Response Commission (SERC).
- The Oil Pollution Act of 1990 33 U.S.C. 2702 to 2761: The Oil Pollution Act (OPA) of 1990 focused the prevention and response to catastrophic oil spills. Congress created a trust fund financed by a tax on oil to clean up spills when the responsible party cannot or will not

carry this out. Oil storage facilities and vessels are required to submit plans on how they will respond to large discharges.

- The Pollution Prevention Act (PPA) 42 U.S.C. 13101 and 13102, s/s et seq. (1990): When Congress passed the Pollution Prevention Act (PPA) in 1990, it established a national policy

  > that pollution should be prevented or reduced at the source whenever feasible; pollution that cannot be prevented should be recycled in an environmentally safe manner, whenever feasible; pollution that cannot be prevented or recycled should be treated in an environmentally safe manner whenever feasible; and that disposal or other release into the environment should be employed only as a last resort and should be conducted in an environmentally safe manner.

  The goal is to get industry, government and the general public to think about reducing pollution cost-effectively by changing production. New production technology would include recycling and source reduction. On top of the requirements of EPCRA, PPA required more reporting about source reduction and recycling activities for chemical releases.

3. POLICY TOOLS

As in many countries, the continuing question in the US is how can federal, state and local regulators align private motives with social objectives to protect the environment better? In general, a regulator has three broad policy tools to help her realign private and public incentives: legal mandates and technological restrictions (for example, specific abatement technology), cooperative institutions to share information between regulators, polluters, and victims (for example, collaborative bargaining), and economic incentive mechanisms to increase the cost of 'environmental shirking' on environmental protection (for example, charges, fees, taxes, tradable permits). Conventional command-and-control approaches still dominate US environmental policy.

Revesz and Stavins (2004) identify several normative factors to help explain the dominance of conventional approaches relative to market-based instruments, despite the evidence which suggests the potential cost savings. On the demand side, they argue that firms prefer regulations that give them a competitive advantage over potential rivals (for example, creates a barrier to entry). Standards are set with input from existing firms in an industry, and frequently 'grandfather' in existing plants from these more stringent future regulations. Environmental groups also lobby for command-and-control instruments over market-based approaches on ethical grounds – we do not want to hand out a 'license to pollute', on practical grounds – too hard to monetize environmental damages and it will create environmental 'hot spots' of concentrated pollution, and strategic grounds – less political leverage to tighten standards in the future. Organized labor also argues for command-and-control approaches to protect jobs. Market-based instruments provide too much flexibility in cost cutting (for example, plant closures), the burden falling on established industries. For instance, in the debates of the amendments to the Clean Air Act, organized labor fought for command-and-control technological solutions (for example, scrubbing) to reduce a coal-fired electric utility's incentive to switch to the cleaner coal in Wyoming, produced by a non-unionized labor force.

Here we consider three policy tools used in US environmental policy – citizen suits, collaborative processes, and market-based economic incentives.

3.1 Citizen Suits

In January 2000, the US Supreme Court upheld one of the most interesting legal tools for environmental protection – the ability of private citizens to use the courts to help enforce federal environmental policy. The Justices voted 7–2 in *Friends of the Earth, Inc. v Laidlaw Environmental Services (TOC), Inc.* (98–822), 149 F.3d 303, to preserve the rights of citizens to act as 'private attorney generals' for nature. Private citizens can use the federal district courts to initiate suits if they can show they have an interest that is or might be adversely affected by violators who damaged the natural environment. The end result of these citizen suits can be injunctive relief or civil penalties imposed on violators to give them an incentive to comply with environmental regulations. The idea is to empower ordinary citizens to take control over their own environmental destiny.

Citizen involvement in the enforcement of federal laws is an old idea. Private citizens helping to enforce laws dates back over 600 years to a 1388 statute in England (Dickinson, 1997). Until the 1970s, US citizens were restricted because most environmental decisions were left in the hands of government bureaucrats and technicians (Sax, 1970). The case for citizen suits was not made so much a case to protect the common man from market failure (for example, externalities), but rather to protect him from administrative failure by the government agencies tasked to address issues with the market misallocation. Administrative complexities, red tape and politics kept the common citizen at arm's length from most environmental decisions. Re-emergence of interest in citizen suits for environmental protection began in earnest in the 1960s, as air and water pollution and threatened species became hotly contested issues. People and legislators began to realize that weak punishment mechanisms in environmental legislation were a problem.

This realization led to the creation of citizen suit provisions in US federal legislation in 1970, that is, section 304 of the Clean Air Act (Miller, 1987). The goal was not to replace legislative process, but rather as 'a means of providing realistic access to legislatures so that the theoretical processes of democracy can be made to work more effectively in practice' (Sax, 1970). This goal of more access was not given much notice until after the Clean Water Act (CWA) was passed in 1972. After the CWA was passed, citizen suits became increasingly popular, and now most citizen suits brought about are a direct result of the Act. Throughout the 1970s and 1980s, as the power to enforce several federal laws was put into citizens' hands as well as the federal government, the number of citizen suits began to multiply and become a useful tool for those interested in environmental protection. Today, although the Supreme Court has raised the bar for the ordinary person to get into court over the past decade, the *Friends of the Earth v Laidlaw Environmental Services* ruling suggests that citizen suits are likely to remain an important tool in the US (Glaberson, 1999). Also, interest in citizen suits probably will continue to spread globally, as suggested by test case suits in less likely places like China, where a Mr Zhang Jinhu sued his local government for compensation from losses suffered due to pollution (Rosenthal, 2000).

Citizen participation went through three waves in the US. The first wave started in the 1970s and 1980s. In the early 1970s, the US Congress enacted several major environmental regulations, including the Clean Air Act and the Clean Water Act (CWA) which included provisions for citizen participation. The CWA, for instance, allows the federal government and states to allocate permits to limit the discharge of pollutants, and establish monitoring and reporting actions. Under §505(a) of the CWA, any citizen has standing to initiate a suit to enforce any limit set by a permit, in which a 'citizen' is 'a person or persons having an interest which is or may be adversely affected' (33 U.S.C. § 1365(a), (g)). But first the citizen must give 60-days notice to the United States Environmental Protection Agency (EPA) of the alleged violation and alleged violator. The notice allows the alleged violator a chance to get into compliance, such that the citizen suit is unnecessary. The CWA authorizes district courts in citizen suits to enter injunctions and to assess civil penalties, payable to the United States Treasury. Plus, the court 'may award costs of litigation (including reasonable attorney and expert witness fees) to any prevailing or substantially prevailing party, whenever the court determines such award is appropriate' (§1365(d)).

Over the last two decades, the first wave ended and a second wave to restrict the power and use of citizen suits started. Most rulings were now coming down in favor of the Restrictive approach. Fear of the outcome of a widespread allowance of citizen suits has a long history. As far back as 1980, fear of the potential damage citizen suits could cause was voiced. Many suits were being brought upon companies that had little or no insurance to pay for the resulting damages from the suits (Terry, 1980). A portion of the public feared firms could not pay the large fees resulting from citizen suits, which could cause firms to file bankruptcy. A key issue in restricting the domain of citizen suits is deciding who has *standing* – the issue of who is entitled to prosecute a particular legal claim in court. The Supreme Court has said that a citizen must meet three constitutional requirements to have standing in court: (a) he must show that he has suffered an 'injury in fact'; (b) he must establish *causation* – the injury 'fairly can be traced to the challenged action'; and (c) he must show that the injury 'is likely to be redressed by a favorable decision' of the court. As we will see, increasing restrictions on standing raises the bar for citizen suits, high enough that some worry that 'the evolution of standing doctrine over the last decade [1990s] has been a case of heads we lose, tails they win' (Echeverria and Zeidler, 1999).

Further rulings kept coming down from the court restricting both the power and frequency of citizen suits. An 8–0 decision from the Supreme Court in *Gwaltney of Smithfield Ltd. v Chesapeake Bay Foundation* ruled that citizens could not file suit for 'wholly past violations'. A violator in a citizen suit had to be either continuously violating pollution laws or had to have shown a threat of doing so in the future from a result of long and steady past violations. If a firm had violated the law in the past but had resolved the dispute in a timely manner, thus showing willingness to comply with the law, the citizen group would not be awarded victory (Johnston, 1999; Leonard, 1995; Taylor Jr., 1987; Young, 1987). Even greater hits were taken when a bill that passed the Senate took away the power of citizens from bringing suit against the government. A Bush–Senate deal took back the power of the citizens from bringing suit against government agencies for failing to supply clean air to the US (Billings, 1990). The federal government was no longer responsible for providing its citizens with clean air. This ruling held up under a different context, when a Florida case *Seminole Tribe of Florida v Florida* ruled that citizens could not bring suit against their state in federal court for failing to comply with federal regulations (Reynolds, 1996). Two more cases reduced citizen suit power. The first case, brought out by the Defenders of Wildlife, saw the Supreme Court uphold a George Bush administration policy that limited the power of the Endangered Species Act to only cases in the United States. United States funded projects that were completed outside the United States could not be brought up with a citizen suit to protect the ESA (Hamburger, 1992). Probably the biggest case in the 1990s was ironically what might have given citizen suits their respectability in the view of society again.

The Supreme Court ruled, in *Bennett v Spear*, that any citizen can bring suit over an Environmental Law; land developers, farmers and ranchers could now use the citizen suit provisions to bring suit that these laws were too restrictive and overprotective of the environment (Savage, 1997). If a person was being harmed by the action of the federal government and felt the actions taken were too severe, they could bring a citizen suit against the government for being too strict with respect to federal environmental law. The ability to have both sides of a protection issue come to court now gave citizen suits a new look. This case was first viewed as another victory against citizen suits brought against developers. Citizen suits found another foe in the 1990s. Lawsuits can be filed on behalf of firms that have citizen suits filed against them. These lawsuits, Strategic Lawsuits Against Public Participation (SLAPP), the phrase coined by George Pring and Penelope Canan, filed in the US, are brought against citizens for speaking out against development or any action that brings a citizen to speak out against the firm. Firms can take citizen groups to court for complaining about development. This action is a preemptive strike against other citizen groups acting to stop others from speaking out.

In the late 1990s, a third wave began. Citizen suits had two notable victories in 1998. The first victory dealt with the issue of 'wholly past violations'. The Fourth Circuit court ruled on remand of *Chesapeake Bay Found. v Gwaltney of Smithfield, Ltd.* that even if the violations were taken care of in the time period between the filing and the time the case went to court, the plaintiff would still be due fees, which was held up in other cases, *Atlantic States Legal Found. v Tyson Foods, Inc.*, *Natural Resources Defense Council v Texaco Ref. & Mktg., Inc.*; now the term 'wholly past violations' only meant if the violations had been cleaned up prior to the filing of the case (Johnston, 1999). The second victory came when the Supreme Court ruled in *Steel Co. v Citizens for a Better Environment* that 'wholly past violations' only dealt with the Clean Water Act, and the Emergency Planning and Community Right to Know Act allowed citizens to sue for past violations (Johnston, 1999). Now, citizen suits could be brought about under other acts beyond the Clean Water Act for violations that occurred at any time.

3.2 Local Collaboration

In an effort to reduce court battles, many US decision makers have begun promoting local control and place-based collaboration as the next step in environmental protection and natural resources management. Collaborative processes encourage local stakeholders to resolve disputes on private and public lands through bargaining and negotiation, rather than through litigation or federal mandate. Devolution of regulation allows communities to try and develop and enforce consensus management plans that adopt specific place-based strategies that complement federal legislation. In principle, such collaboration offers the potential for an efficient Coasean bargaining-type construction of local development and protection of natural resources in which private property rights exist. Collaboration groups trying to capture these potential gains from exchange now number in the hundreds in the west, ranging from informal grassroots meetings to government-mandated advisory councils (see Sabel et al., 2001).

Oates (2001, p. 24) makes a strong case for regulation at the local level:

> My own sense is that where environmental quality is basically a local public good, the case for the setting of environmental standards at an appropriately decentralized level of government is quite compelling. At the same time, one can envision an essential informational and guidance role for the central authority. With the substantial scientific and policy expertise at its disposal, a central agency can effectively provide a menu of options for standards and a choice of policy instruments. Such guidance would become an important resource for state and local officials and their constituencies in the actual design of decentralized environmental programs.

Place-based collaboration is now promoted at both the federal and state levels. A broad range of people now promote collaboration: Secretary of the Interior Gale Norton, the popular press, and academics interested in the underlying structure of these groups. The private sector was already using negotiation, mediation, facilitation and other alternative methods to resolve disputes in the environmental arena. Congress saw this collaboration as having 'yielded decisions that are faster, less expensive, and less contentious' than existing dispute resolution procedures such as litigation (Public Law 101–552, Sec. 2).

At the federal level, for example, Congress enacted the Alternative Dispute Resolution Act of 1990, which moved environmental protection activities away from relying strictly on the federal agencies to a balanced approach that engages local citizen groups.

Local control and place-based collaboration for private property questions is also being promoted at the federal and state levels. At the federal level, Congress enacted the Alternative Dispute Resolution Act of 1990, which moved environmental protection activities away from relying on the federal agencies to a more balanced approach to engage local citizen groups. The implication is that Congress found these alternative means of dispute resolution to produce faster, cheaper, friendlier decisions than existing dispute resolution procedures such as litigation. This legislation authorized and encouraged federal agencies to use alternative dispute resolution techniques for the prompt and informal resolution of disputes, and recognized the benefits of negotiation.

At the state level, more local control and collaboration is reflected in the Western Governors Association's environmental doctrine called Enlibra. The first and second Enlibra principles are 'national standards, neighborhood solutions – assign responsibilities at the right level', and 'collaboration, not polarization – use collaborative processes to break down barriers and find solutions'. The idea behind these principles is that locals who own or use the land also understand local conditions, including landowners, local resource organizations, and state or local governments. The federal government is asked to help locals develop their own plans to define, implement, and enforce accountable targets of conservation.

Some disagree. While noting that collaboration makes sense in theory, they argue that final authority by local groups does not. Michael McCloskey, former executive director and chairman of the Sierra Club, makes the point that delegating final authority 'would effect a massive transfer of power, a repudiation of the progress of the past century, a collapse in environmental gains, and a grievous wound to the practice of democracy'. They fear both local vested interests and outside industries will dominate ordinary citizens in negotiations, leading to either no agreements or to binding, watered-down agreements that promote status quo wealth preservation.

But several reasons explain why collaboration has worked to help promote effective solutions at a local level on both private and public lands. Collaboration reduces the risk that local net benefits will be downplayed relative to national concerns, which encourages local support for the final decision. Locals included in a decision to make a local change are more likely to support or at least understand the suggested policy. Collaboration can also take a broader perspective by promoting cooperation across fence lines of private landowners. Collaboration tries to signal respect for indigenous and anecdotal knowledge that exists in the people most familiar with specific problems, and tries to promote information-sharing between people who might not necessarily trust each other's motives.

Dan Kemmis has taken the idea of local control in the interior west to an extreme. Kemmis, the director of the Center of the Rocky Mountain West at the University of Montana, defines his vision on how local control might actually be codified into a larger and more formal institutional structure. He argues that perhaps the time is right for the west to govern the west. He contends that the mountain west could recapture its democratic roots through authentic self-determination similar to the semi-autonomous relationship that Scotland, Wales and Northern Ireland have with the United Kingdom. He calls for a 'progressive, bipartisan, regional solidarity among western governors and within the Senate . . . for a West-wide compact to transfer responsibility for public lands to western institutions' (Kemmis, 2001, p. 231).

Essentially, such an extreme form of local control would give a lot more final authority over natural resources. But whether such a powerful final authority should or could be allowed depends on whom you ask. Some people believe it is a necessary condition for more effective local control and collaboration. They fear that stakeholders take their negotiation duties lightly if they think their recommendations are advisory rather than binding. Former EPA Administrator William Ruckelshaus, for example, is a prominent supporter of final authority. He stressed 'it is best if the relevant governmental authority signals in unambiguous terms . . . that what comes out of the [collaborative] process will likely prevail as public policy'. US Senate Minority Leader Tom Daschle, for whatever motive, also recently promoted final decision making authority on locals. He added an amendment to legislation that gave final authority through force of law to a consensus agreement struck between the US Forest Service, the logging industry, and two major environmental groups to allow thinning in the Black Hills National Forest. Daschle's amendment maintains final authority for the agreement by shielding it from any future appeal or legal challenge.

A well-known example on final authority is the Quincy Library Group's forest management plan. The Quincy Library Group is a local collaborative group in northern California who asked for final authority for their five-year forest-management experiment developed by their coalition. They sought support for their plan on the national political arena after the Forest Service failed to adopt key aspects of their plan. The forests in their plan were the Plumas, Lassen and Tahoe National Forests in northeastern California. Despite the efforts of national environmental groups like the Wilderness Society, the Quincy group eventually was successful. Congress passed by a 429–1 vote and President Clinton signed their plan into law in 1998; since then they have received nearly $25 million in federal funds to help implement their plan. The Herger-Feinstein Quincy Library Group Forest Recovery Act was signed into law in 1998 and authorizes a five-year pilot project mandating the US Forest Service to manage the Plumas, Lassen and Tahoe National Forests under the plan developed by the Quincy Library Group.

3.3 Market-based Incentives

Economists have long promoted market-based incentive systems as a cost-effective alternative to inflexible command-and-control environmental regulations. The basic idea behind incentives is private flexibility to achieve desired public objectives. Incentives raise the cost of environmental shirking, while allowing people the flexibility to find the least-cost pollution control strategy. By increasing the cost of shirking, the producer has a private incentive to provide the socially optimal level of pollution control. Environmental policy in the US commonly uses economic incentives in the implementation of rules and regulations. For example, federal and state officials use several economic incentive mechanisms to help protect endangered species on private land, including impact fees, subsidies, tradable development rights, conservation banking, fee simple acquisition, and conservation easements in the form of either purchased development rights or donations for tax relief. See, for example, Hanley et al. (1997), Anderson and Leal (2001), Stavins (2000), and Parkhurst and Shogren (2004) for more details.

Price incentives

The regulator can increase the costs of shirking by setting a 'green' charge, tax or subsidy on producer behavior or products. Emission or effluent charges are the most commonly discussed form of pricing for pollution. Emission charges are taxes or fees levied on the discharge of pollutants into air or water, or onto the soil, or on the generation of noise. These charges are designed to reduce the quantity or improve the quality of pollution by making polluters pay at least part of the costs of the harm they do to the environment. Economists favor emission charges over other options because by charging for every unit of pollution released into the environment they induce firms to lower their emissions to account for social damages. Because pollution control costs typically differ among producers, those with lower control costs reduce emission levels further than high cost polluters. Emission charges give producers an incentive to develop and adopt newer and better pollution control technologies as a means of bringing down the charges they must pay. To the degree that individual polluters use pollution control strategies which represent least-cost solutions, the aggregate costs of pollution control are minimized.

Emission charges are widely applied to waste. Since municipal and industrial wastes have to be treated before they are dumped, emission charges on waste take the form of waste treatment charges. Waste-related emission charges tend to vary as a function of the cost of waste treatment. Country experience with the use of emission charges for waste pollution control is also varied. While the United States applies emission charges on municipal and industrial wastes, the available evidence suggests they are more successful in raising revenue than in changing behavior.

While Congress has generally not been too interested in 'green taxes', several tax initiatives had or have environmental consequences. Gaines and Westin (1991) list several examples, including the ability to amortize pollution control facilities; tax-exempt financing for sewage and solid waste disposal facilities and other facilities for the public good; the tax code encouraging timber planting and maintenance (for financial not environmental reasons); charitable contributions of habitat for conservation (for example, preservation of open space); debt-for-nature swaps with developing countries; excise taxes on fuels and motor vehicles; tax relief for alcohol fuels (that is, ethanol); taxes for leaking underground storage tank trust fund; Superfund taxes and trust fund including tax on petroleum, hazardous substances, imported chemicals and corporations; oil spill liability trust fund tax; excise tax on ozone-depleting chemicals (for example, chlorofluorocarbons); excise taxes on coal; excise taxes on fishing equipment; and energy tax credits for renewable energy resources (for example, solar, geothermal).

For land use issues, US regulators use an impact fee as a cash or in-kind payment by a developer to a government as a precondition to receive a development permit. These fees have become popular in the last two decades. Governments frequently require developers to expend resources to finance a local public good like a park, as a precondition to receiving the necessary permits for development (for example, a cash payment, land donation, public parks, streets or other public goods). The goal is to offset the negative consequences of development to the surrounding environment and existing infrastructure. Impact fees are usually paid when the developer obtains his permit, which allows the new public goods to be created before completion of the development project. Impact fees have the additional attribute that those creating the new demand for public goods pay for that demand, allowing existing residents to maintain a level of public good provision by requiring development to 'pay its own way'.

Subsidies or compensation are another form of pricing incentive. While the call for compensation through subsidies is not new, it remains controversial. Compensation has its critics and supporters from both sides of the fence. Citizens who are wary of compensation-for-collaboration see the funds as a wedge that could be used to further open the door for more federal control over their property. Conservationists who oppose compensation see it as unable to fulfill targeted conservation goals such as creating larger habitat reserves and as a backdoor way to sabotage resource policy through federal under-funding. There is also the romantic-conservation ethic mindset toward land conservation promoted by people like Ralph Waldo Emerson, Henry Thoreau and John Muir. These preservationists believed land had other uses than just for human financial gain. Landowners are free to pursue private profits provided they behave as responsible social citizens too, because by definition land is already in public service. Land uses should be viewed as 'harm-preventing' rather than as 'public good providing'.

Conservationists who support subsidies see them as a practical way to buy cooperation. Landowner proponents argue that it is only fair to compensate property owners who are restricted in their ability to protect their investment. They view laws that restrict their autonomy to protect obscure nature as a threat to both the economic system and the broader social order (see for example Epstein, 2002). They view land as capital, and believe capital is the key ingredient that allows people the ability to create, store and share the wealth necessary for national prosperity. These landowners believe their land ethic is valid, and would like their on-going stewardship appreciated. This classical liberal viewpoint takes a Hamiltonian perspective – the government should abdicate to market forces that create wealth by allowing for resources to move freely from low valued to highly valued uses. Rightly or wrongly, they fear that restricting private land for species protection without just compensation is another step down a slippery slope toward collectivism.

Subsidies are financial assistance offered to landowners by regulators. Subsidies create an incentive to encourage landowners to maintain their land in an undeveloped state or to mitigate the environmental impact of development by helping the landowner meet maintenance and restoration costs of environmentally sensitive areas. Subsidies usually take the form of grants, loans, cash payments or tax allowances that are offered by federal, state or non-profit organizations (Hanley et al., 1997). Subsidy programs are funded by numerous methods, including tax revenue, lottery funds and special permits. Consider an example to illustrate how subsidies are used in species protection.

The California Department of Fish and Game (CDFG) administer a subsidy program, called the Timber Tax Credit Program (TTCP). The TTCP induces private landowners to undertake conservation projects voluntarily to improve habitat, and the probability of survival of the coho and chinook salmon, and the steelhead trout. The TTCP provides a tax credit of up to $50 000 to a landowner, upon completion of the approved project (for example, restoration of the stream banks, improvements to the flow of the stream, revegetating the habitat with indigenous plants, and performing upland work to reduce sediment runoff and to improve the timing and distribution of water returning to the stream). A landowner interested in participating submits an application listing the applicant's personal information, a brief description of the proposed project, an estimate of total and qualified project costs, location, directions to the proposed project, estimated time frame, type of fish that will likely benefit from the project, and the tax credit recipient's name(s) and ID number(s). This tax credit information is accompanied by a detailed description of the proposed project and a detailed estimation of the project costs. The CDFG then determines if the proposed project complies with state and federal law (CRA, 2000).

Tax credits can be up to 10 per cent of the estimated qualified costs of the proposed project, which are the costs for labor, materials, and in some instances the rental rate for heavy equipment. The costs must be incurred for purposes that directly increase the survival rate of salmon and steelhead. Costs associated with the installation of water pumps, well drilling, permanent roads and buildings, and services rendered by professional engineers do not qualify. The CDFG sums the estimated qualified costs for all of the completed approved projects, and then divides $500 000 by that summed number to obtain the tax credit percentage, which cannot exceed 10 per cent. The estimated qualified costs are then multiplied by the tax credit percentage, and the landowner is issued a tax credit in that amount. This tax credit is levied against the net tax, and if not completely used in the year issued, the remaining credit can be applied to tax liabilities in future years. The timber tax credit is funded by a tax placed on timber sales outside of the United States and receives approximately $500 000 a year, which is entirely issued in credits. The costs of administering the program are covered by a non–dedicated preservation fund (CRA, 2000).

Tradable permits

Tradable permits specify a pre-determined total level of emissions or emission concentrations within a specified region. Permits equal to the permissible total emissions are distributed among producers in the region. The permits can be traded among plants of a single producer as well as among producers. Producers that keep their emissions levels below their allotted permit level can sell or lease their surplus permits to other producers or use them to offset emissions in other parts of their own facilities. To ensure that such permits serve their purpose as incentives to change pollution control to socially desired levels, total emission levels within a given region are limited, such that the permits are valuable to producers. This scarcity value creates an incentive to trade with permits.

The US makes limited use of tradable permits for pollution control. Probably the most important permit systems are those developed and implemented at the state level to comply with federal ambient air quality standards enacted by the Clean Air Act. A now classic example is the Acid Rain program, which uses tradable permits to reduce emissions of sulfur dioxide (SO_2) from electric utilities. Starting in 1993, the permit program has been a success: many utilities' trade, SO_2 emissions and ambient concentrations have fallen to the target levels, and the costs are lower than expected. As noted by Stavins (2000), the cost saving from the CAA trading program 'was about $250 million savings per year over the 5-years of the lead reduction program, and up to $1 billion per year for the acid rain allowance trading program'.

The main feature of tradable permits is that producers, not regulators, must decide on the design and location of pollution control strategies. Overall, evidence from the US suggests that permits have not achieved significantly more reductions in emissions than standard regulatory systems, but that the unit costs of reductions are reduced (Hahn, 1989). The evidence is ambiguous as to whether tradable permits have stimulated any more innovation in pollution control technology than the command-and-control technological restrictions. Tradable permits have proven to be administratively cumbersome. Their application has been hindered by debates about baseline emission levels, the need for government approval at all stages of policy formulation, and the process in which producers must engage as they exchange proposals for carrying out a permit trade. In addition, the permit trading process has technical, financial and legal dimensions which have to be addressed before each trade in permits occurs.

For land use and endangered species protection, tradable development rights (TDR) programs specify a predetermined maximum level of development within a specified region, and then distribute development rights equal to the permissible total amount of development to landowners within the region. Landowners who keep their development levels below their allotted development rights level can sell their surplus development rights to other landowners, or they can use them to offset development on other properties. To ensure that development rights serve their purpose as an incentive to change development control to desired social levels, total development levels within a given region are limited such that the development rights are seen as a scarce resource, which is valuable to developers (Hanley et al., 1997). TDR programs ensure that development occurs on the properties with the highest development values, but they do not guarantee that the most environmentally sensitive land is left undeveloped (Boyd et al., 1999). This non-targeted result can reduce the net benefits to society when land has a greater habitat value than development value. If this land is still developed under the TDRs, the mechanism has performed poorly. The most common approach to overcome this inefficiency is to combine TDRs with zoning (Miller, 1999).

Government agencies responsible for land use planning determine which properties within a specified region should be protected for their valuable environmental characteristics and qualities. They then restrict development of these properties, and landowners are provided with development rights to compensate them for the loss of economic use. These rights can then be sold to developers in the less restricted properties within the region, where development is more desirable. Those properties that are restricted are called *sending zones*, and development properties are called *receiving zones*. Once sending and receiving zones are determined, the regulator decides on a formula for transferring the development rights from one zone to the other. A key feature that ensures that developers purchase TDRs from sending zones is that the density of development in receiving zones, prior to acquisition of TDRs, is restricted to less than the demanded density (Miller, 1999). The price of a TDR is determined through the open market. To facilitate trading and minimize transaction costs, regulators can establish a *TDR bank* or *exchange*, which brings together willing buyers and sellers such that each can find mutual gains through trade (Tripp and Dudek, 1989).

TDRs have been used by various states for close to three decades to protect historical buildings and landmarks, agricultural and ranch lands, open spaces and view corridors, and to protect riparian areas, forests and other ecologically sensitive lands. One of the earliest programs was New York City's Landmark Preservation Law. The program was initiated in the 1970s to protect historical landmarks by restricting development of air above historical buildings. The law allows the owner to be compensated for the lost right to develop by transferring the development rights for that air space to surrounding buildings that are allowed to build beyond the zoned height restrictions. New York City also allows development rights to transfer hands via *zoning lot mergers* between adjacent landowners. These landowners can combine their allowed floor area without joining ownership of the properties, provided the total floor area between the two buildings does not exceed the zoned maximum amount of floor area of the two properties. This system allows a developer to purchase the floor area not in use by an adjacent landowner and exceed the zoning restriction by that amount (Miller, 1999). Other TDR programs have been authorized by state statute in 22 states, including six in the west. Kansas and Washington have passed legislation that approves the use of TDRs for the purpose of general zoning. In Idaho, TDRs are used to protect 'designated historic properties'. Hawaii has approved use of TDRs for the 'protection, enhancement, preservation, and use of historic properties and burial sites'. Arizona TDRs are used to protect the 'public health, safety, and general welfare' of its citizens. Colorado's TDR programs are to be used for the protection of species, species habitat, agricultural and ranching lands, and open spaces (Miller, 1999).

Conservation banking

Developers undertaking a new project are frequently required to mitigate any adverse effects, which can be onsite, or the developer can purchase development credits to satisfy the regulation on land use. Development credits can be purchased as needed or banked to fulfill future requirements. Developers purchase these credits from private or publicly owned *conservation banks*, which determine the prices of the credits based on demand and supply. The developer purchases credits if and only if the cost of mitigation through credit purchase is less than the costs of alternative approaches to mitigation, such as onsite mitigation or establishing a separate conservation bank. If profits are to be made by bank owners, other conservation bank owners will be attracted into the market, and market competition will lower the price of the credits.

The amount of credits that a conservation bank, or *mitigation bank*, sells depends on the quality and type of habitat, and the number of a specific endangered species supported on a specific parcel of land. Bank owners increase credits by managing land to increase either the quality or quantity of the land to protect endangered species, or both. For example in Georgia, the Southlands Mitigation Bank, owned by the International Paper Company (IP), is an ideal habitat for the red-cockaded woodpecker (RCW). RCWs build nests in pine trees at least a 100 years old, and require stands at least 30 years old for the purpose of foraging, of which IP owns 16 000 acres in the Southlands Forest region. In conjunction with the Environmental Defense Fund, International Paper developed a habitat conservation plan (HCP) covering 5300 of the available 16 000 acres. The HCP established a baseline of two pairs of RCWs, and the HCP had a land management plan to meet a goal of increasing the population of RCWs to 30 pairs through techniques such as prescribed fire, creating new or restoring existing nesting cavities, and relocating young RCWs to the region. As each new pair of RCWs is established in the HCP area, International Paper obtains a permit to offset an incidental take on its own property or it can sell the credit to a third party within a specified region and approved by the FWS. Other examples include the San Vicente Conservation Bank and the Manchester Avenue Conservation Bank (MACB) both in San Diego County, CA (EDF, 1999). By 1998, 43 conservation banks were established in California.

Fee simple acquisition

Fee simple acquisition is the purchase of land, with all of its inherent property rights. Landowners voluntarily enter into an agreement to sell their land, typically at fair market value. Local governments often purchase land for public goods such as playgrounds, nature trails and other park lands

(Boyd et al., 1999; UCLCC, 1997). Sellers are generally private individuals or organizations; land trusts and other non-profit organizations do purchase land and then sell or transfer the land to government agencies (LTA, 1998).

One example of a transfer acquisition is Snake Creek Canyon, located on the east side of the Wasatch Mountains, UT. A local ski resort planned to develop the area. Instead, the ski area sold the land to the Nature Conservancy, acting in the interests of several municipalities, a private industry, citizen groups, and a state agency. This group agreed to reimburse the Nature Conservancy for the initial funds to purchase the land. The land had its development rights severed. The land trust, Utah Open Lands, holds the conservation easement; the Utah State Division of Parks has taken on the management of the property. This acquisition demonstrates how agencies and organizations can work together to accomplish land use goals (UCLCC, 1997). Another example of cooperation between government agencies and non-profit organizations is the California Coastal Conservancy (CCC). The CCC offers a wide array of programs to protect the California coastline and the valuable resources that are found there. Since its inception in 1976, the CCC has helped protect nearly 33 000 acres of wetlands, sand dunes and farmlands by working with non-profit land conservation organizations through the Nonprofit Organizations Assistance Program (NOAP). NOAP provides funding to non-profit organizations for the purpose of acquiring land or interests in land that satisfy CCC objectives, while the ownership and costs of managing the land fall on the shoulders of the non-profit organization (CCC, 2000).

Land trusts and other non-profit organizations use fee simple acquisition as a tool to protect land in ecologically sensitive regions, especially focusing on land threatened by urban sprawl. Land trusts acquire land by fee simple acquisition, donation of land with all property rights intact, and purchased development rights (PDR) and donated easements (Nijhuis, 2000). Purchasing the land or obtaining the land in its entirety through donation gives the land trust more control over land uses. The price of this control is the costs of managing the land, which often requires significant staff and resources. Land trusts try to reduce management costs by serving as a broker or middleman between the landowner and a larger trust or government agency. Land trusts also avoid management costs by acquiring a conservation easement, purchased development rights (PDR) or donated, which allows the landowner to remain on the land and maintain the land according to the terms of the easement. The land trust is still responsible for monitoring and enforcing the terms of the easement.

Conservation easement

A conventional easement is a legal instrument that serves to separate specific rights in the land and transfer those rights from the landowner to another entity (Wiebe et al., 1996). A conservation easement serves the same purpose, except that species and habitat protection is the explicit goal. An easement is generally negotiated between adjacent landowners where both landowners benefit from the agreement. Easements are typically *affirmative* and *appurtenant*. *Affirmative* means the easement holder is given the right to conduct specified activities, such as a right-of-way. *Appurtenant* means the benefits provided by the easement belong to and are typically realized only by the easement holder. Such easements have been used to transfer partial interests in land for thousands of years. A conservation easement severs some of the interests in the land and transfers those interests to another party. In contrast to a conventional easement, a conservation easement tends to be *negative* and *in gross*. Here *negative* means that rather than allowing the holder of the easement to engage in specified activities, the holder of the easement can restrict the landowner from engaging in specified activities; *in gross* means that the easement holder can be someone other than an adjacent landowner. A conservation easement prohibits the landowner from specified uses on his or her land.

In general, conservation easements are classified into two broad categories – *purchased development rights* (PDR) easement and *donated* easements. The type of sellers, the type of buyers, the mode of compensation, and the duration of the contract characterize the difference between the two easements. A PDR easement is typically entered into by profit-maximizing landowners who require full compensation for their forgone opportunity, the land's development value. The purchaser of a PDR easement is often a government agency, which generally has a larger coffer than most non-profit organizations, and is better able to finance the purchase of the easement. The payment for a PDR easement is typically a one-time lump sum payment, and PDR easements can be purchased for limited time periods or in perpetuity.

The donated easement is based on a tax incentive, which typically appeals to landowners who value the preservation of land and are willing to be compensated at less than fair market value for the easement. Federal tax law requires that land must be donated to a non-profit conservation organization and donated in perpetuity to qualify for tax incentives (Weibe et al., 1996: 12). Tax incentives can take the form of a deduction in income taxes, a reduction in the base value for estate or gift taxes, and, if the conservation easement meets certain requirements, an additional reduction in the estate tax base (Small, 2000).

4. ON-GOING POLICY DEBATES

Environmental policy in the US remains contentious. People disagree about how safe is 'safe enough', how regulated is 'too regulated', who should pay what and when, whether accounting for costs and benefits is better or worse than cost-effective targets. We consider the roles taken by federal and state governments.

4.1 Clean Air

The goal of the Clean Air Act (CAA) and subsequent amendments were to bring all US counties into compliance with the NAAQS – the minimum acceptable level of air quality. The key mechanism to control behavior is to designate a county in 'non-attainment' if any ambient concentrations of the six criteria pollutants exceeded the NAAQS limits. Being in non-attainment means that stricter regulatory oversight would apply to this county. One critical on-going policy debate is whether the CAA has truly been responsible for better air quality in the US. For example, consider the case of sulfur dioxide (SO_2) air pollution. During the three decades since the CCA was passed in 1970, SO_2 declined by a dramatic 80 per cent. The open question is whether the passage and enforcement of CAA caused this decline. No consensus has emerged given data limitations and the fact that there is no counterfactual baseline (that is, the road not taken) against which to compare reality. One has to tease out the effect of the CAA relative to other changes that occurred over these three decades (for example, energy prices, technological change).

While some researchers suggest the CAA was the prime reason for the change, there is little agreement. Greenstone (2004), for example, evaluated this question by compiling a comprehensive data base on trends of SO_2 in all counties. Estimating the relationship between SO_2 concentrations and CAA non-attainment regulations, he found the CAA had limited affect on reducing SO_2. He speculates that additional state and local regulations and economic conditions could have been a reason, but little data exist to either confirm or reject this alternative explanation. But one complication emerged that restricts the ability to understand this data – Greenstone found that many counties designated as in non-attainment actually were in compliance, with SO_2 levels below the NAAQS. Two reasons were offered to explain this result – the state failed to ask EPA to reconsider their status due to high costs of proving they were in compliance, or EPA failed to lighten up on the intensity of the regulations given the county was once in non-compliance, that is, the grim strategy in game theory in which one mistake leads to eternal punishment.

Another issue in air quality policy revolves around 'how safe is safe enough', given relative costs and benefits of tighter NAAQS. In 1997, the US Environmental Protection Agency's (EPA) issued rules to tighten the ozone and particulate matter (PM) ambient air quality standards triggered an intense debate in and outside the Administration about the quality of the research used to support these decisions. The debate ranged from the actual health effects to be ameliorated by these standards and the scientific support underlying these standards, to the real economic costs to implement and comply with these standards. In the end, President Clinton supported the tighter federal air pollution standards, stating that 'I think kids ought to be healthy'. The new standards for PM of 2.5 microns ($PM_{2.5}$) in diameter call for daily means not to exceed 65 micrograms per cubic metre of air, and for annual means not to exceed 15 micrograms per cubic metre. The new ozone standards call for concentrations in the air not to exceed 80 parts per billion over an 8-hour period, and areas that exceed the new standard more than four times per year averaged over a three-year period would have to take corrective action.

Among the many contentious issues raised in this debate, consider two points in more detail. First, under the Clean Air Act, the EPA Administrator sets air quality standards to protect public health with an 'adequate margin of safety'. These are *health-based* standards – in principle, the Administrator can and should ignore all economic considerations in setting the degree of stringency. As such, the standards are to be decided based on the current science that considers whether a statistically significant cause-and-effect relationship exists between the feared pollutant and health. But in this debate the underlying science is not at all clear. Even the EPA's science advisory board determined that no 'bright line' existed to separate one proposed standard from another as being more protective of public health, including the current standard. And therefore the choice of a standard is a policy judgment, not a scientific decision (Wolff, 1997).

Health effects associated with ozone are transitory, and a strong link between ozone exposure and long-term human health effects or mortality has not been confirmed by the scientific community. For example, based on the EPA's own risk analysis, the expected reduction in excess hospital admissions of asthmatics in the New York City area is about 30 per ozone season when moving to the proposed standard from the current standard, compared to total hospital admissions of asthmatics of about 15 000 per ozone season. The number of children playing outdoors in the nine urban areas that EPA studied who would experience an ozone-related cough would be reduced by about 5000 – about 0.2 per cent of outdoor children, and 30–40 per cent of children are outdoor children. The changes in health risk are small, uncertain, and overlap from moving to the proposed standard from the current standard so that no clear distinction emerges. The weakness in the scientific evidence with $PM_{2.5}$ is even more evident given the lack of a plausible biological mechanism, the limited number of studies considering $PM_{2.5}$ directly, and the weak correlation in the studies.

Biases associated with measurement and specification errors are prevalent in such health-based standards, especially when self-protection behaviors are left unaccounted for; ambient concentrations are usually taken to be synonymous with exposure, which is not the case when people change behavior to reduce risk. For example, consider the case of the Six Cities study, the most important data in the EPA's case for their $PM_{2.5}$ standard (Dockery et al., 1993). The study examined the relationship between air pollution and premature deaths in six American cities, finding that mortality was 26 per cent higher in Steubenville, Ohio than Portage, Wisconsin, the two cities with the most and least air pollution of the six considered. But the Six Cities findings are subject to criticism that the study did not correct for differences across cities. Key differences left unaccounted for include temperature, humidity and income – median family income in Steubenville is about $7000 less than in Portage. But the missing point is identical to the argument with the children's risk: economic variables affect behavior, which affect the risks faced by people, and exclusion of these variables from risk assessment biases predictions. Studies have shown that people persistently below the poverty line are far more likely to become sick than wealthy people for a variety of reasons including habits, lifestyle, less medical screening, and the ability to self-protect. Ignoring this causality biases the estimated objective risk to these children.

The second point is that although economics is not used to guide standard-setting, EO 12866 requires the agency to prepare an economic analysis of the implementation of the proposed and final rules. These analyses included modeling inventories of known emissions sources to identify the most efficient set of control measures to meet the standards in various geographic areas, the health benefits that would be achieved based on projected air quality improvements, and the costs of these measures. EPA estimated the costs and benefits of implementation with varying degrees of credulity. Consider the cost of the ozone standard. The proposed standards will be a significant burden to states. Under the proposed standard, nearly 200 additional counties with about 50 million people will be out of attainment. The emissions reductions required to meet the standard are substantial for big areas like Los Angeles (90 per cent) and New York (80 per cent), and for smaller areas like Hartford, CT (80 per cent), Portland, OR (25 per cent), and Huntington, WV (50 per cent). The EPA estimated the costs to reach partial attainment of the ozone standard to be about $2.6 billion per year, based on marginal abatement costs between $3000 to $10 000/ton(t) of ozone (see Fumento, 1997).

But the Clean Air Act does not mandate partial compliance; it calls for full compliance, albeit eventually. As such, the appropriate measure is the costs of full attainment, which according to the President's Council of Economic Advisers could be as high as $60 billion per year. The EPA responded by claiming that the $10 000/t is a cut-off on the marginal cost curve for ozone abatement, even if reduction is mandated. Their explanation is that nobody will pay more than $10 000/t to reduce ozone pollution either due to new innovations, tradable emission systems, or delayed compliance. The argument says that these cost figures are exaggerated anyway, and that business estimates of compliance costs are always inflated. Marginal abatement costs exceeding $10 000/t are irrelevant.

This cost cap made it into a Presidential directive, in which the President asks the EPA to encourage ideas like a Clean Air Investment Fund to cap control costs at $10 000/t. A factory or power plant that faces abatement costs greater than $10 000/t can reach compliance by paying into the fund (tons to compliance@$10 000/t), which will then use the money to buy reductions from other sources. If actual costs exceed $10 000/t, the Fund would be insufficient to cover full compliance, implying that full compliance can only be achieved if costs are lower than the cap. The cap creates an ambiguity about the real costs of this policy, since only the degree of compliance that can be afforded will be achieved. Obviously a cap does not remove these costs to the state level in which these targets will have to be achieved.

4.2 Climate Change

The debate over climate change revolves around whether the US federal government should sign onto the Kyoto protocol or continue to go it alone. This question keeps climate change policy as one of the most controversial issues in the US. Federal level involvement is critical, since climate change is a global public good – emissions from all sources accumulate in a common atmosphere regardless of their location. Individual state action to reduce emissions, while important for a leadership role, is a minor drop in the much larger global carbon pool.

A few key events trace out the broad outlines of US climate change policy debates from the mid-1980s to the mid-1990s. The Reagan and Bush 41 administrations were skeptical about the need for substantial reductions in carbon emissions. They advocated 'actions which will have broad-ranging benefits' such as eliminating CFCs and other stratospheric ozone-depleting substances (under the Montreal Protocol); implementing various pollution-control measures that would also promote energy efficiency (under the Clean Air Act); increasing forest sinks; encouraging energy efficiency in buildings, appliances and lighting; and increasing the use of renewable and non-fossil sources of energy. Under President Bush 41, the US negotiated and signed the 1992 United Nations Framework Convention on Climate Change. Article 2 of the convention says the objective is to stabilize GHG concentrations within a time frame that would prevent 'dangerous' human damage to the climate system. In concert with the Framework Convention, advanced industrialized countries pledged to reduce emissions to 1990 levels by 2000. This pledge was not a legally binding international agreement.

The Clinton administration was more enthusiastic about carbon control policies, at least in rhetoric. They initially embraced voluntary technology-based measures promulgated in the 1993 Climate Change Action Plan. This approach was based on a firm conviction that substantial progress toward reducing carbon emissions could be achieved without adverse economic consequences; to the contrary, the administration touted the economic benefits of cleaner and more climate-friendly technology. By 1996, it was clear that the US would fail to achieve the goal of reducing emissions to 1990 levels by 2000. Reasons cited for the failure included less program funding than anticipated from a Republican Congressional majority and, more important, over-optimistic goals and a misspecified baseline (for example, oil prices did not rise as projected).

In 1996, the administration announced its willingness to accept legally binding, long-term emissions reductions goals in the international negotiations without spelling out which goals or policies it would support. As negotiations proceeded toward the 1997 Kyoto Protocol, the US Senate passed, by a vote of 95 to 0, a non-binding resolution offered by Senators Robert Byrd and Chuck Hagel in the summer of 1997. The Byrd–Hagel resolution stated that the US should accept no climate agreement that did not demand comparable sacrifices of all participants. The resolution required the administration to provide an economic justification of any climate change policy regime – a demonstration that the prospective benefits were worth the costs.

The 1997 Kyoto Protocol of the Framework Convention was the next major milestone. The protocol states that the industrialized 'Annex B' countries agreed to legally binding reductions in net GHG emissions that would average about 5 per cent below 1990 levels by 2008–12. Given expected business-as-usual emissions growth in the United States between 1990 and 2010, the actual emissions reductions needed for compliance are substantial (for example, one-third of what otherwise would prevail in the US). No numerical targets for the emissions of developing countries were set in the protocol.

After Kyoto, the Clinton administration pursued a public campaign to increase awareness of climate change risks. A report prepared by the President's Council of Economic Advisers (CEA, 1998), estimated Kyoto would imply an annual GDP decrease of less than 0.5 per cent, about $10 billion dollars; no expected negative effect on the trade deficit; increases in gasoline prices of only about $0.05 a gallon; lower electricity rates; and no 'significant aggregate employment effect'. Critics, however, labeled the report as too optimistic and out of step with mainstream economic analyses. Other observers found more moderate costs; the Kyoto Protocol would neither be painless nor would it destroy national economies. President Clinton stated that the Kyoto Protocol would not be sent to the Senate for ratification until policy makers settled disputes about policies for flexibility in the means of compliance, costs of compliance, and 'meaningful participation' by developing countries. Acrimonious debate erupted sporadically between the administration and Congress, as well as among various non-governmental stakeholders about budgetary priorities related to climate change and the consequences of climate policies for the US economy.

In 2001, the G.W. Bush Administration officially announced its opposition to Kyoto. Their opposition rested on the perception that compliance costs would be excessive without developing country participation. They worried that these firms would have to follow rules ignored by competitors in developing nations, leaving them at a competitive disadvantage. They feared that the extra risk could scare these billion dollar investments to the Middle East or Venezuela, which would cost jobs in Canada. In 2002, the Administration announced its climate policy – a greenhouse gas emission intensity goal. Emission intensity focuses on reducing metric tons of greenhouse gases per million dollars of output (GHGmt/$mo). The Administration's stated target is to reduce the US economy to 151 from 180 GHGmt/$mo by 2012, about a 20 per cent improvement. The administration's plan promotes voluntary measures to meet a unilateral non-binding target of 100 million metric tons GHG abatement, or less if the economy grows faster than expected – a 2 per cent rate of improvement in GHG intensity over the next decade. While policies to make the Bush plan operational are similar to the Clinton Administration's (for example, tax credits, early emissions reduction credits, R&D funding), a sticking point remains developing country participation.

Why are federal level politicians so hesitant to ratify the Kyoto Protocol? 'Job protection' is the simple answer. Senators, be they Republicans or Democrats, have little incentive to ratify a treaty that results in perceived job losses in their states. So even though the Kyoto Protocol includes several flexibility mechanisms that allow nations some latitude as to how they will meet the targets and timetables, the costs to the domestic economy are still argued to be too great. The Bush Administration's reaction to the developing nations' reluctance for binding emission controls is captured in the statement by US Undersecretary of State Paula Dobriansky: 'the [Kyoto Protocol] is costly, ineffective, and unfair. It is also impractical and unrealistic. Climate change is a global phenomenon but the developing countries are not participating' (Associated Press, 2002). Instead of binding commitments based on uncertain net benefits, the G.W. Bush Administration has promoted voluntary abatement actions and carbon sequestration as a least-disruptive-to-the-economy approach to reducing overall carbon concentrations.

At the local level, some states have promoted bottom-up policies to reduce carbon emissions through renewable energy, energy conservation, carbon sequestration in agriculture and forestry, waste management, transportation systems to reduce fossil fuel use, and air pollution control. These are local efforts to address a global risk. These local efforts will be effective only if everyone cooperates toward this common objective. Solving such classic coordination problems, however, is not a trivial policy issue (Schelling, 1960). A sole state can do a lot towards reducing its own emissions, but this effort will ultimately have a significant impact on global climate change if and only if all other players participate (for example, other states, other nations). Nevertheless, state level climate policy will emerge if local decision makers see the policy as an opportunity for economic development (renewable energy sources, carbon sequestration) or policy entrepreneurship (more energy conservation, less traffic congestion, career advancement). See Rabe (2002) for nine detailed case studies on state climate policy, ranging from the promotion of renewable resource policy in Texas, better waste management in North Carolina, and tighter air pollution control in Massachusetts.

4.3 CERCLA (Superfund)

The debate here rests on whether US federal laws on how best to clean up and pay for the clean-up of historic toxic waste sites is too burdensome and unfair for private parties at the local level. The Comprehensive Environmental Response, Compensation, and Liability Act of 1980 (CERCLA), or Superfund, authorizes the federal government to respond to hazardous substance emergencies and to protect the public health and welfare and the environment. Unlike other environmental laws, CERCLA was to be run primarily by the federal government; states would have a limited role. Today, however, states play a key role in waste site clean-up, both in assuming lead responsibility for over 10 per cent of federal Superfund sites and in developing their own state-level policies. Pennsylvania, for example, finances 10 per cent of a remedial action; the federal government covers the rest. The state is responsible, however, for 100 per cent of the operation and maintenance costs after the remedial action is complete. Local officials help negotiate with responsible parties for clean-up actions; they also review remedial investigations and feasibility studies, remedial action design and construction, and cost recovery.

Regardless of whether under federal or state control, considerable criticism has been levied against CERCLA. Industry groups, lenders, environmental groups and legislators have expressed dissatisfaction with how the current law addresses a number of controversial issues (Probst et al., 1995). A point of contention has been the reliance on the 'polluter pays' principle in CERCLA, which assigns liability in cleaning up the nation's hazardous waste sites while partly funding clean-ups with a hazardous waste trust fund. The liability approach found in the current CERCLA program has caused delays in clean-up, and has generated excessive transaction costs (see Dixon, 1994). Criticism has also focused on the possibility that the Superfund program provides incentives to private parties to spend more money litigating than cleaning up hazardous waste sites (Acton and Dixon, 1992).

Why does the current law need reform? Due to the high costs and long time horizons involved in cleaning up hazardous waste sites, and with litigation plaguing the program, observers note that reform is needed in the Superfund program. The average time that lapsed between a site's placement on the National Priorities List (NPL) and completion of clean-up increased from 2.4 years in 1986 to 10.6 years in 1996. Listing times have also increased, as the average time between discovering a site and placing it on the NPL has increased significantly over the life of the Superfund program. In response to these concerns, EPA has adopted many administrative reforms in the Superfund program over the past few years. These reforms include setting priorities for clean-ups, clarifying the role of cost in the remedy selection process, encouraging brownfield redevelopment, and using more reasonable assumptions about current and future land use.

The 'polluter pays' principle in CERCLA allows EPA to force those parties responsible for contributing to the contamination of a hazardous waste site to accept financial responsibility and clean it up. While this notion has been effective in keeping the federal cost to the Superfund down by minimizing direct government implementation of clean-ups, the principle has generated excessive levels of litigation over the assignment of liability. Further, the liability scheme in CERCLA has shifted transaction costs of allocating clean-up shares to the multiple parties and away from the federal government. As a result, the private sector bears the burden of the increasingly substantial transaction costs. Movement away from the status quo of the current system will impose additional up-front costs on EPA, which provides little incentive for the agency to eliminate the principle from the current Superfund law.

The legal history of the current liability system provides insight into why critics of the current law continue to push for an overhaul of how liability is resolved. The courts have held that, under CERCLA, liability is retroactive, strict, and joint and several. Retroactive liability applies since the law addresses contamination that was caused by activities taking place before CERCLA was enacted in 1980. Liability is strict because a responsible party can be found liable even if it was not negligent. When the damage at a hazardous waste site is not divisible, liability is joint and several. Under joint and several liability, the government can hold one or more parties liable for the full costs of the site clean-up, even if other parties at the site are liable. Joint and several liability has created the climate conducive to costly levels of litigation among private parties trying to determine allocation of contribution shares. EPA can determine that a few parties are responsible for contamination of a particular site, and can then force them to pay for the entire cost of clean-up. These parties seek compensation from other responsible parties through contribution litigation. This can cause a firm, forced to pay for clean-up costs given joint and several liability, to pursue contribution from firms that may have played only a minimal role in the contamination of a particular site. Many times, a responsible party lists a large number of businesses in the local phonebook as additional potentially responsible parties (PRPs). These 'phonebook nominations' can cause excessive litigation as the private parties use the courts to settle the liability issue.

Experts agree that the average level of transaction costs per Superfund site is too great. A RAND study examines PRP transaction costs for 108 private-sector firms with annual revenues less than $20 billion. At 18 Superfund sites from 1981 to 1991, RAND estimated that transaction costs made up 32 per cent of total clean-up costs, averaging $32 million per site (see Dixon, 1994). For over 50 per cent of those firms with total expenditures greater that $1000, transaction costs accounted for more than 60 per cent of clean-up costs. A RAND study estimated that for five large industrial firms with average annual revenues of $70 billion between 1984 and 1989, transaction costs averaged 21 per cent of total clean-up costs. In addition, the study examined the total expenditures on hazardous-waste claims of four large insurers from 1986 to 1989, and found that an average of 88 per cent of expenditures were transactional in nature. Finally, a 1994 RAND report uses the results from their previous two studies to estimate transaction costs to be 36 per cent of total private-sector clean-up expenditures through 1991. Using EPA's cost estimate of $26 million per site, and a private-sector transaction cost share of 36 per cent, private party transaction costs total over $9 million at each Superfund site. The total transaction costs generated by the Superfund program would presumably reach even higher with the addition of local, state and federal government transaction costs.

While some federal remedies exist to help reduce these transaction costs, state and local authorities have long demanded more control over CERCLA since the impacts of hazardous waste sites are borne at the state and local levels. The National Governors Association (NGA), for example, has asked that CERCLA be run more like the other environmental laws – EPA should establish program requirements, provide technical assistance and ensuring funding, and then should 'authorize or delegate full or partial management of the remedial and emergency removal programs to all capable states interested in administering cleanups'. The NGA would also like EPA to step back and review overall state performance rather than site-by-hazardous-waste-site. For those interested states, the Governors would like more responsibility for establishing priorities, undertaking remedial investigations/feasibility studies, selecting remedies, selecting contractors, and conducting remedial clean-ups.

4.4 Endangered Species Act

The on-going debate over the Endangered Species Act (ESA) rests on the distribution of benefits and costs from species protection, and whether compensation should be paid for protecting species. The benefits of species protection accrue nationally; the costs are borne by local landowners. About 90 per cent of the nearly 1100 species of plants and animals listed as endangered or threatened under the Act are found on private land. The question then is who is taking what from whom – are local private landowners 'taking' away the national benefits of protecting endangered species by their land use decisions, or is the federal government 'taking' away the local benefits derived from how landowners choose to use their private property. Here 'taking' has two meanings: to 'take' a listed species means to 'harass, harm, . . . wound,' and harm encompasses habitat modification; to 'take' private property rises to the level of a Fifth Amendment 'taking' – private property shall not be taken for a public use, without just compensation.

The intention of the ESA is to save all species; there was no explicit recognition of relative costs and benefits in the original Act. A species with high economic cost of recovery and low economic benefits has the same standing as a species with palpably large economic benefits and small costs. Congress explicitly noted that economic criteria were to be excluded in both the listing and the designation of proposed critical habitat. The Supreme

Court agreed with this view in the 1978 case, *Tennessee Valley Authority v Hill* (437 U.S. 187, 184 (1978)): 'the value of endangered species is incalculable,' and 'it is clear from the Act's legislative history that Congress intended to halt and reverse the trend toward species extinction – whatever the cost'.

Like CERCLA, the ESA was initially meant as a federal policy with limited delegation to the States. The federal funds available to preserve species, however, have been inadequate for the task. Of the over 1200 species listed as threatened or endangered, over 40 per cent have approved recovery plans. Since approval is a separate matter from adequate appropriations for the recovery plan, the status of some of these species has deteriorated and the survival prospects for slightly under 60 per cent are deteriorating. Moreover, the fact is that recovery plans are not developed for years, if at all. Biological analysis of recovery plans and goals suggest that more than half of listed vertebrates would remain in serious risk of extinction even after meeting population targets in their recovery plans (Carroll et al., 1996).

Matters are worse than this. There are nearly 200 species for which sufficient data exist on vulnerability to warrant endangered or threatened status, but the budgets for listing are inadequate to consummate the task. The current budgetary limits allow listing species at a rate of about 100 per year. Moreover, a list of 3600 'indefinite' species designated as possibly threatened or endangered was eliminated two years ago, because the list caused 'confusion about the conservation status of these taxa [species]' (61 Federal Register 7596–7597, 1996). The list of 3600 created a cloud of uncertainty about the economic viability of the habitats affecting the species in limbo. The list was excised because landowners complained to their congressional representatives about the economic costs of this uncertainty.

Funding for the endangered species program of the Fish and Wildlife Service has failed to keep pace with the number of listed species, with the result that the real budget per species is 60 per cent of its 1976 level. Federal and state expenditures increased to about $270 million in 1996 from $44 million in 1989, relative to total government expenditures of over $1.4 trillion (Dawson and Shogren, 2001). Limited budgets and political realities also create conflicts within ESA recovery plans, in which over 50 per cent of expenditures go to ten vertebrates. These species and their 1993–1996 expenditures are: northern spotted owl ($55.8 million); red cockaded woodpecker ($38.7m); bald eagle ($25.2m); desert tortoise ($22.8m); Colorado squawfish ($22.5m); marbled murrelet ($16.9m); gray wolf ($13.8m); American peregrine falcon ($13m); whooping crane ($10.7m); and razorback sucker ($10.6m).

In addition, since owning land which is hospitable to an endangered species can dramatically circumscribe any development plans for that land, local landowners have an incentive to destroy the habitat before listing occurs – the 'shoot, shovel, and shut-up' strategy. The print media routinely report cases of habitat destruction triggered by an anticipation of listing. For example, just ten days before listing of the golden-cheeked warbler by Fish and Wildlife Service, a firm owned by Ross Perot hired migrant workers with chain saws to destroy hundreds of acres of oak and juniper warbler habitat (Mann and Plummer, 1995). Wilcove et al. (1996) cite this incentive as 'one reason why so many species are teetering on the very brink of extinction by the time they receive protection'.

Under the 1978 amendments to the Act, the Secretary of the Interior (Sec. 4) may 'take into consideration the economic impact, and any other relevant impact, of specifying any particular area as critical habitat' for a threatened or endangered species, and can exclude an area from critical habitat designation if the benefits of exclusion outweigh the benefits to specifying the critical habit, 'unless failure to designate leads to extinction'. Under the same set of amendments (Sec. 7), it is possible for a federal agency, the governor of a state, or a permit or license applicant to apply to the Secretary of the Interior for an exemption from the Act. The Secretary then submits a report to a committee, sometimes called the 'God Squad', that discusses, among other things, the availability of reasonable and prudent alternatives to the agency's proposed action, and 'the nature and extent of the benefits' of the action and proposed alternatives. Not surprisingly, the designation of land as 'critical habitat' is controversial and arduous, because private parties seek not to have their lands designated in this way (NRC, 1995). But since nearly 80 per cent of all species have no critical habitat designation, this pathway to account for economic considerations is inactive in many cases.

The power of the Act rests with its provisions to constrain the activities of private parties and public agencies. Parties caught violating the proscriptions of the Act are punished by more than a slap on the wrist. Of those prosecuted on criminal charges for illegal takings, a quarter went to jail for between 10 and 1170 days, a quarter paid fines from \$1000 to \$50 000, and many others were put on probation (US GAO, 1995). Private parties can avoid these perils by requesting an 'incidental take' provision. A person can qualify for an incidental take by submitting and receiving approval of a habitat conservation plan, which specifies how the habitat will be developed in a way that must minimize the 'impact of a taking' and 'not appreciably' impinge on the probability of survival or recovery. Private parties can be affected by how stringently the 'harass' and 'harm' wording is interpreted. In the past, critics of the Act have cited some examples of federal government dedication to the letter of the law that may seem to go beyond common sense (Mann and Plummer, 1995).

Again to bring a federal law closer to the local people affected directly by the ESA, state Governors have argued for more official state authority over its implementation. They contend that the ESA can only be implemented effectively through a full federal–state partnership that recognizes 'the broad trustee and police powers that states possess over fish and wildlife within their borders'. State officials are looking for the ESA to be run like other environmental programs – federal government sets general species standards, and then delegates the implementation of recovery plans to those states interested in more local control.

4.5 Children's Health

Children deserve special attention, no argument there. The debate is how best to incorporate threats to their health in general environmental policy. Evidence suggests that children face disproportionate health risks from environmental hazards (see Wargo, 1996). These unbalanced risks stem from several fundamental differences in the physiologies and activities of children and adults. As children develop, their digestive, nerve, and immune systems are more susceptible to toxic pollutants and other environmental hazards. Children eat, drink and breathe more for their weight, and spend more time outside in exposure to greater amounts of contamination and pollution for their weight than adults. They also face potential exposures over their entire lifetime and they are less able to recognize and to protect themselves. All this supports the idea that children require special attention when designing environmental policy.

In 1997, President Clinton issued Executive Order 13045 'Protection of Children from Environmental Health Risks and Safety Risks' (Federal Register, 1997). The EO directs the federal government to safeguard children from environmental threats through three areas: policy, research coordination and federal regulatory analysis. First, although many agencies thought this was already part of their mission (for example, Federal Drug Administration, Health and Human Services), Section 1 requires all agencies to make the protection of children a high priority in implementing their statutory responsibilities and fulfilling their overall missions. Second, Section 3 creates an interagency task force to define a coordinated research agenda to identify research and other initiatives that the Administration could take to protect children, and to enlist public input for these efforts. Third, Section 5 requires, for the first time, that agencies examine and explain the effects of their rules on children. Agencies promulgating major regulations that may have a disproportionate impact on children now must

(a) evaluate the environmental health or safety effects of the planned regulation on children, and (b) explain why the planned regulation is preferable to other potentially effective and reasonably feasible alternatives considered by the agency. The idea is to link policy decisions to the health science on children, to ensure accountability to the public, and to force agencies to refocus their research agendas. Section 5 is the key to the order and, potentially, the most controversial – it has been called the 'kick me' provision and requires an explanation when actions beneficial to children are passed over. Supporters argue that without Section 5 the order will be merely hortatory and symbolic.

This Executive Order (EO) raises several issues worth more attention. First, by maintaining that environmental risk is exogenous, and beyond the control of children or adults, the EO maintains the false separation of the mechanistic risk assessment and behavioral choice. But risks to children are not derived from autonomous sources, they are functions of both natural science parameters and their parents' self-protection decisions (Crocker and Shogren, 1997). Given the relative marginal effectiveness of different self-protection actions, how people confront risk differs across individuals and situations, even though the natural phenomena that trigger these actions apply equally to everyone. Thus the EO does not address the evidence that suggests the most significant threats to children's health are the behavioral choices frequently associated with poverty, for example, high discount rates. Researchers need more information to determine the bias in assessing risks to children solely in terms of natural science information given that the sources of systematic variation are relative prices, incomes and other economic and social parameters. Omitting private behavioral responses to risk will result in overestimating the risk to children, and underestimating the value of reduced risk.

Second, the EO was designed for a few federal agencies who wanted a potential counterweight to the cost–benefit EO 12866 – the regulatory review order that already requires similar analysis on costs, small business impact, and other issues, and future regulatory reform aimed at a broader accounting of risk–benefit trade-offs in federal regulations. The EO provides a potential wedge to divide-and-conquer regulatory decisions if children's health is played as the trump card in the regulatory debate. Suppose a cost–benefit analysis reveals that a new regulation is a net loser overall but a net gain to children; the decision not to implement is no longer clear. The research need is to reduce the knowledge gap on how society evaluates risks to children, and how explicit distributional weights for children in cost–benefit analysis affect welfare measurement.

Finally, the children's EO could pressure agencies to ratchet up their regulatory standards at the local level, with a corresponding and potentially unjustified increase in the costs and burdens of regulation. Industry continues to criticize this pressure to raise standards across the board. The additional burden of Section 5 may further delay the regulatory process, and add resource demands to agencies already confronted with budgetary constraints. If agencies do not strengthen the relevant regulatory standards, the EO provides a ready basis to mount judicial challenges on decisions. Every supplement to a rule or regulation provides a new avenue to attack and compromise the core focus of the rule. Whether disclosure produces net economic benefits remains an empirical question.

5. CONCLUDING COMMENTS

This chapter provided a brief overview of the political economy of environmental policy in the United States over the last three decades. We conclude with several general observations. Judging the overall success of environmental protection is a challenge – although overall environment quality has improved over the three decades, the open question is whether we paid too much for this achievement. Judging the success of federal policies is challenging due to the lack of data and the lack of a counterfactual baseline and confounding factors of state and local regulations. The federal regulatory framework is large and expanding. Environmental federalism is alive and well, and the debate over a better mix of federal and state power-sharing for environmental protection continues. Cost-effective market-based controls have become more common, but are still relatively rare. Many environmental policy innovations come from the bottom-up regulatory approaches of the state. Officials of state governments constantly demand greater authority in environmental policy making, especially for those federal regulations initially designed to be implemented at the federal level. The demand arises in part because of the relatively blunt performance of these acts (for example, endangered species, Superfund).

BIBLIOGRAPHY

Acton, Jan Paul and Lloyd S. Dixon (1992), 'Superfund and transaction costs: The experiences of insurers and very large industrial firms', Santa Monica, CA: RAND.

Anderson, Terry and Donald Leal (2001), *Free Market Environmentalism*, New York: Palgrave Macmillan.

Andrews, R.N.L. (1999), *Managing the Environment, Managing Ourselves: A History of American Environmental Policy*, New Haven: Yale University Press.

Associated Press (2002), 'Nations approve climate change draft', 1 November.

Billings, L.G. (1990), 'Grading the Clean Air Act: Bush–Senate compromise weakens law', *The San Diego Union-Tribune*, 11 March, p. C-1.
Boyd, James, Kathryn Caballero and R. David Simpson (1999), 'The law and economics of habitat conservation: Lessons from an analysis of easement acquisitions', discussion paper 99-32, Resources for The Future, April.
Brown, Gardner M., Jr. and Jason F. Shogren (1998), 'Economics of the Endangered Species Act', *Journal of Economic Perspectives*, **12** (3), 3–20.
California Coastal Conservancy (CCC) (2000), 'About the Coastal Conservancy', and 'Coastal Conservancy Programs', http://www.coastalconservancy.ca.gov (cited August 2000).
California Resources Agency (CRA), Department of Fish and Game, Inland Fisheries Division (2000), 'Timber Tax Fish (related) Incentives for Sustainable Habitat', www.dfg.ca.gov/timber/ttcp_2.html, (cited 7 September, 2000).
Carroll, R., C. Augspurger, A. Dobson, J. Franklin, G. Orians, W. Reid, R. Tracy, D. Wilcove and J. Wilson (1996), 'Strengthening the use of science in achieving the goals of the endangered species act: an assessment by the Ecological Society of America', *Ecological Applications*, **6** (1), 1–11.
Clinton Administration (1998), 'The Kyoto Protocol and the President's policies to address climate change: administration economic analysis', Washington, DC: The White House.
Council of Economic Advisers (CEA) (1998), '1998 Annual Report of the US Council of Economic Advisers', Economic Report of the President transmitted to the Congress February 1998, Washington, DC: US Government Printing Office.
Crocker, Thomas D. and Jason F. Shogren (1997), 'Endogenous risk and environmental program evaluation', in G. Knaap and T.J. Kim (eds), *Environmental Program Evaluation. A Primer*, Urbana, IL: University of Illinois Press, pp. 255–69.
Dawson, Deborah and Jason F. Shogren (2001), 'An update on priorities and expenditures under the Endangered Species Act', *Land Economics*, **77** (4), November, 527–32
Dickinson, D. (1997), 'Is "diligent prosecution of an action in a court" required to preempt citizen suits under the major federal environmental statutes?', *William and Mary Law Review*, **38** (4), 1545–82.
Dinan, Terry M., Maureen L. Cropper and Paul R. Portney (1999), 'Environmental federalism: Welfare losses from uniform national drinking water standards', in Arvind Panagariya et al. (eds), *Environmental and Public Economics: Essays in Honor of Wallace E. Oates*, Cheltenham, UK and Northampton, MA, USA: Edward Elgar, pp. 13–31.
Dixon, Lloyd S. (1994), Fixing Superfund: The effect of the proposed Superfund Reform Act of 1994 on transaction costs', Santa Monica, CA: RAND.
Dockery, Douglas et al. (1993), 'An association between air pollution and mortality in six US Cities', *New England Journal of Medicine*, **329**, 1753–9.
Echeverria, J. and J. Zeidler (1999), 'Barely standing: the erosion of citizen "standing" to sue and enforce environmental law', Georgetown Environmental Policy Project, http://www.envpoly.org/papers/barely.htm.
Environmental Defense (EDF) (1999), 'Mitigation banking as an endangered species conservation tool', http://www.edf.org/, November.
Epstein, Richard (2002), *Principles for a Free Society: Reconciling Individual Liberty With the Common Good*, Reading, Mass: Perseus Books.

Federal Register (1997), 23 April (Volume 62, Number 78, 19883).
Freeman, A. Myrick III (2000), 'Water pollution policy', in Paul R. Portney and Robert N. Stavins (eds), *Public Policies for Environmental Protection*, 2nd edition, Washington, DC: Resources for the Future Press.
Fumento, Michael (1997), *Polluted Science. The EPA's Campaign to Expand Clean Air Regulations*, Washington, DC: American Enterprise Institute Press.
Gaines, S. and R. Westin (1991), 'Taxation for environmental protection: a multinational legal study', Greenwood, Connecticut.
Glaberson, W. (1999), ' "Citizen suits" losing power as weapon against polluters', *The Plain Dealer*, Section National, 6 June, p. 18.
Greenstone, Michael (2004), 'Did the Clean Air Act cause the remarkable decline in sulfur dioxide concentrations?', *Journal of Environmental Economics and Management*, **47** (3), 585–611.
Hahn, Robert (1989), 'Economic prescriptions for environmental problems: How the patient followed the doctors orders', *Journal of Economic Perspectives*, **3**, 94–114.
Hamburger, T. (1992), 'Court limits citizen suits challenging policies on environment', *Star Tribune*, 13 June, p. 1A.
Hanley, Nick, Jason F. Shogren and Ben White (1997), *Environmental Economics: In Theory and Practice*, New York: Oxford University Press.
Harberger, Arnold (1978), 'On the use of distributional weights in social cost–benefit analysis', *Journal of Political Economy*, **86**, S87–S120.
Johnston, C.N. (1999), '1998: The year in review', *Environmental Law*, **29** (1), 69.
Jones, Laura, Laura Griggs and Liv Fredericksen (2000), 'Environmental indicators' (4th edn), Critical Issues Bulletin, April, Vancouver: Fraser Institute, http://oldfraser.lexi.net/publications/criticalissues/2000/enviridic/.
Kemmis, Daniel (2001), *This Sovereign Land: A New Vision for Governing the West*, Washington, DC: Island Press.
Land Trust Alliance (LTA) (1998), 'Summary of data from the 1998 National Land Trust Census', lta.org/consopt.html.
Leonard, A.R. (1995), 'When should an Administrative Enforcement Action preclude a Citizen Suit under the Clean Water Act?, *Natural Resources Journal*, **35**, 555–624.
Lester, J.P. (1995), 'Federalism and state environmental policy', in J.P. Lester (ed.), *Environmental Politics and Policy, Theories and Evidence*, 2nd edition, Duke University Press.
Mann, C. and M. Plummer (1995), *Noah's Choice*, New York: Alfred Knopf.
Miller, Andrew J. (1999), 'Transferable development rights in the constitutional landscape: Has Penn Central failed to weather the storm', *Natural Resources Journal*, **39**, Summer, 459–516.
Miller, J.G. (1987), *Citizen Suits: Private Enforcement of Federal Pollution Control Laws*, New York: Wiley Law Publications.
Millimet, D. (2003), 'Assessing the empirical impact of environmental federalism', *Journal of Regional Science*, **43**, 711–33.
National Research Council (1995), *Science and the Endangered Species Act*, Washington, DC: National Academy Press.
Neimark, P. and P. Mott (1999), *The Environmental Debate: A Documentary History*, Westport, CT: Greenwood Press.
Nijhuis, Michelle (2000), 'A land-trust toolbox', *High Country News*, **32** (4), 28 February.

Oates, Wallace E. (2001), 'A reconsideration of environmental federalism', Resources for the Future discussion paper 01-54, Washington, DC.
Parkhurst, Gregory M. and Jason F. Shogren (2004), 'An evaluation of incentive mechanisms for conserving habitat', *Natural Resources Journal*, **43**, 1093–149.
Percival, R., A. Miller, C. Schroeder and J. Peape (1992), *Environmental Regulation: Law, Science, and Policy*, Boston, MA: Little, Brown and Co.
Portney, Paul R. (2000), 'Air pollution policy', in Paul R. Portney and Robert N. Stavins (eds), *Public Policies for Environmental Protection*, 2nd edition, Washington, DC: Resources for the Future Press.
Probst, Katherine N., Don Fullerton, Robert E. Litan and Paul R. Portney (1995), 'Footing the bill for Superfund cleanups: Who pays and how?', Washington, DC: The Brookings Institution and Resources for the Future.
Rabe, Barry G. (2002), 'Greenhouse & Statehouse: The Evolving State Government Role in Climate Change', prepared for the Pew Center on Global Climate Change.
Revesz, R. (2001), *Environmental Law and Policy Statutory and Regulatory Supplement*, New York: Foundation Press.
Revesz, Richard L. and Robert N. Stavins (2004), 'Environmental law and policy', NYU Public Law Research Paper 82, 13 September.
Reynolds, J. (1996), 'Court ruling could affect environmental laws', *American City and County*, **1** (8), 65.
Rosenthal, E. (2000), 'China pollution victims starting to fight back', *New York Times*, 16 May.
Sabel, Charles, Archon Fung and Bradley Karkkainen (2001), *Beyond Backyard Environmentalism*, Boston: Beacon Press.
Savage, D.G. (1997), 'Supreme Court lets Species Act foes file suit', *Los Angeles Times*, Home Edition, 20 March, p. 1.
Sax, J.L. (1970), *Defending the Environment: A Strategy for Citizen Action*, New York: Alfred Knopf.
Schelling, T. (1960), *The Strategy of Conflict*, Cambridge, MA: Harvard University Press.
Sigman, Hilary (2000), 'Hazardous waste and toxic substance policies', in Paul R. Portney and Robert N. Stavins (eds), *Public Policies for Environmental Protection*, 2nd edition, Washington, DC: Resources for the Future Press, pp. 215–60.
Small, Stephen J. (1998), *Preserving Family Lands: Book 1, Essential Tax Strategies for the Landowner*, Boston: Landowner Planning Center.
Small, Stephen J. (2000), 'An obscure tax code provision takes private land protection into the twenty-first century', in Julie Ann Gustanski and Roderick H. Squires (eds), *Protecting the Land: Conservation Easements Past, Present, and Future*, Washington, DC: Island Press, pp. 55–66.
Stark, M. (2004), 'Following a busy year, Wyoming tries to cope with coal bed growing pains', *Billings Gazette*, 4 January.
Stavins, R.N. (2000), 'Market-based environmental policies', in P.R. Portney and R.N. Stavins (eds), *Public Policies for Environmental Protection*, 2nd edition, Washington, DC: Resources for the Future, pp. 31–76.
Taylor Jr., S. (1987), 'Supreme Court roundup: citizens suits in pollution cases are limited', *New York Times*, 2 December, p. 24.
Tear, T., J. Scott, P. Hayward and B. Griffith (1993), 'Status and prospects for success of the endangered species act: a look at recovery plans', *Science*, **262**, 976–7.

Terry, S. (1980), 'Citizen suits against polluters increase – but can guilty pay?', *The Christian Science Monitor*, Midwestern Edition, 26 December, p. 11.

Tripp, James T.B. and Daniel J. Dudek (1989), 'Institutional guidelines for developing transferable rights programs', *Yale Journal on Regulation*, **6**, 369–91.

US Environmental Protection Agency (2000), 'Regulatory impact analysis: heavy-duty engine and vehicle standards and highway diesel fuel sulfur control requirements', EPA420-R-00-026, Washington, DC.

US General Accounting Office (GAO) (1995), *Endangered Species Act: Information on Species Protection on Nonfederal Lands*, GAO/RCED-95-16, Washington, DC.

US Geological Survey (2003), 'Coal-bed gas resources of the Rocky Mountain region', USGS Fact Sheet, FS-158-02, Washington, DC, February.

Utah Critical Land Conservation Committee (UCLCC) (1997), 'Land conservation in Utah: Tools, techniques, and initiatives', http://www.governor.state.ut.us/, January.

Wargo, John (1996), *Our Children's Toxic Legacy. How Science and Law Fail to Protect Us from Pesticides*, New Haven: Yale University Press.

Wiebe, Keith, Abebayehu Tegene and Betsey Kuhn (1996), 'Partial interests in land: Policy tools for resource use and conservation', Economic Research Service/USDA, AER-744, November.

Wilcove, D., M. Bean, R. Binnie and M. McMillan (1996), *Rebuilding the Ark*, New York: Environmental Defense Fund.

Wolff, George T. (1997), 'The scientific basis for a new ozone standard', *Environmental Manager* **2** (9), 27–32.

Wondolleck, Julia and Steven Yaffee (2000), *Making Collaboration Work: Lessons from Innovation in Natural Resource Management*, Washington, DC: Island Press.

Wyoming Department of Environmental Quality (2003), 'National pollutant discharge elimination system application for permit to surface discharge produced water from coal bed methane new discharges, renewals, or major modifications', Cheyenne, Wyoming.

Young, L.R. (1987), 'Environmentalists lose clean water suit', *Journal of Commerce*, 2 December, p. 9.

PART II

Non-federal countries

11. Chile: The development–sustainability dilemma

Tommaso Chiamparino, Laura Piazza and Irene Venturello

This chapter is made up of two parts: the first one, entitled 'Environmental legislation and policymaking in Chile', describes the situation of the environment in Chile and the set of norms and bodies with environmental functions; the second one, 'Chilean environmental governance: a critical review' is dedicated to the peculiar issues that, in some way, are unique to the country.

The analysis of Part I begins with a historical review of the decentralization process and offers a parallel description of the evolution of environmental legislation and concern. The study then focuses on the institutional set-up created by the Environmental Framework Law and on the legislation deriving from international agreements. In the last sections of Part I, we introduce Chile's environmental situation, paying particular attention to the tools available to manage it.

Part II is constructed around some key issues that we considered emblematic of Chilean environmental policymaking. First, the anomalous nature of the environmental institutions, the incomplete process of decentralization and its weak participatory support. In addition, we analyse the forms of horizontal cooperation and the limits of the monitoring processes. Finally we underline an aspect of specific relevance for environmental protection in developing countries: the impact on domestic legislation of the environmental rules imposed by international trade agreements.

PART I: ENVIRONMENTAL LEGISLATION AND POLICYMAKING IN CHILE

1. The Decentralization Process

1.1 The authoritarian deconcentration

During the military rule the institutional reforms imposed by General Pinochet's government designed an authoritarian administrative deconcentration (one strictly controlled by the centre). This process culminated in several law decrees put forward by the National Commission of Administrative Rationalization (CONARA), which created new regional and municipal institutions. The model, promoted by the military legislators, took inspiration from the Italian one (its main promoter, General Canessa, was of Italian origin) and it provided for a division of the country into Regions, Provinces and Municipalities, all chaired by persons chosen by the central government.

The rationale for these territorial re-organizations was both geo-political and geo-strategic because the main goal was to control both the national frontiers and internal conflicts. The consequences were not, however, those expected by the military regime. From their inception, a stronger regional consciousness surfaced and some political personalities emerged who were tied up with the Army but who also expressed regionalist aspirations (Ahumada, 1998).

The Constitution of 1980 finally established an ultra-centralized presidential regime and provided juridical support to this authoritarian deconcentration, which was completed by the Municipal Laws ordained by the government in 1988.

1.2 The democratic government reforms

In 1989, during his election campaign, the democratic candidate Patricio Aylwin promised to adopt a strategy of real decentralization instead of what had so far been only an authoritarian devolution. He thought he could reach his goal through a structural reform of local administrations via their democratization and an improvement of their financing system. Nevertheless, this process took rather a long time and went through a number of heated negotiations with the political opposition; the final result was a kind of compromise.

In 1992 the Constitutional Law on Municipalities (*Ley Orgánica Constitucional de Municipalidades*) was promulgated, which provided for democratic elections of mayors and members of the councils and listed in detail the functions of the municipalities. In addition, it established a new body called CESCO (*Consejo Economico y Social Comunal*, a municipal Economic and Social Council) for the participation in municipal activity of social and economic organizations.[1]

The Constitutional Law for the Reform of the Regional Administration approved in 1993 appeared generic and less innovative than the above-mentioned municipal law. The 1993 law sets up a system of regional governments headed by an appointee of the national government (called *Intendente*), with a Regional Council whose members are elected by the Municipal councils.[2]

The responsibilities of the regional institutions match those of the deconcentrated divisions of the central ministers (SEREMIs). The law also institutes a territorial division of the region and recognizes a provincial level of government. Both the regional and the provincial governments are conceived as administrative branches of the central government, strictly dependent on the Presidency of the Republic; their principal duties are to promote investments and to manage funds aimed at increasing the development of the regions, with particular attention to projects dealing with the environment (see Figure 11.1).

As far as the financing system is concerned, the Municipal and the Regional Laws provide both autonomous and state incomes. The Regions only have at their direct disposal the proceeds from taxes (*patentes*) based on the ground space (square metres) occupied by the firms and not on their business volume. The Municipalities' own fiscal incomes derive from driving licences and territorial taxes on commercial activities,[3] but they are still quite small.

The distribution of regional and municipal financial resources, then, is mostly determined by the national government, which divides them

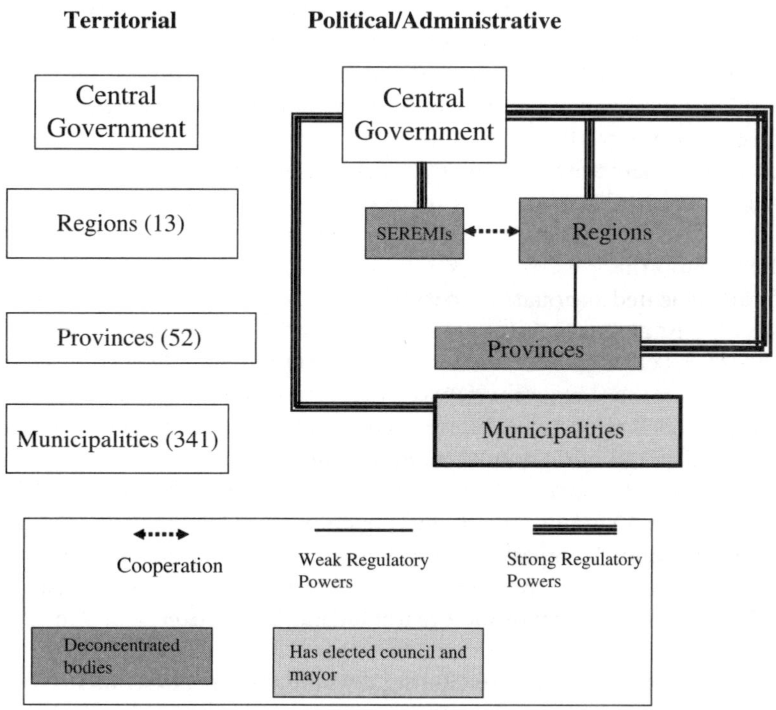

Figure 11.1 Chile's administrative and territorial organization

with compensative criteria between the National Funds for Regional Development (*Fondo Nacional de Desarrollo Regional*) and the Municipal Common Funds (*Fondo Común Municipal*). These funds are allocated to infrastructures and development projects formulated by the regional and municipal authorities; decisions are taken on the basis of socio-economic indicators together with principles of management efficiency and in consideration of potential emergencies.

1.3 Potentials and shortcomings of Chilean decentralization

During the years following the regional reform, the decisional autonomy of the Regions frequently clashed with the interventionist inclination of the central government; this was mostly due to the latter's wide mistrust of local authorities.

Paradoxically the Municipalities, in spite of their inferior political dimensions, benefited from a clearer legislation defining their exclusive jurisdiction, and could act with greater political independence.

In spite of an important evolution, the process of decentralization has not up to now given satisfactory results, for a number of political, cultural and economic reasons. First of all, historically there has not been any clear, generally accepted mechanism for the allocation of responsibilities; consequently, the weakening of trust in local governments on the part of the central one caused a great reduction of the political space at their disposal (Valenzuela Barros, 1996: 14).

Secondly, there are no strong regional identities that could push towards a larger decentralization. Thus the centralism of the political authorities never had to face regional political movements or regionalist requests from public opinion.

From an economic point of view, the insufficient growth of the National Funds for Regional Development, in comparison with other expenditure decisions, received much criticism (Valenzuela Barros, 1996: 21–22).

At the same time inequality between the regions became wider: the Santiago Metropolitan Region (*Región Metropolitana*) acquired enormous political weight and a kind of decisional monopoly in regional expenditure, and now produces almost 50 per cent of Chile's Gross Domestic Product (GDP); by contrast, other Regions, though making an outstanding contribution to the domestic product, have had and continue to have limited bargaining power.

2. Historical Evolution of the Environmental Legislation

2.1 Environmental legislation during the military rule (1973–89)

Chile's economic model during the military rule emphasized exports based on extractive activity in agriculture, fishing, lumber as well as in minerals (principally copper). At the same time it privatized the financial sector, shrank manufacturing, and encouraged international trade. In order to spur restructuring of the economy, the military regime had imposed drastic cutbacks in state-owned enterprises and reduced government regulation of the economy. Chile's economy, after a rocky start, has done quite well. From the mid-1980s onwards, Chile has sustained a positive rate of growth in its gross domestic product, kept its fiscal accounts in order and enjoyed low inflation and a sound financial system. Its external accounts have been kept in order thanks to vigorous exports.

Yet this sustained economic growth came at a significant cost to the environment, among its other negative effects. The impact of rapid, unregulated development, based on intensive agriculture and extraction of natural resources, contributed to the destruction of natural forests, pollution of water resources as well as desertification. Mining of non-renewable natural resources polluted both the air and the water of nearby towns and coastal areas. Air pollution dramatically affects Chile's capital city, Santiago, and other major urban centres.

In this context a higher environmental sensibility started to develop among Chile's population, witnessed by the creation of the first environmental NGO (see section 3.5.2). In spite of these new movements, the military government basically either ignored the environmental impact of its development model or, when pressure mounted, gave it very low priority. The main goal of the government was to promote economic growth as rapidly as possible, at any cost and with minimum intervention by the government. As a result, the country's environmental problems worsened significantly between 1973 and 1984, but no efforts were made to develop laws or institutions to deal with them, while the ministries, themselves weakened in their powers, could not count on the help of any coordinating mechanism. Nevertheless, a combination of the growing world attention to environmental issues and the expansion of Chile's environmental movements induced the military government to respond in two ways. First, it recognized the issue of the environment in the Constitution of 1980, which gave it legal standing and is still the law of the land today. This constitution states that citizens have the right to live in a pollution-free environment and that it is the duty of the government both to ensure such a right and to watch over the preservation of nature. Then, in 1983 an NGO called CIPMA organized the first Scientific Congress for the Environment; despite government control of the media, the latter were able to report to the nation the serious concern expressed by the scientific community regarding the critical state of Chile's environment. In response, the military government created in 1984 the National Commission for Ecology, whose main task was to establish a national environmental policy. That goal, however, was not achieved despite the best efforts of its well-intentioned staff.

2.2 Environmental policies of the democratic government

Chile's military government officially ended in March 1990, with the presidency of Patricio Aylwin, leader of a coalition of political parties known as the *Concertación por la Democracia* (CPD). In the CPD's programme, environmental problems received their share of attention along with the issues of political democracy and social equity. But at the same time there was also a strong commitment to give continuity to the socio-economic model pursued by Pinochet's government. Only marginal and gradual changes took place. Yet domestic forces were not the only ones giving urgency to environmental concerns. External pressures too were acting on the government in support of the development of proper environmental policies. The World Bank, for example, had an impact, by lending expert advisors to the main governmental organization in charge of formulating national environmental policy.

3. The Environmental Framework Law

In order to establish the legal and institutional basis for environmental policymaking, in 1992 the Aylwin administration presented to congress the Environmental Framework Law which, after long and often heated debates, was passed (*Ley de Base de Medio Ambiente No. 19300*) in March 1994.

The law answered two important needs: on the one hand, it created the instruments to make environmental protection effective; on the other, it shaped the institutional structure in charge of managing environmental policies. The policy behind this law originated in the urgency to control two critical cases of pollution, those of the Metropolitan Region, and in the mining area, in the north of the country. The objective was to recover acceptable environmental conditions and, subsequently, to apply the formerly ignored prevention principle. The promulgation of the law increased the awareness that environmental policies have not only to protect the natural environment but they are also important factors in social and economic development.

3.1 Instruments and norms

System of Environmental Impact Assessments Among the set of instruments defined by the Framework Law, the most important is without a doubt the System of Environmental Impact Assessments (SEIA).[4]

The most detailed part of the normative text describes its functioning, and states all the conditions needed in order to apply it.

Article 8 assigns the task of administrating the SEIA and coordinating the State bodies to the Regional Commissions on Environment (COREMA),[5] except for project evaluations regarding areas incorporating two or more regions, in which case the responsibility pertains to the National Commission (CONAMA).[6]

The economic activities that might cause environmental damage are explicitly listed: the law mentions, among others, urban planning, mining projects (in general, projects concerning non-renewable resources), airports, harbours and industrial plants.

Two possible types of environmental assessment are introduced: the Study of Environmental Impact (EIA) and the Declaration of Environmental Impact (DIA). The EIA requires a description of the project or the productive activity, a general description of the environment in which it will take place, and the identification of all positive and negative impacts, as well as of all mitigation, management and monitoring activities. The DIA is a report describing the project, the activity (or the planned modification to it), on which basis the competent authority can judge whether it is compatible with existing environmental regulations.

In addition, a maximum time is allowed for the competent commission to reach a verdict, after which the projects can automatically be considered approved. Given the huge number of studies submitted, many projects end up being approved only thanks to this norm.

When projects are rejected by the COREMAs, they can still be submitted for a final judgement to the National Commission on Environment, which can express a different verdict. This 'emergency exit' allows the central government to retain the ultimate power over the approval of projects that are considered particularly important and of national interest.

Environmental Quality Standards (NCA) and Emission Standard (NE)

The Environmental Framework Law also establishes the procedures needed to set NCAs (the objectives) and NEs (the instruments). In this case again a coordination role was assigned to CONAMA eliminating a great deal of duplication and overlap, especially in regulatory and control fields.

Environmental standards may be primary, that is serve the protection of human health; or secondary, that is preserve other components of the environment. The power to set standards is assigned depending on the seriousness and harmfulness of pollutants. Primary standards must be uniform throughout the country, reflecting the idea that good health is a right to be granted to everybody, independently of where people live. Secondary standards, for pollutants that can damage the environment but that are not directly harmful for people, are assigned to local authorities.

Experience shows that CONAMA has often formulated NEs without a close connection to the NCAs – the objectives they were supposed to achieve. This practice is not efficient, and imposes unnecessary costs and limitations on economic activities with dubious environmental results (Del Fávero and Katz, 2001).

The economic dimension is taken into account in the formulation of NCA and NE, since it is mandatory to perform a cost–benefit analysis before enforcing standards, but paradoxically it is not compulsory to take its results into consideration. A study on emission standards (Del Fávero and Katz, 2000) has shown that in all cases considered, economic analysis has either revealed higher costs than benefits, or it has been unable to yield an evaluation. The economic analysis does not seem to play an important role in the regulatory process as it is usually done at the end of the process, that is when the emission limits levels have already been fixed.

The 'polluter pays' principle The Environmental Framework Law explicitly establishes the 'polluter pays' principle, which places the costs of non-compliance on the perpetrator, rather than on the state, in order to oblige private companies to absorb the costs of the pollution they cause. Any legal person, public or private, that is responsible for environmental damage exceeding the limits prescribed by the laws must bear the cost of remedying the situation.

The appeal for environmental damage can be submitted by any legal or individual person or by the Municipalities, for damages within its territorial boundaries or even by the State through the State Defence Council (*Consejo de Defensa del Estado*).

The Municipalities can institute a civil action if the violation happens in their area; if they fail to do so, and the trial ascertains the damage, condemning the polluter, the Municipality will be condemned as well for joint responsibility.

The civil court in charge of the judicial proceedings is chosen according to the criterion of territoriality (location of the damage). The penalty is determined on the basis of the seriousness of the damage, of the extent of the violation with respect to the limits and of further elements as, for example, the financial resources of the polluter, his recidivism and the compliance with the standards decided in the Study or the Declaration of Environmental Impact.

3.2 Institutional set-up

In addition to establishing norms and sanctions, the Framework Law also instituted the main policymaking body, the *Comisión Nacional de Medio Ambiente* (CONAMA), a decentralized national commission that oversees all issues related to the environment. The CONAMA is set up to serve as a coordinating committee between 13 ministries with environmental functions (among which are Economy, Public Works, Agriculture, Health, Mines, Housing and Urban Affairs) and is chaired by the Minister of the

General Secretariat of the Presidency (SEGPRES):[7] 'That SEGPRES functions as the strategic and tactical nerve centre of the presidency is an indication of how sensitive and politicized environmental issues have become in Chile' (Silva, 1997: 17, our translation).

The Commission's main functions consist in: a) proposing the government environmental policy lines to the Presidency of the Republic; b) administering the System of Environmental Impact Assessment at a national level; and c) coordinating the process of environmental quality policymaking; it also promotes environmental education.

The CONAMA is structured into an Executive Board (*Consejo Directivo*) made up of the 13 Ministers with environmental functions, charged with executive tasks; and a Directive Committee (*Dirección Ejecutiva*), a technical body headed by a General Director, with administrative functions, which entertains all the international relationships with supra-national environmental organizations.

The law also institutes a Consultative Council (chaired by CONAMA's president and comprising academics, enterprises and labour union representatives and one member directly named by the President of the Republic) with the task of formulating opinions on questions coming from the Directive Committee.

Finally, there are deconcentrated bodies, called Regional Commissions on Environment (COREMAs).[8] COREMA's main function is to coordinate environmental management (mainly in the SEIA) at the regional level assuring the participation of the Municipalities and other local social organizations. While COREMAs are decision-making bodies, administrative support is provided by the Regional Divisions of the CONAMA.[9]

CONAMA's budget depends mostly on annual governmental funds, but an important contribution comes from multilateral and bilateral organizations (though they are often linked with specific environmental goals).[10]

The structure of the system is illustrated in Figure 11.2.

3.3 The environmental tasks of the Municipalities

The decentralization of the environmental institutional structure reaches regional level. However, at the smallest political division of the country, the Municipalities, there is no structure corresponding to the COREMAs.

The role of Municipalities in environmental management is defined by the Environmental Framework Law and by the Constitutional Law on Municipalities. The first one, although not implying any modification of municipal institutions, assigns to them a few responsibilities concerning Environmental Impact Assessments (EIA), the assessment of responsibility for environmental damage, and monitoring and enforcement. As far as the EIA system is concerned, the Framework Law requires the Municipalities

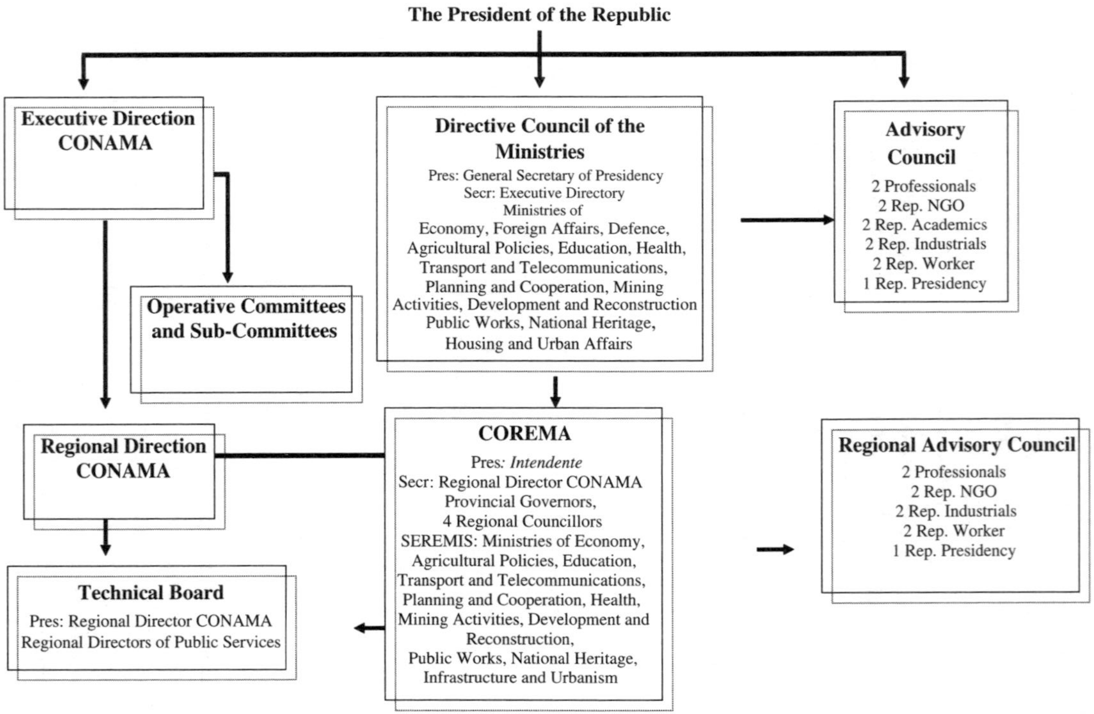

Figure 11.2 The environmental institutional set-up

to 'duly publicize the contents of the projects submitted to environmental impact studies' in order to provide the public with information on such projects and to promote popular participation (see section 3.5.1).

A more relevant role is played by the municipal level in assessing responsibility for environmental damage. The Municipality, within its territory, can represent in court anyone who claims to be a victim of environmental damage. In the event that the Municipality refuses to start a civil action and the damage is subsequently proved, the Municipality could be considered jointly liable for it.[11]

As regards monitoring and enforcement, the role of the local level is not officially recognized and the competences of control are assigned to regional agencies connected with the central Ministers involved. But in practice Municipalities and these agencies often try to cooperate in order to perform the monitoring function more efficiently.

The municipal role and competences are organically listed in the Constitutional Law on Municipalities, which divides the franchise functions – which belong exclusively to municipalities – from the non-franchise ones, for which competences are shared with other institutions. Among the former, some functions are relevant for environment protection: public transport, garbage collection and cleaning of roads and parks. Environmental management in general falls within the latter, with generic duties such as cooperating in monitoring, realizing partnerships with other institutions and enforcing legal dispositions and regulations on environmental issues. Such a vague definition of environmental policymaking responsibilities produces really few practical results.

3.4 An overview on the decentralization of environmental powers

Figure 11.3 provides an overview of the decentralization trends in Chilean environmental policies. What has taken place in Chile is an evolution toward a light form of decentralization, better defined as a deconcentrated system.

Environmental coordination bodies have been set up both at national and at regional level. The regional board is in charge of coordinating the implementation and enforcement activities of public agencies responsible for environmental tools within the regional territory. In addition it has the power to assess the environmental implications of projects (EIA).

Despite the decentralization of some functions, the central government keeps all main decision-making powers. It can interfere discretionally in regional competences.

Local governments are responsible for waste management and for land planning. In addition, Municipalities cooperate with regional and national agencies in monitoring and enforcing. Notwithstanding, poorer rural

Field / Level	Industry Pollution	Agriculture	Ecosystem Protection (biodiversity and fisheries)	Forests	Water	Implementation and enforcement
International	– Montreal Protocol – Kyoto Protocol – Convention on Climate Change	–UNCCD	– Convention on Biological Diversity – Cartagena Protocol – Convention on Climate Change – Protocol to Antarctic Treaty			
National	– Primary NCA – Emission trading – Incentives to cleaner technologies	–Primary NCA	– ITQ (supervision and implementation)	SNAPSE, command and control tools reforestation subsidies	Water rights assessment Water and sewage (politic and regulatory responsibility) Primary NCA	Regulatory powers Implementation Enforcement coordination
Regional	– SEIA – PPDA (enforcement and coordination)	–SEIA				Enforcement
Local	– PPDA and emission trading (control together with other public bodies) – Secondary NCA and NE	– Territorial spatial planning – Secondary NCA and NE	– ITQ (control)		Water supply and sewage system, Secundary NCA and NE	Enforcement
Private sector	– International certification		– VA – APP	– Management plans – International certification	Water supply and sewage system (almost 80% is privatized)	

centralization — decentralization or deconcentration — privatization

Figure 11.3 Centralization/decentralization trends in Chilean environmental governance

municipalities often lack the technical competence and financial resources necessary to implement tools for sustainable management in these fields.

During recent years, the government has implemented an extreme and particular form of decentralization: the privatization of natural resources. Some functions in water and forest management and in air pollution control have now been shifted to the private sector.

3.5 The role of the civil society in environmental protection

3.5.1 The possibilities of participation provided by the Environmental Framework Law In discussing the Municipalities' role within the EIA process we underlined their task of informing citizens about the projects submitted to environmental studies. Such provision is part of a wider will on the part of the legislator to include in the normative text a public discussion of the projects, in order to give the public an active role in local environmental decision-making.

The Framework Law establishes a period of 60 days during which any legal person and members of citizens' organizations discuss the characteristics of the projects, under the supervision and coordination of the CONAMA, which also has the task of recording proposals coming from the public and judging whether to incorporate them into the projects.

Though there is no doubt about the potential of this mechanism for civic participation in environmental issues, it has to be noted that such a process is limited to the discussion of the Studies of Environmental Assessment and is not extended to the Declarations, for which the only requirement is that the public be informed on the main features of the project.

As a consequence, what happened in recent years is that, in order to avoid the public discussion step, many projects have been passed with Declarations (the Framework Law is quite ambiguous in differentiating a Study from a Declaration) thus reducing the possibility for local communities to express their opinions and criticism: 'Nowadays 80% of the projects are passed as Declarations and public participation hardly exists. In Santiago's municipality only 2 Studies of Environmental Impact have been presented since 1998.'[12]

In addition to these arrangements, the Environmental Framework Law creates a Consultative Council within the CONAMA structure (and similar ones within the COREMAs), as described in section 3.2., in order to provide an opportunity for members of society at large to play a role in formulating environmental policy.

3.5.2 The role of environmental NGOs By assigning two seats, within each Consultative Council, to environmental NGOs' representatives, the

Framework Law officially recognizes their role in the environmental policy process.

The Chilean environmentalist movement is quite young. Although the first NGO, the CODEFF (National Committee for the Defence of Flora and Fauna),[13] dates back to 1963, the first important signal of an environmental form of mobilization, denouncing the downsides of indiscriminate economic development, came only 20 years later.

In 1983 the 'Scientific Congress of the Environment' was organized by the Centre for Environmental Research and Planning (CIPMA),[14] and in spite of tight media control, it garnered substantial publicity. However, environmental protection remained a low priority for the military regime, and the movement was unable to grow much until the return to civilian rule, when it was spurred on by a larger and higher-profile gathering, the 1989 'First National Meeting of Environmental Actions Organisations'.

The first years of democratic rule created a climate of optimism and openness, in which the environmental NGOs managed to strengthen ties with educational, women's, indigenous, workers' and peasants' organizations. The resulting influences were visible in the presentation made by Aylwin's government at the 1992 Earth Summit in Rio de Janeiro (Carruthers, 2001: 343–58).

The situation, however, turned rapidly inhospitable for green movements as well as for the other social organizations: all of them suffered from the sudden collapse in popular participation and were not able to respond with concrete actions of mobilization. All the personalities interviewed for the purpose of this study on the actual weight of environmental NGOs were quite forceful in judging that their capacity to raise awareness and organize popular support around environmental conflicts is today low.[15]

4. International Agreements on the Environment

Since the United Nations Conference on the Human Environment held in Stockholm in 1972, Chile has signed all main international environmental agreements. The Chilean environmental legislation evolved thereafter, following the guidelines of the international agreements signed and the decisions taken by International Organizations of which Chile is a member.[16] Both the above Conference of Stockholm and the following Rio Declaration on Environment and Development (approved in 1992 together with the Agenda 21) are now part of Chilean national law.

These agreements try to promote integration between environmental protection and economic development, fostering a system based on the interconnections of trade, environment and growth (Fundación Facultad de Derecho de la Universidad de Chile, 1998).

Chilean environmental policies, however, do not satisfy many of the prescriptions in Agenda 21 (Fundación Facultad de Derecho de la Universidad de Chile, 1998). For example: a) there is still no national plan coordinating environmental policies, strategies and economic sectoral projects and aiming at integrating environment and development; b) there has been no serious investment in strengthening the link between environment and development at all the institutional levels in charge of environmental decision-making; c) mechanisms of social participation in the decision-making process have either not been created or implemented (Montenegro et al., 2001).

The United Nations Convention on Biological Diversity, signed in 1992, was another important step for Chile's environment even though the actual norms in this field are still insufficient to ensure efficient protection.

The CONAMA considers anyway the protection of genetic heritage as one of the most important challenges for future environmental policies. This requires a diversification of protected areas, now mainly in the ice-regions, in order to extend the protection of the biodiversity to the Centre and the north of the country.[17]

In the meantime, Chilean genetic heritage tends to be exploited by foreign companies who do not share profits with the local legitimate owners of the resources (Fundación Facultad de Derecho de la Universidad de Chile, 1998).

In the field of international environmental protection, the important role played by Chile in the Antarctic Region since the Second World War is worth mentioning. Chile, close to the Antarctic both geographically and for historical reasons (Montenegro et al., 2001), participated in the birth and approval of the Antarctic Protocol on Environmental Protection, signed in October 1991, which assigns to Chile important responsibilities for the defence of the Antarctic environment. The Protocol led to the creation within the CONAMA, of the CONAEIA (National Committee for Antarctic Environment Evaluation),[18] in charge of managing the studies of environmental impact and promoting eco-tourism in the Antarctic zones under Chilean sovereignty.

The above-mentioned agreements deal with environmental issues of particular importance for Chile. It is in these fields that the government's will of establishing links with other countries in order to self-impose norms that otherwise could not have been introduced, clearly emerged.[19]

This notwithstanding, the environmental normative process is still unsatisfactory, and the political intention of giving effective implementation to international agreements has often been weaker than the will displayed at the moment of adhesion and ratification (Fundación Facultad de Derecho de la Universidad de Chile, 1998).

5. The Environmental Situation

The importance of environmental problems in Chile is emphasized by the tremendous economic weight of sectors that make an intense use of renewable resources and generate heavy industrial pollution. In recent years, Chile has experienced a period of strong economic growth based mainly on the exploitation of its considerable natural resources. As growth proceeded at a rapid pace, the health and productivity costs of environmental degradation have become more and more apparent. Chile's main environmental problems are urban pollution of air and water, industrial pollution, in particular from mining, and the intensive use of natural resources, such as native forest and fisheries.

In the following sections we analyse the present state of natural resources and the instruments used to deal with environmental problems.

5.1 Air pollution

Urban air pollution is perceived as one of the most alarming problems by the Chilean population, in particular in Santiago. During the winter the capital city experiences a very high level of air pollution, causing great damage to health, such as an increase in premature deaths and serious respiratory diseases (Sanchez et al., 1998). Pollution is caused by industrial and vehicle emissions and is made worse by the city's location in an enclosed valley, with little wind and thermic inversion, limiting pollutants' dispersion.

In June 1996, environmental authorities defined it a saturated zone with respect to four atmospheric pollutants: TSP, PM10, carbon monoxide and ozone, and the so-called 'Santiago's Decontamination Plan'[20] was designed and then implemented. The plan, although often criticized and modified, has achieved some positive results in recent years. It involves a set of environmental control policies and tools. The most innovative is a compensation system for particulate emission, which regulates emissions from different sources and fixes the daily emissions from existent sources. In addition, it allows sources to compensate emissions among themselves.

Although a significant reduction in emissions took place, data on transactions and prices suggest that the emission trading market has not fully developed.[21] The main reason behind such an outcome is a combination of regulatory uncertainty, significant transaction costs and incomplete enforcement due to institutional restrictions (Montero, Sanchez and Katz, 2002). However, this system has provided important advantages over traditional command-and-control regulations, such as speeding up the completion of the inventory of sources and emissions, and providing affected firms with more flexibility to comply in different ways and to better adapt to new market conditions.

5.2 Water resources

Water shortages mostly affect the north, the desert zone which is considered the driest in the world, where the intense mining activity consumes and contaminates the already limited water resources.

River pollution, on the other hand, affects the whole country, except Patagonia. River and groundwater pollution is mainly due to the lack of adequate treatment of domestic and industrial effluents. As a matter of fact, until 1998 the law did not regulate the treatment of the sewage water before it flowed into the sea.

Water management in Chile makes use of two innovative tools: transferable water rights and a water rating system based on marginal costs.

Transferable water rights The 1981 National Water Code, following a neoliberal economic ideology imposed by Pinochet, separates water rights from the land, assigns a fixed quantity of them freely and for a predetermined period of time, makes them tradable and enables them to be registered in the Real Estate Title Office.[22] The initial distribution is based on applications by potential users to the Water Head Office (DGA), the institution in charge of managing, controlling and planning the use of rights.

Given the lack of official data on trading, it is very difficult to evaluate the working of this market, but scholars agree that the volume and frequency of permanent transfers have been low. This is due on the one hand to lack of experience and information, on the other to the failed legalization of rights in conformity with formal process.[23] Bauer (1998)[24] discusses the contradictions implied by the implementation of the National Water Code, which is modelled on neoliberal economics developed with reference to a context, such as the US, with a strong judiciary and a system of precedent. In Chile, the judiciary is formalistic, interprets the law strictly and literally, and is not used to playing a pro-active role, and the lack of precedent and adequate technical knowledge on water issues have caused court rulings to be unpredictable and contradictory. According to Bjornlund and McKay (2002), since the disputes have to be settled in the courts, it appears that they are generally won by those who can afford the best lawyer.

Some scholars agree in identifying the impediments to trade in the rigidity of the water distribution system. Others criticize the strong speculations these rights are subject to and the lack of environmental sustainability of the system, highlighted by the initial free assignation of rights[25] (Leal, 1996). In addition, there are no explicit limits to consumption (that is, the water could be used entirely for human needs) and the regulation of water pollution has been left out.

Water rating system based on marginal costs Chile applies a water rating principle based on marginal costs both for water supply and for disposal of waterborne waste. This system was set up to tackle the scarcity of public financing in this sector. Until 1980, normative, regulatory and operative responsibility were concentrated in the SENDOS, an autonomous public body which regulated the actions of public and private firms and minor municipalities. At the end of the 1980s the sector's reform separated and specified institutional responsibilities, as shown in Table 11.1.

National Water Services were decentralized on the grounds of the regional system, and decentralized units were transformed into autonomous but publicly-owned firms. Rate reform was based on strictly economic considerations aimed at recovering operating costs, while social and redistributive targets were pursued through a direct subsidy. The application of this system involved a marked increase of prices in the last 10 years with relevant price differences among regions. This evolution was considered necessary in order to reflect the real cost of services and to allow firms to self-finance.

The privatization process started in 1998 and more than three-quarters of Chilean households are now served by private water companies. The privatization was justified by the authorities with the need to attract private financing in order to increase the coverage of the urban sewerage system.

According to expectations, privatization was followed by an increase in investments by the privatized companies, with respect to their public counterparts. While private companies invested 70 per cent more in 2001 than in 1998, public companies invested almost 70 per cent less. The decline of the public sector reflects both the growing difficulties the government has in funding its cash flow and the political will to disinvest in public utilities. Sharp differences between the two groups of companies also emerge in pricing behaviour. Between 1998 and 2001, private companies on average

Table 11.1 Powers over the water sector

Body	Functions	Remarks
Ministry of Economy	Political and normative functions.	
SISS, Superintendence of Sanitary Services	Regulatory and fiscal control body. Establishes technical norms. Revises rates. Can impose sanctions.	Under the Ministry of Construction. No political and financial autonomy.
Regional and other minor firms	They supply the service.	Generally autonomous public firms, recently privatized.

raised their rates by 20 per cent more than public ones.[26] Most of the differences in price behaviour stem from the fact that privatized companies invested more and added new services (mostly sewage treatment). As for the remaining gap, a line of thought points to the superior bargaining skills of private management in dealing with issues such as the negotiation of water rates[27] (Bitrán and Valenzuela, 2003).

Increasingly aware of the cost of water, customers reduced their consumption by almost 10 per cent in three years. The change in consumption is not a direct effect of privatization but an indirect one, since the adjustment of water rates was a precondition for private investment in the sector.

Efficiency differences have also become apparent. While private companies have improved their performance as measured by four common indicators of efficiency, public ones have seen their performance worsen by all of them.[28] On the other hand, data show that public companies are more efficient in managing their water losses. However, Bitrán and Valenzuela (2003) argue that this is not due to a greater ecological awareness but to cost-efficiency considerations. Public companies are in fact located in the driest zones, where water is scarce and very expensive, which makes the reduction of water losses the most cost-efficient strategy. By contrast, where water is more abundant, the most efficient way to deal with water losses may be to buy more water rights.

Surprisingly, a social consensus has emerged and made the higher water rates acceptable, given the improvements in service quality and the addition of new services such as sewage treatment.

This sanitary regulation system has also been criticized by some scholars and NGOs. In particular, Leal (1996) claims that this is not a truly environmental instrument, because it has not been designed with this aim, and it doesn't give any incentive to reduce pollution.

5.3 Forest management and biodiversity

Chile is covered by a native forest of extraordinary value, hosting a number of rare species representing a valuable genetic heritage.

In this field, the legislation is inadequate and unclear,[29] based on scarce information. Norms are often not applied or inconsistent due to the lack of cooperation between the different competent bodies (Del Fávero and Katz, 2001). Biodiversity protection represents the most troubling deficiency of Chilean environmental management as highlighted by the Yale University Index.[30] The introduction of exotic species with a different life cycle, so as to increase productivity, has altered the ecosystem balance causing heavy biodiversity loss.

In particular, the commercial timber sector experienced a period of strong economic growth, largely built on fast-growing exotic species. To support this sector, the government implemented a policy of reforestation subsidies disregarding the negative consequences in terms of native forest depletion and of biodiversity loss.[31] Plantation forests of exotic species are always economically more attractive than the plantation of native forest species, and there are no financial incentives in favour of the latter. To address the depletion of native forests, in 1997 the Ministry of Agriculture proposed a draft bill introducing taxes on cutting native forests and incentives for sustainable management of native forests, but both strong economic lobbies and NGOs boycotted it.[32]

Chile is now embarking on increasing public–private cooperation in environmental matters such as collaboration in environmental monitoring and Protected Areas management. In recent years there have been a few cases of private companies managing Protected Areas, but the lack of coordination and connexion with SNASPE (National System of Forest Protected Areas) has widely reduced the potential benefits. In order to improve these Private Protected Areas (APP), the government is studying a draft bill to attract private investments.[33] This new system should give an incentive to private citizens to 'adopt' ecologically strategic zones. These zones, strategic for biodiversity protection, could be expanded, relieving at the same time the financial burden and the work of CONAF, the main forestry development and conservation institution, in charge of the maintenance of SNASPE. It is, therefore, fundamental that a territorial network be created, able to establish and protect biological passages connecting public and private areas between them (Sepúlveda, 1997).

5.4 Soil

The great geomorphic, climatic and hydrologic diversity of Chile provides the country with a large variety of soils. The northern zone is characterized by continuous and worrying desertification[34] and salinization processes, while arable lands are situated in delicate ecosystems unable to support the overexploitation of resources linked to short-run economic needs like fuelwood and farming. In addition, wind and water erosion, the use of end-of-pipe technology and the expansion of human activities make the soil depletion process worse (Centro de Análisis de Políticas Públicas, 2000).

Another serious problem is the overuse of pesticides and fertilizers in traditional cultivation; according to the Yale Center Index, the use of these products is decidedly above the world average. The available information is scarce and not updated; the actions for soil preservation have been inadequate, dispersed, and they have rarely provided new technologies aiming at a sustainable management.

It must also be noted that the loss of arable land is due to urban expansion and production activities often taking place out of any kind of territorial planning or rules. The percentage of municipalities or regions developing according to such planning tools is very low.[35] Despite the good intentions expressed by CONAMA's staff, some scholars[36] point to the unsatisfactory evolution of planning processes, especially visible in the plan for Santiago, recently modified towards less stringent environmental norms.

5.5 Marine resources management

With its 4600 km coastline and its large exclusive economic zone, Chile has access to one of the most productive fisheries in the world. The rapid growth of the fisheries sector is a consequence of the high quantity of fish being caught, one of the highest in the world, after China and Peru.[37] The most commercially important species are now in a position of being fully exploited, and others have been overexploited to the point of causing a clear reduction of biomass.

In order to preserve four species in full exploitation, the 1991 Fisheries Law introduced an individual transferable quotas (ITQ) system, managed by the Secretariat of Fisheries of the Ministry of Economy, in collaboration with some independent research organizations and the National Service of Fishery (SERNAPESCA), in charge of monitoring the system. This tool has proven successful in preserving species, but it has been applied to a very limited range of fisheries[38] that on the whole account for about 1 per cent of total landings by volume and 2 per cent by value (Borregaard and Leal, 2002). In spite of widespread satisfaction with this system, lobbying efforts in opposition succeeded in limiting its application to other species (Borregaard and Leal, 2002).[39] Finally, this field is subject to a strong evaluation uncertainty that prevents scholars from reaching a consensus about the amount of marine fauna and its evolution trends.

5.6 Obstacles to the adoption of market-based instruments and economic evaluation

Tools such as SEIA, NCA and NE are typical of a 'command-and-control' model of public environmental management. Their prevalence reveals some reluctance towards economic policy instruments that could stimulate private sector creativity. In this perspective, the Environmental Framework Law treats market-based instruments for environmental management only incidentally: they are mentioned in the articles concerning the Decontamination Plan. Nevertheless some argue that an implicit mandate in favour of a market-based approach can be found in the key principles of Chilean environmental management, that is the prevention principle, the efficiency principle and the polluter pays principle (Borregaard and Leal, 2002).

In order to introduce environmental considerations in CONAMA studies, to propose market-based instruments and to control the economic analyses, an Environmental Economics Unit was established inside the CONAMA. Anyway, the introduction of market-based instruments has been slow and difficult, with a partial and circumscribed application. Insufficient levels of staffing and budgets have been devoted to market-based instruments with respect to other tools managed by the CONAMA.

According to some scholars (Borregaard and Leal, 2002; Del Fávero and Katz, 2001), one of the main obstacles to the adoption of market-based tools is the lack of political will, expressed by insufficient funding for research, shortage of staff and competences about the use of these instruments, and the lack of data on some environmental components of the country. Research has often merely compiled information without developing any critical analysis. Moreover, economic evaluations don't follow a standardized methodology, and studies and information are dispersed and underused, despite the creation of a National System of Environmental Information (SNIA). Furthermore, it often happens that these economic evaluations are not taken into consideration at the time of the decision.

Evaluation studies are carried out mainly by the Environmental Economic Unit of CONAMA, which often commissions studies to professionals or academics[40] or private consulting firms (Borregaard and Leal, 2002).

In some matters, such as biodiversity classification-lacking official studies, administrative authorities, like CONAF and SAG, use 'red books', which are documents prepared by an informal group of scientists (Del Fávero and Katz, 2000).

PART II: CHILEAN ENVIRONMENTAL GOVERNANCE: A CRITICAL REVIEW

This second part is devoted to highlighting some features that are peculiar to the Chilean case.

The main factors of the evolution of the environmental set-up are strongly linked to the democratic transition started in 1989, and to the rapidity of economic development taking place since the first years of the 1970s that suddenly forced the political elite to deal with the problem of sustainability.

Both environmental legislation and its instruments are extremely recent and still evolving, which explains why many issues regarding the Chilean environment are still unclear and hard to frame.

This causes a frequent discrepancy between the situation *de jure* and *de facto*, between international trends in environmental policymaking and questionable interpretations that they have been given in Chile, which emerges clearly from the key problems analysed in the following.

6. Critical Analysis of the CONAMA

From the outset of the research, the National Commission on Environment emerged as a controversial institution, characterized by many anomalies and around which there is a lively debate. Interviews with NGO members and CONAMA directors provided quite different points of view, contradicting one another.

According to NGOs, the Commission is responsible for the lack of environmental concern in the government agenda;[41] on the contrary, CONAMA's exponents claim that the work of the Commission since its creation has been satisfactory and has led to important improvements in environmental protection.[42]

We analyse below the main controversial characteristics that make the CONAMA the object of such different interpretations.

The first anomaly of the CONAMA stands in its hybrid nature: it is not a ministry but a technical body composed of the 13 Ministers with environmental functions. Such a structure was designed to give a transversal dimension to environmental politics. But in practice this turned it into a mere coordination body (Silva, 1997).

In order to react to the increasing general discredit around CONAMA's role, during the last years an interesting debate has emerged on the possibility of transforming it into a Ministry of the Environment. Although such a change could increase and clarify the CONAMA's competences, nobody within the staff seemed to approve of it.[43] It is argued that, even at the risk of condemning the Commission to a subordinate role in environmental decision-making, CONAMA's task is to take environmental issues to the top of each Ministry's agenda. For this reason, if a Minister of the Environment were created – as in all other Latin American countries, except Peru – this would lead all other Ministries to drop any consideration of the environment. In this way the ecological issues would lose priority in political agenda and in public opinion.[44] Many support CONAMA's coordination role as the only way to deal with the transversal dimension of environmental issues. But this argument becomes sterile if not followed by a strong call for wider powers and competences in order to allow the Commission to play the role of environmental protection body efficiently.[45]

Underlying such an inertial attitude there is the political will of maintaining the status quo. Moreover, the creation of a Ministry of the Environment is opposed by the Ministers actually coordinated by the CONAMA because they would lose power, competences and funds.[46]

On the other hand, the Commission does not benefit either of the potential advantages of its technical nature. The initial decision to entrust CONAMA's direction to the Minister of the General Secretariat of the Presidency was taken in order to guarantee its transversal nature. But as a consequence the body assumed a strong political character; the executive board changed with every change of government, thus hindering a consistent action in the long run (Silva, 1997).

This lack of continuity explains the growing discredit of the CONAMA among local administrations and public opinion. Many Municipalities, after cooperating for a long time with environmental authorities, saw their efforts thwarted by the changing, for example, of a regional director (see also section 8).[47]

In conclusion, from environmental NGOs, from the civil society and from local administrations comes a strong denunciation of CONAMA's lack of independence, which weakens the chance of bringing environmental politics into government agenda.

Inside the CONAMA, instead, a passive acceptance of the marginality of the environmental authority prevails. This is certainly dangerous in a country like Chile in which the strong market-oriented attitude risks ruling out any attention to the environment.

7. Inefficiencies in Monitoring and Control Tasks

As described above, environmental policy in Chile clearly divides design and promotion functions from monitoring and control. The former functions are the responsibility of decentralized public agencies.

Among these agencies, an important role is played by the decentralized services of the Health Minister (*Servicio de Salud*), by the committee for water control (*Dirreción de Aguas*) and by the CONAF (*Corporación Nacional Forestal*), which controls the protection of forestry and woodlands.

Issues related to beaches and coastal waters are dealt with by the DIRECTEMAR (*Dirección General del Territorio Marítimo y de Marina Mercante*), a department of the Chilean Navy. Fishing activities are under the control of SERNAPESCA (*Servicio Nacional de Pesca*). Inspections on the mining activity and energy plants are a task of the SERNAGEOMIN (*Servicio Nacional Geologico y Minero*). Finally, the law allows the Municipalities to cooperate with these committees in order to coordinate the inspections on activities taking place within their boundaries.

There is a strong overlap of functions in this field. At present, out of 13 different environmental bodies, seven are responsible for the water sector while no one is responsible, for instance, for landscape control.

The duplication and overlapping of function in imposing sanctions is due to the lack of internal and external coordination, to a non-regulated inspection activity, and to a lack of human and financial resources. In the opinion of Claudio Nilo, CONAMA environmental policy coordinator, only 20 per cent of the projects are subject to close control while the fragmentation of competence can cause a project to incur several sanctions for the same offence.[48] Moreover the sanctions are too low to provide economic incentives (Borregaard and Leal, 2002).

Local governments play a role in this field, but the law is quite ambiguous. Although monitoring is entrusted to regional bodies, local institutions gained residual legislative power. Municipalities now try to coordinate their actions with *Servicios de Salud*, and other regional public services, dealing in particular with noise pollution and food control.[49]

8. Political Participation and Decentralization

8.1 Citizens' participation in environmental policymaking

With the return to democracy in 1989 the participation in environmental matters was very high.[50] The initial enthusiasm soon decreased and after the first years of democratic government, popular mobilization and activism whittled down and was gradually substituted by an increasing distrust in democratic institutions. The only public figure in whom an acceptable degree of trust was maintained was the President of the Republic. It is quite a discouraging picture that shows the inability of the new political elite to manage the enormous support initially received.

This may be due to several reasons: on one hand there is the individualistic character of Chilean society as a consequence of the economic neoliberal model imposed by the authoritarian regime. Much research shows a high level of competition for personal success and a low reliance of people on their fellow citizens and their ability to associate and organize for common goals.[51] In addition, the legacy of almost 20 years under an authoritarian regime without any freedom of public expression and association caused a tendency to an atomized and passive attitude on the part of society that the return to democracy could not totally reverse. A general distrust in the political system also plays a role. A quarrelsome elite, frequent scandals, and an inefficient electoral system *provoked* in Chilean population a wide sense of apathy and alienation.

Finally it is worth considering the impact of decentralization on the consolidation of democratic life. As explained in Part I, the intentions of the democratic government were to promote a huge process of decentralization of the administrative structure and a progressive democratization of local governments. However, the unsatisfactory way in which this has been accomplished greatly hindered the creation of political spaces for contact between citizenry and institutions and of conditions enhancing social participation.

Two main reasons explain the optimism around the potential role of citizens in environmental matters at the beginning of the 1990s. First, many environmental problems (the air pollution in Santiago and the question of the mines in the north of the country) had reached a dangerous level and affected people directly. The population, helped by active and well-organized environmental NGOs, seemed to have a growing propensity to associate in order to face environmental conflicts. The other reason for optimism came from the Environmental Framework Law, which introduced new procedures for interaction and democratic participation in environmental management.

The results, however, are quite controversial. The tools provided by the Law for citizenship participation in the Studies of Environmental Impact had an initial success with the Santiago Air Pollution Decontamination Plan realized in 1998.[52] Even in cases in which the local struggles didn't succeed, as in the RALCO issue,[53] local communities showed great potential for aggregation that in this case took the shape of a union of the Mapuche indigenous population.

The RALCO case also showed that Chile suffers from an 'agency capture' problem that far exceeds the norm for developed countries. This caused a widespread distrust and frustration among citizens and gradually reduced people's participation, as their efforts have often been defeated by the closed ties between business and political elite (Sabatini et al., 2000).

Moreover, the Framework Law introduces such participation tools only for the Studies of Environmental Impact and not for the Declarations. As already mentioned in section 3.1, in recent years the resort to the studies has gradually decreased, essentially in order to bypass long discussion procedures and potential pressures from public opinion. Finally, public participation is also hindered by the extremely technical nature of the studies.[54]

8.2 The shortcomings of environmental decentralization

As described in Part I, the CONAMA is structured into administrative regional divisions, which support the executive environmental bodies, the COREMAs, composed of regional political and technical members. But the COREMAs' powers (such as the right to approve or refuse the Declarations or Studies of Environmental Impact) have to be seen in the framework of the partial evolution of a Chilean decentralizing process still characterized by a difficult transition from a form of deconcentration to a real decentralization.

The only notable step in this direction was made with the reform of the Municipalities, whose mayors and councils have been elected democratically since 1993.

The direct election of the regional bodies, however, was not introduced, keeping the presidential designation of the *Intendente* and that of the regional councillors by the Municipal correspondents. The *Intendente* even has the right to choose the other members of the regional board (which makes it unlikely that COREMA members will be openly in opposition to the central government).

Moreover, the financial autonomy of local institutions has not been increased, with the regional and municipal budget decisions still being taken essentially by the central government. Such failure invalidates the great part of still innovative legislative proposals in environmental decentralization.

The Municipalities, being directly elected, could appear to offer the best chance for a political opportunity for positive interaction between people and institutions (offering to the former effective chances to participate in environmental management). But as mentioned in Part I, they are assigned very limited functions dealing with the environment and limited executive and normative powers.

Municipalities' only task in the EIA system was to provide citizens with information on the submitted projects. They also lament a lack of involvement by the CONAMA in all the discussions on environmental norms and policymaking: 'To tell you the truth I don't know what kind of coordination with the Municipalities the CONAMA wants to pursue. Nowadays the CONAMA is quite discredited among local administrations essentially because of its substantial discontinuity in the attitude towards us.'[55]

In general, local governments do not have enough resources to undertake concrete environmental interventions beyond the basic policies of street cleaning and garbage collecting. This is particularly true in poorer regional or urban areas, where the share of the budget devoted to environmental policies is extremely small.[56]

8.3 Horizontal cooperation

The de facto limited decentralization in environmental management, together with the scarce municipal and regional financing resources, have not allowed the establishment of forms of competition among these institutions.

At the municipal level we have found some limited experiences in horizontal cooperation, as demonstrated by *Red Municipal de Atención Primaria Ambiental*, a network coordinating 12 municipalities in the metropolitan area of Santiago. Despite the partial success of this project, the network coordinator laments its lack of continuity.

CONAMA's unreliability and discredit make it very difficult to introduce forms of vertical cooperation. Most of the projects studied in cooperation between CONAMA and Municipalities never saw the light.

In current practice, Municipalities mainly rely on personal contacts and friends, exchanging information on the sector involved and adopting forms of cooperation to carry out their control task.

It can be interesting to note that Municipalities have not shown more or less environmental sensibility than higher tiers of government as far as the introduction of environmentally damaging industries is concerned. In general, richer Municipalities appear to be more environmentally-friendly but this is not a rule without exceptions, as shown by the Municipalities of Lota and Coronel, which refused to convert abandoned mines in dangerous waste deposits despite the strong economic crisis of the area.

In general, environmental matters are not regarded as a political priority in local agendas. This is due not only to faults on the part of politicians and administrators, but also to the lack of 'internal demand' for environmental politics from the community. There are also structural limitations, in the framework of a centralized system with no use of incentive policies (Valenzuela, 1999).

In developed countries, national and regional governments finance municipalities directly in order to sustain investment and maintenance costs of environmental technology, necessary for recycling of urban waste, for sanitary services, and for use of clean energy. In Chile there are no incentives in this area, either global programmes helping rural municipalities to set city plans (or EIA), or subsidies for investments in social infrastructure.

8.4 Decentralization and participation in the environmental field: two unfulfilled promises

Citizen participation and decentralization, which were meant as the strongly innovative elements of the Environmental Framework Law, are two deeply correlated and interdependent aspects of social and political dynamics.

At the beginning of the 1990s a new attitude gained ground in Chilean society, and different forms of popular organization and mobilization developed that were focused on issues of welfare, quality of life and sustainability. Policymakers had to respond to this climate in some way. Probably the intention of the legislator was to go beyond the satisfaction of the participation demand from public opinion and to trigger a virtuous circle between decentralization of environmental competences and spaces for participation (Bocchetto, 1993: 18–19). A decentralization process, offering more room for dialogue between citizens and politics, allows a potential increase of public participation and it may constitute a powerful instrument to foster participation and popular initiative, but it can turn out to be inadequate if conditions to encourage self-organization and association are not met.

The decentralized structures established by the Environmental Framework Law aimed precisely at encouraging such a virtuous circle between the vitality of environmental organizations and a new institutional set-up that could offer them the opportunity to express themselves. Such a process would have brought about a more efficient and shared environmental management. The controversial results of this process have been discussed in the previous sections.

The model of environmental decentralization created by the Framework Law remains innovative on its own but loses the great part of its potential if it is not included in a wider decentralization project characterized by deep reforms of local governments.

In conclusion, the institutional framework has kept most of its centralized structure and the political culture has only partially evolved from its centralist and elitist character. This frequently implied interferences by the central government in the activity of regional environmental bodies, generating a widespread sense of dissatisfaction. The actual situation of *impasse* is due to a lack of political will to push forward the decentralization process together with a weaker and weaker 'voice' demanding participation from below, which prevent the innovative potential of the Environmental Framework Law from being realized.

9. The Role of International Trade in the Evolution of Environmental Legislation

Since 1973, the Chilean economy has opened its boundaries to international trade and to the system of norms it imposes. Among these norms, the respect of minimum environmental standards had the undeniable role of starting a process that would otherwise probably have been postponed.[57]

In 1997, together with a Free Trade Agreement with Canada, Chile signed a side agreement on environmental cooperation.[58] This led to important improvements in environmental protection, confirming the significant role that international trade can play in this field. The agreement imposes on Chile a deadline for putting into effect its environmental legislation. This does not mean introducing Canadian norms into Chile's legislation, but activating Chilean laws that have already been approved.

This apparently minor clause had important effects because a large share of Chilean current legislation was still not enforced. Moreover, the Agreement with Canada forced the huge body of norms having a bearing on the environment to be re-organized and streamlined.

As a matter of fact the Chilean legislator had grouped all its 2400 environmental norms into a unique body of laws, arguing that from a juridical point of view 'everything is environment'. The Agreement, instead, gave a stricter and more rational definition of environment (drawing on the one given in the NAFTA), which allowed a major rationalization of the whole legislation produced.

This is only an example of the possible virtuous effects that international trade may have in a country like Chile, where the last decades have been marked by a wild economic liberalism. In this context, in fact, international trade might impose some restraint on the growth model in the name of 'sustainability'.

The environmental effects of international trade on the export sector are interesting. In the forestry and fishing sectors, for example, the stricter rules imposed by trade agreements have deeply modified the production process and the product characteristics. Firms were able to acquire know-how and introduce important technological and organizational innovations. By the way, the inactivity of the state in this field strongly limited an efficient exploitation of comparative advantages deriving from the sustainable management of Chilean natural resources (V Encuentro científico sobre el medio ambiente en la Universidad de la Frontera, 1996).

Nevertheless, Chile's negotiating power in international relationships is widely increased with respect to the time when the mines of the II Region were exploited by foreign firms without any care for environmental sustainability (V Encuentro científico sobre el medio ambiente en la Universidad de la Frontera, 1996).

Although today Chile is able to benefit from the environmental standards introduced by bilateral trade agreements, such norms might be imposed by developed countries with the hidden intention of limiting the competitiveness of the developing countries. Developed countries have too often adopted, even in recent years, protectionist policies towards mining products, justifying them with ecological arguments (the Chilean mining industry has often been accused of 'ecological dumping') but with the aim of defending the lack of competitiveness of their internal production.

International trade may certainly be a great occasion for the evolution of environmental protection in Chile, provided that the norms imposed do not turn into an instrument to keep the country in a situation of marginality and economic dependence.

While trade has played an important role in the harmonization of Chilean environmental legislation, for other reasons it represents a real threat for sustainability. During the last decades, for example, wood exports have increased remarkably, seriously endangering the forests' heritage. This resource has a crucial role in protecting biodiversity and soil quality (which constitutes a benefit for agriculture too) and in stimulating international trade. The current forest law in force does not ensure a sustainable use of forests, and in this sector the supra-national level has not yet provided better incentives.

Another example is provided by the mining sector, where, as reported by all main Chilean NGOs, international trade is causing serious environmental problems. In spite of some relevant improvement in the legislative framework, mines' exploitation is not regulated enough. Because of the domination of foreign investments, the gradual impoverishment of mining resources and environmental damages are not even balanced by real benefits for the Chilean economy.

10. Conclusions

In the light of the actual environmental legislation, tools and institutions created in recent years, and considering the above critical issues, some general conclusions can be drawn about Chile's environmental condition and on its future perspectives.

Improvements made by Chile in the last decades have undoubtedly been remarkable, although there still exist deficiencies in the policy tools provided, as well as in enforcing and monitoring tasks. Duplications and overlapping create inefficiency and coordination problems among institutions, while the discontinuous policy makes it very difficult to introduce forms of vertical cooperation.

The Environmental Framework Law opened the way to a clearer legislation, to the creation of instruments for environmental management and to the institution of an articulated and partially decentralized environmental structure. The international agreements that Chile stipulated, particularly those on international trade, allowed a significant enforcing of environmental rules otherwise inactive.

In spite of this, the unsatisfactory outcomes are principally due to a weak ecological sensibility, both on the part of the political elite and of public opinion.

Even in cases concerning particular attention to environmental problems by local institutions and civil society, the lack of a real decentralization maintains crucial decisional powers at the level of the central government, where economic growth and development concerns too often prevail over those of sustainability.

NOTES

1. *Ley 18695, Orgánica Constitucional de Municipalidades.* Santiago de Chile, 1992.
2. *Ley 19175, Orgánica Constitucional sobre Gobierno y Autoridad Regional.* Santiago de Chile, 1993.
3. Art. 13, *Ley 18695, Orgánica Constitucional de Municipalidades.* Santiago de Chile, 1992.
4. In the law the system is called *Sistema de Evaluación de Impacto Ambiental.*
5. COREMA stands for *Comisión Regional de Medio Ambiente.*
6. CONAMA stands for *Comisión Nacional de Medio Ambiente.* See below, section 3.2.
7. SEGPRES stands for *Secretaría General de la Presidencia.*
8. COREMAs are composed by the regional *Intendente*, the provincial governors, the regional secretaries (SEREMI) of the 13 ministers with environmental functions, four members of the Regional Council and the Director of the CONAMA's regional division. Each region has a Consultative Body made up of nine members among scientific experts and representatives of the civil society, in charge for two years and designated by the *Intendente* from a list provided by their own category associations: two environmental scientists, two from environmental NGOs, two from enterprises, two from labour unions and one is directly nominated by the *Intendente.*
9. It is quite interesting to observe that the law defines the maximum number of CONAMA's staff, that can be no more than 62 (art.88), reflecting the general intention of the lawmaker to reduce to small and lean all government institutions, including the environmental field.
10. The US Agency for International Development, for example, has provided funds to establish a database which can be used to monitor pollution trends. See Silva (1997).
11. However, this seldom happens because of the insufficient definition of 'environmental damage' provided by the Framework Law; environmental responsibility is often hard to recognize and many private entrepreneurs can take advantage of this ambiguity. Personal interview with Paola Escobar (Co-ordinator of Environmental Area of Santiago's Municipality), Santiago de Chile, December 2003.
12. Personal interview with Paola Escobar.
13. CODEFF stands for *Comité Nacional pro Defensa de la Flora y Fauna.*
14. CIPMA stands for *Centro de Investigación y Planificación del Medio Ambiente.*
15. Nowadays, the green groups seem to follow different paths: CODEFF practises a sort of conservative environmentalist action, emphasizing habitat protection and defence of wild areas, rather than an activist attitude. CIPMA, which under military rule headed strong protest activities, is turning into a centre of research and studies, moving away from protesting and closer to a consultative role in CONAMA's activity. Other smaller NGOs, like the 'Casa de la Paz' or the 'Fundación Terram' gained importance during the 1990s through their contribution in specific fields: the former emerged for an intense promotion of environmental education, the latter through research and scientific publications. Interviews with Gabriel Del Fávero, Paola Escobar, Claudia Blanco.
16. Personal interview with Gabriel Del Fávero.
17. Personal interview with Claudio Nilo.
18. *Comité Nacional para la Evaluaciòn sobre Medio Ambiente Antartico.*
19. Personal interviews with Claudio Nilo, Gabriel Del Fávero and Jorge Cáceres.
20. These instruments have been used in particular in the case of atmospheric pollution in Santiago and in mining activities. An area is defined as 'latent' if a pollutant's concentration is between 80 and 100 per cent of the standard limit (NCA), 'saturated' when NCA limits are exceeded. An area ia declared latent or saturated through a Decree of SEGPRES, and countersigned by the Health Ministry if the primary NCA is exceeded, or by another sectional competent ministry in the event of secondary standards.
21. Data show that decontamination efforts have been successful. However, the reductions in emission observed are basically due to the fact that existing sources switched from highly polluting coal and wood to liquid fuels. Additionally, in 1997 natural gas became available in the city, and most of the boilers switched to this new fuel.

22. Seventh Article of National Water Code.
23. Only a relatively small portion (35–50 per cent) of rights have been registered in the Real Estate Title Offices. Water rights have been based on facts rather than on formal law, that is, on the ability to prove that one has used water for many years.
24. Cited in Bjornlund and McKay (2002).
25. The free assignation of water rights is particularly serious in desert zones where water is scarce and mines can obtain as much water as they want, without paying for it.
26. Data from SISS, available on-line at http://www.siss.cl.
27. Water rates are negotiated by private companies and the SISS.
28. The efficiency indicators are: Sales and administrative expenses/Sales ratio; Return on Equity: Return on Assets; Operating income/sales ratio.
29. As demonstrated by lack of clear distinction among commercial, tourism and preservation norms.
30. In this field Chile is not only below world average but also below its 'peer group' average.
31. From an economic point of view, this tool, introduced in 1974, represented a great success for the firms and a profitable business for the government. This incentive can be considered an auto-financed investment to the extent that it generates an income tax revenue which in time could exceed the subsidy, and government could partially regain its contribute (Haltia and Keipi, 2000).
32. On this point, it is interesting to note that NGOs and a few forest companies have achieved a voluntary agreement to preserve native forest, with which the firms have pledged to avoid replacing native forest with exotic species (Fundacíon Terram, 2003).
33. The most emblematic example is the agreement between the Government and the US billionaire Douglas Tompkins for the creation of an enormous 'Santuario de la Naturaleza' in the Pumalin Park.
34. A specificity of the process of desertification in Chile is that it is caused by its agricultural and farming activities.
35. The law prescribes that development plans have to be compulsorily subject to SEIA analysis. Evaluation should give not only a yes/no type of judgement but also produce constructive suggestions. To this point, scholars are studying the introduction Strategic Environmental Evaluation (EAE) defined as the principle of EIA applied to policies, plans and action programmes. Actually, this tool has already been outlined in law but not yet implemented.
36. Personal interview with Federico Arenas (Professor of Geography at Catholic University of Chile) Santiago de Chile, December 2003.
37. See Yale Center for Environmental Law and Policy (2002).
38. These are the 'Squat Lobster Fishery' (*Pleuroncodes monodon*) since 1992; the 'Deep Cod' Fishery (*Dissostichus eleginoides*) since 1992; the 'Yellow prawn' Fishery (*Cervimunida jhoni*) since 1997; the 'Orange roughy' Fishery (*Hoplotethus atlanticus*) since 1999.
39. The body of law is wide and structured, even if some experts complain about the lack of competent courts and judges and a suitable database.
40. For instance, the main study on environmental conditions of Chile, 'Informe País: Estado del Medio Ambiente en Chile' is commissioned every two years to the University of Chile-Centro de Análisis de Políticas Públicas, in collaboration with UNEP.
41. Personal interview with Rosario Vial.
42. Personal interviews with Jorge Cáceres and Claudio Nilo.
43. Personal interviews with Claudio Nilo and Claudia Blanco.
44. Personal interview with Javier García.
45. Personal interview with Rosario Vial.
46. Personal interviews with Claudio Nilo.
47. Personal interview with Paola Escobar.
48. Personal interview with Claudio Nilo (Co-ordinator of Environmental Policies in the Executive Board of CONAMA), Santiago de Chile, November 2003.
49. It is interesting to note that revenues from sanctions are not used for environmental protection but are instead assigned to a Health Fund. Personal interview with Paola Escobar.

50. Personal interview with Oscar Godoy. Statistics on political participation are significant: in the 1989 free elections 88 per cent of the population were registered in electoral lists and went to the polls.
51. Personal interview with Oscar Godoy.
52. Interviews with Jorge Cáceres and Javier García. The Plan was approved after long discussions with citizen organizations, environmental NGOs and groups of scientific experts. Inside the CONAMA it is considered the symbol of the success of the system.
53. The RALCO incident may be taken as evidence of the deep contradiction existing in the realization of the Law's intentions. As a matter of fact, the strong opposition to a hydroelectric plant project by local communities and a great part of CONAMA's directorial board, was by-passed with the intervention of the President of the Republic; using a power assigned by the law, President Eduardo Frei intervened to change the composition and votes of the directorial board, firing project opponents and replacing them with others more sensitive to national business interests. The project envisaged the construction of a hydroelectric generating station in Region VIII by a Spanish enterprise called Endesa. Seven indigenous families of the Mapuche group protested against the construction of the dam, which would flood their ancestral homeland. The project was approved by CONAMA's board in June 1997.
54. Personal interview with Paola Escobar.
55. Personal interview with Paola Escobar.
56. Personal interview with Gabriel Del Fávero.
57. Personal interview with Gabriel Del Fávero.
58. Canada–Chile Agreement on Environmental Cooperation (CCAEC), one of the two Side Agreements to the Canada–Chile Free Trade Agreement (CCFTA).

BIBLIOGRAPHY

Ahumada, J. (1998), *Chile en los 90. El proceso de descentralización*, Santiago de Chile: Dolmen Ediciones/Presidencia de la Republica.

Bauer, C.J. (1998), *Against the Current: Privatization, Water Markets and the State in Chile*, Boston: Kluwer.

Bitrán, G. and E. Valenzuela (2003), 'Water services in Chile: Comparing private and public performance', in *Public Policy for the Private Sector*, no. 255, March, World Bank Group.

Bjornlund, H. and J. McKay (2002), 'Aspects of water markets for developing countries: experiences from Australia, Chile and the US', in *Environment and Development Economics*, Vol. **VII**, October, New York: Cambridge University Press.

Bocchetto, M. (1993), *Descentralización y participación social en la gestion local del medio ambiente*, Programa de Post-grado en Ciencias Sociales – Instituto Latinoamericano de Doctrina y Estudios Sociales, Santiago de Chile.

Borregaard, N. and J. Leal (2002), 'El caso de Chile', in J. Acquatella, *Desafios y propuestas para la implementación más efectiva de instrumentos económicos en la gestión ambiental de América Latina y el Caribe*, in *CEPAL Serie Manuales*, no. 18, Santiago: CEPAL Ed.

Carruthers, D. (2001), 'Environmental politics in Chile: legacies of dictatorship and democracy', *Third World Quarterly*, no. 22.

Centro de Análisis de Políticas Públicas (2000), *Informe País: Estado del Medio Ambiente en Chile – 1999*, Santiago, Chile: LOM Editorial.

Contreras, J.P. (2002), 'Norte de Chile: conservación de humedales altoandinos para un desarrollo productivo sustentable', *Ambiente y Desarrollo*, March, **XVII** (1), CIPMA Ed.
Del Fávero, G. and R. Katz (2000), 'Gestión Ambiental en Chile', in F. Larrain and R. Vergara M. (eds), *La Transformación Económica de Chile*, Santiago de Chile: CEP Ed.
Del Fávero, G. and R. Katz (2001), 'Gestión Ambiental: ¿Como Avanzar?', in H. Beyer and R. Vergara M. (eds), *¿Qué Hacer Ahora? Propuestas para el desarrollo*, Santiago de Chile: CEP Ed.
Dourojeanni, A. and A. Jouravlev (1999), 'El Código de Aguas en Chile: entre la ideología y la realidad', *CEPAL Serie Recursos Naturales e Infraestructura*, no. 3, CEPAL Ed.
Espinoza, G. (1999a), 'Logos, debilidades y Desafíos de la Gestión Ambiental', in *Gestión Ambiental en Chile: ¿Qué Tanto Hemos Avanzado? – Cuaderno del segundo centenario*, no. 9, Santiago de Chile: CED Ed.
Espinoza, G. (1999b), 'Uso de Principales Instrumentos de Gestión Ambiental', in *Gestión Ambiental en Chile: ¿Qué Tanto Hemos Avanzado? – Cuaderno del segundo centenario*, no. 9, Santiago de Chile: CED Ed.
Fundación Facultad de Derecho de la Universidad de Chile (1998), *Derecho del Medio Ambiente*, Congreso Internacional, Santiago de Chile: Editorial Juridica-CONOSUR Ltd.
Fundación Terram (2003), 'Acuerdo forestal: Cuando el mercado incorpora lo ambiental', *Análisis de conyuntura-Recursos Naturales*, no. 11, November, Santiago de Chile: Terrám Ed.
Gomez-Lobo, A. (2003), 'La regulación y la privatización del sector de agua potable y saneamiento en Chile', paper presented at WB Course on *Gestión Integrada de Recursos Hydrícos*, November, Buenos Aires.
Haltia, O. and K. Keipi (2000), 'Financiamiento de inversiones forestales en América Latina: el uso de incentivos', in Kari Keipi (ed.), *Politicas Forestales en America Latina*, Washington: BID.
Hartje, V., K. Gauer and A. Urquiza (1994), *Usos de Instrumentos Economicos en la Política Ambiental Chilena*, Bonn: GTZ.
Leal, J. (1996), 'Aplicación de instrumentos de política económica para la gestión ambiental y el desarrollo sustentable en America Latina y el Caribe', in Sunkel Osvaldo (ed.), *Sustentabilidad del Crecimiento Economico Chileno*, Santiago de Chile: Universidad de Chile.
Maggi, C. and Yoon Kern Soo (2000), 'Competitiveness and environmental policy: The case of Chile and Korea', INEF Report 42, Institut Für Entwichlung und Frieden, Duisborg.
Montenegro, S., D. Hervé and V. Durán (2001), *Los Tratados Ambientales: Principios y Aplicación en Chile*, Santiago de Chile: Imprenta Prograf Ltda.
Montero J.P., J.M. Sanchez and R. Katz (2002), 'A market-based environmental policy experiment in Chile', *The Journal of Law and Economics*, **XLV**(1), Chicago: University of Chicago Press.
Namuncura, D. (1999), *Ralco: Represa o Pobreza?*, Santiago de Chile: Ediciones LOM.
Peña Torres, J. (2002), 'Debates sobre Cuotas Individuales Transferibles: ¿Privatizando el mar? ¿Subsidios? o ¿Muerte anunciada de la pesca extractiva en Chile?', unpublished paper.

Pizarro, G.R. and C. Zolezzi (2003), 'Impactos ambientales del escape de salmonidos', in *Análisis de Politicas Publicas*, November, no. 22, Santiago de Chile: Terrám Publications.
Sabatini, F., C. Sepúlveda and H. Blanco (2000), *Participación ciudadana para enfrentar conflictos ambientales*, Santiago de Chile: CIPMA Ed.
Sanchez, J.M., S. Valdés de Ferari and B. Ostro (1998), 'Estimación de los beneficios en salud del Plan de Descontaminación de Santiago', *El Trimestre Economico*, July, **LXV**(3), Mexico City.
Sepúlveda, C. (1997), 'Incentivos para la creación y el manejo de Areas Silvestres Protegidas Privadas en Chile', *Ambiente y Desarrollo*, September, **XIII**(3), Santiago de Chile: CIPMA Ed.
Sepúlveda, C. (2002), 'Areas privadas protegidas y territorio: la conectividad que falta', *Ambiente y Desarrollo*, Vol. **XVIII**, Santiago de Chile: CIPMA Ed.
Silva, S. (1997), 'Democracy, market economics and environmental policy in Chile', *Journal of Interamerican Studies and World Affairs*, **38**(4), 1–33.
V Encuentro científico sobre el medio ambiente en la Universidad de la Frontera (Temuco) (1996), *Inserción Global y Medio Ambiente*, March, Santiago de Chile: CIPMA Ed.
Valenzuela Barros, J.P. (1996), *Descentralización fiscal: los ingresos municipales y regionales en Chile*, Santiago: CEPAL.
Valenzuela, E. (1999), 'La corresponsabilidad como factor para lograr un municipio con politícas de calidad de vida', in *Ambiente y Desarrollo*, March–June, Santiago de Chile: CIPMA Ed.
World Bank (1994), 'Chile: Managing Environmental Problems: Economic Analysis of Selected Issues', Report 13061-CH, World Bank Document.
Yale Center for Environmental Law and Policy (2002), *Pilot Environmental Performance Index*, New Haven: Yale University.

Interviews

Arenas, Federico, Professor of Geography at Catholic University of Chile, Santiago de Chile, December 2003.
Barrientos, Cristian, Co-ordinator of the Environmental Culture and Human Environment Area of the CONAMA Division in the II Region, Antofagasta, December 2003.
Blanco, Claudia, Chief of the Air Pollution area of CONAMA, Santiago de Chile, November 2003.
Cáceres, Jorge, Technical Director of CONAMA, Santiago de Chile, November, 2003.
Del Fávero, Gabriel, Lawyer specialized in Environmental Law, Santiago de Chile, November 2003.
Escobar, Paola, Co-ordinator of Environmental Area of Santiago's Municipality, Santiago de Chile, December 2003.
García, Javier, Technical Area's Assistant of CONAMA, Santiago de Chile, November 2003.
Godoy, Oscar, Professor of Political Science at the Catholic University, Santiago de Chile, December 2003.
Nilo, Claudio, Co-ordinator of Environmental Policies in the Executive Board of CONAMA, Santiago de Chile, November 2003.
Vial, Rosario, Member of the Fundación Terrám NGO, Santiago de Chile, December 2003.

APPENDIX: LIST OF ACRONYMS

Acronym	English	Spanish
ASPP	Private Protected Forest Areas	Areas Silvestres Privadas Protegidas
CESCO	Municipal Economic and Social Council	Consejo Economico y Social Comunal
CIPMA	Centre for Environmental Research and Planning	Centro de Investigación y Planificación del Medio Ambiente
CODEFF	National Committee for the Defence of Flora and Fauna	Comité Nacional pro Defensa de la Fauna y Flora
CONAEIA	National Committee for Antarctic Environment Evaluation	Comité Nacional para la Evaluación sobre Medio Ambiente Antartico
CONAF	National Corporation on Forestry	Corporación Nacional Forestal
CONAMA	National Commission on Environment	Comisión Nacional de Medio Ambiente
CONARA	National Commission of Administrative Rationalization	Comisión Nacional de Racionalización Administrativa
COREMA	Regional Commissions on Environment	Comisión Regional de Medio Ambiente
CPD	Coalition for Democracy	Concertación por la Democracia
DGA	Water Head Office	Dirección General de Aguas
DIA	Environmental Impact Declaration	Declaración de Impacto Ambiental
DIRECTEMAR	General Direction of the Civilian Navy	Dirección General del Territorio Marítimo y de Marina Mercante
EAE	Strategic Environmental Evaluation	Evaluación Ambiental Estrategica
EIA	Environmental Impact Assessments	Evaluación de Impacto Ambiental
ITQ	Individual Transferable Quotas	Cuotas Individuales Transferibles
NCA	Quality Environmental Standards	Normas de Calidad Ambiental
NE	Emission Standard	Normas de Emisión
NGO	Non-Governmental Organization	Organización No Gubernamental

Acronym	English	Spanish
SEGPRES	Minister of the General Secretariat of the Presidency	Secretaría General de la Presidencia
SEIA	System of Environmental Impact Assessment	Sistema de Evaluación de Impacto Ambiental
SEREMI	Regional Secretaries of the Ministers	Secretaría Regional de Ministerios
SERNAGEOMIN	National Geological and Mining Service	Servicio Nacional Geológico y Minero
SERNAPESCA	National Fishing Service	Servicio Nacional de Pesca
SISS	Superintendency of Sanitary Services	Superintendencia de Servicios Sanitarios
SNASPE	National System of Forest Protected Areas	Sistema Nacional de Areas Silvestres Protegidas
SNIA	National System of Environmental Information	Servicio Nacional de Información Ambiental
SPET	Tradable Permits System	Sistema de Permisos de Emisión Transables

12. China: Seeking meaningful decentralization to achieve sustainability

Changhua Wu and Hua Wang

> Without an understanding of the powers of various actors, the domains in which they exercise their powers, and to whom and how they are accountable, it is impossible to learn the extent to which meaningful decentralization has taken place.
>
> (Agrawal and Ribot, 1999)

1. INTRODUCTION

When China embarked on a process of reforms three decades ago, the country was governed by an extensive, functioning bureaucracy and had a centrally planned economy modeled generally on that of the Soviet Union. With reforming the economic and political system as its core mission, the Chinese leadership started to relax the tight state control in the early 1980s. Economically, the country began the transition from a state-directed, command-and-control economy to an economy that is more market-driven. As a result, significant economic authority was devolved to provincial and local officials; many political constraints were removed from local economic activities; and Beijing's ability to influence those activities and their outcome was greatly diminished. Politically, a similar transformation of institutions and authority also occurred. As Economy (2004) puts it, four distinct processes were set in motion: 1) The traditional culture of 'rule by man' was gradually replaced by a more institutionalized system with a codified system of laws; 2) significant political authority was devolved from Beijing to local officials; 3) China embraced technological assistance, policy advice, and financial support from the international community; and, 4) as government was further separated from the market, it also retreated from its traditional role as social welfare provider, while encouraging private, non-state actors to fill the gap in areas such as environmental protection.

The process of economic and political transformation has been further strengthened with China's integration into the 'global village'. Accession to WTO is the latest milestone where the government has had to agree to a further improvement in the transparency of law-and-policy-making process and to abide by the rules which govern the global trade union.

Against the backdrop of the swift and broad changes in the political and economic landscape is the continued deterioration of the country's environmental quality. This is reflected in the following facts:

- Air quality in many Chinese cities falls well below international and domestic standards. Of the 335 Chinese cities regularly monitored, over 40 per cent fell into Grades IV and V.[1] In other words, almost half of Chinese cities monitored are unsafe by Chinese Air Pollution Index (API)[2] standards.
- Nearly 700 million Chinese lack access to safe water and consume drinking water contaminated with animal and human waste that exceeds the maximum permissible levels for faecal coliform bacteria. The average annual availability of water is merely 2200 cubic meters of fresh water per capita (SEI and UNDP, 2002: 24).
- Over-extraction has reduced forest coverage on the upper reaches of the Yangtze from 30–40 per cent in the 1950s to only 10 per cent by 1998. Every year, over 1.1 million hectares, or about 1 per cent, of forest disappears due to over-extraction (SEI and UNDP, 2002: 19).
- Estimates from China's Red Data Book of endangered species show that more than one-tenth, or more than 500 vertebrate species and about 15–20 per cent, or about 4000–5000 species of higher plants are endangered, due to biotope destruction, pollution and wildlife trade (SEI and UNDP, 2002: 22).

The above-mentioned facts suggest that the reform process has had negative impacts on the environmental situation in China. However, the reforms have also changed the political landscape for environmental protection in positive ways. This is reflected in the increasing level of concern about the country's environmental problems seen amongst both the leaders and the public, efforts by the leaders to develop and improve a formal environmental protection apparatus both at the central and local levels, commitment to building a legal infrastructure for environmental protection, development of increasingly sophisticated laws and regulations, signing of international and regional environmental agreements, and provision of more political space for the development of environmental NGOs and a stronger civil society.

This chapter reviews the changes in environmental governance in China and the development and enforcement of environmental policies under the decentralized government system as well as the country's struggle to find the right mix or balance of decentralization and centralization in environmental governance. The purpose is to better understand the roles of various actors, the domains in which they exercise their powers, and to whom and how they are accountable. The attempt is to assess the extent to which meaningful decentralization has taken place in protecting the environment and natural resources in China and to examine ways to find the balance in the move towards a path of sustainability.

2. THEORETICAL FRAMEWORK FOR ASSESSMENT

The definition of decentralization varies in many cases. In this chapter we use the definition from WRI (2003) which states 'decentralization is the process where a central government relinquishes some of its responsibilities or powers to a local government, local leader, or community institution' (WRI, 2003: 90). Decentralization involves different kinds of power sharing, such as: '1) political or democratic decentralization, 2) administrative decentralization, 3) co-management arrangement, and, 4) community management' (WRI, 2003: 92).

Theoretically, the people who live closest to a natural resource stand to be most affected by its loss or altered state. They have a material interest in managing their environment's sustainability. This provides the rationale for decentralization – the steps that many central governments have been taking to give regional, municipal and local institutions responsibility for certain public sector functions, from forest management to the provision of waste disposal services – which is an important development in environmental governance (WRI, 2003: 89). However, decentralization does not rule out a strong role for the central government in resource management decisions. There are studies from around the world which show that control over natural resources only at the local level is rarely a recipe for environmental success (WRI, 2003, see Boxes). Communities themselves can decimate resources out of desperation, ignorance, through corruption or short-term profit-seeking. Natural resources require the active overseeing of many levels of government across many spatial scales (Larson, 2003: 211–26). This is because even though natural resources are located in specific communities, their management has wider repercussions, for instance as in the case of downstream impacts on water supply, regional air pollution, global climate change, and biodiversity loss. Local communities may overlook these concerns or be incapable of addressing them adequately.

Ideally, decentralization reforms seek to balance central government control and regulation with local input and empowerment. When effective, decentralization should bring government closer to the people and increase opportunities for citizens to take an interest in public affairs. But achieving decentralization's potential depends largely on how the reforms are designed and implemented (World Bank, 2000: 109).

To benefit the environment and improve equity in resource management and environmental protection, WRI (2003) set four minimum criteria that must be met:

1. Decentralization must result in a transfer of meaningful powers – including fiscal powers – to a local institution.
2. The institution to which power is transferred must be representative of the local populace in its diversity – not just elite interests – and have a broad knowledge of local natural resources and people's dependence on them.
3. The local public must be able to hold the institution accountable through elections, hearings or other democratic means.
4. Fiscal and regulatory incentives must be in place to promote sustainable management of natural resources over the long term.

Meeting all the four criteria is not easy. This chapter attempts to apply these four criteria to analyse the decentralization reforms, their implications for environmental governance, and the consequent impacts in China's case.

3. BACKGROUND: MAJOR STEPS IN DECENTRALIZING THE GOVERNANCE SYSTEM

To understand the evolution of environmental governance in China, it is important to fully grasp the changing landscape of overall government restructuring in the last couple of decades.

China has undertaken certain steps towards major reforms (Zhao, 1998) or decentralization reforms (Qiao, 2003) to meet the demands for transition towards a market-oriented economy during the last three decades. Fundamental changes in power structure and roles of actors in the political, economic and social platforms include introduction of the Household Responsibility System, dismantling of the collective ownership of agriculture, de-concentration and transfer of central authority to regional and local centers, and changes stemming from China joining WTO.

In 1978, the Household Responsibility System, in which each household is regarded as a basic economic unit to sign a land lease contract to conduct various economic activities, privatized use rights in rural areas by leasing agricultural land. Farmers initially received leases on their land for one to three years. Leases were lengthened to 30 and later 50 years in the following decades. In the early 1980s, the contract responsibility system was extended to forestlands and in the 1990s to grasslands. This basically dismantled the collective ownership of agriculture and radically altered the functions of government.

In 1982, the government passed legislation that devolved fiscal and economic decision-making responsibilities from the central and provincial to the county, township, and even village levels. Under the Fiscal Responsibility System, each level of government became financially independent, that is, responsible for raising and managing its own revenues. (Before 1980, local governments remitted tax revenues directly to the central government and awaited their partial return which depended on central discretion.) Fiscal decentralization meant new responsibilities for township governments.

In 1988, a new round of government restructuring focused on promoting the change in government responsibilities and functions. Economic management departments of the government were required to replace the direct with mostly indirect forms of management in order to increase administrative efficiency and to speed up administrative legislation.

The year of 1993 witnessed another round of government restructuring. The focus was on separating government from business, rule-making from implementation, strengthening supervision, and less direct management of enterprises. In 1998, the State Council was set up to establish a government administrative system that would effectively support China's socialist economic system. The basic principle guiding the changes in government structure was set forth as 'streamlining, unification and efficiency'. The assignments and divisions of responsibilities were modified in accordance with the principle of 'consistency of power and responsibilities'. And the legal construction of the administrative system has been strengthened according to 'ruling the country by law and governing by law' principle. These reforms were carried out at provincial, municipal and county levels in the following years. Indeed the 1998 reform has been regarded the most dramatic in terms of government restructuring.

The most recent reform in 2003 is one step further to improve the government administrative structure by setting up a much better developed administrative management system that is standardized, coordinated, transparent, clean and highly efficient. The main driving force for this reform was China's accession to the World Trade Organization. One highlight of this reform is separation of decision-making, enforcement and supervision. In addition to internal supervision of the administrative departments, it also emphasizes external input from the society, media, people's congresses and the political consultative conferences.

In comparison with many other countries in the world, China's progress in political democratization may seem limited; however, government restructuring has occurred six times which has had wide-ranging impacts. A closer look at the reforms shows that the number of government agencies has been declining and the functions of government agencies at different levels have changed dramatically. The government has gradually given up its controls over materials allocation, prices, and enterprise operation and management. State-owned enterprises have basically realized shareholder ownership, marketized operation and management. Private sectors have gained rapid growth and have become a strong pillar of national economic development. China has moved closer to a market economy.

Dramatic changes have also occurred at the operational level in the government. Legal forces play a role in all sectors. 'Rule by law' and 'administration by law' has become a basic requirement of government operation. Central government's powers have further devolved, while increasing attention is being paid to public participation in government public services. A government with limited powers, rule by law, multiple public power centers and transparency have undoubtedly created favorable conditions for China to move further towards political democratization.

4. FROM ENVIRONMENTAL AWAKENING TO THE CURRENT ENVIRONMENTAL GOVERNANCE SET-UP

China's environmental awakening came around 1972. In 1972, the country was hit hard by ecological disasters along the coasts of north-east and north China and in suburban Beijing when tainted fish from a polluted reservoir appeared in the city's market. In the same year, the first UN Conference on the Human Environment was held in Stockholm, Sweden. China sent a delegation to the conference. That year, China was still a very much 'closed' society in the middle of the Cultural Revolution turmoil.

4.1 Early Steps toward Environmental Governance

The 1972 UN Conference served to make the Chinese delegation realize that China shared problems of environmental degradation with the rest of the world. It was followed up, a year later, by the convening of the first National Conference on Environmental Protection in Beijing, and in 1974, the establishment of the Leading Group on Environmental Protection by the State Council. The Leading Group included officials from the ministries of planning, industry, agriculture, communications, water conservancy and public health. Its mandate was to study environmental protection issues. In the following nine years, however, the Group met only twice.

In the meantime, all provinces, municipalities and autonomous regions were required to establish organizations for environmental control, research and monitoring. Local governments also formed 'three wastes (waste gases, waste water and waste solids) offices' which had little bureaucratic authority, but nonetheless represented the first foray into institutionalized environmental protection at local level.

Through the mid-1970s, other small steps were taken to improve the environmental situation, including some environmental investigations by local officials. During this period, however, little real progress on environmental protection was made due to the political turmoil and large-scale development campaigns of the Cultural Revolution.

In 1978, the Chinese Constitution was amended to include concern for the environment. Article 26 says 'the state protects the environment and improves the living environment of the people and the ecological environment. The state prevents and controls pollution and other public hazards.' Article 9 states 'the state ensures the rational use of natural resources and protects rare animals and plants; appropriation or damaging natural resources by any organization or individual by whatever means is prohibited.'

In 1979, the National People's Congress (NPC), the country's legislature, approved the draft Law of the People's Republic of China on Environmental Protection. The Law, often regarded as the basic law for environmental protection in China, provided a clear definition of 'the Environment' and established basic principles to safeguard the environment and promoted the development of a legal network for environmental protection (Qu, 1989: 214–16). 'Environment', as defined by the Law, refers to the total body of all natural elements and artificially transformed natural elements affecting human existence and development, which includes atmosphere, water, seas, land, minerals, forests, grasslands, wildlife, natural and human remains, nature reserves, historic sites and scenic spots, and urban and rural areas. The environmental areas of responsibilities, according to the Law, include protection and improvement both of people's living environment and the ecological environment, preventing and controlling pollution and other public hazards and safeguarding human health. The Law further stipulates that 'the plans for environmental protection formulated by the state must be incorporated into the national economic and social development plans; the state adopts economic and technological policies and measures favorable for environmental protection so as to coordinate the work of environmental protection with economic construction and social development.' (Article 4)

Article 5 says that 'the state shall encourage the development of education in the science of environmental protection, strengthen the study and development of the science and technology of environmental protection, raise the scientific and technological level of environmental protection and popularize scientific knowledge of environmental protection.'

According to the Law, the department of environmental protection administration under the State Council shall conduct unified supervision and management of the environmental protection work throughout the country. The departments of environmental protection administration (EPBs) of local people's governments at or above the county level shall conduct unified supervision and management of the environmental protection work within areas under their jurisdiction.

The state administrative department of marine affairs, the harbor superintendency administration, the fisheries administration and fishing harbor superintendency agencies, the environmental protection department of the armed forces and the administrative departments of public security, transportation, railways and civil aviation at various levels shall, in accordance with the provisions of relevant laws, conduct supervision and management of the prevention and control of environmental pollution. The competent administrative departments of land, minerals, forestry, agriculture and water conservancy of the people's governments at or above county level shall, in accordance with the provisions of relevant laws, conduct supervision and management of the protection of natural resources. (Article 7)

With the legislative framework in place, China enacted a series of structural reorganizations designed to strengthen the environmental protection bureaucracy. These include:

- In 1982, the government created a Ministry of Urban and Rural Construction and Environmental Protection that incorporated the Leading Group on Environmental Protection. Many local governments followed suit, merging their environmental protection bureaux (EPBs) into new departments of urban and rural construction; however, during this process jobs were eliminated and the bureaux' already weak authority further diminished.
- In 1984, the State Council in effect acknowledged its mistake in abandoning the Leading Group and established the State Environmental Protection Commission to aid in cross-sectoral coordination. The Commission, composed of participants from more than 30 government ministries and bureaux, reviewed environmental policies, initiated new plans and organized environmental activities,

such as inspection, into local implementation of environmental laws (Qu, 1997: Preface).

- Later in 1984, the State Council also raised the profile of the Environmental Protection Bureau, elevating its status to the National Environmental Protection Bureau within the Ministry of Urban and Rural Construction and Environmental Protection, doubling its staff to 120 people, and enabling the agency to 'issue orders directly to provincial EPBs, decide upon and conduct its own meetings, and receive Ministry of Finance funds directly earmarked for environmental protection, rather than waiting for these funds to be channeled through the Ministry of Construction' (Jahiel, 1998: 769).
- In 1988, the Bureau achieved independent status from the Ministry and was reclassified as an Agency called the National Environmental Protection Agency (NEPA) with a bureaucratic rank below a ministry. It resumed direct reporting to the State Council.
- In 1989, the Standing Committee of the National People's Congress (NPC) formally promulgated the Law on Environmental Protection, which embraced four central principles: (1) coordination of environmental protection; (2) pollution prevention; (3) polluter responsibility; and (4) enhancement of environmental management (Qu, 1997: 7–9).

4.2 The influence of 1992 Rio Summit on Chinese Environmental Institutions

Between 1972 and 1992 when the Rio UN Summit was held, China experienced profound economic, political and social transformation. China achieved a miracle of continued and rapid two-digit economic growth. The 1989 Tiananmen Square event indicated the desire and demand among some leaders and the populace for further political openness and democracy. China increasingly became an important player in the international arena.

The most significant event that triggered certain fundamental changes in China's environmental governance was the 1992 UN summit on environment and development in Rio de Janeiro. The changes include the following:

- 'Sustainable development' was incorporated into the government's planning process, as an ideal and national strategy to guide the country's development.[3] In the aftermath of the UNCED, China became the first country to develop an action plan embodying the ideal of sustainable development.[4]

- The Western ideal of public participation and role of NGOs was recognized by Chinese leaders and merged into their concept of environmental governance. With the setting up of the first 'official' environmental NGO – Friends of Nature – in 1994, China was ushered into a period in which non-governmental organizations were reintroduced into Chinese society. In 1993, the government for the first time in history officially cited public participation as a goal in environmental protection.[5]
- Market-based instruments were reinforced as the basis for environmental policy reform, through such measures as pricing natural resources like coal and water.

Since the Rio Summit, China has undertaken a few other major steps towards strengthening of its environmental governance. These include:

- In 1993/1994, the Committee for Natural Resources and Environmental Protection was set up under the National People's Congress (NPC) to take responsibility for revising and drafting new environmental laws, assuring their rapid promulgation, and supervising their enforcement.
- The 1996 Decision of the State Council on Several Issues Concerning Environmental Protection[6] identifies the importance of public participation and the development of NGOs. It states, 'A mechanism for public involvement shall be established. Social organizations shall play their role. The public shall be encouraged to involve in environmental protection and to charge against or disclose any kind of illegal activities of violating environmental laws and regulations.'
- In 1998, NEPA was upgraded to ministerial status and renamed State Environmental Protection Administration (SEPA). SEPA's elevation to the status of a ministry clarified its position as the agency with overall responsibility for environmental management and protection in China.

5. THE NATIONAL LEVEL: STRUCTURE, ACTORS AND POWER ASSIGNMENTS

The Chinese Constitution sets the structural foundation for the Chinese state and the government. According to the Constitution, the Chinese state is a multi-layered institutional structure with territorial divisions at the center, province, city, county, township and village levels. It is composed of numerous government functional units (commissions, ministries, bureaux and departments), responsible for a diverse range of issues. These functional units exist at the national level and typically replicate themselves (or their functions) in a vertical chain through successively lower territorial levels of government. Individual functional units within this system receive administrative guidance from their parent units above them; and they are also subject to the leadership of the local governments to which they belong.

China has three major categories of governing institutions. First, the National People's Congress is the highest organ of state power in China. The National People's Congress and its Standing Committee exercise the highest power of the state. Second, the State Council, the Central People's Government of the People's Republic of China, is the highest level executive body, the highest organ of state administration. Third, the people's courts are the judicial organs of the state, and the people's procuratorates are state organs of legal supervision. The latter two are set up, supervised and accountable to the National People's Congress (see Figure 12.1).

5.1 Environmental Protection Apparatus

SEPA is a government agency that is directly affiliated to and supervised by the State Council. Environmental Protection Bureaux or Offices (EPBs/EPOs) through successively lower levels of the administrative hierarchy at the provincial, city, county, district, and in some places, township levels, are SEPA's replicas (see Figure 12.2).

The core agencies behind environmental governance in China include:

- The National People's Congress (Environmental and Resources Protection Committee is one of the specialized committees) which is the top lawmaking body.

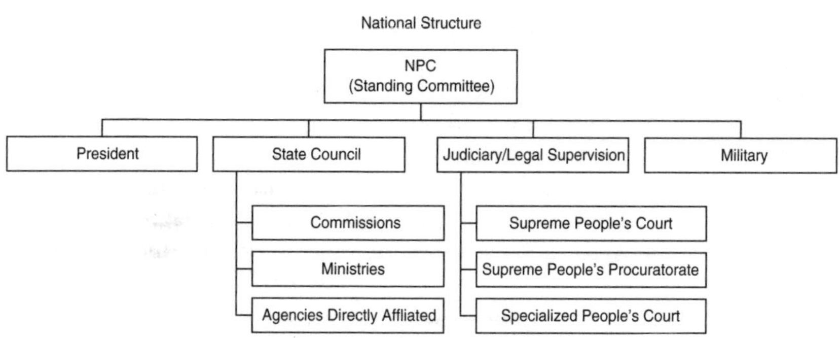

Figure 12.1 National government structure

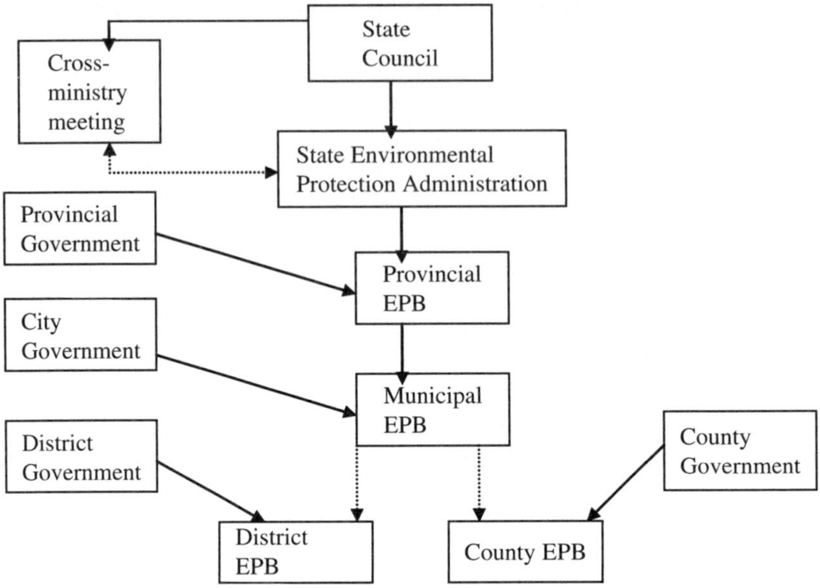

Figure 12.2 Structure of environmental authorities

- SEPA, which is the administrative or executive department with an assigned mandate of environmental protection.
- The Supreme People's Court, which is the judiciary branch.

Together these three agencies assume responsibilities for the full scope of central government activities, including drafting laws, monitoring implementation of laws and regulations, and enforcement.

5.2 Power Assignments among Government Actors

Within the State Council (or the Central Government), different responsibilities are distributed among different ministries and agencies (see Table 12.1). The State Council divides its members into:

1. Macro adjustment coordination and control, such as the State Development and Reform Commission (SDRC) and Ministry of Finance (MOF);
2. Specialized economic management, such as Ministry of Agriculture, Ministry of Construction, Ministry of Railways, Ministry of Communications, Ministry of Water Resources;

Table 12.1 Government agencies with environmental responsibilities under the state council

Responsible Areas	Actors	Examples
Macro coordination/ control	State Development & Reform Commission	State land use and protection Water resources and environment planning Nation-wide ecological/environ. construction Coordinate all economic sectors
	Ministry of Finance	Fiscal policy, control of state-owned
Specialized public agency	State Environmental Protection Administration	Pollution control Ecosystem protection Natural resource management Urban environmental management
Pollution control	SEPA	
	Ministry of Construction	Solid wastes, urban environment
	Ministry of Railways	Railway industrial pollution control
	Ministry of Communications	Marine (shipping) pollution control
	Ministry of Water Resources	Water quality, water body sink Total water pollutant control
	Ministry of Health	Drinking water quality
Ecosystem protection	SEPA	
	Ministry of Agriculture	Grassland, wetlands, agricultural Aquatic wildlife protection
	State Forestry Administration	Terrestrial biodiversity, land use, forest eco-construction Forest resource protection, land
	Ministry of Land and Resources	
Natural resource management	SEPA	
	Ministry of Land and Resources	Land, mineral and marine resources management
	Ministry of Water Resources	Water supply
	Ministry of Agriculture	Fishery, renewable energy, land
	State Forestry Administration	Timber and forest products Terrestrial wildlife resource use, forest farms, plantations

Table 12.1 (continued)

Responsible Areas	Actors	Examples
Others	Ministry of Science and Technology	R&D
	Ministry of Education	Environmental education
	General Auditing Agency	Environmental auditing
	General Customs Agency	
	Taxation	

3. Education, science, technology, culture, social welfare and resource management, of which Ministry of Land and Resources is one; and then,
4. Agencies directly affiliated to the State Council, like SEPA and State Forestry Administration among others.

A main limitation of the institutional framework in China is collaboration across sectors, which is essential for making progress towards environmental goals. As illustrated earlier, mandates run across several agencies, often with unclear division of responsibilities. SEPA, elevated to a ministerial-level agency directly under the State Council's administration, is much less powerful than many other agencies listed earlier. SEPA has a cross-cutting mandate and needs to collaborate to succeed. However, tough battles and competition for funding make horizontal cooperation among Chinese government bureaux difficult (see Box 12.1).

SEPA, since it was elevated to the status of a ministry, falls under the direct leadership of the State Council, from which it receives almost all of its funding. It is supported in its efforts to formulate national policy by the Committee on Natural Resources and Environmental Protection under the chief legislative body – the National People's Congress.

SEPA is replicated as Environmental Protection Bureaux (EPBs) or Offices (EPOs) down through successively lower levels of the administrative hierarchy at the provincial, city, country, district, and in some places, township levels. The chief responsibility of these local environmental units is to enforce laws and implement policies designed by SEPA and to assist in drafting local regulations to supplement central ones. EPBs and EPOs thus work directly with local factories and other polluters, as well as with industrial bureaux and local government actors.

BOX 12.1 SEPA's MANDATES

SEPA is authorized to conduct 'unified supervision and management of environmental protection throughout the country'. SEPA is given the following groups of powers:

A) Policy and Regulatory Functions

- Drafting guidelines, policies, laws, regulations and administrative regulations;
- Environmental assessment for important economic and technological policies, economic and development planning with the endorsement of the State Council;
- Drafting national plan for environmental protection;
- Drafting and supervising implementation of the plan for pollution prevention and control and ecological protection for key regions and basins identified by the state;
- Organizing formulation of the program for environmental function areas.

B) Enforcement

- Organizing enforcement of the pollution prevention and control laws and regulations in case of various pollutants;
- Guiding, coordination and supervising efforts towards marine environmental protection.

C) Supervision

- Supervising the exploitation of those natural resources with impact on ecological environment;
- Overseeing environmental protection efforts in various types of natural reservation zones, scenic and historic sights and forestry parks;
- Supervising biodiversity protection and natural resource management (e.g. desertification prevention and control);
- Making suggestions on establishing various kinds of new national natural reservation areas;
- Supervising national natural reservation areas.

D) Cross-cutting and regional issues' coordination

- Guiding efforts which deal with cross-cutting issues (across department, cross-provincial, etc.);
- Investigating and dealing with major environmental pollution accidents and ecological damage accidents;
- Resolving interprovincial environmental disputes;
- Organizing and coordinating efforts to prevent and control water pollution in national key basins;
- Being in charge of environmental supervision and environmental administrative assessment;
- Organizing assessing of enforcement of environmental protection laws.

E) Standards

- Formulating national standards for environmental quality and discharge;
- Documenting local environmental protection standards;
- Reviewing environmental protection within urban comprehensive plans;
- Publishing annual environmental protection reports and related documents (e.g. national sustainable development profile).

F) Environmental management and EIA

- Formulating and organizing implementation of regulations on environmental protection management;
- Examining and approving the EIA of major new construction events;
- Guiding urban and rural environmental protection comprehensive control;
- Being in charge of efforts of rural environmental protection and guiding the construction of national ecological pilot areas and promoting eco-agriculture.

G) R&D, Certification, and Environmental Industry

- Coordinating environmental science and technology, important research projects and technological pilot engineering;
- Guiding the development of the environmental protection industry;

- Managing the national certification on environmental management system and environmental labels;
- Building and organizing the qualification approval system on environmental protection.

H) Environmental Monitoring and Information Disclosure

- Supervising environmental monitoring, statistics and information, and formulating the regulations and norms on environmental monitoring;
- Organizing the setting up and management of national environmental monitoring network and national information network;
- Organizing, guiding and coordinating the efforts towards environmental education and publicity;
- Promoting the participation of public and non-governmental organizations in environmental protection.

I) Global Environmental Issues and International Conventions

- Formulating national principles for addressing global environmental issues;
- Managing international cooperation on environmental protection efforts;
- Taking part in coordination of major events on environmental protection;
- Participating in the negotiations on international environmental protection agreements;
- Managing and organizing coordination in the implementation of international environmental agreements;
- Coordinating and implementing foreign-funded environmental projects;
- Dealing with foreign affairs in relation to environmental protection with the endorsement of the State Council;
- Communicating with international environmental organizations.

J) Nuclear Safety

- Managing nuclear safety, radioactive wastes, nuclear materials, and formulating related guidelines, policies, laws and standards;

- Participating in emergency measures related to nuclear and radioactive accidents;
- Conducting unified supervision and management of the safety of nuclear facilities and utilization of electromagnetism radioactive effects, and development of mineral resources with radioactive contents;
- Supervising the safety of nuclear pipes and unclear pressure-bearing facilities.

5.3 Supranational Players: International Conventions and Multilateral, Bilateral and Regional Cooperation

China is the largest recipient of environmental aid from the World Bank, the Asian Development Bank, the Global Environmental Facility, and Japan. The international community has supported China in virtually every aspect of its environmental protection work (Economy, 2004: 21–22) – the development of a legal system, monitoring systems for air pollution, exploring energy alternatives to coal, and so on.

China is currently a signatory to nearly 30 international environmental conventions under the auspices of the UN, and has reached cooperative agreements with many countries on multilateral, bilateral and regional bases.

5.4 International and Domestic NGOs

Although China's legal framework does not promote the creation of NGOs in the Western sense, environmentally oriented NGOs, still limited in scale, are beginning to provide Chinese society a medium/forum for expressing environmental concerns and for effecting change. Many Chinese NGOs have official governmental sponsors who guide them through the registration process and provide political cover and support for their work. There are mostly two kinds of environmental NGOs: 1) fairly independent NGOs, and 2) government-organized NGOs.

5.5 Institutes and Think-tanks

Recent years' explosion of international academic exchange and the involvement of Chinese experts in environmental development cooperation projects have helped create an atmosphere of more independent, critical thinking among research institutes and think-tanks. For instance, the Rural Development Institute of the People's University in Beijing is one of many educational institutions that combine academic research and rural development project experience in China's interior.

There are also a number of institutions that play an important role in building and extending environmental management systems within Chinese industry. The China National Cleaner Production Center, under SEPA, is an example of institutions that carry out consultancy business in the field of environmental auditing, cleaner production, and setting up of ISO 14000 systems.

6. THE LOCAL LEVELS

China has a centralized power structure and an administrative hierarchy which runs through from the center to provinces, cities, counties, towns and a number of other organizational units. The central government, however, has far less influence over the provinces than what could be expected from such a highly centralized governance system. We look at local-level governance next.

6.1 Local Governments

Local people's governments are established in provinces, autonomous regions and municipalities directly under the Central Government, counties, cities, municipal districts, townships and villages. They are the executive bodies of the organs of the state powers as well as local organs of state administration at the corresponding levels. Local people's governments at different levels practice the system of overall responsibility by governors, mayors, county heads, districts heads, township heads and village heads (see Figure 12.3).

Local governments at and above the county level conduct administrative work concerning the economic sector, education, science, culture, public health, physical culture, urban and rural development, finance, civil affairs, public security, judicial administration and family planning in their respective administrative areas; issue decisions and orders; remove and train administrative functionaries, appraise their work and reward or punish the staff. They carry out the resolutions by the people's congresses at the corresponding level as well as the decisions and orders of the state administrative organs at the next higher level and conduct administrative work in their respective administrative areas.

Local governments at and above the county level direct the work of their subordinate departments and of people's governments at lower levels, and have the power to annul inappropriate decisions of their subordinate departments and people's governments at lower levels.

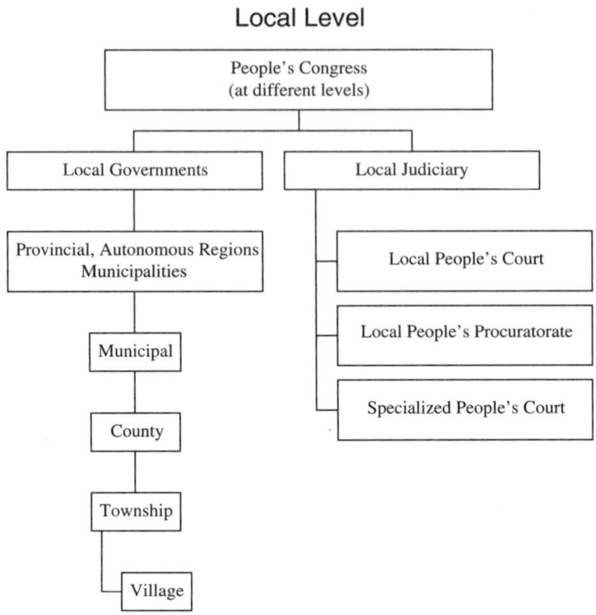

Figure 12.3 Local government structure

People's governments at provincial level, in provincial capital cities and in larger cities approved by the State Council, can stipulate local rules and regulations. Auditing bodies are established by local governments. Local auditing bodies at different levels independently exercise their power to supervize through auditing in accordance with the law and are responsible to the people's governments at the corresponding level and to the auditing body at the next higher level.

6.2 Local Environmental Governance

Local governments have been given not only the authority necessary to reform local industries, but also the power to control financial resources at the local level. As a result, local governments have attained new bargaining powers, which have led to a tendency to sidestep or ignore rules handed down by the central government. Since pressures on local governments to promote economic growth are enormous, central environmental authorities have difficulties imposing environmental regulations, which often, justifiably, are seen as impediments to local economic development. It is not always quite clear who is in authority – the central or the local level – and the picture is further muddled by the existence of various local, provincial, and central regulations, guidelines, standards, and other more or less legal documents. SEPA, being a central authority with limited power, and without provincial or local representatives, has particular difficulties in promulgating environmental regulations. The result is that provincial and local units bluntly ignore SEPA's decrees.

The 1990s saw a significant worsening of the gap between SEPA's declining staff resources and the widening mandate assigned to it. This gap extends to EPBs at the provincial level. None of the reforms of the 1990s addressed the critical issue of budgets and financing to underwrite the operations of SEPA and the EPBs. The funding of supervision and monitoring activities is inadequate. The organizational structure of environmental administration is very susceptible to interference by local leaders.

In 1989, the Law on Environmental Protection established the 'environmental responsibility system'. In theory, this placed the responsibility for environmental protection in the hands of local officials, who would work together with local EPBs to improve local environmental quality. The officials must sign responsibility contracts with local EPBs which outline specific environmental goals and pledge to work jointly to achieve these targets. Investment decisions, experiments with new policy tools, engaging the public, and establishing linkages with international actors all fell within the portfolio of these leaders (Economy, 2004: 117). Further efforts were made to address the so-called 'horizontal–vertical' issue, in which lower-level EPBs report to higher-level EPBs, and ultimately SEPA, but receive their budgetary resources from the local government. Appointments to head local EPBs must now be endorsed by a higher-ranked environmental agency.

Lower-level EPBs were strengthened, either by lifting their bureaucratic status or by giving them independent bureaucratic status. As of 2000, all 31 provincial EPBs were independent agencies and 30 of them were first-tier institutions; all city-level EPBs were independent agencies, and most were first-tier; about 70 per cent of county EPBs were independent; and about 1422 environmental protection units were established at the township level (World Bank, 2001: 99–100).

6.3 Factors affecting Local Environmental Governance

As mentioned at the beginning of the chapter, the goal of decentralization should be to achieve an appropriate level of local input within a strong central framework of national environmental policy. In China's case, despite a highly decentralized system of environmental protection, lack of a strong central apparatus has generated rather wide gaps in environmental governance among different localities. In her research on devolution of authority that affects local environmental governance, Economy (2004: 115–18) identified certain major factors that have deeply influenced how environmental issues are perceived and handled at local levels.

- Environmental awareness of and commitments from local officials – a more environmentally proactive governor or mayor tends to work more closely with local EPBs and make more commitments to improving local environmental quality. For instance, Zhongshan, Shanghai, Dalian and Xiamen have had mayors who have made the environment a top priority and have been recognized for their environmental protection efforts and achievements. Their EPBs also possess enough clout (thanks to mayoral support) to persuade other local bureaux to engage in cooperative activities.
- A province or city's wealth largely determines the resources it can devote to environmental protection. Shanghai with GDP per capita of $4500 and Xiamen with $5000 devoted approximately 3 per cent of their local revenues to environmental protection in 2002. In 2003, Shanghai's mayor was determined to increase the share to 5 per cent of local revenues apportioned to environmental protection. By contrast, Sichuan, a province in southwest China, with a per capita GDP of $576 in 2000, devotes barely 1 per cent of its local revenues to environmental efforts.
- China's top environmental cities are also closely linked with the international community, including various cooperation efforts with the World Bank, Asian Development Bank, and industrialized countries such as Japan, Germany, Norway, the Netherlands, and so on. For instance, Dalian receives a lot of support from Japan to assist its urban planning, establishing environmental priorities and pollution monitoring. Shanghai is now working closely with the World Bank to deal with its water supply and management system.
- The overriding objective of economic growth at the local level fails to provide incentives for local government officials to invest more in environmental protection. Local officials gain legitimacy by increasing incomes, ensuring low unemployment rates, and maintaining stability. Improving the local environment offers few rewards to them. This 'incentive' structure may even apply to EPB staff. The result is that local officials often shun environmental protection responsibilities (Lieberthal, 1997: 3–8).

7. DISTINCT ISSUES AND ENVIRONMENTAL POLICIES IN THE DECENTRALIZED ENVIRONMENTAL GOVERNANCE SYSTEM

7.1 The Household as the Basic Unit to Manage Natural Resources in Rural China

The Household Responsibility System, established in early 1980s, privatized use rights in rural areas by leasing agricultural land. Farmers initially received leases on their land for one to three years. Leases or land tenures were lengthened to 30 and later 50 (or 70) years in the course of the following decades. The farmers now have increased leeway to trade contracts and pass on land tenure rights to heirs. In the early 1980s, the contract responsibility system was extended to forestlands and in the 1990s to grasslands, and households were granted use rights to barren lands (family plots) through an auction system (Zuo and Xu, 2001). This basically dismantled the collective ownership of agriculture and radically altered the functions of government.

The government hoped the System would improve farmers' stewardship of natural resources but it was widely judged as having failed to do so in the early stage. This can be seen in the widespread incidence of grassland destruction and desertification, deforestation, soil erosion, salinization, land pollution and biodiversity loss. For instance, estimates of the level of overgrazing in China range from about 30 per cent above the carrying capacity in northern China as a whole to 15 per cent in Qinghai, 60 per cent in Inner Mongolia, 130 per cent in north Shaanxi, 150 per cent in northwest Shanxi, and a staggering 250 per cent in Ningxia (SEI and UNDP, 2002: 18). Excessive use of chemical fertilizers and pesticides causes serious soil pollution. According to a survey by the Ministry of Agriculture, almost 20 per cent of inspected livestock products fail to meet state contamination standards. Pesticide residues have been found in more than half of the foods grown and produced in suburbs of large cities (Shao and Deng, 2000).

Since the government's agricultural policy has changed many times during the past 40 years, farmers lack confidence that they will retain long-term tenure over the land and therefore are unwilling to invest in long-term improvements. Instead, they concentrate on increasing short-term yields through the heavy application of chemical pesticides and fertilizers. Meanwhile, economic liberalization and market reform, in tandem with the dismantling of collectives and privatization of land rights, have hastened environmental degradation. Farmers hastened to cut trees on their allotted lands to sell on the free market (William, 1994: 13–30).

The abandonment of collectivized agriculture and adoption of the Household Responsibility System which allocates agricultural lands, forestlands and grasslands to individual households on long-term leases, also completely reconfigured the set of actors involved in local resources management and subsequently created new interests that got represented in local decision-making forums.

The Household Responsibility System was followed by a broader strategy of decentralization in decision-making. In 1998, two laws, established for the first time the election of Village Committees and village leaders. These laws provide for new natural resources management responsibilities to be allocated to the Village Committees (Zuo and Xu, 2001). Their purpose is to strengthen the basis for participatory decision-making at the grass-roots level. The Committees may develop their own regulations for community natural resources management as long as they are in full compliance with the Chinese constitution and laws, and with the regulations and policies of the county.

The village is the lowest administrative level in the Chinese system; the next lowest level is the township, followed by the county, prefecture and province. During roughly the same period that village decentralization took place, the central government increased township authorities' power to manage natural resources. In 1994, stations for forestry, agricultural extension, irrigation management, water and soil conservation that were previously at the county level were transferred to the township. A law providing for greater independence in township financing and staff management increased townships' discretion in using their own funds, although such funds are relatively limited compared with the resources available to higher levels of government (Zuo and Xu, 2001).

Barrier: inadequate inter-agency cooperation and inter-jurisdictional coordination

The reforms so far have failed to improve environmental management in many parts of the country because management at the ecosystem level is inadequate. Although these governance problems are not unique to a decentralized policy environment, the national and provincial governments have clearly focused their attention on allocating responsibilities to lower levels without strengthening the coordinating and supporting structure for sound environmental governance at the watershed levels, as shown by a case study in Baoshan of Yunnan Province (Zuo and Xu, 2001).

The case study revealed that government agencies fail to cooperate within the same watershed to preserve and protect clean water flows and appropriate land use. For example, flooding caused by upland soil erosion and deforestation is inadequately monitored and managed. Meanwhile, villages give priority to micro, not macro, issues. Stakeholders lack the capacity to address serious conflicts over natural resources between upland and lowland communities. These failures indicate the need for mechanisms to resolve natural resource-related conflicts.

7.2 Devolving Fiscal Decision-making Responsibilities

In 1982, the government passed legislation that devolved fiscal and economic decision-making responsibilities from the central and provincial to the county, township and even village levels. Under the Fiscal Responsibility System, each level of government became financially independent, that is, responsible for raising and managing its own revenues. Fiscal decentralization meant new responsibilities for township governments. However, the tax structure also ensured that the majority of revenues would accrue to upper levels of government, leaving townships insufficient monies to carry out their development mandates (Zuo and Xu, 2001).

Much upper-level government revenue became available to lower levels through a project-based system. Integrated inter-governmental groups now decide on project priorities. Even counties do not have the capacity to develop projects, so project planning takes place at the prefecture level or above. Given the size of resources at stake in the project system, it could be said that a major part of the development planning process has therefore been decentralized to a level that is still large in its geographic scope.

In the context of fiscal decentralization, the emergence of privately owned Township-and-Village Enterprises (TVEs) has been both economically and environmentally significant. These enterprises create a major source of revenue for cash-strapped local authorities. Therefore, local governments have been willing to turn a blind eye to the heavy pollution they produce. TVE-led mining, food processing, refinery, and paper and pulp making have transformed the landscapes of the country's wide countryside and exacerbated the pollution of air, water and land resources (William, 1994).

After realizing the weaknesses of fiscal decentralization, when the central government could barely collect enough money for its coffer, the national government reversed its previous policy by tightening control over local revenues and expenditures in the late 1980s and early 1990s. Part of the practice now is to assign a percentage to each province in accordance with its economic capacity and capability to collect revenue for the national coffer.

7.3 Strengthening the Framework of National Environmental Policy

Although not quite at the same level as economic growth or poverty alleviation, environment is firmly a national priority. Sustainable development is designated the 'guiding principle and strategy' for the country's social and economic development. Green GDP is gaining popularity over traditional GDP as a measure of real development. The new leadership in China now pursues a coordinated development of economy, society and its citizens.

Over the decades, the government has mostly followed three approaches to addressing environmental challenges. In the early years, the government responded to key national issues, such as acid rain or soil erosion, through targeted administrative and technical measures. This 'campaign' approach was inherited from the Mao era. It was the central policy instrument then, but it has continued to color the way the government perceives how to meet various challenges to this day. However, since China embarked on the reforms since 1979, the leadership has been committed to the second approach, wherein a legislative and regulatory framework forms the basis for government action. The third approach relies on market forces and market-based instruments. This has been growing in importance along with the formulation of the 'socialist market economy' that now constitutes a basic philosophy in the Chinese reform efforts. The government has continually revised and strengthened its institutional framework for environmental management in order to implement these approaches.

Very recently, the government has recognized the value of information and public access to information as a powerful tool to help attain environmental goals. Since the promulgation of the first Environmental Protection Law in 1979, China has adopted and enacted more than 20 statutes on pollution control, natural resource conservation, and human health and safety. In addition, dozens of regulations, procedures and initiatives, as well as hundreds of standards have been passed. On the basis of the legislative and regulatory development, a framework of national environmental policy has emerged in China. Table 12.2 (World Bank, 2001) is an example of various policy instruments employed in China to tackle industrial pollution problems.

Market reform has been the hallmark of the changes that China has undergone over the last couple of decades which has brought about substantial efficiency gains. China's GDP has increased faster than major emissions, reflecting a positive environmental effect from market reform.

The Chinese government sees the value of employing the market to make environmental protection profitable and motivate a knowledgeable population to control compliance and environmental quality. Among the experiments with market-based instruments are the polluter-pays principle and pollution levy system, taxation, pricing energy and water, and emissions trading.

There is still a long way to go before environmental governance through market-based instruments will make its effects widely felt in China. To a

Table 12.2 Current framework for industrial pollution management and control in China

Command-and-control instruments	Economic incentives	Voluntary instruments	Public disclosure instruments
Concentration-based pollution discharge limits Mass-based controls on total pollution discharge EIA Three synchronous policies Limited time treatment Two compliance policies Environmental compensation fees	Pollution levy fee Non-compliance fines Discharge permit system Sulphur emission fees (experimented) Emission trading (experimented) Subsidies for energy-saving products Regulation on refuse Credit for high-polluting firms	Eco-labeling system Promotion of ISO 14000 system Cleaner production	Clean-up campaigns Environment awareness campaigns Information disclosure (mandatory/voluntary)

large extent, the economic boom of the last two decades has occurred at the expense of the environment, and a considerable part of the economic growth has been generated in an economic environment where entrepreneurs have benefited from cheap inputs of materials and labor, without having to pay for effluent discharges or workers' health.

Thus, in a sense, China is trapped in between the worst of two worlds: on the one hand, a socialist heritage of under-priced natural resources and free right to pollute, and, on the other, an unrestrained embrace of a market economy, where, as Deng Xiaoping stated 'it is glorious to be rich' (SEI and UNDP, 2002: 42).

7.4 Building a Checks-and-balances Mechanism of Accountability

The year of 1993 witnessed the beginning of a decade-long, more aggressive, governance reform in China. The legal construction of the administrative system was strengthened according to 'ruling the country by law and governing by law' principle. Similar reforms were carried out at provincial, municipal and county levels in the following years. The governance reform was furthered in 1998 and 2003 with emphasis on standardization, coordination, transparency and high efficiency of government administration.

At the core of the reform is separation of decision-making, enforcement and supervision. In addition to internal supervision of the administrative departments, it emphasizes taking into account 'outside' input from the society, media, people's congresses and the political consultative conferences.

At the community level, the Organizational Law on the Villagers' Committee provided a guiding framework for direct election of Village Committees to oversee village-level natural resources management. The new laws encouraged the development of village regulations for resources management. Overall, the reforms have created a situation in which the highest scope for public participation and representation is at the village level, where almost no financial resources exist. Far more financial resources remain at higher levels of government, where officials are still appointed.

At the national level, in recent years, access to information and participation in decision-making processes has been gradually recognized as important in order to ensure an informed citizenry which is needed to check against corruption and to hold the governors accountable for the governed. For instance:

- The State Council of China issued a Guideline on Implementation of Moving Forward Governing by Law on All Fronts.[7] While identifying the goals of governing by law, which include openness, Article 10 of the Guideline states that except for those that fall within the scope of State secrets, as well as business secrets and personal privacy that shall be protected in accordance with the law, government agencies shall disclose government information and guarantee the public's rights to inspect any of the information disclosed by the government.[8]
- Since 1999, stronger legal guarantees for public access to government information and decision-making have been enacted, in particular, the Administrative Penalty Law, the Administrative Reconsideration Law and the Administrative Permit Law. For instance, the Administrative Penalty Law of China stipulates that an 'announcement system' be implemented in government law enforcement to inform the public of the procedures of law enforcement, working standards and legal liabilities. Without it, the public could simply decline the legal decision.[9] The Administrative Permit Law requires that the government agency publicize any regulations related to administrative permits. Without such a step, the concerned regulation shall not be used as the basis for administrative permit.[10] Except those that fall under State secrecy, business secrets or private privacy,

the implementation and results of administrative penalties, reconsideration and permits shall be made public.[11]

- The development of internet technology has made public access much easier and efficient. All government agencies now in China run websites, which disclose all the information in accordance with law.
- The Administrative Permit Law contains one Chapter on Public Hearing, which promulgates that government agency shall make public announcement and hold public hearings for those matters that shall be decided through hearing in accordance with laws and regulations, or those that the administrative agency thinks important which involve the public's interests.[12] The Law also states that hearings shall be held publicly[13] and the public has the right to inspect and check any records of agencies' oversights and inspections.[14]

The Law of Promoting Cleaner Production mandates polluters to disclose related information to the public through mass media. The upcoming Regulation on Public Access to Information lays the foundation for public access to environmental information. China's State Environmental Protection Administration has also announced its decision on access to government environmental performance and enterprises' disclosure of environmental information. An accountability mechanism of checks-and-balances is now gradually emerging in China.

7.5 Deepening Integration with International Actors

Global changes in ecology and in political economy are beginning to foster devolution of some power and authority away from the nation-state and toward greater reliance on supranational, regional and local levels of governance. International environmental conventions and agreements, and multilateral, bilateral and regional cooperation are a few typical examples of how this works out.

China plays an active and dynamic role in the preparation and implementation of international environmental conventions. China has ratified all relevant environmental conventions – with obligations under more than 80 bilateral and multilateral environmental treaties. Premier Zhu Rongji reinforced China's commitment to assume responsibilities related to the reduction of greenhouse gases when, on 3 September, 2002, at the World Summit on Sustainable Development, he announced that China was moving forward with ratification of the Kyoto Protocol of the Framework Convention on Climate Change. The process of ratifying and implementing global conventions has been influential in placing environmental issues high on the national political and development agenda. Furthermore, these accords often provide needed financial and other support for the development and implementation of domestic environmental laws by domestic institutions.

By signing a convention, China commits to taking measures leading to the protection of environmental resources, including current state assessments, sharing of information, engagement in international cooperation, preparation of national action plans, and integration of environmental protection with general development plans and programs. China is held accountable to the international bodies in charge of the convention implementation, such as UNEP.

Active collaborations are also carried out at multilateral, bilateral and regional levels as well as with NGOs.

8. BEYOND ENVIRONMENTAL GOVERNANCE

The Chinese government has clear environmental policy goals that were most recently articulated in former President Jiang Zemin's speech at the 16th Communist Party Congress in 2003. Sustainable development was identified as one of the three key pillars of the strategy to build a 'well-off society in an all-round way'. An essential element of this objective is to address 'the growing contradiction between the ecological environment and natural resources on the one hand, and economic and social development on the other'.

Over the last three decades, the environment has been given increasing priority. In the 10th Five-Year Plan (2001–2005), sustainable development is designated the 'guiding principle and strategy' for the country's economic and social development. The Plan also identifies environmental protection as a national priority. Although not quite at the same level as economic growth or poverty alleviation, environment is firmly a national priority.

8.1 Interconnections

With sustainable development and environment high up on the national agenda, one would expect an integration or coordination mechanism to be in place between environment and other State policies. However, the reality tells a different story. As indicated earlier, the State Council used to have an Environmental Protection Commission, set up in 1984, to aid in cross-sectoral coordination. But the Commission was disbanded in 1998 when SEPA was elevated to a ministry and the Commission's role of coordination was transferred to SEPA. The dissolution of the Commission removed a potentially important forum for encouraging collaborative work on cross-cutting environmental issues and for resolving jurisdictional disputes.

Experience in other countries also suggests that SEPA, as a second rank (non-cabinet) ministry, will not be able to carry out this role effectively.

In China, SEPA is challenged by its mandate to coordinate, as it is below ministerial level in many respects, and is considered somewhat of a 'newcomer'. Moreover, it is often perceived by enterprises, local governments and production-oriented ministries as an environmental policeman trying to limit economic growth. Faced with these reactions, SEPA often develops a defensive attitude, and sticks to issues it feels most comfortable with – those which can be addressed without collaboration with other agencies.

On paper, it is required that all major economic development policies in China are subject to an environmental impact assessment to minimize adverse impacts on the ecological environment. But in reality this does not happen; questions like who will do it, how to do it, how the assessment will impact on the policies, and so on remain unanswered.

Lack of interconnections can be further explained by an example in the area of ecological conservation. Many government agencies and departments are involved and have a mandate, such as SEPA, SFA, MOA, MOWR, but many of them have conflicting interests and they are, more often than not, driven by the need to promote their own interests. Without the State Council's EPC-like organ in place, there exists no linkage or connection among the plans made by those agencies, let alone that some agencies have conflicting mandates, such as SFA which is in charge of both conservation and exploitation of forests.

8.2 General Powers

As part of its efforts to strengthen environmental law enforcement, the government revised its Criminal Law a few times in order to punish violations of environment and resources protection laws and regulations and damage to the environment, property and public health. The implementation of many environmental policies, such as pollution prevention and control, and natural resources protection, has been strengthened consequently. The current Law's Section 6 of Chapter VI is specifically designated to 'Crimes of Undermining Protection of Environmental Resources'. Three to seven-year prison terms and monetary penalties are specified for any violation of the state's stipulations against discharge, dumping or disposal of radioactive wastes, hazardous wastes, and other dangerous substances into the environment. Violation of laws or administrative regulations on the protection of aquatic resources, illegal hunting and killing of specially protected species, illegal occupation of or serious damage to forestland and cultivated land, illegal logging and mining, and so on is penalized accordingly.

Table 12.3 Import and export of environment-related goods

Name	Agency
List of Goods Prohibited to Be Imported	Ministry of Foreign Trade and Economic Cooperation (MOFTEC)
List of Wastes Used as Raw Materials and Restricted in Importation	MOFTEC, General Administration of Customs, State Administration of Quality Supervision, Inspection and Quarantine, SEPA
List of Waste Used as Raw Materials under Automatic Import License Category	SEPA, MOFTEC, etc.
List of Machinery and Electronic Products Subject to Automatic Import License	MOFTEC, etc.
List of Goods Subject to Import License	MOFTEC, etc.
List of Goods for Which Quota, License and Specific Import Administration Measures are Eliminated	MOFTEC
List of Goods Prohibited to Be Exported	MOFTEC
Announcement on Prohibiting Export of Black Moss	MOFTEC

The Criminal Law has provided law enforcement agencies with stronger teeth and more power. However, facts show that in order to implement the law fully, a tremendous burden falls on the shoulder of victims – to collect proof – in order to make a case. The success of implementation has proved to be patchy so far in China.

Another general power is trade and commerce. Globalization and China's opening up mean that China is increasingly interacting with its neighbors and with the rest of the world. Trade and commerce are growing at an unprecedented rate. All those interactions are playing important roles in driving environmental and social changes in China. China has developed a series of specific laws and regulations on environmental protection in imports and exports, and general trade (see Tables 12.3 and 12.4).

A number of important multilateral environmental agreements include trade provisions (see Box 12.2).

In addition there are a series of environment-related provisions in the legal instruments on China's accession to WTO. Those are China's commitments to abide by various environment-related requirements as a member of WTO. The aim of WTO is to establish international competition globally under equal conditions. To be competitive, Chinese industry

Table 12.4 Import and export of hazardous chemicals

Name	Agency
Circular on Strengthening the Management of Hazardous Chemicals	SEPA, MOFTEC, Ministry of Public Security, etc.
Provisions on Environment Management of the First Import of Chemicals and the Import and Export of Toxic Chemicals	NEPA, MOFTEC
Standards of Registration Fee for Environment Management of Chemical Export and Import	NEPA
Circular on Renewal of Registration of Environment Management of First Import of Chemicals	SEPA

BOX 12.2 TRADE PROVISIONS IN MULTILATERAL ENVIRONMENTAL AGREEMENTS

- Basel Convention on the Control of Transboundary Movement of Hazardous Wastes and their Disposal
- Amendment to the Basel Convention
- Rotterdam Convention on the Prior Informed Consent Procedure for Certain Hazardous Chemicals and Pesticides in International Trade
- Stockholm Convention on Persistent Organic Pollutants
- Framework Convention on Climate Change
- Kyoto Protocol to the UN Framework Convention on Climate Change
- Montreal Protocol on Substances that Deplete the Ozone Layer
- Convention on Biological Diversity
- Cartagena Protocol on Biosafety
- Convention on International Trade in Endangered Species of Wild Fauna and Flora
- Agreement on Fish Stocks
- International Tropical Timber Agreement
- Convention on the Ownership of Cultural Property
- Rio Declaration on Environment and Development
- Agenda 21
- Statement of Principles on Forests

has to become more efficient, which, at least in the long run may lead to improved utilization of resources, conservation, and the import/use of cleaner, efficient technologies.

8.3 Use of Scientific Expertise in the Decision-making Process at Different Levels of Government

The existence of independent and reliable sources of quality advice is crucial to sound decision-making, especially when it comes to the complex issues surrounding sustainable development. In the past, technical and academic institutes were part of or under the supervision of government ministries or agencies, gathering information for those agencies. Not surprisingly, the advice produced in these institutes had been carefully tuned to follow 'their master's voice', with the result that any notion of potentially adverse effects was routinely brushed under the carpet.

Recently, due to the government restructuring and reform, many of these institutes enjoy increased levels of independence. This, combined with strengthened capacities, means they are now in a position to give objective and even challenging advice to decision-makers.

Another aspect of the growing numbers of more independent expert institutions is that a competitive market for environmental knowledge and services is being formed, where government agencies procure decision support such as studies, investigations and feasibility studies on a contractual and, increasingly, also competitive basis.

Finally, the growing pluralism in the technical and academic sectors has improved the opportunities for Chinese institutes to network and collaborate with research institutes and consultancies around the world. Chinese institutes have begun taking part in bids for overseas consulting as well as international research assignments.

Table 12.5 looks at SEPA as an example to illustrate the sources of scientific expertise.

8.4 Offences to Ecosystems across Jurisdictions

The economic activities of China and its enterprises have an impact on both the regional and global environment. Although no detailed studies of China's ecological footprint have been undertaken, five relevant areas can be named: 1) greenhouse gas emissions; 2) biodiversity; 3) transboundary pollution; 4) domestic consumption; and 5) Chinese overseas investment. To cite an example, increasingly severe dust storms resulting, in large part, from desertification occurring throughout China, have played havoc with air quality and transportation in China and neighboring countries such as

Table 12.5 Sources of scientific expertise

Category	Example
Internal Research Center	Policy Research Center of SEPA
General	Chinese Academy of Sciences Chinese Academy of Social Sciences
University	Tsinghua University Beijing University Renmin University Tongji University Fudan University
Environmental Academy	Chinese Academy of Environmental Sciences Chinese Academy of Environ Planning Nanjing Academy of Environ Sciences Wuhan Academy of Environ Sciences Guangzhou Academy of Environ Sciences
Independent Think-Tanks	South North Institute

the Republic of Korea and Japan. Plumes of dust from these storms have even been identified in the mainland United States, reportedly transported via the jet stream.

One positive aspect of these 'global' environmental concerns is that they have served to motivate, in large part, meetings between high-level government officials in the affected countries to discuss possible solutions to China's progressive environmental problems. In 2002, for instance, the environmental ministers of China, South Korea and Japan met in Seoul for the 4th Tripartite Environment Ministers Meeting. The discussions were mostly focused on the problems of 'yellow dust' emanating from China. South Korea initiated the Meeting in 1999 as a means to address transboundary pollution originating in China. Since then, the meetings have evolved to address other environmental issues of mutual concern.

Bilateral and multilateral cooperation has been the typical way that China works with other countries to protect the environment along the border areas. The Mekong River Watershed Management Committee is a regional organization with members from Southeast Asia along the Mekong River. Though China has not become an official member of the Committee, the River has its origins in China's southwest Tibet-Qinghai Plateau and China sits right up there on the upper reaches. What China does along the watershed and how China plans to utilize the water resources at the upper reaches have a major impact on the river itself as well as the development of those countries along the middle and lower reaches of the river. This mechanism brings the stakeholders together to discuss how to work together to protect the watershed while pursuing economic growth.

Other examples include the China/Russia collaborative program to protect the Usuri River; China/Myamur/Laos cooperation on trafficking in endangered species, among others. However, it may be noted that there exist many problems in those mechanisms, such as lack of financial support, weak enforcement, as well as endemic corruption in many countries that negatively affect the outcomes of those mechanisms.

8.5 Incomplete Information

The conventional way of decision-making in China does not really consider much risk, uncertainty or incomplete information. Under the culture of 'rule by man', the decision-making process is more or less influenced or controlled by some individuals instead of a scientifically-based process. The situation is changing these days, with 'rule by law' gradually replacing 'rule by man', and an increasing awareness of the importance of basing decisions on science.

Risk management is gradually being adopted by many policy analysts and scientists when providing policy support and recommendations to the decision-makers. Still relatively new, risk analysis and risk management is now included in many decision-making processes, in particular when there is incomplete information, such as environmental health effects and developing standards.

8.6 Contractual Arrangements

The responsibility system has been used by SEPA to hold local decision-makers accountable for the environmental quality in China. Governors and mayors are evaluated in their performance partly by the environmental improvement and quality of their jurisdictions. Through this kind of contractual power, SEPA seeks to ensure that many environmental policies are successfully implemented at the local level.

9. CONCLUSIONS

There is no doubt that China is facing a major environmental challenge. If GDP growth continues at or near 8 per cent into the short- to medium-term future, urbanization continues and possibly even accelerates, and industrialization continues to move towards production of more highly transformed products, the scope and dimensions of the environmental agenda will continue to grow and become more complex. To grapple with these challenges effectively, China needs to maintain its current decentralization reform process. The reform process, generally, has had a positive impact on the evolution of environmental governance. Though reform in the economic and public administration and governance spheres has progressed unevenly, the environmental payoffs are generally great.

Continued reform of public administration towards good governance for sustainable development is essential in order to stimulate economic reform, and is a required basis for enhancing the environmental legislative framework and ensuring its implementation. The developing cadre of more efficient public officials at the national level and across China, with increasingly clearer duties and responsibilities, and with a commitment to the rule of law, is necessary for safeguarding the environment. A further deepening of this process, with clarifications and separations of duties, from national to local levels, and between agencies at the same level, will yield impressive results. Notably, SEPA's and EPBs' efforts to strengthen capacity need to be maintained.

In the meantime, limited experiments in governance reform show that empowering and liberalizing the will of people, within a regulated and monitored framework, can release a strong and comprehensive positive force for environmental change, which can complement rather than threaten government objectives and actions. Notably, experiences in China and other countries suggest that the media and NGOs could be strong weapons in the future. Related to this, continuing progress on ownership structures – notably the ownership of productive units, of profits and liabilities – is facilitating and stimulating improved behavior within enterprises. Likewise, experiments show that land tenure systems can make or break efforts to safeguard forests, grasslands and agricultural lands.

The reactive approaches of the past will not be sufficient to address the challenge China faces. The government needs to become more proactive on the environmental agenda. Given the substantial and growing tension between development policy and the environmental agenda, the government needs to strengthen the consideration of environmental factors in policy development and comprehensive environmental supervision of all elements of the government's work. The government should maintain its strong commitment to the environmental agenda.

In the particular case of SEPA, it should be further elevated to be a member of the State Council to ensure that the government's environmental concerns are taken into account on all aspects of development policy. SEPA's institutional capacity, including staffing level, should be significantly increased to bring it more into line with relevant international competitors.

An inter-agency coordination body should be established. The lack of cross-sectoral coordination is commonly seen to be at the heart of critical development problems facing the government. This is apparent in water resources management, urban planning, forest sector management, product-related environmental measures, and many other related sectors. This dimension of the government's functioning needs to be significantly strengthened. This body should align its functions more closely with the government's sustainable development objectives.

Conflicts of interest within natural resource management agencies between resource development and resource protection need to be solved. The allocation of environmental regulatory authority between the different levels of government should be reviewed, and measures should be taken to correct oversight at a lower level by higher levels. The good work on ensuring public participation already done by the government needs to be extended to provide a greater role for the people in the formulation of the environmental laws, as well as the EIA process and other relevant environmental decision-making activities.

NOTES

1. World Health Organization (WHO) has developed a set of guidelines for air quality on the basis of health impacts. Chinese government has also developed its own domestic air quality standards from Grade I to V, measuring the level of air pollution from best to worst.
2. The API is developed to indicate general air quality as a function of the levels of sulphur dioxide, nitrous oxides and other suspended particulates. The State standards system is based on the API, with Grades I and II being considered suitable for long-term living conditions, Grade III acceptable for short-term exposure, while Grades IV and V are unsuitable for human life.
3. In China's 5-year planning cycle, sustainable development was adopted as a national strategy to guide the country's economic, political and social development in the medium- and long-term.
4. China's Agenda 21 was modeled on the UNCED's global Agenda 21. It incorporated input from over 300 ministries, commission and local governments, and totaled 128 projects.
5. China in 1993 specifically included public participation in the EIA process for construction projects undertaken with loans from international financial organizations, as stated in the 'Notice on Strengthening Management of Environmental Impact Assessments in Construction Projects Undertaken with Loans from International Financial Organizations' (SEPA, 1993).
6. The State Council, 3 August, 1996.
7. The Guideline is based on two precedents: 1) governing by law was added to the Constitution in 1999; and 2) the State Council issued Decision on Moving Forward Governing by Law on All Fronts in November of 1999.
8. The Guideline is available only in Chinese.
9. The Administrative Penalty Law of China, Article 5.
10. The Administrative Permit Law of China, Article 5.
11. All the three administrative laws contain this provision.
12. Article 46 of the Administrative Permit Law.
13. Article 48 (2) of the Administrative Permit Law.
14. Article 61 of the Administrative Permit Law.

REFERENCES

Agrawal, Arun and Jesse Ribot (1999), 'Accountability in decentralization: A framework with South Asian and West African cases', *Journal of Developing Areas*, **33**(4), 473–502.

Economy, Elizabeth C. (2004), *The River Runs Black: the Environmental Challenge to China's Future*, a Council on Foreign Relations Book, Ithaca and London: Cornell University Press.

Jahiel, Abigail (1998), 'The environmental organization of environmental protection in China', *China Environmental Quarterly*, December.

Larson, Anne (2003), 'Decentralization and forest management in Latin America: Towards a working model', *Public Administration and Development*, **23**(3).

Lieberthal, Kenneth (1997), 'China's governing system and its impact on environmental policy implementation', *China Environment Series*, No. 1.

Qiao, Mu (ed.) (2003), *Interpreting the New Government: Policy Direction of the Crucial Issues Related to National Economy and the People's Livelihood*, Beijing: Chinese Communist Party History Press.

Qu, Geping (1989), *Environmental Management in China*, Beijing: Chinese Environmental Science Press.

Qu, Geping (1997), *We Need A Transformation*, Changqun: Jilin People's Publishing House.

SEPA – State Environmental Protection Administration of China (1993), *Notice on Strengthening Management of Environmental Impact Assessments in Construction projects undertaken with Loans from International Financial Organizations*, Bejing.

Shao, Wenjie and Min Deng (2000), 'Survey found excessive pesticide residues in large Chinese cities', *Guangming Daily*, 13 June.

Stockholm Environment Institute (SEI) and UNDP (2002), *China Human Development Report 2002: Making Green Development a Choice*, Hong Kong: Oxford University Press (China) Ltd.

William, Bridget (1994), 'Environmental concerns as China modernizes', *Journal of Northeast Asian Studies*, **13**(3),13–30.

World Bank (2000), *World Development Report 1999/2000: Entering the New Century*, New York: Oxford University Press.

World Bank (2001), *China Air, Land and Water: Environmental Priorities for a New Millennium*, August, Washington, DC.

World Resources Institute (WRI) (2003), *World Resources 2002–2004: Decisions for the Earth – Balance, Voice, and Power*, Washington, DC.

Zhao, Libo (1998), *Reform of Government Administration, China Perspectives towards the 21st Century*, Jinan: Shandong People's Press.

Zuo, Ting and Jiancu Xu (2001), 'The impact of decentralization and local participation on upland watershed management I Yunnan, Southwest China', *REPSI Working Paper*, Washington, DC: World Resources Institute.

13. The Danish communes: Capacities and constraints in environmental management

Mikael Skou Andersen

> No 'Invisible Hand' can be relied on to produce a good arrangement of the whole from a combination of separate treatment of the parts. It is, therefore, necessary that an authority of wider reach should intervene and should tackle the collective problems of beauty, of air and of light, as those other collective problems of gas and water have been solved.
>
> (Pigou, 1932: 195)

1. INTRODUCTION

Local authorities still play a significant role in the implementation of national environmental policies when looking at the situation in terms of local environmental administrative tasks and resources. Basic services with regard to pollution control (wastewater treatment, waste management, nature protection) administered locally in the majority of EU countries account for 80–90 per cent of total public expenditure directed at environmental policy. Efforts to integrate environmental policy into other policy sectors have, moreover, led to further local authority involvement. For example, the restructuring of EU agricultural policy has been increasingly based on local area planning and has, thereby, been placed within the realm of local and regional authorities.

Having acknowledged this fundamental role, a tendency in favour of new types of management instruments exploiting channels other than those of local authorities is to be observed over the past decade. These comprise market-based instruments, such as environmental taxes, voluntary agreements, producer responsibility schemes, environmental certification, environmental auditing and environmental impact assessment (EIA). These new management instruments have been criticised for pushing genuine local environmental administration into the background. When, for example, a voluntary agreement between the government and one or more industry branches is entered into, local authorities' traditional task of environmental regulation of companies is eroded. Other state-level management instruments represent more a supplement to local authority initiatives. However, introduction of these would seem to a certain extent to reflect that local authorities, in themselves, are not able to secure a satisfactory level of environmental protection.

Some qualification is, however, required as experience and tendencies vary between different countries. While Denmark has moved from a highly decentralised model towards a more centralised one, Swedish and Norwegian environmental reform has tended to move in the opposite direction. In a period where the pendulum swinging between state and local administration in Denmark is out of sync with other Nordic countries, this chapter can be regarded as a collection of reflections and experiences gathered in Denmark, a country which is sometimes described as the EU's most decentralised member state.

Denmark has an administrative tradition for local administration and decentralisation which is stronger than that found in other Nordic countries. As a consequence, the local municipalities enjoy considerable autonomy. They impose their own local income taxes and although they also receive grants from the state, local income taxes represent the most important source of revenue, comprising 35 per cent of total income tax revenue (Strukturkommissionen, 2004). Few other countries in the EU allow local authorities such a significant share. The municipalities and counties also have broad discretionary powers within the realm of the law. While Stockholm decides the books to be used in Sweden's primary schools, this issue has remained a local matter in Denmark, to be decided upon by teachers, school councils and the municipal authorities. In environmental policy, many guidelines do not directly bind the local authorities, and enforcement is primarily a responsibility for the municipal authorities. The tax collection powers provide the municipalities with a clear interest in increasing local employment, so as to increase their own revenues. For the environment such a clear development interest has often led to the sacrifice of amenity values and natural resources. The circumstance that the tax collection powers provide more opportunities for service delivery (for example in waste and sewage control) serves to balance the overall performance of municipalities. A dividing line seems to exist between service delivery (well executed) and regulatory competence (leniently administrated). The latter have more and more been shifted to the regional level, to the counties.

The roots of decentralisation in Denmark are to be found in the constitutional conflict that took place in the late nineteenth century between Copenhagen's ruling class, on the one side, and farmers and smaller landholders struggling for independence and local self-governance, on the other

(Mørch, 1982). The poet, priest and educator, N.F.S. Grundtvig, was a main inspiration for the farmer's movement. A Conservative government dissolved Parliament with a rule by decree in the 1890s; however, the farmers eventually seized power in both Houses of Parliament in 1901. Since that time, profound scepticism among farmers directed against Copenhagen has given way to a marked decentralisation of competencies to local authorities in the majority of public services. A further source of inspiration for decentralisation came from German town governments (Gunlicks, 1986). As workers and Social Democrats had outnumbered farmers by the 1930s, the preference for local self-governance had become institutionalised and the tradition for delegation was continued – also thanks to the influence of the landholders' party, the Social Liberals.

Denmark has been acknowledged to have had a profound degree of environmental change during the 1990s (OECD, 1999). The domestic expansion of windpower, a unilateral carbon energy tax and an activist approach at the international level helped increase Denmark's reputation as a pioneer in sustainable development. Yet, more analytical comparisons on the basis of extensive environmental datasets have frequently ranked Denmark well below other small European states, when attempting to measure environmental performance (Scruggs, 1999). CO_2-emissions per capita in Denmark are in fact similar to the level in the USA, a key reason being the fossil fuel-based power generation sector – with utilities under municipal ownership. That there are strong vested interests at the local level, which tend to counterbalance the pioneering tendencies in national environmental policy-making, will be further spelled out in this chapter.

2. SOME GENERAL REFLECTIONS ON THE CLASSICAL ISSUE OF CENTRALISATION VS. DECENTRALISATION

The question of which roles local and national authorities should play in environmental management represents a classic problem. Environmental problems were from the outset conceived as issues that are inherently *local* in their nature. Pollution affects local watercourses and rivers, and lack of sound waste disposal impacts the countryside. As an area of *low politics* it has been customary to entrust environmental responsibilities to the lowest level of public administration. Yet, factors which challenge the wisdom of this approach have been present long before globalisation of environmental policy-making emerged.

Nigel Haigh (1994) has described how, when England adopted its (and Europe's) first air pollution law in the 1860s, a wide and lively debate unfurled among legislators and experts regarding the appropriate level of authority. One approach was that local authorities should constitute the responsible administrative level, as they had been in relation to the, then, Hygiene Law. Another approach felt that a national air pollution inspectorate should be set up, in the same way that, in 1833, a factory inspection body had been established. A careful compromise resulted; the local authorities were to be the responsible authority except in the case of technically complex installations, for which a national air pollution inspectorate was to be established. In this way, shared responsibility became the norm for air pollution regulation in England.

This discussion and outcome could be interpreted as a result of the rather centralised administrative tradition of imperial Britain, and hence as a deviant case of less relevance for generalisation. Yet, even in countries with a federal/confederate administration, the early assignment of environmental powers was not unequivocally in favour of local municipalities. In the former Prussia, use of the local authority level to regulate sewage discharges into the Rhine and the region's other waterways had, in fact, already been abandoned by the turn of the last century. Towns situated upstream on the larger rivers did not take sufficient interest in establishing treatment works, with the result that surface and drinking water in towns lower downstream was spoiled. This tendency prevailed despite the fact that around 1870 early technologies had been developed for the treatment of wastewater. A landmark court ruling in 1904 against the town of Essen led to a new assignment of competence. Local municipalities were required to hand competencies over to regional administrative structures, and a system of regional water catchment management was established. The new and independent authorities began to manage water pollution financed by discharge levies, moreover in direct cooperation with industry.

These two examples indicate that it may be misleading to conceive the assignment of environmental powers as an issue which has only surfaced in recent years. The lively debate that has taken place in the EU regarding the subsidiarity principle in environmental management has indeed early precedents, though defining reasonable administrative boundaries and distinguishing between which environmental issues should be administered locally and which at regional or national level remains a thorny issue. The subsidiarity principle would seem to imply that local authorities should take responsibility for local environmental problems, regional authorities for regional problems and national authorities for national problems – while the EU as a supranational institution should occupy itself mainly with transboundary environmental problems. Yet, these spatial divisions are challenged by asymmetry between the beneficiaries and the burdened in issues of environmental protection, and may explain why the EU has had relatively limited success with application of the subsidiarity principle in environmental policy-making.

The increasingly transboundary nature of environmental issues is often put forward as a reason describing why local authorities have come under pressure; however, there is, in itself, little new in that environmental problems cross boundaries. The German example above describes how externality conflicts among various local authorities had already existed at the turn of the century, as they also did between countries – with, for example, air pollution coming from England producing black snow in Norway (Reitan, 1997). It is, therefore, not an especially recent experience that allows us to observe that local authorities, despite being assigned responsibility for environmental management, will often choose to allow extra-territorial externalities due to the economic benefits associated with these benefits exceeding the share of the externalities incurred locally.

The learning process in public administration appears to be marked by vicious circles, both in general and in the field of environmental policy. Institutional rigidities are apparent in regulatory policy-making, and in the environmental area this tendency is perhaps being reinforced. The issues relating to the allocation of administrative tasks between authorities are pushed into the background by more acute environmental issues, to which environmentalists prefer to draw society's attention.

Hence, the increased pressure that the local authority level comes under today is hardly a result solely of the existence of more innovative administrative approaches. Nor is it a result of scientific advances in our understanding of the global nature of environmental problems. Pressure on local authorities needs rather to be seen as stemming from two further sources; on the one hand, *financial pressure*, in that local authorities often do not comprise economically effective administrative units and, on the other hand, *market-determined pressure*, as the industrial ecological modernisation process does not thrive in interaction with local authorities. This is hardly an observation that is confined to Denmark alone.

3. STRUCTURED OR ADAPTIVE IMPLEMENTATION

Local authorities are normally charged with ensuring implementation of rules or norms established on a national level. As such, the local authority is subordinated in relation to instructions and regulations from superior authorities. There is, nevertheless, not a traditional subordinate relationship, since local authorities are led by political organs, with a direct mandate from the local electorate. Precisely this political legitimisation leads, through national legislation, to local authorities' being allowed certain discretionary powers to weigh up the national requirement against prevailing local conditions. These discretionary powers can, however, vary a great deal.

In the literature, two types of implementation methods are distinguished from each other; the structured and the adaptive approach (Berman, 1980). In structured implementation, national legislation typically regulates local authority behaviour in detail, for example, via establishment of binding standards, deadlines and procedures. In adaptive implementation, national legislation simply establishes the framework for local authority activities, leaving responsibility for filling in the detail with the local authority, itself.

The structured approach is typical for federal systems and can be illustrated with the USA's Clean Air Act, where Congress, in an attempt to avoid 'capture' of the regulatory authorities, described the legislation in minute detail. The law, in fact, prohibited the American Environmental Protection Agency (EPA) from negotiating with interested parties, and mandated it to establish purely health-based requirements for the air quality level to be achieved locally. In the field of the environment, the structured implementation method is most frequently observed in federal systems, where several layers of regional and local authorities coexist. The approach seems to reflect an attempt on the part of the legislator to minimise the risk for lost focus under implementation. For this reason, the structured implementation method is also apparent in the Federal Republic of Germany, just as a number of detailed EU environmental directives can be seen as an expression of this method.

With adaptive implementation, more popular in small unitary states, only a framework for the local authority's regulatory tasks is legislated for. Legislation establishes an organisation, an allocation of authority between the authorities and some general principles for the local administration, but leaves it with the regional and local authorities, potentially in cooperation with each other, to manage the more detailed implementation and explicit details of the legislation. The Danish Environmental Protection Law represents a typical example of such an adaptive implementation through broad framework legislation, where various stakeholders have also had the opportunity to play a key role in establishment of environmental protection. National standards for emissions of harmful substances have primarily been in the form of optional guidance notes, and it has been left to the local authorities to evaluate these against the prevailing conditions in the local receiving environment. This differs from the German approach, where standards for Best Available Technology are fixed by the regulators at national level, giving rise to the paradox that the German air pollution standards (TA Luft) which are used by the Danish EPA only have guidance status, whereas in Germany they are binding.

Implementation research reveals that implementation problems are to be expected, regardless of which of the two implementation approaches are practised. Pressmann and Wildawsky (1973) showed the determining significance of the implementation process itself. According to the so-termed 'bottom-up' approach, implementation problems can be explained by, amongst other things, the implementing authorities' having their own agenda influenced by issues other than those arising from the law in question. Environmental legislation represents just one among the many sectors of legislation which local authorities are charged with putting into operation. Moreover, local authorities are confronted with specific local problems and considerations. Within this complex implementation scenario, the execution of environmental legislation represents just one aspect of the local authority workload, and attention as well as resource allocation represents only a proportion of total available resources. This consideration can be led further to include considerations of the street-level officer who puts the actual rules and decisions into practice (Lipsky, 1980). The street-level bureaucrat has, similarly, many different tasks within his field of responsibilities. Even where he is employed full-time within a department devoted, for instance, to the environment, inspection will be likely to comprise only one area of his workload, alongside, for example, issuing pollution permits, local planning and rodent control. By way of this, accompanied by lack of resources, a field officer may come to develop survival strategies, for example, to put too much weight on dialogue and compromise in consultations with local polluters. Evidently, this is just as relevant whether a field officer is employed in a decentralised or a deconcentrated administration.

Nevertheless, implementation via local authorities does not simply represent a bureaucratic control problem, but also a political problem. The local authorities have an interest in, amongst other areas, local employment and tax revenues, which means that they can benefit from adapting implementation. Often, this can be done in a way which is not directly illegal, but which scarcely matches the spirit of the legislation. Even under structured legislation there will be a grey area in legal implementation, which makes it possible for a local authority to protect its own interests, while upholding that the law has not been breached. This grey zone is relatively more significant with the adaptive implementation method, however.

With these theoretical distinctions in mind we can now turn to the Danish experience.

4. THE 'MUNICIPALISATION' OF ENVIRONMENTAL MANAGEMENT IN DENMARK

When, in 1973, Denmark passed its first environmental protection act, it was modelled on that in Sweden; however, the Danish version became significantly more decentralised on key points. Firstly, the local authorities, the municipalities, came to play a more significant role in Denmark, while Miljøstyrelsen (the Environmental Protection Agency) came to enjoy fewer powers than its counterpart, Naturvårdsverket, in Sweden. Tasks originally intended for the regional level were awarded to the municipalities. The guidelines and instructions issued by the Environmental Protection Agency were not to be binding for the municipal environmental permit and licensing system, and even the largest companies would obtain their environmental permits from the municipalities. Municipal decisions could be appealed against in an Environmental Appeal Board, with the Minister for the Environment being afforded an additional 'call-in' authorisation to reverse decisions made locally. During the legislative decision-making process, though, he had to promise not to use this tool and, in practice, the appeals body has been seen to guard the autonomy of the municipalities.

This 'municipalisation' of the environment was an innovative feature of the reforms of the 1970s. Previously, local commissions for hygiene and agriculture had responsibility for environmental tasks, according to the watercourse law of 1949, among others. The new powers awarded to municipalities occurred in extension of the 1968 municipal reform, where larger and more powerful municipal units were created. The newly established Ministry of the Environment acquired its top civil servants from the Ministry of the Interior, where the work on municipal reform had just ended. The driver in this process was the widespread consensus which prevailed in Danish society on the role municipalities should play in the building up of the welfare state, and in Parliamentary debates leading up to the new legislation, no one raised questions about the potential conflict between local economic interests and environmental interests. On the contrary, the Environmental Protection Act was equipped with a special paragraph explicitly charging local authorities with balancing the environment with the economic interests of both companies and society.

The role of municipalities was apparent in all areas of pollution control, from water and air to waste management. Even in chemical policy, one of the innovative features of reform in the 1970s was a collection system for hazardous waste, to be organised by the municipalities under the umbrella of their national association. As a result of this development, a national incinerator for hazardous waste was established under municipal control.

Only forest management remained administered by a deconcentrated state management system, relying on the Agency for Forest and Nature Protection and its local districts. This tradition dates to the forest law of 1805, passed as Denmark had lost its entire fleet in wars with England, and the state needed control with wood production.

In the early years of environmental reform it soon became apparent that municipalities, first and foremost, regarded their environmental duties as confined in particular to the establishment of sewage treatment works and waste disposal – in a way, this was well in line with extension of the welfare state's traditional service institutions. It is fair to say that the municipalities were fairly successful with this service delivery, although sewage treatment was not at the most advanced level. Waste disposal by incineration was seen as a lever for self-reliance in energy supply.

However, broader regulatory tasks, such as control and approval of pollution from local companies, were not tasks that the municipalities were experienced with. According to the law, permits were required in connection with companies who expanded production or established new facilities; however, the efforts on the part of the municipalities were notably reactive. Permits were given to those companies which approached the municipalities themselves, and inspection took place mainly in response to complaints.

A general problem soon arose in connection with the steady stream of rules and guidance on environmental issues from the state authorities, which the local authorities lacked the capacity to deal with. The following quotes stem from a report prepared for the Danish Environmental Protection Agency, but not formally published – it surveyed the role of municipalities in environmental administration, and quoted local officials as stating:

> If we should be able to read all the material we receive from the EPA, we would almost have to employ a person exclusively for reading. He would not then be able to be disturbed with enquiries, and so it wouldn't matter if he read it or not.
>
> Yes, we put it straight up on the shelves – otherwise we would drown in it. We are not in a position to make use of everything they produce.

It took nearly a decade, however, before the public began to realise some of the disappointing aspects of local environmental administration. By making use of rules on rights regarding access to information, environmentalists gained access to the records on the environmental inspection by municipalities of a wide range of large companies. They found inspection activities to be relatively poor. The municipal inspection process was found to be lacking, and response to breaches was either to turn a blind eye or to legalise them. A range of spectacular cases were brought to light in the press (for an overview, see Larsen and Christensen, 1985). This led to Parliament's application of a somewhat unusual decision in relation to the municipalities – that environmental permits issued according to environmental protection law should also be complied with!

Developments in the 1990s were marked by a certain crisis for municipal powers in environmental protection. New policy instruments were introduced, which helped circumvent the implementation shortfalls at local level, but although some competencies were shifted from municipal to regional level (the counties), there was no major restructuring of the administrative set-up, nor of the powers allocated to municipalities in environmental legislation. Some of the new policy instruments followed from EU policy initiatives, such as Environmental Impact Assessment, which was novel for Denmark. It helped establish mandatory procedures for the local authorities. Voluntary agreements with industry, although strongly advocated by some administrators, never really achieved broader acceptance or application. Environmental taxes were more popular, both with administrators and environmentalists, and an introduction of a broad range of such taxes was one of the more significant elements of developments in the 1990s. Denmark now has more than 25 different environmental taxes and they contribute approximately 10–12 per cent to the total tax base.

Another driver of change was the so-called 'green majority' in the Danish parliament during the 1990s; a coalition of parties sympathetic to environmental issues. Although many far-reaching environmental reforms were introduced, no real questioning or attempts to introduce changes on the issue of municipal authority took place. There was a quiet devolution of competencies to the regional level, the counties, which took over regulatory competencies in pollution control and nature protection, and which became responsible for monitoring the state of the aquatic environment. In 2001 the parliamentary majority was wiped out by landslide elections, where the political right gained momentum. The present liberal–conservative government has discontinued several environmental expenditure programmes, but has tended to reinforce the role of municipalities and local decision-making in environmental administration.

The implementation problem can be summarised in the question: do municipalities comply with the state's requirements and the politicians' will? The latest status report of municipal environmental inspection activities demonstrates that municipalities fall short even of the goals set out and put into force by their own national association. On average, environmental management is allotted just three employees in a typical municipal administration, with relatively wide variation, in that in 50 (of 277) municipalities, there is less than one employee! Even though the municipalities have had the opportunity to finance staff for certain environmental management tasks via a special charging scheme, the report reveals that only a small group of municipalities charged what was required for inspection. The Environmental Protection Act foresees concurrent inspections of highly polluting companies; however, with more than 500 companies per inspection officer, several years can go between inspection visits. Municipalities also have responsibility for controlling farms' compliance with national regulations on the storage and application of fertiliser. In this area, it can be especially difficult for rural municipalities to apply an effective agricultural inspection, as farming interests will often feature strongly in the respective municipal board and its technical committee. It has been reported that current status with regard to agricultural regulation is characterised by 'black spots' on the map, where municipal inspection shortfall has reduced implementation of fertiliser regulations.

In my study of water pollution control policies in four European states, the municipal approach in Denmark was contrasted with the Waterboard approach in the Netherlands. In the latter case, responsibility was delegated to single-purpose entities, founded on stricter application of the polluter-pays principle. In terms of environmental change from 1970 to 1990, the Netherlands were far more successful than Denmark in reducing pollution at source. The municipalisation of environmental responsibility had led to over-investments in expensive end-of-pipe treatment in Denmark, and in a slow and modest curbing of water pollution discharges as compared to the Netherlands (Andersen, 1994, 1999). A recent update of the study has largely confirmed the findings of the initial analysis (EEA, 2005).

Table 13.1 provides an overview of the outcomes of centralisation/decentralisation trends in Danish environmental politics in recent years (1990s). Danish membership of the European Union has favoured a certain centralisation, due to the large number of EU directives that have to be implemented in national legislation. Yet, the local authorities (either municipalities or counties) remain largely in control of inspection and enforcement at the local level. The only real exception to this pattern is forest policy. Implementation and enforcement, above all, is a task for local authorities, where the state mainly becomes involved in cases of judicial complaints.

5. THREE ASPECTS OF THE LOCAL MANAGEMENT PROBLEM

The implementation problem of the local administration can be related to three analytically distinct issues; the problem of scale, the subsidy issue and the capacity challenge. While the first two types of problems have been

Table 13.1 Assignments in Danish environmental governance

	Industry	Ecosystems	Agriculture	Forests	Water	Implementation and enforcement
International	IPPC	Habitat and Birds Directive	Nitrate Directive	Rio	Water Framework Directive	ECJ
National	Green accounting, voluntary agreements, eco-taxes	National Parks	Plan for Aquatic Environm.	Forest extension plan	Plan for Aquatic Environm.	
Regional	Permits, inspection	Nature plans	EIA; agro-env. subsidies	State Forest Districts		Planning, monitoring
Local	Permits, inspection	Green guides	Permits, enforcement	*No role*	Advanced sewage treatment	Inspection

discussed extensively in economics literature, the problem of capacity requires consultation of political science and public administration literature. In the following, the character and extent of the problem of scale, the subsidy issue and the capacity problem, will be briefly sketched – in relation to Danish environmental management.

5.1 Problem of Scale

The problem of scale concerns whether the authority has the necessary reach or size to solve the task it faces technically and economically efficiently. Several European countries have launched reforms of the local authority structure in order to adapt size to the economic and technical conditions, and in order to produce public services effectively. Development has taken place in favour of larger units, both on the local authority and the regional level. (A notable exception is France, where reform of local authority divisions has not been altered since the time of Napoleon. As a result of this, France still has more than 36 000 local municipalities, said to be more than in the rest of the EU-15 (Wright, 1989).)

In Denmark the problem of scale in environmental management is apparent especially in relation to management of the public utilities within water and waste. While in waste management it has been realised that it is necessary to coordinate or operate jointly in cooperative units, the municipalities are rather reluctant to give up operation of sewage treatment plants. This tendency prevails, and in many cases the plants are not staffed with sufficiently competent personnel. A report has revealed that as many as 25 per cent of plants were not fulfilling the emission/discharge requirements they were designed to reach. Privatisation has been considered, but remains an option limited to just one or two communes.

5.2 The Subsidy Problem

The subsidy problem essentially has two aspects;

- whether local authorities are capable of producing collective environmental goods at prices that imply that 'true costs' are passed on – that is, whether they can live up to application of the 'polluter-pays' principle,
- whether local authorities in a wider sense can manage to produce environmental goods cost-effectively.

As in most other EU member states, in Denmark it is the local authorities which are responsible for sanitation, waste collection and disposal, as well as water supply. Despite these tasks typically being financed by independent user fees, financing out of the general tax base as well as cross-financing between the different consumer groups is not unusual, to minimise or distort the user payment to protect or attract certain companies. Local authorities can exploit the advantages of scale, with responsibilities in many different areas, drawn together in a common management unit. As a significant part of polluters' fixed environmental costs consist of charges to service providers in the areas of waste and water, the local authorities can attract companies, jobs and tax revenues by offering discounts in these basic cost areas.

The derived effect, however, is that environmental services are produced inefficiently because subsidisation leads to increased demand for these services, where prices reflecting real costs would rather lead to a reduction in demand. A second effect is that local companies do not undertake internal production adjustments to reduce environmental impact, which at a truer cost level would be cost efficient. As a result of this, the overall company and socio-economic costs are driven up.

The 'polluter-pays' principle is, according to the OECD's official definition, a 'no-subsidy principle', as use of subsidies in national environmental policies can undermine competitiveness in international markets (OECD, 1975). Subsidisation of polluters, nevertheless, takes place in the majority of countries, and is without doubt most subtle at local level, where the international free-trade organisations are not able to detect this defensive use of trade-distorting methods. The subsidy problem is also apparent in that municipalities can cross-subsidise treatment of industrial discharges, by transferring costs onto households.

5.3 The Capacity Problem

The capacity problem concerns local authorities' knowledge and resource capacity to process existing information and data for use in the on-going administration of national legislation. The capacity problem is particularly a function of the local environmental administrations' personnel resources and specialisations, or lack thereof.

Environmental issues are, in themselves, complex, and administration of national legislation usually requires a high information level regarding production methods as well as established or potential technologies in a large number of companies and branches. Even adapting and continually being updated with this information requires a solid pre-existing knowledge, not to mention time. As resources in this area are limited, local environmental authorities often prefer standardised and routine licensing procedures, based on established technologies, which can apply to a wide range of polluters regardless of their specific production processes. In this way, a bias can easily arise in favour of expensive and problematic end-of-pipe solutions. According to the mass-balance approach, end-of-pipe technologies which do not reduce effort factors, but rather focus exclusively on treatment of waste products, will merely involve conversion of liquid or volatile substances into solid waste products (for example, sludge, slag). These types of conversion do not solve many environmental problems, but represent more a displacement of the problems. As this type of public problem-solving mechanism becomes institutionalised, the over-capacity often developed in public utilities may be seen as a physical indication of the capacity problem of local environmental administration.

The capacity problem can also be expressed as the municipalities' lack of ability to carry out strategies for a process and product-integrated environmental policy. Since the mid-1990s, municipalities have been charged with putting a cleaner technology standard into practice in connection with the system of environmental permits; however, an evaluation has revealed that municipalities have not managed to live up to this requirement. The regulatory system did not significantly influence introduction of cleaner technology, whereas green company strategies played a more dominant role in this regard (Andersen and Jørgensen, 1997).

The capacity problem also surfaces as a resistance towards the increased market influence in environmental policy. The EU's Waste Directive allows for greater freedom of choice with regard to which treatment sites commercial waste can be delivered to. A study of municipal waste regulations, however, reveals that as many as 95 per cent of municipalities hold this information back from citizens, in so doing safeguarding the local treatment monopoly.

These insights into the municipal implementation of environmental protection law do not bear witness, in my view, so much to a wilful and cynical avoidance of requirements and norms, as to that local municipalities are complex organisations with many tasks and interests which need to be brought together under day-to-day management. Municipalities still have to adapt implementation to available resources and to the local political circumstances they are confronted with. It is in the light of these pressures that municipal implementation problems need to be understood.

6. THE CAPACITY PROBLEM AND ECOLOGICAL MODERNISATION

The capacity problem concerns the more general problem for local as well as state authorities of finding a language for administration that is adequate where a large part of industry has, on its own initiative, undertaken ecological modernisation. This ecological modernisation process has, itself, a significant dynamic in that one of the driving forces is companies' own desire to win strategic advantage by operating at the cutting edge of public regulatory requirements.

Classic command-and-control regulation is built partly on technology-specific norms and standards, set down by authorities from their knowledge of what is available and possible, and partly, to a large extent, on public authorities' taking the responsibility on themselves to treat and neutralise residual outputs from production focusing chiefly on point sources. Use of local authorities as implementation bodies was part of this reactive, end-of-pipe regulatory paradigm. Local authorities could put passive solutions into action to treat the industrial stream of residuals, but not put in place a preventative environmental policy.

During the 1990s, more focus has been on the significance of diffuse pollution sources and, in the same vein, broader circulation and life-cycle schools of thought have developed. As Albert Weale puts forward in his characterisation of this 'new politics of pollution', which builds upon a realisation that the causal interaction and the effects of pollution problems are wide-reaching and complex, necessitating a preventative, anticipatory approach rather than clean-up and reparative approach. This new view of environmental regulation builds on the mass balance approach where the environment is not regarded as a sectoral problem, but as an element which needs to be integrated into other policy areas. In a narrow sense, the ecological modernisation process would dictate that environmental protection should be directed at the source and be integrated into production processes, but in the wider sense it implies a need for structural changes in industrial society (Weale, 1992).

The concept of ecological modernisation has been interpreted in different ways; however, it refers basically to the necessary modernisation of industrial society on the basis of sustainability (Mol, 1995; Andersen, 2002). The concept has developed over time as it has become clear that the 'old' environmental policy – where concern for the environment was regarded as being in conflict with economic development – has been replaced with new environmental policy, where environmental concern is regarded as a necessary precondition for a viable economic development. The realities of pollution, as well as the economic perspectives tied up with development of new environmentally-friendly technologies, have probably been equally significant for the advance of the new environmental strategic approach. Instead of regarding environmental policy as a potential economic burden, it is seen by the ecological modernisation school of thought as a source for continued development, although within a certain, not clearly defined, ecological utilisation space. This perception of environmental policy was quite clearly put forward in Commission President Jacques Delors' White Paper from 1993, and caught on in several European countries, including Denmark – here championed by the green majority in parliament.

The capacity problem differs qualitatively from the classic scale and information problems within local environmental administration and fundamentally concerns the potential roles played by state and local authorities in the ecological modernisation process. A change has taken place largely at the central level, where authorities have begun to regulate using economic management instruments, voluntary agreements, environmental audits, environmental certification, and so on. Efforts, here, are aimed at creating favourable frameworks and institutions able to ensure the ecological modernisation process a free run with actors in the market. The state has an important role to play, the fundamental aspect being that the state defines the frameworks and institutions for transactions in the market economy; however, what capacity applies to local authorities in this new environmental policy development? The role of local authorities as, to a greater or lesser extent, the implementation body for national decisions, has been eroded in connection with the selection of market-based and self-regulatory strategies introduced at national level. Local authorities lack the expertise to enter into dialogue with the companies, as well as the capacity – with the exception of certain isolated measures, such as use of public purchasing as a management instrument. Local authorities' only and most important capacity is considered to consist of their democratic foundations and the opportunity they have to foster a locally-rooted debate on sustainable development. All things being equal, this must be regarded as a considerable curtailment in relation to the role they played under the 'old' environmental regulatory paradigm.

7. TECHNOLOGICAL CHANGE AND INSTITUTIONAL RIGIDITIES

Let me end this critical review of Denmark's decentralised environmental management system with an extensive reference to the famous welfare economist Arthur C. Pigou, who was a predecessor to Keynes as professor at Cambridge. On the issue of scale, Pigou remarked nearly 75 years ago that despite rapid technological change, for example in water, electricity and gas, leading to boundaries for the most efficient organisations continually being shifted, institutional rigidity at a local level led to a failure to adapt to these changes:

> These changes in the area proper to management have not, however, in general, been followed by the transference of the public utility industries to new public authorities created ad hoc; for the task of ousting the municipalities is opposed by an immense amount of friction, and is, therefore, little likely to be successfully undertaken. Hence, in practice, public operation often implies that industries, whose most economical area of management is intermediate between the areas representative of the central authority and of local authorities respectively, will, in fact, be worked by local authorities; and this, of course, implies a reduction of the unit of management below what is commercially best. (Pigou, 1932: 402–3)

Efforts on the part of local authorities to retain the tasks they had won or had been awarded led to 'diseconomies of scale', and many tasks were, therefore, gathered on a more local level than would otherwise have been economically and technically desirable. Pigou took, therefore, a rather critical view of local authority organisation where local authority utilities, for example supplying water, gas and electricity, were concerned. This, in his view, did not result simply from local politicians' short-term outlook, determined by the next election or the potential to export externalities out over local authority boundaries, but first and foremost from the local authorities' lack of *ability* to produce collective goods efficiently in a bureaucratic organisation.

Pigou's favoured alternative to the bureaucratic organisation was special authorities managed by experts 'for the express purpose of industrial operation or control', who, in being appointed for a longer period of time, would be protected from blackmail from influential electoral groups. Among his favourite examples were such companies as the London Port Authorities, London's Waterboard and the United States' Interstate Railway Commission (Pigou, 1932: 334).

Pigou's discussion of the scale problem can be thought to constitute a direct parallel to the situation in 1960's United States water resource economics, where Kneese and Bower (Kneese and Bower, 1968; Kneese and Schultze, 1975) criticised the local authorities' inefficiency, here in the more recent fight against pollution, not simply in Pigou's discussion relating to the classic utility company scenario. Use of special authorities was also advocated, founded on the basis of hydrological boundaries in the case of environmental protection. Kneese, who at the same time can be regarded as one of the instigators of the modern mass balance approach to environmental regulation, was aware of the German Wasserverbände in the Ruhr district, and put forward that these regional special authorities were more effectively suited to management of water resources than were local authorities and municipalities, whose boundaries were often arbitrary in relation to natural resources.

In the context of a modern environmental policy the patterns for integration of science and expertise in the policy-making process, and in the day-to-day environmental management, deserve careful study. In Denmark the building of the National Environmental Research Institute during the 1990s is one of the cornerstones of these patterns, as were the extensive strategic environmental research programmes funded by the government, which involved many universities and research institutes. The reports from the environmental experts are often at odds with sectoral and local interests, and are perceived as one of the key drivers in the policy process; perhaps for this reason the budget reductions were particularly severe for research following the government change in 2001.

8. OUTLOOK

When it is taken into consideration how much has been researched and how problematic it has been to verify theories on local authorities' expenditure behaviour, there is little ground for optimism with regard to the potential for verifying theories on local authorities' environmental behaviour, especially if the theories are to be valid for industrialised countries (for an overview of theory and empirical analysis concerning local authority's role in the public sector, see Bruun, 1994).

A surprising amount of the knowledge generated on the behaviour of local authorities in the field of the environment is based on case studies. One of the few comparative studies on implementation of environmental policy at the local level is Knoepfel and Weidner's classical study of air pollution legislation in six European countries (Knoepfel and Weidner, 1985). This said, it must be expected that there be certain, supposedly systematic variations in the scope of the above-mentioned problems between various countries, and that more universal reasons for these differences can be identified, relating to the local authority's placing and role with society.

- Problems in implementation must be expected to vary according to local authority autonomy in relation to the state measured by the local authority share of tax revenues. The greater autonomy, the greater the interest vested in local employment and tax revenues and, as a result, relatively significant implementation problems.
- Efficiency problems must be expected to vary according to the local authority structure and division, in that the problems may generally increase in significance the smaller the average municipal size. This can, however, potentially be offset through delegation of competencies

out to regional authorities or by contracting out, or use of special authorities.

- Capacity problems must, on the other hand, be expected to be rather universal to local authorities and, therefore, particularly dependent on the extent to which a given country has adopted a market-orientated approach to its ecological modernisation process.

Within the context of this chapter, the opportunity has not arisen to carry out a more systematic deliberation of these simple hypotheses. Since these hypotheses are derived from a case study of Denmark, they would also require analysis in a broader international context. Although Denmark is a small country, the size of municipalities is not different from what is found in many other countries. This suggests that the problem of local authority management deserves more scrutiny elsewhere.

Postscript

On June 24 2004 the Danish liberal–conservative government agreed with its coalition partner, the Danish People's Party, on a structural reform of local government. As a result of this reform the counties will be abolished from 2007. Most environmental responsibilities previously with the counties, will be entrusted the municipalities. A new regional level, without tax collection powers or democratically elected councils, will oversee municipal environmental management.

BIBLIOGRAPHY

Andersen, Mikael Skou (1994), *Governance by Green Taxes: Making Pollution Prevention Pay*, Manchester and New York: Manchester University Press.

Andersen, M.S. (1999), 'Governance by green taxes: implementing clean water policies in Europe 1970–1990', *Environmental Economics and Policy Studies*, **2**, 39–63, Tokyo.

Andersen, Mikael Skou (2002), 'Ecological modernisation or subversion: the effect of Europeanization on Eastern Europe', *American Behavioral Scientist*, **45**(9), 1394–416.

Andersen, Mikael Skou and Ulrik Jørgensen (1997), 'Evaluation of the cleaner technology programme', *Environmental Review*, no. 14, Copenhagen: EPA.

Berman, Paul (1980), 'Thinking about programmed and adaptive implementation', in Helen M. Ingram and Dean E. Mann (eds), *Why Policies Succeed or Fail*, California: Sage Publications.

Bruun, Finn (1994), 'Kommunernes rolle i den offentlige sektor: teori og empiri', *Økonomi og Politik*, no. 3, pp. 32–9.

Danish EPA (1995), 'Environmental administration in Denmark', *Environment News*, no. 17, Copenhagen: Ministry of Environment and Energy.

Danish EPA (2000), *Economic Instruments in Environmental Protection in Denmark*, Copenhagen.

European Environment Agency (2005), *Effectiveness of Urban Waste Water Treatment Policies in Selected Countries*, EEA-report 2/2005, Copenhagen.

Gunlicks, Arthur B. (1986), *Local Government in the German Federal System*, Durham, NC: Duke University Press.

Haigh, Nigel (1994), 'The environment as a test case for subsidiarity', in Mark Dubrulle (ed.), *Future European Environmental Policy and Subsidiarity*, Brussels: European Interuniversity Press, pp. 55–62.

Kneese, A. and B. Bower (1968), *Managing Water Quality; Economics, Technology, Institutions*, Baltimore: Resources for the Future.

Kneese, Allan V. and Charles L. Schultze (1975), *Pollution, Prices and Public Policy*, Washington DC: Brookings Institution.

Knoepfel, Peter and Helmut Weidner (eds) (1985), *Luftreinhaltepolitik im Internationalen Vergleich*, volumes 1–6, Berlin: Edition Sigma.

Larsen, Vagn Juhl and Per Christensen (1985), *Håndbog for Kratluskere: Bvordan man Afslører en Miljøforbryder*, Harlev J.: Niche.

Lipsky, Michael (1980), *Street Level Bureaucracy*, New York: Russel Sage Foundation.

Mol, A. (1995), *The Refinement of Production: Ecological Modernization Theory and the Chemical Industry*, Utrecht: Van Arkel.

Mørch, Søren (1982), *Den nye Danmarkshistorie 1880–1960*, Copenhagen: Gyldendal.

OECD (1975), *The Polluter Pays Principle*, Paris: OECD.

OECD (1999), *Environmental Performance Review: Denmark*, Paris: OECD.

Pigou, A.C. (1932), *The Economics of Welfare*, London: Macmillan & Co.

Pressmann, J.L. and A. Wildawsky (1973), *Implementaion: How Great Expectations are Dashed in Oakland: Or Why It's Amazing that Federal Programs Work at all*, Berkeley, CA: University of California Press.

Reitan, M. (1997), 'Norway – A case of splendid isolation', in M.S. Andersen and D. Liefferink (eds), *European Environmental Policy: The Pioneers*, Manchester: Manchester University Press.

Scruggs, L. (1999), 'Institutions and environmental performance in 17 western democracies', *British Journal of Political Science*, **29**(1), 1–31.

Strukturkommissionen (2004), *Betænkning nr. 1434*, chapter 14, Copenhagen: Indenrigsministeriet.

Weale, Albert (1992), *The New Politics of Pollution*, Manchester: Manchester University Press.

Wright, Vincent (1989), *The Government and Politics of France*, London: Unwin Hyman.

14. France: Forces shaping centralization and decentralization in environmental policymaking*

Albert Breton and Pierre Salmon

1. INTRODUCTION

Among the many decision-makers who play a role in France's environmental governance, some are located at the central, some at the regional, municipal and other subnational levels of government. The present balance between centralization and decentralization is the result of permanent structural features of the French governmental system on the one hand, and of recent developments both in that system and in environmental concerns and priorities on the other. Several structural features combine to enable the central government to adapt and tailor its policies to local needs and conditions. The policies of central governments are never compelled to be uniform as is sometimes asserted (Tocqueville, 1835/1969: 161; Oates, 1972: Chapter 2), but the capacity to adapt to spatial heterogeneity is particularly strong in the case of France for reasons that we examine. This is a general statement, applicable in varying degrees across all policy areas, but it is particularly pertinent to environmental policies.

We look into the usefulness of that capacity and into the various forms that it can take. We argue that the recent developments mentioned above tend to profoundly alter the setting in which the central government's capacity to adapt to local circumstances takes place. One important change is the substantial decentralization that took place in France in the early 1980s. The motive behind the change had little to do with the environment (Salmon, 2000). Decentralization nonetheless affects environmental policymaking. By enhancing the responsibilities, authority, and ambitions of subcentral governments, it has changed the context in which the central government historically engaged in spatially non-uniform policies. Because many tasks, with important local dimensions, can now be undertaken by subcentral governments and not only by the central government, the rationale for the latter to undertake those tasks must now often be sought in the logic of vertical competition or of concurrency.

Another set of important developments relates to demand. Populations are still to a degree concerned with the environment inasmuch as it is seen to have an effect on their health and safety. In many cases the perception of who or what threatens health and safety has changed in a way which modifies what is expected from governments. A few decades ago, threats in the form of industrial hazards and of pollution were perceived to originate mainly in industrial activities and facilities, especially those of large-scale industries such as iron and steel, pulp and paper, and petrochemicals. In addition, the ill effects of industrial activities that most worried the public had a territorial span which was relatively limited: a city or part thereof, and at the limit a region.[1] It was also felt that the causal relation between industrial practices and their local environmental effects was variable, depending on a host of factors such as population density and weather conditions. This suggested a need for tailor-made control. In France, for reasons that we underline, the machinery of government was relatively well equipped to satisfy such a need. Thus, unlike countries such as Germany and Switzerland (Knoepfel, 1998: 165), the attention given to air pollution could focus on dealing with 'immissions' (that is, trying to achieve ambient standards) rather than on regulating 'emissions' (that is, making sure that uniform constraints on practices were respected).[2]

If not all, at least much of this has changed. We list here some of the main changes (we return to them in Section 3). First, scientific information has persuaded many individuals that human activities have ill effects, notably on health and safety, that are global more than local. This change returns the focus from immissions or ambient standards to emissions. In the case of some important substances, what counts is their aggregate emission, possibly at the world level. Second, in Western Europe at least, the main culprits are no longer sought in industrial processes, especially those of large firms, but rather in consumers' activities, mainly transportation, domestic waste, heating and air-conditioning.[3] Third, for reasons both related and unrelated to these changes, the main drive to deal with environmental problems in France and in the other member countries originates in the European Union. The EU is in effect almost compelled to implement uniform regulation. One reason is that it is not well equipped to monitor the implementation of tailor-made policies. Another relates to the goals, pursued in the wake of the 1987 Single European Act, of eliminating market distortions and establishing a 'level-playing field'. These goals make any tailor-made interventions highly suspect. As a consequence the member states are constrained to follow suit and to rely on uniform regulation more than they otherwise would. Fourth, in part because of external influences, public opinion in France has steadily become less prone to perceive all environmental problems in terms of hazards to people's welfare and in particular to their health. Public opinion now pays more attention to matters such as nature preservation, landscapes and biodiversity.

These changes, related to decentralization and to changes in demand, have had important effects on the ability of the French central government to vary its policies locally. Policy variation is perhaps less important in some areas than it was in the past, but it remains essential in others. The role of subcentral governments, however, has become essential in all areas. Where local considerations dominate, the central government tends to disengage itself, even though in some areas it has both an incentive and the ability to intervene in a way fully adapted to local circumstances. Where, however, global results originating in demands from the EU and from international commitments must be achieved, the central government does not have the capacity to act alone. The cooperation and involvement of subcentral governments is needed. The central government has had to find ways of achieving those global results without jeopardizing the benefits, in terms of innovation and competition, of the decentralized system that it itself helped to establish in the early 1980s.

In the foregoing discussion, mainly as a convenient classificatory device, we have applied the traditional distinction between supply and demand to the case of environmental policies. We also touched upon changes in both supply and demand which have led to changes in the outcomes of their interaction. The organization of the chapter follows the same line. We study supply in Section 2 and turn to demand in Section 3. Section 4 concludes.

2. THE SUPPLY OF ENVIRONMENTAL POLICY

2.1 An Introduction to Section 2

As just noted, we are concerned in this section with matters that are conveniently lumped together as pertaining to the supply of environmental policies. The section begins by identifying the large number of decision-makers involved in the process of designing and implementing these policies. It then describes how these actors interact with each other and with institutions that are not principally preoccupied with environmental issues but, for reasons that are spelled out, have to be brought in the decision-making process. Throughout the section, the decentralized nature of some parts of the French governmental system is underlined, and attention is paid to the complex mode of interaction that characterizes a system in which governments at all four jurisdictional levels need each other to be effective suppliers of environmental policies. Of necessity, the section pays attention to coordination and to the institutions that promote and nurture it.

2.2 Institutional Decision-makers

Decision-makers involved in the elaboration and implementation of environmental policies are so numerous and heterogeneous that several authors have used words such as complexity and fragmentation to depict the French governmental system. Indeed, a single ministerial department in charge of the whole array of policies does not exist.

When the Ministry of Environment was created in 1971, it was in effect an *administration de mission*, that is, a small department not expected to have a managerial role, but contributing, in a given area, to the design and coordination of the policies followed by all other departments inasmuch as they have or might have significant effects in that area. In the course of time the Ministry became more of an *administration de gestion*, that is, more like an ordinary department, but it never acquired a really dominant standing in that function.[4] Other larger and more powerful departments at the national level have continued to have a very substantial influence on environmental policies. Those which have the larger responsibilities in that domain are industry, agriculture, public works and health. The policies of these departments and others concerning each environmental set of issues are coordinated by a number of 'interministerial' councils chaired by representatives of the Prime Minister.

Eventually a number of national agencies were nominally or effectively brought under the formal supervision of the Ministry of Environment. The main ones are the *Agence de l'Environnement et de la Maîtrise de l'Energie* (ADEME), the *Conservatoire du Littoral*, and the *Office National des Forêts*. The six *Agences de bassin* (watershed agencies) dealing with water, and the six national parks have also been made dependants, in principle at least, of the Ministry of Environment.[5] There are many other agencies involved in environmental policies. More are created each year. To mention a few: *Agence Nationale pour la Gestion des Déchets Radioactifs* (ANDRA), *Agence Française de Sécurité Sanitaire des Aliments* (AFSSA), *Agence Française de Sécurité Sanitaire Environnementale* (AFSSE).

An important and general feature of the French governmental system is the often extensive presence, at the level of the regions and of the *départements*, of most ministerial departments and of some agencies. We will be particularly interested in the regional directorates of the Ministry of Environment (DIREN) and of the Ministry of Industry (DRIRE), the regional offices of ADEME, and of course in the prefects at the regional and *départemental* levels.

As mentioned earlier, the decentralization reform of the early 1980s has increased considerably the relevance of subcentral governments in environmental as well as in other policy areas. There are three levels of subcentral governments in France whose fully democratic machinery includes bodies akin to an executive and a 'legislative' branch. They are the communes or municipalities, the *départements* and the regions. There is no hierarchy among the three levels, in the sense that none is subservient to another, and, as we will see, each is competent to deal with the environment or some parts thereof. We must mention a fourth intermediary level which is especially important in the area of environmental implementation. It consists of various kinds of intercommunal bodies entrusted by the communes with common activities within metropolitan areas. They are not, however, democratically elected governments as are governments at the other levels and thus they are not as independent.

Finally, as already noted, 'Brussels' plays a crucial role. That role can be rationalized as a surrogate demand addressed to the French institutional system as a whole; we discuss that role in Section 3. Another set of actors, not mentioned so far, but to which we devote some attention, is made up of the various courts (civil, criminal and administrative) involved in environmental litigation.

2.3 Locally-tailored Policies of the Central Government

The central government has – and has had for centuries – the capacity and, to a lesser degree, the incentive to adapt its national policies to local conditions. Its resources for that purpose consist first of the prefects, successors of the powerful *intendants* on whom the *Ancien Régime* largely relied to govern the provinces since the days of Richelieu and Colbert in the seventeenth century. In each region and *département* there is a prefect representing the central government as a whole. A second resource consists of the *field* or *territorial services* of the various departments of the central government.[6] Practically all ministerial departments (foreign affairs is an obvious exception) have sizeable field services, some at the level of the regions only, most at the level of the *départements* also. The prefects have some authority over all these field services as a matter of principle. In practice, the latter, however, also report directly to their superiors in Paris. There is in addition the *cumul des mandats*, a peculiar characteristic of the French political system, whereby the main political actors at the center also have important responsibilities at the subcentral level. Due to recent reforms, this phenomenon is less pervasive than it used to be, but it remains important. Does the *cumul des mandats* enhance or hinder the capacity of the central government to adapt to local conditions? It is clear that it brings local concerns directly into the decision-making process of the central government. On the other hand, it may weaken the independence and authority of the local representatives of the central administration, and thus provide an incentive for more rigid, less spatially varied, policies. Whatever results from the *cumul des mandats* depends on the characteristics of the prefects and of the field services. It would appear that on the whole the *cumul des mandats* is favorable to flexibility.

Both the prefects and the staff of some of the field services in each *département* and region enjoy a relatively high and independent status, based first of all on technical competence but also on the security provided by affiliation to a *grand corps*.[7] The prefects are typically graduates of the *Ecole Nationale d'Administration*. Their technical competence lies mostly in the field of administrative law (the *intendants* also drew most of their strength from their training in law). Prefects can be appointed, displaced, or dismissed *ad nutum* (at will) by the government but in fact they get substantial protection as a result both of tradition and of their affiliation to the *corps préfectoral* (one of the *grands corps*). The ministerial departments of public works and of industry are staffed both at the central level and in each region by *ingénieurs des ponts et chaussées* and *ingénieurs des mines* respectively – in both cases largely recruited among the top graduates of the *Ecole Polytechnique* – that is, by highly qualified, scientifically-trained technocrats who are members of prestigious and powerful *grands corps*.[8] Because these officials, including to a lesser extent the prefects, are both highly qualified professionals and relatively independent, they are usually trusted to resist at least moderate pressure from politicians and lobbies. This explains that in these areas policymaking, rather than being based on uniform regulations, is focused on management and seeks solutions to concrete problems that are reasonable and highly dependent on space and time (Larrue, 2000). It is not a sufficient reason, however, to ensure optimal policymaking. For this to obtain, the perspective and concerns adopted by these officials also have to be considered. To what extent, in particular, are they concerned with environmental issues, rather than exclusively with, say, employment and economic development?

The question is particularly relevant since the only field service exclusively specialized in environmental matters does not share the favorable characteristics mentioned above. Created as recently as 1991 by the consolidation of various services (the largest of which was involved in the administration of water), the *Directions Régionales de l'Environnement* (DIREN) are still sparsely staffed by medium-rank civil servants unconnected to a *grand corps* (see Lascoumes and Le Bourhis, 1997).[9] Dedicated to environmental issues, the DIREN suffer from a lack of strength and credibility. Moreover, the Ministry of Environment shares, at the level of the regions, a field service with the Ministry of Industry: the *Directions Regionales de l'Industrie, de la Recherche et de l'Environnement* (DRIRE). Because of its link with the Ministry of Industry, which is staffed by *ingénieurs des mines*, the DRIRE are stronger and more prestigious than the DIREN. Moreover, the DRIRE are largely if not wholly concerned with industrial development. This 'double-tasking' creates a potential conflict of interests.[10] The seriousness of that problem is mitigated by the fact that, at some point, the *ingénieurs des mines* decided collectively that the environment is valuable and raises scientifically interesting issues, well worth the deployment of their technical skills (see Lascoumes, 1994: 144–45). This has led them to seek necessarily context-dependent and concrete compromises between concerns with the environment and industrial development objectives. In areas like industrial waste and air pollution in which such compromises seem, or seemed, justified, their role has been compared by some authors to a kind of technical *magistrature*. The foregoing facts support the point we stress in this subsection, to wit, the capacity of the central government to adapt its policies to local circumstances. We address later the question of whether the particular environmental issues we have mentioned above are as relevant today as they were some decades ago.

In the field services of the Ministry of Agriculture, serious problems are raised by the plurality of tasks included in the same job, to use the language of the multi-task literature (Holmstrom and Milgrom, 1991). Until 2002, that ministry encompassed not only one *corps*, the *ingénieurs agronomiques*, but two if we count the less numerous but more prestigious *ingénieurs des eaux et forêts* (some of them being prior graduates of *Ecole Polytechnique* as *ingénieurs des mines* and *ingénieurs des ponts et chaussées*). All the personnel of that very large ministry, whether located in Paris or in the regions and *départements*, has for a long time, however, been educated and socialized to perceive their role as consisting of two main tasks: the protection of farmers (enhanced by a formal sharing of responsibilities with farmers' unions in the management of agriculture) and the promotion of increased agricultural productivity measured as quantity produced per hectare. As is now well known, success in meeting the second objective has been achieved at a very large cost to the environment. The ministry as a whole, and its field services in the *départements* and regions in particular, are now entrusted with the task of finding and implementing solutions to environmental problems, whether or not these are caused by agricultural activities. The difficulties involved in combining this new set of tasks with the entrenched modes of thought – the prevailing culture – and the enduring objectives that have contributed to creating most of the problems in the first place are likely to persist. As a consequence, in this area, the main rationale for modes of intervention based on compromise, negotiation and flexibility is to be sought in politics of both the lobbying and electoral kinds.

To summarize the main point of this subsection we, as many others, have observed a tendency for the environmental policies of the central government not to be imposed by a command system but to be implemented unevenly and flexibly through a process of negotiation.[11] This allows a large variation in the way the policies are made to reflect local circumstances across regions and other subcentral jurisdictions. Contrary to at least some of these authors, however, we have not explained this state of affairs by the weakness of the governmental apparatus, but by its strength, that is by the capacity of the central government to adopt such an approach whenever it deems appropriate to do so.

2.4 Powers of Subcentral Governments

As a result of the decentralization laws of 1982–1983, there are three levels of elected subcentral governments. At each of these levels, governments are made up of an elected deliberative branch ('deliberative' being more appropriate here than 'legislative'), which elects the head of the executive branch. Thus in each of the 36 000 communes, the municipal council elects a mayor; in each of the 96 *départements*, the 'general' or *départemental* council elects a 'president'; and so does the regional council in each of the 22 regions.[12] The offices of mayor and of president are far from being purely formal. They confer considerable authority on their incumbents, akin, relatively speaking, to that of prime ministers in parliamentary systems. Even though, in spatial terms, communes are enclosed in *départements* which in turn are enclosed in regions, the three levels are completely independent – none subordinated to any other. Governments at each level have responsibilities largely specified in laws enacted by the Parliament in Paris. Whatever these specifications, what is essential is that each level has substantial freedom regarding budgets, borrowings, and the setting of rates on a number of local taxes that constitute part of their revenue.

Mayors, however, have powers that *départemental* and regional presidents (with some exceptions) do not have. In addition to their status as democratically chosen representatives of the inhabitants of the communes, mayors are the delegates of the central government in their respective communes. As a rule, the heads of the executive in *départements* and regions do not have this double role because, at those levels, the authority of the center is delegated to the prefects. This difference is one of the main reasons why the mayors, by themselves or with the explicit approval of their municipal councils, and charged with the 'tranquility and safety of the inhabitants', can do such things as regulating, forbidding and authorizing that do not fall within the powers of the regional and *départemental* councils or of their presidents.[13] At the regional and departmental levels, the authority to do these things, in spite of the decentralization laws of 1982–83, still belongs essentially to the regional and *départemental* prefects.

We have insisted on this point because, as we will see, it has a bearing on practically all the policy issues pertaining to the environment. There are policy instruments that elected governments at all the three subcentral levels do use; they consist of planning, spending, taxing, borrowing, financing or granting, producing and investing. Many objectives can be achieved by the use of such tools. When the activities involve regulating, policing, authorizing and forbidding, however, the only remaining actors are the mayors, on the one hand, and the representatives of the central government, under the authority of the prefects, on the other. The regional and *départemental* governments are unable to act in this way[14] (nor can the *Agences de l'eau* for that matter, in spite of the importance of their role).[15] French communes are numerous, which means that most of them are small; whether spontaneously or induced to do so by various programmes, most of them have decided to act collectively in some domains and for that purpose have joined various kinds of intercommunal bodies. Even though these bodies play a large and increasing role in many policy areas, including the environment, they are subject to the same limitations as are the regional and *départemental* governments and the *Agences de l'eau*. The prefects and the other representatives and external services of the central government under their authority, thus remain actors that any serious analysis of subcentral governments cannot bypass.

The preceding remarks on the distribution of powers must be considered together with the following principle concerning the assignment of environmental responsibilities. Article 1 of the relevant decentralization law, that of 7 January 1983, says: '*Les communes, les départements et les régions concourent avec l'Etat à la protection de l'environnement et du cadre de vie*.' This principle allows the four levels of government to use their powers for environmental purposes. In other words, generalized concurrency is, so to say, desired or even prescribed. Two qualifications, however, must be noted. First, as just explained, some types of powers are not available to some levels. Second, though the law imposes obligations to act, these obligations are often imposed unevenly across levels. For instance, communes are responsible for the provision of drinking water and sewerage, the collection of household waste, and the enforcement of water, air and noise regulations. Communes have an obligation to comply, that is to act, and this obligation can be enforced by the courts. It sometimes is (see Romi, 1998). But *départements*, regions and the central government are not prevented from intervening in the same areas. Actually, the prefects are also responsible for enforcing water, air and noise regulations. *Départements* and regions cannot regulate water, air and noise pollution, but as combating pollution is not only a matter of regulation, *départements* and regions can contribute a great deal by granting subsidies and other forms of financing, which they are fully entitled to do by the principle cited above.

Another example is the assignment (much reinforced in a law of 1995, the so-called *Loi Barnier*) to the *départements* of the responsibility to protect '*espaces naturels sensibles*' (sensitive natural areas). For that purpose, *départements* can raise a special tax – the *Taxe Départementale des Espaces Naturels Sensibles* – which provides them with the means to buy land. The council of a *département* can determine the exact limits of these *espaces sensibles*, and it has a preemptive right to buy land located in these areas whenever it comes on the market. The delimitation of *espaces sensibles* effected by the *départemental* council must, however, be approved by the prefect and, as a consequence, *départements* still, on the whole, lack regulatory power. In any case, the same *départements* can devote other sources of funds to the same objective or undertake to buy land without using their right of preemption. Furthermore, other levels of governments as well as agencies such as the *Conservatoire du Littoral* also contribute in various ways to the protection of natural resources.

There are other ways in which all levels of government concur in the task of protecting the environment. Many laws compel subcentral governments to pay attention to the environmental dimensions of the decisions they take on issues independent or distinct from the environmental domain. For instance, since the decentralization laws, municipalities have the authority to establish more or less alone an important document, now called the *Plan Local d'Urbanisme* (PLU), which sets, for some time ahead, the uses to which the land can be put on the territory of the communes. Among other functions, this document is the basis on which mayors deliver construction and demolition permits. In the process of deciding on these issues, the law obliges them to consider a number of environmental consequences of their decisions. For instance construction permits must include a discussion of the consequences on the landscape (the *volets paysagers* of the permits). Another contribution of subcentral governments to environmental policies lies in their representation in various institutions that play a role in these policies. They are represented for instance in the national and regional natural parks and in the *Agences de l'eau*. The number of boards, committees or commissions in which all levels of government and many subsets of the central administration are represented is large and reflects a need for coordination. We turn to that issue in the next subsection.

As noted, there are many circumstances in which environmental objectives cannot be achieved without recourse to regulations and policing. At the level of the *départements* and to a lesser degree at that of the regions, this endows the prefects and the other territorial services of the central government under their authority with a major function. Admittedly, as a consequence of the decentralization laws, the prefects' monitoring of decisions made by subcentral governments has become lighter (becoming *a posteriori* instead of *a priori*). It has not become unsubstantial, however. For instance, prefects can impose changes in the decisions regarding urban planning and construction made by the municipalities. More importantly, prefects retain the main responsibility in many policy areas, a phenomenon which has sometimes been interpreted as reflecting a generalized distrust of subcentral governments with regard to environmental matters (Szarka, 2002: 92). To illustrate, the prefects remain responsible for the establishment of inventories of resources and/or medium-term programmes of public works in domains such as landscapes and other natural resources, household waste, industrial waste, industrial hazards, air protection and water management. The prefects are in charge of the elaboration and enforcement of the *département*'s sanitary regulations (to which mayors can add regulations of their own). They can pass 'biotope orders' (*arrêtés de biotopes*) to protect eco-systems, hedges for instance. Private forest owners must seek their permission to 'deforest'. Prefects regulate the use of water during droughts, the use of cars during peaks of air pollution, traffic of any kind (including on foot) when there is a risk of forest fires, and so on.

Their most important function, it is claimed by many ecologists, should be policing and enforcement of the existing laws and regulations within their jurisdictions. For that purpose, the human resources available to the prefects consist of the external services of the central government under their authority (a prefect represents in his or her jurisdiction the prime minister and all the ministers): the personnel of the prefects' bureau (the prefecture), that of the DIREN and the DRIRE, the external services of other ministries such as agriculture and public works, various bodies of inspection, and most importantly the police forces, including, in the countryside, the *gendarmerie*. Whether these resources, which are also used for many other tasks, are sufficient to enforce the enormous corpus of regulations dealing with the environment is doubtful. Fortunately, as we will see, ways to enforce existing regulations are increasingly used that have the potential to do more than complement what the central government in the *départments* and regions can achieve.

2.5 Coordination and Initiative at the Subcentral Levels

Coordination is required by several features of the situation described above. An effort is being made to codify the laws and, as a second step, the regulations dealing with the environment.[16] Whether spontaneous or imposed by Directives from Brussels, the annual legislative and regulatory output of the central government in that policy area is large and multifaceted. Its interpretation and implementation at the subcentral level require various kinds of specialized knowledge that no single bureau can master by itself. The problem arises within the territorial services of the central administration, but it is especially serious at the level of subcentral governments which, without external help, are in general ill-equipped to deal with the technological and scientific aspects of all the issues they are or should be concerned with.

This deficiency is mitigated to some extent by a feature of the organization established by the 1982–83 laws of decentralization: the central government and the *départements* share a number of services. This is the case, in particular, of the territorial services of the Ministry of Public Works – the *Directions Départementales de l'Equipement* (DDE) – which employ a relatively large number of people and are run by the *ingénieurs des ponts et chaussées*. The services of the DDE are now shared between the central government and the *départemental* councils and their presidents. Something similar exists in the case of the Ministry of Agriculture – whose services at the level of the *départements* are the *Directions Départementales de l'Agriculture et de la Forêt* (DDAF) – but not in the case of the ministries of industry and of the environment.

The territorial services of the latter two share not only the characteristic of being completely independent of subcentral governments – a feature which they tend to consider as an asset for the fulfillment of their missions – but also that of having no bureau of their own at the level of the *départements*, which the administration of the Environment at least considers as an impediment.[17] Thus, to act at the level of the *département*, the DIREN must rely officially on the DDAF (and in practice on the DDE also), whose philosophy and networks are quite different from theirs (and always somewhat suspect from an environmental perspective). In each region, as a consequence, the DIREN or the regional prefect undertakes to coordinate environmental programmes with the policies – whose environmental dimensions are seldom the main ones – of the DDE and DDAF, and possibly other services (Health, Culture, and so on). This arrangement may be satisfactory depending on the issues on the agenda and on the personalities involved, in particular on the attitudes adopted by the prefects (see the panel discussion in chapter 10 of Lascoumes, 1999). For instance, some prefects consider as essential that the central government presents a unified front. Others acknowledge the existence of informal networks that transcend the limits of the central administration, extending beyond the personnel of subcentral governments to environmental associations, academics and other individuals particularly concerned with ecological or environmental matters. Conflicts will then focus on substantive concerns rather than on institutions.

A second reason for the necessity of coordination follows from the specialization of powers noted in the preceding subsection. It is often the case that for a project to succeed, a whole array of contributions must be mobilized. To create a natural regional park, for instance, some regulations are needed that only the prefects can provide, some acquiescence or even support must be awarded by the communes and the *départements* involved, and technical expertise must be given by the territorial services of the central administration as well as by various associations. The projects that succeed have often benefited from the existence of informal networks transcending the border of public and *a fortiori* central administrations (see Micoud, 1999). More generally, many projects require a level of funding which exceeds the capacity of any single actor, the central government excepted. Co-financing is thus needed, which of course requires coordination. In fact, most projects are co-financed by several levels of government as well as arm's length agencies such the *Agences de l'eau* and ADEME, and even sometimes by the European Union.

Coordination is needed mainly because of the dissonance that arises from the co-existence of two facts. The priorities of the central government and of the subcentral governments are generally quite different, whereas the means to satisfy the objectives of the former, in the domain of the environment particularly, are to a large extent in the hands of the latter.[18] Coordination is a way for the central government to obtain from subcentral governments the support for its policies without which the latter cannot be put in place. The establishment of contractual relationships is the major way to achieve coordination.[19] But some convergence may be obtained simply by the participation, in many forums of coordination at the subcentral level, of representatives both of subcentral governments and of the territorial services of the central government. These forums provide an opportunity for the central government to explain its policies and for serious discussions of their transposition to the setting of each particular subcentral jurisdiction. It is often the case that the objectives set at the national level are much more environmentally-friendly than are the main concerns of subcentral governments. As a consequence, the participation (which we discuss in Section 3) in many forums of the representatives of various groups particularly concerned with environmental and ecological objectives is of great help to the central government, which explains why the latter tends to favor or impose their participation. But it also happens, perhaps as frequently, that the central government supports projects that are opposed both by some subcentral governments and by environmental associations. That situation often arises in the domain of transportation.

Completing a motorway, building a new railway line, enlarging an airport, or constructing a transborder tunnel may be considered indispensable by the central government though it is the source of serious inconvenience to the inhabitants of some subcentral jurisdictions. The temptation of the central government is to cut discussions short and have recourse to its authority to impose a solution. Still there are quite a few examples of dialogues that have led to solutions mitigating the inconvenience inflicted on locals without seriously reducing the benefits derived from the projects. An example is the set of discussions which followed, in the early 1990s, the strident protests raised initially by the projected extension of the TGV from Lyons to Marseilles (Lascoumes, 1994: 233–34).

As noted, the most powerful means of coordination to obtain convergence is by the use of financial inducements. In the French case, the central mechanism is that of the *Contrats de Plan Etat Région* (CPER). In their basic structure, they have evolved relatively little since their creation by the decentralization laws of 1982–83, but the government decided in December 2003 to undertake their reform. In each region, the negotiation leading to a CPER is formally one between the regional prefect and the president of the regional council. Many other actors are of course involved. The negotiation leading to the contract takes about two years and the contract must be approved by the Council of Ministers in Paris as well as by the regional council concerned. CPER are different across regions because each region is free to formulate proposals in agreement with its own priorities and expectations about the preferences of the central administration. The central government, however, also announces its own priorities (whether they are genuine is another matter). The CPER currently in progress are for the period 2000–2006. At the beginning of their negotiation, that is in 1998, the central government announced four priorities, one of which was sustainable development, and in 1999, within that priority, the government spelt out a particular emphasis on the limitation of emissions of gas contributing to global warming. Some regions – for example Poitou-Charentes – responded by putting to the fore a comprehensive set of measures addressing that subject.[20]

Disregarding contracts involving lower-level jurisdictions (communes and *départements*) and the funds provided by the European Union, the regions as a whole and the central government earmarked 17.5 billion euros each to the 2000–2006 CPER. The principle of equal funding was thus respected at this aggregate level but the share of the central government in individual CPER varied from 40 per cent (for Ile-de-France) to 63 per cent (for Limousin), reflecting in part a concern with equalization (*péréquation*). The above aggregates represent 15–20 per cent of capital formation by the central government (excluding military expenditures) and 25–30 per cent of capital formation by the regional councils. From a legal perspective, the status of a CEPR is that of a real contract but, because it concerns planning, all claims about instances of non-implementation have been rejected by the administrative courts. Still, and perhaps amazingly, the commitments subscribed to in the CPER since their beginnings in the 1980s have on the whole been respected by both parties.

Many specific agreements are covered by the CPER. An example is the agreements concluded in 1999–2000 between ADEME and the regions for the purpose of promoting more energy-efficient housing and industrial buildings, and introducing new techniques for recycling waste and reducing air pollution. A great number of contractual relationships between governments at different levels are distinct from the CPER, however, which means that contractual relationships are even more important, in quantitative terms, than what the aggregates above suggest. The contracts signed outside the CPER are mostly between the central government on one side and cities, intercommunal bodies and *départements* on the other, although regions and various agencies are often also parties to the contracts. An example is the set of contracts between the central government and particular cities for the purpose of building noise-abating equipment, with regions and *départements* also participating in some cases. In the wake of the Rio Conference, all levels of subcentral government have been encouraged to develop projects for enhancing sustainable development, and the central government has signed contracts with some of them. This program of *Agendas 21 locaux*, however, seems to have had limited success.[21] By contrast, many cities have found ways to fund part of the cost of new modes of clean-air public transportation by way of contracts with other levels of government. Tramways (not that new, by the way), in particular, are currently extended, introduced or reintroduced in many medium-sized towns – larger cities creating or extending underground systems, also with some co-financing.

In this complex system, a lot depends on individual initiatives on the part of officials (mayors, presidents of regional and *départemental* councils, members of the territorial services of the central government and of semi-autonomous agencies), but also of members of associations and of individual citizens. When induced to do so, many of these individual agents or small networks can imagine or conceive, and then develop, environmental or ecological projects that will find support, financial in particular, at some level of government. Thus, despite the many shortcomings that we have noted and contrary to other policy domains (education for instance), in the area of environmental policy, the structure of supply, admittedly somewhat messy, is endowed with flexibility and capacity to respond to demands. If this proposition is granted, the real question concerns the kinds and the weights of the demands that may be forthcoming.

3. THE DEMAND FOR ENVIRONMENTAL POLICIES

3.1 An Introduction

As in the previous section on supply, we use the notion of demand as an organizing principle that makes it convenient and easy to assemble some of the more important factors that in effect point to where a demand for environmental policies originates. We first pay attention to various environmental groups – pressure groups or demand lobbies – that promote policies aimed at curing what are perceived as environmental problems. We then turn our attention to public opinion and political parties as forces that serve to articulate the demands of the public. Finally, we focus on the European Union in its role of 'demander' of environmental policies.

3.2 Environmental Groups

The number of groups active in the environmental and ecological domain lies somewhere between 5000 and 20 000, depending on how strictly one defines that domain. This is an impressive number. It is generally agreed, however, that these groups are relatively weak compared to groups in some other countries. As a rule, they have fewer staff, are less science-based, less disciplined, and less embedded in the population than is the case in several other countries. Still, in France perhaps more than elsewhere, the role of environmental groups in the design and especially in the implementation of environmental policies is essential. The reason for this is simple: groups make up for some of the shortcomings of public decision-makers alluded to in the last section. Before describing the tasks that the groups fulfill, and asking whether these tasks are mutually consistent, two general points must be stressed.

First, the role of groups is more crucial at the local and regional levels than it is at the central level, not that the actions of national environmental organizations are insignificant. The difference in importance will become apparent when we analyze the various ways in which groups help mitigate the shortcomings of public decision-making with regard to environmental and ecological issues. At this point, we need only emphasize the particular weakness in France of environmental groups at the national level. This weakness must be assessed in relation to the policy agenda. For a long time there was no real discrepancy between the groups at the national level and the policy agenda because that agenda was relatively limited and easily dealt with. The main form of group action at the central level were the *sociétés savantes* (learned societies) working toward the conservation of various types of natural resources that were not endangered by economic development as they have come to be. These societies, whose scope and membership could be local or national, were already active in the nineteenth century if not before, and they secured significant results in the first half of the twentieth century: the creation in 1912 on the North coast of Brittany of the bird sanctuary of Sept Iles, the protective status given in 1924 to the Camargue (the area formed by the Rhone delta). Many of the members of these societies were either civil servants in the central administration or elected office-holders at some level of government, and therefore the groups were more like networks than traditional pressure groups or demand lobbies. Their influence on conservation legislation is thus difficult to disentangle from spontaneous initiatives coming from within the administration, or from elected politicians.

In 1969 most of these societies, at all levels of government, became affiliated to an organization called *Fédération Française des Sociétés de Protection de la Nature*, now known as *France-Nature-Environnement* (FNE). Today FNE claims to assemble 3000 associations (with an aggregate membership of 300 000 individuals) and to be present in 50 national forums of consultation.[22] Indeed, consultation and representation are the main activities of FNE, whose structure and resources are ill-adapted to exerting overt pressure. To find more active militancy, one must turn to FNE's affiliates, especially those working at the regional, *départemental* and local levels. Some of the affiliated national organizations, however, also act as pressure groups with regard to special issues. An instance is the extended battle fought by the *Ligue Française de Protection des Oiseaux* to protect birds, in agreement with EU Directives and the French *Conseil d'Etat* rulings, against the mostly illegal deeds of the very influential hunters' groups and the almost unanimous support they get from the French Parliament. Currently there is not much else to mention at the national level. Anti-nuclear actions continue, though on a small scale in no way comparable to the large demonstrations of the mid-1970s. The only issue that generates action, albeit on the part of relatively small constituencies close to José Bové and the *Confédération Paysanne*, is experimentation with GMOs. The French branches of international organizations such as Greenpeace, WWF and Friends of the Earth, are notoriously underdeveloped.

The second general point is that a very large proportion of the activities of environmental groups are financed with public funds. This runs counter to the view that the French state, heir to the French Revolution and faithful to the doctrine of the general will, distrusts pressure groups and does everything it can to undermine their influence. This view, endorsed by many authors, is often expressed by the groups themselves, presumably to explain away their weakness. A more sophisticated and even conspiratorial interpretation of the central government's behavior is that, by financially supporting the groups and entrusting them with productive tasks, it renders them docile and unwilling to question its policies. There may be some truth in the analysis of the consequences of governmental support to the groups, but these consequences can be seen as side-effects of the government's strategy rather than as its intended objectives. What seems to motivate support to environmental groups is the awareness on the part of the central government, and in particular of its Ministry of Environment, of the essential role these groups play in the realization of governmental objectives. This is true at any rate of the support by the central government and most of its territorial services in charge of the environment. The conspiratorial interpretation may have some plausibility in regard to some of the support granted by subcentral governments.

Support takes many forms other than outright subsidies, and their quantitative significance is difficult to gauge. A main form of support is legal. A law passed in 1976 has created, between the ordinary associations and the more prestigious *associations reconnues d'utilité publique*, a new category, the '*associations agréées*' (an expression meaning something like 'accredited' or 'licensed' associations). The powers of the *associations agréées* were extended by a 1995 law. Depending on their scope, these *associations agréées de protection de l'environnement* (this is now their exact name) can be accredited by the prefects or by the Ministry in Paris. This accreditation can be reversed in the same way, and both kinds of decisions may be brought before the courts. According to Jacqueline Morand-Deviller (1987 [2002]: 28), there are about 200 national *associations agréées*, 200 in the region of *Ile-de-France*, and about 30 to 40 in each of the other regions. Being singled out in this way confers some new powers and opens up some new possibilities as we will illustrate.

What are the tasks that environmental groups can accomplish? First, some groups are able to bring valuable information to decision-makers who need it. We noted in Section 2 the difficulties encountered by many decision-makers at the subcentral levels in mastering the highly technical information required to address many environmental and ecological issues. Exclusive reliance on the information provided by the personnel of the territorial services of the central government has its dangers, especially when these services are not wholly dedicated to the pursuit of environmental goals, as is the case in agriculture, public works, and to a lesser degree industry. The problem is that groups themselves often lack the necessary technological knowledge. Where they have the required knowledge, however, their contribution can be quite substantial. It is an important function of national and international organizations such as those mentioned earlier to improve the technical capacity of local environmentalists. This is also a function of a number of public institutions such as the *Institut Français de l'Environnement*, ADEME, and so on.

Second, many groups, especially but not exclusively *associations agréées*, are entrusted by governments at all levels, including the EU, with quasi-productive tasks.[23] Often, the main reason why governments 'outsource' some of their responsibilities to groups is that governments lack the resources, in particular human resources, to do the job themselves. This is particularly true of subcentral governments. In turn, both for economic and motivational reasons, the organizations chosen are environmental groups rather than private firms. Groups are cheaper because they mostly rely on unpaid labor, and they are particularly efficient and reliable in accomplishing ecological tasks because the motivation of their members to perform such tasks well is difficult to match in other forms of organization. This comparative advantage of groups is particularly apparent with regard to the management of bird and other natural reserves, biotopes, forests, and so on. It is not absent, however, from the many other kinds of work entrusted to groups: thus groups are asked to provide an ecological education to children, to raise the awareness of subsets of the population regarding ecological issues, and to promote responsible behavior such as saving energy and recycling waste. They also receive contracts to study and monitor a number of variables. Regional, general and municipal councils rely on groups to design programs to deal with particular environmental and ecological issues and sometimes with the environment as a whole. Groups are attracted to these tasks because they confirm their social usefulness and because they provide financial resources that can be allocated to other purposes.

The third task of environmental groups is obvious. By their militancy, which is expressed in many ways, some of them violent, environmental groups mitigate a natural tendency among decision-makers to give insufficient attention and weight to environmental and ecological issues. Militant groups are mostly situated in the provinces and, as a consequence, their activities are geographically limited in scope. Their action usually targets decisions of subcentral governments, particularly those affecting land use, but it can be addressed to the central government when it is at this level that decisions, though local in their effects, are made. We have already mentioned the South-East TGV project of the 1990s. In this instance, the environmentalists won a partial victory. A recent example is the re-opening (after a spectacular accident) of the Mont-Blanc Franco-Italian Tunnel to truck traffic. In that case the local environmentalists in the valley in which the French entrance is situated, even though they fought with some vehemence, eventually lost almost completely in the short run on which they had focused. The French government could not escape the fact that a way had to be found in the very short run to allow truck traffic in and out of Italy – closing one tunnel would only have displaced the pressure onto another.[24] A third illustration refers to the episode that gave stamina to the budding environmental movement in France. This was the case of a ski station planned within the Vanoise National Park in the Alps. After a long fight, President Pompidou himself decided that the project had to be abandoned.

The most critical function fulfilled by environmental groups is the fourth one – the use of the courts to enforce the rules. Again, this activity takes place mainly in the provinces. There are technical reasons for that, in particular the procedure that has to be used for bringing matters to the courts. The main reason, however, is that subcentral governments are among the major violators of rules, while the field services of the central government are unreliable enforcers of the rules that these subcentral governments as well as private firms and individuals tend to violate.[25] In fact, in as much as both the local governments and the territorial services of the central government other than those, like the DIREN, which report exclusively to the Ministry of Environment, are chiefly concerned with economic development, employment and similar objectives, militant environmental groups, where they exist, can constitute a counter-force and mitigate this bias. In addition to insufficient motivation, the lack of resources constrains the enforcement of environmental rules by territorial services. A correct enforcement of safety and anti-pollution regulations, for instance, tends to be very time-consuming while available time for doing the job is typically scarce.

The three main types of courts in the French system are relevant in matters that pertain to the environment. We summarize a somewhat complex judiciary organization as follows. To bring a matter to a court, an association must have a collective object or interest, defined in its by-laws, that sufficiently justifies its active concern in the matter. If this condition is met – courts are quite strict on this – and if the author of the violation is a private agent, the rule has always been at least since the law of 1901 that any association can bring the matter to a 'civil' court (a *tribunal de grande instance*, and especially its segment for urgent matters, the *juge des référés*) and ask it to impose immediately the cessation of the illegal act and/or grant a financial compensation (which takes more time). If the violation is the outcome of a decision or a rule made by a public authority – a subcentral government in particular or the executive branch of the central government – then an association must bring the case to an administrative court (*tribunal administratif*). Finally, *associations agréées* have the power to bring cases against private agents to a criminal court (a *tribunal correctionnel*). In many circumstances, associations can choose among the three types of courts. This would be possible, for instance, if a public authority has allowed the infringement of a rule by a private agent (a frequent case), and if this seriously harms some protected object (human, animal, historical, and so on). This explains that the strategies adopted by environmental groups vary considerably. In Brittany, the very active federation of groups called *Eaux et Rivières de Bretagne* has adopted a particularly aggressive strategy: according to Raymond Léost (1998: 85), it brings 60 per cent of cases to the criminal courts and 20 per cent to each of the other two types (in the case of civil courts mainly to the *juge des référés*, to obtain immediate injunctions). The main rationale is that obtaining rulings from the administrative courts takes too long.

It is sometimes claimed that the four tasks undertaken by environmental groups are not compatible with each other because there is a conflict between working for public administrations and questioning their decisions and at the limit bringing them to court. Though this is true to a large extent, there are many groups which manage to overcome this difficulty (see the case studies in Lascoumes, 1994). Associations entertain different relationships with different public administrations – for instance, they may take mayors to court while simultaneously cooperating with central or regional governments. Also, because it is relatively costless to create an association, barriers to entry in the world of environmental groups are low. Thus discontented members of a group can easily secede and create another which is more militant and independent of public subsidies.

The main limitation of the contribution of groups is elsewhere. As their strength is mostly at the subcentral level, they tend to focus on issues whose geographical scope is less than that of the country, and *a fortiori* less than that of the world. This means that in France the contribution of groups to issues like global warming and the depletion of the ozone layer is limited. These global issues, however, have become those that most worry public opinion. We now turn our attention to that matter.

3.3 Public Opinion and Political Parties

There has been a considerable increase over the long run in the attention given to environmental issues everywhere. The main structures of policymaking in France were designed and implemented in the late 1960s and early 1970s in a context of 'low ecological pressure' (Theys, 1998: 24). The thrust came from a few civil servants and politicians. At the time, public opinion was largely unconcerned with the environment. (This was to change shortly afterwards with the build-up of nuclear generators and the rise of the anti-nuclear movement.) This is not the case any more, though the increase has not been uniform and smooth. There have been large fluctuations over time in the rank occupied by the environment in people's priorities. To a large extent these fluctuations are common to European, and perhaps worldwide, public opinion (Boy, 1999). These fluctuations are, no doubt, also related to the political context. According to Herbert Kitschelt (1990), an increase in support given to the environmental cause in France tends to follow disillusionment with the performance of the Left when it is in power, while when the Right is in power, the cause loses some of its appeal. The relative importance given to the environment is also different across locations at any point in time. One reason for these differences seems to be a negative correlation between the level of unemployment and the priority given to environmental issues (Bonnetain and Boy, 1995). A correlation between these same variables is probably also a factor in the fluctuations over time.

The level of concern for the environment as expressed in polls is now extremely high. In a 2002 poll, nine persons out of ten declared themselves to be 'fairly' or 'very' concerned. A majority, however, were not ready to accept reductions in their standard of living and their comfort, or any slowing down of the economy for the sake of preventing the degradation of the environment. In that poll, 62 per cent indicated they would refuse to pay 10 per cent more to buy 'green products' and again 62 per cent of the active population (including students) said they used their car to go to work (IFEN, 2003a). There is also a difference on these matters between the public at large and various kinds of decision-makers. A recent poll documents this with regard to members of the two houses of the French Parliament: on all the issues and possible remedies, the answers of the members of Parliament reflect much less concern with the environment than do polls that measure public opinion in general.[26]

An interesting characteristic noted in Joseph Szarka (2002) and in the IFEN study is that for some time, public opinion has been more worried about the state of the planet than about that of their own country or region. In the IFEN study, the proportion of respondents who judged the state of the environment to be bad at the level of the planet, of France, and of their region, are 63, 19 and 15 per cent respectively. This fact must be considered together with two others previously noted. One is that groups are more active with regard to local and regional than with national issues. The other is that dealing with global effects at this point in time requires putting pressure on consumers and small producers rather than on large industrial units. These facts taken together suggest that politics is essential regarding environmental matters, and that voters rather than interest groups must be relied upon to press governments to adopt policies that target global issues and befit their seriousness. This poses a difficult question. Should the required electoral mobilization take place primarily at the subcentral or central levels of government? It is understandable that political parties geared to ecology have hesitated between the two strategies.

The main ecology party today is *Les Verts* (hereafter the *Verts*) created in 1984.[27] Officially, it is strongly in favor of decentralization both in general and in terms of environmental policies.[28] Decentralization is key to the movement's general philosophy and approach to society which is reinforced by a belief in linguistic and cultural regionalism. The rationale for the *Verts*' view regarding environmental decentralization is that the largest and most active environmental groups operate mainly at subcentral levels.

Yet, in practice, the attitude of the *Verts* with regard to decentralization is ambivalent, which may reflect electoral imperatives as they are a small party representing between 3 and 10 per cent of the vote. Given the current fragmentation of the French electorate (in the first round of the 2002 presidential election, the representatives of the two main parties each polled less than 20 per cent), the higher limit of this range is not negligible, even though it tends to be reached only in elections for the European Parliament and for regional councils, both based on proportional representation and belonging to a category called in Szarka (2002: 56) 'second-order elections'. A greater constraint is that at the last count (2003), the *Verts* numbered only 10 000 regular members. Moreover, they have not been able to attract the kind of candidates who can win under systems based on a two-stage majority in single-member districts, which is the traditionally dominant system in France, governing in particular both national elections (legislative and presidential) and elections for the councils of the *départements*. The consequence is that the *Verts* in the latter case are completely absent from *départemental* councils. The *Verts* entered Parliament for the first time in 1997 with six seats, and obtained three seats in 2002, in both cases thanks to their alliance with the Socialist Party. In the case of municipal elections, based on a mixed system with a majority premium, the same alliance allowed the *Verts* to obtain seats in many municipal councils, but very seldom the job of mayor – some 30 mayors out of 36 000, none in main cities. However, in many municipalities held by the Left, especially in large cities, members of the *Verts* were entrusted with significant responsibilities. A case in point is Paris where a coalition of the Left which included the *Verts* was followed by significant pro-environment policy changes. As for the presidential elections, each of them since 1974 has been an occasion for the views of ecologists to be communicated to the electorate by candidates who, since 1981, have obtained between 3 and 5 per cent of the vote in the first round.[29]

To sum up, at no level have elections granted much satisfaction to the *Verts* or for that matter to any other ecology party. The most unfavorable elections for them are those at the levels of the *départements* and small communes. In both cases, the *Verts* do not have candidates who can be elected. Malicious observers could relate this handicap to a salient aspect of their current platform, which proposes the elimination of the *département* level and the assembling of small communes into larger units governed by councils elected under proportional representation. A more charitable way of saying the same thing is that the *Verts*, unlike the main parties, do not let their selfish electoral interests prevent them from offering reasonable solutions to long-standing problems.

In spite of their electoral weakness, the ecology parties, the *Verts* among them, have had an important impact on policymaking through the incentives they have provided other political parties to 'green' their platforms and agendas. The Socialist Party, however, has been prevented from moving significantly in that direction by its alliance with the Communist Party, on the whole hostile in practice to environmental policies. The Right, on the other hand, has not been constrained in that way, and Jacques Chirac has not shied from making bold promises such as his 2002 electoral one of adding to the French Constitution a 10-article *Charte de l'Environnement* which is, at the time of writing, being debated in Parliament.[30]

The ecology parties have also found a more direct way to influence policymaking, by having their leader or one of their other members, appointed as Minister of the Environment. This has occurred twice; in 1988–1991 with Brice Lalonde, and in 1997–2002 with Dominique Voynet. To these two cases, both under Socialist Prime Ministers, one could add that of Corinne Lepage, a well-known environmental lawyer who was given in 1995–1997 the environment portfolio in a center-right Cabinet. These periods have been marked by particularly active environmental policymaking and by a degree of re-centralization – a positive relation between the two being perhaps unavoidable. We give two examples. One is the creation of the DIREN through which Lalonde, even though very favorable to decentralization in principle, nonetheless strengthened the authority of the Ministry of Environment at the level of the regions.

The other illustration is the policy followed by Voynet with regard to important arm's length agencies such as the ADEME and the six *Agences de l'eau*. The twin ideas underlying the creation of such agencies were firstly to make environmental policies completely self-financing in some specific sectors and secondly, for that purpose, to provide some authorities with a large degree of autonomy, in particular with regard to financial resources and the allocation of funds. In the case of water, the *Agences de l'eau*, created in 1964, were given the power to levy a charge on private users of water – that is, on consumers and industrial firms, but not on farmers – and to use the proceeds to subsidize improvements in water treatment. The central government appoints the head of each *Agence*, but subcentral governments and users of water are also represented in the governance structure and in practice are closely involved in decision-making. The *Agences* have been able to assemble very considerable sums of money and to finance more or less all capital spending on water treatment and sewerage, thus implementing a kind of 'water pays for water' principle. They are vigorously supported by the main users of their funds, that is by industrialists and subcentral governments.

Both welfare economists and ecologists, however, have strongly objected to a mechanism in which the proceeds of environmental charges are recirculated as subsidies or as loans to the same population of polluters. This, the argument goes, is not a correct application of the 'polluter pays principle' which requires a complete separation between pollution taxes fixed so as to internalize externalities, and public spending on environmental policies.[31] Voynet endorsed that argument, but she was not successful in changing the system with regard to water. She did succeed, however, with regard to a much less politically difficult case, the ADEME. That agency, in charge of promoting energy conservation, environment-friendly treatment and management of waste, and ways to diminish air and noise pollution, was mainly financed by several specific taxes related to pollution. In 1999, these taxes were replaced by a single 'general tax on polluting activities', whose proceeds were not given to ADEME but were earmarked to finance something completely outside its domain, to wit the implementation of the law on the *Réduction du Temps de Travail* (also called *loi sur les 35 heures* or *loi Aubry*). This, it was argued, yielded a 'double dividend'. As a consequence, the ADEME is now financed from the general budget. Its autonomy is reduced and its funding less secure (see Adnot, 2001).

3.4 The European Union

Even though the European Union's responsibilities in environmental matters officially begin with the Single European Act of 1987, the influence of the EU on the environmental policies of member countries started much earlier and is now widely acknowledged as being pervasive as well as decisive. It is important for our purpose to stress at the outset three characteristics of the environmental action of the European Union.

First, in that domain the European Union rules by way of directives rather than by regulations. Unlike regulations which apply directly in each member country, directives oblige countries to 'transpose' EU prescriptions in their own corpus of laws and regulations. To varying degrees, this gives member states some discretion. As a consequence, we can treat the European Union's decisions in this area – as well, as a matter of fact, as the obligations formulated in international treaties such as Kyoto – as making demands on the French governmental system.[32] Another consequence is that the directives that influence French laws and regulations are not directly visible and the population is aware of them only when their role is publicly acknowledged. Although such acknowledgements are not lacking, a tendency to underestimate the magnitude of the role of the European Union persists. In fact, many of the environmental policies, laws and regulations referred to in the foregoing discussion implement directives adopted in Brussels.

Second, in part because the European Union has no money, it produces a regular flow of often very demanding directives but does almost nothing to ease compliance by way of subsidies, grants and loans.[33]

Third, nowadays, environmental policymaking by the EU has clearly something to do with the global nature of the problems to be addressed. Inasmuch as the required collective action to tackle these global problems (global warming, the depletion of the ozone layer, sustainable development, biodiversity) requires decisions at something like the world level, the EU seems more apt to be influential than are single-member countries. One should then expect EU commitments to be made operational by directives. This, however, is not the whole story. The EU's involvement in environmental matters predates by several decades the emergence of the global concerns referred to above. Moreover, much of the content of the directives has little to do with these concerns. In reality the main long-standing motive for the involvement of the EU is the goal, central to European integration since its beginnings with the Treaty of Rome, of creating a single competitive market, and for that purpose of eliminating barriers to trade and distortions to competition (see Breton and Salmon, 2001). Environmental regulation by member states has the potential to fragment the common market and to distort competition among firms; regulation at the EU level mitigates that possibility. In many respects, this logic is carried further in the EU than it is in federal countries such as Canada, Switzerland and the United States.[34]

To these three characteristics of EU environmental policy, we may add a feature of the French governmental system noted previously, which is that subcentral governments at the three levels have no or little power to make rules. This explains that one important issue raised in some countries, in particular federal ones, does not arise in the French case. That issue is the adaptation of the rules made by subcentral governments to the obligation of the central government to transpose in its laws and regulations prescriptions and directives decided at a higher level – at the level of the EU but more generally at that of various international conferences and treaties. We will see, however, that a variant of the problem may be relevant in France.

How do the demands emanating from the EU, generally in the form of directives, affect the various relationships described in the preceding sections and subsections? Before endeavoring to answer that question, one more point should be stressed. Some directives require little or no response from the French government because the rule or regime they prescribe is already in force in France. A case in point is the directive, enacted in 1984, which requires that air-polluting industrial facilities cannot open without an authorization. As noted by Corinne Larrue (1999: 189), this rule has been in effect in France for more than a century. Many directives, however, have compelled the French government to modify substantially the legal framework and other features of its policies. This is the case, for example, of the directive of 1980 on the quality of drinking water and of the ozone directive of 1992.

One important effect of the EU's intense involvement in environmental matters is to reinforce the role and influence of the Ministry of Environment within the central government as well as vis-à-vis private agents and subcentral governments. We noted that directives do not apply directly, but must be 'transposed' in French laws and regulations. The Ministry of Environment is mainly responsible for that task, and later for the implementation of the new rules. At the subcentral level, this enhances the authority of the DIREN. Another effect of EU rule-making, noted by many observers, is that it has compelled the French system to move toward a more 'command and control' mode of governance (Larrue, 1999: 183). As we saw, the way of dealing with environmental problems in France tends, or tended, to be relatively flexible, relying more on dialogue, negotiation, assessment of particular circumstances by trusted civil servants, and most importantly on financial incentives, rather than on stiff impositions of precise uniform rules. Many EU directives fix precise uniform rules, constraining directly activities or characteristics that are judged harmful to the environment. The French system has had to adapt. French legislation transposing EU directives necessarily includes the same prescriptions. It is difficult, however, to appraise how strong is the effect of these directives because that effect cannot be fully disentangled from that of other forces working in the same direction, in particular the increased responsibility in environmental problems deemed the most serious, of consumers, farmers, and small entrepreneurs compared to the responsibility of large industrial firms. Even without EU directives, negotiations with the individuals making up these large categories, or rather with their representatives, are necessarily different from negotiations with the smaller number of large firms.

This notwithstanding, one can argue that the philosophy underlying environmental governance in France endures. EU norms are still typically implemented in a framework of negotiation and, when consistent with EU prescriptions, with financial incentives of various sorts. The involvement of subcentral governments remains essential. To reduce air pollution and save energy as prescribed by EU directives, the powers of mayors to introduce speed limits and material devices that contribute to their enforcement, to exclude cars altogether from some portions of cities, to develop public transportation, to encourage environmental associations and so on, are essential. The councils of the *départements* and the regions make use of some of these powers and others falling in the same category. Moreover, as stressed in Section 2, finance is possibly as decisive a tool as regulation to achieve environmental policies. Some financial support is given out of its budget by the central government, which also creates financial incentives in the form of tax relief and manipulation of the tax structure (unleaded petrol being less taxed than leaded, for instance). Subcentral governments, those of the regions in particular, are important providers of funds, especially to finance capital investment. So are the *Agences de l'eau*. The considerable financial effort undertaken in the 1990s to modernize water supply and sewerage facilities so as to respect the water and sewerage EU directives, involved first of all the *Agences de l'eau* and the communes, but also all the other levels of government as well as specialized banks and the financial market.

To encourage different actors to implement EU prescriptions – adopted by the central government as its own so to say – the main tools are the contractual policy discussed earlier and a host of planning obligations and consultative forums and procedures. This, however, does not prevent subcentral governments from using their resources for environmental purposes unrelated to the objectives and obligations decided at the EU level. This raises the problem alluded to above of subcentral public authorities heeding the obligations agreed to by the central government. As one of the major concerns of the EU is preventing environmental policies of member countries from becoming obstacles to trade and distortions to competition, there must be limits to the constraints that these policies of subcentral governments impose in addition to those set at the EU level. To avoid distorting competition, there is also a need for a close scrutiny of financial grants and loans awarded to private agents. Moreover, to avoid obstacles to trade, norms fixed at the EU level are sometimes interpreted as ceiling requirements – no member country being authorized in these cases to impose stricter norms (see Vogel et al., 2003). This last point is irrelevant to our discussion because, as noted, subcentral governments in France do not impose in any significant way norms of their own. The freedom of subcentral governments, however, may be constrained by the same principle with regard, not to regulation, but to grants and loans to private firms. It is difficult to deny that such financing distorts competition – this also applies to financing by arm's length authorities such as ADEME and *Agences de l'eau*. It appears that so far these constraints on the initiatives of subcentral governments have remained more potential than effective. In fact, it seems that as yet the EU has not significantly constrained the financial efforts of subcentral governments which are targeted at plausible environmental objectives.

4. CONCLUSION

The realities we have been concerned with in the foregoing discussion – environmental and ecological problems and policies, and governance systems and policymaking – are not only multifaceted and therefore complex, they are also deeply rooted in the history and culture of people. This is certainly true of France. The most common practice among economists, well illustrated in the organization of most textbooks, is to pay attention first to demand on the general assumption, broadly valid over the long-term, that supply is a response to demand. We have begun our chapter with a discussion of supply – that is, with a discussion of the institutions of governance and their mode of interaction – because, in France, as we hope we have made clear, the endogenous demand for environmental policies is to a considerable degree shaped by the supply side.

In the mind of most scholars, decentralization is classically associated with the division of powers or responsibilities among governments located at different jurisdictional levels. One of the reasons for this is that work on decentralization has often been related to discussions of federalism and of federal problems. France is a unitary state, but at least since the reforms of the early 1980s, it is decentralized in that classical sense, even though all the powers continue to be formally owned by the central government in Paris. But France is additionally decentralized in a different way. Through the institution of the prefects and through its field or territorial services, the central government is itself decentralized (a reality sometimes called *déconcentration*). The importance of coordination has been stressed by students of federalism as an essential component of decentralization. The point is simply that without coordination, decentralization will be wasteful. We have abundantly documented the need for and the broad incidence of coordination institutions and activities throughout the French governmental system.

Not all powers related to the environment are assigned to all jurisdictional levels in France. This notwithstanding, the division of environmental responsibilities is carried sufficiently far to produce a considerable degree of concurrency in assignments. Concurrency need not and does not beget uniformity in policies, even if it calls for, and receives, coordination. Concurrency will, however, stimulate competition among the various actors concerned with the environment, to the benefit of the latter and of the citizenry in general.

The increasing saliency of the environment in general, consequent on the emergence of new environmental problems such as global warming and the depletion of the ozone layer, has found a counterpart in changes in the demand for public environmental policies. In France, this has taken place more through the workings of political competition as structured by electoral rules at the various levels of jurisdiction than by the agency of environmental groups. At the same time, we have enquired into whether these changes in demand have affected the relative influence of central and subcentral governments in the shaping of environmental policies.

The Achilles heel of even generally approved and supported policies is often located at the level of monitoring and especially of enforcement. We have mentioned and described the actions of institutions of various sorts at that level of activity, and remarked that these were probably not sufficient to guarantee optimal implementation. We have also noted the role that groups of citizens, acting through the courts, can and do play in this all-important area.

We have noted the influence of directives from the EU on environmental policies and regulations in France, and on the heightened status that the environmental and ecological concerns of Brussels confer on the Ministry of Environment. As with most things that originate at a more senior tier of governance, there is a resulting tendency toward increased centralization, but by stimulating more activity at junior levels, that centralization is matched by a compensating decentralization that may be smaller or larger that the increased centralization.

We are aware that many dimensions of the question of optimal governance still have to be addressed. We hope that our discussion and the framework in which it is embodied can serve as a basis for future research and elaboration.

NOTES

* We wish to thank Jean-Marc Callois for his comments on an earlier draft of the chapter. The usual disclaimer applies.

1. The nuclear industry was a major exception for a number of years.
2. Among the factors that explain the capacity to make use of tailor-made prescriptions, we include a lesser concern in France with the legal norm of equality of treatment than that which obtains in a country such as Germany (Knoepfel, 1998: 166).
3. Small firm and agricultural activities are also important. We consider them later.
4. The department changes its name each time there is a change of Prime Minister (see Szarka, 2002: 73–6). At the time of writing, with Jean-Pierre Raffarin as Prime Minister, it is called *Ministère de l'Ecologie et du Développement Durable*. For convenience, we refer to it as Ministry of Environment.
5. *Agences de bassin* are now referred to as *Agences de l'eau*.
6. A field or territorial service is the part of the personnel of a ministry which is located in a region and/or *département* and is in charge of implementing the policies of the ministry in those jurisdictions.
7. The French administration is divided into *corps*, that is into sets of persons whose recruitment, status, career and function are supposed to be the same. The *grands corps* are the elite part of this system. They are recruited mainly from the best graduates of either the *Ecole Polytechnique* or the *Ecole Nationale d'Administration*. On the ground that they must be independent, they have kept the privilege, inherited from the *Ancien*

Régime corporations, to govern themselves. The best known are the *Inspection des Finances*, the *Cour des Comptes*, the *Conseil d'Etat*, the *Corps des Mines* and the *Corps des Ponts et Chaussées*. The *corps diplomatique* and the *corps préfectoral* are somewhat less autonomous and exclusive than the foregoing, and have lost ground over the last decades (for more detail, see Kessler, 1994).

8. To be exact, only those among the *ingénieurs des mines* who come from the top graduates of *Ecole Polytechnique* belong to the *Corps des Mines* (their official title is *Ingénieur du Corps des Mines*). The same is true, *mutatis mutandis*, for the *ingénieurs des ponts et chaussées*.
9. The creation of a *corps de l'environnement* was contemplated by the government in the late 1980s and early 1990s. The idea was eventually dismissed on a variety of grounds (see Kessler, 1999). In any case, one should recall that most, if not all, the *grands corps* are one or even two centuries old.
10. It must be said that the environmental responsibilities of the DRIRE are limited to industrial and nuclear installations and are entrusted to an inspection division which is largely separated from the part of the DRIRE concerned with development.
11. According to Szarka (2003: 93), French policymaking combines in the environmental domain 'a statist top-down mode of policy formulation' and 'a pragmatic, bottom up mode of implementation, based on "humdrum" compromises with polluters'. Szarka also cites a paper by Larrue and Chabason (1998) in which it is noted that 'the main characteristic of the implementation of French environmental policy is that it is based on consensus rather than on imposition of constraints'.
12. These figures apply to metropolitan France only, excluding Guadeloupe, Guyane, Martinique and Réunion. The 'general council' is to the *département* what the regional council is to the region; for the sake of clarity, we refer to it as '*départemental* council' or as 'council of the *département*'.
13. To be exact, one should distinguish among the regulatory powers of the mayors those that are linked to the role of representative of the center, and as such are submitted in principle to some hierarchical monitoring by the prefects, and the powers that are assigned by law to the mayors as representatives of the population. The prefects can question decisions authorized by the latter only by way of bringing these decisions before the courts.
14. This may change as a result of the revision of the French Constitution which took place in March 2003. It will now be possible for a subcentral government to seek the right, as an experiment limited in time, to adopt rules that are contrary to laws and regulations in force in the whole country.
15. The limitations to which the *Agences* are subjected are important in explaining the complexities of the French system of water management. The *Agences de l'eau* are a significant aspect of the decentralized governance of environmental policies. See Appendix A.
16. The first part of the *Code de l'Environnement*, synthesizing 39 laws, was published in 2000.
17. The DRIRE, however, have *départemental* sections and are, in principle, subject to the hierarchical authority of the *départemental* and regional prefects.
18. A problem, incidentally, which is not dissimilar *mutatis mutandis* from that encountered in the relations between governments at different levels in federal countries.
19. Even though the imposition upon subcentral governments of new obligations is also a method used. For instance, cities and metropolitan areas over a certain size are now compelled to establish *Plans de Déplacement Urbain* (PDU), the purpose of which is to plan ways of making transportation more energy efficient and less polluting.
20. The mechanism is not unlike the better-known one of matching grants. One difference perhaps is the contractual framework within which the relationship develops and its capacity to incorporate different contents across regions.
21. As is well known, Chapter 28 of the 'Agenda 21' program adopted in the wake of the Rio Conference recommends that, in all countries, each local government should build up, through a process involving all the individuals, firms and associations concerned in its jurisdiction, a program of sustainable development at its level. According to data collected in 2001 by the International Council for Local Environmental Initiatives, there were more than 2000 local Agenda 21 in Germany, more than 400 both in Italy and in

the United Kingdom, and 69 in France. These figures are uncertain: local *chartes de l'environnement* are sometimes counted as first-generation local Agenda 21 and sometimes treated as something different; the population concerned by each Agenda 21 varies enormously within and across countries (IFEN, 2003b: 124–25). It is also true that the local Agenda 21 program has been imposed on local governments in countries such as the United Kingdom and Sweden, whereas in France the program relies on voluntary initiatives of local governments, with only weak financial incentives provided by the central government. Thus, in France, local programs are not necessarily recorded at the central level. The whole program lags in France because, so far, it has been given a relatively low priority, not only by the central government and its territorial services, but also by most subcentral governments (see at http://www.association4d.org/article.php 3?id_article=39 the judgment formulated by D4, an association created in 1993 to help implement the Rio sustainable development program). The central government decided in 2003 to target 500 local Agenda 21 in 2008.

22. These figures are about twice as high as those, cited by Szarka (2002, p. 39, note 11), that applied to the early 1990s.
23. This function is more explicit in the case of the *associations agréées de protection de l'environnement*, however, since the law says that they 'will be called upon to participate in the actions of the public bodies that concern the environment' (article L141-2 of the *Code de l'Environnment*).
24. What will happen in the long run is another matter.
25. Violation of European Union Directives by laws adopted by the French Parliament can be redressed both in France by the *Conseil d'Etat* and, at the European level, by the European Court of Justice. A case in point is the still pending issue of bird protection.
26. *Le Monde*, 3 March 2004, p. 9.
27. Its full name is: *Les Verts. Confédération Ecologiste – Parti Ecologiste*. See Szarka (2002: 5–7) for a useful explication of the difference between ecologism and environmentalism.
28. The platform of *Génération Ecologie*, the party created in 1990 by Brice Lalonde and for a while a serious competitor to the *Verts*, was also strongly in favor of decentralization.
29. Even though the *Verts* can now claim on average more voters than the Communist Party, the strength of the latter lies in the large number of its members, the large number of experienced and well-known office-holders in the communes and the *départements*, and, above all, the concentration of its electoral support in some strongholds. As a consequence, the Communist Party has more seats in Parliament and is a more compelling electoral ally of the Socialist Party than the *Verts* can seriously pretend to have been or to be. Ile-de-France, Alsace, Brittany and Rhone-Alpes are four regions in which the *Verts* are more electorally successful than elsewhere, but these regions are far from constituting strongholds. To some extent, the difference between the Communist Party and the *Verts* may be a consequence of the former having been in the past, over many decades, one of the major French parties, in power in the councils of quite a few *départements* and in many cities, including large ones, whereas the latter remains a young party, with a relatively short experience of being associated with decision-making while in office.
30. In a rather inconspicuous way, except for its Article 5 on the hotly debated 'precautionary principle'.
31. See *Commissariat Général du Plan* (1997); OECD (1997); Vourc'h and Lenain (2001).
32. There is a close relation between international commitments and EU prescriptions: in March 2002, the EU decided to oblige member states to ratify the Kyoto Protocol.
33. The sums specifically devoted to the environment by the European Union, in the form of programs such as LIFE or projects financed by the European Investment Bank, are quite modest. Progressively, a substantial part of the structural and cohesion funds, whose purposes are broader, has been reallocated to environmental programs. This amounts to something like 10 per cent of the budget of the EU (see Larrue, 1999; London, 2001). That budget, however, is notoriously small and France's share in the 10 per cent that goes to the environment is particularly tiny.
34. On this point, on the comparison between the EU and the United States, see Vogel et al. (2003).

REFERENCES

Adnot, Philippe (2001), *ADEME: la grande illusion*, Rapport du Sénat no. 236, Paris: Sénat.

Barraqué, Bernard (1999), 'Water institutions and management in France: An overview', paper presented at the *Semana Internacional de Estudios sobre Gestão de Recursos Hidricos*, Foz de Iguaçu, 19–23 April, URL:http://www.ufrgs.br/iph/**barraque**_water_institutions_and_management_in_france.pdf.

Bonnetain, Philippe and Daniel Boy (1995), 'Electorat écologiste et risque industriel', *Revue Française de Science Politique*, **45**(3), 454–75.

Boy, Daniel (1999), 'L'évolution de la préoccupation environnementale en France dans les vingt-cinq dernières années', in P. Lascoumes (ed.) (1999), *Instituer l'environnement: Vingt-cinq ans d'administration de l'environnement*, Paris and Montreal: L'Harmattan, Ch. 13.

Breton, Albert and Pierre Salmon (2001), 'External effects of domestic regulations: Comparing internal and external barriers to trade', *International Review of Law and Economics*, **21**(2), 135–55.

Commissariat Général du Plan (1997), *Evaluation du dispositif des Agences de l'eau*, Paris: la Documentation Française.

Defeuilley, Christophe and Olivier Godard (1998), 'La nouvelle politique de gestion des déchets d'emballages: quand concertation et décentralisation ne riment pas avec incitation', in Bernard Barraqué and Jacques Theys (eds), *Les Politiques d'environnement: Évaluation de la première génération 1971–1995*, Paris: Editions Recherches, pp. 180–208.

Holmstrom, Bengt and Paul Milgrom (1991), 'Multitask principal–agent analyses: Incentive contracts, asset ownership, and job design', *Journal of Law, Economics and Organization*, **7**(Special Issue), 24–52.

IFEN (Institut Français de l'Environnement) (2003a), 'Les Français et l'environnement: opinions et attitude au début de 2002', *Etudes et Travaux*, **39**, December.

IFEN (2003b), '45 indicateurs du développement durable: une contribution de l'IFEN', *Etudes et Travaux*, **41**, December.

Kessler, Marie-Christine (1994), *Les Grands Corps*, Paris: Presses Universitaires de France.

Kessler, Marie-Christine (1999), 'Pourquoi n'y a-t-il pas de corps de l'environnement?', in Lascoumes (ed.) (1999), *Instituer l'environnement: Vingt-cinq ans d'administration de l'environnement*, Paris and Montreal: L'Harmattan, Ch. 5.

Kitschelt, Herbert (1990), 'La gauche libertaire et les écologistes', *Revue Française de Science Politique*, **40**(3), 339–65.

Knoepfel, Peter (1998), 'Remarques d'un observateur étranger sur la lutte contre la pollution atmosphérique en France', in Bernard Barraqué and Jacques Theys (eds), *Les Politiques d'environnement: Évaluation de la première génération 1971–1995*, Paris: Editions Recherches, pp. 153–70.

Larrue, Corinne (1999), 'Le ministère de l'environnement et la mise en oeuvre en France de la politique européenne de l'environnement', in P. Lascoumes (ed.), *Instituer l'environnement: Vingt-cinq ans d'administration de l'environnement*, Paris and Montreal: L'Harmattan, pp. 179–93.

Larrue, Corinne (2000), *Analyser les politiques publiques d'environnement*, Paris and Montreal: L'Harmattan.

Larrue, Corinne and Lucien Chabason (1998), 'France: fragmented policy and consensual implementation', in Kenneth Hanf and Alf-Inge Jansen (eds), *Governance and Environment in Western Europe: Politics, Policy and Administration*, New York: Addison Wesley Longman, pp. 60–81.

Lascoumes, Pierre (1994), *L'éco-pouvoir: environnement et politiques*, Paris: Editions La Découverte.

Lascoumes, Pierre (ed.) (1999), *Instituer l'environnement: Vingt-cinq ans d'administration de l'environnement*, Paris and Montreal: L'Harmattan.

Lascoumes, Pierre and Jean-Pierre Le Bourhis (1997), *L'environnement ou l'administration des possibles: La création des Directions Régionales de l'Environnement*, Paris and Montreal: L'Harmattan.

Léost, Raymond (1998), 'La stratégie contentieuse d'une association de protection de la nature en Bretagne', in Patrice Le Louarn (ed.), *Décision locale et droit de l'environnement*, Rennes: Presses Universitaires de Rennes, pp. 85–106.

London, Caroline (2001), *Environnement et instruments économiques et fiscaux*, Paris: Librairie Générale de Droit et de Jurisprudence.

Ménard, Claude and Stéphane Saussier (2002), 'Contractual choice and performance: the case of water supply in France', in Eric Brousseau and Jean-Michel Glachant (eds), *The Economics of Contracts: Theories and Applications*, Cambridge and New York: Cambridge University Press, pp. 440–62.

Micoud, André (1999), 'Associations et environnement: une "histoire" pleine d'enjeux', in P. Lascoumes (ed.), *Instituer l'environnement: Vingt-cinq ans d'administration de l'environnement*, Paris and Montreal: L'Harmattan, Ch. 9.

Morand-Deviller, Jacqueline (1987), *Le droit de l'environnement*, 5th edn, 2002, Paris: Presses Universitaires de France.

Oates, Wallace E. (1972), *Fiscal Federalism*, New York: Harcourt, Brace Jovanovich.

OECD (1997), *Environmental Performance Reviews: France*, Paris: OECD.

Romi, Raphael (1998), *Les collectivités locales et l'environnement*, Paris: Librairie Générale de Droit et de Jurisprudence.

Salmon, Pierre (2000), 'Vertical competition in a unitary state', in Gianluigi Galeotti, Pierre Salmon and Ronald Wintrobe (eds), *Competition and Structure: The Political Economy of Collective Decisions: Essays in Honor of Albert Breton*, Cambridge and New York: Cambridge University Press, pp. 239–56.

Szarka, Joseph (2002), *The Shaping of Environmental Policy in France*, New York and Oxford: Berghahn Books.

Szarka, Joseph (2003), 'The politics of bounded innovation: "New" environmental policy instruments in France', *Environment Politics*, **12**(1).

Theys, Jacques (1998), 'Vingt ans de politique française de l'environnement: les années 70–90: un essai d'évaluation', in Bernard Barraqué and Jacques Theys (eds), *Les Politiques d'environnement: Évaluation de la première génération 1971–1995*, Paris: Editions Recherches, pp. 17–40.

Tocqueville, Alexis de (1835/1969), *Democracy in America*, Garden City: Harper and Row, Anchor Books.

Vogel, David, Michael Toffel and Diahanna Post (2003), 'Environmental federalism in the European Union and the United States', paper prepared for the International Conference on *Globalization and National Environmental Policy*, Veldhover: The Netherlands, September, URL:http://www.tilburguniversity.nl/globus/activities/ conference/papers/**vogel**.pdf.

Vourc'h, Ann and Patrick Lenain (2001), 'Comment organiser une croissance écologiquement durable en France?', OECD, Département des Affaires Economiques, working paper no. 314.

APPENDIX A: WATER AND SEWAGE[1]

Water has been regulated for environmental purposes at least since the beginning of the nineteenth century but the two main laws governing it have been enacted in 1964 and in 1992. The latter law has made it even clearer that water cannot be privately owned. The 36 000 French communes are in charge of the provision of water and sewage collection. They can act in common, and as a consequence there are 15 000 communal and intercommunal units in charge of water, and 10 000 units in charge of sewage collection. Communes remain the owners of most drinking water works and sewage treatment plants. The majority of them, however, outsource under a variety of contractual arrangements the construction of new facilities and their operation to private firms, although some cities and intercommunal bodies prefer not to have recourse to any form of delegation and do everything themselves.[2] The three main private companies distribute 85 per cent of drinking water in France and they also operate a large part of sewerage. The central government and most *départements* provide financial support to small rural communes, while some regions finance or co-finance special programs.

The six *Agences de l'eau*, corresponding to the six main watersheds or river basins, were created by the law of 1964, whose object was 'the regime and distribution of water and the fight against its pollution'. They impose abstraction and pollution levies on the use of water by certain categories of agents, and give loans and subsidies ultimately to the benefits of those agents of the same categories who undertake improvements in water conservation. The main categories of users are consumers and industries. Farmers are not charged, and consequently are not helped to reduce pollution. The process is one whereby the representatives of users decide on a five-year program, assess its cost, and set the level of the levies in proportion to the cost. As noted in the main body of the text, subcentral governments and industrial firms have come to perceive the system as congruent with their interest.

The law of 1992 created two levels of long-term water planning, one at the level of basins and the other at the level of smaller rivers making up sections of river basins. Subcentral governments are involved in both types of planning. Policing, however, remains essentially the responsibility of the central administration – that is, formally of the prefects, but in practice of the territorial services of the ministries of public health, agriculture, industry, public works and environment. The price of water charged to users (except farmers) has increased substantially over the last decade. As mayors collectively refused to allow that the communes (or intercommunal bodies) collect the price of water and sewage themselves, these prices are typically charged to the users by the private companies.

APPENDIX B: HOUSEHOLD WASTE[3]

With regard to household packaging waste, the French system is relatively complex and involves several actors. Legally, communes are responsible for dealing with household waste in general. About half the communes outsource this task to private firms, most of which are affiliates of the large companies which play an essential role in the treatment of water and sewage. The task of organizing the treatment of household waste on a more aggregate level is entrusted to the *départements*. An agency, originally the *Agence Nationale pour la Récuperation et l'Elimination des Déchets* (ANRED), later absorbed in ADEME, was in charge of research, technical assistance, collection of a specific tax and payment of subsidies to promote new modes of treatment. As noted in the text, ADEME does not collect environmental taxes any more. The central government does, and finances ADEME from the general budget.

Packaging waste has become a major component of household waste (more than half when measured in volume). Since 1992, the private firms (both producers and importers) which are responsible for used packaging are compelled either to take care of it themselves or to contribute to their treatment. Most firms have chosen the second alternative. A private non-profit firm called *Eco-Emballages* was created in the early 1990s and accredited by the central government to collect the contributions of the packaging providers (two smaller firms play a similar role for particular kinds of packaging). *Eco-Emballages* is owned 70 per cent by industrial firms, 20 per cent by recycling firms, and 10 per cent by large retailers. It receives on average 0.06 euros per packaging from about 10 000 industrial firms. The contributing firms can place a green point or marker on the packaging of the products they produce or sell which helps households to sort the packaging. *Eco-Emballages* uses the proceedings (its budget was 365 million euros in 2003) mainly to subsidize the recycling operations of the 29 000 communes with which it has established contractual relations. These subsidies are conditional on commitments by the communes, commitments which have had to evolve somewhat in the course of time, in particular on the occasion of the two negotiations with the central government that *Eco-Emballages* had to engage in for the renewal of its accreditation. The communes also transact directly with industrial users of recycled material. As a consequence of contractual commitments made by the communes, their inhabitants have been encouraged to sort their packaging waste. In 2003 as a result, 58 per cent of household packaging waste was recycled rather than ending in landfills or incinerators.

APPENDIX C: INDUSTRIAL HAZARDS

On 21 September, 2001, the AZF fertilizer factory (belonging to Total-Elf), located in the suburbs of Toulouse, exploded, killing 31 people, injuring 2400, making 500 dwellings inhabitable and damaging 85 schools. The AZF factory was one of 1250 factories in France classified as high-risk and falling under the EU Seveso Directive.

The first inquiry revealed no clear-cut violation of any of the – in principle meticulous – procedures imposed by French and EU rules where industrial hazards are concerned. The cause of the explosion, involving a reaction between several chemicals, was difficult to ascertain and did not point to an obvious act of negligence on the part of the factory's management. The main issue then was whether a factory such as the AZF Toulouse factory should operate in the surroundings in which it was located. It was opened in 1924, in what was then the countryside. In 2001, except for its immediate neighbors – two other chemical plants, one of which belonged to the *Société Nationale des Poudres et Explosifs* and made ammunition – it was surrounded by dwellings, offices, stores, university departments, schools and hospitals.

The Prime Minister asked Philippe Essig, a well-known public manager formerly in charge of the French Railways, to write a report on the monitoring of industrial hazards in the wake of the Toulouse blast. The analyses developed in the report are summarized and commented on in Essig (2002). Essig's main point is that it is useless and even illusory to employ a precautionary principle interpreted to force zero damage from industrial hazards. Serious hazards are not confined to Seveso sites but are present wherever there are economic activities. The problems these activities raise are pervasive. Reliance on decisions of a purely technical nature about what level of risk is or is not acceptable should be abandoned, because they lack an objective basis. The economic pressure underlying urban sprawl is unavoidable. Economic and social considerations cannot be dismissed. For instance, before the explosion, the displacement of the AZF factory, which employs several hundred workers, had been seriously considered, but deemed to be socially unacceptable.

The solution according to Essig lies in further decentralization and democratization of decision-making in that domain. It is imperative that a trade-off be sought between industrial risks and social and economic benefits linked to a given location and to the extension of activities in the neighborhood of dangerous sites. The search for this trade-off, however, should not be entrusted to public officials at various levels of government (*inspecteurs des installations classées*, mayors, prefects and so on) but to democratic decision-making by the people concerned. In his paper, Essig does not discuss the informational requirements that such a solution entails, as his preoccupation is to separate decisions about the level of risk the concerned population is willing to accept from whatever technical knowledge exists about that risk. Nonetheless, Essig's recommendation does clearly raise many issues pertaining to the origin, reliability and distribution of information.

NOTES

1. For analyses in English of the French system, see Barraqué (1999), Ménard and Saussier (2002), and Szarka (2002).
2. Ménard and Saussier (2002) conclude, on the basis of their empirical analysis, that the choice made among these solutions largely reflects their comparative advantage in purely economic terms.
3. See Defeuilley and Godard (1998); Szarka (2002: 178–84); *Le Monde*, 2 March 2004, p. 16.

REFERENCES

Essig, Philippe (2002), 'Toulouse et suites: les risques industriels en France', paper presented at the joint conferences of CPGSC, CRAIM and DRIE, Montreal, 4–5 November, URL:http://www.drie-montreal.org/documents/congres_2002/Toulouse.pdf.

15. Capacity constraints on local government environmental policies in Ghana

Felix Ankomah Asante

1. INTRODUCTION

Decentralization, a potential and effective way of enhancing the quality of public administration, is defined as the de-concentration and devolution of power and responsibility to local levels. Decentralization helps to generate good contacts with citizens, brings decision-making to the level where events generally take place, helps to strengthen the democratic process and lays the foundation for the emergence of autonomous institutions of governance within the structure of the national state (Ayee, 2003a).

Tremendous shifts have been experienced under the current decentralization policy in Ghana. These shifts would not have been possible without a relatively high degree of political commitment on the part of the government. Not only is power – planning, administrative, financial, legislative and executive – being transferred, the ingredients to operationalize local government and decentralization are also being provided side by side. However, the pace of transfer of resources, means and competencies has not been appreciable due to administrative, financial, manpower, infrastructural and institutional reasons.

The ability to achieve successful transfer of power depends, amongst others, on building administrative capacity at all levels of society, both by involving a wider range of organizations and by decentralizing authority and responsibility. It is essential to develop institutional capacity not only within the government structure, but also the institutional capacity of local organizations, and most importantly to construct both horizontal and vertical linkages between these organizations and the national political economy framework. Evidence abounds that the creation of a legal framework for transferring power does not necessarily ensure effective decentralization. Without a multi-dimensional approach to decentralization focusing on capacity-building initiatives, provision of basic infrastructure and transfer of competencies and financial resources, effective decentralization and local governance will be a hoax.

This chapter concentrates on one of the most important factors driving the implementation of decentralization programmes: the capacity and constraints of local governments in implementing environmental policies in Ghana.

2. HISTORICAL PERSPECTIVE OF DECENTRALIZATION IN GHANA

A nationwide effort towards decentralization of the administrative machinery in Ghana was first made in the colonial era. The earliest attempts based on the overall colonial political strategy of 'Indirect Rule' were made with the native authorities, which centred on a traditional leader (chief or some member of local royalty). In those early days, the colonial government sought to buttress local government on what it believed to be the indigenous political institutions. The municipal ordinance of 1859 established municipalities in the coastal towns. In 1943, a new ordinance set up elected town councils for selected cities in Ghana. The Municipal Councils Ordinance was passed in 1953, followed by the Local Government Act, 1961, Act 54, which was passed after independence in 1957. In all these pieces of legislation, the distinction between central and local government institutions was maintained, in line with the Dual Hierarchy Model. In terms of this distinction, two separate organizational structures for the administration of Ghana exist: one based in the capital with branches in the local (district) level and the other separate and distinct, based in well-defined localities and referred to as Local Government.

Long before the attainment of independence in 1957 and some time thereafter, commissions and committees had been appointed at various times to enquire into the administration of the country. The reports by these bodies made conclusive recommendations for the devolution of central administrative authority to the local levels. In spite of the far-reaching nature of the recommendations, most of which were accepted, attempts at decentralization could not materialize until 1974.

Though passed in 1971, the local Administration Act, 1971, Act 359, was not implemented until 1974 due to a change of government in 1972. Significant changes were made to the 1971 Act before it was introduced as the Local Administration (Amendment) Decree, 1972, NRCD 258.

The 1974 Local Government structure, described as the 'Single Hierarchy Model', sought to abolish the distinction between Local and Central Government at the local level and to create a common monolithic structure (District Councils) to which was assigned the responsibility of the totality of government at the local level. The legal framework was provided by a Decree for decentralization to the local (district) level, the sectors of Agriculture Administration, Education, Survey and Town Planning, Social Welfare and Community Development, Public Health, Engineering, Fire Service and Sports. Some of the hitherto smaller local council areas were merged to create large districts, resulting in the creation of 65 District Council areas with all-appointed District Councils.

The Councils were on a purely non-elective basis; two-thirds of the councillors were central government nominees, while the other third represented chiefs. The structure that evolved could be termed nominal because the personnel of the so-called decentralized departments retained membership of their parent ministries and departments for technical guidance, transfers, training, promotions and postings. The Councils had no control whatsoever over the civil service personnel and this contributed largely to most of the problems faced by them. While the Councils were supposed to integrate departments in the district, the departments still maintained control over departmental financial estimates for central government projects. Below the District Councils were Municipal/Urban/Local Councils, and Town and Village Committees (GTZ and SNRD, 1996).

Though the legal framework provided a degree of decentralization to the districts and a fusion of government activities at the local level, the Single Hierarchy Model instituted in 1974 did not work satisfactorily. A number of factors militated against the effective and efficient performance of the local government system. They include the following (Asante, 2003):

i. No effective, accountable and legitimate (in terms of electoral legitimacy) political structure was established at the district level to oversee the structure. Its implementation was left to bureaucrats who were the same persons who had looked up to Accra (the capital) all along.
ii. In deciding to start decentralization from the regional level, the regions were given more authority, but that only led to additional bureaucratic hurdles in the attempt to decentralize to the local (district) level. Under the 1974 structure, decentralization was to begin with the regions; in practice, it ended with the regions!
iii. The functions which were transferred to the District Councils were not accompanied by a simultaneous transfer of competence and means which are a requisite for effective decentralization.
iv. Very little effort was made to address the infrastructural, staffing and other logistic needs of the District Councils.
v. Some of the districts were so large that the administration could not reach all the parts.

vi. Rather curiously during the period, moves were successfully made to centralize even further in Accra. Functions which had hitherto been exercised with moderate success by the District Councils were taken over by the central government. Examples include the Ghana Education Service and the Omnibus Services Authority.

The lack of strong political will and commitment on the part of successive governments and the reluctance of the bureaucratic class to give up power to lower levels of administration also contributed to the undesirable situation.

2.1 The New Local Government System

The current local government reforms and decentralization policy could be traced to many converging factors (GTZ and SNRD, 1996) including the following:

a. macro-economic policies pursued under the Economic Recovery Programme (ERP);[1]
b. urge of the international donor community to establish democratic structures and strengthen Local Government and ensure bottom-up decision-making to achieve greater participation in the development processes;
c. demand (internal and external) for a devolution of power on a subsidiary basis;
d. shortcomings of the pre- and immediate post-independence local government systems (Dual Hierarchy Model and the Single Hierarchy Model);
e. favourable political conditions, for example, the Government's genuine commitment to decentralization and grassroots participation in development-related activities.

Administrative arrangements

The structure of decentralization in Ghana (see Figure 15.1) has a 'mixed' or 'fused' decentralized authority – a system in which institutions extending from the central government (like the District Chief Executive (DCE) and de-concentrated departments and organizations) and locally-based institutions (like District Assemblies) are linked into one organizational structure at the local level (Ayee, 2003b). The Metropolitan, Municipal and District Assemblies are the political and administrative authorities in the district and they exercise deliberative, legislative and executive functions.

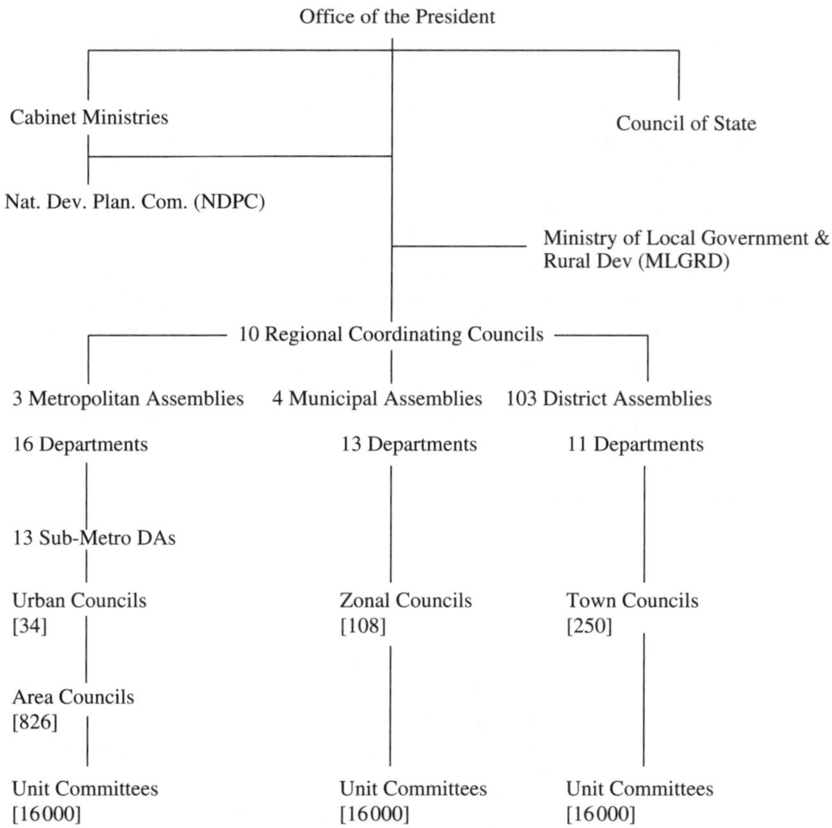

Figure 15.1 The structure of decentralization in Ghana

The new local government system is made up of a Regional Coordinating Council and a four-tier Metropolitan and three-tier Municipal/District Assemblies structure. A total of 110 District Assemblies, of which 45 are new, have been created under the new local government system (28 new districts have just been created, bringing the total number to 138). The Regional Coordinating Council (RCC) consists of the Regional Minister as Chairman and his Deputy, the Presiding Member of each District Assembly and the District Chief Executive of each district in the region, two chiefs from the Regional House of Chiefs, and the regional heads of the decentralized ministries without voting rights. The District Assembly is comprised of elected representatives, Member(s) of Parliament from the constituencies that are within the district as non-voting members, the District Chief Executive (DCE) and other members (not more than

30 per cent of the membership appointed by the President in consultation with chiefs and other interest groups). The functions of the District Assemblies are outlined in the Local Government Act of 1993, Act 462 (see Box 15.1 for the functions of the District Assemblies).

The DCE is appointed by the President with prior approval of two-thirds of the members of the District Assembly present and voting. His term of office is four years, and he/she is eligible for a second term of office. He may be removed if two-thirds of the members of the District Assembly pass a vote of no confidence in him. A system of checks and balances at the district level exists under which the head of the executive, the DCE, is separated from the head of the legislature, the Presiding Member. The Presiding Member is elected by two-thirds of the members and may be removed by two-thirds of the members. His/her term of office is two years and he/she is eligible for re-election.

District Assemblies are either Metropolitan (population over 250 000), Municipal (one-town Assemblies with a population over 95 000) or District (population 75 000 and over).

The Sub-Metropolitan District Councils are directly below the Metropolitan Assemblies. There are 13 of these structures established. This arrangement takes into consideration the complex and unique socio-politico-economic characteristics and management problems associated with the three metropolises. Urban Councils are created for settlements of a particular nature with populations above 15 000 and which are cosmopolitan in character with urbanization and management problems, though not of the scale of the metropolises. Thirty-four such councils have been established.

The Zonal, Town/Area Councils and Unit Committees are the other levels in the new local government structure. Unit Committees form the base structure of the new system. A unit is normally a settlement or a group of settlements with a population of between 500 and 1000 in the rural areas, and a higher population, 1500, for urban areas. The Zonal Councils are the 'one town' Municipal Assemblies of Cape Coast, New Juaben, Tamale and Tema. Town/Area Councils are found in the Metropolitan and District Assemblies. In the District Assemblies, Town Councils are established for settlements with populations of between 5000 and 15 000, and Area Councils for a number of settlements/villages which are grouped together but whose individual settlements have populations of less than 5000. Town Councils in the Metropolitan assemblies are greatly different in size, sometimes exceeding 50 000 people.

The Local Government Act, 1993, Act 462, establishes 11 departments for a District Assembly, 13 departments for a Municipal Assembly and 16 for a Metropolitan Assembly (see Appendix for the list of decentralized departments).

BOX 15.1 FUNCTIONS OF THE DISTRICT ASSEMBLIES

The Local Government Act, 1993 (Act 462) Section 10 provides details of functions of the District Assemblies as follows:

a. be responsible for the overall development of the district and ensure the preparation and submission through the Regional Co-ordinating Council –
   (i) of development plans of the district to the National Development Planning Commission for approval; and
   (ii) of the budget of the district related to the approved plans to the Minister for Finance for approval.
b. formulate and execute plans, programmes and strategies for the effective mobilization of the resources necessary for the overall development of the district;
c. promote and support productive activity and social development in the district and remove any obstacles to initiative and development;
d. initiate programmes for the development of basic infrastructure and provide municipal works and services in the district;
e. be responsible for the development, improvement and management of human settlements and the environment in the district;
f. in co-operation with the appropriate national and local security agencies be responsible for the maintenance of security and public safety in the district;
g. ensure ready access to courts in the district for the promotion of justice;
h. initiate, sponsor or carry out such studies as may be necessary for the discharge of any of the functions conferred by this Act or any other enactment; and
i. perform such other functions as may be provided under any other enactment.

Other functions of the District Assemblies are as follows:

a. A District Assembly shall be responsible for the preparation and approval of its annual budget.
b. District Assemblies as planning authorities shall perform planning functions assigned to them under any enactment for the time being in force.

Successes

The successes of Ghana's decentralization programme can be measured against the main objectives for which it was implemented in the first place. One of the objectives of the decentralization programme is to ensure that people living in the rural areas have access to basic services and infrastructure. Indeed, the District Assemblies (DAs) have undertaken development projects such as the construction and maintenance of classroom blocks, feeder roads, clinics, public toilets, markets and provision of street-lights in previously neglected rural areas that were denied access to these services. Some of these projects were undertaken in collaboration with local as well as international non-governmental organizations. The projects have in turn opened up new opportunities for development in the districts. The improved infrastructure development has improved health and sanitation infrastructure and thereby removed some of the barriers to social and economic development. This notwithstanding, there have been complaints from some rural people that most of these services and infrastructure have been concentrated mainly in the district capitals to the detriment of the rural areas (Ayee, 1992; 1996; 2003a).

Another main objective of the decentralization programme is to allow for participation of the people in their own affairs and their empowerment. The activities of DAs have enabled the local people to show some interest in their own affairs. A spirit of voluntarism and awareness to develop one's community was clearly seen among the local people, especially during the initial period of the programme. However, people's interest declined when they realized that their expectations could not be fulfilled because the DAs lacked the human and financial resources to implement their set development objectives. Furthermore, most district plans are subjected to public hearing at the sub-district level but the hearing is not patronized by most people mainly because of apathy and/or the absence of sub-district structures in some districts due to composition problems. In spite of these hiccups, the DAs have no doubt created a high level of political awareness which has injected some political dynamism, with some functionaries of the DAs and the electorate demanding even greater accountability from the District Chief Executive and Presiding Member and DA members respectively (Ayee, 2004).

The issue of poverty reduction is central to the decentralization programme. However, there is a perception[2] amongst some people that poverty reduction was not part of the original objectives of decentralization in Ghana but rather an objective added later on by the government under pressure from the donors. Whatever it may be, a number of poverty-reduction strategies were introduced. They include the Programme of Actions to Mitigate the Social Costs of Adjustment (PAMSCAD)[3] in 1987, the Productivity and Income Generation Fund popularly called the 'District Assembly Poverty Alleviation Fund' in 1996 and the Highly Indebted Poor Countries (HIPC) Fund in 2002. The Poverty Alleviation Fund in particular is to give the poor access to credit facilities to use in investment in job creation. Even though this is a laudable scheme and has assisted hitherto vulnerable groups like women in small-scale industries, it has not been well implemented for a number of reasons. First, the modalities for selection of beneficiaries are not too clear. There is the perception, whether rightly or wrongly, that most of the beneficiaries are selected on their political affiliations and not on their levels of deprivation and vulnerability. Second, there has been a high default rate in the re-payment of the loans given out because the beneficiaries have not invested them rightly to create the expected job but rather regarded them as booty to meet personal commitments such as paying children's school fees. In addition, apart from the smallness of the loan (500 000 cedis),[4] the credit facility was not distributed on schedule so it was not made available to the people when they needed it most.

The development import of the so-called 'Poverty Alleviation Fund' appears lost in some District Assemblies. The returns show that some District Assemblies have even failed to allocate the funds. However, despite unsuccessful attempts to politicize the issue, the rationale for this Fund is unquestionably valid especially when it is aimed at increasing rural productivity and generating urban employment through support to private sector, small, micro and medium scale enterprises. At the same time, it is important to keep in mind that the 'Poverty Alleviation Fund' is the taxpayer's money and it should be disbursed and recovered within the framework of the regulations that govern the use of public funds.

From the foregoing, it is clear that the decentralization programme in Ghana has achieved marginal successes. This notwithstanding, 51.6 per cent of people in 12 districts[5] of Ghana have faith in the DAs not only as the appropriate institution for solving community problems, but also to ensure effective delivery of services and solutions to problems at the grassroots level (Ayee and Amponsah, 2003).

Challenges

Since 1988, the challenges facing decentralization have been daunting in spite of efforts being made by the successive governments to address them. In the Ministry of Local Government and Rural Development's (MLGRD) *Status of Decentralization Implementation* paper there is a daunting list of constraints and challenges as well as a number of factors that have impeded previous attempts to strengthen local government capacities and performance. They include the following:

- agitations for more districts which have led to the creation of 28 districts in addition to the current 110 districts;
- sectoral conceptual differences in the interpretation of the decentralization policy and transfer of powers, functions, responsibilities and resources;
- absence of maps to firmly identify boundaries that will enable DAs to plan for the development of their areas of jurisdiction;
- shortage of adequately trained human resources at the local level;
- inability to make the sub-district structures function because of their size and lack of funds to pay core staff;
- lack of participatory bottom-up planning;
- lack of fiscal decentralization as a result of the centralization of the management of public finance due to existing legislation (Financial Administration Decree, 1979 and Financial Administration Regulations, 1979) and administrative procedure concerning local government public finance;
- the lack of management of interface between decentralized public institutions, private sector enterprises and civil society mainly because of the absence of clear-cut regulation, procedure and boundaries of good practices, consultation and communication on the roles of NGOs, Civil Society Organizations (CSOs) and Community-Based organizations (CBOs) (MLGRD, 2002).

Apart from the above-mentioned constraints, a number of challenges face the decentralization programme.[6] They include the following:

- Lack of strong leadership at all levels of decentralization. The absence of an authoritative institution/centre which plays the role of coordinating, overseeing and monitoring individual and collective efforts of stakeholders across government along with the planning and implementation of decentralization-related initiatives has led to the lack of a common vision and plan for the decentralization process. In other words, there has not been a home-grown action plan to promote Ghana's version of decentralization. This problem may seem to have been resolved with the recent appointment of an eleven-member Presidential Oversight Committee on Decentralization in November 2003.
- Loss of institutional memory as a result of the change in government in January 2001, which resulted not only in the massive transfer of staff but also the replacement of one-third government appointees to the DAs. A further loss of institutional memory also occurred after the August 2002 District Assembly and Unit Committees

elections. This has undermined the process of capacity-building for decentralization.

- Unpredictability and lack of transparency of District Assemblies Common Fund (DACF) and lack of discretion afforded to district authorities over the allocation of funds coupled with weak financial position of DAs vis-à-vis their 86 assigned functions.
- Non-partisanship of the DA is a mirage because in the 1994, 1998 and 2002 District Assemblies and Unit Committees elections it was an open secret that most, if not all, political parties either sponsored or supported individual candidates to win seats in all the DAs, contrary to the constitutional provisions. In actual practice Ghana's DAs are not free from partisan politics. This is because the political parties want to retain control at the grassroots level in order to boost their chances of winning national elections.
- The formal integration of the 11 line departments or organizations of central government at the district level into the decentralized local government system remains one of the unresolved issues that have stalled the implementation of Sections 37, 38 and 161 of Act 462. Associated with this problem is the apparent conflict between certain decentralized departments or organizations and the line departments or organizations, namely, Ghana Education Service created by Act 506, 1995; Ghana Health Service and Teaching Hospital created by Act 525, 1996; Ghana National Fire Service created by Act 537, 1997; Forestry Commission created by Act 571, 1997; Ghana Library Board established under Act 327; and National Disaster Management Organization (NADMO) established under Act 517. All these Services and Organizations are listed among the decentralized departments of Metropolitan District Assemblies (MDAs) under Act 462. The apparent conflict between Act 462 and the enactments referred to raises issues of both policy and law – whether these Services could and should be decentralized. The creation of these Services seems to have undermined the speedy establishment of a Local Government Service, the related Act having been passed by the Parliament in September 2003. It is a means towards re-centralization (Ayee, 1997; 2003a; 2003b).

3. ENVIRONMENTAL POLICY FRAMEWORK

Attempts over the years to address environmental problems in Ghana had been largely ad hoc and cosmetic, or at best sector-oriented and therefore limited in scope. It had become evident that the body of existing legislation on various aspects of the environment was inadequate and unimplemented, and many provisions had no bearing on present-day realities or on the aspirations of the people in Ghana. There was the need for a new direction and thrust in national development efforts to ensure that plans aimed at improving the standard and quality of life take due cognizance of environmental considerations. 'Environment' comprises the whole set of natural or biophysical and man-made or socio-cultural systems, in which man and other organisms live, work and interact.

The ultimate aim of the National Environmental Policy of Ghana is to improve the surroundings, living conditions and the quality of life of the entire citizenry, both present and future. It seeks to ensure reconciliation between economic development and natural resource conservation and also to make environmental sustainability a key element supporting the country's economic and social development.

Specifically, the policy seeks to:

i. maintain ecosystems and ecological processes essential for the functioning of the biosphere;
ii. ensure sound management of natural resources and the environment;
iii. adequately protect humans, animals and plants, their biological communities and habitats against harmful impacts and destructive practices, and preserve biological diversity;
iv. guide development in accordance with quality requirements to prevent, reduce and as far as possible, eliminate pollution and other adverse environmental consequences;
v. integrate environmental considerations in sectoral, structural and socio-economic planning at the national, regional, district and grassroots levels; and
vi. arrive at common solutions to environmental problems in West Africa, Africa and the world at large.

For effective implementation of the National Environmental Policy the following principles are applied:

i. optimum sustainable yield in the use of resources and ecosystems;
ii. use of most cost-effective means to achieve environmental objectives;
iii. use of incentives in addition to regulatory measures;
iv. delegation of decision-making and implementation to the most appropriate level of government;
v. polluter pays for the cost of preventing and eliminating pollution and other environmental impacts caused by him/her;
vi. public participation in environmental decision-making; and
vii. international cooperation.

3.1 Issue-specific Policies

Management of environmental resources

Conservation of forest, fishery and wildlife resources The need to protect nature and habitat, landscape, flora and fauna from the threat of further degradation and depletion is an area of concern to many Ghanaians. There is an increasing awareness of the direct economic benefits of forests and wildlife to the people, and the linkages between these resources and the environment.

Protection of the soil Protection of the soil has been recognized as an important aspect in the management of natural resources in Ghana. This arises from an awareness of adverse impacts on the soil from increasing agricultural, mining and manufacturing activities. The 'threats' to the soil can be classified as follows: (a) contamination by harmful substances from various sources; (b) degradation of the chemical, biological or physical structure; and (c) misuse and waste as a result of space-consuming activities.

Energy resources Woodfuel constitutes the primary energy source of most Ghanaian households, while the industrial sector is almost entirely dependent on hydro-power. This situation poses a serious threat to economic development and the environment. To reduce the pressure on forests for woodfuel, the development of alternative energy sources has been promoted, while the efficiency of production, conversion and use of woodfuel has been improved.

Water resources Water is used for various purposes, including domestic, industrial, agriculture, recreation and transportation. Measures have been instituted to ensure that conflicts between the different uses of water are avoided or reduced to the minimum. Also measures are taken to protect the various watersheds and also to employ environmentally sound methods of disposing of waste water and to prevent pollution of fresh water bodies.

All water resources (the property and control) are vested in the President on behalf of and in trust for the people of Ghana. Nobody can use water without authority. In order to (i) divert, dam, abstract or use water resources or (ii) construct or maintain any works for the use of water resources, an application for a water use permit is first filed with the Water Resources Commission (the body to oversee water resources on behalf of the President of the Republic). The Commission, upon receipt of the completed application form, publishes a notice of the application in the mass media. The Commission, prior to granting a permit, publishes in the

Gazette and in at least one national newspaper a notice (a) stating the purpose of the application, and (b) inviting objections from the public within three months from the date of the first publication.

In considering an application, an investigation is conducted to ascertain whether the proposed use of the water (a) is in accordance with the established water use policies and plans and (b) does not cause irreparable damage to water resources, public health and the environment. A public hearing in respect of an applicant is held in those cases where (i) there is adverse public reaction to the proposed use; (ii) the use of the water involves the dislocation, resettlement or in any manner causes the destruction of the natural water resources of the community; or (iii) the Commission considers that the particular use of the water would have an impact on the natural resources of the basin. The Commission collaborates with the following institutions when conducting a public hearing: (i) the Environmental Protection Agency (EPA); (ii) the traditional authorities of the community; and (iii) the relevant government institutions and agencies.

Water abstracted by mechanical means and used for any purpose where the abstraction level does not exceed five litres per second, and subsistence agricultural water use for land areas not exceeding one hectare, are exempted from the permit requirement but have to be registered. Application for registration in this respect is submitted to the relevant District Assembly. If the District Assembly is satisfied with the application, it registers the water use and issues the applicant with a registration number. The District Assembly furnishes the Commission quarterly with a list of all registered water users in its locality.

Urban areas and waste management The volume of waste generated in the urban centres is rapidly increasing. Although a substantial percentage of the urban waste in Ghana is readily biodegradable and therefore potentially re-usable or recyclable for materials or energy, the appropriate and necessary resources are not readily available. Much of the urban waste (solid) is disposed of on the land and some (liquid) is dumped into the sea with little or no treatment.

Prevention and control of pollution

Atmospheric pollution The atmospheric pollution control strategy under the national environmental policy is geared towards an overall long-term objective to reduce air pollution within Ghana as well as beyond its boundaries. The main objectives of the strategy are to: (a) identify the atmospheric pollutants which are currently and potentially of greatest concern for the protection of human health and the environment; (b) determine the most appropriate means for handling pollution problems identified, without transferring air pollution to water or soil; (c) set and implement national standards for specific sources discharged into the air; (d) reduce, in the longer term, the ambient air concentrations of the most crucial pollutants to levels considered acceptable for the protection of sensitive ecosystems; and (e) define and implement preventive measures against indoor pollution.

Water bodies The environmental policy on water is aimed at sustainable development and use of water resources. In this regard, particular quality standards have been set for (a) specific uses of water and (b) pollution caused by the discharge of certain dangerous substances into the aquatic environment.

Chemicals The increasing number of chemicals used in the country needs to be controlled. A procedure is established for regulating potentially dangerous chemicals by enacting appropriate legislation regarding the export, import, marketing and use of chemicals that are banned or severely restricted in other countries or where local experience makes such control necessary.

Noise Noise pollution, a by-product of industrialization and modernization, can be avoided using present-day state-of-the-art technology. Appropriate standards and legislation on noise control, both ambient and industrial, need to be enacted and enforced to prevent the worsening of the noise problem as the national economy gains momentum and the standard of living for a large section of the population improves.

3.2 Challenges

The major environmental problems facing Ghana in recent years centre around land use, forestry and wildlife, human settlements, water quality, coast and wetlands, industrial pollution, mining, hazardous waste and chemicals and environmental displacements (Boon, 1998).

Land use, forestry and wildlife
Forestry and land use practices continue to have a hazardous effect on the Ghanaian environment, with its consequent effects on wildlife. Some of the problems in relation to forest and land use are deforestation and land degradation driven by the following factors:

- agricultural and construction activities;
- bush fires;
- uncontrolled grazing;

- inappropriate use of agricultural chemicals and fertilizers; and
- timber exploitation and illegal chainsaw lumbering.

Since 1981, the annual rate of deforestation in Ghana has been around 2 per cent/year or 750 hectares each year. The consequence of deforestation in the semi-arid regions is the threat of desertification, as seen in Northern Ghana, where 35 per cent of the total land area is estimated to have been affected (EPC, 1991). Deforestation has led to many environmental consequences such as local climatic changes, soil erosion, land degradation, instability in hydrological regimes and loss of biodiversity.

Coast, wetlands and water quality

Industrial and mining activities, improper use of agro-chemicals and rapid urbanization have led to increasing effluent discharge into existing water bodies. In addition, soil erosion caused by poor agricultural practices is causing increased sediment loads in rivers and suspended particles in water bodies. The pollutants in the coastal zone include industrial effluent discharge, household garbage and sewage, agricultural, fishing and household chemicals and oil waste. Pollution of surface waters directly affects aquatic biota, reduces biodiversity and increases treatment costs of water supplies for domestic and industrial use.

Fishing has also caused many problems directly and indirectly. The use of poison and dynamite in fishing, for example, is still going on even though there is a ban on this practice. Indirectly, pollution of the water bodies results from the engine oil which is used to run the outboard motors used for fishing.

Sewage and domestic waste

The generation of huge volumes of waste from domestic and commercial activities in the cities is fast becoming a health problem. Littering and dumping of household waste in unauthorized areas are also contributing to the environmental problem. These problems occur as a result of overcrowding and unauthorized construction of structures.

4. INSTITUTIONAL SET-UP FOR ENVIRONMENTAL GOVERNANCE

4.1 Public Agencies and Specialized Bodies

Environmental Protection Agency (EPA)

The EPA was established under an act of Parliament, Environmental Protection Agency Act, 1994, Act 490. This replaced the Environmental

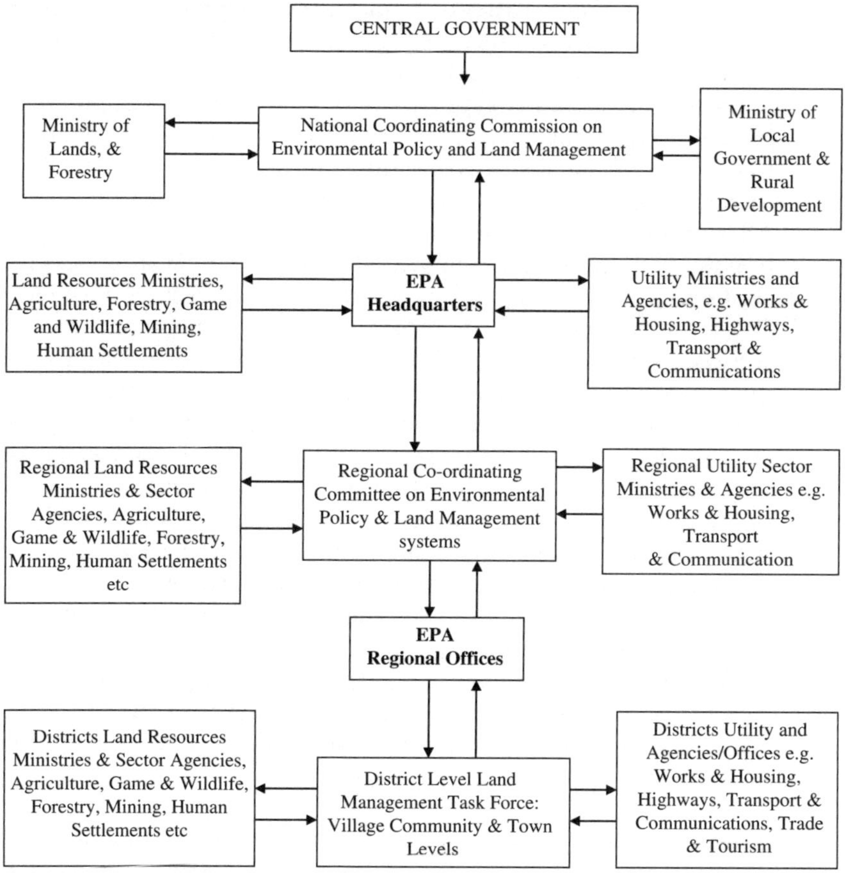

Source: EPA, Ghana.

Figure 15.2 An integrative institutional framework for environmental management and policy

Protection Council of 1974. The Agency is primarily an advisory and research organization, which is expected to coordinate the activities of other bodies concerned with environmental matters, but with little enforcement (see Figure 15.2). Specifically its functions include the following:

i. to advise the Minister for Environment on the formulation of policies on all aspects of the environment and in particular to make recommendations for the protection of the environment;

ii. to coordinate the activities of bodies concerned with the technical or practical aspects of the environment and to serve as a channel of communication between such bodies and the Ministry;
iii. to coordinate the activities of such bodies as it considers appropriate for the purposes of controlling the generation, treatment, storage, transportation and disposal of industrial waste;
iv. to collaborate with such foreign and international agencies as the Agency considers necessary;
v. to issue environmental permits and pollution abatement notices for controlling the volumes, types, constituents and effects of waste discharges, emissions, deposits or other sources of pollutants and of substances which are hazardous or potentially dangerous to the quality of the environment or any segment of the environment;
vi. to issue notices in the form of directives, procedures or warnings to such bodies as it may determine for the purpose of controlling the volume, intensity and quality of noise in the environment;
vii. to prescribe standards and guidelines relating to the pollution of air, water, land and other forms of environmental pollution including the discharge of wastes and the control of toxic substances;
viii. to ensure compliance with any laid down environmental impact assessment procedures in the planning and execution of development projects, including compliance in respect of existing projects; and
ix. to act in liaison and cooperation with government agencies, District Assemblies and other bodies and institutions to control pollution and generally protect the environment.

Membership of the Agency is made up of the Ministries for Environment, Local Government, Finance, Health and Education. It also has representatives from the Ghana Standards Board, Council for Scientific and Industrial Research and the Association of Ghana Industries.

Water Resources Commission (WRC)

This body formulates comprehensive national water policy regulations to control and manage water resources in the country. It also issues rights for the abstraction of water. Specifically, the Commission (a) proposes comprehensive plans for the utilization, conservation, development and improvement of water resources; (b) initiates, controls and coordinates activities connected with the development and utilization of water resources; (c) grants water rights; (d) collects, collates, stores and disseminates data or information on water resources in Ghana; (e) requires water user agencies to undertake scientific investigations, experiments or research into water resources in Ghana; (f) monitors and evaluates programmes for the operation and maintenance of water resources; (g) advises the government on any matter likely to have an adverse effect on the water resources of Ghana; (h) advises pollution control agencies in Ghana on matters concerning the management and control of pollution of water resources; and (i) performs other such functions as are incidental to the foregoing.

Forestry Commission
The Forestry Commission, established under Act 571 of 1999, is the main implementing body of Ghana's forest and wildlife policy. It is a corporate body integrating the activities of all the public agencies that were previously individually responsible for the management and regulation of utilization of forest and wildlife resources in Ghana. Under the Forestry Commission, the right to harvest and utilize timber is awarded in the form of a 'timber contract'. This is contained in Act 617, Timber Resources Management (Amendment) Act 2002. Under this Act, the contract holder enters into a contract with the Government to utilize and manage the timber resource on stated Terms and Conditions.

4.2 District Assemblies

In line with the government's policy of decentralization and the concept of local institutional arrangement under the Local Government Law, Act 462 of 1993, District Assemblies have a central role to play in the implementation of the environmental policies. The Local Government Law makes the District Assemblies responsible for the development, improvement and management of human settlements and the environment in the district. They also, under the law, have responsibility for monitoring the impact of projects on people's development, the local, district or national economy, and the environment. The Assemblies also have the responsibility of enforcing legislations and making by-laws.

Each Assembly is recommended to have a District Environmental Management Committee made up of the assembly members and representatives of the decentralized departments with the overall responsibility for monitoring and coordinating environmental protection and improvement activities in the district.

4.3 Non-Governmental Organizations (NGOs) and Community Groups

In recent years, religious groups, professional associations and other groups especially concerned with the promotion of sound environmental practices have gained prominence at both local and national levels. A number of such groups render active support in the implementation of programmes by both the Environmental Protection Agency and other agencies like the Forestry Commission especially at the local level where they have been proved most effective.

5. IMPLEMENTATION OF POLICY TOOLS

The Environmental Protection Agency (EPA) is the institution that advises and coordinates all environment-related issues in the country. It is the overall coordinating body for the implementation of the environmental policies. However, other institutions and bodies like the District Assemblies play very important roles.

5.1 Role of Sectoral Agencies/Institutions

Various ministries and agencies which deal with some aspect of the natural and built environment implement some of the environmental policies. Notable among these are the Ministry of Food and Agriculture, Water Resources Commission, Energy Commission, the Land Commission and some research institutions.

5.2 Role of the District Assemblies

District Assemblies have a central role to play in the implementation of the environmental policies. This is because national policies and programmes on the environment can best be translated into action at the local and district levels. To this end, District Environmental Management Committees with an overall responsibility for monitoring and coordinating environmental protection and improvement activities in the districts were to be established within each District Assembly but currently are not in place or operational. One problem identified for its non-establishment is that members are not paid, and also it is an additional responsibility imposed on the Assemblies. There are also no documented Terms of Reference for the Committee in the Local Government Law and thus no budget for its operations. Some specific actions implemented by the District Assemblies include:

i. to sustain and enforce bushfire legislation and strengthen control organization (training by the National Fire Service and monitoring by EPA is required);
ii. to establish protected areas to be managed for multiple uses in the coastal zone (by collaboration with NGOs);

iii. to control agricultural development in the coastal zone, with particular attention to the use of agro-chemicals and the implementation of soil conservation programmes (with technical support from District Agricultural Officer); and
iv. to enforce standards and regulations on waste water discharges, emissions, and disposal of solid wastes.

5.3 Role of Community Groups

Community Environmental Committees (CECs) are the organizations through which the environmental programmes of the District Assemblies are carried out at the community (town and village) level. The members are selected from the community. The CECs are responsible for mobilizing the people and resources in the community, provide forums for discussions on the environment, promote energy conservation and generally serve as the local environmental watch-dog by reporting to the appropriate authority in the district any activity deemed to violate the integrity of the local environment.

5.4 Role of Non-Governmental Organizations (NGOs)

The role played by NGOs in the past and currently in the area of environmental management is greatly appreciated. Some NGOs are undertaking tree planting and community forestry projects. Apart from specific projects and programmes they may undertake jointly with the District Assemblies and the CECs, NGOs are also encouraged to promote non-formal environmental education programmes, afforestation and agroforestry projects, and projects for the management of woodlands, watersheds and wildlife in collaboration with local authorities and community groups.

NGOs like the World Vision in Dangme West District of the Greater Accra Region organize a stakeholders meeting with the District Assembly and the decentralized departments at the end of the fiscal year to plan for the following year. This is to enable the NGO to include the needs and priorities of the district into their programme(s) the following year.

6. ENFORCEMENT AND CONTROL

6.1 Powers of the Environmental Protection Agency (EPA)

The EPA may, by issuing a notice in writing, require any person responsible for any undertaking which in the opinion of the Agency has or is likely to have an adverse effect on the environment, to submit to it in respect of the undertaking an environmental impact assessment containing such information within such period as shall be specified in the notice. When the Agency issues a notice it informs the organ or department of government that has responsibility for the issue of any licence, permit, approval or consent in connection with any matter affecting the environment that the notice has been issued, and the organ or department will not grant the licence, permit, approval or consent unless it has been notified by the Agency that the notice has been complied with.

Where it appears to the Agency that the activities of any undertaking pose a serious threat to the environment or to public health, the Agency may serve on the person responsible for the undertaking, an enforcement notice requiring him or her to take steps as the Agency thinks necessary to prevent or stop the activities. An enforcement notice specifies the following: (a) the offending activity; (b) the steps required to be taken; and (c) the time span within which the steps shall be taken. Any person who acts contrary to an enforcement notice issued commits an offence liable on summary conviction to a fine not exceeding 2 million cedis and in default to imprisonment for a term not exceeding one year.

Where a person to whom a notice has been served fails to comply with the directives contained in the notice within the stipulated time or such further period as the Agency may grant, the Minister for Environment may take steps as he considers appropriate to ensure compliance with the notice. Where authorized by the Minister, a police officer, an officer of the Agency or any public officer authorized by the Minister may use force as may be necessary for the purpose of ensuring compliance with the enforcement notice. Any person who hinders or obstructs this, commits an offence and is liable on summary conviction to a fine not exceeding 500 000 cedis or to imprisonment for a term not exceeding six months.

6.2 Powers of the District Assemblies

The District Assembly, like the EPA, also has the power to impose fines. The power of the District Assemblies lies in their ability to make by-laws. A District Assembly may make by-laws for the purpose of any function conferred upon it, for example, for controlling noise pollution. A District Assembly may, in terms of by-laws:

a. specify as penalty a fine not exceeding 200 000 cedis or a term of imprisonment not exceeding six months, or both;
b. specify a further penalty not exceeding 2000 cedis for each day on which the offence is continued after written notice of the conviction

has been served on the offender in the case of a continuing offence; and

c. make provision for the payment of such fees or charges as the Assembly may think fit.

Fines are, in general, the main policy tool used by the Assemblies. For example, in the Dangme West District, the Assembly budgeted an amount of 800 million cedis for the 2004 fiscal year as revenue to be generated from sand, stones and gravel collection either through permits or fines. A fee of 15 million cedis, for example, is required to be paid as a permit fee which is used to reclaim degraded land.

6.3 Challenges for EPA and the District Assemblies

Environmental Action Plan (EAP) for Ghana (EPC, 1991) was formulated by the Environmental Protection Council to address the nation's environmental problems in a comprehensive and integrated manner. Its objective was to provide a technical, institutional and legal framework for dealing with the problems of land and water degradation, diminishing forest and wildlife resources, and problems associated with mineral extraction and other industrial activities (Benneh, 1998).

The District Assemblies are also empowered by law to come out with by-laws to address the environmental problems at the local level. However, most districts have problems in enforcing these by-laws because most locally generated revenue for the Assemblies comes from activities which have negative environmental impacts, such as charcoal production and sand winning, among others. In the Dangme West District, for example, taxes from sand winning are one of the biggest sources of locally-generated revenue.

A big challenge for the Environmental Protection Agency (EPA) is how to come to grips with waste management, not only in Accra but also in all other parts of the country. The District and Metropolitan Assemblies do not see protection of the environment, including sound waste management practices, as their core function, nor do they have sufficient resources to undertake this function.

Another key challenge the EPA is facing is how to mainstream environmental issues into national, sectoral, regional and district level policies, programmes and plans. As a step towards this goal, the Agency in collaboration with the National Development Planning Commission (NDPC) initiated a pilot study to undertake a Strategic Environmental Assessment (SEA) on the Ghana Poverty Reduction Strategy (GPRS).

The EPA has been granted the power to prosecute environment-related cases in the courts. However, there is concern over the fact that a large number of environment-related cases which are being prosecuted by the Agency's legal officers are pending in the law courts because of frequent adjournments. A successful decentralization of the Agency's activities to the regional and district offices is the key to raising community awareness at the local level. This requires infusion of huge resources, both human and capital.

7. CONCLUSIONS

Effective environmental control requires a 'holistic' knowledge reflecting a synthesis of the biological and physical factors. Environmental assessments must also include social and economic factors within an institutional arrangement that permits appraisal of alternatives in terms of anticipated consequences. However, this is often not possible because of limitations, which we may summarize as follows.

Data Availability and Gathering

A fair amount of environment-related data already exists in the country. However, this is scattered and to a large extent not coordinated, having been gathered by different organizations at different times for specific purposes. Water quality data appears to be quite adequate, although gaps exist in time series data. Generally, an extensive monitoring of the air and water quality is required in Ghana so that a base period can be set to serve as basis for comparison in the future.

A major shortcoming of the overall monitoring system is the lack of a common framework. Also the scope of data collected does not provide information on social, cultural and economic aspects of the development process in a method which permits determination of inter-relationships.

Most of the lead institutions responsible for data collection in the area of land and water resources lack basic facilities for efficient operation. Most observation and ancillary equipments have broken down, are insufficient or non-existent.

Environmental Protection Agency (EPA)

EPA acts as a catalyst for change by working through partnerships at the national, regional, district and local levels in order to achieve results. EPA's partnership with the district, municipal and metropolitan assemblies is of particular importance because these institutions form the level of government closest to the people and therefore are in a better position to know local concerns and to develop and implement practical action programmes for addressing these concerns. However, this vital link in the case of environmental governance is weak in terms of handling environmental issues.

District Assemblies

It is difficult for the District Assemblies to fulfil their responsibility in implementing environmental policies because they are not strong enough, and the decentralized departments are still not firmly established in the districts due to problems of space and housing for the officials. The District Assemblies and especially the key departments would have to be strengthened in order to enable them to discharge their responsibilities effectively.

NGOs and Community Groups

NGOs, with the advantage of being free from bureaucratic problems facing government agencies, are able to gain easy access to the grassroots level to engage in developmental activities. Against this background, the NGOs could play a valuable role in sensitizing the local population to environmental issues and environmental restoration and enrichment programmes. It would be necessary to bring all the NGOs together to explore their full participation in implementation of the environmental policies.

NOTES

1. Ghana's Economic Recovery Programme (ERP) initiated in 1983 proceeded in two distinct phases. The first phase, 1983–1986, had economic stabilization as its main focus, halting the economic decline of the previous years; and ERP II, 1987–1989, sought to embark on a programme of growth and development, with special emphasis on the social services. This involved institutional reforms, amongst which decentralization was given prominence by the Government under the Local Government Sector Reform programme. The involvement of the private sector and the populace, especially at the grassroots level in the development process, was given a high premium.
2. This perception may be right or wrong. The Ministry of Local Government and Rural Development's paper 'Decentralization in Ghana: Implementation Status and Proposed Future Directions', published in March 2002, does not mention poverty reduction as an achievement or problem of decentralization. This notwithstanding, the fact that the decentralization programme was meant to give 'power to the people' (empowerment) and redress the rural–urban drift suggests that the element of poverty reduction is implicit in the objectives.
3. For a review of the PAMSCAD, see Hutchful (2002), Chapter 7, pp. 116–39.
4. Exchange rate of 9000 cedis to US$1.
5. The 12 districts are Bolgatanga, Bawku East, East Gonja, Wa, Kintampo, Nkoranza, Kwahu South, Akwapim North, Mfantsiman, Kommenda-Edina-Eguafo-Abirem, East Nzema and Kpandu. These were the study districts in which pre- and post-district assemblies and

unit committee elections surveys were conducted in July and August 2002. The surveys were conducted by the Department of Political Science, University of Ghana and covered 3600 respondents in the 12 districts.

6. For an extensive discussion of the problems and constraints see Ayee (2003a) Chapter 2: pp. 45–81; Ayee (2003b) pp. 1–27; Ayee (2004) Chapter 6: pp. 125–54.

BIBLIOGRAPHY

Asante, F.A. (2003), *Economic Analysis of Decentralisation in Rural Ghana*, Germany: Peter Lang.

Ayee, J.R.A. (1992), 'Decentralization and effective government', *Africa Insight*, **22**, 49–56.

Ayee, J.R.A. (1996), 'The measurement of decentralization: The Ghanaian experience', *African Affairs*, **95** (378), 31–50.

Ayee, J.R.A. (1997), 'Local government reform and bureaucratic accountability', Regional Development Dialogue, (UNCRD Nagoya, Japan), **18** (2) (Autumn), 86–104.

Ayee, J.R.A. (2003a), 'Local government, decentralization and state capacity in Ghana', in Wisdom Tettey, K.P. Puplampu and B. Berman (eds), *Critical Perspectives on Politics and Socio-Economic Development in Ghana*, Leiden: Brill.

Ayee, J.R.A. (2003b), 'Towards effective and accountable local government in Ghana', *Critical Perspectives*, **13** (March), 1–27, Ghana: Ghana Centre for Democratic Development.

Ayee, J.R.A. (2004), 'Ghana: A top-down initiative', in Dele Olowu and James Wunsch (eds), *Local Governance in Africa: The Challenges of Democratic Decentralization*, Boulder, CO./London: Lynne Rienner, Chapter 6, pp. 125–54.

Ayee, J.R.A. and N. Amponsah (2003), 'The district assemblies and local governance: Reflections on the 2002 local elections' in N. Amponsah and K. Boafo-Arthur (eds), *Local Government in Ghana: Grassroots Participation in the 2002 Local Government Elections*, Accra: Department of Political Science, Chapter 3.

Benneh, G. (1998), 'Institutional issues on the environment and resource management with reference to Ghana', http://www.unu.edu.unupress/unupbooks/80918e/80918Eoz.

Boon, E.K. (1998), 'Monitoring, evaluation and control of environmental policy and programmes in developing countries: Lessons from Ghana', in L. Hens, R. Borden, S. Susuki and G. Caravallo (eds), *Case Studies in Applied Human Ecology – An International Overview*, Brussels: VUB-Press.

Environmental Protection Council (EPC) (1991), *Ghana Environmental Action Plan*, Volume 1. Accra, Ghana.

GTZ and SNRD (1996), 'Decentralization and local government in Ghana', Decentralization and Rural Development, Working Paper No. 3. Ghana: SNRD Working Group.

Hutchful, E. (2002), *Ghana's Adjustment Experience: The Paradox of Reform*, Oxford; Accra: UNRISD/Heinemann/James Currey.

Ministry of Local Government & Rural Development (MLGRD)(2002), *Decentralization in Ghana: Implementation Status and Proposed Future Directions*, March: pp. 1–28. Accra: Ministry of Local Government and Rural Development.

Republic of Ghana (1992), 'Constitution of the Republic of Ghana', Accra.
Republic of Ghana (1993), 'Local Government Act, 1993. Act 462', Accra: Ghana Publishing Corporation.
Republic of Ghana (1994), 'Environmental Protection Agency Act, 1994', Accra: Ghana Publishing Corporation.

APPENDIX: DECENTRALIZED DEPARTMENTS UNDER THE METROPOLITAN, MUNICIPAL AND DISTRICT ASSEMBLIES

Metropolitan	Municipal	District
1. Central Administration Department	1. Central Administration Department	1. Central Administration Department
2. Finance Department	2. Finance Department	2. Finance Department
3. Education, Youth and Sports Department	3. Education, Youth and Sports Department	3. Education, Youth and Sports Department
4. Metropolitan Health Department	4. Municipal Health Department	4. District Health Department
5. Waste Management Department	5. Agriculture Department	5. Agriculture Department
6. Agriculture Department	6. Physical Planning Department	6. Physical Planning Department
7. Physical Planning Department	7. Social Welfare and Community Development Department	7. Social Welfare and Community Development Department
8. Social Welfare and Community Development Department	8. Natural Resources Conservation Department, Forestry, Game and Wildlife Division	8. Natural Resources Conservation Department, Forestry, Game and Wildlife Division
9. Natural Resources Conservation Department, Forestry, Game and Wildlife Division	9. Works Department	9. Works Department
10. Works Department	10. Industry and Trade Department	10. Industry and Trade Department
11. Industry and Trade Department	11. Transport Department	11. Disaster Prevention Department
12. Budget and Rating	12. Disaster Prevention Department	
13. Legal Department	13. Urban Roads	
14. Transport Department		
15. Disaster Prevention Department		
16. Urban Roads		

16. Italy: Towards responsibility-sharing in environmental protection

Ivana Capozza* and Giovanna Garrone

1. INTRODUCTION

In Italy, environmental concerns have prompted effective actions only in relatively recent times, in spite of the high pressures determined by the country's economic and social features, such as the high density of population, mostly concentrated in coastal areas and in the plains.

Environmental governance is affected by the overall government system. Italy is a regional (quasi-federal) state with a four-tier system of government: the country is divided into 20 Regions (to five of which the Constitution grants an increased autonomy),[1] 110 Provinces and, at the sub-provincial level, 8102 Municipalities and a number of several different local authorities, such as Mountain Communities. It is undergoing a significant, albeit slow and somewhat bumpy, evolution towards a proper federal set-up such that the current system is not easy to classify (Crosetti et al., 2002). The assignment of powers over the environment is evolving accordingly, with a general tendency towards an increasing role of local authorities at different levels. However, the allocation of competences among levels of government is not always clear.

This chapter reviews the current institutional setting for environmental governance in Italy, focusing on the ongoing decentralisation process and on the evolution of the policy instruments. Section 2 retraces the evolution in time of the institutional set-up leading to the current system of actors and assignments. This is described in section 3, which also deals with the role of the environmental protection agencies and the evolution of the planning activity for sustainable development. Section 4 is devoted to the policy tools, and focuses specifically on the few economic instruments and the development of voluntary approaches. Conclusions follow.

2. THE DEVELOPMENT OF THE INSTITUTIONAL SETTING FOR ENVIRONMENTAL GOVERNANCE

All levels of government are presently involved in environmental policy, if not in formulating it (at the legislative level), at least in its implementation and management. The ways functions and responsibilities are assigned between different governments – and other intermediate/specialised bodies – have been the object of some relevant transformations. Table 16.1 presents the main steps of this transformation.

Until almost 1986, when the Ministry of Environment was created, Italy lacked specific environmental legislation. The protection of the environment was mainly delegated to the ordinary Courts of the civil and criminal law (Civil Code and Criminal Code). Civil law was used to indirectly recognise the obligation to compensate environmental damage arising from illegal acts, but only when associated with negative effects for other personal rights (for example property rights). Criminal law defined environment-related crimes and prescribed penal sanctions for causing events such as fires, epidemics (for human beings, flora and fauna), floods and landslides, poisoning of water and food, damages to cultural or natural heritage.[2] Hence, this was an ex post environmental protection, taking place only after the occurrence of a damaging event (Postiglione, 1988) and mainly linked to the protection of public health.

Although the 'environment' as such was never mentioned in the Constitution, the protection of the environment was based on the combination of the Constitution articles relating to the protection of human rights, health and landscape and cultural heritage[3] and it was interpreted as falling under the responsibility of the central government. Nonetheless, environmental governance at the national level was shared among several ministries (for example health, agriculture, infrastructure). The effectiveness of such a multiple reference system was poor, as is shown by the low number of environmental acts issued in this period.

The situation improved considerably during the 1980s, with the introduction of the regulations on urban waste, sea protection, landscape protection and the transposition of the 'Seveso directive'.[4] This improvement of the legislative framework went along with an increasing concern by public opinion and a growth of the green movement,[5] both spurred on by some environmental emergencies, such as the 1976 Seveso chemical accident (Lewanski, 1998).

Local authorities played an increasing role in taking environmental measures (Lewanski, 1998). Regions were instituted in 1972, though they had to wait until 1977 to acquire effective powers, either directly assigned or delegated. The areas left to regional legislation, within the boundaries of national framework laws,[6] included several fields connected with the environment such as urban planning, hunting and fishing, agriculture and forestry. Administrative powers tended to parallel legislative ones, and the State could delegate to Regions additional administrative responsibilities on matters that fell under its exclusive legislative competence. Such administrative power was then shared with provincial and municipal governments, partly by direct assignment, partly by delegation. The role of Municipalities was particularly relevant in this period, as their local dimension allowed them to register earlier citizens' needs and to respond to them, either directly or by stimulating the search for solutions at a higher government level (Lewanski, 1998). As we will see (in section 'Local Agenda 21'), Municipalities still play a very active and propulsive role for environmental policy.

The establishment of the Ministry of Environment in 1986 marked a turning point for the environmental governance model. The Ministry was set up with the general task of assuring a coherent organisational structure for the conservation and enhancement of natural resources and the preservation of safe environmental conditions. The law establishing the Ministry was a sort of environmental framework act. In particular, it transposed the EU directive on environmental impact assessment, appointing the Ministry as the national authority responsible for it. Moreover, it defined environmental damage for the first time, identifying public and private bodies allowed to resort to Courts. Environmental associations were acknowledged as having the right to call for the intervention of inspection bodies and to participate in trials. However, this right was limited to those associations certified by the Ministry. Finally, primary inspection powers were assigned to the *Carabinieri* Division for Environmental Protection, which responds directly to the Ministry.

The new Ministry was assigned responsibilities and powers previously attributed to distinct central bodies. In particular, it was transferred functions relating to water and waste that had previously been assigned to inter-ministerial committees. It also gained responsibilities over nature protection from the Ministry of Agriculture and Forestry. The other environmental themes were air pollution, industrial risk, contaminated sites, noise, sea protection, soil, and environmental impact assessment. For most of these fields of activity, the Ministry had to cooperate with other central authorities, mainly the same ones involved in the suppressed inter-ministerial committees for water and waste. Such coordination was not an easy task, especially because the Ministry was an 'infant' compared to other long-established Ministries, which were interested in keeping their powers. Moreover, the Ministry lacked both financial and human resources, the former being largely devoted to managing environmental emergencies.

The following years saw a marked increase in the legislative production, mainly under the impulse from the European Community and the international context: themes such as water quality, ozone layer, air pollution, noise, wastes, natural habitats, flora and fauna were regulated.

The general political crisis of the early 1990s contributed to putting the environment aside until the second half of the 1990s. With Mr Edo Ronchi as the first Green Minister of the Environment (within the 1996–1998 centre-left government), the role of the Ministry was strengthened, in terms of functions and resources.[7] Other responsibilities were transferred to the Ministry, and the required agreement with other central authorities was gradually limited to some specific areas, such as environmental impact assessment.

The legislative framework substantially improved, and activity at international level increased. In 1997 (Rio+5 review of Agenda 21), the Parliament adopted a sustainable development agenda (*Agenda per lo Sviluppo Sostenibile*).

Together with the strengthening of environmental governance and institutions at the central level, a decentralisation process was pushed forward.

The evolution towards a federal structure has so far taken place in two main stages:

1. The so-called 'Bassanini Acts', introducing administrative federalism (Act n. 59/1997 and its implemental decree n. 112/1998).
2. The reform of the Title V of the Constitution (Constitutional Law n. 3/2001).

The 'Bassanini Acts' aimed at bringing a substantial change in the relationships between the State and the system of local governments within the framework of the existing Constitution, anticipating to a great extent the subsequent Constitutional Reform. The subsidiarity principle, extrapolated from the supranational (European Union) context, was applied to orientating the assignment of powers between the State and the Regions but also between the latter and the local governments. On the one hand, the 'Bassanini Acts' devolve to the Regions all administrative functions and responsibilities that relate to the development of the respective community and located on the respective territory. On the other hand, they also state that all functions that do not require to be performed at a unitary regional level are to be transferred to local governments.[8]

These principles apply to environmental matters as well.

A reform of the Constitution was passed in 2001. It concerns almost exclusively intergovernmental relations. The reform introduces the word 'environment' into the Constitution for the first time, assigning the 'protection of the environment, of the ecosystem and of cultural heritage' to the exclusive power of the national parliament.

However, legislative power over other relevant matters connected with the environment is either shared between the State and the Regions or assigned to the exclusive competence of Regions.

Although both administrative and legislative decentralisations had not been fully implemented, a further constitutional reform, designed and approved by Parliament vote in 2005, never came into force as it was rejected by a national referendum. Whereas such reform was explicitly aimed at creating a federal State, it entailed the recentralisation of some powers (for example industrial safety, energy production and distribution, general norms on health protection). Hence, in recent years, progress in the institutional capacity of regional and local governments and federalist pressures (mainly the expression of the northern regions) coexist with attempts at fixing a fragmented legislative framework, which sometimes result in a recentralisation of responsibilities.[9]

Summing up, the alternate trends towards centralisation or decentralisation of environment-related powers have not been determined by environmental governance considerations, but have followed mainly the politically-driven development of the overall institutional setting.

The reader will note that the European Union is included among the main drivers/actors reported in Table 16.1. Indeed, the European Union has always played a propulsive role in terms of defining new environmental legislation and policy tools.[10] Nonetheless, the Community rules and guiding principles have not been of sufficient impulse for the definition of a coherent and comprehensive legislative framework for the environment. Firstly, Italy has often been late in transposing EU legislation, and this transposition has mostly been carried out through emergency procedures, either directly by the Government (*decreto legge*) or through delegation of the legislative power from the Parliament to the Government (*decreto legislativo*).[11] Secondly, the production of environmental legislation in Italy has usually been driven by 'emergency' and has often been directly prompted by natural disasters or events raising public awareness.[12] This is a peculiarity of the Italian political system, in which even technical decisions offer grounds for political conflicts and only emergencies bring political parties to reach consensus easily (Lewanski, 1998).

Only in recent years has an increasing media attention been devoted to environmental themes and in some cases has been a driver of environmental decision-making. For example, media attention on climate change

Table 16.1 The development of the institutional setting

Phase	Features	Main drivers/actors of environmental policy
Before 1986	–Plurality of actors (Ministries) at the central level. –Environmental protection based on Civil and Criminal Codes. –Weak public opinion and political will. –Initial (and insufficient) legal discipline of air, water, urban waste, sea, landscape and industrial risk.	–Regional and local government (particularly Municipalities). –EU (late 70s – early 80s). –Environmental emergencies.
1986–1992	–Establishment of the Ministry of Environment (1986). –Initial weakness of MoE. –Uncertain evolution of intergovernmental relations. –Electoral success of the Greens (protest vote), but still low political influence.	–Central government. –EU.
1992–1997	–*Tangentopoli*, institutional crisis and the beginning of the Second Republic: environment is not a priority (1992–1995). –Greens in the cabinet (1995–2001). –Strengthening of MoE. –Creation of a Commission for Sustainable Development. –Establishment of a network of environmental protection agencies. –Marked increase in the legislative production.	–Central government. –EU.
1997–2001	–Administrative decentralisation (Bassanini Acts 1997–1998). –Political decentralisation (Constitutional Reform 2001). –Strengthening of regional and local governments.	–Central government. –EU. –Regional and local governments.
2001–2007	–New Constitutional reform towards federalism approved by Parliament (2005), but rejected by referendum (2006). –Further progress in institutional capacity of regional and local authorities to deal with environmental matters. –Worsening of local conflicts over localisations of plants and increased media attention. –Greens back in the cabinet (2006).	–EU. –Regional and local governments. –Environmental protection agencies. –Mass-media.

paralleled a renewed role of the central government on this issue, with the allocation of financial resources and the introduction of specific energy efficiency measures in the Financial Law 2007. On the other hand, mass-media have somehow hindered decision-making, by reinforcing environmental conflicts over localisation choices for infrastructures (such as landfills, waste incinerators, power plants and high-speed railways). Blanchetti and Conti (2006) report a high increase in coverage of such conflicts in 2005–2006 with respect to previous years (over 4000 press articles on 171 disputed projects) but also a tendency to overrepresent the opponents' contentions and to privilege emotional arguments over accurate information.

3. THE MAIN ACTORS AND THE CURRENT ASSIGNMENT FRAMEWORK

3.1 Legislation

As mentioned above, the constitution assigns exclusively to the national parliament the 'protection of the environment, of the ecosystem and of cultural heritage'. At first sight environmental matters could appear to be strongly centralised. However, other relevant environment-related matters are assigned to the concurrent national and regional legislation, meaning that the legislative power resides with the Regions within 'fundamental principles' determined by the central State. Areas that are not explicitly listed as exclusively assigned to the national parliament or concurrent legislation are assigned to the exclusive legislation of Regions (see Table 16.2).

The new art. 116 of the Constitution provides for the possibility of 'asymmetric federalism', that is granting further forms of autonomy to 'ordinary' Regions that ask for them. This will allow concurrent matters to be transferred to the exclusive competence of Regions, or matters that are the exclusive competence of the State to concurrent legislation. The protection of the environment, of the ecosystem and of cultural heritage is explicitly included in the latter case.

The interpretation of the assignment of powers resulting from this reform has not always been straightforward. Nonetheless, on practical grounds, Regions retain powers that they have been acquiring for years.

The legal framework is still excessively fragmented (OECD, 2002). The devolution process has in some ways increased this fragmentation, because of the local disparities in the formulation and implementation of legislation, technical standards and administrative procedures.

Table 16.2 Assignment of legislative powers over environment and related areas

Exclusive competence of the State	Concurrency (State–Region)	Exclusive competence of Regions
• Protection of the environment, of the ecosystem and of the cultural heritage.	• Protection of health. • Enhancement of environmental and cultural heritage. • Food. • Environmental services (civil protection). • Land management. • Main transportation networks. • Production, transport and distribution of energy (national scale). • Workplace safety.	• Agriculture. • Production and distribution of energy (regional scale). • Water resources, water main, mineral and thermal waters. • Hunting and fishing (rivers and lakes). • Building and town planning. • Regional transportation networks, road systems.

3.2 Administration

At the central level, the main actor is the Ministry of Environment and Territory (MATT), although some powers still rest with other ministries, mainly the Ministry for Cultural Heritage (as regards environmental impact assessment and landscape protection), the Ministry of Productive Activities (energy), the Ministry for Infrastructure and Transport (transport and environmental infrastructure), the Ministry for Agriculture and Forestry (organic farming and genetically modified organisms, fisheries and forests) and the Ministry of Domestic Affairs (civil defence).

MATT is a member of the Commission for Sustainable Development. The Commission includes representatives of several Ministries, and of local authorities when needed. It has powers over the environmental component of sustainable development, and its main objective is to coordinate the decision-making among all the involved administrations. The Commission worked intensively at its beginning, especially towards meeting the deadlines of some international conventions (climate change and desertification), but its activity has been slowing down since 2002 (La Camera, 2003).

Other central agencies provide technical support to the various levels of government, such as the National Agency for Energy and Environment

(ENEA), the National Health Institute, the National Statistical Institute (ISTAT), the National Research Council and the National Sea Research Centre. Moreover, since 1993 a system of Environmental Protection Agencies has been established (see section 3.3).

All in all, the central government maintains coordination and control functions, together with supervision and oversight powers. It issues guidelines, defines thresholds and limit values. It is exclusively assigned a number of 'responsibilities of national relevance' (see Tables 16.2 and 16.3) and maintains powers of substitutive intervention.

The Regions have a fundamental role both in planning (identification of priorities for environmental action and coordination of environmental intervention) and in issuing technical norms that adapt to the regional context the above-mentioned guidelines and values determined through the national legislation.

Provinces are active in planning and monitoring. They take part in all regional plans (on waste and landfills, air and noise pollution). The Territorial Coordination Plan identifies land use, location of major infrastructures, intervention lines for hydro-geological matters, areas for natural parks and reserves. Many monitoring and authorisation powers reside with the Provinces, as emphasised by the law instituting ARPAs, whose technical departments are to this purpose made functionally dependent on Provinces (see section 3.3).

The role of the Municipalities is defined mainly by sectoral laws. Following the 'Bassanini Acts', the amended Constitution assigns all administrative functions to the Municipalities unless they need to be allocated to higher tiers (Metropolitan Areas, Provinces, Regions or State) for the sake of efficiency or territorial homogeneity (in accordance with the subsidiarity principle).

Coordination problems among administrations at the same or different levels can be solved through contractual agreements. Contractual agreements between administrations serve as a link between different fields and levels of planning activity. They are explicitly prescribed as the tool for coordination and integration (also on the financial front). As far as environmental matters are concerned, a number of sectoral environmental laws refer to contractual agreements between administrations. These agreements have played a role since the late 1980s, becoming increasingly important through the 1990s and they seem to have received a strong impulse from the decentralisation process (Bobbio, 2000).[13]

Examining public expenditure by level of government offers additional evidence of the increasing role that local administrations play in environmental governance. According to Regional Public Accounts data for years 2003–2005, overall central government expenditure amounted

Table 16.3 Assignment of administrative powers over environment and related areas

Exclusive competence of the State	Concurrency (State–Region)	Provincial or inter-municipality	Municipality
• Implementation of international conventions and EC directives. • Conservation of natural areas of international relevance, of biodiversity, of species protected by treaties and conventions. • Report on the state of the environment. • Protection, safety and monitoring of marine environment. • Setting of standards, quality and safety objectives and technical norms needed for an adequate level of environmental protection in the national territory. • Technical support to environmental planning on matters of national competence. • Identification of animal huntable species. • Identification of species at risk of extinction. • Supervision of the national environmental protection agency.	• Environmental information and education. • Fostering of clean technology and sustainable development policies. • Coastal protection.	• Land protection, environmental protection and enhancement. • Protection and improvement of water and energy resources. • Enhancement of cultural heritage. • Road system and transports. • Flora and fauna protection, natural parks and reserves. • Hunting and fishing (rivers and lakes). • Waste management and emission controls. • Public health, hygiene, and prevention.	• Locations of production activities (involving issues of urban planning, health, environmental protection and safety). • Public health. • Traffic. • Green areas. • Waste collection and disposal. • Sewage water treatment. • All residual functions.

to over a half of total public expenditure, whereas the weight of the central government on environmental expenditures averaged just 4.5 per cent. Local governments, which among other authorities include Municipalities and Provinces, accounted for the largest share (47 per cent), followed by national public enterprise and local public utilities (37 per cent). In this period, waste management and water services accounted for the largest share of expenditures by local entities (nearly 70 per cent) and by public utilities (55 per cent) respectively. Whereas in these sectors Regions played a marginal role, regional expenditures were higher in other environmental fields (such as hydrological and soil protection, pollution abatement, nature and biodiversity conservation, support for agriculture and forestry, environmental monitoring). However, data show sharp disparities between the Centre-North and the South of the country, where the expenditure share by public utilities was considerably lower, partly as a consequence of the incomplete implementation of sectoral reforms.

3.3 The System of Environmental Protection Agencies

The current system of environmental protection agencies was designed in 1993, following the outcome of a referendum called to remove monitoring and inspection activities in environmental matters from the Ministry of Health.[14] This system appears almost to mirror the territorial structure of the government system.

The role of the National Agency

APAT, the National Agency for Environmental Protection and Technical Services, is the central authority for environmental monitoring, and it was created as a technical agency abreast of the political authority.[15] However, its independence from the Ministry is not absolute, and oversight and orientation powers rest with the MATT.

The functions attributed to APAT comprise:

1. Carrying out technical and scientific activities of national relevance related to environmental protection, such as basic and applied scientific research, collection, processing and publishing of environmental data, cooperation with EEA and other international agencies.
2. Providing coordination and orientation to ARPAs (the regional agencies, see below) in order to ensure that uniform methodologies are used across the country.
3. Providing technical advice and support to MATT and (through ad hoc agreements) other administrative and public bodies.

Objectives, priorities and resources for APAT's activities are set out in three-year plans, reviewed annually, which implement MATT's directives.

ARPAs: functions and organisation

Regional agencies (ARPAs)[16] are intended as the 'operational arms' of the Regions, to whom they provide support for planning, regulatory and pre-trial activities. Inspections, monitoring and analyses are carried out on behalf of all levels of local administrations, Provinces, Municipalities and Local Health Authorities (ASL).

The tasks assigned to the ARPAs can differ to some extent across Regions, as well as the internal organisation of the agencies. ARPAs are generally organised in functional areas and provincial departments. The latter are the structures actually carrying out the services in the field. Regions can stipulate agreements with the Provinces to place provincial departments under their functional dependence.

A strengthening of the role of the Provinces in environmental matters is taking place to different degrees across the country, both through the devolution of functions from the Regions and the functional dependence of ARPA's operational departments.

ARPAs play a relevant role in the collection and production of environmental data. A network of Environmental Information Systems (SINA) is articulated in regional focal points (a structure that recalls the national focal points of the European EIONET). However, such information networks have taken a long time to become operational, partly because of the high implementation costs. The whole picture of the flow of environmental data involves many steps. At the central level, the MATT is in charge of transmitting data to European institutions (European Commission, EEA); transmitting them to the national agency is the responsibility of the Regions, who may or may not choose to devolve it to ARPAs. Anecdotal evidence shows that communication failures can occur in some of the steps.

ARPAs: implementation and territorial disparity

Setting up the ARPAs took much longer than the six months initially allowed for (see Figure 16.1). The implementation process was slow and showed dramatic territorial differences, which can be roughly depicted as a North/South division. The last ARPA to be created was the Sardinian one (September 2002).[17] A survey conducted by ARPAV (the Veneto agency) of 18 agencies operational as of 31 December 2001 provides data on human resources (Cadrobbi, 2002). While these cannot be used directly for a cross-region comparison, they do reveal that human resources employed by ARPAs were at the time well below their expected fully-fledged staffing level. The results of a 'benchmarking project' (APAT-ONOG, 2003, 2006)

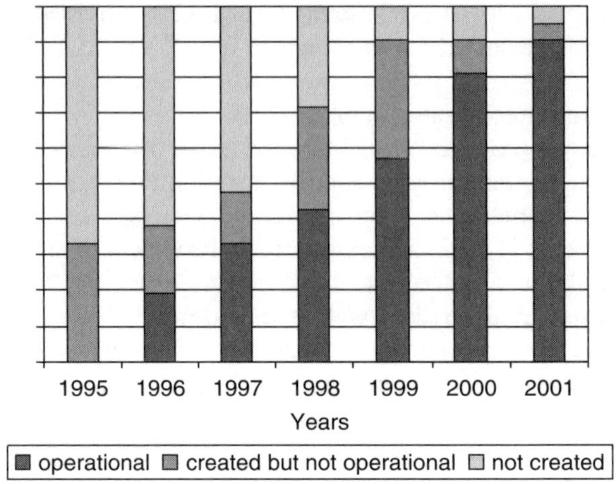

Source: APAT-ONOG (2003).

Figure 16.1 State of implementation of the ARPAs/APPAs system

show a high degree of similarity among agencies as regards the monitoring and inspection activities, while the situation is more diversified as regards the technical and scientific support to local governments.[18]

The huge regional differences in the actual setting up and performance of ARPAs has prompted APAT to undertake initiatives aimed at overcoming disparity and achieving coordination between the peripheral agencies. An interesting one is the 'twinning' project launched towards the end of 1998 with the aim of completing the setting up of the agencies. Ad hoc agreements defined the terms of a close cooperation between a 'good' ARPA with a 'laggard' one. This involved exchanging regulatory and technical documents, training activities and workshops, exchanges of visiting staff. These twinnings were later renewed under the A.G.I.R.E POR programme, financed with Structural Funds.

Overall, the Italian system of agencies seems sensibly designed, and its set-up certainly marks a step forward in environmental governance, especially considering that the laboratories previously in charge of environmental controls (PMPs), which the ARPAs replaced and absorbed, acted in a completely decentralised and uncoordinated way.

The negative valuation certainly concerns the delays and incompleteness of the network implementation. The setting up of the agencies system took place in the years of the administrative and constitutional reforms. ONOG (APAT-ONOG, 2003) argues (somewhat self-defensively) that this created some uncertainty in the interpretation of the agencies' mandate, and accounts for some of the difficulties in implementation. It also calls for a revision of the institutive laws, and a greater emancipation from the legacy of the health sector.

3.4 Planning for Sustainable Development and Environmental Management

Since 1989, there have been several attempts at developing a comprehensive programmatic framework for environmental policy. However, they failed in harmonising the planning instruments at various governmental levels and in imposing mid-term strategies (OECD, 2002).

The latest step towards sustainable development planning was the adoption by the central government of the Environmental Strategy for Sustainable Development in 2002, as a contribution to the Johannesburg World Summit on Sustainable Development. It is articulated in four priority areas, which reflect those involved in the Sixth EU Environment Action Plan (EAP). Unlike previous planning experiences, the Strategy states specific objectives and targets, and identifies implementation instruments (partially recalling the 6th EAP).

The Strategy is the first example of wide participation in environmental decision-making, since it was discussed both with other central and local administrations and with stakeholders, such as environmental NGOs and consumer, worker and enterprise organisations. However, some stakeholders, particularly environmental NGOs, argue that they were involved at a too advanced stage of the process. The participatory approach was meant to be extended to the implementation of the Strategy, through the establishment of a Forum bringing together public authorities and civil society.

The Commission for Sustainable Development is in charge of assessing the achievement of the Strategy goals. The monitoring is carried out by means of an annual report presented by the MATT.

The implementation of the Strategy has been limited to the approval of the national programme for curbing GHG emissions, even though the two planning documents followed two separate and parallel paths. Although the Strategy tried to avoid the mistakes of past planning experiences (for example by setting objectives, targets, indicators, monitoring and participation procedures), once the Johannesburg Summit was over its implementation apparently lost momentum.

In the late 1990s, following the administrative decentralisation reform, Regions were assigned the overall planning of environmental protection, together with the land use and sectoral planning that was already their responsibility. However, the definition of sectoral plans has incurred severe delays, especially in Southern regions, thus hindering the investments and the effective management of environmental services. In particular, this was the case for waste and water management, hydrogeological risk, reclaiming of polluted sites and management of natural protected areas. Since 2003 significant progress has taken place in Southern regions, which have succeeded in completing most of their pending plans. A contribution to this acceleration in the planning process was given by the overall system of rules for the allocation of financial resources linked to the Community Structural Funds programming 2000–2006 (see Box 16.1).

BOX 16.1 INTEGRATION OF ENVIRONMENTAL CONCERNS INTO REGIONAL PROGRAMMES: THE CASE OF COMMUNITY STRUCTURAL FUNDS FOR OBJECTIVE 1 REGIONS

Italian Southern regions were included in Objective 1 of the EU structural policy,[19] receiving an overall financial aid for about euro 46 billion in the period 2000–2006, for the promotion of development and structural adjustment. The implementation of institutional and sectoral reforms and the strengthening of technical and administrative processes were deemed to be a basic requirement for the achievement of structural policy development objectives in Italian Objective 1 regions. To this end, the access to funds for waste, water and soil protection investments was made dependent upon a prior definition of related plans. Moreover, Italy set up a 'performance reserve' incentive scheme, conditioning an amount of Structural Funds to the achievement of fixed targets in the fields of administrative practices, by 2003. Four out of ten indicators and targets of institutional improvement concerned the environment: preparation and approval of territorial and landscape programming documents; implementation of integrated water services; urban waste management through optimal service areas; and creation and operativeness of ARPAs. This 'sanction and award' system fostered progress in sectoral reforms (Anselmo et al., 2006).

Within this framework, environmental governance was also enhanced by establishing Environmental Authorities (EAs) at national and regional level, pursuant to the general requirement of the EU. EAs are linked in a Network involving also Managing Authorities (MAs), that is the bodies in charge of managing structural funds programmes. To our knowledge, only Italy and Spain have activated this kind of network. EAs have the mission of cooperating with MAs and participate in the supervision of the programming and implementation processes. The overall aim is to overcome a sectoral approach to environmental governance, moving towards a greater coordination of economic, social and environmental measures.

EAs have been supported by a Task Force created in 2001 under a six-year project financed by Structural Funds (Environment Operational Project), seeking to improve environmental expertise and effectiveness of central and local administrations in Southern Italy. According to OECD (2002), this was 'a very innovative capacity-building project', because it has provided for the first time an adequate number of staff units exclusively dedicated to the integration of environmental concerns into regional programmes. The Task Force has been essential to enable EAs to carry out their activities and to comply with their institutional role.

4. ENVIRONMENTAL REGULATION AND POLICY TOOLS

Italian environmental policy still relies heavily on the command-and-control approach. Market-based instruments amount mainly to a number of environment-related taxes, while an element of novelty is introduced by voluntary instruments, which have been used increasingly in recent years.

4.1 The Command-and-control Approach

There is a large number of norms stating emission and concentration limits and thresholds for air, water and wastes, pesticides and chemicals, mainly consistently with and/or resulting from EU regulations. These standards have been usually defined at the central level and applied uniformly throughout the country, thus limiting the possibility of local governments to adapt them to the local environmental context (Lewanski, 1998). The operative part of these norms is the licensing and permitting system, which provides an example of the Italian fragmented regulation framework. Many different authorities are in fact involved in permitting, both at the national level (MATT and Ministries of Health, Cultural Heritage, Agriculture and Forestry, Productive Activities, Infrastructures) and at the local one (Regions, Provinces, Municipalities, fire brigades, local health authorities). The network of ARPAs is often involved for technical consultation and to assist the body in charge of the authorisation process.

Construction and operation of industrial plants require licences concerning water discharge and abstraction, waste production and disposal, air emission, and soil and land use (see Table 16.4). Some of these plants are also subject to environmental impact assessment (EIA): though EIA is

Table 16.4 Authorities issuing environmental permits

Air	• Refineries and thermoelectric power plants: MAP, after consultation of the Regions. • Plants with low pollution potential: either Regions or Provinces (if delegated) and Municipalities. • Plants different from the above: either Regions or Provinces (if delegated) and after consultation with the Municipalities. • Application for the use of regulated fuels in thermoelectric plants: Municipalities. • Application for building, modifying or enlarging thermoelectric plants: provincial fire brigades/Prefects.
Waste	• Waste disposal in marine water: MATT, after consultation of MPAF. • Regions: – building of new special waste treatment plants and modification of existing plants; – operation of plants for special waste disposal and recovery; – building of plants for urban waste treatment, recovery and/or disposal (in agreement with the Province). • Provinces: – project of plants for urban waste disposal and/or recovery, already included in provincial waste plans; – stocking of special waste at the production place. • CONAI: compulsory association to the consortium for all the producers and users of packaging materials.
Water	• Direct discharge in marine water: Regions. • Direct discharge in marine water by ships and aircrafts: MATT, on proposal either by the head of the marine department or of the nearest harbour. • Discharge in river basins: Provinces. • Discharge in soil and subsoil: Municipalities. • Sewage discharges: Municipalities. • Water abstraction: Municipalities.
Hazardous industrial activities ('Seveso')	• Notification of the activity to MATT, Ministry of Health and Regions (when production or storage exceed the limits). • Fire brigades. • MAP. • Mayors.

originally intended to integrate environmental concerns into decision-making and project selection processes (see below under section 4.3), in Italy it becomes an instrument of the command-and-control approach.

The 'Bassanini Acts' introduced a simplified permitting procedure, by reuniting all the administrative licences for construction, enlargement and restructuring of plants in the hands of Municipalities, through the establishment of one-stop shops (*Sportello Unico per le Attività Produttive*).[20] The *Sportello* collects the requests for authorisation and passes them to the competent bodies, including those responsible for EIA.[21] Special permitting and notification procedures are required for environmentally hazardous activities.

For those economic activities covered by the EU IPPC directive,[22] procedures have been made more effective, through an integrated authorisation for all kinds of discharges (wastes, atmospheric emissions and wastewater). The network of environmental agencies is responsible for collecting plant emission data (air and water) and keeping the Italian pollution emission register (*Inventario nazionale delle emissioni e loro sorgenti* – INES). IPPC authority is either the MATT or the Regions or other authorities appointed by Regions, depending upon industrial activity and plant size. As of 2006, the share of authorised IPPC plants is quite small, due to delays in setting up the system (the directive was fully transposed only in 2005). A further permit is needed to emit greenhouse gases for plants involved in the EU emissions trading scheme for CO_2.

The effectiveness of permitting for the protection of the environment depends upon the functioning of the inspection system. Italy has a persistent problem of non-compliance with regulation, despite the improvement in the monitoring and control activities.

4.2 Market-based Instruments

Market-based instruments consist mainly in environment-related taxes concerning energy, transport, waste and water (discussed in the following subsections).

Energy and transport

In Italy, as in the EU, taxes and charges on energy and fuel are considerably high. These taxes take the form of excises on mineral oils, carbon, and generally on fuel for household heating, industrial use and transport. In particular, a carbon tax on carbon, coke and orimulsion used by large combustion plants was introduced in 1998, but was rapidly phased out; proceeds were intended to be earmarked for the reduction of payroll social security contributions and for compensation measures (curbing GHG emissions and promoting energy efficiency and energy production by renewable sources).

From 1998, taxes on sulphur dioxide and nitrogen oxides emissions were also imposed on large combustion plants to combat acidification, eutrophication and ground-level ozone. Italy is in line with its international commitments for SO_2 and NO_X,[23] but this can be attributed to the overall modernisation of the energy production system, rather than to the effectiveness of the above-mentioned charges, since the decreasing trend in emissions of SO_2 and NO_X started in 1980 and in 1992, respectively.

Both productive plants and households pay a tariff on electricity consumption, which is obviously affected by fuel prices (including the tax elements).[24]

Taxes and charges do not meet the requirement of efficient environmental taxation, as they are in general set at a level too low to induce producers and consumers to modify their behaviour, and sometimes provide incentives in the wrong direction.[25] Moreover, the rigidity of the demand for electricity and petrol limits the effectiveness of these tax instruments. Hence, taxes and charges end up working essentially as a source of revenue. This provides fresh support to the idea that high energy and fuel charges are driven mainly by non-energy considerations.

In Italy, the only example of an economic instrument other than taxes (apart from the EU CO_2 emission trading scheme) is provided by 'green' and 'white' certificates. The former are issued for the production of electricity from renewable sources and can be freely traded. A fixed share of energy production/import of each producer/importer must come from renewable sources; alternatively, a producer/importer must hold an equivalent number of green certificates. The system has supported the steady growth of production from renewable sources, and especially from wind, waste and biomass.

'White certificates' are tradable licences assigned to energy distributors and energy service companies to give evidence of their energy saving achievements. The system was introduced in 2005 and in the first year of implementation certified savings were higher than expected. Yet, Southern regions have been less involved in the system, due to both insufficient interest by operators and lower customer awareness (AEEG, 2006).

Water and waste

During the 1990s local charges on both water use[26] and waste management[27] were introduced. The latter is levied and collected by Municipalities, while the level of the water charge is determined by Local Water Authorities and collected by the water management service providers. In both cases, the charges are used to cover the whole cost of the service rather than as environmental measures. A prerequisite for the application of the tariff in both sectors is the setting up of their respective Optimal Management Areas. This process has suffered from severe delays, especially in the Southern regions. As a result, tariffs have hardly been based on economic efficiency considerations, though some steps have been taken in this direction. Nonetheless, the level of charges is too low to provide incentives to modify behaviour and there is no clear link between resource use and payment. For example, the household waste charge is composed of two parts: a fixed one for common waste management costs, and a variable part related to effective waste generation. However, since waste generation is determined with a 'presumptive' calculation, based on house size and number of household members, consumers gain no direct (easily determinable) monetary benefit from reducing the amount of waste (Capozza and D'Amato, 2004). While the regulation provides for tax discounts for separately collected wastes, this requires setting up specific facilities (the so-called 'ecological islands'), which has been experiencing delay, especially in Southern Italy. Nonetheless, some experiences of charges linked to undifferentiated waste weight have been taking place.

Other economic instruments related to the waste sector are the regional landfill tax and the CONAI contribution.[28] The former is charged to the user of a landfill facility according to the weight of disposed wastes, though the effective payment is made by the landfill operator. The latter is faced by producers and users of packaging, on the basis of weight and types of material (the highest for plastic and the lowest for glass). Since its purpose is mainly cost recovery (for collecting and recycling packaging), it fails to encourage producers to use more environmental friendly packaging (Gerelli, 2002).

In general, fiscal measures play a secondary role with respect to the specific (financial) support to some activities (eco-incentives) (La Camera, 2003). Direct financial and administrative incentives appear to be more effective in guiding producers' and consumers' choices (as will also emerge from section 4.4).

On the other hand, some economic sectors benefit from financial support that might represent environmentally harmful subsidies (OECD, 2002). For example, it was estimated that the removal of direct financial aid and tax benefits in the energy sector would potentially lead to a reduction in CO_2 emissions up to 5.3 per cent (OECD, 2002). Agriculture and fishery are also subsidised at both EU and national level. In particular, the Common Agricultural Policy (CAP) has led to more resource-intensive practices, though its 2003 reform is expected to drive the sector towards more environmentally-friendly farming methods.

4.3 Integration of the Environmental Dimension into Decision-making

Environmental impact assessment

Environmental impact assessment (EIA) has been introduced through a convoluted process in Italy. As a result, there are currently three types of procedure: national EIA, regional EIA and special EIA for strategic infrastructures and productive plants. The Italian regulation is the direct consequence of the introduction of EIA at the European level. Italy transposed the first EIA directive in 1986, with the law establishing the MATT.[29] MATT is responsible for this procedure; the assessment is carried out by the Environmental Impact Assessment Commission in cooperation with the Ministry for Cultural Heritage and after consultation with the Region involved in the project. However, Regions have traditionally had a residual role in national EIA. The recommendation of the EIA Commission is binding[30] and the MATT has power of surveillance over the execution of projects. The activity of the EIA Commission has been somehow cyclical (Figure 16.2).

However, the 1986 transposition of the EIA directive left unregulated those types of projects that might be subject to EIA if the Member State so decides (Directive 85/337/CEE, Annex II) and this led to an infringement procedure in 1993. Following the Community's decision, Regions have been vested with legislative and management powers on Annex II interventions.

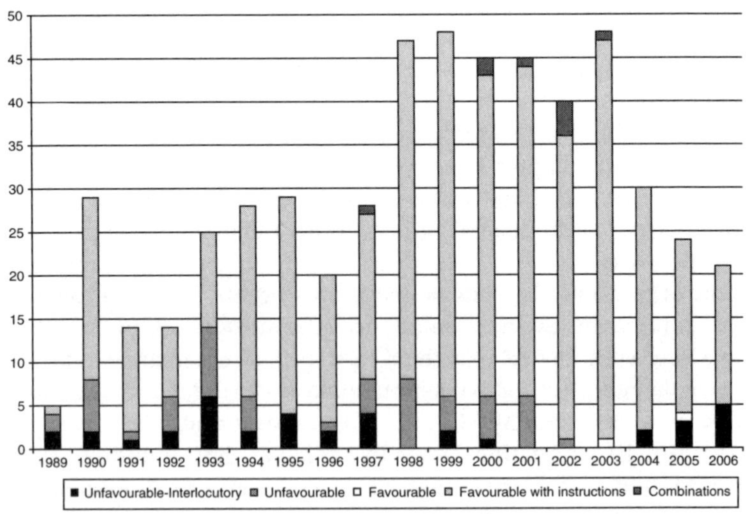

Figure 16.2 Activities of the EIA Commission (number of assessed projects)

The result of this process has been a heterogeneous framework,[31] which has often fed conflicts between the project proponent and the evaluating authority, on the one hand, and between the central and the local level, on the other. In this respect, the norm delegating part of the regulation to the Regions allowed them to use a special consultation procedure (*Conferenza dei Servizi*) for solving the possible conflicts arising between all the public and private actors involved or interested in a project. However, not all of them have defined a clear role for this 'conflict solving' tool. Furthermore, popular participation is still a critical aspect of the EIA procedure, because of the difficult access to documents and the short time allowed for observations (30 days), which must be produced in written form (Vittadini, 2003).

Starting from 2001, further exceptions have been introduced in the EIA standard procedure, in order to simplify and expedite it. These exceptions concern public and private infrastructures and productive plants having national strategic importance, and large electric power plants, considered of fundamental importance for the safety of the national energy system.[32]

Strategic Environmental Assessment

The Directive 2001/42/CE introduced the Strategic Environmental Assessment (SEA) of plans and programmes in the European legislation. Severe delays have been experienced in transposing the directive into the national legislation.

Nonetheless, several Regions have introduced the SEA procedure for the evaluation of some territorial and sectoral programmes of regional interest, anticipating the directive itself. Regions have integrated the environmental dimension into either the urban and territorial planning legislative framework or the regional EIA legislation, or a combination of the two (Arcari, 2003). It might be surprising that so many Regions have regulated SEA, while EIA had to wait for a long time. One possible explanation is that the SEA of a plan provides a reference framework for both the EIA and other authorisations of projects included in the plan, thus expediting the permitting procedures. The relationship between SEA and EIA is clearly defined only by a few regional legislations.

The initial applications of SEA have been carried out mainly at local level and have essentially consisted in an EIA procedure applied to a plan.[33] More recently, SEA has been increasingly applied, for example to Structural Funds Programmes 2007–2013. The effectiveness of the procedure in terms of assuring informed public participation and influencing decisions remains an open question.

4.4 The Voluntary Approach

In recent years, the voluntary approach has been gaining an increasingly important role in Italian environmental policy. The National Environmental Strategy for Sustainable Development (2002) emphasises both the voluntary approach and the participation of civil society in the decision-making process, particularly at the local level. Furthermore, it stresses the synergies between these two dimensions.

This new course of environmental policy in Italy follows the EU's pathway, characterised, *inter alia*, by the primary position acquired by the voluntary approach among the instruments set out in the 6th Environment Action Plan.

In what follows, we distinguish between the voluntary instruments involving the business community (environmental audit, ecological labelling and voluntary agreements), and those aimed at stimulating participation of local entities and civil society in environmental policy (Local Agenda 21 and related local sustainability processes). As we will see, the growing use of these instruments is also the result of financial and administrative incentives.

Environmental management systems

There is no regulated environmental certification scheme set up at the national level. We refer here to the two available schemes through which an organisation or a firm can voluntarily commit to the improvement of its environmental performance: the European Eco-Management and Audit Scheme (EMAS) and the international standard UNI-EN ISO 14001.

The number of registered organisations has been steadily increasing for both schemes in the last decade, though with the usual North–South disparity. ISO 14001 certifications are by far more widespread than EMAS.[34] Data from December 2006 show that the number of firms certified under ISO 14001 is 9825, nearly 14 times higher than it was in 2000. As regards EMAS, 566 organisations were registered at the end of 2006, with a decisive increase over the past three years, bringing Italy among EU leaders. Interestingly the public administration has been increasingly involved in EMAS, accounting for over 8 per cent of overall registrations. Hence, Italy made up for its initial delay in EMAS implementation, which can be ascribed to several factors, relating to both the structure of the Italian economy (especially to the small average dimension of Italian firms and their insufficient innovative capacity), and the delay in the setting up of authorities and bodies responsible for the EMAS procedure.[35]

The increase in both types of certifications can be partly due to the effect of promotion campaigns and of financial incentives, which mainly take two forms: the direct financial assistance for the implementation of an environmental management system, and some administrative advantage or some priority in accessing financial aid granted to organisations either already registered under EMAS/ISO 14001 or committing to do so.[36] There is evidence that firms, especially in the South, have adopted environmental certifications for increasing their chance of accessing public subsidies (Ascani and Falcitelli, 2006). Incentives have also been assigned in cooperation with the private sector, through an extensive use of voluntary agreements (see below) involving central and local administrations, and mainly taking the form of memorandum of understanding (*protocolli d'intesa*).

Firms registered under EMAS or ISO 14001 have improved their environmental and economic performance, in terms of both reduction in the use of natural resources and waste production (Allegro et al., 2007).

Ecological labelling of products

Italy has never introduced a national ecological label for products with reduced environmental impacts, in terms of both pollution and use of natural resources. However, the European label of ecological quality is quite widespread. Ecological quality is defined at the European level on the basis of scientific criteria for sets of products. Producers, importers, service suppliers, wholesalers and retailers may voluntarily apply for the label. The competent body (national level) responsible for issuing the licences is the Ecolabel-Ecoaudit Committee, with the technical support of APAT and of authorised laboratories, in charge of technical tests on products.

As of July 2006, 96 licences were assigned in Italy for a total of 1380 products. Italy is the Member State with the highest number of licences in Europe, followed by France and Denmark. This increase in the number of Ecolabel products may reflect a higher environmental awareness on the part of Italian consumers, who are responding well to the 'ecological' marketing strategy of producers and sellers (mainly big retail chains, such as Esselunga and COOP). However, the impulse role of European market and consumers has to be taken into account, especially for those products (such as shoes and textiles) destined for export and for tourist accommodation services. Furthermore, ecological certification of products benefits from promotional campaigns and financial incentives, mainly offered by local authorities through agreements with the private sector, regarding environmental certification of both products and organisations.

In this context, the labelling of organic farming products is particularly important. Italy has a leading role in Europe with 8 per cent of the Utilised Agricultural Area dedicated to bio-agriculture. Organic products receive a label reporting the name of the private certification agency authorised to verify that production complies with the regulation requirements. The system of organic farming falls under the shared responsibility both of the Regions, which keep the registers of firms, and the Ministry for Agriculture and Forestry (MPAF), which authorises and monitors the certification agencies, and coordinates the transfer of data and registers from the Regions to the EU.

The diffusion of organic farming began in the mid-1980s, when the first national self-regulatory standards were developed by the National Commission for Organic Farming, created by regional associations of farmers and consumers. In the early 1990s, the introduction of both the European label for organic products and the EU policy supporting agri-environment measures boosted the conversion of agricultural land to organic practices.[37] Moreover, in consideration of the economic weight of both agriculture and food industry, organic farming benefits from several national financial aid schemes (for example the Fund for the Organic and High Quality Farming created with the Financial Act 2001 and funded by a 2 per cent charge on synthetic pesticide and fertiliser sale proceeds) and from research, education and training programmes. The support for organic farming also represents an example of green public procurement at national level, with the provision of a share of public schools' and hospitals' catering expenditures reserved for organic and local products (Financial Act 2000).

Green public procurement (GPP) can provide a powerful stimulus to the diffusion of green products and of ecological labelling.[38]

At the national level, GPP was introduced in 1997 with the Ronchi Decree on waste: at least 30 per cent of overall requirement by public offices must be covered by goods coming from recycling activities. This rule became effective in 2003 and procurement procedures have been further opened to environmental considerations in the following years. Nonetheless, green criteria are still hardly included in procurement procedures and monitoring is lacking, with some virtuous exceptions at the local level.[39]

Sound technical analyses are still needed to assess environmental performance of organic farming as well as of ecological labelling and GPP.

Voluntary agreements

Through voluntary environmental agreements (VAs), public authorities and the private sector (one firm, a group of firms or a whole industrial sector) negotiate their commitments towards some environmental quality and/or performance goal. Praised as potentially more flexible and less costly than 'command-and-control' instruments, VAs often meet the favour of both the public administration and the business community. However, it is debatable whether (and under which circumstances) they can achieve environmental improvements beyond 'business-as-usual' (see for example OECD, 2003).

Compared to other European countries, environmental VAs have had a late start in Italy (late 1980s), partly because of the delay in the establishment of the Ministry of the Environment, which has indeed usually been the public counterpart in agreements of national relevance with large enterprises, though local authorities are becoming increasingly active, especially in Central and Northern regions. In the Italian context, VAs have to be considered in the light of the general governance framework, characterised by an increasing usage of contractual agreements also between public bodies.

The key document is the Ronchi Decree, which has explicitly introduced VAs as a policy instrument for waste and packaging. VAs were then extended to both the water and energy sectors. After a first burst of enthusiasm in the late 1990s, the process has slowed down (Energieverwertungsagentur, 2001). In some cases, the Government failed in meeting its obligations (Lewanski, 1998), with a consequent partial loss of credibility. VAs have involved mostly those economic sectors having high environmental impacts, such as chemicals and energy, aimed at reaching results in the following areas: climate change, water, waste and environmental management schemes. These VAs have usually had multiple purposes: on the one hand integrating and/or implementing environmental regulations, and on the other hand anticipating and/or replacing forms of regulation. In most cases these agreements have produced the expected results (Amadei et al., 1998; Camera and Tamborra, 2002). However, the real impact on the environment remains unclear as it depends upon the ambitiousness of the objectives and target set out in the agreements.

General oversight and promotion powers over VAs are assigned to the MATT. However, agreements are not systematically surveyed and there is no complete and updated census.[40] Each directorate of the Ministry directly and autonomously manages its own agreements, without any formal obligation of information. Moreover, the MATT has no oversight power over local agreements. Consequently, a constant monitoring of results is not carried out, and data about the performance of these instruments is not available. At the local level, VAs seem to achieve their targets because of the active participation and interest in implementation by both the local authorities and the business community, which can be seen as the result of the typical Italian industrial structure characterised mainly by small and medium enterprises localised in bounded geographical areas (industrial districts).

The obstacles to VA implementation can be summarised as follows: unclear legal framework, inadequate technical and scientific expertise on the part of the public administration, low degree of trust between the public administration and the business community and fragmented interest of very dispersed producers. Furthermore, the agreements do not usually provide for a clear monitoring system, a non-compliance procedure and a deadline for achieving the objectives.

Local Agenda 21

Local Agenda 21 (LA21) is both a voluntary and participative policy instrument, aiming at improving sustainability at the local level, particularly in urban areas: local governments voluntarily commit to the definition and implementation of an action plan for sustainable development involving the local community, which is called to participate in the process.

Italian local governments are actively involved in LA21 processes and in promotional campaigns at both the European and international level. In recent years, an increasing number of local governments have joined the European Sustainable Cities and Towns Campaign by signing up to the Aalborg Charter (1994), which implies a formal commitment to engage in LA21 processes. In 2006, Italy is the country with the second highest number of signatories (821), representing around 35 per cent of the total.[41] This is mostly the result of the co-financing offered to LA21 by MATT in 2000, which was conditional on the signature of the Charter: the signatories increased from 105 in 2000, to 482 in just one year. The administrations involved in the process are mainly Municipalities (over 70 per cent), followed by Provinces, Mountain Communities, Parks, Municipality Associations and Regions. According to data for 2006, some 40 per cent of the signatories have effectively started the process; 17 per cent of activated LA21 are implementing a Local Action Plan (LAP), considerable progress with respect to 2002, when only 4 per cent (the 'pioneers') had reached the action plan stage.[42] Advanced LA21 projects are mainly driven by Provinces, which have larger financial and human resources than Municipalities, as well as better management capacity of a complex participative process. Most LA21 projects relate to aspects of the environment such as energy, urban planning, sustainable mobility and waste management. The implementation of the LAPs has improved local governments' performance in waste management, urban planning, water and sustainable mobility (Coordinamento Agende 21 Locali Italiane, 2006).

Before 2000, LA21 processes were activated only by a few pioneering local administrations, mainly in the North-Centre of the country and led by the Municipality of Ferrara, which in 1999 created the Italian Local Agenda 21 Coordination (now Association). The Association plays a fundamental role in the promotion of LA21 initiatives, by disseminating the principles, practices and results of the process, and by favouring the exchange of information and representing a reference point for local authorities.

The first initiative MATT took to promote LA21 was to establish the 'Sustainable Cities for Children' (in 1998) and 'Sustainable Cities' (in 1999) awards, assigning money prizes to those Municipalities that had implemented sustainable measures (according to predefined indicators).[43] The turning point was 2000, with MATT's first call offering financial support to LA21. A second one followed in 2002. In both cases, a web-based forum was used for purposes of information and public participation in the definition of the call itself, as well as for providing technical assistance to the design of project proposals. These were the first experiences of this kind in Italy.

These initiatives generated a large response and induced local governments to autonomously support sustainability plans, including in the South of Italy. Nonetheless, the geographical distribution of LA21 remains biased towards the North-Centre of the country (Figure 16.3) and after the 2000–2002 boom, the activation of LA21 has slowed down.

The role of the MATT is limited to financing and monitoring the supported projects, without any responsibility of national coordination, oversight or guidance, which are left to the Italian LA21 Association and APAT. Local governments remain the main actors, not only for the management, but also for initiating and activating the process, which is an Italian peculiarity: the large majority of LA21 projects are proposed by public bodies, particularly by environment departments, and their political representatives, rather than by citizens' groups or by green associations. The consequence is twofold. If the initiative is mainly political, the process risks being halted by a change in the local council's governing party. Where the initiative is mainly in the hands of environment departments rather than of local councils, LA21 tends to be seen in the narrower focus of an environmental

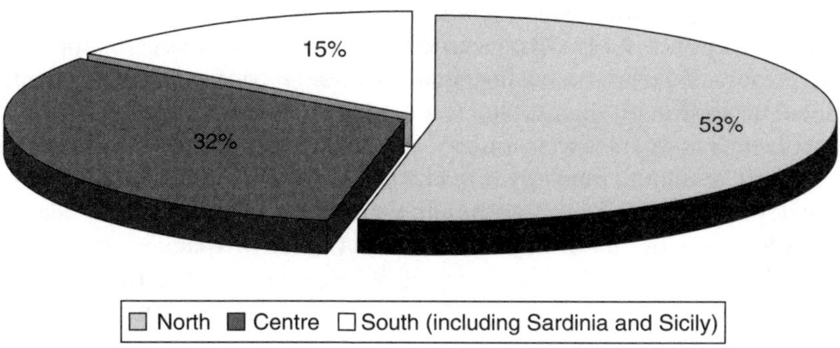

Source: Coordinamento Agende 21 Locali Italiane (2006).

Figure 16.3 Geographical distribution of activated LA21 (2006)

initiative, rather than in the more ambitious one of a sustainable development plan. The integration between LAP and the other territorial and sectoral programmes is thus still lacking, and sectoral approaches prevail.

5. CONCLUDING REMARKS

Environmental policy in Italy has had a relatively late start. Indeed very little was done before the institution of the Ministry of Environment in 1986. It has traditionally been marked by unclear assignment of responsibilities, and fragmented legislation, which has often been prompted by situations of 'emergency'. Moreover, implementation and enforcement remain weak. A system of environmental protection agencies has been set up only over the last decade.

Nonetheless, recent years have seen significant transformations. On one hand, the Ministry has strengthened its role, becoming the main point of reference for environmental matters at the central level. On the other hand, an ongoing process of decentralisation has to some extent 'rationalised' environmental governance, especially by enhancing the role of intermediate local administrations (Provinces). However, some ambiguities remain in the assignment of powers between the central government and the Regions. Persistent regional disparities in institutional capacity, which affect among other things environmental performance, are also reflected in the slow and uneven development of regional environmental agencies.

The increased autonomy of peripheral administrations has increased the resort to contractual agreements, which on environmental matters can respond to a need for both simplification and integration.

The EU plays a fundamental role as impetus to environmental policy, compensating, to some extent, relatively weak pressure from public opinion.

As far as policy tools are concerned, a command-and-control approach still prevails. Market-based instruments mainly consist in environment-related taxes, though their design is not adequate to provide effective incentives. In recent years, the voluntary approach has become more relevant. Ecological audit and labelling, Local Agenda 21 and voluntary agreements have developed significantly, although their success can be partly explained by several forms of financial and non-financial incentives.

NOTES

* The views expressed here are those of the author and do not necessarily reflect those of the Italian Ministry of Economic Development.

1. Friuli Venezia Giulia, Sardinia, Sicily, Trentino Alto Adige and Valle d'Aosta.
2. These provisions of the Criminal and Civil Codes are still valid.
3. Articles 2 (human rights), 9 (landscape and cultural heritage) and 32 (human health) of the Italian Constitution.
4. Directive 1982/501 ('Seveso I', which followed the serious toxic release from a chemical plant which took place on 10 July 1976 in Lombardy, and was named after the municipality that was most severely affected).
5. *Legambiente*, the first purely Italian environmental association, was founded in 1980. Other groups were *Italia Nostra*, mainly involved in protection of cultural heritage, and the Italian branch of WWF.
6. The delay by the State in issuing such framework laws had the effect of virtually blocking the Regions' legislative power for a long time.
7. Financial resources allocated to the MATT substantially increased in the period 1997–2000: a steady increase was registered in financial resources touching euro 1684 million in 2000. Moreover, a Sustainable Development Fund was established within the MATT budget in 2000.
8. The allocation of administrative responsibility to local governments is thus twofold: by the national legislator for matters pertaining to the State, and by individual Regions for matters regulated by regional legislation.
9. A central government's attempt at handling the fragmented environmental legislation system led to the so-called 'Environmental Code' (Legislative Decree 156/2006), which deals with several environmental matters (environmental assessment, IPPC, water, soil protection, waste, reclaiming of polluted sites, air emissions, compensation for environmental damage) and transpose a number of EU directives. Since the Code brings about a recentralisation of competences that had not been previously agreed with Regions, it has encountered immediate and strong opposition from regional and local authorities, as well as from environmental organisations. As a result, the entry into force of many parts of it was postponed, awaiting reformulation.
10. As an example of the EU's role of stimulus to Italian legislation, it is interesting to note that out of the 96 environmental acts selected for the period 1966–2001 and listed in the Environmental Performance Review of Italy (OECD, 2002), 33 transpose EU directives. This is particularly evident as far as the waste and water sectors are concerned. Furthermore, 27 acts directly stem from ratification of international commitments, especially in the sectors of air quality and nature protection.
11. Italy is one of the Member States that have been most frequently caught as being non-compliant with EU environmental Directives (European Commission, 2006).
12. For example, the first identification of areas at high risk of landslide and flood (1988) was a consequence of the landslide in Valtellina in 1987; the landslide in Sarno in 1998 and the flood in Soverato in 2000 prompted the further identification of risky sites and the adoption of a new approach based on prevention and civil protection. Moreover, in 2001, responsibilities over land and soil protection were transferred from the Ministry of Public Works to the Ministry of Environment (which was then transformed into MATT). The adoption of the framework Act on electromagnetism pollution in 2001 is linked to public protests for the aerials of Radio Vaticana near Rome. The framework Act on forest fires in 2000 is associated with the recurrent criminal fires in summertime in that year and in previous years. Regulation of noise and air pollution in the largest cities (1992), which enables local authorities and Mayors to take several emergency measures, followed repeated situations of crisis mostly linked to urban traffic in the early 1990s. Similarly, the Presidents of the Regions may take emergency measures in the waste sector, where crises are dramatically frequent, especially in Southern Italy (Campania being the 'black sheep'). This list is not meant to be exhaustive.
13. Bobbio (2000) noted that, on the one hand, contractual practices might lead to decisions that are less equitable, less wise and less transparent, but on the other, they represent a chance for integrating different (albeit not necessarily incompatible) interests, thus responding to a federalist and pluralistic discourse. Still, he argues that the increase of contractual arrangements in Italy is due – rather than to a cultural

transformation – mainly to the need of overcoming decisional impasses, powers of veto and bureaucratic inertia, and of compensating for the informal adjustments between administrations.

14. Lewanski (1998) notes that until then the monitoring and inspection system was biased towards protection of public health rather than the environment in itself. The outcome of the referendum is not necessarily a sign of increased environmental concern in Italian public opinion. In 1993, citizens were called to vote on several questions at one time. As usually happens, the result was the same for all of them, and was driven by the question(s) on which the public debate mainly focused or that aroused stronger views, which in that instance (the year after the *Tangentopoli* turmoil) was the question concerning the law on the public financing of political parties.
15. The Agency was initially established as an ANPA (National Agency for Environmental Protection) and was replaced in 2002 by APAT, which incorporates the functions of ANPA and most of the national technical services that previously depended directly on the Prime Minister's office (hydrographical, mareographic, dams, geological, but not the national geo-seismic service).
16. There are 19 regional agencies and two provincial agencies (APPAs) for the Autonomous Provinces of Trento and Bolzano. 'ARPAs' is used to refer to all.
17. 'Creation' only implies that a general director is nominated, while the lag between the establishment of an agency and the moment it becomes operational can be significant (see Figure 16.1).
18. The project was launched in February 2002 by ONOG (Observatory on the Staff and the Organisation of the ARPA/APPA System), with the aim of systematically comparing data and experiences in order to identify organisation problems and good practices. Only 11 agencies participated in first phase of the project (2001–2002). These agencies were mainly from Northern regions, and all are among the best performing ones: Campania, Emilia Romagna, Friuli Venezia Giulia, Lazio, Liguria, Lombardy, Marche, Piedmont, Tuscany, Umbria, Veneto. Nineteen (all except Sardinia and Abruzzo) took part in the third phase (2005–2006).
19. Council Regulation (EC) No. 1260/1999 of 21 June 1999 laying down general provisions on the Structural Funds.
20. This procedure is applied in those Municipalities that have established the Sportello and in those that operate the service jointly with other Municipalities and/or permitting authorities. Otherwise the normal procedure applies.
21. The *Sportello Unico* in some ways has made things more complicated, since it does not re-assign licensing powers, but creates only a 'marshalling yard'.
22. The sectors covered by the IPPC include (with some specification of productive capacity and/or pollution potential): non-renewable energy industry, production and processing of metals, mineral and chemical industries, waste management, pulp and paper, fibres or textiles, food products, milk, animal waste, intensive rearing of poultry or pigs.
23. Helsinki Protocol (1985), Oslo Protocol (1994), Sofia Protocol (1994) and Göteborg Protocol (1999).
24. Interestingly, a share of the tariff is intended to finance investments in renewable energy sources.
25. For example: the tax rate on unleaded petrol is higher than on diesel, despite the fact that polluting emissions and health risks (PM_{10}) associated with diesel are deemed to be higher (OECD, 2002).
26. Galli Act 36/1994.
27. Ronchi Decree 22/1997.
28. CONAI is the National Packaging Material Consortium, a private organisation bringing together producers and users of packaging materials. The Ronchi Decree mandated CONAI to coordinate activities related to separate collection, recovery and recycling of packaging waste.
29. However, this was a formal transposition of the Community legislation, delegating the definition of technical procedures to a subsequent Governmental Act. This Act was issued only two years later, identifying the projects compulsorily subject to EIA

according to Annex I of the Directive (national EIA) and the steps of the so-called 'assessment of environmental compatibility' procedure.

30. Only the Ministry interested in the project can oppose the EIA recommendation, mandating the final decision to the Council of Ministers, and shifting it to a political level.
31. The so-called 'Environmental Code' (Legislative Decree 152/2006) is deemed to define a comprehensive regulatory framework for EIA, Strategic Environmental Assessment and IPPC, but its entry into force was postponed beyond 2006.
32. For these strategic interventions the procedure is faster, with a shorter time available for public consultation. The technical evaluation is the responsibility of a Special EIA Commission, composed of members appointed by both the central government and the interested Region; the object of their environmental compatibility assessment is the preliminary project, rather than the definitive one, and the final judgement is mandated to the CIPE (rather than the MATT). This shift of powers might lead to an increase in weight for the political aspects of the process, at the expense of the technical aspects: the strategic (political) feature of the project is likely to dominate, limiting the role of EIA to an assessment of feasibility rather than of environmental compatibility (Vittadini, 2003).
33. Among these, the SEA of the programme for the Winter Olympic Games of Turin 2006 is often recalled as the very first application, also because it was decided by a national law.
34. Reasons for this might be that ISO certification is valid beyond EU borders and that it implies a weaker commitment than EMAS does. Furthermore, the EMAS registration process is longer (varying from 12 to 24 months, compared to the 4 to 12 months needed for ISO 14001) and it involves a public authority, whereas ISO certificates are issued by a private organisation (Sincert).
35. In particular, the Ecolabel-Ecoaudit Committee was set up in 1997, with four years' delay on the approval of the first EMAS regulation. The Committee is in charge of issuing the EMAS registration and of accreditation of environmental verifiers, with the technical support of APAT. The APAT also represents the national 'focal point' of the network promoting the diffusion of EMAS; the network consists of about 100 points involving the Ecolabel-Ecoaudit Committes, ARPAs and APPAs (regional 'focal points'), the local industrial organisations and the Chambers of Commerce. ENEA is also involved in environmental audit in terms of research and promotional activities.
36. One example of direct financial assistance is the Sustainable Development Fund, set up in 2000, which allocates 12.5 million euros to the promotion of EMAS, through financial assistance to small and medium enterprises willing to implement this system. As for the administrative advantage for ISO 14001 or EMAS certified sites, one important example is the use of the information regarding the environmental management system for obtaining the integrated authorisation under the IPPC regulation. Finally, an example of advantages to certified sites in accessing public funds is the Law 488/92, granting financial assistance to industrial firms: priority is given to firms that, *ceteris paribus*, commit to environmental certification.
37. In 2002, the number of organic farms decreased as a consequence of the end of Community financial aid.
38. GPP consists in the introduction of environmental criteria in the purchase process by public authorities, agencies and administrations, requiring them to buy a certain share of green products and services. The overall aim is to support the demand for ecological products by adding up the demands coming from the private and public sector.
39. The first local administration to implement GPP was the Municipality of Ferrara, in 1994. Examples of administrations actively involved in GPP projects are the Provinces of Cremona, Ferrara and Turin, the Municipality of Florence and the APPA Trento. According to a Legambiente study on 2000 Municipalities, only 2.2 per cent has adopted a GPP plan (Legambiente, 2007). Results from an EU survey on a sample of tenders show that around 35 per cent include environmental specifications, placing Italy far away from the top EU countries (Bouwer et al., 2006).
40. An overview is presented in MATT (2001) on data provided by APAT. Another partial and insufficiently updated survey of Italian VAs managed at the central level is provided by the OECD/EEA database on economic instruments and voluntary approaches.

41. http://www. aalborgplus10.dk.
42. Data reported in the text is the result of a web-based survey (Coordinamento Agende 21 Locali Italiane 2006). Therefore, non-respondents are not taken into account.
43. Five and two editions (respectively) of the two awards have been held (up to 2002).

BIBLIOGRAPHY

AEEG (2006), 'Primo rapporto annuale sul meccanismo dei titoli di efficienza energetica', Rome.

Allegro, R., M. Mason, A. Mazzi and A. Scipioni (2007), 'Costi, benefici e aspettative della certicazone ISO 14001 per le imprese italiane', Universitá degli Studi di Padova – Centro Studi Qualitá Ambiente, Padova.

Amadei P., E. Croci and G. Pesaro (1998), *Nuovi Strumenti di Politica Ambientale. Gli Accordi Volontari*, Milan: Franco Angeli.

Anselmo, I., M. Brezzi, L. Raimondo and F. Utili (2006), 'Structural funds performance reserve mechanism in Italy in 2000–2006', Materiali Uval n. 9, Ministero dell'Economia e delle Finanze, Rome.

APAT-ONOG (2003), *Primo Rapporto Benchmarking – Le Agenzie ambientali a confronto*, Rome.

APAT-ONOG (2006), *3° Rapporto Benchmarking – Le Agenzie ambientali a confronto*, Rome.

Arcari, S. (2003), 'Il quadro di riferimento legislativo nazionale e regionale in materia di integrazione della dimensione ambientale in piani e programmi', *Valutazione Ambientale*, **II**(3).

Ascani, P. and F. Falcitelli (eds) (2006), 'Imprese, ambiente ed agevolazioni pubbliche: Indagine statistica sul comportamento delle aziene italiane', Ministero dell'Economia e delle Finanze, Rome.

Blanchetti, E. and E. Conti (eds) (2006), *Nimby Forum – Infrastrutture, energia, rifiuti: L'Italia dei sì e l'Italia dei no*, Milan.

Bobbio, L. (2000), 'Produzione di politiche a mezzo di contratti', *Stato e Mercato*, no. 58.

Bouwer, M., M. Jonk, T. Berman, R. Bersani, H. Lusser, V. Nappa, A. Nissinen, K. Parikka, P. Szuppinger and C. Viganò (2006), *Green Public Procurement in Europe 2006: Conclusions and Recommendations*, Haarlem: Virage Milieu & Management bv.

Cadrobbi, P. (2002), *Il Sistema Italia APAT/ARPA/APPA*, A.R.P.A.V. (Agenzia Regionale per la Prevenzione Ambientale del Veneto).

Camera, R. and M. Tamborra (2002), 'Gli accordi volontari in Italia: risultati di un'indagine empirica', Rapporto sullo sviluppo sostenibile 3.2002, Fondazione Eni Enrico Mattei.

Capozza, I. and A. D'Amato (2004), 'I rifiuti come esternalità negative: dal teorema di Coase alla tariffa rifiuti in Italia', in M. Letizi (ed.), *Comportamento Criminale, Ecomafie e Smaltimento dei Rifiuti. Strumenti e Proposte per un Approccio Analitico*, Soveria Mannelli: Rubbettino Editore.

Coordinamento Agende 21 Locali Italiane (2006), *Indagine 2006 sullo stato di attuazione dei processi di Agenda 21 Locale in Italia*, Modena.

Crosetti A., R. Ferrara, F. Fracchia and N. Olivetti Rason (2002), *Diritto dell'ambiente*, Rome, Bari: Editori Laterza.

Energieverwertungsagentur (2001), *Implementation of Long Term Agreements (LTA) in industry: improving LTA schemes in Austria, Italy and Norway. Final Report*, Vienna.
European Commission (2006), 'Seventh Annual Survey on the implementation and enforcement of Community environmental law – 2005', Commission Staff Working Paper, 8 September, Brussels.
Gerelli, E. (2002), 'La Tariffa dei Rifiuti: uno Strumento dell'Economia Ambientale', Convegno 'La tariffa dei rifiuti urbani – Esperienze a Confronto', Scuola Grande di S. Giovanni Evangelista, Venice, 27 September 2002.
Grassi, Stefano (2001), 'Nuove prospettive per il riordino della normativa a tutela dell'ambiente dopo la riforma del titolo V della Costituzione', *Ambiente e Sviluppo*, no. 7, December, pp. 11–17.
La Camera, F. (2003), *Sviluppo Sostenibile. Origini, Teoria e Pratica*, Rome: Editori Riuniti.
Legambiente (2007), *Green Public Procurement: Acquisti veridi nella pubblica amm-nistrazione italiana*, Rome.
Lewanski, Rudolf (1998), 'Italy: Environmental policy in a fragmented state', in Kenneth Hanf and Alf-Inge Jansen (eds), *Governance and Environment in Western Europe. Politics, Policy and Administration*, Essex: Addison Wesley Longman.
MATT (2001), *Relazione sullo Stato dell'ambiente*, Rome.
MATT (2002), *Strategia d'azione ambientale per lo Sviluppo Sostenibile in Italia*, Rome.
Ministry of Economic Development, Department for Development and Cohesion Policies, Regional Public Account database, http://www.dps.tesoro.it/cpt-eng/cpt.asp.
OECD (2002), *Environmental Performance Reviews: Italy*, Paris: OECD.
OECD (2003), *Voluntary Approaches for Environmental Policy. Effectiveness, Efficiency and usage in Policy Mixes*, Paris: OECD.
OECD/EEA database on economic instruments and voluntary approaches: http://www1.oecd.org/scripts/env/ecoInst/index.htm
Postiglione A. (1988), *Manuale dell'ambiente*, Rome: La Nuova Italia Scientifica.
Vittadini, M.R. (2003), 'VIA e VAS: non facciamo gli stessi errori', *Valutazione Ambientale*, **II**(3).

APPENDIX: LIST OF ACRONYMS

Acronym	Italian	English
AEEG	Autorità per l'Energia Elettrica e il Gas	Regulatory Authority for Electricity and Gas
ANPA	Agenzia nazionale per la Protezione Ambientale	National Environmental Protection Agency
APAT	Agenzia per la Protezione dell'Ambiente e per i Servizi Tecnici	National Environmental Protection Agency (new denomination)
APPA	Agenzia Provinciale per la Protezione Ambientale	Provincial Environmental Protection Agency

Acronym	Italian	English
ARPA	Agenzia Regionale per la Protezione Ambientale	Regional Environmental Protection Agency
ASL	Azienda Sanitaria Locale	Local health unit (new denomination)
BAT		Best Available Technologies
CAP		Common Agricultural Policy
CIPE	Comitato Interministeriale per la Programmazione Economica	Inter-ministerial Committee for Economic Planning
CONAI	Consorzio Nazionale Imballaggi	National Packaging Material Consortium
Confindustria		Organisation of industrial businesses
CSF		Community Support Framework
CTS	Commissione Tecnico Scientifica	Scientific and Technical Commission of the MATT
DPEF	Documento di Programmazione Economica e Finanziaria	Document of Economic and Financial Planning
EAP (6th)		Sixth Environment Action Plan of the European Community
EEA		European Environment Agency
EIA		Environmental Impact Assessment
EMAS		Eco-Management and Audit Scheme
ENEA	Ente per le Nuove Tecnologie, l'Energia e l'Ambiente	Organisation for new technologies, energy and environment
GDP		Gross domestic product
GHG		Greenhouse Gas
GPP		Green Public Procurement
INES	Inventario nazionale delle emissioni e loro sorgenti	National pollution emission register
IPPC		Integrated Pollution Prevention and Control
ISTAT	Istituto Nazionale di Statistica	National Statistical Institute
LA21		Local Agenda 21
LAP		Local Action Plan
LIFE		Financial Instrument for the Environment
MAP	Ministero delle Attività Produttive	Ministry of Productive Activities
MATT	Ministero dell'Ambiente e della Tutela del Territorio	Ministry of Environment and Territory

Acronym	Italian	English
MPAF	Ministero delle Politiche Agricole e Forestali	Ministry of Agriculture and Forestry
MUD	Modello Unico di Dichiarazione (rifiuti)	Uniform annual waste declaration
ONOG	Osservatorio Nazionale Organizzazione e Gestione delle ARPA-APPA	Observatory on the Staff and the Organisation of the ARPA/APPA System
PMP	Presidi Multizonali di Prevenzione	Multi-zone Prevention Facility
SEA		Strategic Environmental Assessment
SF		Community Structural Funds
SINA	Sistema Nazionale Informativo e di monitoraggio Ambientale	National System for Environmental Information and Monitoring
VA		Voluntary Agreements

17. The Netherlands: An integrated, participatory approach to environmental policymaking

Duncan Liefferink and Mark Wiering[1]

1. INTRODUCTION

The Netherlands has a reputation of being one of the more progressive states in Europe when it comes to its environmental policy. The ambitious National Environmental Policy Plan (1989) was one of the first plans that tried to internalise environmental issues in society and used 'sustainable development' as an encompassing strategy to integrate different policy fields. Over the years the Dutch have played an active role on the European playing field too, sometimes exporting their own environmental policy concepts to Europe and frequently standing firm in all kinds of negotiations on environmental matters (Liefferink, 1997a: 210). These ambitions and activities cannot only be reduced to an overly strong Dutch engagement in environmental issues, but also stem from the fact that the Dutch confront huge environmental problems. The Netherlands is a small and extremely densely populated country, with large industries, an extensive road and rail infrastructure, one of the biggest harbours in the world and a major European airport. And, maybe most remarkably for such a small country, it is the third largest exporter of agricultural products in the world.

In the next section, we will briefly characterise Dutch environmental policy by way of its history and the policy strategies that the main governmental bodies have employed. We will do so from the point of view of institutionalisation. For the remainder of the chapter, our main interest is to analyse which types of policy arrangements evolved in certain periods and to explain how and – if possible – why. Which policy instruments can be evaluated as effective and efficient? Which governmental layer fits which environmental problem best? And, is environmental policy heading towards a 'systemic view of the environment'?

Obviously we cannot answer these questions for all possible environmental issues in the Netherlands. We will concentrate on a selection of them in the domains of industrial pollution (section 3), agricultural pollution (section 4), ecosystem protection, especially nature policy (section 5), and natural resource management, especially water management (in section 6). We will conclude with a reflection on the observed trends in Dutch environmental policy arrangements and the opportunities and constraints resulting from these trends.

2. AN INSTITUTIONAL HISTORY OF DUTCH ENVIRONMENTAL POLICY

Before digging into the history of environmental policy in The Netherlands it is useful to explain our perspective. By 'institutionalisation' we mean the social process in which agencies make agreements, make rules, use language, use expressions and so on, in short, produce social structures that start to 'live their own lives' and that, in turn, partly determine the actions of these same agencies (Giddens, 1984). In our domain, social practices are about environmental policy and politics. Our focus is to explain continuity and change in what we call policy arrangements, that is policy actors and coalitions, discourses, rules of the game, and resources (Van Tatenhove et al., 2000: 54).

The Netherlands is usually described as a decentralised unitary state. It has three general governmental layers (the national level, the provinces and the municipalities) and one functional governmental layer, namely that of the water boards (see section 6). Autonomy of the lower layers is limited, but the precise extent depends on the policy field. The environmental field is a relatively centralised policy domain, while spatial planning is more decentralised.

Environmental policy as an independent policy domain starts its history at the end of the 1960s. However, to do justice to the day-to-day policy practices in environmental policy nowadays we must go back further. We claim that Dutch environmental policy consists of different layers of rules, laws, conducts, concepts, views on the environment, and so on that stem from *all* different periods of institutionalisation, dating back to the first nuisance legislation in the nineteenth century. From that moment on, new policy practices were introduced, and at the same time old ones lived on, so we can speak of a 'layering of institutions'. That is why we choose to describe the evolution of the central policy concepts and instruments of Dutch environmental policy chronologically.

The first period is that of the industrialisation in the nineteenth century, when 'danger, damage and nuisance' from industrial sites became increasingly disturbing. Back in 1810 a first decree was announced, which eventually led to the Nuisance Act (*Hinderwet*) of 1875, known as the first centralised environmental law in the Netherlands. This law remained in place until 1993(!), when it was finally included in the Environment Act (*Wet Milieubeheer*). Important elements of the original Nuisance Act live on in today's Environment Act. The central policy instrument remains the environment permit for business. The traditional 'nuisance permit' is now a more integrated environmental permit, but 'danger, damage and nuisance' is still part of the core framing of 'environment' (ECWM, 2003). As we will see (section 5), however, the institutionalisation of nature conservation followed its own course.

In the 1970s, the interest in environmental problems increased, both in the political domain and in Dutch society. There is a strong parallel with institutional developments in other Western countries. The Ministry of Public Health and Environmental Hygiene (*Ministerie van Volksgezondheid en Milieuhygiëne*) was established in 1971, and a series of compartment-based legislation was produced in the following period (for example water pollution, air pollution, noise and waste). There were several reasons to use a sequence of direct regulations that were confined to particular environmental compartments or sectors. First of all, the environmental problems were conceived of as highly urgent. Differentiated legislation was a strategy to deal with these problems rapidly. Constructing an integrated Environment Act would simply have taken too long. There was an alternative, by extending the existing Nuisance Act with other subjects and policy instruments, but the experiences with this Act gave reasons for concern. The implementation of the Nuisance Act by (mainly) municipalities was on a very low level. Moreover, the local level would not be appropriate for the 'new' environmental issues. So, by using direct regulation on the basis of new legislation, environmental policy was in fact centralised and was not infected by bad experiences of low implementation at the local level.

Political division was the second main reason for the 'fragmented institutionalisation' of Dutch environmental policy in the 1970s and 1980s. Because environmental policy had no (strong) political position by then, other departments regulated parts of the environmental domain. Surface water pollution was 'captured' by the Ministry of Transport, Public Works and Water Management (*Ministerie van Verkeer en Waterstaat*, V&W). Agricultural pollution gradually became the concern of the Ministry of Agriculture (Ministry of Agriculture, Nature Management and Fisheries; *Landbouw, Natuurbeheer en Visserij*, LNV). Energy matters were dealt with by the Ministry of Economic Affairs (*Economische Zaken*, EZ).

During the 1980s, we witness a process of both internal institutionalisation of the environmental domain and an external focus on new actor coalitions, new discourses, and new policy instruments. This can best be illustrated by the so-called 'environmental management philosophy' promoted by the liberal Minister Pieter Winsemius, appointed at the (renamed) Ministry of Housing, Spatial Planning and Environment (*Volkshuisvesting, Ruimtelijke Ordening en Milieubeheer*, VROM) in 1982–86. Internally, he introduced new management models such as the 'regulation chain' and the 'policy life cycle'. For the sake of better communication, environmental problems were presented as (seemingly) coherent clear-cut issues like 'acidification', 'disposal' or 'disturbance'. Externally, Winsemius focused on environmental awareness and 'internalisation' among very divergent groups in society. This focus was very explicit in the policy of 'target groups' (*doelgroepen*, that is more or less homogeneous categories of polluters such as agriculture, traffic and transport, refineries, gas and electricity suppliers; Van Tatenhove and Goverde, 2002: 55). One of the ideas behind this approach was to get to grips better with groups otherwise associated with other policy domains. As a further example of the penetration of environmental policy into other domains was the important position of the environmental impact assessment in spatial planning and public works. In a relatively short period environmental policy moved from a highly fragmented set of legislation to a domain with inspiring and encompassing policy strategies and concepts.

In the 1990s most of the aforementioned policy developments were generally continued. Although the historical institutional layers still exist (the nineteenth century permit, the 1970s compartmental legislation, and so on), nowadays environmental policy is more and more integrated with domains such as water quantity, agriculture, nature conservation, spatial planning and transport. In the more recent period, we see institutional changes influenced by three related trends: the trend from government to governance ('multi-actor'), the trend from compartmentalisation and differentiation to integration ('multi-sector'), and the trend towards multiple governmental levels, notably the growing role of the EU, combined with a certain shift of responsibilities in some areas from the national towards the regional and local levels ('multi-level'). In the next sections we will discuss these changes in four environmental domains in more detail.

3. INDUSTRIAL POLLUTION CONTROL

Industrial pollution control in the Netherlands can be characterised by two types of government intervention: traditional 'command-and-control' regulation and an approach based on co-operation between the state and polluters. The origins of the two arrangements, which now co-exist, can be associated with two phases in the development of Dutch environmental policy.

3.1 Command-and-control

As we have seen, early environmental policy in the Netherlands was based on the Nuisance Act of 1875. Its main instrument to control danger, damage and nuisance caused by industry was a licensing procedure. In that sense, the Nuisance Act was the direct precursor of the specific, so-called 'sectoral' laws dealing with water pollution, air pollution, waste and noise, among others, that were enacted from the late 1960s in response to growing environmental concern.

Competent authorities as well as procedures were different for each of these Acts. While municipalities remained responsible for granting licences to a large number of small polluters, predominantly under the Nuisance Act, competences with regard to larger and more complex installations and processes were concentrated at the provincial level. Authority for the Air Pollution Act (1970), for instance, lay entirely with the provinces.

The Surface Water Pollution Act (1969) is an exceptional case in two respects. First, it is administered jointly by the semi-autonomous water boards (mainly regarding the smaller water courses) and the regional branches of the Ministry of Transport, Public Works and Water Management (larger water courses). Second, it was the first, and for a long time the only, environmental law that made use of a substantive regulatory levy, which was highly successful in curbing organic discharges into surface water (cf. Bressers, 1983; Andersen, 1994; Liefferink, 1997b: 87–92). Only from the second half of the 1990s were 'green' taxes applied more widely in the Netherlands (Vermeulen, 2002: 74–75).

3.2 Co-operation with Target Groups

In the beginning of the 1980s it became apparent that the almost exclusive reliance on direct regulation was neither effective nor efficient. For industry, in particular, it was highly impractical to have to deal with several different licensing authorities in parallel. A programme was developed for rendering licensing procedures more efficient, but in practice it led to 're-regulation' rather than deregulation (Hanf, 1989; Liefferink and Mol, 1997).

In 1982, Pieter Winsemius was appointed Minister of VROM. The key concept of his new approach, which was set out most consistently in the 1989 National Environmental Policy Plan (Ministerie van VROM, 1989) was the internalisation (*verinnerlijking*) of environmental responsibility. On the one hand, assuming responsibility for the environmental consequences of their actions was to become part of the daily practice of firms – or other polluters, for that matter. On the other hand, policy makers should better take into account the needs and wishes of what were now called the 'target groups' of policy. This was to be accomplished by closely involving industrial sectors in the design of measures and the setting of standards, and by stimulating various forms of 'self-management' such as environmental management systems and eco-auditing.

The internalisation approach can be interpreted as the return of the environmental policy field, after a more contentious period in the 1970s and early 1980s, to the neo-corporatist style of negotiation and consensus which has been a core feature of Dutch politics throughout the past century (Liefferink, 1999; cf. Lijphart, 1968). Neo-corporatism is characterised by the exchange of influence on government policy against positive commitment on the part of private actors. This is exactly what we observe here. Alternatively, and not necessarily in contradiction with the former interpretation, internalisation has been associated with ecological modernisation (Liefferink and Mol, 1997; Mol et al., 2000).

3.3 Today's Practice: Co-operation and Licensing Combined

Voluntary agreements (VAs), or covenants, are the central instrument of the internalisation approach. Typically, such agreements are negotiated between the state and industry, usually represented by the relevant branch organisation. For that reason, well-organised business sectors are an important pre-condition for working with VAs (Mol et al., 2000).

Since the late 1980s, well over one hundred environmental VAs have been concluded in the Netherlands. They can deal with a wide range of environmental issues within one industrial sector, for example the dairy industry (Liefferink and Mol, 1997: 189–92). Alternatively, they can focus on one specific problem covering several sectors, for example packaging waste (Haverland, 1998). Yet another group is specific both regarding substance and sector, for example the series of Long Term Agreements (LTAs) on Energy Efficiency Improvement concluded between the Ministry of Economic Affairs and various sectors individually (Enevoldsen, 2000).

Sometimes VAs have been used as a fully independent policy instrument. This was the case, for instance, with the 1991 Packaging Covenant, which established targets for the reduction of various types of packaging waste. In the context of the implementation of the EU's Packaging Waste Directive of 1994, however, the European Commission required the covenant to be replaced by formal regulation. Interestingly, this was followed by a second covenant in 1997, containing more ambitious targets than the Directive in exchange for relaxation of certain procedural requirements (Haverland,

1998; Lauber and Ingram, 2000). In most cases, however, VAs are linked to more traditional regulation. Obligations agreed in covenants tend to be 'affirmed' afterwards, either by way of formal legislation or in the conditions of individual licences, not least in order to limit the risk of free riding (Liefferink and Mol, 1997: 193; Enevoldsen, 2000: 74).

This said, and despite the apparent success of the approach based on negotiation and consensus with target groups, it is clear that traditional instruments, that is formal law and licensing, are still important in the Netherlands. Since the first attempts in the early 1980s, much has been done to further streamline licensing procedures. With the Environment Act (*Wet Milieubeheer*) of 1993, a number of formerly separate licensing procedures were eventually integrated into a single licence. It must be noted, though, that the somewhat exceptional Surface Water Pollution Act (see above), as well as adjacent fields like nature protection and spatial planning, still have their own laws and procedures. Recently, the intention has been expressed to integrate these as well into a single 'environmental' licence in the broadest sense of the word (Ministerie van VROM, 2003).

Also from the early 1990s, standard requirements were established at the central level for an increasing number of frequently occurring, 'uncomplicated' sources of pollution. Their operation no longer requires a licence, but only has to be notified to the authorities (Backes and Nelissen, 2000). A further step in this direction is the recent development of a 'framework licence' (*vergunning op hoofdzaken*), specifying only general environmental targets. How these targets are reached is to a large extent left to industry. In order to qualify for a 'framework licence', the company must, among other things, operate a certified environmental management system (ISO 14001 or EMAS) (Van Loosbroek and Klaver, 2001). This approach, which may be qualified as 'conditioned self-management', provides another link between the traditional 'command-and-control' instrument of licensing with the more flexible and open arrangement based on internalisation and self-management.

What is the implication of present-day practice for lower levels of government? In fact, most of the developments we have just sketched appear to lead to less room for manoeuvre for sub-national government. Provinces or municipalities in the Netherlands have never had any significant rule-making competence in the environmental field, but the first generation of environmental laws granted a certain discretion to them in establishing the precise conditions of licences coming under their authority. Considering the division of formal competences as such, this has not changed much. Although most of the 'old' laws, including the Nuisance Act, have been integrated into the Environment Act, municipalities remain responsible for the vast amount of small polluters, while provinces generally take care of the more complex installations. Already about half of the 'small polluters', however, have now become subject to standard requirements (Backes and Nelissen, 2000: 289). For the remaining sources, moreover, much of the room for discretion for the lower levels of government has been pre-empted by centralised VAs with industry (Driessen, 2000: 170). Provinces, and especially municipalities, are thus increasingly left with the task of monitoring and enforcing policies defined by others.

4. AGRICULTURAL POLLUTION CONTROL

The Netherlands is one of the main exporters of agricultural products in the world. It hosts an important intensive livestock industry (pigs, poultry, cattle), mainly in the South and East of the country, and intensive horticulture in the West. This, of course, has great environmental consequences. The predominant sources of agricultural pollution are the manure surpluses and the use of chemicals, such as pesticides and fertilisers. Other problems are the drying out of soils through drainage and irrigation, and, in horticulture, the intensive use of energy in glasshouses. We will focus, though, on the problem of manure surpluses, because it was long viewed as one of the most 'wicked' problems, and perfectly illustrates the key policy developments in the Dutch agro-environmental domain.

4.1 The Rise of National Agro-environmental Regulation

As in the industrial sector, the classical environmental permit formed the initial basis for regulating pollution by farmers. Besides this, there existed traditional regulations for agricultural sources at the local level, for example for odour, and some at the national level, for example instructions for pesticides. In the 1960s and 1970s, Dutch livestock farming grew enormously, and the pollution that accompanied the production and intensive use of manure as well as fertilisers gradually gained more attention. It was realised that the practice of intensive manuring is an important source of acidification and has great impact on the quality of the soil, ground water and surface water.

After a long period of problem denial by the agricultural policy community, the Minister of Agriculture in 1984 surprised friend and foe with a set of volume regulations for livestock farmers to reduce the manure surpluses. Initially this did not have the effect environmentalists had hoped for, because the livestock farming industry continued to grow. Soon, however, the centralised manure legislation became one of the strictest and most complex regulatory regimes in the environmental domain. The manure legislation covered the livestock production (by way of manure production quota), the spreading of manure that was applied to the land and the disposition of surplus manure by so-called Manure Banks, accompanied by all kinds of administrative procedures. Later, after the disastrous pig disease in 1997, this was supplemented with 'pigs quota'. At the end of the 1990s, livestock farmers were obliged to use a system to administer their mineral flows (*mineralenboekhouding*) with strict norms for loss of minerals at farm-level. This system originated from the agricultural community itself, to prevent other and more stringent policy measures.

What makes the domain of agricultural pollution slightly different from other environmental domains is the important accent on penal law and law enforcement. The General Inspectorate of the Ministry of Agriculture, although sympathetic towards its agricultural clientele, has a relatively stringent enforcement style (Wiering, 1999).

4.2 Agro-environmental Policy at a Regional Level

One of the recent strategies of the Ministry of VROM has been to take up environmental issues at a regional level. The Ministry had no direct entrance to the relatively closed neo-corporatist agricultural community, but through participation in regional spatial-environmental projects the agricultural target group could be reached. Some of these projects strongly focused on agro-environmental problems (Frouws and Van Tatenhove, 1993). But although the 'regionalisation strategy' certainly was successful as a policy concept, it consituted an addition rather than a replacement of the command-and-control regulations of the central level, more so because the European obligations for ground water pollution of agricultural sources (Nitrates Directive) pushed the central level towards even stricter norms and legislation.

4.3 Stalemate and Breakthrough in Manure Policy

The problem of manure surpluses subsisted despite – or, as some say, thanks to! – the extended regulatory framework. The existing manure legislation succeeded in changing farming practices and 'freezing' the total volume of livestock, but did not manage to reduce it. The agricultural community and its representatives took a defensive stand, partly because they saw little room to manoeuvre, chained as they were by strict regulations, and partly due to the overwhelming series of animal diseases.

A remarkable deal broke the stalemate in 2000. Provinces, municipalities, the Ministry of Agriculture and the Ministry of the Environment agreed to combine the 'wicked' manure problem and the need to 'reconstruct' livestock farming with another hot issue, that is the wish of municipalities to build more houses in rural areas. A trade-off was made by which the Ministry of Agriculture paid for livestock farmers to be bought out and the provinces paid for the demolition of stables. The provinces could compensate the financial costs by allowing municipalities to build new houses in (attractive) rural areas. Many livestock farmers in fact signed up for this so-called 'Room for Room' deal.

Since the outbreak of pig disease, furthermore, it became clear that it was necessary to use zoning as an instrument to prevent the carrying of diseases in intensive livestock areas. The idea of reconstructing rural areas was extended to other policy domains, like nature policy, spatial planning and water management. The original spatial-environmental projects thus evolved from a narrow focus on agricultural pollution to an integrated restructuring of the Dutch countryside in multifunctional rural areas.

All in all it is difficult to draw conclusions on the effectiveness of the different (centralised and regional) policy arrangements that we discussed – all the more because they existed side by side – but a few suggestions can be made. The manure problem was for a long time high on the political agenda but it is no longer. Manure surpluses have been reduced both by autonomous developments in agriculture and by a succession of events and policy measures, most notably the mineral bookkeeping system (RIVM, 2004). It made farmers more aware of their pollution and their ability to prevent it. More generally, the command-and-control regulation made it unattractive to make a career in intensive livestock farming, and demotivated farmers. The different animal diseases exacerbated the situation for farmers and confirmed the bad public image of agriculture; many farmers were reaching the point where they wanted to get out. The 'Room for Room' programme made this possible and that explains its success. So, different contextual factors explain the success of single policy instruments.

The general trends in policymaking for agricultural pollution are, firstly, a more integrated way of policymaking: agricultural developments are now (more) evaluated together with nature policy, water management, spatial planning, housing and so on. Secondly and strongly related, the political and economic position of agriculture has changed dramatically. The special relation with the Ministry of Agriculture and the neo-corporatist setting disappeared. Thirdly, the national level regulation is no longer the central level of regulation – it has to share the regulatory space with both European regulation and regional initiatives – but still functions as the 'big stick' for regulation and enforcement. The European legislation on nitrate is a heavy burden for Dutch agriculture, not only due to its ambitions, but also because of the inflexible way it is implemented.

It recently turned out that the successful minerals bookkeeping system will have to be exchanged for a system that more closely resembles the European template.

5. ECOSYSTEM PROTECTION

The development of nature policy in the Netherlands presents itself in three phases. The first phase, starting in the late nineteenth century, was driven by private initiatives. State involvement increased only gradually. During most of the second half of the twentieth century, the field was dominated by spatial planners at the central government level. Around 1990, a certain degree of decentralisation was carried through, leading to more active participation of private actors at the local and regional level. At the same time, crucial elements of the previous phases remained in place.

5.1 A Late Start

The Netherlands was a late starter in nature protection. Reasons commonly given for this are the comparatively late industrialisation of the country, and the lack of a strong romantic tradition (Van der Windt, 1995; Van Koppen, 2002: 151).

Private initiatives date back to the last decades of the nineteenth century and focused on the purchase and protection of predominantly 'unspoilt' areas (De Jong, 1999: 80–86). Substantive state involvement in the field of nature protection only started in the 1920s and 1930s. In 1928, the Netherlands was among the last industrialised countries to enact a Law for the Protection of Natural Beauty (*Natuurschoonwet*). Its main purport was to establish financial mechanisms for the support of private landowners (De Jong, 1999: 85). In the same period, the first national parks were established. Also here, private initiative played an important role.

5.2 Increasing State Involvement and Nature Conservation by Spatial Planning

After the end of the Second World War, public and political attention was directed at rebuilding the country, followed by massive economic development and a rapid growth of the population in the 1950s and 1960s. However, urban and industrial development and a strong intensification of agriculture also led to a renewed interest in protecting the last remaining bits of nature in the Netherlands, not least to accommodate the growing demand of urban dwellers for 'green' recreational areas. Private purchase of natural areas continued, now with increasing state subvention. At the same time, biologists started to appreciate the value of what was called 'half-nature', that is cultural landscapes shaped by centuries of human intervention, but nevertheless supporting highly characteristic communities of plants and animals (Van der Windt, 1995: 74–93; De Jong, 1999: 58; Van Koppen, 2002: 158).

Significantly, nature protection as an area of government policy was allocated in the Ministry of Culture, Recreation and Social Work (*Cultuur, Recreatie en Maatschappelijk Werk*, CRM). The Ministry of CRM, however, was not endowed with many powers and entered into a long-standing coalition with the (then) Ministry for Housing and Spatial Planning (*Volkshuisvesting en Ruimtelijke Ordening*, VRO). This Ministry had a strong and legally well-established range of spatial planning instruments at its disposal. It effectively functioned as the main protector of natural areas in the Netherlands until well into the 1980s (Gersie and Horlings, 1995: 146).

The 1970s were the high-days of the idea of 'half-nature' in Dutch government policy. Under the catchword of 'interweaving' (*verweving*), the government attempted to combine natural, agricultural and recreational functions, among others, within particular areas. The main instrument to do so was financial compensation to be granted to farmers in exchange for adapting farming methods to the requirements of nature and landscape protection. With its voluntary character, this approach in principle fitted well into the Dutch policy culture of co-operation and consensus (see above). At the time, however, the very idea of nature conservation was still highly controversial among Dutch farmers. Thus, one of the main conditions for a successful application of voluntary instruments – the existence of basic agreement among the parties involved – was not fulfilled. As a result, the policy of so-called 'management contracts' (*beheersovereenkomsten*) never realised its original ambitions (Gersie and Horlings, 1995: 138–41).

The 1980s saw a gradual re-appraisal of the idea of 'wilderness'. Apart from the apparently limited success of the efforts to 'interweave' nature and agriculture, two other factors played a decisive role in this shift (De Jong, 1999: 93–4). First, new scientific ideas fuelled a renewed interest for more 'natural', 'undisturbed' ecosystems (Van Koppen, 2002: 164–6). These ideas, secondly, found an unexpected and very visible expression in the spontaneous coming-into-being of a major wetland (*Oostvaardersplassen*) in the new polder of South Flevoland, created in the 1960s. The area came close to how the low countries must have looked before human habitation. The event confirmed ideas about the self-(re)generating capacity of ecosystems. It made an increasing number of people believe that a development back to a supposedly 'original' state might be accomplished in other areas as well, if only the necessary conditions were created. The latest 'state of the environment' report, however, points out that the general quality of the environment is not yet sufficient to support this fully (RIVM, 2004).

5.3 Nature Conservation and Nature Development as an Independent Policy Field

The objective of deliberate 'nature development' was first taken up in the influential Fourth Memorandum on Spatial Planning of 1988 (Ministerie van VROM, 1988). The Memorandum distinguished four possible 'courses' for the development of rural areas. In zones where the ecological, or 'green', course applied, restoration to an 'original' state was one of the options (De Jong, 1999: 95–7).

On the basis of the Fourth Memorandum, the policy field of spatial planning would probably have continued to take the lead in nature protection, if a major institutional reshuffle had not taken place in The Hague in the meantime. In 1982, environmental management had been added to the Ministry of VRO (now renamed *Volkshuisvesting, Ruimtelijke Ordening en Milieubeheer*, VROM), whereas nature policy had been moved from the Ministry of CRM to what was now called the Ministry of Agriculture, Nature Management and Fisheries. The latter ministry now had an even stronger interest in strengthening its influence in the important area of strategic spatial planning. Apart from that, the Ministry had suffered from a broadly publicised internal crisis shortly before, and wanted to improve its public image. Nature policy may have given the Ministry, or at least some of its directorates, an excellent opportunity to accomplish both goals at the same time (Leroy and Gersie, 2004), particularly since public attention for 'green' issues happened to be peaking at the time (Liefferink, 1997a: 218). It did so by publishing its own Nature Policy Plan in 1990 (Ministerie van LNV, 1990). Significantly, the Plan contained a new set of policy concepts, most notably that of establishing a National Ecological Network (*Ecologische Hoofdstructuur*, EHS), consisting of a number of core areas and buffer zones, connected by ecological 'corridors'. The EHS only partly overlapped with VROM's 'green course' areas (Gersie and Horlings, 1995: 151) and can be seen as an offensive – and in fact quite successful – attempt by the Ministry of Agriculture to shape nature policy according to its own logic (Gersie and Horlings, 1995: 148; Van Koppen, 2002: 168; Leroy and Gersie, 2004).

The EHS was to be implemented by a wide range of instruments. Areas owned by the traditional private nature organisations were brought under the EHS. A state programme for the purchase of new areas was set up (suffering from severe budget cuts in recent years), and it was sought to influence the function and use of land owned by others, for instance by using the 'management contracts' of the 1970s (Gersie and Horlings, 1995: 158). In order to give central guidance to this process, a detailed set of targets, largely based on scientific criteria and relating to types of ecosystems and species, accompanied the EHS. The targets, however, coupled with the lack of co-ordination with VROM's four courses, soon turned out to be too rigid. Provinces, in particular, required more flexibility. In the wake of a more general trend towards decentralisation in this period, substantiated among others by an agreement between the state and the provinces in 1993, the so-called Decentralisation Impulse, more room was created for discussion and negotiation about a much broader range of considerations than just scientific ones (Gersie and Horlings, 1995: 151). The direct involvement of provinces and municipalities as well as various interests in co-ordinating committees at the sub-national level led to a certain differentiation in the ways the EHS was implemented on the ground.

Nevertheless, two types of problem still exist. First, conflicts between the different levels of government continue to occur. On the one hand, provinces and other sub-national actors still complain about the restrictive, 'top-down' limits imposed upon regional implementation by the central government. The Ministry of Agriculture, on the other hand, may have been successful in wresting nature policy largely from the hands of the spatial planners, but in doing so, it has also lost the strong legal planning instruments of that field (Leroy and Gersie, 2004). The relatively weak instrumentation of nature policy may help to explain why progress in the implementation of the EHS is slow (RIVM, 2003). Second, the problem is enhanced by the increasing role of the EU in the field. The ecological network approach and the scientific, species-oriented foundation of the 1992 Habitats Directive and the Natura 2000 programme, in particular, were strongly and actively inspired by the Dutch EHS, but by the time their implementation was due, Dutch nature policy had already moved on to the more interactive, decentralised practice described above. This made it increasingly difficult to cope with the requirements of the Directive, which were now experienced as inflexible (Van den Top and Van der Zouwen, 2000). Thus, the Ministry of Agriculture is currently squeezed between EU requirements, its own great ambitions, the modest degree of decentralisation that was carried through during the past decade, and a lack of strong central powers to resolve serious conflicts. A new balance in this situation is yet to be found (cf. Leroy and Gersie, 2004).

6. NATURAL RESOURCE MANAGEMENT/WATER MANAGEMENT

Lastly we will discuss natural resource management in the Netherlands, focusing on a resource that is of special importance to the Dutch: water. Being a country located in the Rhine Delta – for a substantial part below sea level – the necessity of forms of water management in the Netherlands goes back at least a thousand years. Water management organisations were in fact the first 'governmental' layer of what we now call The Netherlands.

The content of water management can be divided into a set of tasks concerning the quantitative and the qualitative 'water household'. Quantitative water management concerns traditional hydraulic engineering like flood control or hydro-electric power dams as well as the day-to-day practice of inspection and maintenance of water works. Qualitatively, there is the cleaning and the pollution control of surface water amongst other ecological matters. First we will draw some historical lines about Dutch water organisations, concentrating on quantitative water management. Next we will discuss the 'ecological turn' in water management and the growing attention for water quality. Thirdly, integrated water management will be illustrated on the basis of two new policy instruments.

6.1 Quantitative Water Management

The first initiatives in water management came from associations of farmers as well as nobles and monasteries that co-operated in drainage works and building dikes or mounds. By the late Middle Ages the first 'water experts' entered the stage. These institutionalised in the functional governmental layer of the water boards (*waterschappen*). This layer still functions today, next to the three general governmental layers, that is the nation state (Ministry of Transport, Public Works and Water Management and its central agency), the provinces and the municipalities. Executive tasks are divided over all four governmental layers. The major rivers and lakes are dealt with at the national level. Ground water policy and general water planning systems belong to the provincial level. The regional water boards are generally in charge of surface water quality, engage in dike reinforcement operations and have supervision and maintenance tasks. Sewerage and city water management, finally, are dealt with at the local level.

Quantitative water management has long been relatively immune to changes in governance. Historically, the autonomous water agents used to work in a closed policy environment. Applying a typology on executive agencies by Wilson (1989), the political environment of water managers could long be positioned as 'majoritarian politics'. Both the costs and the benefits of water policy were spread over many groups of civilians, so there were no important (hostile or benefiting) societal groups in the political environment.[2] Therefore water politics was, overall, not polarised. Furthermore, the policy field was strongly dominated by expert (hydraulic engineering) knowledge, and was not easily accessible for citizens or other policy agents. However, internal developments in water management and the growing interest of the public media, politics and science have recently influenced the traditional institutional arrangements in the water policy domain.

6.2 Qualitative Water Management: an 'Ecological Turn'

Along with the societal concern for environmental problems in the 1960s, water quality gradually became a part of water management. At an early stage the Ministry of Transport, Public Works and Water Management launched the Surface Water Pollution Act (1969), which regulates surface water discharges and promotes the treatment of waste water, either at the source or in large regional treatment facilities (see section 3). The law does not require central co-ordination, but activates provinces and especially water boards, who are involved in inspection of discharges and operating sewage treatment plants. The existing water agencies picked up environmental issues, though water quantity and quality remained two separate expert domains.

On the national level the different planning reports on 'water household' nicely show the evolution in environmentalism in water management. While the first report (Ministerie van V&W, 1968) emphasised the quantity of freshwater as the key issue, the second report (Ministerie van V&W, 1984) cautiously introduced the concept of integrated water management (water quantity and quality). It reacted to the general environmental concern, on new insights and conflicts concerning the Delta Works and on the (relatively new) problems of drought that led to vast scientific reports on the freshwater distribution. In the third report, five years later, integrated water management and water-based ecosystems had become central concepts. This third report on water household also sets water quality norms, differentiated by function (like shipping, swimming, fishing, drinking, recreation, nature), media (water, bottom, shores) and aspect (physical, chemical, biological) (Ministerie van V&W, 1989). In these reports an 'ecological turn' is visible, and part of it is explained by changes in profession of policy makers and the role of key persons that bring in new ideas and concepts (Disco, 2002: 232). Gradually there is a transition from a 'hydraulic engineering' focus, not least stemming from the large and long term Dutch infrastructure works, like the Delta Works, to concepts of ecosystem-based river management and integrated water management.

6.3 Integrated Water Management and New Policy Instruments

Since the near-flooding of the major rivers in The Netherlands (1993 and 1995), quantitative water management has undergone important changes, and this has also had repercussions for environmental and nature policies. The dominating ideas and convictions of water policy actors seem to be in motion, as well as the institutional arrangements that guide them. It looks as if there is a major shift in policy discourse, from 'defending against water' to 'accommodating water'. Historically, the focal point of Dutch flooding risk management had always been to divide water and land use, by building ever higher and stronger dikes (Wiering and Driessen, 2001). Since the late 1990s the focus has been on 'giving room to the river', trying to combine all sorts of societal activities and desires with resilient and sustainable water systems. New solutions to problems of flooding risk management in the great rivers, combined with problems of regional water supply, are openly discussed. The debate is about retention basins, emergency areas for water surpluses (where rivers can occasionally flow) or 'green' rivers. This radical change has also led to a renewed attention for the organisational structure of Dutch water policy, including the introduction of new policy instruments and new roles for policy actors.

We shall discuss two instruments to illustrate these new policy developments. The first is 'water impact assessment' (*watertoets*), which may to some extent be compared with environmental impact assessment. This is a new instrument in The Netherlands and, as we believe, in Europe. The second, the river basin approach, partly results from the European Water Framework Directive, thus experiences will be recognisable for other Europeans.

'Water impact assessment' is a set of rules to judge spatial plans (new housing locations, infrastructure, and so on) and related policy decisions on their effects on water in a certain area, both qualitative (clean water) and quantitative (high water, water systems). It is a process instrument to secure water issues to be part of the considerations in planning, measures and alternatives as early as possible. The assessment can be seen as a serious attempt to bring water management and spatial planning agencies closer together. It empowers water agencies, and at the same time it changes their role from reactive to proactive in planning issues. Problems are the differences in discourse, especially the conflicting framing of water as '*the* fundamental ordering principle' versus 'one of the ordering principles'. Besides this, there are differences in policy styles of water managers (technical standards, the ruler as metaphor) and spatial planners (the charcoal drawing as metaphor).

The second instrument that illustrates actual policy developments is the river basin approach, which integrates different water aspects in the wider context of other policy fields and policy in other countries. It is an example of both regionalisation and internationalisation. Within the context of Dutch water policy the river basin approach is applied to create 'room for the rivers' and 'room for water'. A threefold strategy is being implemented: first to retain water as much as possible in the soil and in regional water systems, secondly to store water, for example in retention basins, and finally to discharge water through the major rivers to the North sea. This policy has put the focus on regional water systems and their relation with the major rivers, and is worked out in 17 different sub-river basin areas.

Besides these national initiatives, The European Water Framework Directive (WFD) has put a river basin approach to the fore and also influences water management, but the WFD is expected predominantly to have an impact on water quality matters. As far as the organisation of water management is concerned, it is still too early to see the effects of the WFD. The WFD asks for co-operation in the four river basins that The Netherlands is part of (Meuse, Rhine, Scheldt and Eems), and thus for international water management, but does not prescribe how to co-operate. On the part of the Dutch, the WFD has not led to new institutional arrangements, but to continuation of the co-operation between the existing water agencies (on four different levels) and co-operation within existing international agencies, like the Rhine Commission. Both internal policy developments and the WFD have stimulated territorial shifts towards the region and sub-river basins.

To conclude, we are witnessing a growing importance of integrated water management in various aspects. Water quality and water quantity are more and more integrated in policy plans and in river basin approaches. Water policy and spatial planning are connected to each other in early stages of the planning process through instruments like the water impact assessment. Water aspects are taken far more seriously since the 'shock event' of high water levels in 1993–1995, and are now a fundamental part of regionally oriented environmental policies.

Though the different governmental layers continue to exist and to have their separate tasks, there is a trend towards regionalisation and internationalisation, as we have seen in other policy domains. Currently, the efficiency of the fourth governmental layer of the water boards is being discussed, but changes are not likely to take place in the short term. It is generally acknowledged that the water boards have special technical expertise and take good care of their functional tasks.

7. CONCLUSIONS

In the foregoing, we have discussed four key areas of Dutch environmental policy: industrial pollution, agricultural pollution, nature conservation and water management. To a considerable extent, to be sure, these areas show their own specific dynamics. At the same time, however, at least three common trends can be discerned. They deal with: (1) the framing of the questions at stake; (2) the actors; and (3) the levels of government involved in environmental policy processes. For all three of those, the 1980s appear to have been of key importance. In that period, shifts were initiated that continue to have an impact up to the present day. In the following section we will briefly review these shifts and try to pin down some of their underlying causes.

First, as in most other industrial countries, early environmental policy in the Netherlands had a strong 'anthropocentric' focus. Pollution control was aimed at the protection of human health by limiting the emission of specific pollutants. Water management was primarily viewed as a 'fight against the water' to prevent the Low Countries from flooding. And nature conservation, particularly in the 1950s to 1970s, found much of its legitimisation in the demand for recreational areas by a growing and increasingly wealthy population.

Only gradually has the very complexity of environmental problems become apparent. It was recognised that human health and well-being was determined by complexes of environmental factors rather than by individual pollutants. It was recognised, moreover, that the scale of environmental problems might range far beyond national borders and that pollution could shift from one medium to another, for example from air to water, or from water to soil. The problems of acidification, especially in the 1980s, and climate change, mainly from the 1990s, were exemplary for these new insights. Parallel to that, the idea spread that nature might deserve protection in its own right. As a result, a broader, more encompassing, 'systemic' – or even 'ecocentric' – view on environmental problems evolved. There was an attempt to develop integrated policies for connected sets of environmental problems across environmental media. From a totally different perspective, this shift was also motivated by the wish to make administrative procedures, for example licensing, more coherent and efficient. Water policy witnessed its own 'ecological turn' by the growing integration of quantitative and qualitative concerns. Nature conservation, finally, moved on from protecting individual reserves to managing ecological networks, while taking into account an ever-broader range of environmental factors.

The introduction of a 'multi-sector' view of environmental policy, however, did not (and does not) proceed without problems. The institutional stabilisation, particularly of the idea of integrating previously separate parts or sectors of the policy field, continues to be difficult and contentious. Water policy, as we have seen, although 'integrating' internally and despite attempts to develop cross-links with other environmental sectors, still very much functions on its own. The integration of environmental licensing has now been going on for about twenty years, but its completion still has to take some serious administrative hurdles. Interestingly, the EU has played a mixed role in these processes. Sometimes, as observed in the case of the Water Framework Directive, it has clearly stimulated and supported domestic developments in the Netherlands. Other EU policies, for instance the Packaging, Habitats and Nitrates Directives, have interfered more negatively with Dutch policies and to some extent have even frustrated novel, integrative approaches such as an encompassing VA, the EHS and the rural Reconstruction project (see above; see also: Liefferink and Van der Zouwen, 2004).

As a second general trend, we can point to the active involvement of a growing number of actors in environmental policy. Examples of the evolution towards 'multi-actor' involvement have featured in all areas discussed in the foregoing sections, such as the target group approach and VAs in pollution control and the various regional spatial-environmental projects in the agricultural policy field, as well as in the implementation of the EHS. Even the relatively closed area of water management now appears to be opening up to a wider variety of interests under the influence of the river basin approach and the now dominant discourse of 'accommodating' rather than 'defending against' water. The trend towards involving a broader range of actors was initiated by Environment Minister Winsemius in the mid-1980s with the idea of the 'internalisation' of environmental policy (see section 2). By that time, it was recognised that traditional 'command-and-control' regulation often led to sub-optimal outcomes in terms of both effectiveness and efficiency. The closer involvement of the 'target groups' in the making of policies should, on the one hand, pave the way for more 'tailor-made' solutions and, on the other, increase the legitimacy of those policies. As we have seen, however, today's popularity of various types of interactive and participative arrangements has by no means ruled out the use of allegedly 'old' instruments. Traditional direct regulation still has an important position in Dutch environmental policy, either independently (for example licensing of various industrial activities) or accompanying and legally framing VAs or regional agreements.

Third, we can observe changes in the levels of government involved in environmental policy making (see Figure 17.1). It is hard if not impossible, however, to discern a consistent trend here. In some areas, either decentralisation or Europeanisation – or a combination of both! – appears to

Field/ Level	Industry pollution	Ecosystem protection	Agriculture	Rural areas & spatial planning	Water	Enforcement
International/ EU	IPPC	Habitat and Birds Directive	Nitrate Directive		Water Framework Directive	European Commission
National	target groups; conve-nants; general rules	ecological network (EHS)	Manure Policy; pesticides	plans & co-ordination	water household planning; infrastructural works	National inspectorates
Provincial/ regional	permits financial instruments	integrated planning	'room for room' & reconstruction areas	plans & coordination 'director-function'; region oriented policies	water household planning; sub-river basins; surface water pollution	Provincial and regional inspectorates
Local	permits		permits	local spatial planning	sewerage	Local inspectorates

Figure 17.1 Centralisation/decentralisation trends in Dutch environmental governance

result in a certain degree of erosion of state-level powers. Cases in point are the areas of ecosystem protection, water, and rural and spatial planning, where the implementation of (respectively) the EHS, river basin management, and most notably various types of spatial-environmental projects in rural areas all lead to enhanced sub-national activity. Upon closer inspection, however, central control over such projects, for instance in the form of basic goals to be achieved, budgets, and co-ordination with adjacent policy areas, continues to be strong. Increasingly, moreover, the national government is itself bound by targets and frameworks set by the EU, for instance in the fields of ecosystem protection and agricultural pollution (Habitats Directive, Nitrates Directive). This effectively leads to further centralisation rather than de-centralisation. Other areas appear to be less dynamic, at least as far as power shifts between levels of government are concerned. Despite major changes in instrumentation over the last decades, the important field of industrial pollution control in particular appears to remain firmly in the hands of the national government, probably even more than a few decades ago. How and by whom exactly policies are enforced, finally, depends very much on the issue at stake (see sections 3–6), but in general terms no major shift in the organisation of environmental inspectorates in the Netherlands can be detected. Considering this fairly mixed picture, in short, we cannot single out a clear trend towards either centralisation or decentralisation in Dutch environmental policy. Therefore, we would rather prefer the more neutral term of increasing 'multi-level' policy making, that is increasing differentiation of environmental policy powers over distinct levels of government, dependent on the policy issue at stake, but without a clear overall direction.

Finally, what is the net result of all these changes? Have they resulted in an improvement in the quality of Dutch environmental policy? This question is difficult to answer in absolute terms, as effects of policies are difficult to separate from each other and from other, 'non-policy' factors. Unfortunately, a counter-factual situation is lacking. Nevertheless, the most recent Dutch 'state of the environment' report (RIVM, 2004) claims that the emissions of several major pollutants have decreased in absolute terms over the past few decades. Thus, a 'de-coupling' of economic growth and environmental pressure seems to have taken place. According to the report, this is largely due to policy and technical measures (*ibid.*, pp. 10–11). To what extent can this finding be related to our three trends? Amongst them, the increasing involvement of 'target groups' in environmental policymaking stands out most clearly. As a now fully-fledged alternative either next to or in combination with other policies, it can be seen as the 'coming-home' of the environmental policy field into the neo-corporatist heartland of Dutch politics. The strong 'fit' of VAs and other public–private agreements with the dominant Dutch political culture alone explains part of their success, especially when compared with other countries (Liefferink, 1999; Vermeulen, 2002: 82–3). In contrast with this, sector integration can be regarded as a necessity dictated to a large extent by the complex and persistent problems of the environmental policy field itself. In addition, the Environment Ministry's strategy, mainly from the 1980s, to extend its influence over other policy areas played a role. Their can be little doubt that present-day 'integrated' policies allow for a much more comprehensive approach, and thus 'work better', than the earlier narrow and fragmented policies. At the same time, co-ordination problems remain immense. The slow pace of bringing further together, for instance, policies regarding pollution, water and spatial planning or, more specifically, licensing procedures, seems to suggest that the trend towards a more 'systemic' way of environmental policymaking has almost reached its intellectual and institutional limits. The increasing differentiation of environmental policy powers over the European, the state and the sub-national level, finally, is to some extent linked to the other two. If one wishes to discuss and negotiate with a wide range of actors an ever more encompassing set of problems, one almost has to do this at a regional or local level. Things may otherwise get overly complex or abstract, or both. As we have seen, this need is evident for instance in the fields of rural spatial planning and water management, but less so in pollution control. In these fields, the increasing role of harmonised EU policies is sometimes awkward. In the light of the transboundary character of many environmental problems as well as their internationalised economic ramifications, however, it is also recognised that the EU is essential for setting the scene in which fine-tuned domestic policies can in any way become effective.

NOTES

1. We would like to thank Jaap Gersie and Mariëlle van der Zouwen for their support as well as the editors of this volume for their valuable comments on an earlier draft of this chapter.
2. The position of farmers can be seen as an exception to this, because historically farmers are important stakeholders in Dutch water boards.

REFERENCES

Andersen, M.S. (1994), *Governance by Green Taxes: Making Pollution Prevention Pay*, Manchester: Manchester University Press.

Backes, C.W. and N.J.M. Nelissen (2000), 'Juridische sturing van milieu-vraagstukken', in P.P.J. Driessen and P. Glasbergen (eds), *Milieu, Samenleving en Beleid*, The Hague: Elsevier, pp. 281–303.

Bressers, J.T.A. (1983), *Beleidseffektiviteit en Waterkwaliteit. Een Bestuurskundig Onderzoek*, Enschede: Technische Hogeschool Twente, dissertation.

De Jong, D. (1999), *Tussen Natuurontwikkeling en Landschaftsschutz. Sociaal-cognitieve Configuraties in het Grensoverschrijdende Natuurbeleid*, Delft: Eburon.

Disco, C. (2002), 'Remaking nature: The ecological turn in Dutch Water Management', *Science, Technology and Human Values*, **27**(2), Spring, 206–35.

Driessen, P.P.J. (2000), 'Provincies als regionaal regisseur', in P.P.J. Driessen and P. Glasbergen (eds), *Milieu, Samenleving en Beleid*, The Hague: Elsevier, pp. 163–85.

ECWM (2003), *Het Brede Begrip 'Milieu'*, 'Advies van de Evaluatiecommissie Wet Milieubeheer over de reikwijdte van het begrip milieu in de Wet Milieubeheer, nr. 2003/15', The Hague: ECWM.

Enevoldsen, M. (2000), 'Industrial energy efficiency', in A.P.J. Mol, V. Lauber and D. Liefferink (eds), *The Voluntary Approach to Environmental Policy. Joint Environmental Policy-making in Europe*, Oxford: Oxford University Press, pp. 62–103.

Frouws, J. and J. van Tatenhove (1993), 'Agriculture, environment and the state, the development of agro-environmental policy-making in the Netherlands', *Sociologia Ruralis*, **XXXIII**(2), 220–39.

Gersie, J. and I. Horlings (1995), 'Landbouw en natuur samen in één hoofdstructuur?' in K. Bouwer and P. Leroy (eds), *Milieu en Ruimte*, Meppel: Boom, pp. 128–63.

Giddens, A. (1984), *The Constitution of Society. Outline of the Theory of Structuration*, Cambridge: Polity Press.

Hanf, K. (1989), 'Deregulation as regulatory reform: the case of environmental policy in the Netherlands', *European Journal of Political Research*, **17**, 193–207.

Haverland, M. (1998), *National Autonomy European Integration and the Politics of Packaging Waste*, Amsterdam: Thela Thesis.

Lauber, V. and V. Ingram (2000), 'Packaging waste', in A.P.J. Mol, V. Lauber and D. Liefferink (eds), *The Voluntary Approach to Environmental Policy. Joint Environmental Policy-making in Europe*, Oxford: Oxford University Press, pp. 104–55.

Leroy, P. and J. Gersie (2004), 'Een historisch tegendraadse ambitie: de vermaatschappelijking van het natuurbeleid in Nederland', in G. Overbeek and S. Lijmbach (eds), *Medeverantwoordelijkheid voor Natuur*, Wageningen: Wageningen Academic Publishers.

Liefferink, D. (1997a), 'The Netherlands: a net exporter of environmental policy concepts', in M.S. Andersen and D. Liefferink (eds), *European Environmental Policy. The Pioneers*, Manchester: Manchester University Press, pp. 210–50.

Liefferink, D. (1997b), 'New environmental policy instruments in the Netherlands', in J. Golub (ed.), *New Instruments for Environmental Protection in the EU*, London: Routledge, pp. 86–106.

Liefferink, D. (1999), 'The Dutch national plan for sustainable society', in N.J. Vig and R.S. Axelrod (eds), *The Global Environment. Institutions, Law and Policy*, Washington DC: CQ Press, pp. 256–78.

Liefferink, D. and A.P.J. Mol (1997), 'Voluntary agreements as a form of deregulation? The Dutch experience', in U. Collier (ed.), *Deregulation in the European Union: Environmental Perspectives*, London: Routledge, pp. 181–97.
Liefferink, D. and M. van der Zouwen (2004), 'The Netherlands. The advantage of being "Mr. Average" ', in A. Jordan and D. Liefferink (eds), *The Europeanization of National Environmental Policy. EU and Member State Perspectives*, London: Routledge.
Lijphart, A. (1968), *The Politics of Accommodation. Pluralism and Democracy in the Netherlands*, Berkeley: University of California Press.
Ministerie van LNV (1990), *Natuurbeleidsplan*, 's Gravenhage: SDU Uitgeverij.
Ministerie van V&W (1968), *Nota Waterhuishouding*, The Hague: Ministerie van V&W.
Ministerie van V&W (1984), *Tweede Nota Waterhuishouding*, The Hague: Ministerie van V&W.
Ministerie van V&W (1989), *Derde Nota Waterhuishouding*, The Hague: Ministerie van V&W.
Ministerie van VROM (1988), *Vierde Nota Ruimtelijke Ordening*, Tweede Kamer 1988–1989, 20490, no. 9–10.
Ministerie van VROM (1989), *Nationaal Milieubeleidsplan*, Tweede Kamer 1988–1989, 21137, no. 1–2.
Ministerie van VROM (2003), *Herijking van de VROM-regelgeving*, 's Gravenhage, Brief van de Minister van VROM aan de Voorzitter van de Tweede Kamer der Staten-Generaal, no. SB/RB/2003101212.
Mol, A.P.J., V. Lauber and D. Liefferink (eds) (2000), *The Voluntary Approach to Environmental Policy. Joint Environmental Policy-making in Europe*, Oxford: Oxford University Press.
RIVM (Rijksinstituut voor Volksgezondheid en Milieu) (2003), *Natuurbalans 2003*, Bilthoven: RIVM.
RIVM (Rijksinstituut voor Volksgezondheid en Milieu) (2004), *Milieubalans 2004. Het Nederlandse milieu verklaard*, Bilthoven: RIVM.
Van den Top, M. and M. van der Zouwen (2000), 'Europees natuurbeleid in Nederland: een pionier die zichzelf in de weg loopt', *Landschap*, **17**(2), 81–96.
Van der Windt, H. (1995), *En dan: wat is Natuur nog in dit Land? Natuurbescherming in Nederland 1880–1990*, Meppel: Boom.
Van Koppen, C.S.A. (2002), *Echte Natuur. Een Sociaaltheoretisch Onderzoek naar Natuurwaardering en Natuurbescherming in de Moderne Samenleving*, Wageningen: Wageningen University, dissertation.
Van Loosbroek, R.G.M. and J.C.M. Klaver (2001), 'Vergunningverlening op hoofdzaken: van regulering naar zelfregulering? Gevolgen voor derden', *Milieu*, 4–5, pp. 209–22.
Van Tatenhove, J. and H. Goverde (2002), 'Strategies in environmental policy – A historical institutional perspective', in P.P.J. Driessen and P.Glasbergen (eds), *Greening Society. The Paradigm Shift in Dutch Environmental Politics*, Dordrecht etc.: Kluwer Academic Publishers, pp. 47–63.
Van Tatenhove, J., B. Arts and P. Leroy (eds) (2000), *Political Modernisation and the Environment. The Renewal of Environmental Policy Arrangements*, Dordrecht: Kluwer Academic Publishers.
Vermeulen, W.J.V. (2002), 'Greening production as co-responsibility', in P.P.J. Driessen and P. Glasbergen (eds), *Greening Society. The Paradigm Shift in*

Dutch Environmental Politics, Dordrecht etc.: Kluwer Academic Publishers, pp. 67–90.

Wiering, M.A. (1999), *Controleurs in Context: Handhaving van Mestwetgeving in Nederland en Vlaanderen*, Lelystad: Koninklijke Vermande.

Wiering, M.A. and P.P.J. Driessen (2001), 'Beyond the art of diking: interactive policy on rivermanagement in the Netherlands', *Water Policy*, no. 3, 283–96.

Wilson, J.Q. (1989), *Bureaucracy: What Government Agencies do and why they do it*, New York: Basic Books.

18. United Kingdom: Environmental policymaking in a centralised, market-driven system*

Stephen Smith

1. INTRODUCTION

Three key features characterise the context of environmental policy in the United Kingdom; a high degree of centralisation of political authority, a substantially market-driven economy, and, over the past 25 years or so, a growing influence from the European Union.

Despite the recent devolution measures, which have established a Scottish Parliament and Welsh Assembly with significant control over many areas of policy, the UK remains a highly-centralised political system. Apart from the 'territorial' devolution to Scotland, Wales and Northern Ireland, there is no regional level of democratic government. Local governments are responsible for significant expenditures (especially on education, social services, transport, and so on), but are entities created by statute, and, likewise, vulnerable to abolition by statute. Local authorities are heavily constrained in how they exercise their assigned powers by detailed, discretionary regulation by central government. At the same time the political system delivers considerable decisive power to the government of the day, as a result of a two-party system, an electoral system which generally gives a single party an absolute majority of legislative seats, and a single democratically-elected legislative chamber (mildly inconvenienced by the delaying powers of the non-elected second chamber).

Second, in comparison with most other west European countries the UK has a more market-driven economy, especially since the privatisations of the 1980s and 1990s. The general tenor of microeconomic policy in many areas – labour market and employment protection, the housing market, industrial policy, and so on – has favoured market-based solutions, and has increasingly distrusted consensual, corporatist approaches based on discussion and negotiation between representative organisations. This tone is increasingly characterising environmental policy too, and the emerging approach to environmental policy is sharply different from that previously thought of as defining the UK policy approach.

Third, the international dimension is becoming increasingly important in UK environmental policymaking, because of the growing role of the European Union in matters of environmental policy. Indeed it is becoming increasingly the case that the national agenda in UK environmental policy is governed by the European agenda. Developments in domestic policy are either driven by requirements originating in Europe, or are designed with the intention of influencing the future shape and direction of European Union policy.

Nevertheless, despite the growing Europeanisation of UK policy, the context for many environmental policies in the UK is more self-contained than in most other west European countries, reflecting the UK's geographical position. Of course, many of the most pressing environmental problems which UK policymakers are now addressing – including global warming, the depletion of the ozone layer, the maintenance of global biodiversity, and so on – have an international or, indeed, global dimension, and call for international coordination. But in other areas of environmental policy, the UK is relatively less exposed than most other EU countries to the consequences of other countries' policies. With the exception of Northern Ireland, the UK has no land frontiers with other European countries, and there are no major rivers or shared aquifers that require joint management. The prevailing winds across the UK are from the Atlantic, so that the UK is less affected than most in Europe by airborne transboundary pollution.

This chapter describes the structure of environmental governance in the UK, focusing on those aspects that raise particular and distinctive issues. The main focus is on institutions within the UK. The interaction between UK and EU policies will frequently be important in the analysis, but issues of environmental governance at the EU level, and the structure of decentralisation in the EU are the subject of a separate chapter for this volume by Anthony Zito.

The chapter is in two main sections. Following this introduction, section 2 sets out a primarily-descriptive review of the institutional arrangements for environmental governance in the UK. Section 3 selects and discusses a number of distinctive features about the structure of decentralised environmental governance in the UK. Section 4 highlights some conclusions.

2. INSTITUTIONAL ARRANGEMENTS FOR ENVIRONMENTAL POLICY IN THE UK

This section provides a review of the institutional context of environmental policy in the UK, focusing on four broad areas: the structure of central government departments with environmental responsibilities, the role of central government agencies including the Environment Agency, 'information' institutions providing a range of feedback on policy options and policy performance, and territorial decentralisation to local government.

2.1 Government Departments

A central government 'Department of the Environment' (DoE) was first established in the UK in 1970 by the Conservative government under Prime Minister Heath (see Box 18.1). This combined the functions of the former Ministry of Housing and Local Government and the Ministry of Transport, and consequently had a wide-ranging set of responsibilities, of which narrowly-defined 'environmental' policies were a rather minor part.[1] The new department's major areas of activity included responsibility for local government finance, for housing policy and for transport policy. Drawing together transport and the supervision of local government into a single ministry would have had some logic in terms of better coordination of policies concerning land use and spatial planning, but this had little time to develop before the incoming Labour government in 1974 once again separated transport functions into a Department of Transport.

The departmental location of environmental policy responsibilities within the UK national government then remained largely unaltered for a period of two decades until 1997, when the newly-elected Labour government merged the Departments of Environment and of Transport into a new 'Department of the Environment, Transport and the Regions' (DETR), headed by Deputy Prime Minister Prescott. A subsequent departmental reorganisation in June 2001 took environmental functions away from DETR. These were combined with the former Ministry of Agriculture, Fisheries and Food (MAFF) in a new Department for the Environment, Food and Rural Affairs (DEFRA), and the remaining parts of DETR were renamed the Department for Transport, Local Government and the Regions (DTLR). Less than a year later, the large and unwieldy DTLR was dismantled. The functions relating to local and regional government, housing policy and planning were located in a new 'Office of the Deputy Prime Minister' (ODPM), and transport policy was once again assigned to a separate department, the Department for Transport (DfT).

BOX 18.1 ENVIRONMENTAL POLICY RESPONSIBILITIES IN UK CENTRAL GOVERNMENT

1970
Department of the Environment (DoE): *local government finance, housing policy, land use planning, transport policy, environmental pollution*

1974
Department of the Environment: *local government finance, housing policy, land use planning, environmental pollution*
Department of Transport (DoT): *transport policy*

1997
Department of the Environment, Transport and the Regions (DETR): *local government finance, housing policy, land use planning, transport policy, environmental pollution / sustainable development*

June 2001
Department for the Environment, Food and Rural Affairs (DEFRA): *agricultural sector, the rural economy, environmental pollution / sustainable development*

Department for Transport, Local Government and the Regions (DTLR): *local government finance, housing policy, land use planning, transport policy*

May 2002
Department for the Environment, Food and Rural Affairs: *agricultural sector, the rural economy, environmental pollution / sustainable development*

Office of the Deputy Prime Minister (ODPM): *local government finance, housing policy, land use planning*
Department for Transport (DfT): *transport policy*

The principal motivation for the 2001 restructuring seems to have been to promote a fundamental shake-up of agricultural policymaking, which was perceived as excessively dominated by producer interests in the former MAFF, and incapable of handling wider issues such as food safety and the development of rural communities. With responsibilities for food safety, the environment and rural development, as well as agricultural policy in the narrower sense, it was hoped that the new department would be able to develop its agricultural policies in a wider context than simply the promotion of the sectional interests of the farming industry.

In common with other government departments, the activities of DEFRA are governed by a Public Service Agreement (PSA), negotiated with the Treasury in the context of the three-yearly Spending Review. These departmental PSAs, which set out broad Aims for the department and more specific Objectives and (where practicable) measurable Performance Targets, provide a good overview of the scope of the department's activities and of its current priorities (Box 18.2). DEFRA's PSA indicates some of the areas of cross-departmental responsibility: energy efficiency policies need to be integrated with the energy sector responsibilities of the Department of Trade and Industry (DTI), and vehicle emissions policies are coordinated with DfT. In addition, of course, there are environmental dimensions to the range of land use and planning policies which are the responsibility of the ODPM and the local and regional authorities which it supervises.

BOX 18.2 PUBLIC SERVICE AGREEMENT (2002) FOR THE DEPARTMENT FOR ENVIRONMENT, FOOD AND RURAL AFFAIRS

AIM

Sustainable development, which means a better quality of life for everyone, now and for generations to come, including:

- a better environment at home and internationally, and sustainable use of natural resources;
- economic prosperity through sustainable farming, fishing, food, water and other industries that meet consumers' requirements; and
- thriving economies and communities in rural areas and a countryside for all to enjoy.

OBJECTIVES AND PERFORMANCE TARGETS

1. Promote sustainable development across Government and the country as a whole as measured by achieving positive trends in the Government's headline indicators of sustainable development.

Objective I: Protect and improve the rural, urban, marine and global environment, and lead integration of these with other policies across Government and internationally.

2. Improve the environment and the sustainable use of natural resources, including through the use of energy saving technologies, to help reduce greenhouse gas emissions by 12.5% from 1990 levels and moving towards a 20% reduction in carbon dioxide emissions by 2010.

3. Care for our natural heritage, make the countryside attractive and enjoyable for all, and preserve biological diversity by:

- reversing the long-term decline in the number of farmland birds by 2020, as measured annually against underlying trends;
- bringing into favourable condition by 2010 95% of all nationally important wildlife sites; and
- opening up public access to mountain, moor, heath and down and registered common land by the end of 2005.

Objective II: Enhance opportunity and tackle social exclusion in rural areas.

4. Reduce the gap in productivity between the least well performing quartile of rural areas and the English median by 2006, and improve the accessibility of services for rural people.

Objective III: Promote a sustainable, competitive and safe food supply chain which meets consumers' requirements.

Objective IV: Promote sustainable, diverse, modern and adaptable farming through domestic and international actions.

5. Deliver more customer-focused, competitive and sustainable food and farming as measured by the increase in agriculture's gross value added per person excluding support payments; and secure CAP reforms that reduce production-linked support, enabling enhanced EU funding for environmental conservation and rural development.

Objective V: Promote sustainable management and prudent use of natural resources domestically and internationally.

6. Enable 25% of household waste to be recycled or composted by 2005–06.

7. Reduce fuel poverty among vulnerable households by improving the energy efficiency of 600 000 homes between 2001 and 2004.

Objective VI: Protect the public's interest in relation to environmental impacts and health, and ensure high standards of animal health and welfare.

8. Improve air quality by meeting our National Air Quality Strategy objectives for carbon monoxide, lead, nitrogen dioxide, particles, sulphur dioxide, benzene and 1-3 butadiene. Joint target with DfT.

9. Protect public health and ensure high standards of animal welfare by reducing:

- the annual incidence of Bovine Spongiform Encephalopathy (BSE) to less than 30 cases by 2006; and
- the time taken to clear up cases of poor welfare in farmed animals by 5% by March 2004.

Value for Money

10. Achieve a reduction of 10% of the unit cost of administering CAP payments by 2004–05 and an increase to 95% electronic service delivery capability for such payments by 31 March 2005.

Who is responsible for delivery?

The Secretary of State for Environment, Food and Rural Affairs is responsible for the delivery of this PSA. The Secretary of State for Transport is jointly responsible for the delivery of target 8. The Secretary of State for Trade and Industry is jointly responsible for the delivery of target 2.

Source: HM Treasury (2002) Spending Review, Chapter 13. http://www.hm-treasury.gov.uk/Spending_Review/spend_sr02/psa/spend_sr02_psadefra.cfm

2.2 Government Agencies

Three executive non-departmental public bodies (NDPBs) under the supervision of DEFRA play a central role in environmental policy in England, the Environment Agency, the Countryside Agency and English Nature. Arrangements for Scotland, Wales and Northern Ireland are somewhat different, and not uniform. In some cases, there are separate institutions, in other cases these institutions extend beyond England alone. In the case of the Environment Agency, for example, this covers England and Wales, while separate arrangements exist for Scotland (SEPA) and Northern Ireland.

The Environment Agency was established under the 1995 Environment Act as an integrated environmental regulator, in succession to earlier regulatory bodies covering water, air and other environmental issues. The EA is responsible for regulating air pollution from industrial processes (except for small-scale industrial activities, whose emissions are regulated by local authorities), for regulating water pollution, and for managing water resources and flood defence. It has an annual budget of some £800 million, and a staff of some 11 000. Water resource and flood management accounts for about half of the EA's total spending, and about 6450 employees.

The Countryside Agency (CA) was established in 1999 in succession to the earlier Countryside Commission and its precursor bodies, the Rural Development Commission established in 1909 and the National Parks Commission set up in 1949. It aims to conserve and enhance the landscape, biodiversity and heritage of the countryside, to promote the rural economy and living standards of people who live in the countryside, and to promote recreational use of the countryside, including rural areas on the urban fringe. It has an annual budget of some £100 million and a staff of 600. It does not deliver services directly, but conducts research on issues affecting the countryside, and promotes its recommendations for good practice through information dissemination, and through grants and support to voluntary organisations and other bodies.

English Nature[2] was established as the Nature Conservancy Council in 1973, to provide conservation advice to government and to manage national nature reserves. The 1990 Environmental Protection Act split the NCC into separate bodies for England, Wales and Scotland, and the first of these was renamed English Nature in 2001. In addition to its initial functions, EN is responsible for the notification (designation) and enforcement of Sites of Special Scientific Interest (SSSIs), and for providing management advice to their owners. There are a number of areas (such as countryside access) where EN has responsibilities which lie close to those of the CA. EN has an annual budget of some £170 million, and a staff of 900.

Each of these agencies has an executive role, in the sense of having defined activities and responsibilities to discharge. In addition, these executive NDPBs have a significant role in the processes of policy discussion and development within the UK government. This role in policy development is not limited to consultation about the practicality of central government proposals which the NDPBs would then be asked to administer, but is potentially a wider matter of advocacy in relation to policies affecting the aspects of the environment for which each NDPB is responsible. Thus, for example, the Deputy Prime Minister has been quoted as saying that the Countryside Agency should act as a 'champion' for the countryside, and, likewise, the House of Commons' Environment, Transport and Regional

Affairs Committee argued that the Environment Agency should act as a 'champion' for the environment and sustainable development.

Nevertheless, the activities of the Environment Agency and the other NDPBs are circumscribed by the statutory duties and powers which each has been assigned. Each has an arm's-length relationship to government, in relation to their day-to-day functioning, but the framework of objectives, duties and powers which defines their legitimate sphere of action is set out in statutory guidance from the sponsor department, DEFRA.[3] In the case of the Environment Agency, the most recent statutory guidance was issued in 2002, after an extensive process of consultation both with the agency and with other interested parties, and it sets out objectives over a five-year horizon. The main mechanism for central government influence in the operations of the Agency then arises through the annual corporate planning process, which, amongst other things, determines the budgetary allocation to the agency. This must inevitably restrict the extent to which any of the three NDPBs can become an independent advocate of the interests which it represents, taking positions at odds with those of the sponsoring department and the government of the day.

About one third of the Environment Agency's total expenditures are incurred on its flood defence functions, and a further 20 per cent on water resources, fisheries, navigation and recreation. The EA's environmental protection functions account for about one third of the total budget. Within the EA's Environmental Protection budget, the pattern of spending on regulatory activities is as follows:

Water quality	45%
Waste regulation	34%
Process Industries Regulation (PIR)	8%
IPPC	6%
Radioactive substances Regulation (RSR)	5%
Land quality	2%
Contaminated land	1%

It is evident that the 'water' side of the EA's functions accounts for the overwhelming proportion of both expenditures and staff; air quality regulation accounts for only some 15 per cent of environmental protection expenditures, and only about 5 per cent of the overall EA budget.

About one quarter (27 per cent in 2003/04) of the EA's total budget is contributed by grants from central government (DEFRA and the National Assembly of Wales). A much larger part is obtained in the form of 'own revenues', including flood defence levies (36 per cent), and charges for permitting and other regulatory functions (34 per cent). Charges aim to recover the full costs of delivering regulatory regimes, identifying and allocating costs systematically and 'fairly', but until now have not included any element designed to perform an incentive role. However, the current EA Corporate Strategy includes mention of an aim of a more 'risk-based' approach to regulation, with 'rewards and incentives for good performance', and this may imply changes to the current structure of charges.

2.3 Audit and Scrutiny Institutions

Public institutions of three sorts play a role in auditing, monitoring and scrutinising environmental policies and performance.

Firstly, within the UK parliamentary system, Select Committees of both the House of Commons and the House of Lords monitor government policies and emerging policy issues. In the House of Commons, departmental Select Committees monitor the activities of each of the major departments: DEFRA is currently covered by the Environment, Food and Rural Affairs Committee, which has a remit 'to examine the expenditure, administration and policy of the Department for Environment, Food and Rural Affairs and its associated public bodies'. The predecessor departments to DEFRA (DETR and DoE) were covered by committees reflecting the structure of responsibilities of the department at the time.

Typically, these committees select a limited number of topics for study in each parliamentary session. The normal procedure adopted by these Committees is that, having selected a topic, a broad range of interested parties (government departments and agencies, businesses and industry organisations, academic experts, and so on) are invited to submit written evidence. A smaller number of organisations and individuals are then invited to give oral evidence in hearings of the Committee, which are normally held in public. The final report of the Committee (often in practice drafted with the assistance of an external adviser as well as the administrative staff of the Committees – the 'clerk') is published, along with a selection of the written evidence and transcripts of the oral evidence.

Given the wide-ranging responsibilities of the Department of the Environment and its successors, the number of topics investigated annually by the departmental select committee that related to environmental policy as conventionally defined has been relatively modest. However, the incoming Labour government in 1997 established a new, non-departmental Select Committee, the House of Commons Environmental Audit Committee, to provide a specific focus for investigation of policies affecting environmental protection and sustainable development, especially those which raise issues crossing departmental boundaries. This new committee, which operates in parallel with the existing departmental Select Committee (and to a certain extent duplicates its responsibilities), has raised the profile of environmental policy subjects substantially in Select Committee investigations.

In the House of Lords, the select committee structure differs. Much of the committee work of the House of Lords is involved in monitoring European Union legislation, and environmental issues are primarily covered by Subcommittee D of the Committee on the European Communities, which has responsibility for Environment, Agriculture, Public Health and Consumer Protection.

Second, the National Audit Office has a remit to analyse the effectiveness of policy decisions and implementation by central government departments and central government agencies, through 'value-for-money' audits as well as conventional accounting audit operations. NAO reports on environmental policy matters are listed in Box 18.3.

Third, in the area of environmental policy, the UK has a distinctive institution in the form of the Royal Commission on Environmental Pollution (RCEP). This was set up in the late 1960s by the then Labour government

BOX 18.3 NATIONAL AUDIT OFFICE REPORTS ON ENVIRONMENTAL POLICY MATTERS

Control and Monitoring of Pollution: Review of the Pollution Inspectorate (1991)

Buildings and the Environment (1994)

Protecting and Managing Sites of Special Scientific Interest in England (1994)

National Rivers Authority: River Pollution from Farms in England (1995)

MAFF: Protecting Environmentally Sensitive Areas (1997)

The Home Energy Efficiency Scheme (1998)

DETR: Grants to Voluntary Bodies (1998)

Vehicle Emissions Testing (1999)

Policy Development: Improving Air Quality (2001)

Dealing with pollution from ships (2002)

Environment Agency: Protecting the Public from Waste (2002)

Protecting England and Wales from plant pests and diseases (2003)

under Prime Minister Wilson, with instructions 'to advise on matters, both national and international, concerning the pollution of the environment; on the adequacy of research in this field; and on the future possibilities of danger to the environment'. The Royal Commission consists of about a dozen members, drawn from scientific and other backgrounds – typically about half are prominent researchers from the natural sciences. Members are appointed, formally, by the Queen on the advice of the Prime Minister, which is based on recommendations from the environment department; a recent innovation has been that such posts are publicly advertised. All members of the Royal Commission serve in an individual capacity, rather than as representatives of particular interests, and many members serve on the Royal Commission for considerable periods of time.

The members of the Royal Commission are responsible for selecting the topics which they will investigate; only on a couple of occasions has the government specifically requested the Committee to turn its attention to a particular topic. The mode of operation is very similar to that of the parliamentary Select Committees. Once a subject has been selected, written and oral evidence is requested from interested parties and those with relevant expertise. Over the 35-year period since its inception, around 25 investigations have been conducted, each leading to a published report (Box 18.4). The range of topics investigated by RCEP covers most major areas of environmental policy; the reports include general reviews (for example reports 1, 4, 10), sectoral reviews such as those of agriculture (report 7) and transport (reports 18 and 20), discussions of general environmental policy principles (for example reports 5, 12, 21), and specific issue investigations (for example, lead in report 9, GMOs in report 13, waste incineration in report 17, chemicals in products in report 24).

2.4 Territorial Decentralisation – Local Government

Local government in England consists of two basic layers, lower-tier districts and higher-tier counties (typically covering the area of six or so adjacent districts). There is, however, considerable variable geometry. There are single-tier authorities in some areas, including metropolitan areas, and some rural areas. Arrangements in Scotland and Wales are also different.

Local government in the UK is responsible for significant expenditures, with its main expenditure areas including education, social services, and roads/transport. Its financial resources include a local domestic property tax ('Council Tax'), contributing about 25 per cent of revenues, with the remainder being provided in the form of a population-based share of a nationally-determined business property tax, plus equalising grants from central government. Local governments are elected, but their discretion is

BOX 18.4 ROYAL COMMISSION ON ENVIRONMENTAL POLLUTION REPORTS

1. First Report (1971)
2. Three Issues in Industrial Pollution (1972)
3. Pollution in some British Estuaries and Coastal Waters (1973)
4. Pollution Control: Progress and Problems (1974)
5. Air Pollution Control: an Integrated Approach (1976)
6. Nuclear Power and the Environment (1976)
7. Agriculture and Pollution (1979)
8. Oil Pollution of the Sea (1981)
9. Lead in the Environment (1983)
10. Tackling Pollution – Experience and Prospects (1984)
11. Managing Waste: The Duty of Care (1985)
12. Best Practicable Environmental Option (1988)
13. The Release of Genetically Engineered Organisms to the Environment (1989)
14. GENHAZ – A System for the Critical Appraisal of Proposals to Release Genetically Modified Organisms into the Environment (1991)
15. Emissions from Heavy Duty Diesel Vehicles (1991)
16. Freshwater Quality (1992)
17. Incineration of Waste Eighteenth Report (1993)
18. Transport and the Environment (1994)
19. Sustainable Use of Soil (1996)
20. Transport and the Environment – Developments since 1994 (1997)
21. Setting Environmental Standards (1998)
22. Energy – The Changing Climate (2000)
23. Environmental Planning (2002)

(special) The Environmental Effects of Civil Aircraft in Flight (2002)

24. Chemicals in Products (2003)

(special) The Use of Biomass for Heat and Power Production (2004)

25. Environmental Effects of Marine Fisheries (due 2004)

severely circumscribed. They are created by statute, and can be (and have been) abolished by statute if the central government disapproves sufficiently strongly of their actions. More routinely, and pervasively, local authorities are subject to detailed, discretionary regulation by central government.

The environmental responsibilities of local government in the UK cover the following principal areas:

- Waste management
- Land-use planning and building control
- Local nuisance and disamenity regulation (noise, litter, etc)
- Small-scale pollution control
- Parks, etc
- Road maintenance, improvements, planning
- Public transport regulation

Waste management

The arrangements for waste management are complex, and vary in different parts of the UK. In England, the normal division of responsibilities is that district councils (lower-tier) are responsible for household waste collection, while the higher-tier local authorities, the counties, have responsibility for waste disposal, and planning of municipal waste management facilities. In metropolitan areas and unitary authorities both functions are combined in a single authority, and this is the case in Scotland and Wales, too. This division of responsibility gives rise to some evident coordination problems between waste collection and management; districts are, for example, in effect required to adapt their collection arrangements to whatever disposal and recycling arrangements have been selected at the county level. There are important issues, too, of inter-layer externalities. Efforts by districts to increase the collection of recyclables yield disposal cost savings (in terms of lower landfill charges, and so on) to the counties. To ensure that districts have an appropriate incentive to increase recyclables collection rates, an economic instrument has been established, in the form of a system of recycling credits. The primary function of this is simply to reward districts for recyclables collected, with a payment reflecting the marginal disposal costs thereby avoided.

Planning and development

District councils are responsible for planning and regulation of development, subject to national guidelines, including regional and county 'structure plans'. The planning system makes a functional classification of land and buildings ('agricultural', 'residential', and so on) based on existing use, and case-by-case 'planning permission' is needed for change-of-use and development. Affected residents have the right to submit objections to any planning application, and planning refusals are common, especially where they would involve development outside existing settlements, or major changes to the character of an area. While planning decisions are made by district councils, planning approvals and refusals must be consistent with structure plans, and other central guidance. The applicant developer can appeal to central government if refused, and may be able to claim compensation where refusal of planning permission on inappropriate grounds has resulted in costs.

The outcome of the planning system is a tight constraint on the supply of development land, especially for new housing in the South East of the country, and on industrial developments in many areas. The government appears to believe that there is significant pressure for change to the system, to reduce housing shortages, and to facilitate development.

3. DISTINCTIVE FEATURES AND ISSUES

This section of the chapter highlights a number of issues raised by the governance structures and organisation in the UK, with particular attention to issues relating to questions of centralisation/decentralisation. The first is the role of the European Union in shaping UK environmental policy and institutions. The second and third concern aspects of the organisation of central government and its agencies, while the fourth has to do with the management of information and expertise within these structures. The theme of the fifth is that government organisation and instrument choice are to a certain extent interdependent. Particular forms of organisation will tend to be suited to particular types of policy instrument, while an effective shift towards greater use of market-based instruments and other approaches under the heading of 'ecological modernisation' will typically have certain preconditions in terms of the organisation of government.

3.1 Europeanisation

The most dramatic change in the operation of UK environmental policy over the past two decades has been in the role played by the European Union. This has had a number of dimensions. The EU has been instrumental in initiating more stringent environmental protection in a number of key areas, and in requiring other key changes in aspects of environmental policy (such as improvements in public access to information). Second, the EU has exerted substantial influence on the regulatory style of UK environmental policy, especially an important shift to a more rule-based, uniform and transparent form of regulation. Third, the EU has developed significant powers of compliance, which are forcing the UK – like other member states – to pay closer attention to ensuring that policy decisions and commitments are implemented in practice. Fourth, a recognition of the significant influence of the EU is increasingly leading the UK national government to take initiatives in environmental policy design with the aim of influencing the Brussels agenda.

The role of the EU in environmental policy developed, initially, through the 'backdoor' route provided by the EU's powers to regulate the internal market. A number of environmental policy initiatives were justified by the potential impact of environmental policies on the internal market, especially where environmental policies restricted the characteristics of goods that could be legitimately produced and marketed within the EU. Subsequently, Treaty amendments from the Single European Act onwards have carved out an explicit, and increasingly broadly-defined role for the EU in relation to environmental policy. EU Directives have played a decisive role in a number of areas of environmental policy, in forcing the UK to develop policies to achieve more stringent levels of environmental protection. Some examples include the Drinking Water Directive of 1980, the Large Combustion Plant Directive of 1988, the Landfill Directive of 1999, and so on. In each case, the requirements of the Directive forced the UK to adopt much more stringent policies, with the existence of the Directive effectively preventing ruling out less stringent approaches from public and policy debate.[4]

From the outset, it was clear that there was a major difference in approach to pollution regulation in the UK and in some other EU countries. The UK's tradition, as discussed in section 3.3 below, had been based on case-by-case negotiation between the environmental regulator and individual enterprises, to determine the conditions that would be stipulated in the regulatory consent for polluting emissions. Typically, this negotiation took account both of the competitive situation facing the individual enterprise, and the physical vulnerability of the environment into which the pollution was discharged (Ashby and Anderson, 1981). The tension between this approach and that of other EU member states, and of the Commission, is discussed by a number of authors (see, for example, Haigh, 1989; Weale et al., 2000), and there has been a significant shift over the past two decades towards a more rule-based regime, with less case-by-case discretion. This partly reflects the requirements of EU Directives, but, as Macleod (2000) observes, the shift has also been encouraged by domestically-generated pressures, including moves towards more explicit target-setting and performance measurement for government agencies.

Compliance with the requirements of EU environmental policies is increasingly being encouraged by provisions introduced through the 1993 Maastricht Treaty which provide for the European Court to impose financial penalties for persistent non-compliance. The scale of potential penalties provides member states with an incentive, not only to legislate but to take action to comply with the requirements of EU Directives. The effect is perhaps most significant on policy decisions relating to the achievement of medium-term emission-reduction targets, where forecasts have to be made of the adequacy of a package of measures, and where concern about the risk of being judged non-compliant is encouraging realistic appraisals of the potential impact of policy measures, and, indeed, may be leading to some risk aversion.

Furthermore, it is possible to detect a change in the nature of the UK's involvement in EU environmental policy, from an essentially reactive stance, in which the UK responded to policy initiatives developed elsewhere in the EU, to a more proactive approach. Jordan (2004) describes how, within the EU, the UK has predominantly 'taken' policies shaped elsewhere in the UK, rather than 'shaped' EU policy towards the UK model. Examples can now be found where the UK is clearly trying to shape the design of future EU policies. For example, the emissions trading arrangements introduced within the UK Climate Change programme (see section 3.5 below) were clearly intended to provide a model for a later EU-wide emissions trading regime.

3.2 The Organisation of Central Government

Over the past four decades there have been frequent alterations to the departmental structure of government in respect of the location of various 'environmental' responsibilities, and their co-location with each other, and with related areas of policy. These have included:

- the initial formation of a Department of the Environment in 1970, drawing together land use planning, housing, transport, and, less-systematically, pollution control;
- repeated integration of transport functions in the environment department, and subsequent separation;
- the creation of DEFRA in 2001, separating narrowly-defined environmental policy (pollution control, and so on) from its erstwhile partners (land use planning, transport, and so on), and combining it instead with the former Ministry of Agriculture, Fisheries and Food.

Most of these changes might be partly explicable in terms of short-term pressures on Prime Ministers, to find the right number of posts of Cabinet rank to suit the abilities and ambitions of particular politicians. In addition, the frequent changes of mind about a separate Department of Transport do not suggest that any considered, systematic view about the desirable long-term evolution of the structure of Whitehall departments underlies every change that has been made. Nevertheless, the combination and separation of policy responsibilities has implications for the efficient functioning of government, which may partly be reflected in the choices made, or which may arise despite the need to make changes for other reasons.

The original Department of the Environment was seen as drawing together a range of activities affecting the spatial environment – land use planning, housing development, transport – in a grouping which could have implied effective long-run coordination of choices on development and transport. Whether the departmental separation of transport seriously undermines this kind of strategic decision-making is unclear. In practice, the kinds of tradeoffs involved may be made just as effectively in interdepartmental committees as internally within a combined department (and, indeed, most of the major choices of this sort probably have to involve many other interests, both within government and outside).

The location of pollution control functions in relation to the initial Department of the Environment is perhaps more significant for the operation of policy. Shortly after the department's creation, the main pollution inspectorate, which operated within the institutions directed at employee health and workplace safety (Health and Safety Executive), was transferred out of the DoE and located in the Department of Employment, where it remained until the mid-1980s. This move was of considerable significance, given the emphasis at the time on unemployment problems, and it gave rise to an obvious risk that environmental objectives would be traded off against objectives of creating and maintaining employment in particular sectors, locations and enterprises.

The recent relocation of environmental policy through the creation of DEFRA is widely understood to have been a response to long-term policy and management failures of the agriculture department, which became particularly evident during the Foot and Mouth crisis of early 2001. The department was perceived as unduly captured by producer interests, especially by the interests of large farmers, and its relocation within a department with a conspicuously broader remit of 'environment, food, and rural affairs' was intended to reorientate the department's agricultural policies towards a broader set of public interest objectives, reflecting the interests of food consumers as well as producers, the broader rural economy instead of the declining numbers of people actually employed in agriculture, and the broad range of interests concerned with the environmental management of agricultural activities.

3.3 The Role of the Environment Agency

The Environment Agency was formed through the merger of the former National Rivers Authority (NRA) and HM Inspectorate of Pollution (HMIP) in 1995. It has inherited traditions of regulation deriving from these institutions and their precursors. In particular, a distinctive UK tradition in environmental regulation, dating back to the Alkali Inspectorate established in the late nineteenth century, is frequently observed to have continuing influence on the style of UK regulation. This tradition, based on the principle of 'Best Practical Means' introduced in the 1874 Alkali Act (Box 18.5), involved a discretionary, consultative approach to regulation, conducted by individual inspectors, in dialogue with individual regulated firms. The standard of pollution control demanded at a particular location took account of the circumstances of the local environment, and of the ability of each enterprise to bear the costs of abatement measures. Inevitably, such a system carries risks of capture, as the discretionary judgements being made by individual inspectors are dependent on information derived from the firms, and the continuing, cooperative relationship between regulator and subject demands a non-confrontational, accommodating approach to both pollution control requirements ('consents') and to enforcement. As Jordan et al. (2003: 181) observe, 'Curiously, this style of working had many similarities with the way in which some negotiated agreements are negotiated today.'

Over the past three decades, environmental regulation in the UK has been moving away from this tradition, in three important respects. This

BOX 18.5 CONCEPTS IN UK POLLUTION POLICY

- **Best Practical Means (BPM).** Introduced in the 1874 Alkali Act.
- **Integrated Pollution Control (IPC).** 1990 Environmental Protection Act
- **Best Practical Environmental Option (BPEO).** 1990 Environmental Protection Act
- **Best Available Techniques Not Entailing Excess Cost (BATNEEC).** 1990 Environmental Protection Act
- **Integrated Pollution Prevention and Control (IPPC).** 1999 Pollution Prevention and Control Act
- **Best Available Technology (BAT).** 1999 Pollution Prevention and Control Act

shift has been partly prompted by pressures arising from EU directives, but also from greater public awareness of environmental issues. The key changes are as follows:

Development of an integrated institution for environmental regulation, the Environment Agency, instead of the earlier media-specific regulators. This reflected the shift to a principle of Integrated Pollution Control, which sought to achieve the Best Practical Environmental Option for dealing with particular problems, so as to avoid the risk that a pollution problem in one medium (for example air pollution) might be 'solved' through displacement to other media (for example by shifting wastes to water or landfill instead).

A shift towards more rule-based regulation, away from the extensive discretion assigned to individual inspectors in their negotiations with regulated firms. The 1990 White Paper stipulated the use of the criterion of 'Best Available Techniques not Entailing Excess Cost' (BATNEEC) in the choice of pollution control measures to be required. While in principle this still leaves scope for case-by-case negotiation on the basis of whether costs would be 'excessive' for a particular enterprise to bear, the establishment of this system was accompanied by measures designed to provide clearer guidance to inspectors and regulated firms as to the techniques which would normally be required in particular types of installation. The 1999 Pollution Prevention and Control Act appears to have sharpened this shift to rule-based regulation of individual firms still further, by the requirement to use Best Available Technology (BAT), without any qualification relating to cost.

A shift – albeit still gradual – to a more assertive policy towards non-compliant enterprises, and to greater recourse to legal enforcement action. Until recently, prosecutions for violations of regulatory requirements were rare, reflecting the cooperative approach taken by the regulatory agencies, but, partly under pressure from the public and from select committee reports, the EA has been increasing the use of prosecution. A problem remains – as in many countries – that the effectiveness of prosecution as a deterrent is seriously weakened by the relatively mild sanctions imposed by the courts.

An issue discussed in recent years has been the relationship between the EA, which has responsibility for environmental regulation of the water industry, and the economic regulator of the industry. To meet the requirements of EU Directives on water quality, massive investment in better wastewater treatment is required, and this will imply higher water charges to households and industry. Economic regulation of the privatised water industry is the responsibility of the Office of Water Services (OFWAT), which aims to restrict the industry's ability to earn monopoly profits through price regulation, taking the form of a price cap[5] set by the regulator in five-yearly reviews. OFWAT sees its role as guardian of consumer interests (that is, low prices), and OFWAT has lobbied strongly against the EA's proposals for the required level of water quality investments. The dispute between OFWAT and the EA was natural, given the tight definition of the goals assigned to each institution. Exposure of the conflict, and the policy tradeoff that was at stake, was a clear and constructive aspect of the system. Ministers were required to resolve the issue, and the choice made on the tradeoff between low prices and environmental quality was thus resolved openly and transparently by the political process, rather than hidden, as it would be liable to be, if OFWAT were instructed to take account of environmental considerations in its regulatory decisions, or the EA to take account of consumer interests.

3.4 The Use of Information in Environmental Policy

In all systems of government, discussion, audit and evaluation occurs through a range of channels, including:

- internal audit and evaluation within institutions. Governments may be concerned about aspects of the effectiveness of their own policies,[6] inter-Ministerial competition may lead to internal challenges, and, in some areas of policy, the independent professional ethos of particular groups of employees may provide some semi-independent check on functioning.
- public institutions with an explicit information-gathering or audit function. In the UK these include the parliamentary select committees, the National Audit Office, and the Royal Commission on Environmental Protection discussed above.
- challenges from sectional interests affected by the operation of policy, including industry groups, trades unions, and so on.
- informal public audit and evaluation. Newspapers, academics, NGOs, and political parties may generate some external discussion and challenges to particular policy actions or programmes. In the environmental area, the UK government faces informed challenge, in particular, from strong environmental NGOs such as Friends of the Earth and Greenpeace.

In the UK's highly-centralised political system, which gives central government substantial and decisive power, the development of effective institutions for monitoring and, where appropriate, challenging the central government's environmental policies and their implementation, becomes a matter of considerable significance, for a number of reasons:

- Open discussion and debate can help good ideas to surface, and can provide a mechanism for exposing and discarding bad ones. In contrast to political systems in which governments have to persuade and negotiate with competing centres of power, the UK system permits quick and decisive action, but at the risk that poorly-considered government action can also be taken quickly and decisively.
- Public exposure of the reasoning behind policy judgements, and *ex post* audit and scrutiny of the effectiveness of policies, can provide some defence against the capture of environmental policymaking by particular sectional interests.
- Public confidence may be enhanced where policies are subject to independent scrutiny, and where the informational basis of policymaking is validated by independent experts with no obvious sectional axe to grind.

The role played by the UK's Royal Commission on Environmental Pollution has been assessed by Owens and Rayner (1999). They point out that it performs a number of different functions – as knowledge broker, policy entrepreneur and advocate – and that the trust and authority deriving from its expert, non-representative composition have been crucial to its ability to exert influence. Measuring the influence is harder. Owens and Rayner suggest that there has been some, but limited, direct linkage, in the form of immediate government actions in response to a report, but that the main influence of the Royal Commission arises through more indirect routes – for example, by forcing civil servants to think about a particular issue when giving evidence to the Commission. One area where RCEP may have had long-term influence is through its sustained advocacy of policy integration, and the related case that it made for the establishment of an Environment Agency. In contrast to some of the theorising about the role of expert commissions, Owens and Rayner emphasise that in their view the Royal Commission has not simply functioned as a mechanism for legitimation.

3.5 Institutions and Environmental 'Modernisation'

A further aspect of the UK system which may be of interest is the relationship between institutional structure and the pace and pattern of adoption of the range of policy measures sometimes grouped under the heading of 'ecological modernisation'.[7] This term is somewhat flexible, but can be understood to include the adoption of the range of incentive-based 'economic instruments', including environmental taxes and charges, tradeable permits, and so on, and also the use of 'voluntary' or 'negotiated' agreements between government and individual sectors of industry over matters such as emissions control or waste management.

In the UK, the following aspects may be noted:

1. A relatively early statement of the potential contribution that could be made by 'market mechanisms' in environmental policy, contained within the 1990 White Paper, and subsequently reiterated in other DoE and Treasury documents.
2. A disastrous attempt to extend the standard rate of VAT to domestic energy, previously zero-rated. This was proposed purely for revenue reasons (Crawford et al., 1993), but met intense political opposition, mainly on the grounds of the adverse distributional impact, and was abandoned at the half-way stage. The tax rate was subsequently reduced to the current level of 5 per cent, and political fall-out from the episode has meant that governments have since been very wary of introducing any environmental tax measures that would bear clearly on households.
3. Negligible use of voluntary agreements,[8] with the (very substantial) exception of the agreements negotiated with energy-intensive sectors as part of the Climate Change Programme. As Jordan et al. (2003) note, such agreements appear to be vulnerable to many of the criticisms of the discretionary tradition of plant-level pollution regulation, which the UK has in recent years been modifying.
4. Limited, but significant, environmental tax measures introduced by central government (Box 18.6), including a landfill tax and aggregates levy, both on wholly-new tax bases.

BOX 18.6 ENVIRONMENTAL TAXES IN THE UK, 2004

Landfill tax Introduced in 1996, at a standard rate of £7 per tonne on waste delivered to landfill sites. A lower rate of £2 per tonne applies to inactive waste (building rubble, etc). The standard rate was raised to £10 in 1999, and an annual escalation of £1 per tonne applies for five years from April 2000, leading to a final level of £15 per tonne in 2004. The initial tax rate was determined with reference to landfill externality estimates; subsequent increases have been designed to achieve greater behavioural change. Revenues in 2001/

02 were £502 million (net of contributions to the accompanying voluntary Landfill Tax Credit Scheme), used to finance a 0.2 percentage point cut in employers' National Insurance contributions. The scheme is estimated to have led to a 60% reduction in the volume of inactive waste sent to landfill, but to have had negligible impact on landfilling of other wastes. A Cabinet Office Strategy Unit paper in 2002 concludes that 'a rise to £35 a tonne is required over the medium term'.

Motor fuel differentiation

Tax differential in favour of ***unleaded petrol*** introduced in 1987 at 0.96 pence per litre, subsequently widened to 4.8 pence per litre by 1995. Initial aim was to offset the higher cost of unleaded petrol, and subsequently to provide an incentive for fuel switching. Leaded petrol was removed from normal sale in the UK market in 2000.

Tax differential between ***petrol and diesel fuel*** was eliminated in November 1994 Budget, which raised the excise duty on diesel to equal that on unleaded petrol. This followed a 1993 report of the Quality of Urban Air Review Group, which drew attention to the rapidly-growing problem of particulates emissions from diesel vehicles in urban areas. Diesel duty (conventional diesel) is now taxed more heavily (51.82 pence per litre) than conventional unleaded petrol (48.82 pence per litre).

Ultra-low sulphur petrol and diesel benefit from duty advantage of 3 pence per litre and 6 pence per litre respectively.

Lower rates of duty apply to ***alternative road fuels***, including biofuels, gas used as a road fuel, and, shortly, bioethanol.

Vehicle excise duty differentiation

From June 1999, a annual vehicle excise duty differential was introduced to favour cars with small engines; this now applies only to vehicles registered before March 2001. Currently vehicles below 1550cc receive £55 discount on £160 annual vehicle excise duty. For cars first registered after 1 March 2001 VED has been graduated

	according to the CO_2 emissions performance of the vehicle model, in five bands of charges ranging from £70 to £155 annually for petrol cars, £80–160 for diesel cars, and £60–150 for alternative-fuel vehicles.
Climate Change Levy	A tax on energy use by business and industry, introduced in April 2001 as part of the government's Climate Change Programme. Rates of levy are equivalent to 0.15 pence per kWh for natural gas and coal, 0.43p per kWh for electricity, and 0.07p per kWh for liquefied petroleum gas (LPG). The tax does not apply to domestic energy use, or to energy used in the transport sector. Exemptions include fuels used in electricity generation, fuels used for non-energy purposes, and electricity generated from new renewable energy (e.g. solar and wind power). An 80% discount from the levy applies to energy-intensive sectors that negotiate Climate Change Agreements with DEFRA. Full-year revenues approx. £1 billion, partly used to finance energy efficiency schemes, and the remainder returned to business through an offsetting 0.3 percentage point reduction in employers' National Insurance contributions.
Aggregates Levy	Introduced in April 2002. Intended to reflect the environmental costs associated with quarrying. Applies to sand, gravel and rock subject to commercial exploitation in the UK and UK territorial waters. Exemptions for coal and metal ore mining, for materials used to produce lime and cement, for industrial spoil and waste, highway evacuation and marine dredging. Export tax relief, and corresponding taxation of imports. The levy is charged at £1.60 per tonne, normally payable by the quarry operator. Full-year revenues approx. £305 million, part to be used to finance a Sustainability Fund (to promote local environmental benefits in areas affected by quarrying), and the remainder to finance a 0.1 percentage point cut in employer NICs.

Central London Congestion Charge	Introduced February 2003, by the Greater London Authority. Exemptions include taxis, buses, emergency services vehicles, vehicles used by the registered disabled, etc. Vehicles using gas, electric, fuel cells and bi/dual fuel sources are exempt. The charge is £5.00 per day, for driving within a 21-square kilometre area of central London. The charge is monitored and enforced through cameras able to read vehicle registration numbers, sited at entry points to the zone, and at other locations within the zone. Annual revenues net of running costs are expected to be around £130 million, and must be reinvested in transport in London.

5. A failure by central government to persuade the Environment Agency of the merits of a system of water pollution charges.
6. A substantial market-based element in the UK's Climate Change Programme, including a Climate Change Levy on industrial energy use, partly rebated for firms in energy-intensive sectors that have concluded Climate Change Agreements with central government, and supplemented by a system of carbon trading. An overt objective of the carbon trading scheme is to establish the London financial markets as the global location for environmental permit trading.
7. Indications of recent vigour in the design of new market mechanisms, in particular tradeable-permit type mechanisms. These have included two applications in the energy sector, for carbon, and to stimulate electricity generation from renewable sources, and two waste management applications, for compliance with packaging waste recovery obligations and for landfill of biodegradable municipal waste (Box 18.7).

Fundamental to the pattern of adoption of these measures is that none has grown out of existing regulatory approaches. Indeed, the technology-based form of command-and-control regulation (and the UK's past tradition of ill-defined negotiated regulation of individual enterprises) is unsuited to incremental adaptation to accommodate market mechanisms, as compared with the regulatory approach used in some areas by the US EPA, which has set quantitative limits on emissions at the enterprise level. Incremental modification to make these limits tradeable is a relatively modest step, compared with the wholly-new arrangements that would be required in the UK.

BOX 18.7 TRADEABLE PERMITS IN UK ENVIRONMENTAL POLICY, 2004

Packaging Waste Recovery Notes	A tradeable compliance credit scheme, which began in 1998. UK targets for recovery and recycling of packaging waste place obligations on firms producing and using packaging materials, typically taken on by collective compliance schemes. Environment Agency guidance in 1997 defined a standardised form of evidence (Packaging Waste Recovery Notes, or PRNs) that would be issued by accredited reprocessors and accepted as compliance evidence by the EA. Collective schemes and individual firms can use PRNs as evidence that they have met their obligations for recovery and recycling. Most obligations are met by direct contracts between compliance schemes and reprocessors, but compliance through transactions in PRNs has been growing; such transactions and pricing efficiency in the PRN market are stimulated by electronic trading services. Salmons (2002c) argues that the scheme functioned well in the initial years when the obligations were not very demanding, achieving stable prices broadly consistent with underlying compliance costs; a more severe test for the scheme would be the increase in recovery and recycling rates required from 2001.
Emissions trading (carbon dioxide)	Launched in April 2002, with an initial five-year lifespan (2002–06). Two groups of potential participants: the 5000 firms covered by Climate Change Agreements (CCAs) who can generate and sell allowances by exceeding their negotiated emission-reduction targets, and 'direct participants' who entered the scheme through the ETS auction. In the ETS auction it was open to any organisation to offer abatement of its UK emissions. The auction aimed to 'buy' as much abatement as possible, using a fixed budget of

£215m. A market-clearing price was established of £53 per tonne of CO_2-equivalent, and 34 direct participants were assigned abatement commitments totalling 4 million tonnes of CO_2 (1.1 million tonnes C) annually by 2006. The first three years of the scheme saw some 1400 trades, involving more than 6 million allowances (Smith and Swierzbinski, 2007). Prices were substantially lower than those paid in the ETS auction, starting at around £35 per tonne CO_2 in May 2002, but declining to about £3 by the end of the first year.

Renewables Obligation Certificates

The Renewables Obligation, introduced in April 2002, requires all electricity suppliers to demonstrate to the energy market regulator (the Office of Gas and Electricity Markets, OFGEM) that they have sourced a specified percentage of their output from renewable sources. For 2002 the required percentage was set at 3%, to rise in stages to 10.4% by 2010. Compliance is demonstrated through Renewables Obligation Certificates (ROCs), which are tradeable. Each ROC represents 1MWh of electricity generated from renewable sources (e.g. landfill gas, wind power, biomass, some hydro, etc). Firms have the option of 'buying out' their obligation at a set price of £30 per MWh in 2002, indexed for subsequent years, which places an upper bound to the cost per MWh of complying with the Renewables Obligation; buyout revenue is redistributed to suppliers sourcing renewable energy, in proportion to their use of renewables. ROCs can be banked to a limited extent, and can be converted to Emissions Trading allowances at 0.43 allowances per ROC. ROC prices are not public data.

Landfill Allowance Trading Scheme

A system of tradeable permits designed to restrict landfill disposal of biodegradable municipal waste (BMW), in order to ensure UK compliance with the targets set under the EU Landfill Directive (Salmons, 2002c; Barrow 2003). The scheme will start on 1 April 2005. Permits will be allocated without charge to Waste Disposal Authorities (local governments) according to a formula based on current landfilling and total current waste quantities, and will relate to a particular target year. The first allocation will be for the period up to 2010, by which date the UK must have reduced its landfilling of BMW to 75% of the 1995 level. Permits will be tradeable, with banking permitted up to but not into or across the target year. Some anticipatory borrowing of permits will be allowed.

It is also significant that, so far, the drive for greater use of economic instruments in the UK has come from central government, concerned about the efficiency and economic impact of environmental policy, than from the environment agency. A number of factors probably enter into the EA's comparative reluctance to explore the potential for innovative mechanisms, including the strong professional stake that current EA staff have in the nature of current regulation, and the absence of any direct financial incentive (in the form of any expectation of earmarked revenues). The latter factor is far from undesirable, and indeed, earmarked revenue can potentially have undesirable effects on the pattern of regulation, if it encourages market mechanisms to be designed with revenue considerations, rather than environmental goals, in mind.

4. CONCLUSIONS

This chapter has described the structure and decentralisation of environmental governance in the UK, focusing on those aspects that raise particular and distinctive issues. Section 2 of the chapter has highlighted institutional arragements under four headings – the structure of departments within the central government, the role of decentralised agencies including the Environment Agency, the various institutions for audit and scrutiny of environmental policies and performance, and the role of local government. The UK is a highly-centralised political system, in which central government has substantial decisive power. Territorial decentralisation (with the exception of the recent devolution in Scotland and Wales) is very limited, with no democratically-elected regional level of government, and a system of local government under tight central control. The mechanisms which might generate public responsiveness, effectiveness and accountability in environmental policy arise differently in the UK than in systems of government with more decentralised and dispersed authority. The role of audit and scrutiny institutions assumes considerable significance within such a centralised system. In addition, the EU plays an important role, both as a generator of initiatives, and as a check on performance.

Figure 18.1 summarises the broad division of UK environmental policy across levels of government, and the directions of change observed over the past 20 years or so. (Strictly, the table relates to England rather than the UK as a whole, and does not attempt to represent the position in Scotland and Wales, where devolution has shifted many responsibilities for UK government departments to the devolved assemblies.) At the level of detail shown in the table, there have been relatively few general trends, with the exception of the increasing significance of the international level of government (international agreements and the EU) in most areas of policy. Privatisation of the water industry has led to the creation of a separate water regulator, a form of functional decentralisation to a specialised regulatory agency. Also, there has probably been some general tendency for greater centralisation of land use and planning decisions, especially through appeals against local authority decisions. However, in most areas, the interesting changes in the assignment of policy responsibility have been more complex, and more subtle, than this summary table can represent.

Section 3 of the chapter has identified a number of key issues about the context and assignment of UK environmental policy, and the implications of the organisational structures for the nature of UK environmental policy. One striking feature of the central government institutions responsible for environmental policy in the UK is how frequently these have changed. The last 30 years have seen a succession of reorganisations of the environment-related functions of the UK central government, culminating in the recent creation of DEFRA, which combines environmental regulation with the former agriculture department MAFF. In principle, these reorganisations might have been expected to have had implications for the efficient functioning of environmental policies, especially in areas where it might be important to have good coordination with other related areas of policy, such as transport policy. In practice, there is little evidence on how far different configurations have affected the efficient functioning of environmental policy in the UK.

A second feature of the UK over the past 20 years has been the move towards specialised agencies created by central government, and away from direct implementation of policy by central government departments themselves. These agencies operate with a defined set of responsibilities, an

	Industrial pollution	**Ecosystem protection**	**Agriculture**	**Spatial planning**	**Water**	**Global environment**
International	EU IPPC Directive	Habitat and Birds Directive	Nitrates Directive, Set-Aside provisions of CAP		Water Framework Directive	Kyoto Protocol, EU Emissions trading
National government	Pollution Prevention and Control Act	National legislation	National legislation; support for set-aside	National legislation; appeals against local planning decisions	National legislation. Budgetary allocations to EA for spending.	UK Climate Change Programme; UK Emissions Trading
Central government agencies	Environment Agency Operate IPPC, issue permits, etc	English Nature (wildlife)		Countryside Agency (landscape protection and rural development)	Environment Agency (water quality). OFWAT (economic regulation)	Environment Agency
Local government	Regulate emissions of small-scale enterprises not covered by EA	Local spending on nature reserves, etc		Development planning (buildings, land use, spatial development)		Agenda 21 actions

Figure 18.1 Trends in centralisation/decentralisation in UK environmental policy

allocated budget, and an agreed programme; their performance is monitored against measurable targets. In the area of environmental policy, the key agencies include the Environment Agency, responsible for pollution control and water management, English Nature, responsible for wildlife protection, and the Countryside Agency, responsible for landscape protection and rural development.

The structure of institutions has affected the nature of environmental regulation in a number of ways, of which two may be particularly significant. Recent years have seen a significant shift in the style of UK environmental policy, away from case-by-case negotiation of pollution consents between the regulator and individual enterprises, taking account of local environmental circumstances and the competitive position of the enterprise, towards a more rule-based regulatory approach. Part of the pressure for this has come from the EU; the nature of EU directives has reflected the more rule-based regulatory traditions in other member states. The move towards more rule-based regulation has also reflected the privatisation of key industries, and the shift towards explicit statements of objectives, and quantitative performance measurement, for the agencies responsible for economic and environmental regulation.

A further interaction between institutional structure and policy design can be seen in the pattern of 'modernisation' in UK environmental policy, including the adoption of a limited number of incentive-based regulatory mechanisms. The Environment Agency has played a very minor role in innovation in UK environmental policy, and most of the initiatives towards 'modernisation' of regulatory approaches have come from central government. There are a number of reasons for this, including the nature of existing technology-based command-and-control regulation, which cannot easily be adapted through incremental adaptation to accommodate market mechanisms, and the strong professional stake that current EA staff have in the nature of current regulation. Central government, on the other hand, while initially slower than some other countries to experiment with market-based approaches, has in recent years been a vigorous innovator in environmental policy. The UK Climate Change programme is perhaps the clearest example, containing an environmental tax, emissions trading, and sectoral negotiated agreements.

NOTES

* The author is grateful to Anthony Zito for a useful discussion at an early stage of the research.

1. Indeed, as Weale et al. (2000) note, the DoE did not have departmental responsibility for the national air pollution inspectorate from 1974 to 1987.

2. Since this chapter was written, a further reorganisation in October 2006, under the Natural Environment and Rural Communities Act, has created a new agency 'Natural England', combining English Nature, the landscape, access and recreation responsibilities of the Countryside Agency, and the environmental land management functions of the Rural Development Service. Other functions of the former Countryside Agency have been placed with a new Commission for Rural Communities which has an explicit advocacy role, focusing in particular on issues of rural disadvantage.
3. In the case of Environment Agency activities in Wales, the sponsor is the National Assembly for Wales.
4. There are, of course, interesting questions which this raises about the UK's role in the discussion and adoption of these Directives.
5. The price cap, 'RPI-plus-k', took the form of a maximum permitted percentage increase in prices, made up of two elements, general inflation (RPI) and a permitted annual increase in real price, k, set by the regulator. In other areas where similar price caps are applied in the UK, k is negative and aims to force efficiency improvements, but in the water industry the formula permits a real increase in prices over time, reflecting the increasing costs of environmental obligations (Helm and Rajah, 1994).
6. In the UK, the tax-cutting agenda of the Conservative government of the 1980s and 1990s led to considerable internal pressure for assessments of 'value for money', and individual departments were increasingly pressed by the Treasury to provide evidence to back up requests for continuing financial allocations for particular programmes. This source of pressure, however, acts unevenly across policy fields. Those involving substantial amounts of government expenditure (such as subsidy-based labour market measures) are subject to greater scrutiny than those (such as environmental regulation) where the burdens of policy are largely borne by other agents in the economy.
7. This issue is discussed at some length by Jordan et al. (2003).
8. Jordan and Salmons (2000) identify about ten such agreements, not all of them lasting. Most took the form of codes of good practice, rather than formally-negotiated commitments. Salmons (2002a, 2002b) documents and evaluates two UK Voluntary Restraint Agreements (VRAs), the Farm Films Recovery Scheme, and the Energy Efficiency Agreement with the UK Chemical Industries Association.

BIBLIOGRAPHY

Ashby, E. and M. Anderson (1981), *The Politics of Clean Air*, Oxford: Clarendon Press.

Barrow, Michael (2003), 'An economic analysis of the UK landfill permits scheme', *Fiscal Studies*, **24**(3), 361–81.

Crawford, Ian, Stephen Smith and Steven Webb (1993), *VAT on Domestic Energy*, Institute for Fiscal Studies, Commentary No 39.

Glachant, Matthieu (ed.) (2001), *Implementing European Environmental Policy. The impacts of Directives in the Member States*, Cheltenham, UK and Northampton, MA, USA: Edward Elgar.

Grant, Wyn, Duncan Matthews and Peter Newell (2000), *The Effectiveness of European Union Environmental Policy*, Basingstoke: Macmillan Press Ltd.

Haigh, Nigel (1989), *EEC Environmental Policy and Britain*, London: Longman.

Helm, Dieter and Najma Rajah (1994), 'Water regulation: the periodic review', *Fiscal Studies*, **15**(2), 74–94.

Jordan, Andrew (1993), 'Integrated Pollution Control and the Evolving Style and Structure of Environmental Regulation in the UK', *Environmental Politics*, **2**, 405–27.

Jordan, Andrew (2004), 'The Europeanisation of British environmental policy: from policy "taking" to policy "shaping"', in Andrew Jordan and Duncan Liefferink (eds), *Environmental Policy in Europe: The Europeanisation of National Environmental Policy*, London: Routledge, pp. 205–23.

Jordan, Andrew and Roger Salmons (2000), *The Use of Voluntary Agreements in the UK*, UEA, Norwich: CSERGE.

Jordan, Andrew, Rüdiger Wurzel, Anthony Zito and Lars Brückner (2003), 'Policy innovation or "muddling through"? "New" environmental policy instruments in the United Kingdom', in Andrew Jordan, Rüdiger Wurzel and Anthony Zito (eds), *'New' Instruments of Environmental Governnance. National Experiences and Prospects*, London: Frank Cass Publishers, pp. 179–98.

Knill, C. (1998), 'European policies: the impact of national administrative traditions', *Journal of Public Policy*, **18**, 1–28.

Macleod, Calum (2000), 'Continuity versus change: Enforcing Scottish pollution control policy in the 1990s', *Journal of Environmental Policy and Planning*, **2**, 237–48.

OECD (2002), *Environmental Performance Reviews. United Kingdom*, Paris: Organisation for Economic Co-operation and Development.

Owens, Susan (2000), 'Engaging the public: Information and deliberation in environmental policy', *Environment and Planning A*, **32**, 1141–8.

Owens, Susan and Tim Rayner (1999), 'When knowledge matters: The role and influence of the Royal Commission on environmental pollution', *Journal of Environmental Policy and Planning*, **1**, 7–24.

Salmons, Roger (2002a), 'The UK Farm Films Producers Group', in Marc de Clercq (ed.), *Negotiating Environmental Agreements in Europe. Critical Factors for Success*, Cheltenham, UK and Northampton, MA, USA: Edward Elgar, pp. 197–217.

Salmons, Roger (2002b), 'The energy efficiency agreement with the UK Chemical Industries Association', in Marc de Clercq (ed.), *Negotiating Environmental Agreements in Europe. Critical Factors for Success*, Cheltenham, UK and Northampton, MA, USA: Edward Elgar, pp. 241–66.

Salmons (2002c), 'New areas for application of tradeable permits – solid waste management', in OECD, *Implementing Domestic Tradeable Permits. Recent Developments and Future Challenges*, Paris: OECD, pp. 187–226.

Smith, Adrian (2000), 'Fitting in with Brussels: Implementing the Urban Waste Water Treatment Directive in England and Wales', *Journal of Environmental Policy and Planning*, **2**, 115–34.

Smith, Stephen and Joseph Swierzbinski (2007), 'Assessing the performance of the UK Emissions Trading Scheme', *Environmental and Resource Economics*, **37**(1), 131–58.

Sorrell, Steve (2002), 'The meaning of BATNEEC: Interpreting excessive costs in UK industrial pollution regulation', *Journal of Environmental Policy and Planning*, **4**, 23–40.

Weale, Albert, Geoffrey Pridham, Michelle Cini, Dimitrios Koinstadakopoulos, Martin Porter and Brendan Flynn (2000), *Environmental Governance in Europe. An Ever-Closer Ecological Union?*, Oxford and New York: Oxford University Press.

19. Trends in environmental governance: Evidence from seventeen countries and sundry reflections thereon

Albert Breton, Giorgio Brosio, Silvana Dalmazzone and Giovanna Garrone

In virtually all developed countries, though to a varying degree, the 1970s have seen the concrete appearance and the spread of environmental policies. With a lag of about a decade, developing countries have undergone a similar process but with less intensity, reflecting local circumstances of other urgently felt priorities of human development. Air and water pollution have typically been the prime objectives of regulation. An awareness of the complexity of the interactions between economic activities and ecological systems and the consequent need for integrated sustainable development strategies, however, required another two decades before finding a place on the policy agenda. An examination of the development of governance structures for environmental protection in the 17 countries included in our sample allowed us to bring to light differences and peculiarities, a few interesting trends, and a number of remaining challenges.

1. ECOLOGICAL MODERNIZATION AND MARKET-BASED INSTRUMENTS

A need for 'ecological modernization', intended as a shift from command-and-control policy tools towards both voluntary approaches and market-based instruments, is perceived in most countries. Interestingly, even China has experimented with several market-based tools, which have grown in importance along with the 'socialist market economy' reform process.

The call for such a shift is usually motivated by concerns regarding both the effectiveness and the cost-efficiency of more traditional environmental policy instruments. In Germany, in the 1990s, command-and-control approaches appeared to be increasingly unable to achieve environmental goals, especially as far as pollution problems from diffuse sources were concerned. In Canada, increased use of economic instruments and non-regulatory strategies, at both the national and provincial levels is, among other things, a result of budgetary restraints and concern for competitiveness. Fiscal instruments including environmental taxes, charges and subsidies are now used in a large number of countries in sectors as varied as land conservation, waste management, water extraction and air pollution control. Tax differentials are used in the energy sector to promote energy efficiency, renewable energy and cleaner fuels. In Canada, part of the recent efforts in the realm of taxation are aimed at levelling the playing field by correcting distortions due to pre-existing subsidies to resource extraction activities.

The most common problem with environmental taxes (noted in the studies on India, Italy and Russia) is that often these are designed to generate revenue, or cost recovery in the cases of water and waste charges, rather than to pursue environmental objectives. Moreover, they often allow exemptions which weaken their scope and may entail undesirable distributional outcomes.

Quantity instruments such as tradable permit schemes are less commonly employed than price incentives. The US is undoubtedly the country where they are most widespread. Apart from the well-known and successful case of the Acid Rain programme, other important schemes are implemented at the state level in order to comply with federal regulation (the Clean Air Act). Transferable development rights programmes are also commonly employed for land use and the protection of endangered species.

In the UK, a number of market mechanisms of the tradable permit type have been developed and applied in the energy and in the waste management sectors. The UK is also among the countries that have introduced a carbon trading scheme in their strategies for meeting their Kyoto Protocol commitments, anticipating the implementation of the EU Emission Trading System for carbon emissions, the only case of European-level tradable permits.

A tradable water rights system is being set up in Australia, in the context of a separation between land ownership and water rights in which the environment is formally recognized as a legitimate user of water.

Despite the above summarized trends, command-and-control methods (standard-setting, licensing, zoning) still prevail not only in less developed countries (such as Brazil and Chile, where a central role in environmental policy is played by mandatory Environmental Impact Assessments) but also in most of the OECD countries covered in the preceding chapters.

Some considerations emerging from the country studies contribute to explain the limited adoption of market-based instruments. As regards environmental policy formulated at the EU level, the prevalence of command-and-control tools is due to the fact that the limited budgetary powers of the EU induce a bias in favour of instruments which do not require any budgetary expenditure. Most market-based systems, while reducing abatement costs, imply higher administrative costs than plain command-and-control methods. This does not contradict the fact that the EU has pressured its member states to adopt economic instruments.

Other factors that influence the limited development of market-based instruments include (i) the professional composition of staff in relevant environmental bodies, where there are more natural scientists and lawyers than environmental economists; (ii) the fact that traditional tools are more easily understood by, and visible to, the public; (iii) a preference on the part of firms for instruments such as technological standards which can work as barriers to entry; and (iv) the history (tradition) of regulation: a technology-based regulation style is less apt to accommodate the introduction of economic instruments than the type of regulation prevailing in the US which is based mostly on quantitative limitations.

2. VOLUNTARY AGREEMENTS

The growing incidence of voluntary agreements (VAs) in environmental governance since the early 1990s is another common trend in Western countries, a development that takes place in the context of a more general trend of ecological modernization. Broadly speaking, voluntary agreements include all agreements between companies or umbrella organizations and governments. They can take the form of unilateral industry declarations, bilateral agreements that may be either legally binding or not, and state-granted exemptions from regulations if industries can demonstrate that their compliance with environmental standards is reached with alternative means.

The diffusion of VAs is not uniform: within Europe, for instance, they have become important in Germany, the Netherlands, Italy and France, much less so in the UK and Denmark. Environment Canada has made extensive use of voluntary agreements in its attempt to reduce the emissions of the chemical industry. Since 2002, the US has had a plan to promote voluntary, non-binding measures for greenhouse gases abatement. The energy sector is the main field of application of VAs at the EU level. In fact, even in countries that make negligible use of voluntary agreements, climate change programmes are often an exception. Because countries find it difficult to adopt the costly restrictions on energy-intensive sectors necessary to comply with the Kyoto Protocol, they often have recourse to VAs.

The EU, in its *SAVE II* Programme, encourages member states to promote VAs as instruments for achieving carbon dioxide limitations.

EU directives that set environmental standards must be translated into formal regulations by every member state, even if those standards are already met by pre-existing voluntary agreements. VAs are not simply a policy instrument like, say, taxes and emissions permits, but a way to set standards. As a consequence, their use in matters that are regulated by EU directives is not at the discretion of member states. Voluntary instruments can, however, be used within member states to achieve more ambitious objectives. These elements in the relationship between EU and national regulations were brought to the fore in 1994 when the European Commission required a covenant for the reduction of packaging waste stipulated in the Netherlands to be replaced with formal regulation. Subsequently, in 1997, the Dutch industries entered into an agreement that further tightened the EU target in exchange for relaxation of certain procedural requirements.

The relationship between the use of voluntary agreements and decentralization is not univocal. When negotiated by the central government, VAs may erode the environmental powers of local authorities: Denmark provides evidence in that direction. In Italy, on the other hand, VAs are increasingly negotiated by subnational governments, paralleling the decentralization process, and the ministry does not have power of oversight over local agreements.

On the whole, our comparative research confirms the general patterns recognized in the literature on voluntary approaches as summarized, for example, in the OECD (2003) report, and allows us to derive some further considerations on their effectiveness.

Voluntary agreements appear to have been effective in countries and at times when there was a widespread perception of both the existence of a strong political will and of the feasibility of implementing stringent environmental policies. The late 1980s Netherlands is a case in point. In most other countries they spread in connection with a loss of momentum of environmental concerns, as a means of circumventing the costly trade-offs imposed by more traditional instruments. When the use of voluntary instruments follows a downgrading of the environment in the political agenda, the evidence is that their effectiveness is low.

In addition, the evidence from the country studies is that VAs are often not effectively monitored and that, as a consequence, the extent to which they are actually executed is uncertain. More severe problems arise with 'voluntary challenges', such as the Canadian 'Accelerated Reduction/Elimination of Toxics' and 'National Climate Change Voluntary Challenge and Registry Programme', in which governments invite polluters to reduce emissions below regulated limits and report their progress. Their failure to achieve noticeable results is the consequence of the lack of third party verification and of sanctions for non-compliance.

Voluntary agreements appear to work better, *ceteris paribus*, when they are negotiated between government and industries rather than with individual firms. Hence well organized business sectors are a favourable condition for them to be successful. In some instances VAs are appealing to industries as an opportunity to participate in the formulation of legislation. In these cases, the obligations of VAs are affirmed afterwards either in formal regulations, or by including them among the conditions that firms have to meet for obtaining individual licences (as happens in the Netherlands). A weaker incentive is present when they become a condition for membership in producers' associations (as within the Canadian chemical industry).

Finally, a complete evaluation of voluntary agreements, as of voluntary approaches in general, requires a proper analysis of their targets. Where the actual results of negotiations do not exceed the 'business-as-usual' level of environmental protection, these instruments are no more than indirect forms of (ineffective) subsidization.

3. CONTRACTUAL UNDERTAKINGS

Decentralization has offered new governance instruments to central, regional and local governments, of which contractual agreements between administrations are a significant example. Contracts – a reality that is almost totally absent from the literature on federalism and decentralization, except indirectly in some of the literature on conditional intergovernmental grants – are important instruments in ordering intergovernmental relations. Contractual agreements are sometimes prescribed by the legislation (in the German case, explicitly by the Federal Constitution) as a tool for coordination. The diffusion of contracts to govern the environment has been enhanced by the Agenda 21 plans of action, launched following the Rio 1992 Earth Summit and reaffirmed in Johannesburg in 2002. Under the terms of such plans, sub-central governments have been encouraged to develop projects for sustainable development often implemented through contracts with central governments.

In France there are agreements between the regions and the national *Agence de l'Environnement et de la Maîtrise de l'Energie*, operating under the supervision of the Ministry of the Environment, for the purpose of promoting energy-efficient housing and industrial buildings, as well as introducing new techniques for recycling waste and less polluting modes of public transportation. These agreements involve co-financing, and are real contracts in that breaches are subject to litigation. In Italy, paralleling the decentralization process which began in the early 1990s, most sectoral environmental laws explicitly refer for their implementation to contractual agreements between governments.

There is evidence that intergovernmental contracts have been effective as instruments for overcoming decisional impasses and bureaucratic inertia, but at some cost in terms of a reduction in transparency of the policy-making process and in the equity of its outcomes.

4. PRIVATIZATIONS IN THE PROVISION OF ENVIRONMENTAL SERVICES

Since the mid-1980s we have been witnessing a worldwide trend towards privatizations in the provision of services such as water distribution, sewage and waste disposal. The potential for increased cost-efficiency and the attraction of private financing are typical arguments put forward in favour of delegating to private bodies some of the functions pertaining to the provision of environmental services. Privatization is on the agenda in many countries, accompanied by debates on its distributional implications and on the potentially negative environmental and public health consequences.

Evidence from the countries considered in our research highlights important cases of privatization of forest resources and of services such as the management of protected areas (for instance in Chile and in India). Those eco-labelling and certification schemes that are established and run by NGOs and private companies can also be seen as a form of privatization of an environmental governance function (standard-setting). The largest share of attention, in the realm of the privatization of environmental services, is captured, however, by the provision of water.

Germany has been developing alternative organizational forms of water supply and wastewater disposal, including models of cooperation between municipalities and private firms, and forms of complete privatization. The latter, however, are rare, and private companies must adhere to strict regulations in order to obtain a permit from water authorities.

In France, drinking water is owned by the communes, though some 85 per cent is distributed and sold by private companies through outsourcing agreements. These resolve a problem of scale in the management of waste and water utilities inherent in the existence of 36 000 communes.

In Denmark, despite a similar scale problem, municipalities have been reluctant to privatize, an option chosen by only one or two communes.

The 1988–89 privatization of the British water industry led to an increase in the tax-exempted profits of water companies of 147 per cent between 1990 and 1998, with sewerage and water prices rising respectively by 42 and 36 per cent (PSIRU, 2001). Price increases, together with concerns about the quality of service delivery, led the Office for Water Services (whose main mandate is to restrict the industry's ability to earn monopoly profits) to tighten, in the second regulatory cycle, the price cap which is reviewed every five years.

Privatization can also be motivated by a desire to attract private capital to finance infrastructure investments. This has been the case in Chile. In 1998, the government privatized a fraction of water companies with the aim of channelling resources toward the urban sewerage system. Between 1998 and 2001, investment by the privatized companies increased by a significant amount, while investment by the public firms, because of difficulties in securing funds, fell by an equally important amount. Private companies were able to, and did, improve the quality of their services, whereas the public sector firms were unable to do so. In spite of the fact that the price of water supplied by private firms increased by 20 per cent over that of public suppliers, a social consensus emerged which made the high price of water acceptable to the population at large.

It is difficult to generalize on the virtues and faults of privatization and of the closely related practices of outsourcing and contracting-out. If privatization, outsourcing, and/or contracting-out are accompanied by a reduction in the degree of competition among suppliers, the outcome, over the longer term, may be worse than public provision. In some instances, in order to increase the value of the assets that the government intends to privatize, such assets are assembled into a single portfolio and sold as a package. This typically gives rise to monopolistic behaviour, so that generally, after a few years, the government must implement a basket of regulations to curtail the abuses.

In the case of outsourcing and contracting-out, it is easy to limit access to selected applicants or to allocate contracts on the basis of political rather than economic considerations. When this happens, in-house production and delivery may be superior.

5. THE DIFFUSION OF ENVIRONMENTAL PROTECTION AGENCIES

A salient feature of the evolving structure of environmental governance worldwide is the diffusion of agencies located outside traditional administrations. In 1970, President Nixon established the first Environmental Protection Agency. Because it is not a Cabinet agency, the US EPA is assumed to be an arm's length agency.[1] One must, however, keep in mind that the head of the agency – the Administrator – is appointed by the

President as are all departmental secretaries, is usually given cabinet rank, and represents the United States at international meetings of Ministers of the Environment.

The US Environmental Protection Agency and its equivalents at the state level have been widely imitated though with considerable differences in design, purpose, structure, and length of the arm.

Among the countries we analysed, most have established an Environmental Protection Agency, which provides technical information and generally works in connection with the Ministry of the Environment (Brazil, Denmark, Ethiopia, the EU, Germany, Ghana, France, Italy and the UK are examples). In the US, there is no Ministry or Department of the Environment, but an EPA with a very wide mandate. In Canada the choice has been to deal with most functions pertaining to environmental regulation within the Ministry, without creating an EPA. There appears to be some correlation between the arm's length status as well as the powers assigned to the agency and whether or not it co-exists with a Ministry. Although with significant variations across cases, the length of the arm between government and the agency appears shorter in countries where the Agency is a substitute for a Ministry and its tasks are more incisive. Coherently, among EPAs, those in the US have the broadest responsibilities ranging from research, the establishment and enforcement of environmental protection standards, the drafting of environmental regulations, their implementation and monitoring.

Like the US, Brazil and Chile have created environmental agencies (formally called committees or commissions, but with structures that mimic those of some other EPAs) at every level of government, from the federal to the municipal. These EPA-like commissions also act as forums for the creation of a consensus among stakeholders. Other countries, such as Australia, have EPAs at the state level only and their responsibilities are restricted to monitoring and implementation.

A variant of the model has been established in the EU, with the Union's agency located in Copenhagen charged mainly with providing environmental information. Data on the environmental performance of member states collected by the European Environment Agency play a significant role in monitoring and enforcement, but the agency's limited mandate in comparison with the US EPA has dashed the hopes of its original proponents. EPAs are also being created in a growing number of other member states (in addition to those listed above) including Austria, Ireland, Slovakia, Slovenia and Sweden. In the UK there is one for England and Wales and one for Scotland.

Some transition and developing countries, such as Russia and Ethiopia, are in the early stages of developing environmental agencies. China created an Environmental Protection Agency in 1988, by giving the pre-existing Environmental Protection Bureau an independent status from the Ministry. Ten years later, however, the agency was given ministerial status, assuming overall responsibility for environmental protection in China but returning under the direct control of the State Council and thus losing its arm's length status. Without provincial or local representatives and endowed with declining resources, China's State Environmental Protection Authority has been encountering serious difficulties in promulgating effective regulations as well as in securing their enforcement.

There are wide differences not only in the responsibilities, but also in the vertical structure of EPAs. In the United States, Congress has given the federal EPA broad discretion to implement the environmental statutes. The relationship between the federal agency and the state agencies varies with the medium being regulated. Air pollution is based on somewhat hierarchical links, with federal standards and state implementation plans subject to the approval of the central EPA. A much more decentralized institutional structure deals with water pollution. In European and Latin American countries, subnational EPAs, where present, depend only on the subnational governments situated at their level. Relations may vary: in some cases the central EPA provides guidance and financial resources, with a consequent reduction in the independence of subnational agencies.

There are several motivations behind the creation of EPAs. Certainly, the importance of scientific and technical information for environmental regulation and a consequent need for specialized research have played a role. A second motivation is an attempt to introduce distance between environmental decision-making and lobbying pressures, by transferring some of the functions concerning environmental regulation to an agency independent from voters and funders of electoral campaigns. Interestingly, in the US, the law prohibits the EPA to negotiate with interested parties. Thirdly, arm's length agencies may favour public acceptance of regulations by giving them scientific authority. A further reason behind the creation of EPAs may have to do with a desire to avoid, in a field that requires highly specialised technical competence, the loss of expertise that a spoil system could cause within a government department at every executive turnover. On the other hand, some argue that transferring the responsibility over environmental regulation to an arm's length agency may pose a problem of democratic accountability. Another interesting, still unanswered question is whether developing environmental regulation through an EPA, rather than within traditional government administration, has an impact, and of what sign, on the difficulties encountered by all countries in their attempts to integrate environmental policy across policy sectors (energy, transports, industry, and so on).

6. THE ROLE OF THE JUDICIARY

In a number of countries the judiciary is a major environmental player. Courts act in three distinct ways: (i) they assign and/or re-assign powers to different levels of government; (ii) they fill vacuums in environmental regulation; and (iii) they remedy executive and bureaucratic failures.

As regards (i), supreme courts, at least in the EU and the US, have centralized environmental legislation. The European Court of Justice has constantly supported the right of the EU to regulate the environment.[2] A similar process has taken place in the US: the consequence of judicial decisions has been to diminish any constitutionally protected sphere of state and local regulation by authorizing virtually unlimited (and sometimes exclusive) centralization. Neither the EU nor the US have acted to solve interstate pollution problems, but instead have introduced community or nationwide uniform standards concerning issues of local relevance such as water quality and urban air pollution. This is contrary to what one would expect from the normative theory of fiscal federalism. However, this outcome can be easily explained. EU and US legislators have acted to promote competition in their respective internal markets. Creation and enhancement of the internal market have been the main tasks of the EU since its inception, while the American Supreme Court and the Federal Courts have made extensive use of the dormant commerce clause to extend federal powers with a view to fostering interstate competition. In other countries, such as Germany, the Supreme Court has not played such a role. A federalization of legislation has become possible only after constitutional amendments that have explicitly recognized the right of the federal legislature to regulate in environmental matters.

As for (ii), the role of courts in filling vacuums in environmental legislation and regulation is mentioned in some of the studies included in this volume. While this is the *modus operandi* of the common law systems, this mode was active, with reference to regulation of the environment, mostly before World War II. The aftermath of this war witnessed the emergence, in virtually all of the 17 countries examined, of national legislation in most environmentally relevant sectors. As is well illustrated in the Mandal and Rao study, the Indian Supreme Court has banned the felling of trees in forests without prior permission from the central government, thus creating problems for states that derive substantial royalty revenues from forest leasing. The Indian Supreme Court has also forced the local government of New Delhi to mandate the use of compressed natural gas instead of diesel for heavy vehicles, including those used in the local public transport system, thus imposing additional costs on that government. The Court has through these measures filled regulatory voids, thus protecting in one case forests and in the other the health of citizens against serious threats deriving from air pollution.

The case of India could serve as an example to other countries where environmental legislation is still weak. Unfortunately, executive and bureaucratic failure tend to be present in countries where the judiciary system is also weak and inefficient. The authors of the studies on Chile and Italy rightly point out how bureaucratic slack in enforcing environmental regulations could have, but have not, been countered, at least in the short term, by judicial activism. The temporal limitation is due to the recognition, explicit in Mandal and Rao, of the fact that courts provide ad hoc solutions that, by their very nature, cannot evolve.

As regards (iii), we note that the courts in a number of (mostly developed) countries have fostered the implementation of legislation. Citizens' suits are generally more frequent and thus the role of courts more important in countries that have a system of divided government. This is a finding of the so-called theory of regulatory federalism and it applies to cases such as the EU and the US. When government is divided, the legislative body has a limited impact on the implementation of its legislation. This applies particularly to federal and strongly decentralized systems, where – as illustrated by most cases included in this volume – legislation is the responsibility of the federal or central government, and implementation is the duty of state and/or subnational governments. In these cases, legislation tends to be very detailed in order to limit the discretion of the implementing government units. Detail in turn encourages citizens' suits. The US, particularly since the 1970s, offers many illustrations of the ability of private citizens to help enforce environmental regulation by bringing suits before the courts.

In this respect, courts are less crucial in Canada, confirming the finding of regulatory federalism. Canada does not have a divided government, being a Westminster-type parliamentary democracy with a bicameral system dominated by the lower house. In fact, in a parliamentary system of that type, the Legislative and Executive branches are fused, and legislation tends to give much discretion to the executive.

Germany has elements of both divided and non-divided government systems. Overall, courts do not play a major role in environmental policy-making even though administrative courts are responsible for the implementation of emission standards, that is for compliance with administrative regulation. In France, the role of courts is important, even if the country is not federalized and the central government has, in principle, authority vis-à-vis its subnational governments. Environmental groups have played an important role in bringing violations of environmental regulations to the courts. Due to the complexities of the French judicial system and the length of the administrative courts' decision-making process, environmental groups have also brought their cases to civil and criminal courts.

7. THE ALLOCATION OF ENACTMENT AND ENFORCEMENT POWERS

If a government was to enact laws, regulations, rules, by-laws and so on related to environmental protection but decided *not* to enforce them, it would in effect decide to rely on what has come to be known as the *expressive power* of enactments, that is on the guidelines which laws and regulations contain that can affect behaviour. The decision not to enforce enactments may also be motivated by a tacit political will to loosen the rules. In most of the literature that pertains to this matter, the expressive power of enactments is not recognized – nor is hypocritical behaviour on the part of the government. As a consequence, all enactments are assumed to be enforced by the country's government.

If, however, there is more than one level of government in the country, that is if the governmental system is decentralized – whether the country is federal or unitary – the enacting government need not and, in general, will not be the enforcing agent. Indeed, enforcement requires that the compliance – the actions and behaviours – of citizens be monitored. When citizens do not comply with the enactments, enforcement also requires that they be penalized. In decentralized systems of government, compliance may be monitored by agencies located at one jurisdictional level and the penalties imposed and administered by agencies inhabiting another level.

It is remarkable that, given the near complete lack of attention in the literature paid to the division of enactments and compliance, evidence from the country studies reveals that in a number of these countries – Canada, Denmark, the EU, France, the US for example – these functions are often undertaken by governments at different levels.

In some of these studies, it is recognized that compliance must be monitored, but little attention is paid to the fact that compliance must also sometimes be induced. Both monitoring and inducing can be achieved through the activities of supervision or alarms (marshalling the citizenry) and of enforcement or (monetary and/or in kind) assistance.

Monitoring and inducing activities appear to often cluster within one level of government. In the presence of intergovernmental competition, the reason why they do can be searched in the notion of complementarity, initially formulated by Francis Edgeworth (1881), which says that 'activities are *Edgeworth complements* if doing (more of) any one of them increases the returns of doing (more of) the others' (Milgrom and Roberts, 1995: 181).

8. ENVIRONMENTAL MANAGEMENT BY INDIGENOUS PEOPLE AND LOCAL COMMUNITIES

A growing number of countries are in the process of recognizing the citizenship rights of indigenous peoples. Associated in part with that process is the discovery by the 'establishment' that in many instances indigenous peoples can make contributions capable of increasing the efficiency of environmental management. These contributions stem from the secularly acquired understanding of indigenous populations of the ways and means of exploiting the environment on a sustainable basis, as well as from the deep knowledge they possess of species and their growth, utility and medicinal value.

It appears that the contribution to management can take one or both of two forms. A first form is co-management agreements between governments and indigenous communities pertaining to local natural resources. In Canada, within such agreements, land and water use, wildlife management and environmental impact assessment are generally planned and implemented by joint committees that include a guaranteed number of Aboriginal seats, but wherein the federal or provincial minister retains the responsibility over final decisions. In India, Joint Forest Management programmes are based on a similar participatory approach, with the State government retaining supremacy of decision-making power. In Australia, the management of the large wilderness areas included in the Kakadu National Park, jointly shared by the Aboriginal traditional owners and the central government, is closer to self-government because of the majority of Aboriginal representation in the Board of Management.

The second form of contribution of indigenous communities to environmental management is their formal representation in decision-making bodies at the national or regional level. The only case mentioned in this volume is the Indigenous Advisory Committee that advises the Australian Department of the Environment and Water Resources and takes into account indigenous knowledge of land, conservation and biodiversity.

9. INTEGRATION OF ENVIRONMENTAL POLICY-MAKING WITH OTHER POLICY SECTORS: THE LONG WAY TO A SUSTAINABILITY APPROACH

It is now widely accepted, in principle, that a comprehensive approach to protecting the environment from the disruption caused by unregulated economic growth needs 'to improve or restructure the decision-making process so that consideration of socio-economic and environmental issues is fully integrated' (UNCED, 1992, Agenda 21 §8.3), as asserted by the United Nations' plan of action adopted by more than 178 governments at the Rio de Janeiro summit. In the long-term, the conflict between economic and ecological objectives can only be attenuated if the effects of different policies are considered in an integrated way within an overall policy coordination framework. A majority of the countries that subscribed to Agenda 21 have tried to fulfil their obligations by developing some form of national sustainable development strategy. In most instances, however, such strategies are 'not sufficiently linked to existing government planning, reporting and budgeting processes' (Swanson and Pintér, 2006: 2), with the result that environmental concerns are insufficiently integrated in the policy-making of other departments.[3] As long as this obtains, actual achievements are rather marginal.

In some countries the process of integration has been managed within the Environment Department and the central Environmental Protection Agency, with the involvement of stakeholders (enterprises, trade unions, environmental NGOs, and more junior levels of government) through consultation processes. In others, it has led to the development of ad hoc governance structures.

One such structure is a national council (in most instances called 'Council for Sustainable Development') meant to provide a venue for exploring common grounds for environmental and economic objectives, for conflict mediation and consensus building, and for proposing and implementing initiatives to raise awareness about sustainability among the public. In the German case, the Council also regularly analyses the sustainability of different industries by commissioning studies (Schlicht, n.d.). These councils can be internal to the government and include external stakeholders (the Brazilian Commission for Sustainable Development is an example), or be non-government advisory bodies (such as those created, for instance, in Canada, the UK, Germany and France). Government councils are generally chaired by the Prime Minister and often vice-chaired by the Ministry of Environment. Members typically include ministers (or representatives of ministers) of finance, industry, agriculture, foreign trade, social affairs and health, labour and/or other relevant departments. Non-government councils generally consist of nominated or appointed commissioners from local administrations, business, academia, NGOs and so on and report to the office of the Prime Minister.

Other ad hoc structures are 'Green Cabinets', established in the UK and Germany. Formally called 'Secretary of State Committee for Sustainable Development', the German body was created by the government in 2000, and consists of several Secretaries of State from different areas of policy (environment, foreign affairs, finance, economy and labour, education and research, consumer protection, food and agriculture, health, economic development and cooperation, and transport). It is coordinated by the Chancellor's Office. Its scope includes preparing the government strategy for sustainability in cooperation with the Council for Sustainable Development, and fostering and coordinating the activities of the ministries regarding sustainability. The UK's 'Cabinet Committee on the Environment' possesses an analogous structure and similar objectives.

On the whole, the bird's eye view of this volume tells us that a sustainability approach to environmental issues has not had a profound impact on the design and formulation of policies. Several studies indicate that policy-makers, both in developed and developing countries, are, however, aware of the problems and have adopted a more sophisticated framework that acknowledges the linkages between different environmental issues. The development of governance structures specifically aimed at fostering coordination between policy sectors on matters relevant for the environment is at once a result of such growing awareness and an important factor in diffusing information and concern. Until now, however, policy integration has mostly remained on paper. Many crucial achievements in matters of environmental protection are contingent on policy sectors such as energy, transport and agriculture, whose priority over the environment is rarely called into question.

NOTES

1. Arm's length agencies are bodies created and financed by governments under provisions aimed at avoiding direct government influence over them. They are function specific. Some independently formulate rules and regulations under terms of reference that are part of the legislative acts creating them, and are responsible for implementing these regulations. Such agencies include, among many, central banks, public broadcasters, public granting bodies, and intelligence services.
2. See Kelemen (2004) for a review.
3. The IISD report prepared by Swanson and Pintér (2006) for the OECD evaluates in detail the National Sustainable Development Strategies of 21 countries, according to criteria such as the number of departments and levels of government involved, the embeddedness of the strategy in legislation, the involvement of the Prime Minister or the President's office, the integration of the strategy with the plans and budgets that departments submit to planning and finance departments, and so on.

REFERENCES

Edgeworth, Francis Y. (1881), *Mathematical Psychics*, London: Kegan Paul.

Kelemen, Daniel R. (2004), *The Rules of Federalism. Institutions and Regulatory Policy in the EU and Beyond*, Cambridge, MA: Harvard University Press.

Milgrom, Paul and John Roberts (1995), 'Complementarities and fit: Strategy, structure, and organizational change in manufacturing', *Journal of Accounting and Economics*, **19**, 179–208.
OECD (2003), *Voluntary Approaches for Environmental Policy: Effectiveness, Efficiency and Usage in Policy Mixes*, Paris: OECD.
PSIRU (2001), 'UK water privatisation – a briefing', Public Services International Research Unit, University of Greenwich, UK.
Schlicht, Anja (undated), 'German policy on sustainability and the Council for Sustainable Development (RNE)', *Corporate Seeds*, http://www.hillandknowlton.be/HK/pressoffice/corporate_seeds/18/germany.html.
Swanson, Darren and Pintér, Laszlo (2006), 'Governance structures for national sustainable development strategies. Study of good practice examples', International Institute for Sustainable Development, Winnipeg, Manitoba, Canada.
UNCED (1992), *Agenda 21: Earth Summit – The United Nations Programme of Action from Rio*, New York: United Nations Publications. Available online at http://www.un.org/esa/sustdev/documents/agenda21/index.htm.

Index